Arthur Banks

of the
First World War

 **LEO COOPER**

First published in 1975 by Heinemann Educational Books Ltd
Republished by LEO COOPER (an imprint of Pen & Sword Books)
in 1989, Reprinted in 1997
Reprinted in this format in 2001
by Pen & Sword Books Ltd
47 Church Street
Barnsley
South Yorkshire S70 2AS

A CIP record for this book is available
from the British Library

Copyright Maps © Arthur Banks 1975, 1989, 1997, 2001
Commentary © Alan Palmer 1975, 1989, 1997, 2001

ISBN 0 85052 791 0

Printed and bound by CPI UK

A Military Atlas of the First World War

A map history of the War of 1914–18 on land, at sea and in the air

A Military Atlas

commentary by ALAN PALMER

PREFACE

It is now nearly a quarter of a century since I entered the specialised field of cartography and during that time I have been able to direct much of my effort into the fascinating, but technically complicated, area of military and historical map-production.

I soon discovered that the research material I needed was very widely scattered through many different libraries and military institutions and that much of my time would be spent in sifting through material and consulting veterans of past campaigns. At one time I longed to find some clear, reasonably-priced atlases of battles accompanied by succinct texts, tables, and diagrams. No such volumes seemed to exist, so far as I could discover. The idea of producing such an atlas myself took shape; from my researches and discussions with those who planned and took part in some of the actions I decided to compile my own cartographical record. This was the genesis of this present book.

In these times economy seems to dictate much that we do; therefore, my original plan to give detailed coverage to most of the important military campaigns has had to be modified. As a result, this book is necessarily briefer than the one I originally designed.

However, I hope that the book will be a convenient reference work which deals with those areas where a more detailed examination in cartographical terms has long been demanded.

Arthur Banks
1975

The original version of this atlas has been out-of-print for some years. Nevertheless, demand for it has been steadily increasing with so much media presentation of events in the First World War. Accordingly it has been decided to reprint the work to cater for all the various interests in the war that changed the future for so many millions of people.

1989

ACKNOWLEDGEMENTS

During the research involved in the preparation of this atlas, I consulted some 1,300 historical reference works, examined and cross-checked 4,000 large- and small-scale maps (many of them of German or French origin), inspected several hundred technical manuals plus individual drawings, and attended numerous discussions with experts and veterans of the First World War.

Consequently, this must of necessity be a blanket appreciation of all those who were interested enough in my project to proffer advice and information in order to advance my work at various stages of the scheme.

In particular, I should like to thank General Sir James Marshall-Cornwall, Mr Michael Willis, and Mr Alan Palmer; all three went to enormous lengths to assist me and I am tremendously indebted to them.

In addition, the following persons deserve special mention and my gratitude: Dr R. Banks, Captain G. Bennett, Rear-Admiral P. Buckley, Captain L. Boswell, Captain E. Bush, Mrs J. Campbell, Miss R. Coombs, Major-General P. Essame, Miss S. Glover, Mr R. Holmes, Dr I. Nish, Mr V. Rigby, and Mr R. Welsh. Mr P. Richardson, Mr A. Hill, and Mr D. Heap of Heinemann Educational Books Limited extended endless encouragement and support to aid me in my task.

The librarians and staffs of the following organisations were generous in the facilities they placed at my disposal:

Imperial War Museum, Ministry of Defence, Royal Science Museum, Royal United Services Institute for Defence Studies, Royal Air Force Museum, H.M.S. *Vernon*, Hydrographic Department of the Admiralty, l'École Royale Militaire (Brussels), Turkish Naval Attaché's Office (London), United States Embassy (London), Belgian Embassy (London), and Surrey County Council Headquarters (Study and Information Department).

Finally, and above all, my wife deserves my deepest thanks: her devotion to my cause succoured me on so many occasions during the years of toil entailed in the research and preparation of this volume.

BIBLIOGRAPHICAL NOTE

Owing to the enormity of the research involved, it has proved impossible to itemise every reference work consulted, and the author feels that it would be unfair to specify particular accounts for recommended reading. However, he states that an essential first step for the serious student is to inspect the various military, naval, and aerial official histories of the belligerent powers. Usually these can be obtained from a central reference library or inspected at museums and institutions which specialise in military history and warfare.

CONTENTS

THE PRE-WAR SITUATION

WAR ON THE WESTERN FRONT IN 1914

WAR ON THE EASTERN FRONT IN 1914

THE WAR IN 1917

THE WAR IN 1918

THE PERIPHERAL CAMPAIGNS

WEAPONS

THE WAR AT SEA

THE WAR IN THE AIR

THE PRE-WAR SITUATION

The coming of the Great War took the European peoples by surprise. In the spring of 1914 the nations of western and central Europe had been at peace with each other for forty-three years, a longer period free from conflict than ever before in their histories. Except in the south-eastern corner of the continent, where the Balkan peoples still sought complete independence from Turkish rule, frontiers had remained inviolate since the Franco-Prussian War. Two traditional battle cockpits, the Polish plains and the low-lying fields of Flanders, had escaped war not merely for forty years, but for a full century. Small wonder if the long European Peace lulled ordinary people into a false sense of security. Economists argued war was commercially so disruptive that no industrialised nation would resort to it; intellectuals maintained that international society was enlightened enough to scorn its folly.

Statesmen and generals remained less sanguine. There had, after all, been colonial campaigns throughout the armed peace. By 1914 the army of every European Great Power, except Germany and Austria-Hungary, had already been engaged in fighting since the turn of the century. If colonial disputes had not led to a general conflict it was because, as yet, they had never affected the vital interests of more than two Great Power rivals at the same time; but potentially they were dangerous, as the Agadir Crisis showed in 1911. Moreover no one could ignore the significance of the arms race. Naval and military expenditure by the Great Powers doubled in the last twenty years of the nineteenth century; it doubled again in the first decade of the twentieth. Where could the arms race finish, if not on the battlefield?

There was, too, uncertainty over the ability of the diplomats to safeguard peace much longer. By 1900 Europe was divided by rival alliances, with the Central Powers (Germany, Austria-Hungary, Italy) on one side and with France and Russia on the other. So long as potential opponents seemed equally strong, these alliances made for continuance of the peace rather than war. But by 1905 Russia, defeated in the Far East by Japan and weakened by the threat of revolution, had ceased to be militarily formidable. There was no genuine balance of strength between the Powers. Too many imponderables accumulated. What would the British do? The Liberal Government gave diplomatic support to its Entente partners, France and Russia, but evaded formal military obligations: in the last resort, only the 1839 pledge to uphold Belgium's neutrality counted in British reckoning. What, too, of Italy? Rivalry with Austria over territorial interests in the Adriatic made the Italians uncomfortable members of the Triple Alliance. Was Italy still a 'Central Power'? There was no doubt that the diplomatic system of 1900 had changed by 1914.

Yet mutual antagonism was growing in intensity rather than diminishing. The French still sought recovery of Alsace-Lorraine; the British were increasingly suspicious of Germany's naval shipbuilding programmes; Russian Pan-Slavism seemed to threaten the integrity of Austria-Hungary; and the Germans resented the web of encirclement which they believed others were weaving around them. Already these issues had provoked diplomatic crises, for which solutions were improvised by statesmen unready for war. But everyone in authority knew that once orders were given for mobilisation, the alliance system would work against any localisation of the conflict. Peace was fragile: the Sarajevo crime was to show it lay ultimately at the mercies of chance. The heir to the Austrian throne and his consort were assassinated in the Bosnian capital by a Serbian student on 28 June 1914. By the middle of August five European Great Powers and two of lesser standing were locked in battle from the Flanders Plain to the eastern foothills of the Carpathians.

1

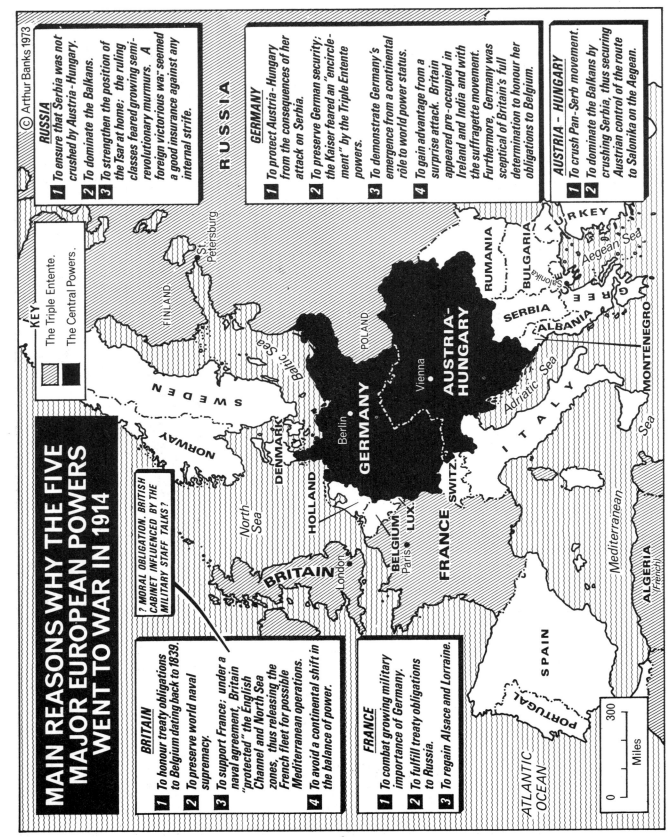

MAIN REASONS WHY THE FIVE MAJOR EUROPEAN POWERS WENT TO WAR IN 1914

© Arthur Banks 1973

RUSSIA
1. To ensure that Serbia was not crushed by Austria-Hungary.
2. To dominate the Balkans.
3. To strengthen the position of the Tsar at home: the ruling classes feared growing semi-revolutionary murmurs. A foreign victorious war "seemed a good insurance against any internal strife.

GERMANY
1. To protect Austria-Hungary from the consequences of her attack on Serbia.
2. To preserve German security: the Kaiser feared an "encirclement" by the Triple Entente powers.
3. To demonstrate Germany's emergence from a continental role to world power status.
4. To gain advantage from a surprise attack. Britain appeared pre-occupied in Ireland and India and with the suffragette movement. Furthermore, Germany was sceptical of Britain's full determination to honour her obligations to Belgium.

AUSTRIA - HUNGARY
1. To crush Pan-Serb movement.
2. To dominate the Balkans by crushing Serbia, thus securing Austrian control of the route to Salonika on the Aegean.

KEY
The Triple Entente.
The Central Powers.

BRITAIN
1. To honour treaty obligations to Belgium dating back to 1839.
2. To preserve world naval supremacy.
3. To support France: under a naval agreement, Britain "protected" the English Channel and North Sea zones, thus releasing the French fleet for possible Mediterranean operations.
4. To avoid a continental shift in the balance of power.

? MORAL OBLIGATION. BRITISH CABINET INFLUENCED BY THE MILITARY STAFF TALKS ?

FRANCE
1. To combat growing military importance of Germany.
2. To fulfill treaty obligations to Russia.
3. To regain Alsace and Lorraine.

RUSSIA

St Petersburg

FINLAND

SWEDEN

NORWAY

DENMARK

North Sea

Baltic Sea

POLAND

GERMANY

Berlin

Vienna

AUSTRIA-HUNGARY

HOLLAND

BELGIUM LUX.

Paris

FRANCE

SWITZ.

ITALY

Adriatic Sea

RUMANIA

BULGARIA

SERBIA

ALBANIA

MONTENEGRO

GREECE

Salonika

Aegean Sea

TURKEY

BRITAIN

London

Mediterranean Sea

SPAIN

PORTUGAL

ALGERIA
(French)

ATLANTIC OCEAN

0   300

Miles

2

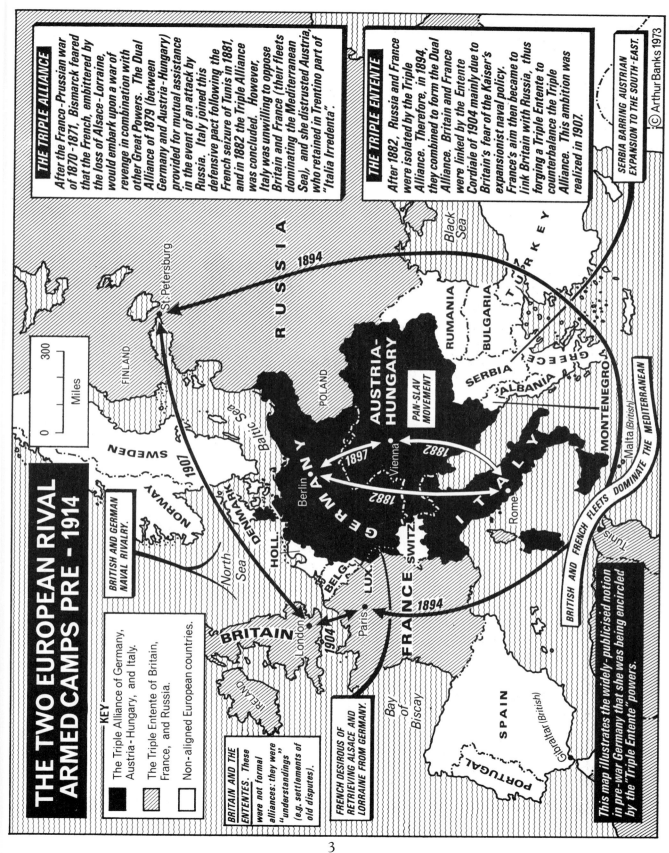

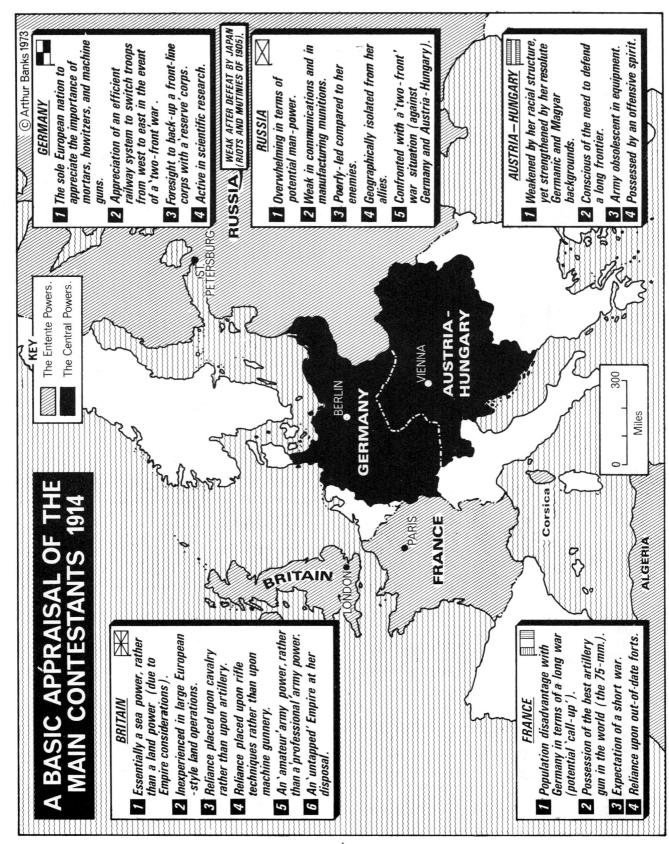

A BASIC APPRAISAL OF THE MAIN CONTESTANTS 1914

© Arthur Banks 1973

KEY

The Entente Powers.

The Central Powers.

GERMANY

1 The sole European nation to appreciate the importance of mortars, howitzers, and machine guns.

2 Appreciation of an efficient railway system to switch troops from west to east in the event of a 'two-front' war.

3 Foresight to back-up a front-line corps with a reserve corps.

4 Active in scientific research.

RUSSIA
WEAK AFTER DEFEAT BY JAPAN (RIOTS AND MUTINIES OF 1905).

1 Overwhelming in terms of potential man-power.

2 Weak in communications and in manufacturing munitions.

3 Poorly-led compared to her enemies.

4 Geographically isolated from her allies.

5 Confronted with a 'two-front' war situation (against Germany and Austria-Hungary).

AUSTRIA-HUNGARY

1 Weakened by her racial structure, yet strengthened by her resolute Germanic and Magyar backgrounds.

2 Conscious of the need to defend a long frontier.

3 Army obsolescent in equipment.

4 Possessed by an offensive spirit.

BRITAIN

1 Essentially a sea power, rather than a land power (due to Empire considerations).

2 Inexperienced in large European-style land operations.

3 Reliance placed upon cavalry rather than upon artillery.

4 Reliance placed upon rifle techniques rather than upon machine gunnery.

5 An 'amateur' army power, rather than a professional army power.

6 An 'untapped' Empire at her disposal.

FRANCE

1 Population disadvantage with Germany in terms of a long war (potential 'call-up').

2 Possession of the best artillery gun in the world (the 75-mm.).

3 Expectation of a short war.

4 Reliance upon out-of-date forts.

ST. PETERSBURG

BERLIN

VIENNA

GERMANY

AUSTRIA-HUNGARY

BRITAIN

LONDON

PARIS

FRANCE

Corsica

ALGERIA

0   300

Miles

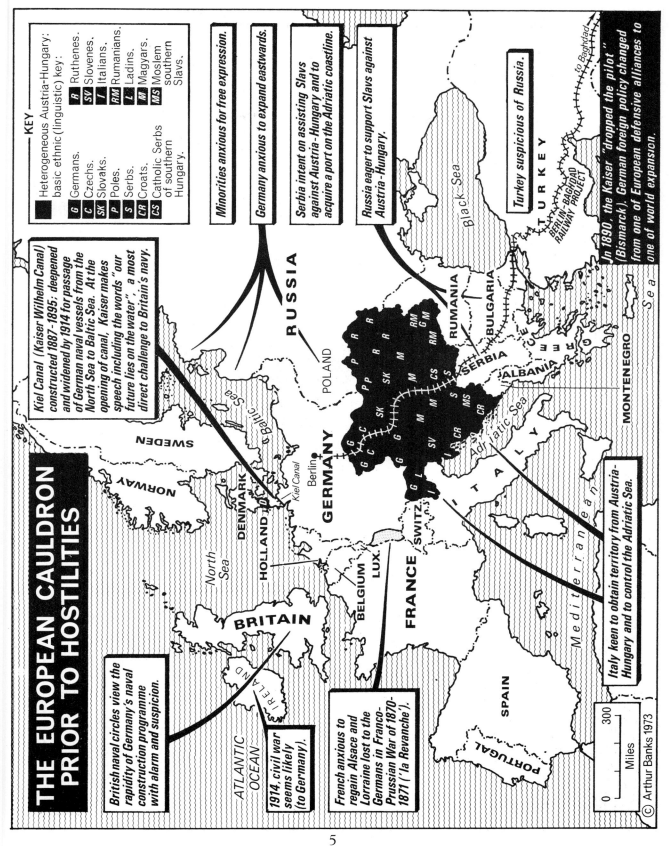

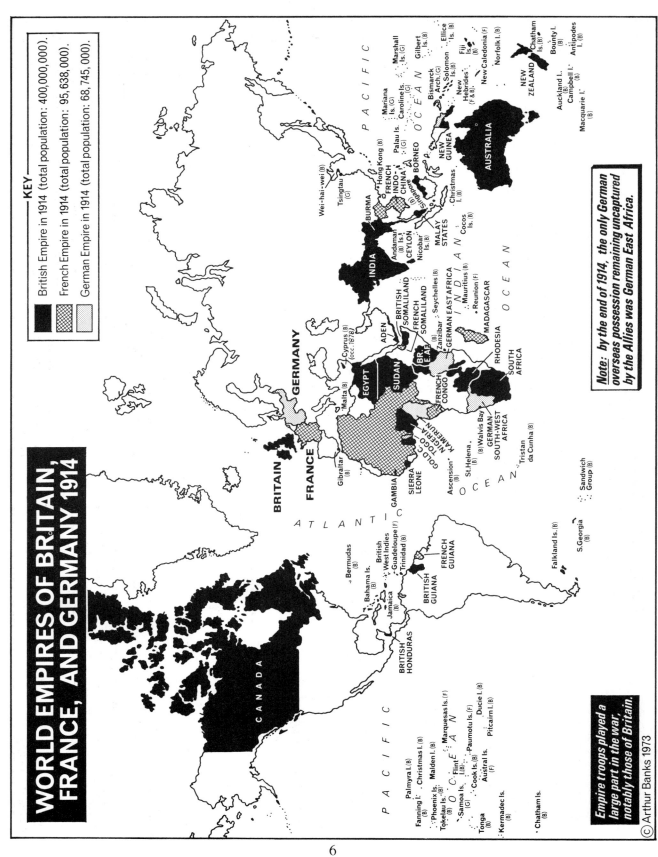

WORLD EMPIRES OF BRITAIN, FRANCE, AND GERMANY 1914

KEY

■	British Empire in 1914 (total population: 400,000,000).
▨	French Empire in 1914 (total population: 95,638,000).
▦	German Empire in 1914 (total population: 68,745,000).

Note: by the end of 1914, the only German overseas possession remaining uncaptured by the Allies was German East Africa.

Empire troops played a large part in the war, notably those of Britain.

© Arthur Banks 1973

6

CRISES IN NORTH AFRICA AND THE BALKANS 1905-1912

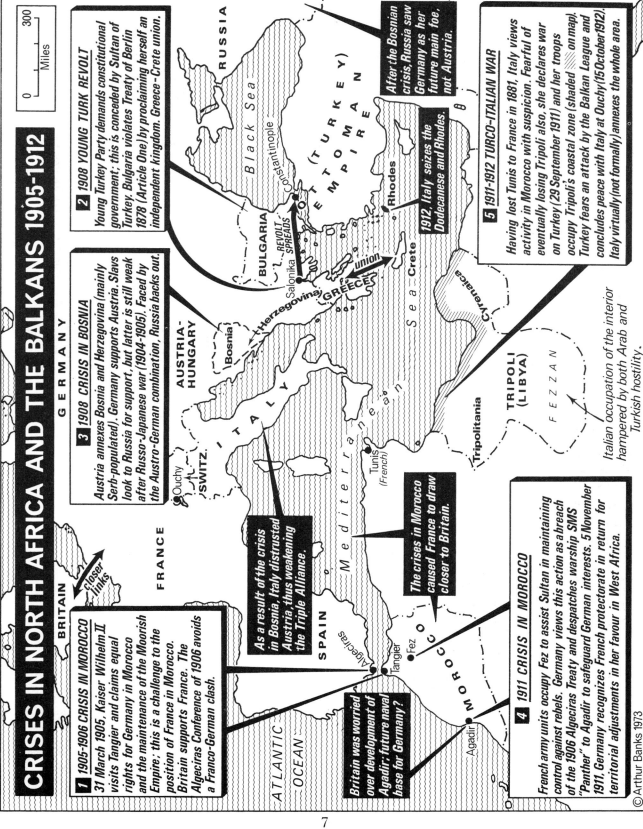

2 *1908 YOUNG TURK REVOLT*

Young Turkey Party demands constitutional government; this is conceded by Sultan of Turkey. Bulgaria violates Treaty of Berlin 1878 (Article One) by proclaiming herself an independent kingdom. Greece–Crete union.

After the Bosnian crisis, Russia saw Germany as her future main foe, not Austria.

5 *1911-1912 TURCO-ITALIAN WAR*

Having lost Tunis to France in 1881, Italy views activity in Morocco with suspicion. Fearful of eventually losing Tripoli also, she declares war on Turkey (29 September 1911) and her troops occupy Tripoli's coastal zone (shaded ░ on map). Turkey fears an attack by the Balkan League and concludes peace with Italy at Ouchy (15 October 1912). Italy virtually (not formally) annexes the whole area.

1912, Italy seizes the Dodecanese and Rhodes.

3 *1908 CRISIS IN BOSNIA*

Austria annexes Bosnia and Herzegovina (mainly Serb-populated). Germany supports Austria. Slavs look to Russia for support, but latter is still weak after Russo-Japanese war (1904-1905). Faced by the Austro–German combination, Russia backs out.

REVOLT SPREADS

union

Italian occupation of the interior hampered by both Arab and Turkish hostility.

As a result of the crisis in Bosnia, Italy distrusted Austria, thus weakening the Triple Alliance.

The crises in Morocco caused France to draw closer to Britain.

1 *1905-1906 CRISIS IN MOROCCO*

31 March 1905, Kaiser Wilhelm II visits Tangier and claims equal rights for Germany in Morocco and the maintenance of the Moorish Empire; this is a challenge to the position of France in Morocco. Britain supports France. The Algeciras Conference of 1906 avoids a Franco-German clash.

Britain was worried over development of Agadir; future naval base for Germany?

4 *1911 CRISIS IN MOROCCO*

French army units occupy Fez to assist Sultan in maintaining control against rebels. Germany views this action as a breach of the 1906 Algeciras Treaty and despatches warship SMS "Panther" to Agadir to safeguard German interests. 5 November 1911, Germany recognizes French protectorate in return for territorial adjustments in her favour in West Africa.

closer links

RUSSIA

Black Sea

Constantinople

BULGARIA

T U R K E Y
(O T T O M A N)
E M P I R E

Rhodes

Salonika

Herzegovina

GREECE — Crete

Bosnia

AUSTRIA-HUNGARY

GERMANY

Ouchy

SWITZ.

FRANCE

BRITAIN

ITALY

S e a

Cyrenaica

TRIPOLI
(LIBYA)

F E Z Z A N

Tripolitania

Mediterranean

Tunis
(French)

SPAIN

Algeciras

Tangier

Fez

M O R O C C O

Agadir

ATLANTIC
OCEAN

0   300
Miles

© Arthur Banks 1973

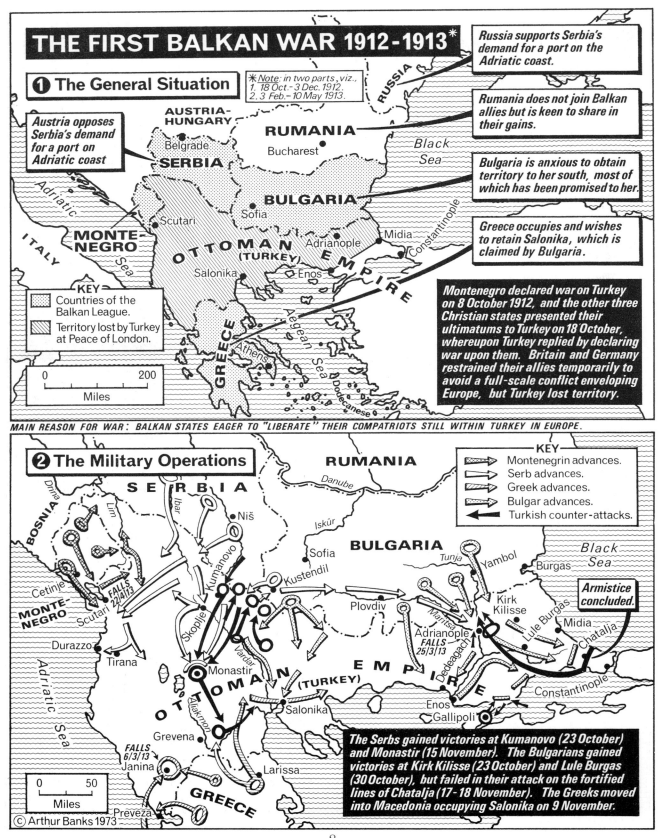

THE FIRST BALKAN WAR 1912-1913*

❶ The General Situation

Note: in two parts, viz.,
1. *18 Oct.- 3 Dec. 1912.*
2. *3 Feb.- 10 May 1913.*

Russia supports Serbia's demand for a port on the Adriatic coast.

Austria opposes Serbia's demand for a port on Adriatic coast

Rumania does not join Balkan allies but is keen to share in their gains.

Bulgaria is anxious to obtain territory to her south, most of which has been promised to her.

Greece occupies and wishes to retain Salonika, which is claimed by Bulgaria.

RUSSIA

AUSTRIA-HUNGARY

RUMANIA

Belgrade

Bucharest

SERBIA

Black Sea

BULGARIA

Scutari

Sofia

Adriatic Sea

MONTE-NEGRO

Midia

Adrianople

Constantinople

ITALY

OTTOMAN (TURKEY) EMPIRE

Salonika

Enos

KEY

▨ Countries of the Balkan League.

▨ Territory lost by Turkey at Peace of London.

GREECE

Aegean Sea

Athens

Dodecanese

0 — 200 Miles

Montenegro declared war on Turkey on 8 October 1912, and the other three Christian states presented their ultimatums to Turkey on 18 October, whereupon Turkey replied by declaring war upon them. Britain and Germany restrained their allies temporarily to avoid a full-scale conflict enveloping Europe, but Turkey lost territory.

MAIN REASON FOR WAR: BALKAN STATES EAGER TO "LIBERATE" THEIR COMPATRIOTS STILL WITHIN TURKEY IN EUROPE.

❷ The Military Operations

KEY

⇒ Montenegrin advances.
⇒ Serb advances.
⇒ Greek advances.
⇒ Bulgar advances.
← Turkish counter-attacks.

RUMANIA

SERBIA

Danube

Drina

Lim

Ibar

Niš

Iskûr

BOSNIA

Sofia

BULGARIA

Tunja

Yambol

Burgas

Black Sea

Cetinje

Kumanovo

Kustendil

Plovdiv

Kirk Kilisse

MONTE-NEGRO

FALLS 22/4/13

Scutari

Skopije

Maritsa

Adrianople FALLS 25/3/13

Lule Burgas

Midia

Durazzo

Vardar

Dedeagach

Chatalja

Tirana

Monastir

OTTOMAN (TURKEY) EMPIRE

Constantinople

Aliakmon

Salonika

Enos

Grevena

Gallipoli

FALLS 6/3/13 Janina

Larissa

0 — 50 Miles

GREECE

Preveza

The Serbs gained victories at Kumanovo (23 October) and Monastir (15 November). The Bulgarians gained victories at Kirk Kilisse (23 October) and Lule Burgas (30 October), but failed in their attack on the fortified lines of Chatalja (17-18 November). The Greeks moved into Macedonia occupying Salonika on 9 November.

Armistice concluded.

© Arthur Banks 1973

8

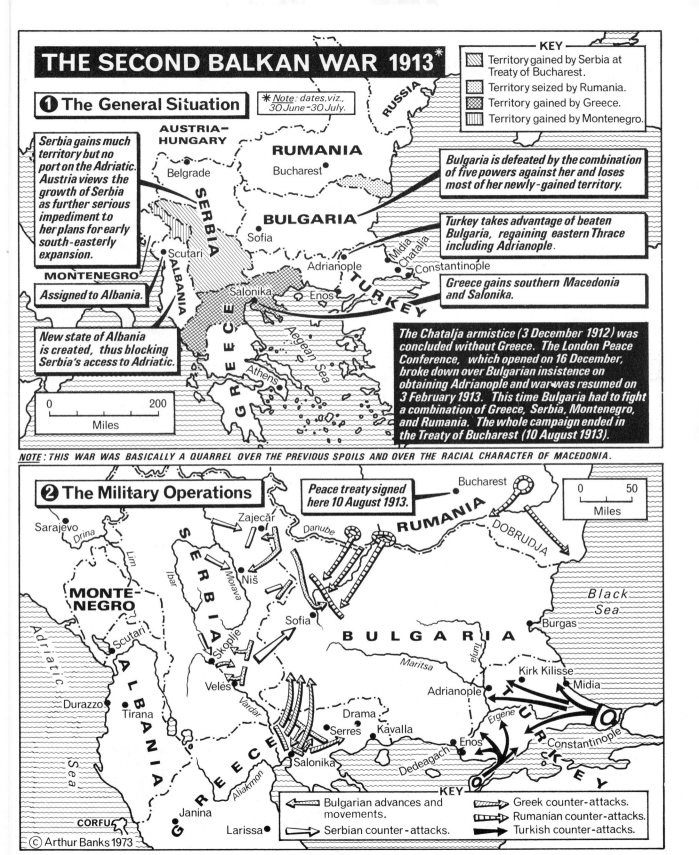

THE SECOND BALKAN WAR 1913*

KEY
- Territory gained by Serbia at Treaty of Bucharest.
- Territory seized by Rumania.
- Territory gained by Greece.
- Territory gained by Montenegro.

❶ The General Situation

Note: dates, viz., 30 June – 30 July.

Serbia gains much territory but no port on the Adriatic. Austria views the growth of Serbia as further serious impediment to her plans for early south-easterly expansion.

Assigned to Albania.

New state of Albania is created, thus blocking Serbia's access to Adriatic.

Bulgaria is defeated by the combination of five powers against her and loses most of her newly-gained territory.

Turkey takes advantage of beaten Bulgaria, regaining eastern Thrace including Adrianople.

Greece gains southern Macedonia and Salonika.

The Chatalja armistice (3 December 1912) was concluded without Greece. The London Peace Conference, which opened on 16 December, broke down over Bulgarian insistence on obtaining Adrianople and war was resumed on 3 February 1913. This time Bulgaria had to fight a combination of Greece, Serbia, Montenegro, and Rumania. The whole campaign ended in the Treaty of Bucharest (10 August 1913).

RUSSIA · AUSTRIA–HUNGARY · RUMANIA · Bucharest · Belgrade · SERBIA · BULGARIA · Sofia · Midia · Chatalja · Adrianople · Constantinople · MONTENEGRO · Scutari · ALBANIA · Salonika · Enos · TURKEY · GREECE · Aegean Sea · Athens

0 — 200 Miles

NOTE: THIS WAR WAS BASICALLY A QUARREL OVER THE PREVIOUS SPOILS AND OVER THE RACIAL CHARACTER OF MACEDONIA.

❷ The Military Operations

Peace treaty signed here 10 August 1913.

0 — 50 Miles

Sarajevo · Drina · Zaječar · Danube · RUMANIA · Bucharest · DOBRUDJA · Lim · SERBIA · Ibar · Morava · Niš · MONTE-NEGRO · Scutari · Sofia · Black Sea · Burgas · Skoplje · BULGARIA · Durazzo · Tirana · ALBANIA · Velés · Vardar · Maritsa · Tunja · Kirk Kilisse · Midia · Drama · Adrianople · Ergene · Serres · Kavalla · Enos · Constantinople · Salonika · Dedeagach · TURKEY · Aliakmon · GREECE · Janina · Adriatic Sea · CORFU · Larissa

KEY
- ⬅ Bulgarian advances and movements.
- ⬜⬜➡ Serbian counter-attacks.
- ▨➡ Greek counter-attacks.
- ⬛⬛➡ Rumanian counter-attacks.
- ➡ Turkish counter-attacks.

© Arthur Banks 1973

9

THE 'SPARK'—ASSASSINATION OF FRANZ FERDINAND 28 JUNE 1914

The assassination of Archduke Franz Ferdinand (heir to the throne of Austria-Hungary) and his wife at Sarajevo, capital of Bosnia, was the spark igniting a chain reaction sequence that led to the outbreak of war in 1914. A group of conspirators associated with two Balkan Slav societies (the 'Black Hand' and the 'Young Bosnia') were involved in the plot, which was put into operation on St. Vitus' Day (a Serbian festival).

The first attempt failed, but the Archduke, who was on an official visit to Sarajevo, went on to the Town Hall as arranged. The return route was altered but the driver of the Archdukes car misunderstood the change of plan (due to poor briefing) and followed the leading car into Franz Josef Street. Princip, one of the conspirators, saw the car reversing into Appel Quay, ran into the road and shot the Archduke and Duchess.

THE TRAGIC FAMILY HISTORY OF FRANZ JOSEF (EMPEROR OF AUSTRIA)

1867. His brother, Emperor of Mexico, was executed.
1889. His son, Crown Prince Rudolf, died mysteriously.
1898. His wife, Empress Elizabeth, was assassinated.

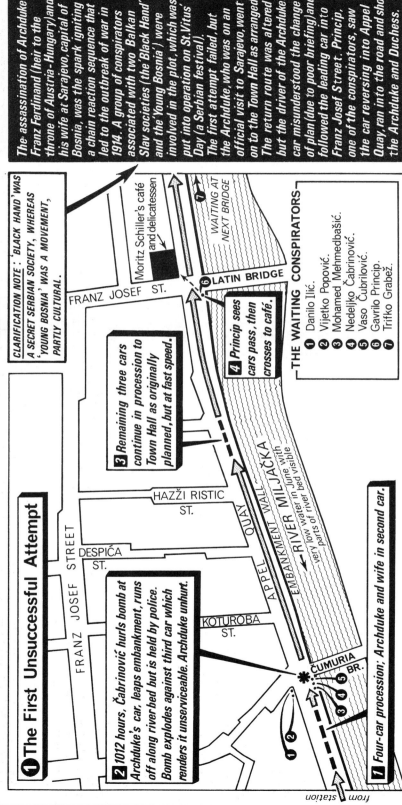

① The First Unsuccessful Attempt

2 1012 hours, Čabrinović hurls bomb at Archduke's car, leaps embankment, runs off along river bed but is held by police. Bomb explodes against third car which renders it unserviceable. Archduke unhurt.

3 Remaining three cars continue in procession to Town Hall as originally planned, but at fast speed.

4 Princip sees cars pass, then crosses to café.

1 Four-car procession; Archduke and wife in second car.

THE WAITING CONSPIRATORS

① Danilo Ilić.
② Vijetko Popović.
③ Mohamed Mehmedbašić.
④ Nedeljko Čabrinović.
⑤ Vaso Čubrilović.
⑥ Gavrilo Princip.
⑦ Trifko Grabež.

Moritz Schiller's café and delicatessen

FRANZ JOSEF ST.

LATIN BRIDGE

WAITING AT NEXT BRIDGE

RIVER MILJAČKA with very low water in June, parts of river bed visible

EMBANKMENT WALL

APPEL QUAY

HAZŽI RISTIC ST.

DESPIĆA ST.

FRANZ JOSEF STREET

KOTUROBA ST.

CUMURIA BR.

from station

② The Second Successful Attempt

Princip (positioned at Schiller's store) fires two shots from Browning automatic at five yards range (1045 hours). Archduke and wife mortally wounded.

visit to museum

FRANZ JOSEF STREET

APPEL QUAY

LATIN BR.

RIVER

MILJAČKA

KEY

- - - Return route from Town Hall as originally planned (before Čabrinović's bomb action).
······· Revised return route (after bomb action).
⑤ Moritz Schiller's delicatessen/café shop.
Ⓖ Position of car during Princip's action.

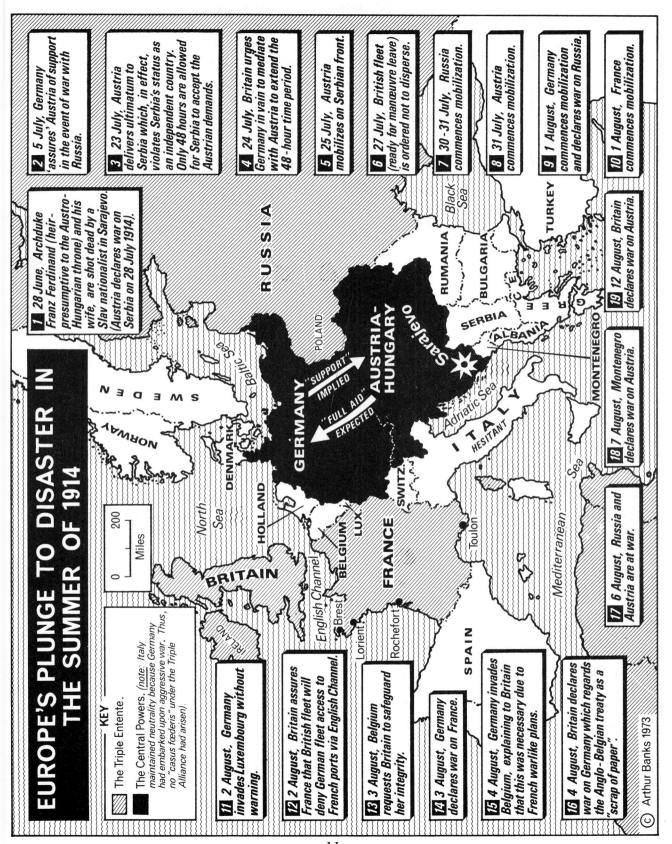

EUROPE'S PLUNGE TO DISASTER IN THE SUMMER OF 1914

KEY

The Triple Entente.

The Central Powers. (*note:* Italy maintained neutrality because Germany had embarked upon aggressive war. Thus, no "casus foederis" under the Triple Alliance had arisen).

0   200
Miles

1 28 June, Archduke Franz Ferdinand (heir-presumptive to the Austro-Hungarian throne) and his wife, are shot dead by a Slav nationalist in Sarajevo. (Austria declares war on Serbia on 28 July 1914).

2 5 July, Germany 'assures' Austria of support in the event of war with Russia.

3 23 July, Austria delivers ultimatum to Serbia which, in effect, violates Serbia's status as an independent country. Only 48 hours are allowed for Serbia to accept the Austrian demands.

4 24 July. Britain urges Germany in vain to mediate with Austria to extend the 48-hour time period.

5 25 July, Austria mobilizes on Serbian front.

6 27 July, British fleet (ready for manoeuvre leave) is ordered not to disperse.

7 30-31 July, Russia commences mobilization.

8 31 July, Austria commences mobilization.

9 1 August, Germany commences mobilization and declares war on Russia.

10 1 August, France commences mobilization.

11 2 August, Germany invades Luxembourg without warning.

12 2 August, Britain assures France that British fleet will deny German fleet access to French ports via English Channel.

13 3 August, Belgium requests Britain to safeguard her integrity.

14 3 August, Germany declares war on France.

15 4 August, Germany invades Belgium, explaining to Britain that this was necessary due to French warlike plans.

16 4 August, Britain declares war on Germany which regards the Anglo-Belgian treaty as a "scrap of paper".

17 6 August, Russia and Austria are at war.

18 7 August, Montenegro declares war on Austria.

19 12 August, Britain declares war on Austria.

GERMANY "SUPPORT" IMPLIED

AUSTRIA-HUNGARY

"FULL AID" EXPECTED

© Arthur Banks 1973

WAR ON THE WESTERN FRONT IN 1914

There had never been so great a concentration of military forces as in August 1914. A little over a century before, Napoleon (who, with Voltaire, believed fortune favoured 'the big battalions') staggered his contemporaries by gathering a Grand Army of 500,000 men to invade Russia. Yet, within a fortnight of the outbreak of war in 1914, the Germans had three times that number in France and Belgium alone. At the same time there were over a million Frenchmen on the Western Front, with three million reservists on call; both the Russians and the Austrians had more than a million and a quarter field troops along their frontiers; and by the end of the year a million volunteers in Britain had come forward for Kitchener's 'New Army'. Napoleon's Marshals counted their big battalions in hundreds of thousands; the commanders of 1914 thought in millions.

These huge numbers determined the character of the war. Military theorists in both France and Germany had long believed victory would come to the nation able rapidly to mobilise its mass of manpower and deploy its forces effectively in the field. It was assumed that the key to success lay in an offensive spirit and that the outcome of the war would be decided by a single campaign on each Front. Kitchener warned the British Cabinet the war would last for at least three years, but his colleagues doubted his powers of judgment. In Berlin that August the Kaiser told departing troops, 'You will be home before the leaves have fallen from the trees'; and few public figures in London, Paris or St Petersburg (soon to be renamed Petrograd) believed the fighting would continue for more than six months. The great tragedy for Europe is that when rapid victory eluded the combatants, the armies—still massive in numbers—became deadlocked in trench warfare, the big battalions checked by the unexpected defensive power of machine guns and exposed to the fury of weapons which the authorities had underrated. It was this transformation of the battlefield which wasted so many lives. Casualties were heavy during the 'war of movement': they were heavier still during the long agony of the 'war of attrition'. At a conservative estimate over the world as a whole—with land fighting in three continents and with warships engaged on every

ocean—one sailor, soldier or airman was killed for every ten seconds the war lasted; and it continued in the end for fifty-one months.

Yet, at the outset, it seemed as if the fighting would indeed 'all be over by Christmas'. The Schlieffen Plan, finally adopted by the German General Staff at the end of 1905, proposed a holding operation against the Russians (who, it was assumed, would be slow to mobilise) in the East while the bulk of the German Army struck against France with an enveloping movement through Flanders and Picardy which would invest Paris from the west and south and thus force the French armies eastwards on to their own defences from Nancy to Belfort. British intervention, though regarded as probable once Belgium was invaded, was discounted as negligible. France defeated, the Germans planned to use the network of railways to move their forces eastwards and destroy the Russian menace. This plan, which was modified by Moltke (Chief of the German General Staff since 1906) in the three years immediately preceding the war, came within an ace of success. The French grand design—Plan XVII—to some extent played into German hands, for it committed two armies to an attack on Lorraine, away from the principal threat to the heart of France. Even when amended after the German invasion of Luxembourg, Plan XVII still ignored the strength of the enemy's thrust into western Belgium. So successful were the Germans that on 30 August the readers of *The Times* in England were startled to learn that 'the investment of Paris cannot be banished from the field of possibility'. What the public was not told was that the French, exhausting themselves by courageous counter-attacks in the spirit of Napoleonic battle panoramas, had already suffered nearly a third of a million casualties (dead, missing, wounded). One out of every ten officers in the whole French army (not merely the regiments in the field) was killed or incapacitated before the end of August 1914.

Moltke's variation on the Schlieffen Plan failed for three principal reasons. He lost touch with his army commanders, who showed excessive independence of manoeuvre; he was so worried by reports of the

Russian advance into East Prussia that he weakened his right wing by detaching troops to the East (compare pages 19, 88 and 89); and he failed to see that three weeks of forced marches in intensive heat and blazing sunshine had reduced the efficiency of the invading armies. When General von Kluck began to move his tired troops south-eastwards, exposing the right flank of the German First Army to the Paris garrison (page 54), the fate of the whole war was in the balance. The French commander-in-chief, Joffre, supported by the Military Governor of Paris, General Gallieni, ordered the French Sixth, Fifth and Ninth Armies (Generals Maunoury, Franchet d'Espèrey and Foch) together with the British Expeditionary Force (Field-Marshal Sir John French) to counter-attack across the lower Marne and its tributaries on 5–6 September. There followed the series of inter-related engagements, the legendary 'miracle of the Marne', fought along a front of more than 125 miles. Momentarily the nerve of the German High Command seemed to crack; Paris and France were saved; the German knock-out blow—which had stunned France in 1870 and which was to stun France again in 1940—was thrust aside.

If the Allies had not themselves been so weary and cautious that September, they might well have turned the German retreat from the Marne into a sensational defeat. As it was, the Germans found they could stabilise their line north of Rheims and along the river Aisne. Moltke retired from active service and was replaced as Chief of the German General Staff by General von Falkenhayn, who at once determined to consolidate the German hold on Belgium, through which the invaders had passed like a scythe in the first weeks of war. When Brussels was occupied on 20 August five divisions of the Belgian Army (80,000 men) fell back on Antwerp, the great fortress-port on the Schelde. So long as the Belgians held Antwerp (from which they made a number of sorties to relieve pressure on the French and British on the Marne and the Aisne) there was a possibility of using the city as a point from which to attack the German right flank. This threat the Germans were determined to eradicate. The First Lord of the Admiralty, Churchill, sought to stiffen resistance in Antwerp by a personal visit and by sending from England a naval division, which was hastily trained and inadequately armed. In the event, the Belgians placed excessive reliance on outdated forts and redoubts which could not withstand the pounding of German artillery. Antwerp duly surrendered to General von Beseler on

9 October, but the main Belgian army withdrew by way of Ghent and Bruges to the line of a canalised small river, the Yser. There, inspired by their courageous King Albert, the Belgians resisted a German advance towards Dunkirk, eventually opening the sluices of Nieuport and bringing the North Sea in flood to the aid of the defenders.

While Beseler was besieging Antwerp, both the Germans and the Allies were engaged in a complicated movement from the Aisne to cover the Channel ports. At times during this 'race for the sea' it seemed as if both sides were risking envelopment by the other during their outflanking operations. Briefly there was hope that the British would capture Lille and open up a route towards Brussels, but they failed to penetrate the town in strength. All six divisions of the B.E.F. were moved northwards from the Aisne to Flanders. By the end of the second week in October they had established a salient around Ypres, Armentières and Neuve Chapelle. It was here that they faced Falkenhayn's principal attempt to break through the Allied positions and take Calais and Boulogne.

The first battle of Ypres (October–November 1914) virtually destroyed the old peacetime British regular army and began to take heavy toll of the new territorial infantry battalions as well. 50,000 British soldiers fell at Ypres that autumn, one division losing two-thirds of its infantry in three weeks of combat. Hardest hit were the original 'old contemptibles', the men who had gone forward to Mons in August (page 47) and retreated for a gruelling fortnight before turning back south of the Marne and forcing the Germans northwards to the Belgian frontier. By the end of November over half of the men who had crossed to France three months previously were casualties, one in ten of them dead. The Germans lost twice as many soldiers as the British at Ypres, yet they never broke through. They penetrated the British line at Gheluvelt on the Menin Road (31 October) but were ejected in a surprise counter attack by the 2nd Battalion of the Worcestershire Regiment, subsequently supported by French units. The city of Ypres was never captured by the Germans, even though fighting raged continuously around the ruined mediaeval cloth town for four years. Ypres and its salient acquired a symbolic significance for the British which was out of all proportion to its strategic value. There were two later battles within the Ypres Salient: in the spring of 1915 (pages 138–143) and from June to November 1917 (pages 172–173); and a final

14

penetration of the German positions in September 1918 (page 196).

Winter set in before the First Battle of Ypres was over. There was no longer any danger of an outright German victory, but equally there was little prospect of an Allied breakthrough. First Ypres marked the end of open warfare: henceforth the opposing armies on the Western Front were paralysed by barbed wire, by entrenchments, by minefields, and by machine-gun emplacements. In another sense, too, First Ypres marked a change of character in the war. The first month of fighting had shown divisions and suspicion between the Allied commanders, especially between the British and the French. The close proximity of British, French and Belgian lines around Ypres helped to weld together the Allied command, although it was difficult to forget old prejudices. The mud-filled disease-ridden trenches bred a sense of communal adversity. At the same time First Ypres showed the extent of Allied resources, for in the line were not only the first battalions of Kitchener's 'new army', but Zouave regiments from French Algeria and Indians from Lahore. Before the fighting died away at the salient in 1918, they were to be joined by units from Canada, Senegal and finally the United States. The cemeteries around Ypres, and the great monument to those 'with no known grave', bear silent testimony to the world-wide character of this most wasteful of wars.

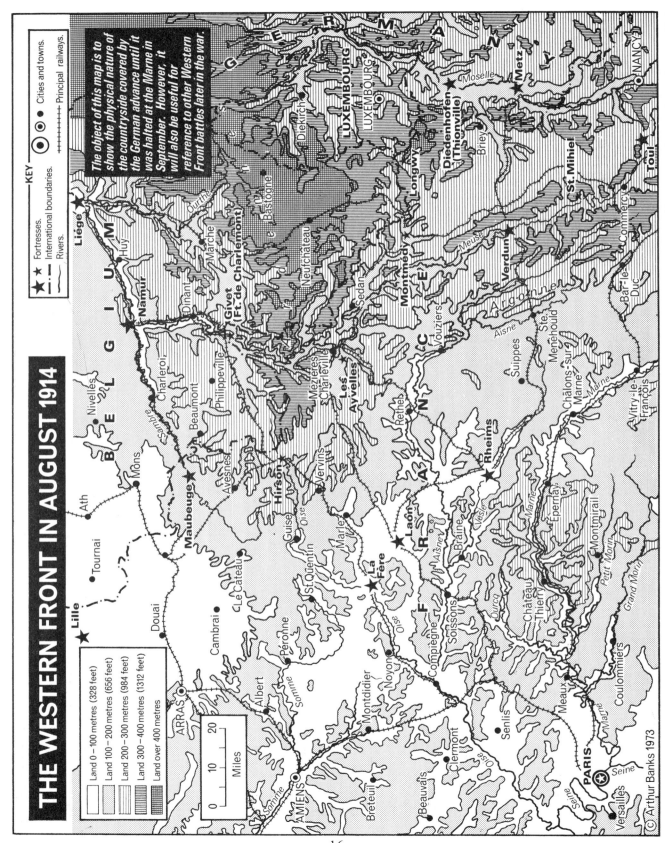

THE WESTERN FRONT IN AUGUST 1914

KEY

★ Fortresses.
-·- International boundaries.
~~ Rivers.

◎ ⊙ ● Cities and towns.
⊕ ⊙ • Principal railways.

The object of this map is to show the physical nature of the countryside covered by the German advance until it was halted at the Marne in September. However, it will also be useful for reference to other Western Front battles later in the war.

Land 0 – 100 metres (328 feet)
Land 100 – 200 metres (656 feet)
Land 200 – 300 metres (984 feet)
Land 300 – 400 metres (1312 feet)
Land over 400 metres

Miles
0   10   20

© Arthur Banks 1973

16

THE WESTERN FRONT IN OUTLINE 1914–1918

The campaign was really one prolonged battle involving territorial gains and losses completely disproportionate to the casualties involved. The basic stages were: the initial German advance of 1914 which was halted at the Marne and Aisne battles: the resulting "race to the sea" (a series of outflanking moves): the fairly stabilized trench line being established: the Allied gains and fights at the Somme and Verdun: the German offensives in the spring of 1918: the Allied advance towards Germany that halted with the Armistice on 11 November 1918.

KEY

- ⋯⋯ Limit of German advance in September 1914.
- ╏╏ General front from end of 1914 to 30 June 1916 (prior to Somme battles).
- ▢ Allied gains in 1916 and 1917.
- ▨ German gains during 1918 offensives.
- ▊ Armistice line on 11 November 1918.
- ·—·— Frontiers in 1914.
- ● Capital cities.
- ● ● Other cities and towns.

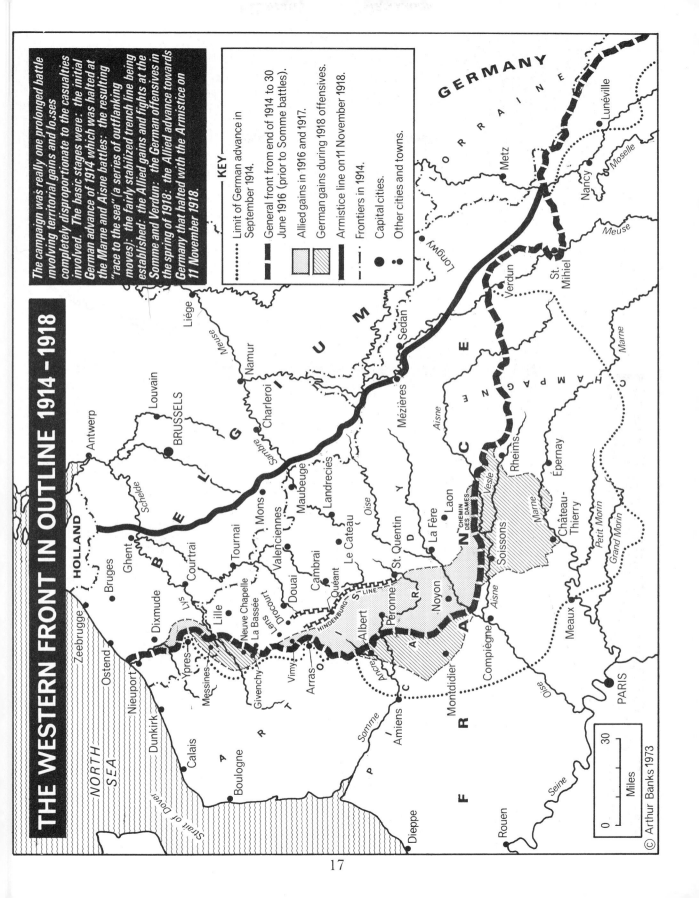

GERMANY

LORRAINE

NORTH SEA

Strait of Dover

HOLLAND

BELGIUM

FRANCE

CHAMPAGNE

ARTOIS

PICARDY

Antwerp
Bruges
Ghent
Zeebrugge
Ostend
Nieuport
Dunkirk
Calais
Boulogne
Dieppe
Rouen
Dixmude
Ypres
Messines
Lille
Neuve Chapelle
La Bassée
Givenchy
Vimy
Arras
Courtrai
Tournai
Lens
Drocourt
Douai
Cambrai
Quéant
Le Cateau
Landrecies
Maubeuge
Valenciennes
Mons
Louvain
BRUSSELS
Namur
Charleroi
Liège
Sambre
Schelde
Lys
Somme
Ancre
Albert
Péronne
Noyon
St. Quentin
La Fère
Laon
HINDENBURG LINE
CHEMIN DES DAMES
Montdidier
Compiègne
Amiens
Meaux
PARIS
Château-Thierry
Soissons
Rheims
Épernay
Mézières
Sedan
Aisne
Vesle
Marne
Petit Morin
Grand Morin
Seine
Oise
Verdun
St. Mihiel
Metz
Nancy
Lunéville
Longwy
Moselle
Meuse

30
Miles
0

© Arthur Banks 1973

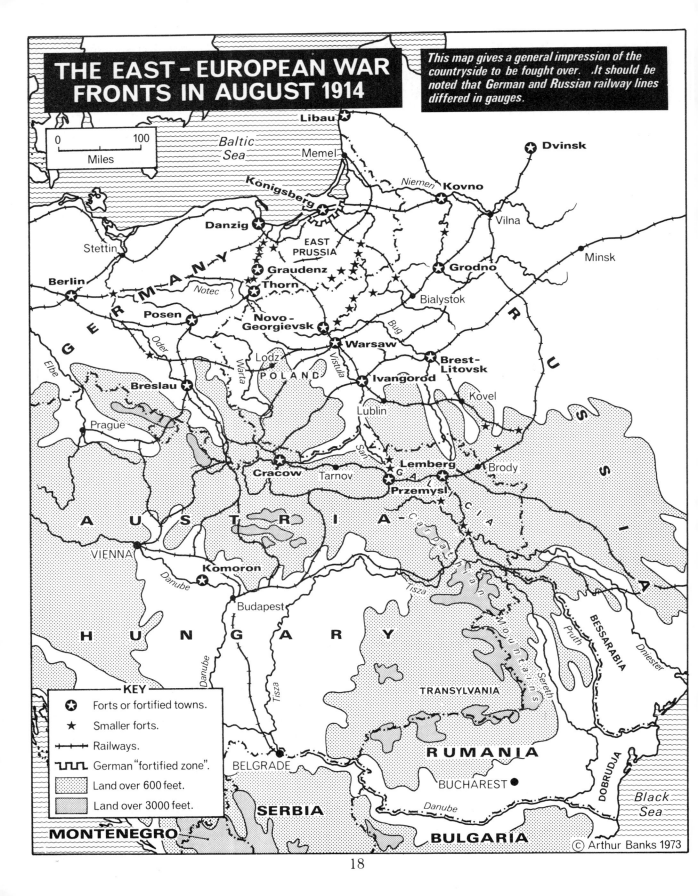

THE EAST-EUROPEAN WAR FRONTS IN AUGUST 1914

This map gives a general impression of the countryside to be fought over. It should be noted that *German* and *Russian* railway lines differed in gauges.

0 — 100
Miles

Baltic Sea

Libau

Memel

Dvinsk

Königsberg

Niemen

Kovno

Vilna

Danzig

EAST PRUSSIA

Graudenz

Thorn

Grodno

Bialystok

Minsk

Stettin

Notec

Berlin

Posen

Novo-Georgievsk

Bug

Warsaw

Brest-Litovsk

GERMANY

Oder

Lodz

POLAND

Vistula

Ivangorod

Kovel

Elbe

Warta

Lublin

Breslau

San

Prague

Kovel

Lemberg

Brody

Cracow

Tarnov

GALICIA

Przemysl

Carpathian

AUSTRIA-

VIENNA

Komoron

Danube

Budapest

Tisza

Mountains

Bessarabia

RUSSIA

Pruth

Dniester

HUNGARY

Danube

Tisza

TRANSYLVANIA

Sereth

RUMANIA

BELGRADE

BUCHAREST

DOBRUDJA

SERBIA

Danube

Black Sea

MONTENEGRO

BULGARIA

© Arthur Banks 1973

KEY
- ✪ Forts or fortified towns.
- ★ Smaller forts.
- ┼┼┼ Railways.
- ⊔⊔⊔ German "fortified zone".
- Land over 600 feet.
- Land over 3000 feet.

18

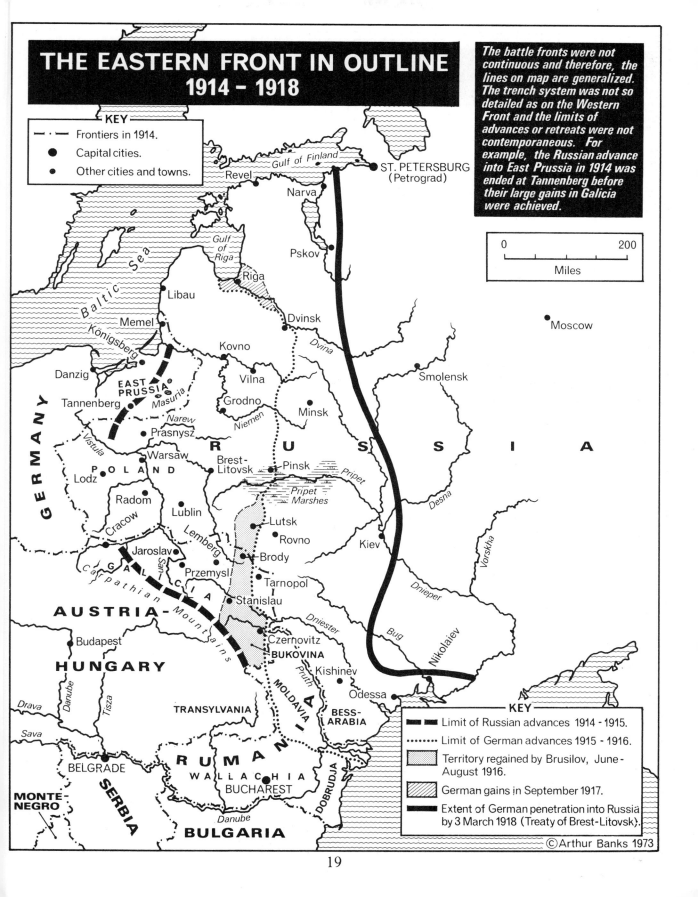

THE EASTERN FRONT IN OUTLINE 1914 - 1918

The battle fronts were not continuous and therefore, the lines on map are generalized. The trench system was not so detailed as on the Western Front and the limits of advances or retreats were not contemporaneous. For example, the Russian advance into East Prussia in 1914 was ended at Tannenberg before their large gains in Galicia were achieved.

KEY

- —·— Frontiers in 1914.
- ● Capital cities.
- • Other cities and towns.

0 ____ 200

Miles

Gulf of Finland

Revel

Narva

● ST. PETERSBURG (Petrograd)

Baltic Sea

Gulf of Riga

Pskov

Riga

Libau

Dvinsk

● Moscow

Memel

Königsberg

Dvina

Danzig

Kovno

EAST PRUSSIA

Masuria

Vilna

Smolensk

Tannenberg

Narew

Grodno

Niemen

Minsk

Prasnysz

Vistula

R U S S I A

Warsaw

Brest-Litovsk

Pinsk

Pripet

Lodz

POLAND

Pripet Marshes

Desna

Radom

Lublin

Cracow

Lutsk

Lemberg

Rovno

San

Jaroslav

Brody

Kiev

Vorskha

GALICIA

Przemysl

Tarnopol

Carpathian Mountains

Stanislau

Dniester

AUSTRIA - HUNGARY

Czernovitz

Bug

Nikolaiev

Budapest

BUKOVINA

Dnieper

Kishinev

HUNGARY

MOLDAVIA

BESS- ARABIA

Odessa

Drava

Danube

Tisza

Pruth

Sava

TRANSYLVANIA

R U M A N I A

KEY

BELGRADE

WALLACHIA

DOBRUDJA

BUCHAREST

- ▬ ▬ Limit of Russian advances 1914 - 1915.
- ······· Limit of German advances 1915 - 1916.
- Territory regained by Brusilov, June - August 1916.
- German gains in September 1917.
- ▬▬▬ Extent of German penetration into Russia by 3 March 1918 (Treaty of Brest-Litovsk).

MONTE-NEGRO

SERBIA

Danube

BULGARIA

©Arthur Banks 1973

GERMANY

MONTE-NEGRO

© Arthur Banks 1973

❶ The Elder Moltke's Appraisal (1879)

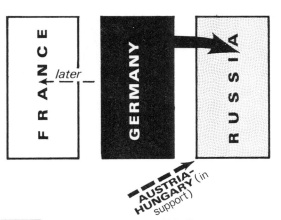

RUSSIA *must be dealt with FIRST.* Count von Waldersee (Moltke's successor) agreed with this provided that the offensive against Russia be conducted in summer weather.

❷ Schlieffen's Appraisal (1905)

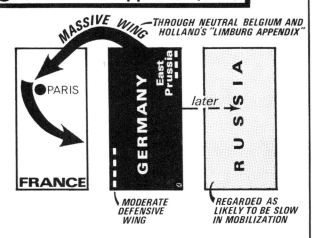

MASSIVE WING — THROUGH NEUTRAL BELGIUM AND HOLLAND'S "LIMBURG APPENDIX"

MODERATE DEFENSIVE WING

REGARDED AS LIKELY TO BE SLOW IN MOBILIZATION

FRANCE *must be dealt with FIRST in a rapid campaign while Russia is kept at bay by means of a holding or delaying operation in East Prussia. Austria in support.*

❸ Schlieffen's Revised Appraisal (1912)

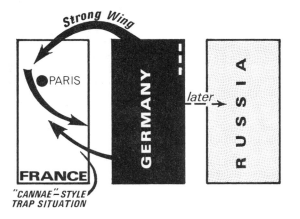

Strong Wing

"CANNAE"-STYLE TRAP SITUATION

Apparently Schlieffen studied Hannibal's victory at Cannae (216 B.C.) in detail and, as a consequence, revised his own plan. But the German right wing was to be kept strong.

❹ The Younger Moltke's Appraisal (1914)

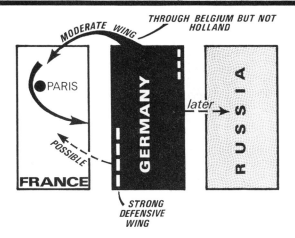

THROUGH BELGIUM BUT NOT HOLLAND

MODERATE WING

POSSIBLE

STRONG DEFENSIVE WING

Moltke (nephew of Bismarck's general) strengthened his defensive wing at the expense of his right wing: he omitted ersatz "back up" formations at rear of right wing armies.

In all plans, Germany had to attack first to obviate her fighting an all-out war on two fronts simultaneously: the two potential enemies had to be fought in sequence to avoid splitting Germany's main effort. Everything hinged upon her ability to switch troops from front to front with speed and precision. Even in August 1914, Germany was not powerful enough to launch two major offensives at the same time. Her fear was that SHE might be attacked first!

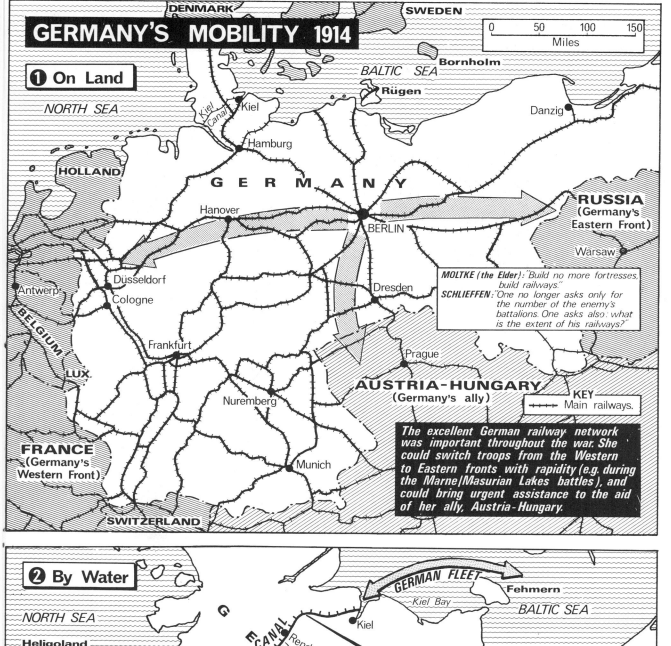

GERMANY'S MOBILITY 1914

❶ On Land

DENMARK

SWEDEN

0 — 50 — 100 — 150
Miles

BALTIC SEA

Bornholm

Rügen

NORTH SEA

Kiel Canal

Kiel

Danzig

Hamburg

HOLLAND

G E R M A N Y

RUSSIA
(Germany's
Eastern Front)

Hanover

BERLIN

Warsaw

Antwerp

Düsseldorf

Cologne

Dresden

MOLTKE (the Elder): "Build no more fortresses,
build railways."
SCHLIEFFEN: "One no longer asks only for
the number of the enemy's
battalions. One asks also: what
is the extent of his railways?"

BELGIUM

LUX.

Frankfurt

Prague

Nuremberg

AUSTRIA-HUNGARY
(Germany's ally)

KEY
—|—|— Main railways.

FRANCE
(Germany's
Western Front)

Munich

SWITZERLAND

The excellent German railway network
was important throughout the war. She
could switch troops from the Western
to Eastern fronts with rapidity (e.g. during
the Marne/Masurian Lakes battles), and
could bring urgent assistance to the aid
of her ally, Austria-Hungary.

❷ By Water

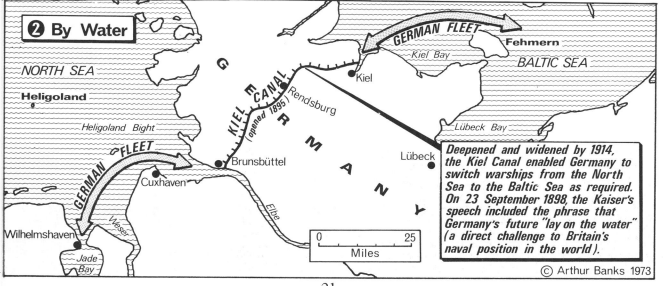

NORTH SEA

G

GERMAN FLEET

Fehmern

Kiel Bay

BALTIC SEA

Heligoland

KIEL CANAL
(opened 1895)

Rendsburg

Kiel

E
R

Heligoland Bight

M

Lübeck Bay

GERMAN FLEET

A

Brunsbüttel

Lübeck

Cuxhaven

N

Y

Elbe

Deepened and widened by 1914,
the Kiel Canal enabled Germany to
switch warships from the North
Sea to the Baltic Sea as required.
On 23 September 1898, the Kaiser's
speech included the phrase that
Germany's future "lay on the water"
(a direct challenge to Britain's
naval position in the world).

Wilhelmshaven

Weser

Jade
Bay

0 — 25
Miles

© Arthur Banks 1973

21

GERMAN MILITARY PLANS 1905-1914

In the years before 1914, German military planners were haunted by fear of an all-out war on two fronts simultaneously (that is, against Russia and France). In 1905, Field-Marshal Graf Alfred Schlieffen prepared a plan based on an assumption that Russia (calculated to be slower in mobilization than France) could be held temporarily at bay, while the bulk of German military power be directed at securing a rapid victory over France. Thus, Schlieffen's plan dealt almost exclusively with the Western Front. Moltke, Schlieffen's successor as Chief of the German General Staff, modified the scheme on several occasions before the war, and an amended version was put into operation in August 1914. Despite initial successes, the plan failed to produce the expected quick victory, and the Western Front became a scene of almost rigid trench warfare until 1918.

① A War on Two Fronts

GERMANY
(efficient rail network linking both fronts)

Holland

Poland

RUSSIA

Belgium

Lux.

• Paris

FRANCE

Austria-Hungary
(Allied with Germany)

Switz.

0   200
Miles

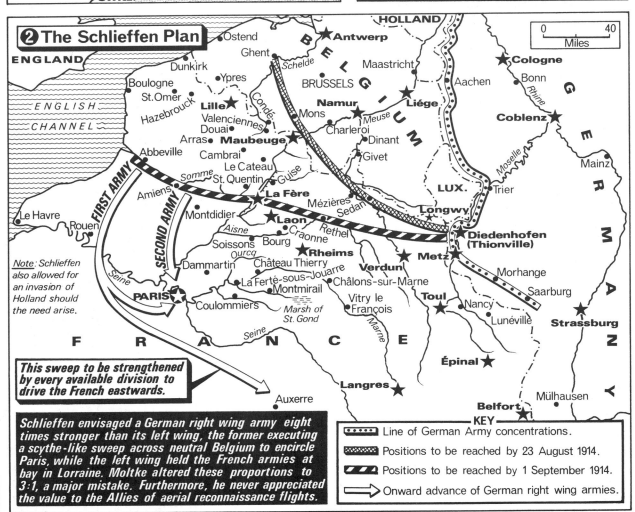

② The Schlieffen Plan

ENGLAND

HOLLAND

0   40
Miles

Ostend

Antwerp

BELGIUM

Maastricht

Cologne

Ghent

Schelde

Aachen

Bonn

Rhine

GERMANY

Dunkirk

Ypres

BRUSSELS

Liége

Boulogne

St.Omer

Lille

Namur

Coblenz

Hazebrouck

Valenciennes

Mons

Charleroi

Meuse

ENGLISH CHANNEL

Douai

Condé

Dinant

Arras

Maubeuge

Givet

Moselle

Mainz

Abbeville

Cambrai

Le Cateau

Guise

LUX.

Trier

FIRST ARMY

Somme

St. Quentin

La Fère

Mézières

Sedan

Longwy

Le Havre

Amiens

Montdidier

Laon

Rethel

Diedenhofen
(Thionville)

Rouen

SECOND ARMY

Aisne

Craonne

Bourg

Soissons

Rheims

Metz

Morhange

Ourcq

Château Thierry

Verdun

Dammartin

La Ferté-sous-Jouarre

Châlons-sur-Marne

Saarburg

Seine

PARIS

Montmirail

Vitry le François

Toul

Nancy

Coulommiers

Marsh of St. Gond

Lunéville

Strassburg

Seine

FRANCE

Marne

Épinal

Note: Schlieffen also allowed for an invasion of Holland should the need arise.

This sweep to be strengthened by every available division to drive the French eastwards.

Auxerre

Langres

Belfort

Mülhausen

Schlieffen envisaged a German right wing army eight times stronger than its left wing, the former executing a scythe-like sweep across neutral Belgium to encircle Paris, while the left wing held the French armies at bay in Lorraine. Moltke altered these proportions to 3:1, a major mistake. Furthermore, he never appreciated the value to the Allies of aerial reconnaissance flights.

KEY

•••••• Line of German Army concentrations.

▨▨▨▨ Positions to be reached by 23 August 1914.

▰▰▰▰ Positions to be reached by 1 September 1914.

⟹ Onward advance of German right wing armies.

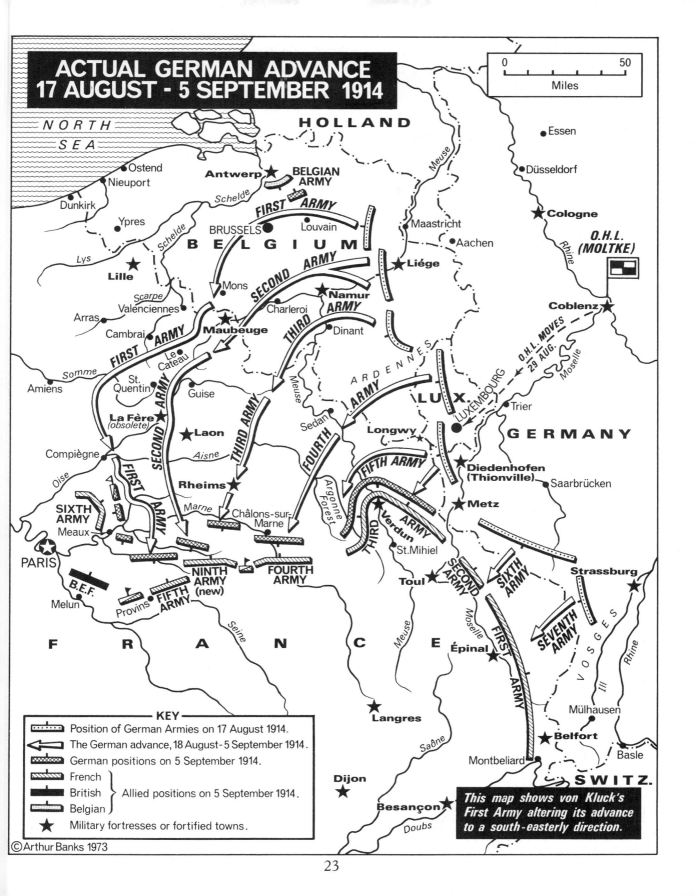

ACTUAL GERMAN ADVANCE
17 AUGUST - 5 SEPTEMBER 1914

0 — 50
Miles

NORTH SEA

HOLLAND

• Essen

• Ostend
Nieuport

• Düsseldorf

Dunkirk

Antwerp ★ **BELGIAN ARMY**

Schelde

FIRST ARMY

BRUSSELS • Louvain

• Maastricht

★ Cologne

Ypres

BELGIUM

Schelde

SECOND ARMY

★ Liége

• Aachen

O.H.L. (MOLTKE)

★ Lille

Lys

Mons

★ **Namur ARMY**

Charleroi

Coblenz ★

Scarpe

Valenciennes

THIRD

★ **Maubeuge**

• Dinant

ARDENNES

Rhine

Arras

Cambrai

FIRST ARMY

Le Cateau

O.H.L. MOVES 29 AUG.

Somme

St. Quentin

Guise

I ARMY

LUX. LUXEMBOURG

• Trier

GERMANY

Amiens

La Fère (obsolete) ★

SECOND ARMY

★ **Laon**

Aisne

Sedan

FOURTH

Longwy

FIFTH ARMY

★ Diedenhofen (Thionville)

• Saarbrücken

Moselle

Compiègne

FIRST ARMY

Rheims ★

THIRD ARMY

Argonne Forest

★ Metz

Oise

Marne

Châlons-sur-Marne

ARMY

Verdun

• St.Mihiel

SIXTH ARMY

Meaux

NINTH ARMY (new)

FOURTH ARMY

SECOND ARMY

Toul ★

SIXTH ARMY

Strassburg ★

PARIS ★

B.E.F.

FIFTH ARMY

FIRST ARMY

SEVENTH ARMY

VOSGES

Melun

Provins

Seine

F R A N C E

Meuse

Épinal ★

Moselle

Rhine

Ill

• Mülhausen

★ Langres

Saône

★ Dijon

★ Belfort

Montbeliard

Basle

KEY
- ┅┅┅ Position of German Armies on 17 August 1914.
- ⟵ The German advance, 18 August-5 September 1914.
- ▨▨▨ German positions on 5 September 1914.
- ▨ French
- ▬ British } Allied positions on 5 September 1914.
- ▭ Belgian
- ★ Military fortresses or fortified towns.

© Arthur Banks 1973

Doubs

S W I T Z.

Besançon ★

This map shows von Kluck's First Army altering its advance to a south-easterly direction.

23

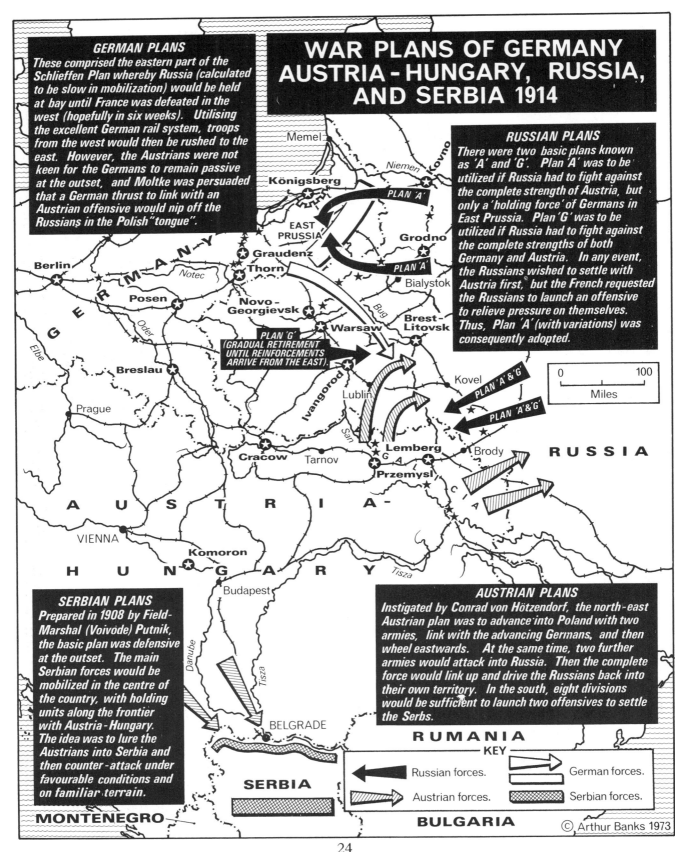

WAR PLANS OF GERMANY AUSTRIA - HUNGARY, RUSSIA, AND SERBIA 1914

GERMAN PLANS

These comprised the eastern part of the Schlieffen Plan whereby Russia (calculated to be slow in mobilization) would be held at bay until France was defeated in the west (hopefully in six weeks). Utilising the excellent German rail system, troops from the west would then be rushed to the east. However, the Austrians were not keen for the Germans to remain passive at the outset, and Moltke was persuaded that a German thrust to link with an Austrian offensive would nip off the Russians in the Polish "tongue".

RUSSIAN PLANS

There were two basic plans known as 'A' and 'G'. Plan 'A' was to be utilized if Russia had to fight against the complete strength of Austria, but only a 'holding force' of Germans in East Prussia. Plan 'G' was to be utilized if Russia had to fight against the complete strengths of both Germany and Austria. In any event, the Russians wished to settle with Austria first, but the French requested the Russians to launch an offensive to relieve pressure on themselves. Thus, Plan 'A' (with variations) was consequently adopted.

SERBIAN PLANS

Prepared in 1908 by Field-Marshal (Voivode) Putnik, the basic plan was defensive at the outset. The main Serbian forces would be mobilized in the centre of the country, with holding units along the frontier with Austria-Hungary. The idea was to lure the Austrians into Serbia and then counter-attack under favourable conditions and on familiar terrain.

AUSTRIAN PLANS

Instigated by Conrad von Hötzendorf, the north-east Austrian plan was to advance into Poland with two armies, link with the advancing Germans, and then wheel eastwards. At the same time, two further armies would attack into Russia. Then the complete force would link up and drive the Russians back into their own territory. In the south, eight divisions would be sufficient to launch two offensives to settle the Serbs.

PLAN 'A'

PLAN 'A'

PLAN 'G'
(GRADUAL RETIREMENT UNTIL REINFORCEMENTS ARRIVE FROM THE EAST).

PLAN 'A & G'

PLAN 'A & G'

0   100
Miles

Memel
Niemen
Kovno
Königsberg
EAST PRUSSIA
Grodno
Bialystok
Berlin
Notec
Graudenz
Thorn
GERMANY
Posen
Novo-Georgievsk
Warsaw
Bug
Brest-Litovsk
Oder
Elbe
Breslau
Ivangorod
Lublin
Kovel
Prague
San
Kracow → Cracow
Tarnov
Lemberg
Brody
RUSSIA
Przemysl
AUSTRIA-
VIENNA
Komoron
HUNGARY
Budapest
Tisza
Danube
Tisza
BELGRADE
RUMANIA
SERBIA
MONTENEGRO
BULGARIA

KEY

Russian forces.	German forces.
Austrian forces.	Serbian forces.

© Arthur Banks 1973

FRENCH PRE-WAR MILITARY PLANS 1914

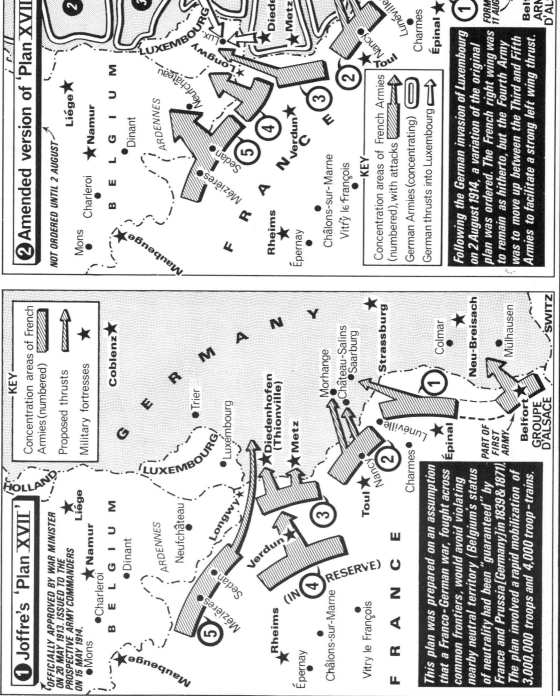

① Joffre's 'Plan XVII'

OFFICIALLY APPROVED BY WAR MINISTER ON 20 MAY 1913. ISSUED TO THE PROSPECTIVE ARMY COMMANDERS ON 15 MAY 1914.

KEY —
- Concentration areas of French Armies (numbered)
- Proposed thrusts
- ★ Military fortresses

This plan was prepared on an assumption that a Franco-German war, fought across common frontiers, would avoid violating nearby neutral territory (Belgium's status of neutrality had been "guaranteed" by France and Prussia (Germany) in 1839 & 1871). The plan involved a rapid mobilization of 3,000,000 troops and 4,000 troop-trains.

② Amended version of 'Plan XVII'

NOT ORDERED UNTIL 2 AUGUST

— KEY —
- German Armies (concentrating)
- Concentration areas of French Armies (numbered), with attacks
- German thrusts into Luxembourg

Following the German invasion of Luxembourg on 2 August 1914, a variation of the original plan was ordered. The French right wing was to remain as hitherto, but the Fourth Army was to move up between the Third and Fifth Armies to facilitate a strong left wing thrust.

The basic weakness of both plans lay in the fact that Germany could strike first, a position which the French felt morally unable to assume in 1914.

0 20 40 Miles

© Arthur Banks 1973

25

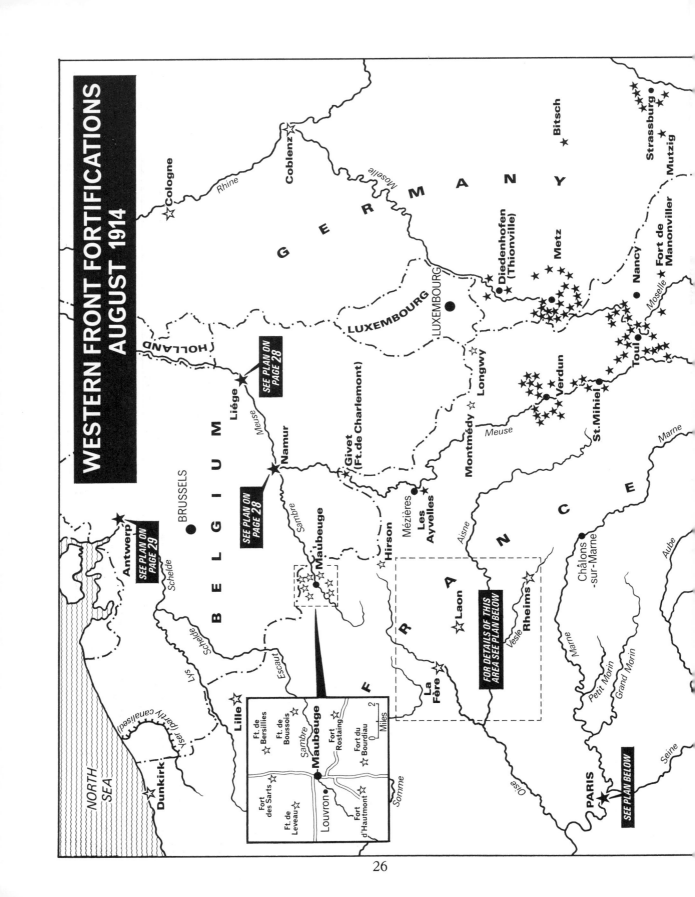

WESTERN FRONT FORTIFICATIONS AUGUST 1914

NORTH SEA

Dunkirk

Antwerp

SEE PLAN ON PAGE 29

Cologne

Rhine

Coblenz

Moselle

G E R M A N Y

Bitsch

Strassburg

Mutzig

HOLLAND

SEE PLAN ON PAGE 28

Liège

Meuse

BRUSSELS

B E L G I U M

Schelde

Lys

Lille

Ft. de Bersillies
Ft. de Boussois
Maubeuge
Fort Rostaing
Fort du Bourdiau
Fort des Sarts
Ft. de Leveau
Louvron
Fort d'Hautmont
Sambre
Somme
Miles

Escaut

Ysergely partly canalised)

Namur

SEE PLAN ON PAGE 28

Sambre

Maubeuge

Givet (Ft. de Charlemont)

Hirson

Mézières
Les Ayvelles

LUXEMBOURG

LUXEMBOURG

Longwy

Montmédy

Diedenhofen (Thionville)

Metz

Verdun

St. Mihiel

Meuse

Nancy

Fort de Manonviller

Moselle

Toul

Aisne

Laon

La Fère

Oise

F R A N C E

Vesle

Rheims

FOR DETAILS OF THIS AREA SEE PLAN BELOW

Marne

Châlons -sur-Marne

Aube

Marne

Petit Morin

Grand Morin

Seine

PARIS

SEE PLAN BELOW

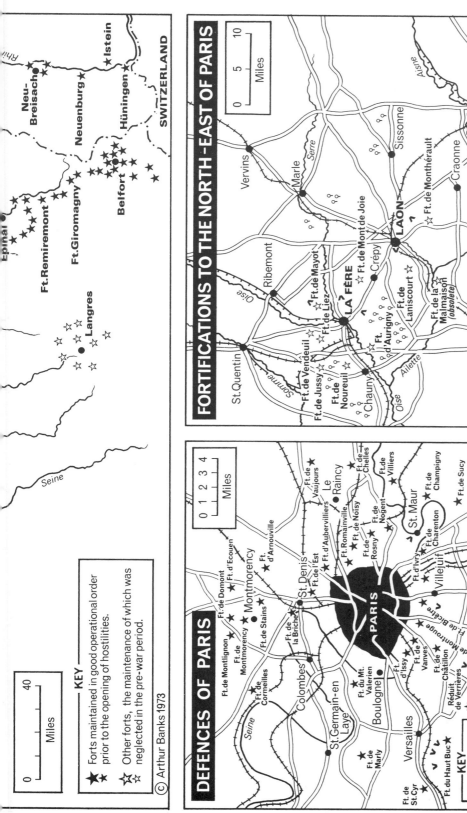

FORTIFICATIONS TO THE NORTH-EAST OF PARIS

Miles
0   5   10

Ft. de Fresnes
Ft. de Vitry
Ft. de la Vigie de Berru
Ft. Nogent l'Abbesse
Ft. de Montbré
Ft. de Brimont
RHEIMS
Ft. de la Pompelle
Moulin
Ft. de St. Thierry
Chenoy
Ft. de Vrigny
Fismes
Vesle
Veste
Ft. de Condé (obsolete)
Soissons
KEY
Aisne
Aisne

Sissonne
Craonne
Ft. de Monthérault
LAON
Ft. de Mont de Joie
Crépy
Ft. de la Malmaison (obsolete)

Vervins
Marle
Serre
Ribemont
Oise
Ft. de Mayot
Ft. de Liez
LA FÈRE
Ft. de Laniscourt
Ft. d'Aurigny
Ft. d'

St. Quentin
Somme
Ft. de Vendeuil
Ft. de Jussy
Ft. de Noureuil
Chauny
Oise
Ailette

KEY
☆ Forts
∨ Redoubts and batteries
ρρ Forests and woods
══ Roads
╫╫ Railways
---- Canals

DEFENCES OF PARIS

Miles
0 1 2 3 4

Ft. de Vaujours
Le Raincy
Ft. de Chelles
Ft. de Villiers
Ft. de Champigny
Ft. de Sucy
Ft. de Noisy
Ft. de Nogent
St. Maur
Ft. de Charenton
Ft. de Villeneuve-St. Georges
Ft. de Limeil
Ft. de Montlignon
Ft. de Domont
Ft. d'Ecouen
Montmorency
Ft. de Montmorency
Ft. de Stains
Ft. d'Arnouville
Ft. d'Aubervilliers
Ft. de Romainville
St. Denis
Ft. de l'Est
Ft. de Rosny
Ft. d'Ivry
Villejuif
Ft. de Bicêtre
Ft. de Montrouge
Ft. de la Briche
Ft. de Cormeilles
Colombes
Seine
Ft. du Mt. Valérien
Boulogne
St. Germain-en-Laye
Ft. d'Issy
Vanves
Ft. de Châtillon
Réduit de Verrières
Ft. de Palaiseau
Versailles
Ft. de Villeras
Ft. de Marly
Ft. du Haut Buc
Ft. de St. Cyr
Seine
PARIS

KEY
★ Forts
∨ Redoubts
══ Roads
╫╫ Railways

This map depicts the system of fortifications that adorned the Western Front area prior to the commencement of hostilities. Many of the northern French fortresses were virtually obsolete or in a state of disrepair and the three Belgian fortresses had been designed in the 1880's and 1890's, long before the advent of "Dicke Bertha" and "Schlanke Emma".

Neu-Breisach
Neuenburg
Istein
Hüningen
SWITZERLAND
Rhine
Rhine
Épinal
Ft. Remiremont
Ft. Giromagny
Belfort
Langres
Seine

KEY
★ ★★ Forts maintained in good operational order prior to the opening of hostilities.
☆ ☆☆ Other forts, the maintenance of which was neglected in the pre-war period.

Miles
0   40

© Arthur Banks 1973

27

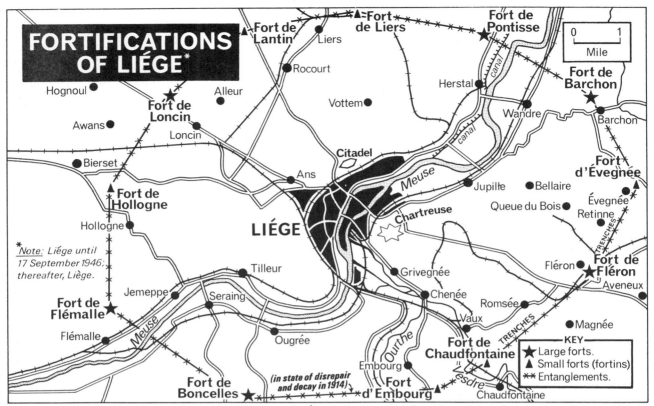

FORTIFICATIONS OF LIÉGE*

Hognoul • Awans • Hollogne • Bierset • Alleur • Rocourt • Liers • Vottem • Herstal • Wandre • Barchon • Jupille • Bellaire • Queue du Bois • Évegnée • Retinne • Fléron • Aveneux • Romsée • Magnée • Vaux • Chenée • Grivegnée • Ougrée • Seraing • Jemeppe • Tilleur • Flémalle • Flémalle • Embourg • Chaudfontaine

Fort de Lantin
Fort de Liers
Fort de Pontisse
Fort de Barchon
Fort de Loncin
Fort d'Évegnée
Citadel
Chartreuse
Ans
LIÉGE
Fort de Hollogne
Fort de Fléron
Fort de Flémalle
Fort de Chaudfontaine
Fort de Boncelles
Fort d'Embourg

(in state of disrepair and decay in 1914)

Note: Liége until 17 September 1946; thereafter, Liège.

Meuse / Ourthe / Vesdre / canal

0 — 1 Mile

KEY
★ Large forts.
▲ Small forts (fortins).
✷✷ Entanglements.

The main forts were pentagonal in shape, whereas the smaller 'fortins' were triangular. All consisted of works beneath ground level, with the guns being housed in steel cupolas which could be raised and lowered again at will. The designer was Henri Brialmont.

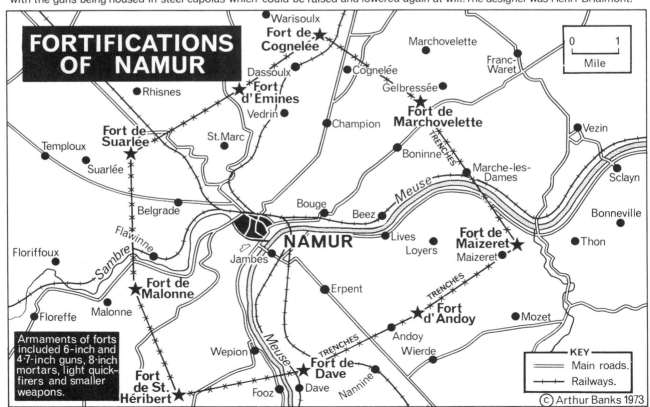

FORTIFICATIONS OF NAMUR

Warisoulx • Marchovelette • Franc-Waret • Dassoulx • Cognelée • Gelbressée • Rhisnes • Vedrin • Champion • Vezin • St.Marc • Boninne • Marche-les-Dames • Sclayn • Temploux • Belgrade • Bouge • Beez • Bonneville • Suarlée • Flawinne • Jambes • Lives • Loyers • Maizeret • Thon • Floriffoux • Malonne • Erpent • Mozet • Floreffe • Wepion • Andoy • Wierde • Fooz • Dave • Nannine

Fort de Cognelée
Fort d'Émines
Fort de Marchovelette
Fort de Suarlée
Fort de Maizeret
Fort de Malonne
Fort d'Andoy
NAMUR
Fort de Dave
Fort de St. Héribert

Meuse / Sambre / Meuse

TRENCHES

0 — 1 Mile

Armaments of forts included 6-inch and 4·7-inch guns, 8-inch mortars, light quick-firers and smaller weapons.

KEY
══ Main roads.
┼┼┼ Railways.

© Arthur Banks 1973

28

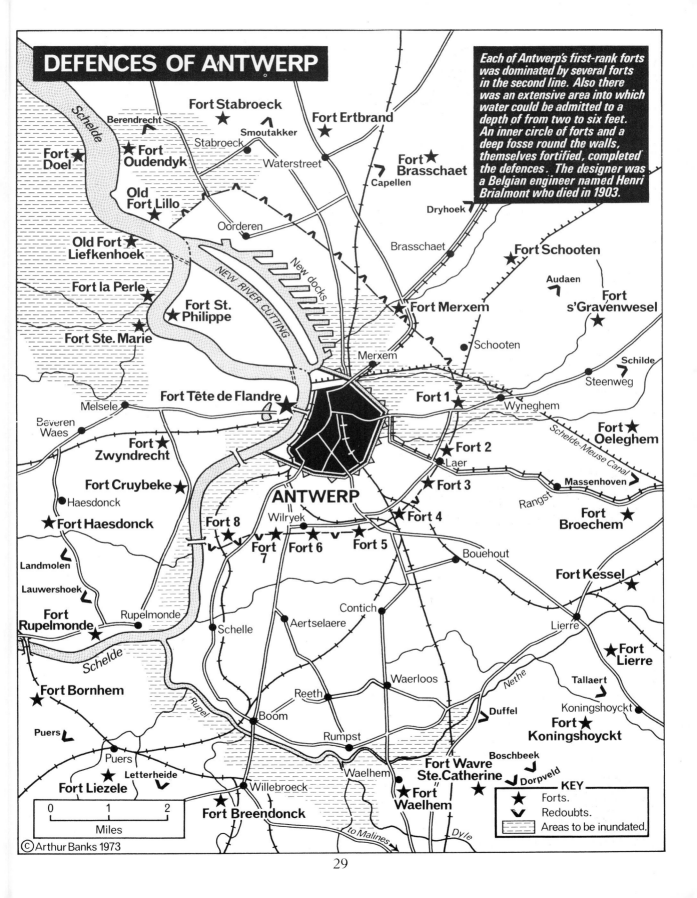

DEFENCES OF ANTWERP

Each of Antwerp's first-rank forts was dominated by several forts in the second line. Also there was an extensive area into which water could be admitted to a depth of from two to six feet. An inner circle of forts and a deep fosse round the walls, themselves fortified, completed the defences. The designer was a Belgian engineer named Henri Brialmont who died in 1903.

Schelde

Fort Stabroeck
Berendrecht
Stabroeck
Smoutakker
Waterstreet

Fort Ertbrand

Fort Brasschaet
Capellen

Dryhoek

Brasschaet

Fort Doel
Fort Oudendyk

Old Fort Lillo

Oorderen

Fort Schooten

Audaen

Fort s'Gravenwesel

Old Fort Liefkenhoek

NEW RIVER CUTTING

New docks

Fort la Perle

Fort St. Philippe

Fort Ste. Marie

Merxem

Fort Merxem

Schooten

Schilde

Steenweg

Fort Tête de Flandre

Melsele

Beveren Waes

Fort Zwyndrecht

Fort 1
Wyneghem

Fort Oeleghem

Schelde-Meuse Canal

Fort Cruybeke

Haesdonck

ANTWERP

Fort 2
Laer

Fort 3

Rangst

Massenhoven

Fort Broechem

Fort Haesdonck

Fort 8
Wilryek

Fort 4

Fort 7 Fort 6

Fort 5

Bouehout

Fort Kessel

Landmolen

Lauwershoek

Fort Rupelmonde

Rupelmonde

Schelde

Contich

Aertselaere

Lierre

Fort Lierre

Schelle

Waerloos

Nethe

Tallaert

Koningshoyckt

Fort Bornhem

Rupel

Reeth

Boom

Rumpst

Duffel

Fort Koningshoyckt

Puers

Puers

Letterheide

Fort Liezele

Willebroeck

Fort Breendonck

Waelhem

Boschbeek

Dorpveld

Fort Wavre Ste. Catherine

Fort Waelhem

to Malines

Dyle

KEY
★ Forts.
⌄ Redoubts.
▭ Areas to be inundated.

0   1   2
Miles

© Arthur Banks 1973

29

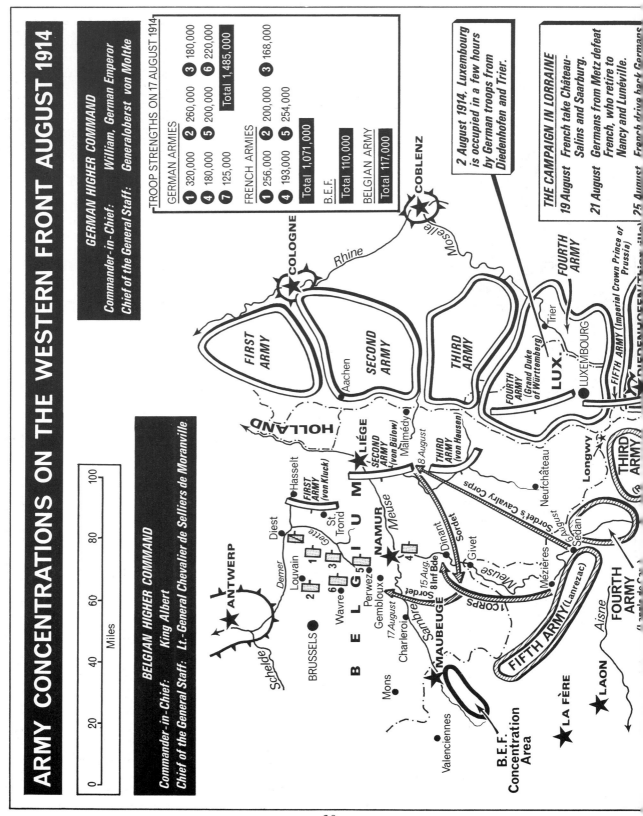

ARMY CONCENTRATIONS ON THE WESTERN FRONT AUGUST 1914

GERMAN HIGHER COMMAND

Commander-in-Chief: *William, German Emperor*
Chief of the General Staff: *Generaloberst von Moltke*

TROOP STRENGTHS ON 17 AUGUST 1914

GERMAN ARMIES

① 320,000	② 260,000	③ 180,000
④ 180,000	⑤ 200,000	⑥ 220,000
⑦ 125,000		Total 1,485,000

FRENCH ARMIES

| ① 256,000 | ② 200,000 | ③ 168,000 |
| ④ 193,000 | ⑤ 254,000 | |

Total 1,071,000

B.E.F. Total 110,000

BELGIAN ARMY Total 117,000

2 August 1914. Luxembourg is occupied in a few hours by German troops from Diedenhofen and Trier.

THE CAMPAIGN IN LORRAINE

19 August French take Château-Salins and Saarburg.

21 August Germans from Metz defeat French, who retire to Nancy and Lunéville.

25 August *French drive back Germans*

BELGIAN HIGHER COMMAND

Commander-in-Chief: *King Albert*
Chief of the General Staff: *Lt.-General Chevalier de Selliers de Moranville.*

0 20 40 60 80 100

Miles

COBLENZ

COLOGNE

Rhine

Moselle

FIRST ARMY

SECOND ARMY

THIRD ARMY

Aachen

FOURTH ARMY (Grand Duke of Württemberg)

FOURTH ARMY

Trier

FIFTH ARMY (Imperial Crown Prince of Prussia)

LUX.

LUXEMBOURG

HOLLAND

ANTWERP

Schelde

Demer

BRUSSELS

Louvain

Diest

Gette

St. Trond

Hasselt

FIRST ARMY (von Kluck)

LIÉGE

SECOND ARMY (von Bülow)

Malmédy

18 August

THIRD ARMY (von Hausen)

B E L G I U M

Wavre

Perwez

Gembloux

Sambre

Charleroi

17 August

Mons

Valenciennes

NAMUR

Meuse

Dinant

Givet

Sordet

Sordet's Cavalry Corps

Neufchâteau

Sedan

Mézières

Meuse

Longwy

THIRD ARMY

MAUBEUGE

8 Inf Bde

15 Aug.

I CORPS

FIFTH ARMY (Lanrezac)

B.E.F. Concentration Area

LA FÈRE

LAON

FOURTH ARMY (de Langle de Cary)

Aisne

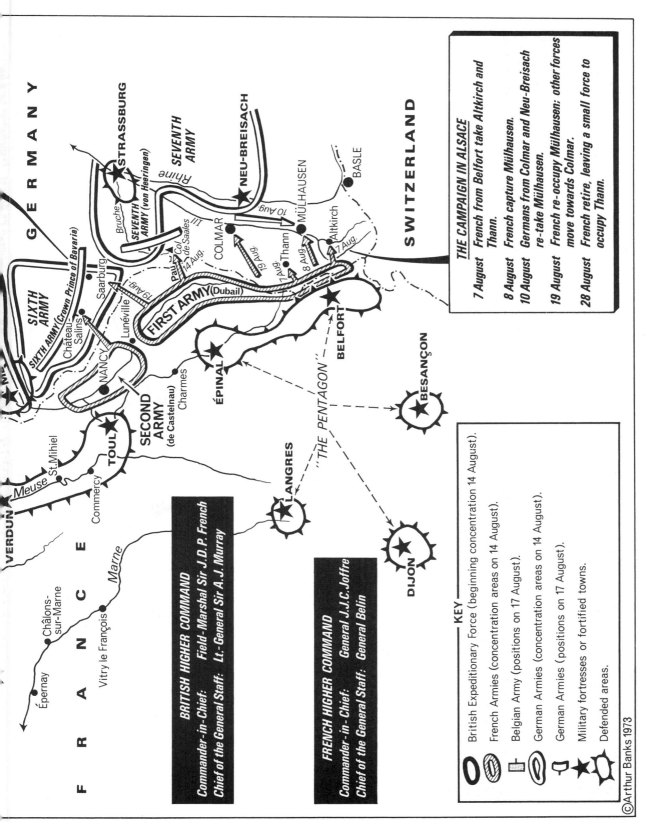

KEY

- British Expeditionary Force (beginning concentration 14 August).
- French Armies (concentration areas on 14 August).
- Belgian Army (positions on 17 August).
- German Armies (concentration areas on 14 August).
- German Armies (positions on 17 August).
- Military fortresses or fortified towns.
- Defended areas.

THE CAMPAIGN IN ALSACE

7 August	French from Belfort take Altkirch and Thann.
8 August	French capture Mülhausen.
10 August	Germans from Colmar and Neu-Breisach re-take Mülhausen.
19 August	French re-occupy Mülhausen: other forces move towards Colmar.
28 August	French retire, leaving a small force to occupy Thann.

BRITISH HIGHER COMMAND

Commander-in-Chief: Field-Marshal Sir J.D.P. French
Chief of the General Staff: Lt.-General Sir A.J. Murray

FRENCH HIGHER COMMAND

Commander-in-Chief: General J.J.C. Joffre
Chief of the General Staff: General Belin

©Arthur Banks 1973

31

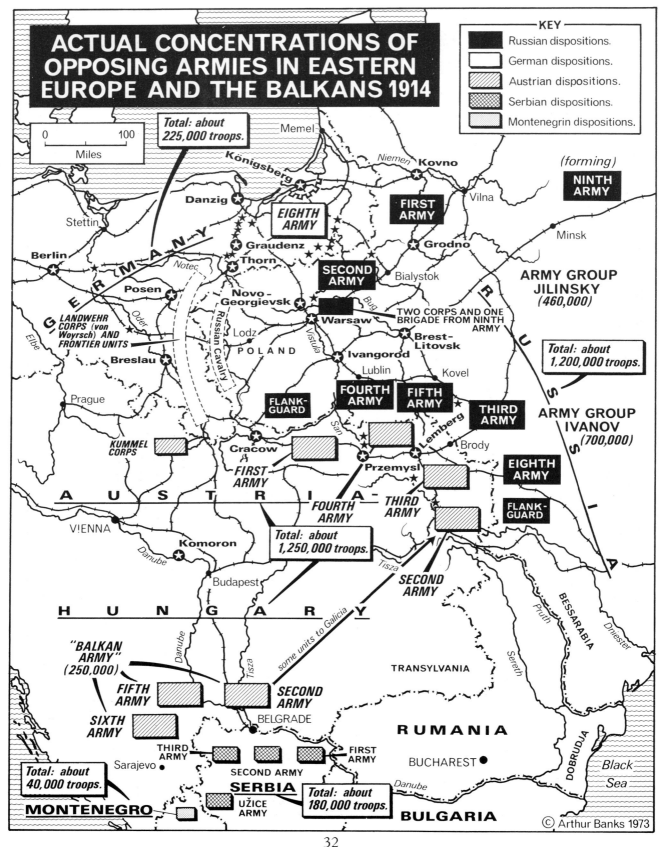

ACTUAL CONCENTRATIONS OF OPPOSING ARMIES IN EASTERN EUROPE AND THE BALKANS 1914

KEY
- Russian dispositions.
- German dispositions.
- Austrian dispositions.
- Serbian dispositions.
- Montenegrin dispositions.

Total: about 225,000 troops.

Memel

Niemen   Kovno

Königsberg

NINTH ARMY (forming)

Danzig

Vilna

FIRST ARMY

Stettin

EIGHTH ARMY

Graudenz

Grodno

Minsk

Berlin

Thorn

SECOND ARMY

Bialystok

ARMY GROUP JILINSKY (460,000)

Posen

Novo-Georgievsk

Warsaw

Bug

TWO CORPS AND ONE BRIGADE FROM NINTH ARMY

LANDWEHR CORPS (von Woyrsch) AND FRONTIER UNITS

Oder

Russian Cavalry

Lodz

POLAND

Vistula

Ivangorod

Brest-Litovsk

Total: about 1,200,000 troops.

Elbe

Breslau

Lublin

Kovel

Prague

FLANK-GUARD

FOURTH ARMY

FIFTH ARMY

THIRD ARMY

ARMY GROUP IVANOV (700,000)

KUMMEL CORPS

San

Cracow

FIRST ARMY

Lemberg

Brody

EIGHTH ARMY

Przemysl

THIRD ARMY

FLANK-GUARD

A U S T R I A -

FOURTH ARMY

THIRD ARMY

VIENNA

Total: about 1,250,000 troops.

Komoron

Danube

SECOND ARMY

Tisza

Budapest

H U N G A R Y

TRANSYLVANIA

Prut

BESSARABIA

some units to Galicia

Sereth

Dniester

"BALKAN ARMY" (250,000)

Danube

Tisza

FIFTH ARMY

SECOND ARMY

SIXTH ARMY

BELGRADE

R U M A N I A

THIRD ARMY

SECOND ARMY

FIRST ARMY

BUCHAREST

Sarajevo

Total: about 40,000 troops.

SERBIA

UŽICE ARMY

Total: about 180,000 troops.

Danube

DOBRUDJA

Black Sea

MONTENEGRO

BULGARIA

© Arthur Banks 1973

32

THREE IMPORTANT GUNS IN 1914

French 75-mm. field gun (Model 1897)

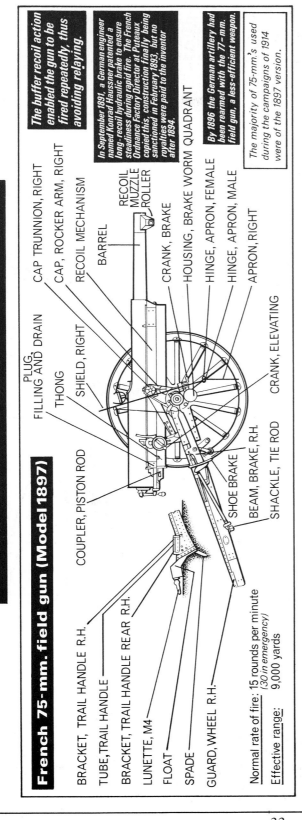

BRACKET, TRAIL HANDLE R.H.

TUBE, TRAIL HANDLE

BRACKET, TRAIL HANDLE REAR R.H.

LUNETTE, M4

FLOAT

SPADE

GUARD, WHEEL R.H.

PLUG, FILLING AND DRAIN

THONG

SHIELD, RIGHT

COUPLER, PISTON ROD

CAP TRUNNION, RIGHT

CAP, ROCKER ARM, RIGHT

RECOIL MECHANISM

BARREL

RECOIL MUZZLE ROLLER

CRANK, BRAKE

HOUSING, BRAKE WORM QUADRANT

HINGE, APRON, FEMALE

HINGE, APRON, MALE

APRON, RIGHT

CRANK, ELEVATING

SHOE BRAKE

BEAM, BRAKE, R.H.

SHACKLE, TIE ROD

Normal rate of fire: 15 rounds per minute
(30 in emergency)

Effective range: 9,000 yards

The buffer recoil action enabled the gun to be fired repeatedly, thus avoiding relaying.

In September 1891, a German engineer named Konrad Haussner patented a long-recoil hydraulic brake to ensure steadiness during rapid fire. The French Ordnance Factory Director at Puteaux copied this, construction finally being sanctioned in February 1893, but no royalties were paid to the inventor after 1894.

By 1896 the German artillery had been rearmed with the 77-mm. field gun, a less-efficient weapon.

The majority of 75-mm.'s used during the campaigns of 1914 were of the 1897 version.

Austrian 30·5-cm. howitzer (Model 1911)

Normal rate of fire: 1 round every 6 minutes

Effective range: 13,000 yards

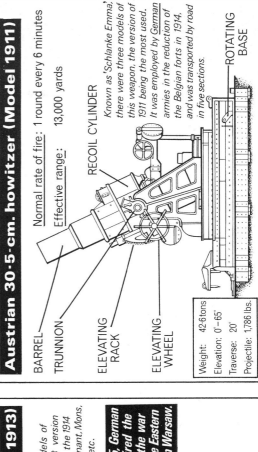

BARREL

TRUNNION

ELEVATING RACK

ELEVATING WHEEL

RECOIL CYLINDER

ROTATING BASE

Known as 'Schlanke Emma', there were three models of this weapon, the version of 1911 being the most used. It was employed by German armies in the reduction of the Belgian forts in 1914, and was transported by road in five sections.

Weight:	42·6 tons
Elevation:	0°–65°
Traverse:	20°
Projectile:	1,786 lbs.

German 15-cm. field howitzer (Model 1913)

Normal rate of fire: 5 rounds per minute

Effective range: 9,300 yards

BARREL

SHIELD

SIGHT BRACKET

ELEVATING WHEEL

BOX TRAIL

SPADES

There were four models of this weapon. The 1913 version was employed during the 1914 battles at Charleroi, Dinant, Mons, the Marne, the Aisne, etc.

On 3 January 1915, German 15-cm. howitzers fired the first gas shells of the war near Bolimow on the Eastern Front, 40 miles from Warsaw.

RIVAL INFANTRY DIVISIONAL ORGANIZATIONS IN 1914

The infantry division was the standard component of corps and armies. These diagrams give approximate comparisons between the main contending forces.

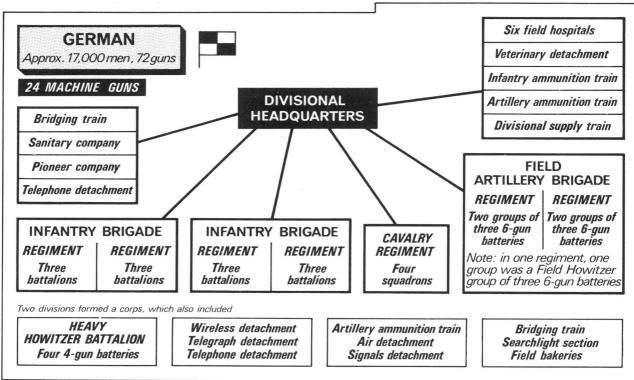

GERMAN
Approx. 17,000 men, 72 guns

24 MACHINE GUNS

- Bridging train
- Sanitary company
- Pioneer company
- Telephone detachment

DIVISIONAL HEADQUARTERS

- Six field hospitals
- Veterinary detachment
- Infantry ammunition train
- Artillery ammunition train
- Divisional supply train

FIELD ARTILLERY BRIGADE

REGIMENT	REGIMENT
Two groups of three 6-gun batteries	Two groups of three 6-gun batteries

Note: in one regiment, one group was a Field Howitzer group of three 6-gun batteries

INFANTRY BRIGADE
REGIMENT	REGIMENT
Three battalions	Three battalions

INFANTRY BRIGADE
REGIMENT	REGIMENT
Three battalions	Three battalions

CAVALRY REGIMENT
Four squadrons

Two divisions formed a corps, which also included

HEAVY HOWITZER BATTALION Four 4-gun batteries	Wireless detachment Telegraph detachment Telephone detachment	Artillery ammunition train Air detachment Signals detachment	Bridging train Searchlight section Field bakeries

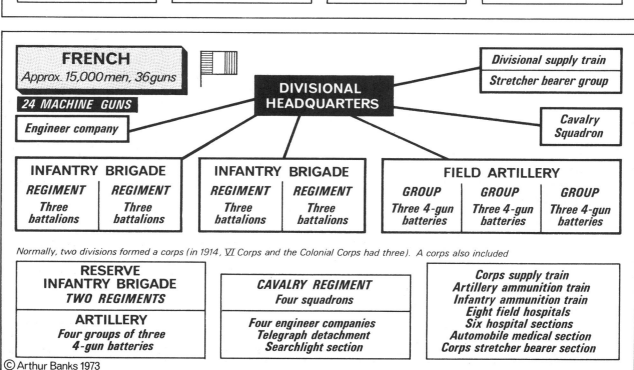

FRENCH
Approx. 15,000 men, 36 guns

24 MACHINE GUNS

- Engineer company

DIVISIONAL HEADQUARTERS

- Divisional supply train
- Stretcher bearer group

Cavalry Squadron

INFANTRY BRIGADE
REGIMENT	REGIMENT
Three battalions	Three battalions

INFANTRY BRIGADE
REGIMENT	REGIMENT
Three battalions	Three battalions

FIELD ARTILLERY
GROUP	GROUP	GROUP
Three 4-gun batteries	Three 4-gun batteries	Three 4-gun batteries

Normally, two divisions formed a corps (in 1914, VI Corps and the Colonial Corps had three). A corps also included

RESERVE INFANTRY BRIGADE TWO REGIMENTS ARTILLERY Four groups of three 4-gun batteries	CAVALRY REGIMENT Four squadrons Four engineer companies Telegraph detachment Searchlight section	Corps supply train Artillery ammunition train Infantry ammunition train Eight field hospitals Six hospital sections Automobile medical section Corps stretcher bearer section

© Arthur Banks 1973

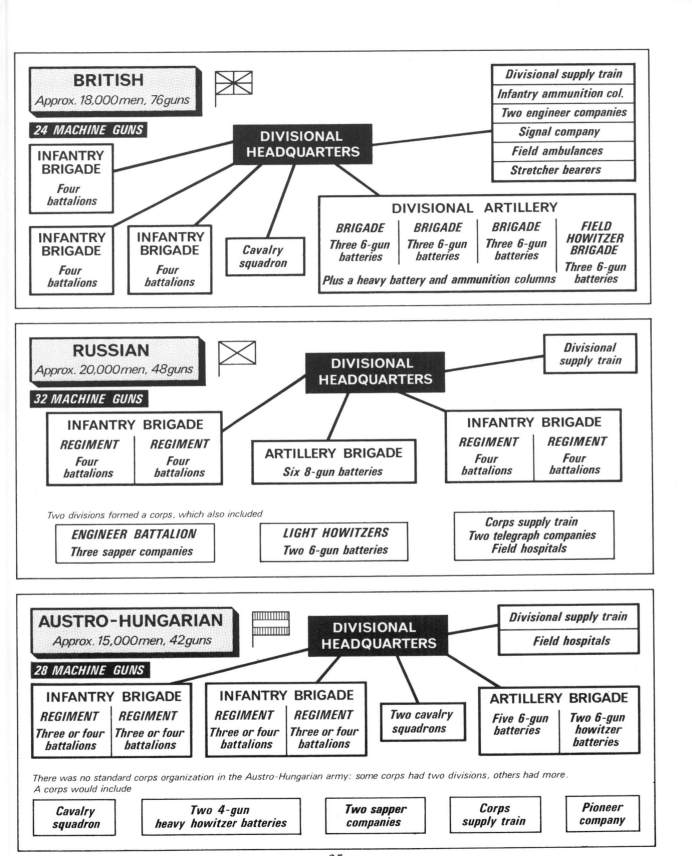

BRITISH
Approx. 18,000 men, 76 guns

24 MACHINE GUNS

DIVISIONAL HEADQUARTERS

- Divisional supply train
- Infantry ammunition col.
- Two engineer companies
- Signal company
- Field ambulances
- Stretcher bearers

INFANTRY BRIGADE
Four battalions

INFANTRY BRIGADE
Four battalions

INFANTRY BRIGADE
Four battalions

Cavalry squadron

DIVISIONAL ARTILLERY

BRIGADE	BRIGADE	BRIGADE	FIELD HOWITZER BRIGADE
Three 6-gun batteries	Three 6-gun batteries	Three 6-gun batteries	Three 6-gun batteries

Plus a heavy battery and ammunition columns

RUSSIAN
Approx. 20,000 men, 48 guns

32 MACHINE GUNS

DIVISIONAL HEADQUARTERS

Divisional supply train

INFANTRY BRIGADE

REGIMENT	REGIMENT
Four battalions	Four battalions

ARTILLERY BRIGADE
Six 8-gun batteries

INFANTRY BRIGADE

REGIMENT	REGIMENT
Four battalions	Four battalions

Two divisions formed a corps, which also included

ENGINEER BATTALION
Three sapper companies

LIGHT HOWITZERS
Two 6-gun batteries

*Corps supply train
Two telegraph companies
Field hospitals*

AUSTRO-HUNGARIAN
Approx. 15,000 men, 42 guns

28 MACHINE GUNS

DIVISIONAL HEADQUARTERS

- Divisional supply train
- Field hospitals

INFANTRY BRIGADE

REGIMENT	REGIMENT
Three or four battalions	Three or four battalions

INFANTRY BRIGADE

REGIMENT	REGIMENT
Three or four battalions	Three or four battalions

Two cavalry squadrons

ARTILLERY BRIGADE

Five 6-gun batteries	Two 6-gun howitzer batteries

There was no standard corps organization in the Austro-Hungarian army: some corps had two divisions, others had more. A corps would include

Cavalry squadron	Two 4-gun heavy howitzer batteries	Two sapper companies	Corps supply train	Pioneer company

RIVAL CAVALRY DIVISIONAL ORGANIZATIONS IN 1914

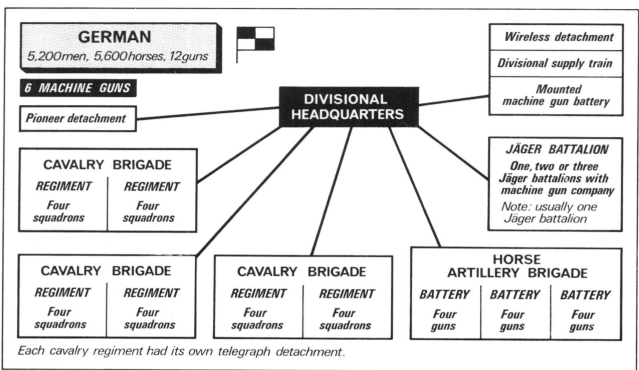

GERMAN
5,200 men, 5,600 horses, 12 guns

Wireless detachment

Divisional supply train

Mounted machine gun battery

6 MACHINE GUNS

Pioneer detachment

DIVISIONAL HEADQUARTERS

CAVALRY BRIGADE

REGIMENT	REGIMENT
Four squadrons	Four squadrons

JÄGER BATTALION
One, two or three Jäger battalions with machine gun company
Note: usually one Jäger battalion

CAVALRY BRIGADE

REGIMENT	REGIMENT
Four squadrons	Four squadrons

CAVALRY BRIGADE

REGIMENT	REGIMENT
Four squadrons	Four squadrons

HORSE ARTILLERY BRIGADE

BATTERY	BATTERY	BATTERY
Four guns	Four guns	Four guns

Each cavalry regiment had its own telegraph detachment.

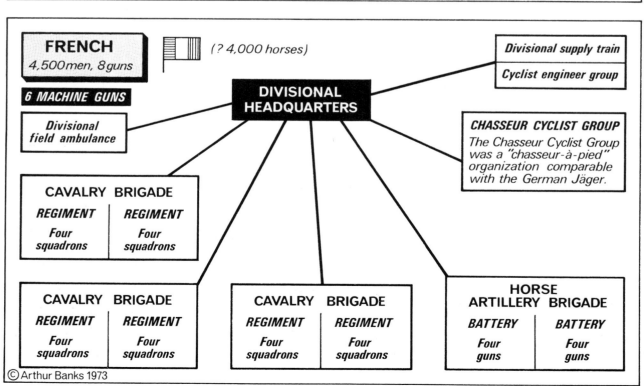

FRENCH
4,500 men, 8 guns

(? 4,000 horses)

Divisional supply train

Cyclist engineer group

6 MACHINE GUNS

Divisional field ambulance

DIVISIONAL HEADQUARTERS

CHASSEUR CYCLIST GROUP
The Chasseur Cyclist Group was a "chasseur-à-pied" organization comparable with the German Jäger.

CAVALRY BRIGADE

REGIMENT	REGIMENT
Four squadrons	Four squadrons

CAVALRY BRIGADE

REGIMENT	REGIMENT
Four squadrons	Four squadrons

CAVALRY BRIGADE

REGIMENT	REGIMENT
Four squadrons	Four squadrons

HORSE ARTILLERY BRIGADE

BATTERY	BATTERY
Four guns	Four guns

© Arthur Banks 1973

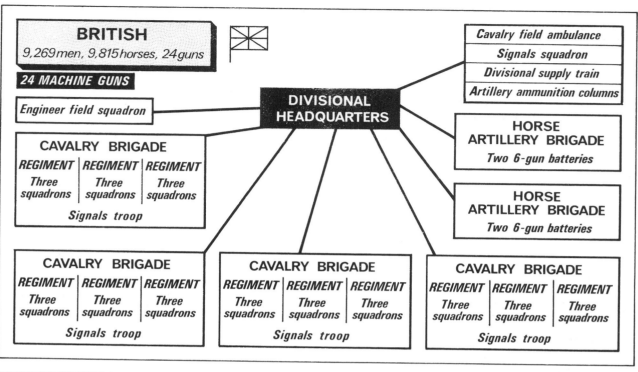

BRITISH
9,269 men, 9,815 horses, 24 guns

24 MACHINE GUNS

Engineer field squadron

DIVISIONAL HEADQUARTERS

Cavalry field ambulance
Signals squadron
Divisional supply train
Artillery ammunition columns

HORSE ARTILLERY BRIGADE
Two 6-gun batteries

HORSE ARTILLERY BRIGADE
Two 6-gun batteries

CAVALRY BRIGADE

REGIMENT	REGIMENT	REGIMENT
Three squadrons	Three squadrons	Three squadrons

Signals troop

CAVALRY BRIGADE

REGIMENT	REGIMENT	REGIMENT
Three squadrons	Three squadrons	Three squadrons

Signals troop

CAVALRY BRIGADE

REGIMENT	REGIMENT	REGIMENT
Three squadrons	Three squadrons	Three squadrons

Signals troop

CAVALRY BRIGADE

REGIMENT	REGIMENT	REGIMENT
Three squadrons	Three squadrons	Three squadrons

Signals troop

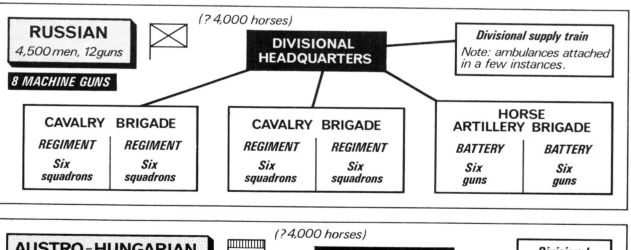

RUSSIAN
4,500 men, 12 guns

8 MACHINE GUNS

(? 4,000 horses)

DIVISIONAL HEADQUARTERS

Divisional supply train
Note: ambulances attached in a few instances.

CAVALRY BRIGADE

REGIMENT	REGIMENT
Six squadrons	Six squadrons

CAVALRY BRIGADE

REGIMENT	REGIMENT
Six squadrons	Six squadrons

HORSE ARTILLERY BRIGADE

BATTERY	BATTERY
Six guns	Six guns

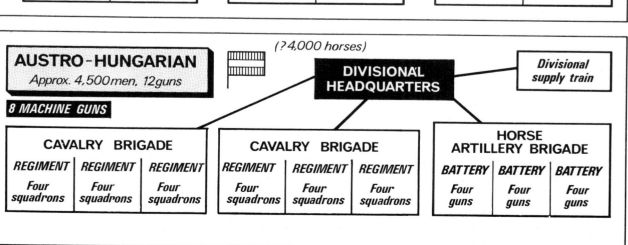

AUSTRO-HUNGARIAN
Approx. 4,500 men, 12 guns

8 MACHINE GUNS

(? 4,000 horses)

DIVISIONAL HEADQUARTERS

Divisional supply train

CAVALRY BRIGADE

REGIMENT	REGIMENT	REGIMENT
Four squadrons	Four squadrons	Four squadrons

CAVALRY BRIGADE

REGIMENT	REGIMENT	REGIMENT
Four squadrons	Four squadrons	Four squadrons

HORSE ARTILLERY BRIGADE

BATTERY	BATTERY	BATTERY
Four guns	Four guns	Four guns

THE GERMAN INVASION OF BELGIUM AUGUST 1914

Situation 17-24 August

NORTH SEA

H O L L A N D

●OSTEND

●BRUGES

Nieuport

DUNKIRK

●Dixmude

Yser

Bergues

81 Territorial Division

●Roulers

GHENT

Schelde

Schelde

Dendre

B

●Ypres

E

●Courtrai

Lys

●Oudenarde

L

G

II

Cassel

Hazebrouck

Warneton

Lys

Armentières

LILLE

Cysoing

82 Territorial Division

●Béthune

GROUP D'AMADE (Reserve)

●Lens

88 Terr. Div.

23 August

24 Aug.

●Douai

Scarpe

ARRAS

HQ, GROUP D'AMADE

F R A N C E

II Cav. Corps

Schelde

24 Aug.

II Cav. Corps

TOURNAI

Antoing

Leuze

24 Aug.

●Renaix

Grammont

II

II

II

II

II

Ath

Dendre

Enghien

FIRST ARMY

II

IV

III

IX

II Cav. Corps (von der Marwitz)

24 Aug.

Peruwelz

Condé

84 Terr. D.

St. Amand

Marchiennes

●Valenciennes

Schelde

IV

III

III

IX

Canal

IV

III

IX

IX

19 Inf. Bde.

II

MONS

B. E. F.

Cav. Div.

5 Cav. Bde.

●Bavai

MAUBEUGE

53 & 69 R.Ds.

53 R.D.

I C
Co

Canal
Binch

XVIII

●Le Quesnoy

●Solesmes

Le Cateau

GHQ, B.E.F.

●Cambrai

Sambre

Helpe

Landrecies

●Avesnes

KEY TO ALLIED DISPOSITIONS

French Fifth Army, 21 August position.

French Fifth Army, 22 August positions.

French Fifth Army, 24 August positions.

British Expeditionary Force, 22/23 August.

Note: Corps are shown by Roman numerals

Royal Flying Corps HQ was at Maubeuge aerodrome. It consisted of 63 aeroplanes and 860 personnel.

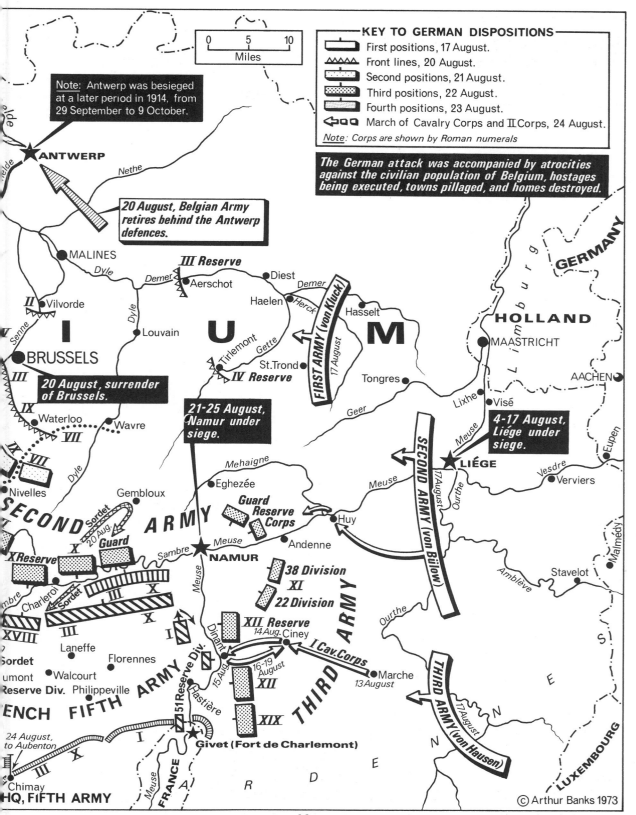

KEY TO GERMAN DISPOSITIONS

First positions, 17 August.
Front lines, 20 August.
Second positions, 21 August.
Third positions, 22 August.
Fourth positions, 23 August.
March of Cavalry Corps and II Corps, 24 August.

Note: Corps are shown by Roman numerals

The German attack was accompanied by atrocities against the civilian population of Belgium, hostages being executed, towns pillaged, and homes destroyed.

0 5 10
Miles

Note: Antwerp was besieged at a later period in 1914, from 29 September to 9 October.

20 August, Belgian Army retires behind the Antwerp defences.

ANTWERP

Nethe

MALINES

Dyle

Demer

III Reserve

Aerschot

Diest

Demer

Haelen

Herck

Hasselt

HOLLAND

Limburg

GERMANY

MAASTRICHT

II Vilvorde

Dyle

Louvain

Tirlemont

Gette

St.Trond

IV Reserve

FIRST ARMY (von Kluck)

17 August

Tongres

AACHEN

BRUSSELS

20 August, surrender of Brussels.

III

IX

Waterloo

Wavre

VII

21-25 August, Namur under siege.

Geer

Lixhe

Visé

4-17 August, Liége under siege.

Eupen

Mehaigne

Eghezée

LIÉGE

Vesdre

Verviers

IX

VII

Nivelles

Dyle

SECOND

ARMY

Gembloux

Sordet

20 Aug.

Guard Reserve Corps

Meuse

SECOND ARMY (von Bülow)

17 August

Ourthe

Malmédy

X

Guard

Sambre

Meuse

NAMUR

Andenne

Huy

Stavelot

Amblève

X Reserve

Sordet

Charleroi

III

X

X

38 Division

XI

22 Division

Ourthe

S

E

XVIII

III

Laneffe

Florennes

I

XII Reserve

14 Aug.

Ciney

I Cav. Corps

Marche

13 August

THIRD ARMY

N

Sordet

umont

Walcourt

Philippeville

Reserve Div.

FRENCH

FIFTH

ARMY

Dinant

51 Reserve Div.

15 Aug.

Hastière

16-19 August

XII

XIX

THIRD ARMY (von Hausen)

17 August

N

24 August, to Aubenton

X

III

I

Givet (Fort de Charlemont)

Meuse

FRANCE

A

R

D

E

LUXEMBOURG

Chimay

HQ, FIFTH ARMY

© Arthur Banks 1973

39

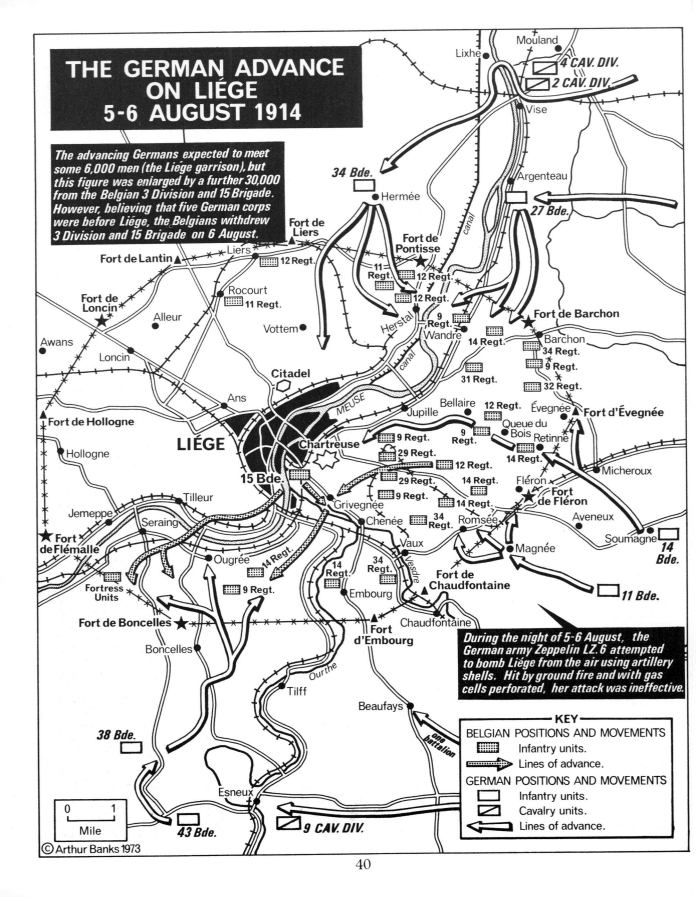

THE GERMAN ADVANCE ON LIÉGE 5-6 AUGUST 1914

The advancing Germans expected to meet some 6,000 men (the Liége garrison), but this figure was enlarged by a further 30,000 from the Belgian 3 Division and 15 Brigade. However, believing that five German corps were before Liége, the Belgians withdrew 3 Division and 15 Brigade on 6 August.

During the night of 5-6 August, the German army Zeppelin LZ.6 attempted to bomb Liége from the air using artillery shells. Hit by ground fire and with gas cells perforated, her attack was ineffective.

Mouland

Lixhe

4 CAV. DIV.

2 CAV. DIV.

Vise

34 Bde.

Hermée

Argenteau

27 Bde.

Fort de Liers

Fort de Pontisse

Liers

12 Regt.

11 Regt.

Fort de Lantin

Fort de Loncin

Rocourt

11 Regt.

12 Regt.

12 Regt.

Herstal

9 Regt.

Wandre

Fort de Barchon

Barchon

34 Regt.

9 Regt.

32 Regt.

Alleur

Vottem

14 Regt.

31 Regt.

Awans

Loncin

canal

Citadel

Ans

MEUSE

Jupille

Bellaire

12 Regt.

Queue du Bois

Évegnée

Fort d'Évegnée

Fort de Hollogne

9 Regt.

Retinne

14 Regt.

Hollogne

LIÉGE

Chartreuse

9 Regt.

29 Regt.

12 Regt.

Micheroux

15 Bde.

29 Regt.

9 Regt.

14 Regt.

14 Regt.

Fléron

Fort de Fléron

Tilleur

Grivegnée

Chenée

34 Regt.

Romsée

Avenux

Jemeppe

Seraing

34 Regt.

Vaux

Magnée

Soumagne

14 Bde.

Fort de Flémalle

Ougrée

14 Regt.

14 Regt.

34 Regt.

Vesdre

Fort de Chaudfontaine

11 Bde.

Fortress Units

9 Regt.

Embourg

Chaudfontaine

Fort de Boncelles

Fort d'Embourg

Boncelles

Ourthe

Tilff

Beaufays

one battalion

38 Bde.

Esneux

0   1
Mile

43 Bde.

9 CAV. DIV.

© Arthur Banks 1973

KEY
BELGIAN POSITIONS AND MOVEMENTS
Infantry units.
Lines of advance.
GERMAN POSITIONS AND MOVEMENTS
Infantry units.
Cavalry units.
Lines of advance.

40

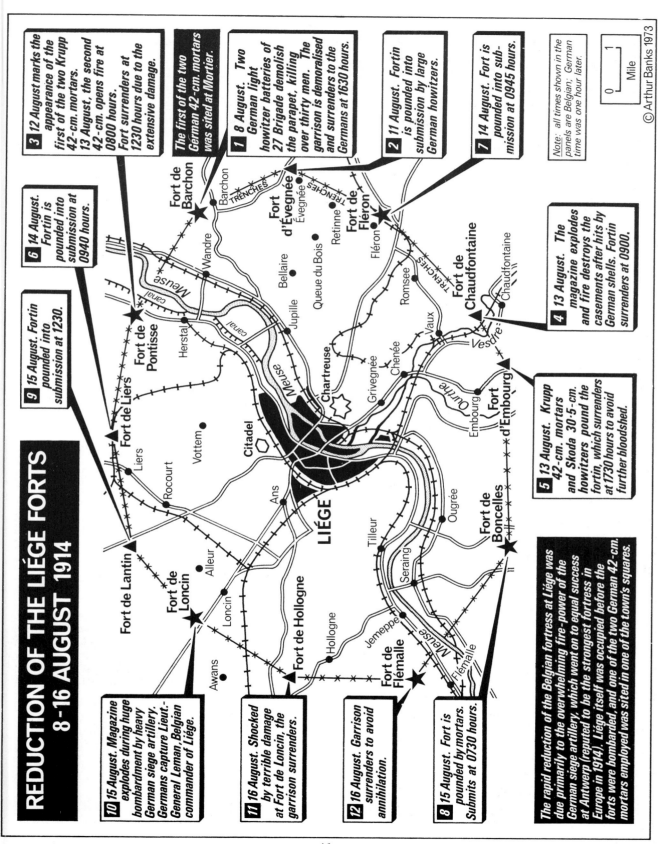

REDUCTION OF THE LIÉGE FORTS 8-16 AUGUST 1914

3 12 August marks the appearance of the first of the two Krupp 42-cm. mortars. 13 August, the second 42-cm. opens fire at 0800 hours. Fort surrenders at 1230 hours due to the extensive damage.

The first of the two German 42-cm. mortars was sited at Mortier.

1 8 August. Two German light howitzer batteries of 27 Brigade demolish the parapet, killing over thirty men. The garrison is demoralised and surrenders to the Germans at 1630 hours.

2 11 August. Fortin is pounded into submission by large German howitzers.

7 14 August. Fort is pounded into submission at 0945 hours.

Note: all times shown in the panels are Belgian; German time was one hour later.

0 1
Mile

© Arthur Banks 1973

6 14 August. Fortin is pounded into submission at 0940 hours.

9 15 August. Fortin pounded into submission at 1230.

TRENCHES

Barchon

Fort de Barchon

Évegnée

Fort d'Évegnée

Retinne

TRENCHES

Fléron

Fort de Fléron

Fort de Chaudfontaine

Chaudfontaine

4 13 August. The magazine explodes and fire destroys the casements after hits by German shells. Fortin surrenders at 0900.

Canal

Meuse

Wandre

Bellaire

Queue du Bois

Jupille

Fort de Pontisse

Herstal

Romsee

Vaux

Vesdre

Chartreuse

Grivegnée

Chenée

Fort de Liers

Liers

Vottem

Citadel

Meuse

Ourthe

Embourg

Fort d'Embourg

Fort de Lantin

Rocourt

Ans

LIÉGE

Tilleur

Ougrée

Fort de Boncelles

5 13 August. Krupp 42-cm. mortars and Skoda 30·5-cm. howitzers pound the fortin, which surrenders at 1730 hours to avoid further bloodshed.

Awans

Alleur

Fort de Loncin

Loncin

Fort de Hollogne

Hollogne

Seraing

Jemeppe

Flémalle

Fort de Flémalle

Meuse

10 15 August. Magazine explodes during huge bombardment by heavy German siege artillery. Germans capture Lieut.-General Leman, Belgian commander of Liége.

11 16 August. Shocked by terrible damage at Fort de Loncin, the garrison surrenders.

12 16 August. Garrison surrenders to avoid annihilation.

8 15 August. Fort is pounded by mortars. Submits at 0730 hours.

The rapid reduction of the Belgian fortress at Liége was due primarily to the overwhelming fire-power of the German siege artillery, which went on to equal success at Antwerp (reputed to be the strongest fortress in Europe in 1914). Liége itself was occupied before the forts were bombarded, and one of the two German 42-cm. mortars employed was sited in one of the town's squares.

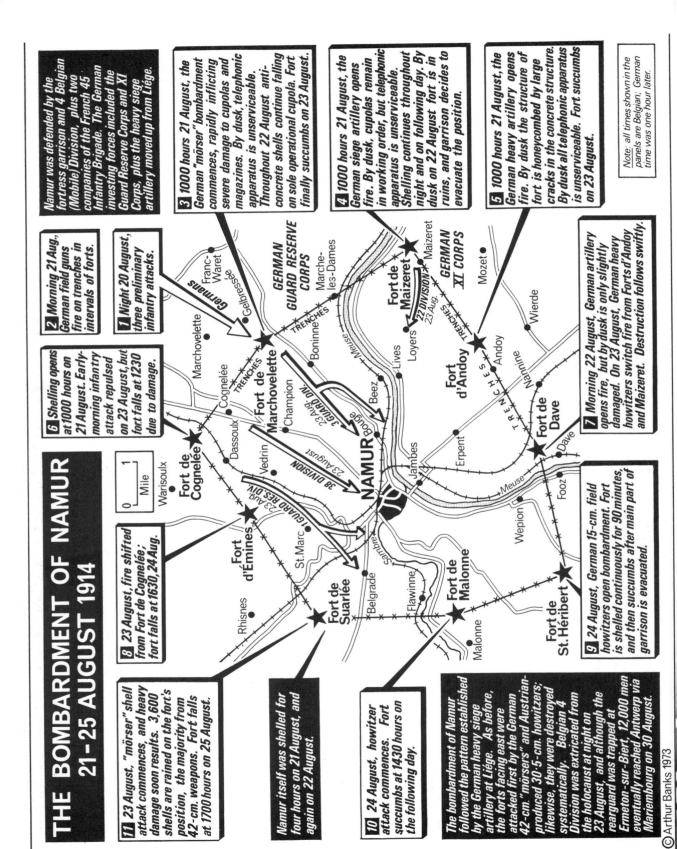

THE BOMBARDMENT OF NAMUR 21-25 AUGUST 1914

Namur was defended by the fortress garrison and 4 Belgian (Mobile) Division, plus two companies of the French 45 Infantry Brigade. The German investing forces included the Guard Reserve Corps and XI Corps, plus the heavy siege artillery moved up from Liége.

1 Night 20 August, three preliminary infantry attacks.

2 Morning 21 Aug., German field guns fire on trenches in intervals of forts.

3 1000 hours 21 August, the German "mörser" bombardment commences, rapidly inflicting severe damage to cupolas and magazines. By dusk, telephonic apparatus is unserviceable. Throughout 22 August anti-concrete shells continue falling on sole operational cupola. Fort finally succumbs on 23 August.

4 1000 hours 21 August, the German siege artillery opens fire. By dusk, cupolas remain in working order, but telephonic apparatus is unserviceable. Shelling continues throughout night and on following day. By dusk on 22 August fort is in ruins, and garrison decides to evacuate the position.

5 1000 hours 21 August, the German heavy artillery opens fire. By dusk the structure of fort is honeycombed by large cracks in the concrete structure. By dusk all telephonic apparatus is unserviceable. Fort succumbs on 23 August.

Note: all times shown in the panels are Belgian; German time was one hour later.

6 Shelling opens at 1000 hours on 21 August. Early-morning infantry attack repulsed on 23 August, but fort falls at 1230 due to damage.

7 Morning 22 August, German artillery opens fire, but by dusk is only slightly damaged. On 23 August, German heavy howitzers switch fire from Forts d'Andoy and Maizeret. Destruction follows swiftly.

8 23 August, fire shifted from Fort de Cognelée; fort falls at 1630, 24 Aug.

9 24 August, German 15-cm. field howitzers open bombardment. Fort is shelled continuously for 90 minutes, and then succumbs after main part of garrison is evacuated.

10 24 August, howitzer attack commences. Fort succumbs at 1430 hours on the following day.

11 23 August, "mörser" shell attack commences, and heavy damage soon results. 3,600 shells are rained on the fort's position, the majority from 42-cm. weapons. Fort falls at 1700 hours on 25 August.

Namur itself was shelled for four hours on 21 August, and again on 22 August.

The bombardment of Namur followed the pattern established by the German heavy siege artillery at Liége. As before, the forts facing east were attacked first by the German 42-cm. "mörsers" and Austrian-produced 30.5-cm. howitzers; likewise, they were destroyed systematically. Belgian 4 Division was extricated from the holocaust at night on 23 August, and although the rearguard was trapped at Ermeton-sur-Biert, 12,000 men eventually reached Antwerp via Mariembourg on 30 August.

© Arthur Banks 1973

42

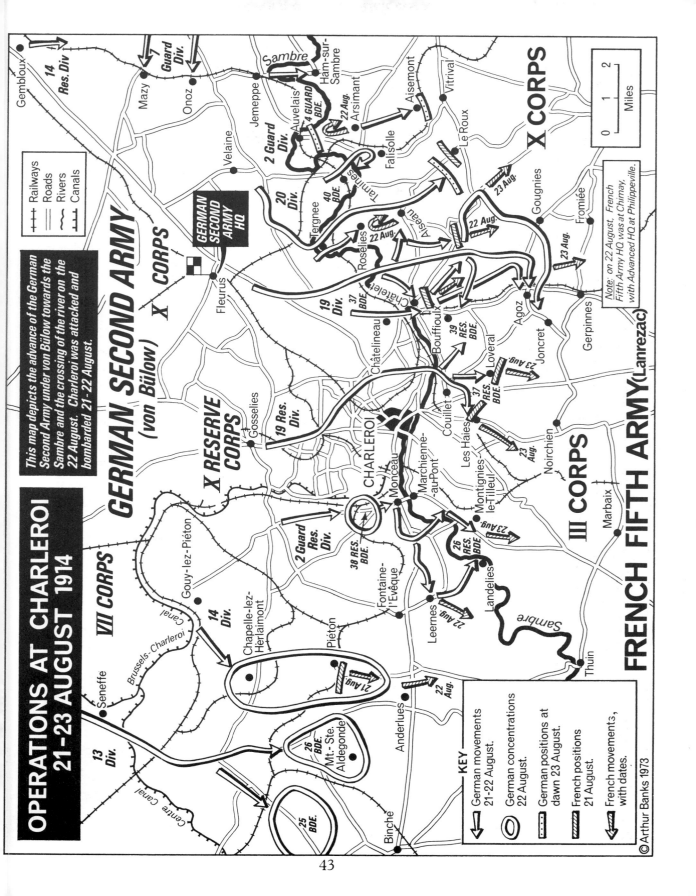

OPERATIONS AT CHARLEROI 21–23 AUGUST 1914

This map depicts the advance of the German Second Army under von Bülow towards the Sambre and the crossing of the river on the 22 August. Charleroi was attacked and bombarded 21–22 August.

GERMAN SECOND ARMY (von Bülow)

X CORPS

X RESERVE CORPS

VII CORPS

X CORPS

X CORPS

III CORPS

FRENCH FIFTH ARMY (Lanrezac)

GERMAN SECOND ARMY HQ

Note: on 22 August, French Fifth Army HQ was at Chimay, with Advanced HQ at Philippeville.

Railways
Roads
Rivers
Canals

0   1   2   Miles

KEY
- German movements 21–22 August.
- German concentrations 22 August.
- German positions at dawn 23 August.
- French positions 21 August.
- French movements, with dates.

© Arthur Banks 1973

Gembloux
Mazy
Onoz
14 Res. Div.
7 Guard Div.
Sambre
Ham-sur-Sambre
Jemeppe
Auvelais
4 GUARD BDE.
22 Aug.
Arsimant
Aisemont
Vitrival
Le Roux
2 Guard Div.
Velaine
Falisolle
20 Div.
40 BDE.
Tamines
Aiseau
22 Aug.
23 Aug.
Gougnies
Fromiée
Roselies
22 Aug.
37 BDE.
19 Div.
Châtelet
Bouffioulx
39 RES. BDE.
Agoz
23 Aug.
Gerpinnes
Joncret
Fleurus
Châtelineau
Loveral
37 RES. BDE.
23 Aug.
Gosselies
19 Res. Div.
Couillet
Noirchien
CHARLEROI
Monceau
Marchienne-au-Pont
Les Haies
Montignies-le-Tilleul
23 Aug.
Marbaix
Seneffe
13 Div.
Gouy-lez-Piéton
Brussels-Charleroi Canal
14 Div.
Chapelle-lez-Herlaimont
2 Guard Res. Div.
38 RES. BDE.
Piéton
Fontaine-l'Évêque
26 RES. BDE.
Landelies
22 Aug.
Leernes
23 Aug.
Sambre
Thuin
21 Aug.
26 BDE.
Mt.-Ste.-Aldegonde
Anderlues
22 Aug.
Centre Canal
25 BDE.
Binche

43

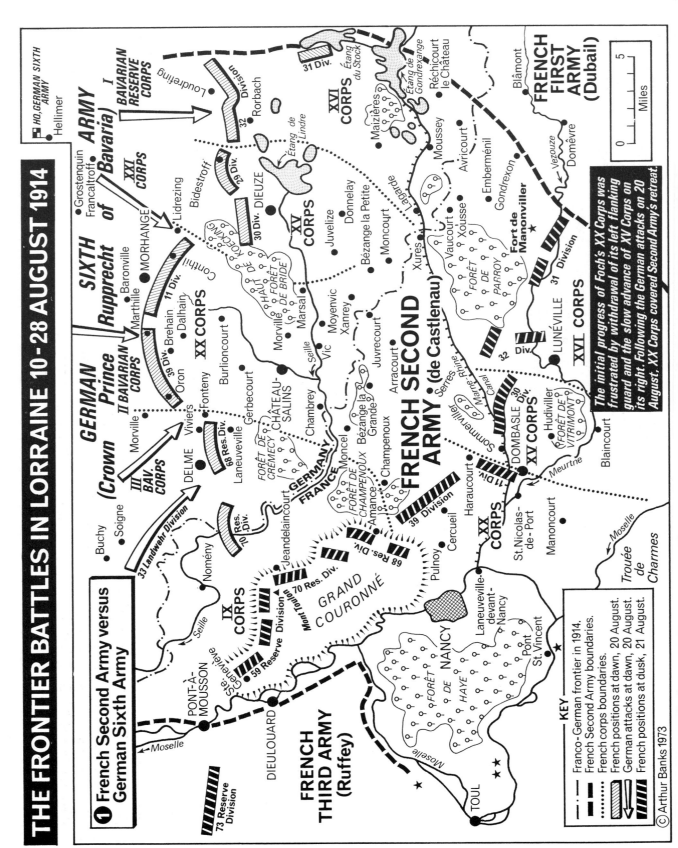

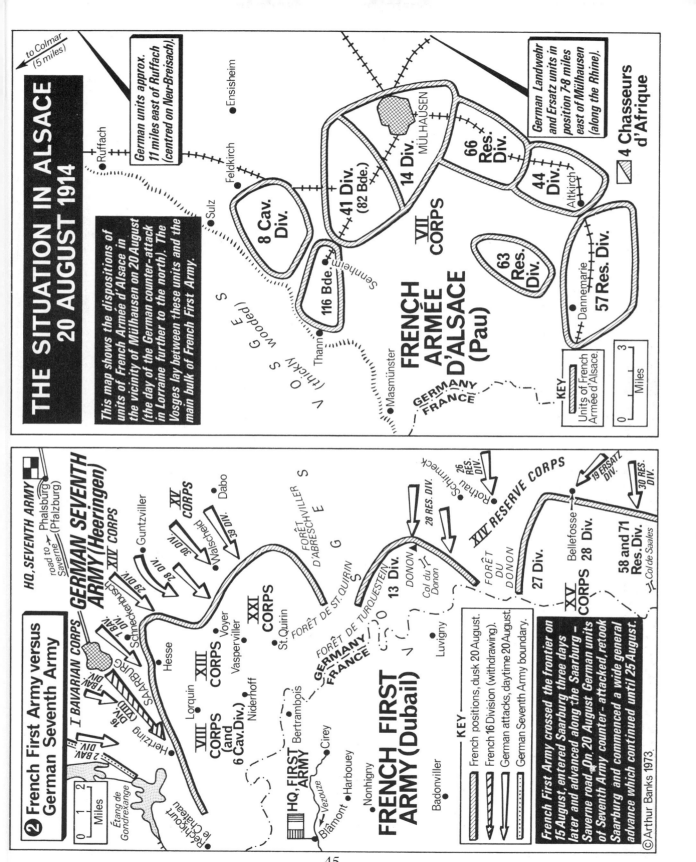

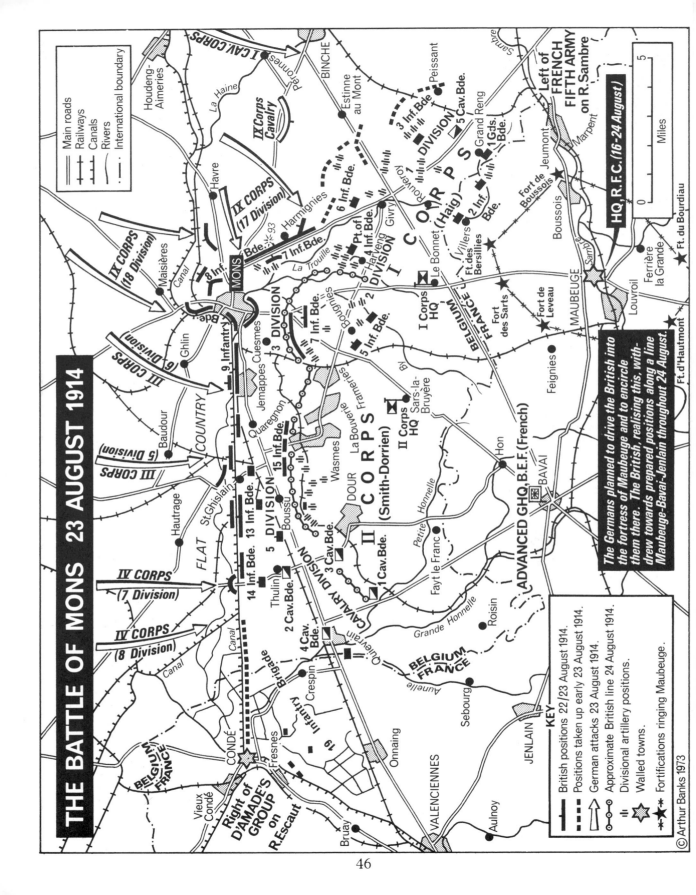

THE BATTLE OF MONS 23 AUGUST 1914
Main roads
Railways
Canals
Rivers
International boundary
IV CORPS (8 Division)
IV CORPS (7 Division)
III CORPS (5 Division)
III CORPS (6 Division)
IX CORPS (18 Division)
IX CORPS (17 Division)
IX Corps Cavalry
I CAV. CORPS
BELGIUM FRANCE
Vieux Condé
CONDÉ
Right of D'AMADE'S GROUP on R.Escaut
Fresnes
19 Infantry Brigade
Crespin
Canal
Hautrage
Baudour
FLAT COUNTRY
St.Ghislain
Ghlin
Maisières
Houdeng-Aimeries
Havre
La Haine
MONS
9 Infantry Bde.
8 Inf. Bde.
14 Inf. Bde.
13 Inf. Bde.
5 DIVISION
15 Inf. Bde.
Thulin
2 Cav. Bde.
Boussu
Quaregnon
Jemappes
Cuesmes
3 DIVISION
7 Inf. Bde.
93
Harmignies
La Trouille
Péronnes
BINCHE
Estinne au Mont
4 Cav. Bde.
CAVALRY DIVISION
3 Cav. Bde.
1 Cav. Bde.
Wasmes
DOUR
La Bouverie
Frameries
Bougnies
II CORPS (Smith-Dorrien)
II Corps HQ
Sars-la-Bruyère
By
5 Inf. Bde.
2 DIVISION
Harveng
Pt. of 4 Inf. Bde.
6 Inf. Bde.
Givry
Rouveroy
1 DIVISION
3 Inf. Bde.
Peissant
5 Cav. Bde.
I CORPS (Haig)
I Corps HQ
Le Bonnet
Villers
2 Inf. Bde.
Grand Reng
1 Gds. Bde.
Bruay
Onnaing
VALENCIENNES
Quievrain
Aunelle
Grande Honnelle
Petite Honnelle
Fayt le Franc
Sebourg
Roisin
Aulnoy
JENLAIN
Hon
ADVANCED GHQ, B.E.F. (French)
BAVAI
Ft. des Bersillies
Fort des Sarts
Fort de Leveau
Feignies
Fort de Boussois
Jeumont
Boussois
MAUBEUGE
Sambre
Marpent
Left of FRENCH FIFTH ARMY on R. Sambre
HQ, R.F.C. (16-24 August)
Louvroil
Ferrière la Grande
Ft. d'Hautmont
Ft. du Bourdiau
0 5 Miles
KEY
British positions 22/23 August 1914.
Positions taken up early 23 August 1914.
German attacks 23 August 1914.
Approximate British line 24 August 1914.
Divisional artillery positions.
Walled towns.
Fortifications ringing Maubeuge.
The Germans planned to drive the British into the fortress of Maubeuge and to encircle them there. The British, realising this, withdrew towards prepared positions along a line Maubeuge-Bavai-Jenlain throughout 24 August.
© Arthur Banks 1973

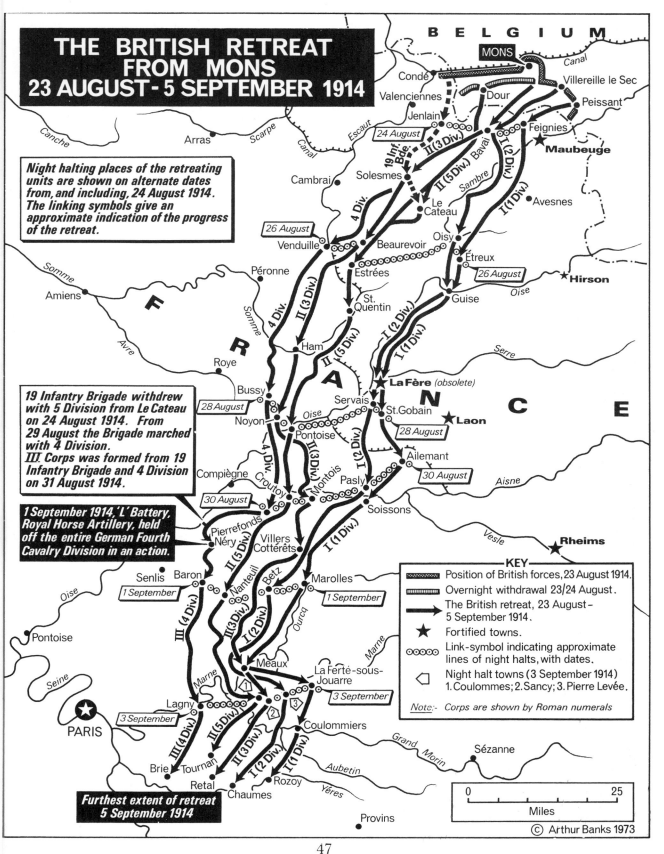

THE BRITISH RETREAT FROM MONS 23 AUGUST – 5 SEPTEMBER 1914

BELGIUM

MONS
Condé
Villereille le Sec
Valenciennes
Dour
Peissant
Jenlain
Feignies
24 August
19 Inf. Bde.
II (3 Div.)
II (5 Div.) Bavai
I (2 Div.)
Maubeuge
Arras
Scarpe
Escaut
Canal
Canche
Canal
Cambrai
Solesmes
4 Div.
Le Cateau
I (1 Div.)
Avesnes
Sambre
Péronne
26 August
Venduille
Beaurevoir
Oisy
Étreux
Amiens
Somme
4 Div.
II (3 Div.)
Estrées
St. Quentin
Guise
26 August
Oise
Hirson
Somme
Avre
F
Roye
Ham
II (5 Div.)
Serre
Bussy
La Fère *(obsolete)*
28 August
Servais
St.Gobain
Laon
Noyon
4 Div.
Pontoise
II (3 Div.)
II (2 Div.)
28 August
Compiègne
Croutoy
Montois
Pasly
Ailemant
30 August
A
Aisne
30 August
Soissons
I (1 Div.)
Pierrefonds
Néry
Villers Cotterêts
II (5 Div.)
Vesle
Rheims

1 September 1914. 'L' Battery, Royal Horse Artillery, held off the entire German Fourth Cavalry Division in an action.

Senlis
Baron
Nanteuil
Betz
Marolles
1 September
III (4 Div.)
II (3 Div.)
I (2 Div.)
1 September
Oise
Ourcq
Marne
Pontoise
Seine
Meaux
La Ferté-sous-Jouarre
3 September
PARIS
Marne
Lagny
3 September
III (4 Div.)
II (5 Div.)
II (3 Div.)
I (2 Div.)
I (1 Div.)
Coulommiers
Brie
Tournan
Retal
Rozoy
Chaumes
Yères
Aubetin
Grand Morin
Sézanne
Provins

Furthest extent of retreat 5 September 1914

Night halting places of the retreating units are shown on alternate dates from, and including, 24 August 1914. The linking symbols give an approximate indication of the progress of the retreat.

19 Infantry Brigade withdrew with 5 Division from Le Cateau on 24 August 1914. From 29 August the Brigade marched with 4 Division. III Corps was formed from 19 Infantry Brigade and 4 Division on 31 August 1914.

KEY
- Position of British forces, 23 August 1914.
- Overnight withdrawal 23/24 August.
- The British retreat, 23 August – 5 September 1914.
- ★ Fortified towns.
- ○○○○○ Link-symbol indicating approximate lines of night halts, with dates.
- ◁ Night halt towns (3 September 1914) 1. Coulommes; 2. Sancy; 3. Pierre Levée.

Note:- Corps are shown by Roman numerals

0 ————— 25
Miles

© Arthur Banks 1973

47

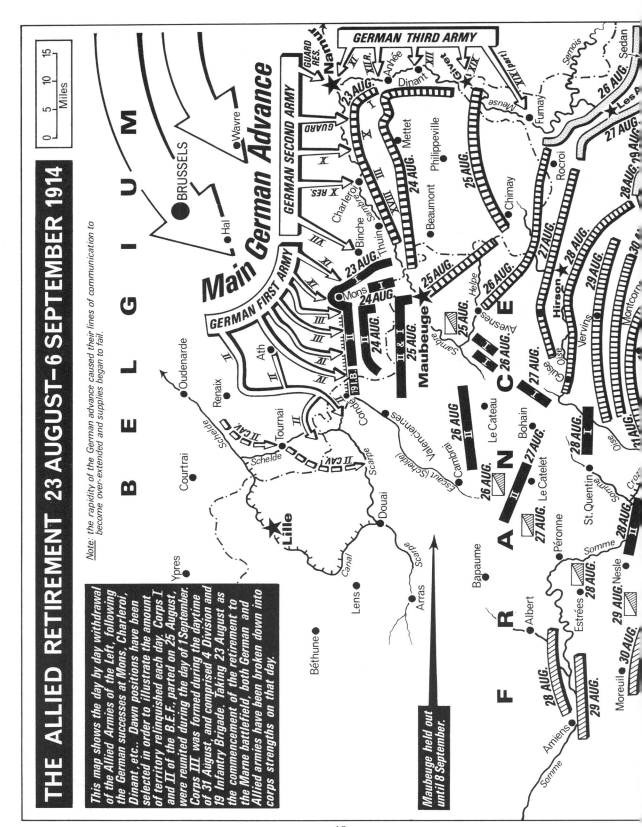

THE ALLIED RETIREMENT 23 AUGUST–6 SEPTEMBER 1914

This map shows the day by day withdrawal of the Allied Armies of the Left, following the German successes at Mons, Charleroi, Dinant, etc.. Dawn positions have been selected in order to illustrate the amount of territory relinquished each day. Corps I and II of the B.E.F. parted on 25 August, were reunited during the day of 1 September. Corps II was formed during the daytime of 31 August, and comprised 4 Division and 19 Infantry Brigade. Taking 23 August as the commencement of the retirement to the Marne battlefield, both German and Allied armies have been broken down into corps strengths on that day.

Note: the rapidity of the German advance caused their lines of communication to become over-extended and supplies began to fail.

B E L G I U M

Main German Advance

BRUSSELS

Hal

Wavre

GERMAN THIRD ARMY

GUARD RES.

Namur

Anhée

Dinant

GERMAN SECOND ARMY

GUARD

Mettet

Philippeville

Chimay

Charleroi

Sambre

Binche

Thuin

Beaumont

GERMAN FIRST ARMY

Ath

Mons

Maubeuge

Oudenaarde

Renaix

Schelde

Tournai

Schelde

Compi

Valenciennes

Escaut (Schelde)

Cambrai

Le Cateau

Bohain

Aulnoye

Avesnes

Helpe

Hirson

Vervins

Guise

Oise

Le Catelet

St. Quentin

Somme

Péronne

Nesle

Estrées

Moreuil

Amiens

Somme

Bapaume

Albert

Arras

Lens

Béthune

Ypres

Lille

Courtrai

Douai

Canal

Scarpe

Scarpe

Scarpe

F R A N C E

Sedan

Semois

Fumay

Givet

Rocroi

Montcornet

Crozat

Meuse

23 AUG.
24 AUG.
25 AUG.
26 AUG.
27 AUG.
28 AUG.
29 AUG.
30 AUG.

Maubeuge held out until 8 September.

Miles
0 5 10 15

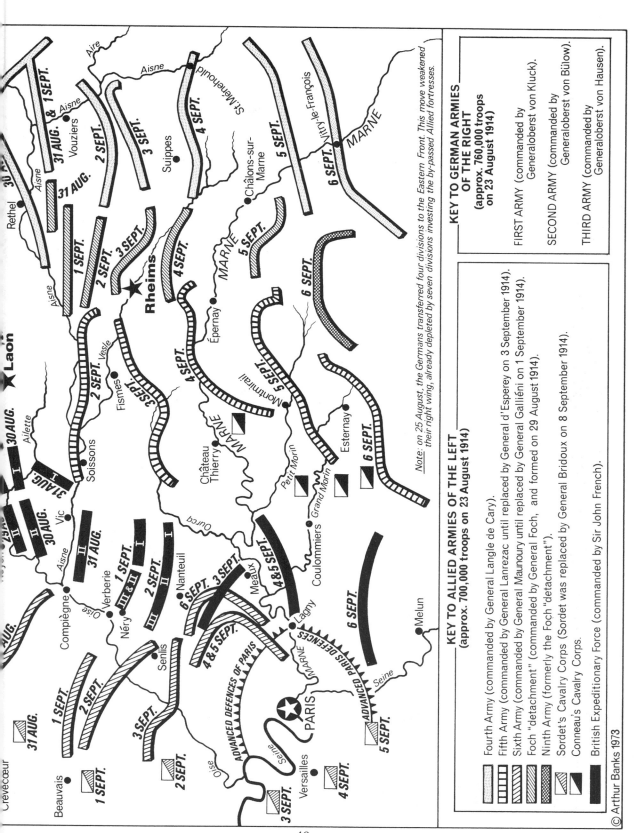

Laon

Rethel

Vouziers

Suippes

Rheims

Épernay

Châlons-sur-Marne

Vitry-le-François

St.Menehould

Soissons

Fismes

Château Thierry

Montmirail

Esternay

Coulommiers

Meaux

Lagny

Nanteuil

Néry

Verberie

Compiègne

Senlis

PARIS

Versailles

Melun

Vic

Beauvais

Crèvecœur

MARNE

Aisne

Aire

Aisne

Vesle

Ailette

Ourcq

Oise

Seine

Petit Morin

Grand Morin

ADVANCED DEFENCES OF PARIS

ADVANCED PARIS DEFENCES

30 AUG. & 1 SEPT.

31 AUG.

31 AUG.

1 SEPT.

2 SEPT.

3 SEPT.

2 SEPT.

3 SEPT.

4 SEPT.

4 SEPT.

5 SEPT.

5 SEPT.

6 SEPT.

6 SEPT.

2 SEPT.

3 SEPT.

4 SEPT.

5 SEPT.

6 SEPT.

30 AUG.

31 AUG.

30 AUG.

31 AUG.

1 SEPT.

2 SEPT.

6 SEPT.

3 SEPT.

4 & 5 SEPT.

4 & 5 SEPT.

6 SEPT.

31 AUG.

1 SEPT.

2 SEPT.

3 SEPT.

4 SEPT.

I   I   II   II   III & II   III

Note: on 25 August, the Germans transferred four divisions to the Eastern Front. This move weakened their right wing, already depleted by seven divisions investing the by-passed Allied fortresses.

KEY TO GERMAN ARMIES OF THE RIGHT
(approx. 760,000 troops on 23 August 1914)

FIRST ARMY (commanded by Generaloberst von Kluck).

SECOND ARMY (commanded by Generaloberst von Bülow).

THIRD ARMY (commanded by Generaloberst von Hausen).

KEY TO ALLIED ARMIES OF THE LEFT
(approx. 700,000 troops on 23 August 1914)

Fourth Army (commanded by General Langle de Cary).

Fifth Army (commanded by General Lanrezac until replaced by General d'Esperey on 3 September 1914).

Sixth Army (commanded by General Maunoury until replaced by General Galliéni on 1 September 1914).

Foch "detachment" (commanded by General Foch, and formed on 29 August 1914).

Ninth Army (formerly the Foch "detachment").

Sordet's Cavalry Corps (Sordet was replaced by General Bridoux on 8 September 1914).

Conneau's Cavalry Corps.

British Expeditionary Force (commanded by Sir John French).

© Arthur Banks 1973

49

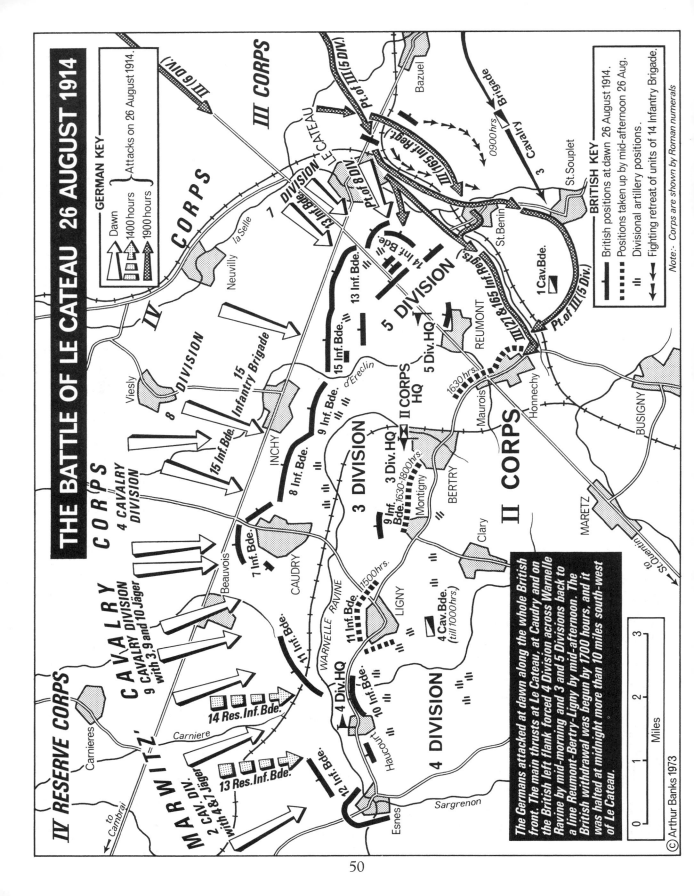

THE BATTLE OF LE CATEAU 26 AUGUST 1914

GERMAN KEY

Dawn
1400 hours
1900 hours

Attacks on 26 August 1914.

BRITISH KEY

British positions at dawn 26 August 1914.

Positions taken up by mid-afternoon 26 Aug.

Divisional artillery positions.

Fighting retreat of units of 14 Infantry Brigade.

Note:- Corps are shown by Roman numerals

The Germans attacked at dawn along the whole British front. The main thrusts at Le Cateau, at Caudry and on the British left flank forced 4 Division across Warnelle Ravine by mid-morning and 3 and 5 Divisions back to a line Reumont-Bertry-Ligny by mid-afternoon. The British withdrawal was begun by 1700 hours, and it was halted at midnight more than 10 miles south-west of Le Cateau.

Miles

0   1   2   3

© Arthur Banks 1973

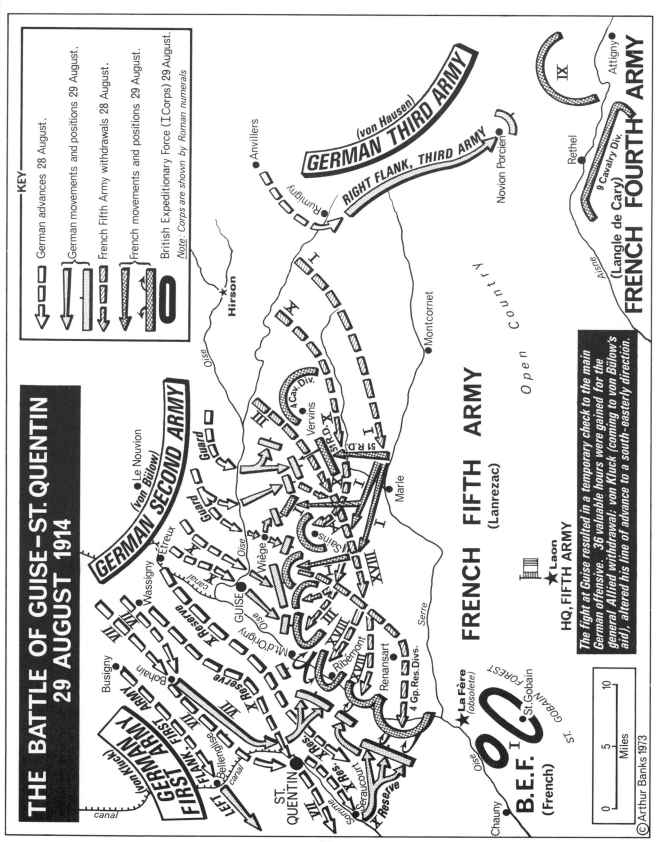

THE BATTLE OF GUISE–ST. QUENTIN 29 AUGUST 1914

— KEY —

German advances 28 August.

German movements and positions 29 August.

French Fifth Army withdrawals 28 August.

French movements and positions 29 August.

British Expeditionary Force (I Corps) 29 August.

Note: Corps are shown by Roman numerals.

GERMAN THIRD ARMY
(von Hausen)

RIGHT FLANK, THIRD ARMY

Anvillers

Rumigny

Novion Porcien

Attigny

Rethel

IX

FRENCH FOURTH ARMY
(Langle de Cary)

9 Cavalry Div.

Aisne

Hirson

Oise

Le Nouvion

GERMAN SECOND ARMY
(von Bülow)

Guard

Guard

4 Cav. Div.

Vervins

5 R.D.

5 T R.D.

Montcornet

Open Country

Étreux

Wassigny

X

Oise

Wiège

Sains

Marle

I

FRENCH FIFTH ARMY
(Lanrezac)

Serre

★ Laon

HQ, FIFTH ARMY

Busigny

Bohain

X Reserve

Guise

Mt. d'Origny

Oise

XVIII

Ribemont

Renansart

4 Gp. Res. Divs.

Bellenglise

canal

canal

GERMAN FIRST ARMY
(von Kluck)

LEFT FLANK

Somme

St. Gobain Forest

La Fère (obsolete)

St.

Oise

Chauny

B.E.F. I
(French)

ST. QUENTIN

Séraucourt

X Res.

X Reserve

VII

The fight at Guise resulted in a temporary check to the main German offensive. 36 valuable hours were gained for the general Allied withdrawal: von Bülow (coming to von Kluck's aid), altered his line of advance to a south-easterly direction.

0	5	10

Miles

© Arthur Banks 1973

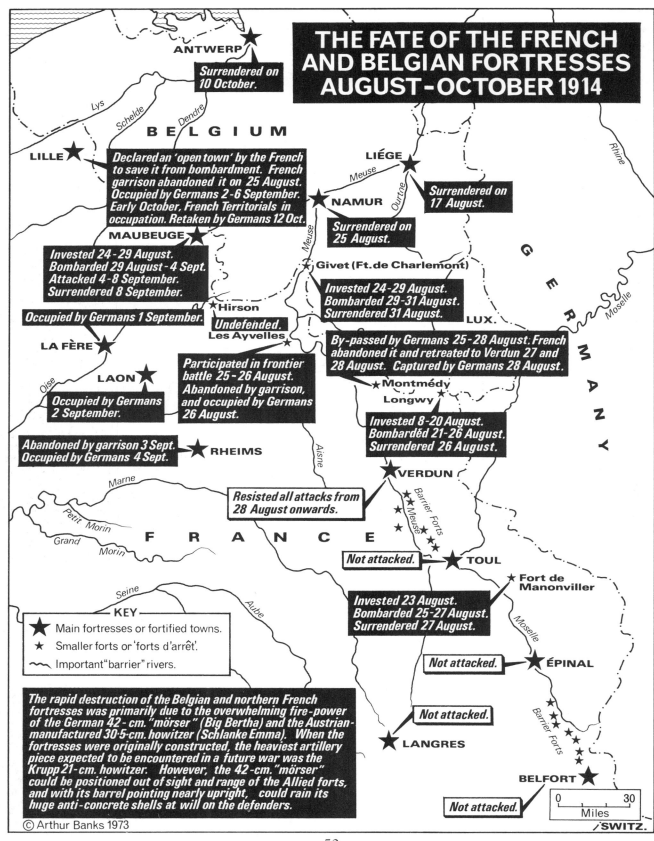

THE FATE OF THE FRENCH AND BELGIAN FORTRESSES AUGUST-OCTOBER 1914

ANTWERP
Surrendered on 10 October.

BELGIUM

LILLE
Declared an 'open town' by the French to save it from bombardment. French garrison abandoned it on 25 August. Occupied by Germans 2-6 September. Early October, French Territorials in occupation. Retaken by Germans 12 Oct.

LIÉGE
Surrendered on 17 August.

NAMUR
Surrendered on 25 August.

MAUBEUGE
Invested 24-29 August. Bombarded 29 August-4 Sept. Attacked 4-8 September. Surrendered 8 September.

Givet (Ft.de Charlemont)
Invested 24-29 August. Bombarded 29-31 August. Surrendered 31 August.

LUX.

Occupied by Germans 1 September.

Hirson

Undefended. Les Ayvelles

By-passed by Germans 25-28 August: French abandoned it and retreated to Verdun 27 and 28 August. Captured by Germans 28 August.

LA FÈRE

LAON
Participated in frontier battle 25-26 August. Abandoned by garrison, and occupied by Germans 26 August.

Montmédy
Longwy
Invested 8-20 August. Bombarded 21-26 August. Surrendered 26 August.

Occupied by Germans 2 September.

Abandoned by garrison 3 Sept. Occupied by Germans 4 Sept.
RHEIMS

VERDUN
Resisted all attacks from 28 August onwards.

Barrier Forts

FRANCE

Not attacked.
TOUL

Fort de Manonviller

Invested 23 August. Bombarded 25-27 August. Surrendered 27 August.

KEY

★ Main fortresses or fortified towns.

✦ Smaller forts or 'forts d'arrêt'.

〰 Important "barrier" rivers.

Not attacked.
ÉPINAL

Not attacked.

Barrier Forts

The rapid destruction of the Belgian and northern French fortresses was primarily due to the overwhelming fire-power of the German 42-cm. "mörser" (Big Bertha) and the Austrian-manufactured 30·5-cm. howitzer (Schlanke Emma). When the fortresses were originally constructed, the heaviest artillery piece expected to be encountered in a future war was the Krupp 21-cm. howitzer. However, the 42-cm. "mörser" could be positioned out of sight and range of the Allied forts, and with its barrel pointing nearly upright, could rain its huge anti-concrete shells at will on the defenders.

LANGRES

BELFORT

Not attacked.

0   30
Miles

© Arthur Banks 1973

SWITZ.

GERMANY

Rhine
Moselle
Meuse
Ourthe
Lys
Schelde
Dendre
Oise
Aisne
Marne
Petit Morin
Grand Morin
Seine
Aube
Moselle

52

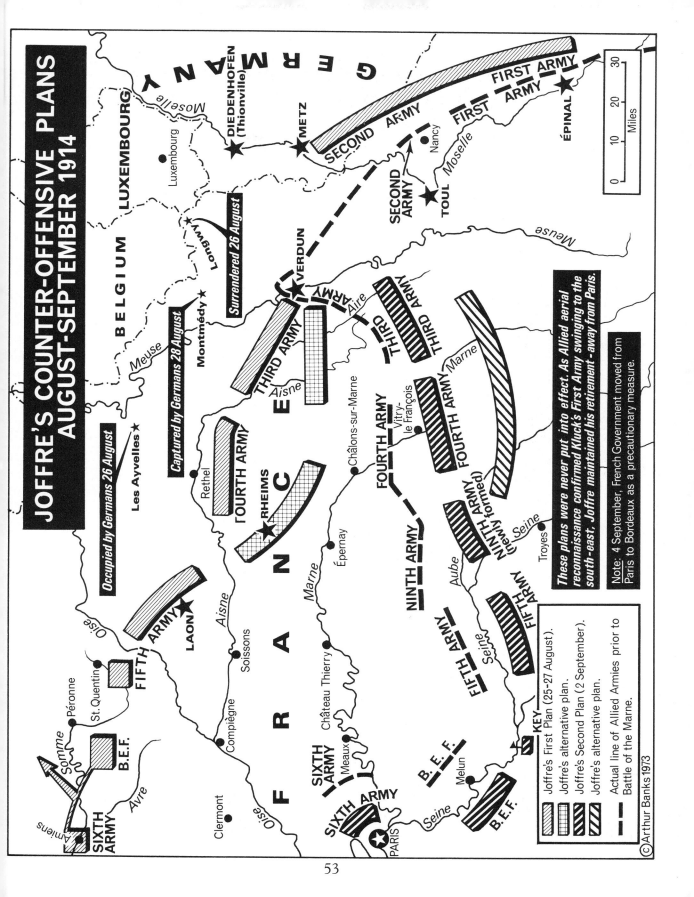

JOFFRE'S COUNTER-OFFENSIVE PLANS AUGUST-SEPTEMBER 1914

GERMANY

LUXEMBOURG

BELGIUM

FRANCE

Occupied by Germans 26 August

Les Ayvelles

Captured by Germans 28 August

Montmédy

Surrendered 26 August

Longwy

VERDUN

DIEDENHOFEN (Thionville)

METZ

SECOND ARMY

FIRST ARMY

FIRST ARMY

Nancy

Moselle

SECOND ARMY

TOUL

ÉPINAL

Meuse

THIRD ARMY

THIRD ARMY

THIRD ARMY

Aire

Aisne

FOURTH ARMY

RHEIMS

Rethel

Aisne

FOURTH ARMY

Châlons-sur-Marne

Marne

Vitry-le-François

FOURTH ARMY

FIFTH ARMY

LAON

Oise

Soissons

Épernay

NINTH ARMY

Aube

NINTH ARMY (Newly formed)

Troyes

Seine

FIFTH ARMY

FIFTH ARMY

Seine

Péronne

St. Quentin

B.E.F.

Compiègne

Clermont

Château Thierry

SIXTH ARMY

Meaux

Seine

SIXTH ARMY

PARIS

Melun

B.E.F.

B.E.F.

Somme

Avre

Amiens

SIXTH ARMY

Oise

Luxembourg

Moselle

Meuse

Marne

These plans were never put into effect. As Allied aerial reconnaissance confirmed Kluck's First Army swinging to the south-east, Joffre maintained his retirement - away from Paris.

Note: 4 September, French Government moved from Paris to Bordeaux as a precautionary measure.

KEY:

	Joffre's First Plan (25-27 August).
	Joffre's alternative plan.
	Joffre's Second Plan (2 September).
	Joffre's alternative plan.
— — —	Actual line of Allied Armies prior to Battle of the Marne.

Miles
0 10 20 30

© Arthur Banks 1973

THE FIRST BATTLE OF THE MARNE 5-10 SEPTEMBER 191

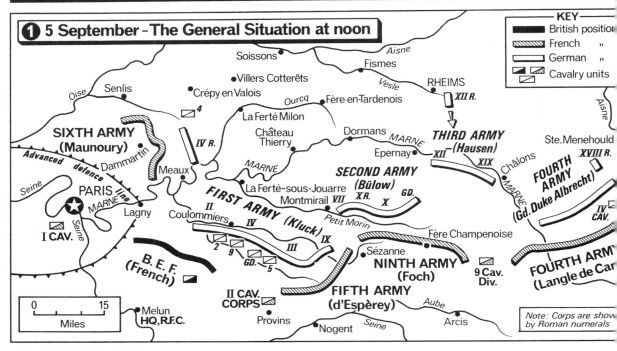

① 5 September – The General Situation at noon

Soissons

Aisne

Villers Cotterêts

Fismes

Vesle

RHEIMS   XII R.

Senlis

Oise

Crépy en Valois

Ourcq   Fère-en-Tardenois

⊠ 4

La Ferté Milon

Dormans

MARNE

THIRD ARMY

Ste. Menehould

SIXTH ARMY
(Maunoury)

IV R.

Château Thierry

Epernay

(Hausen)

XII   XIX

Châlons

FOURTH ARMY

XVIII R.

Advanced defence line

Dammartin

Meaux

MARNE

La Ferté-sous-Jouarre

Montmirail

SECOND ARMY
(Bülow)

VII   X

X R.   GD.

MARNE

(Gd. Duke Albrecht)

IV CAV.

Seine

PARIS ★

MARNE

Lagny

FIRST ARMY (Kluck)

II

Coulommiers

IV

Petit Morin

III   IX

Fère Champenoise

FOURTH ARMY

I CAV. ◩

Seine

2   9

GD.   5

Sézanne

NINTH ARMY
(Foch)

9 Cav. Div.

(Langle de Car

B. E. F.
(French) ▭

0   15
Miles

Melun
HQ, R.F.C.

II CAV.
CORPS ◩

FIFTH ARMY
(d'Espèrey)

Provins

Aube

Arcis

Nogent   Seine

Note: Corps are show by Roman numerals

② 6 September – Withdrawal of the German First Army's Right Wing

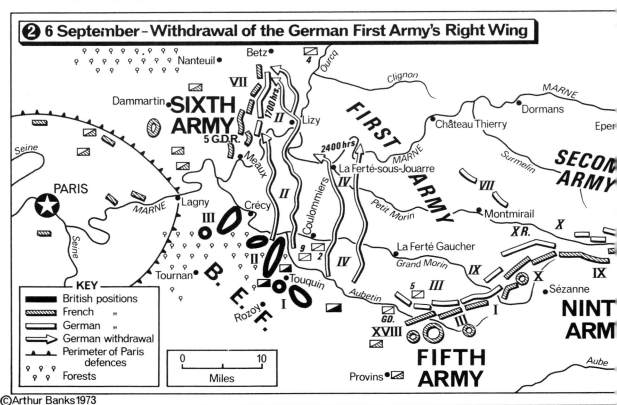

Betz

Ourcq

Nanteuil

⊠ 4

Clignon

MARNE

VII

Dormans

Dammartin

SIXTH
ARMY

II

1700 hrs.

Lizy

FIRST

Château Thierry

SECON
ARM

5 G.D.R.

Meaux

2400 hrs

La Ferté-sous-Jouarre

Surmelin

Eper

Seine

IV

ARMY

VII

PARIS ★

MARNE

Lagny

III

Crécy

II

Coulommiers

Petit Morin

Montmirail

X

X R.

II

9   2

IV

La Ferté Gaucher

Grand Morin

IX

X

IX

Tournan

B.

I

Touquin

Aubetin

5   III

Sézanne

E.

Rozoy

F.

GD.

I

III

NINT
ARM

XVIII

0   10
Miles

Provins ◩

FIFTH
ARMY

Aube

© Arthur Banks 1973

54

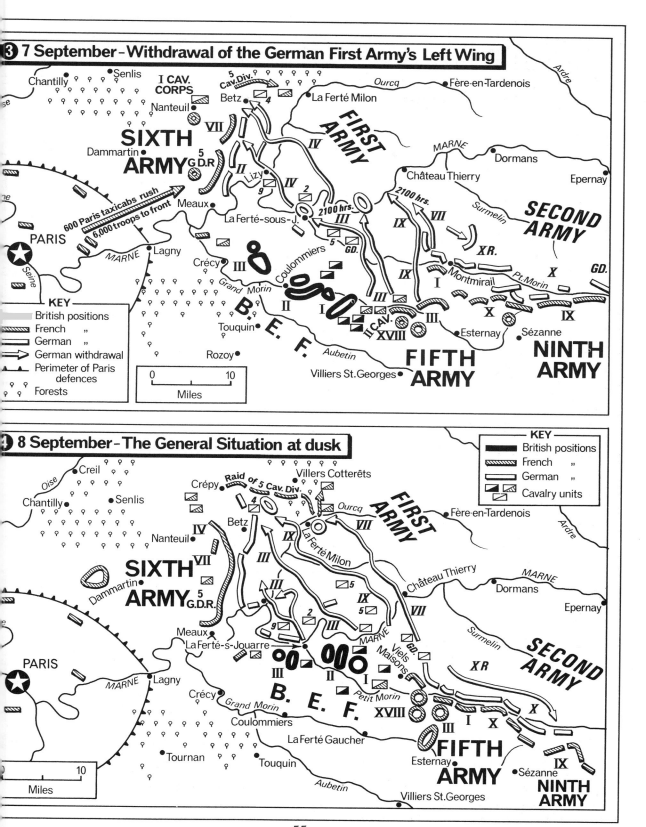

3 **7 September – Withdrawal of the German First Army's Left Wing**

Chantilly • Senlis
I CAV. CORPS
5 Cav.Div.
Betz
Ourcq
La Ferté Milon
Fère-en-Tardenois
Ardre

Nanteuil
VII
SIXTH ARMY
Dammartin
5 G.D.R.
II
Lizy
9
IV
2
FIRST ARMY
IV
MARNE
Château Thierry
Dormans
Epernay

600 Paris taxicabs rush
6,000 troops to front
Meaux
La Ferté-sous-J.
III
2100 hrs.
5 G.D.
IX
2100 hrs.
VII
XR.
SECOND ARMY
Surmelin

PARIS
Seine
MARNE
Lagny
Crécy
III
Grand Morin
Coulommiers
II
I
III
III
III
XVIII
I CAV.
I
Montmirail
X
Pt.Morin
X
GD.
IX

KEY
British positions
French "
German "
German withdrawal
Perimeter of Paris defences
Forests

Touquin
B. E. F.
Aubetin
Esternay
Sézanne
FIFTH ARMY
NINTH ARMY

Rozoy
Villiers St.Georges

0   10
Miles

---

4 **8 September – The General Situation at dusk**

KEY
British positions
French "
German "
Cavalry units

Oise
Creil
Crépy
Raid of 5 Cav. Div.
Villers Cotterêts
Ourcq
FIRST ARMY
Fère-en-Tardenois
Ardre

Chantilly • Senlis
Betz
4
IX
VII
La Ferté Milon
Château Thierry
MARNE
Dormans
Epernay

Nanteuil
IV
SIXTH ARMY
VII
Dammartin
5 G.D.R.
III
III
III
5
IX
5
VII
Surmelin
SECOND ARMY

Meaux
La Ferté-s-Jouarre
9
2
III
III
Viels Maisons
GD.
XR

PARIS
MARNE
Lagny
Crécy
III
Grand Morin
Coulommiers
II
I
Petit Morin
XVIII
I
IX
X
X
IX

Tournan
B. E. F.
La Ferté Gaucher
Touquin
Aubetin
Esternay
III
FIFTH ARMY
Sézanne
IX
NINTH ARMY

10
Miles
Villiers St.Georges

55

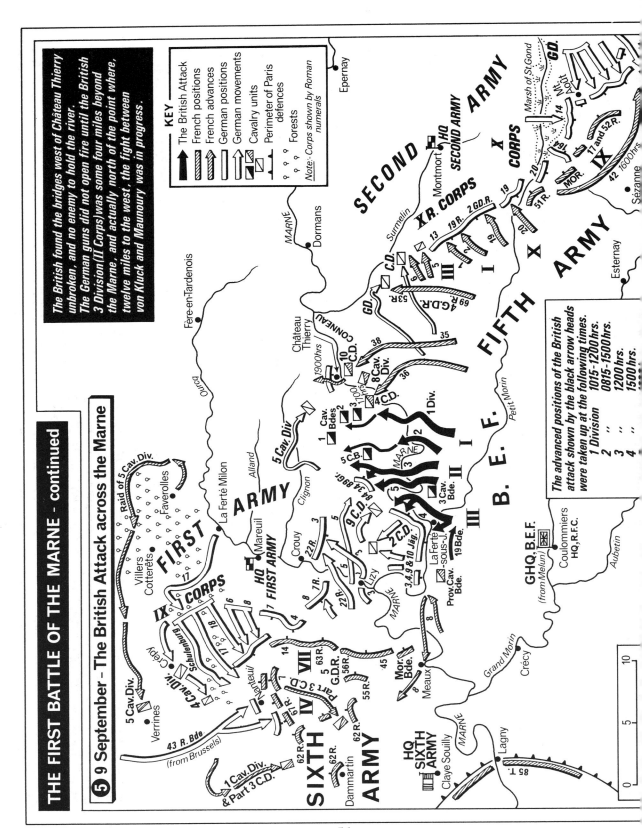

THE FIRST BATTLE OF THE MARNE - continued

⑤ 9 September – The British Attack across the Marne

KEY

The British Attack
French positions
French advances
German positions
German movements
Cavalry units
Perimeter of Paris defences
Forests

Note:- Corps shown by Roman numerals

The British found the bridges west of Château Thierry unbroken, and no enemy to hold the river. The German guns did not open fire until the British 3 Division/II Corps)was some four miles beyond the Marne. and actually north of the point where, twelve miles to the west, the fight between von Kluck and Maunoury was in progress.

The advanced positions of the British attack shown by the black arrow heads were taken up at the following times.

1 Division	..	1015-1200hrs.
2 "	..	0815-1500hrs.
3 "	..	1200 hrs.
4 "	..	1500 hrs.

SECOND ARMY

FIFTH ARMY

B. E. F.

FIRST ARMY

SIXTH ARMY

56

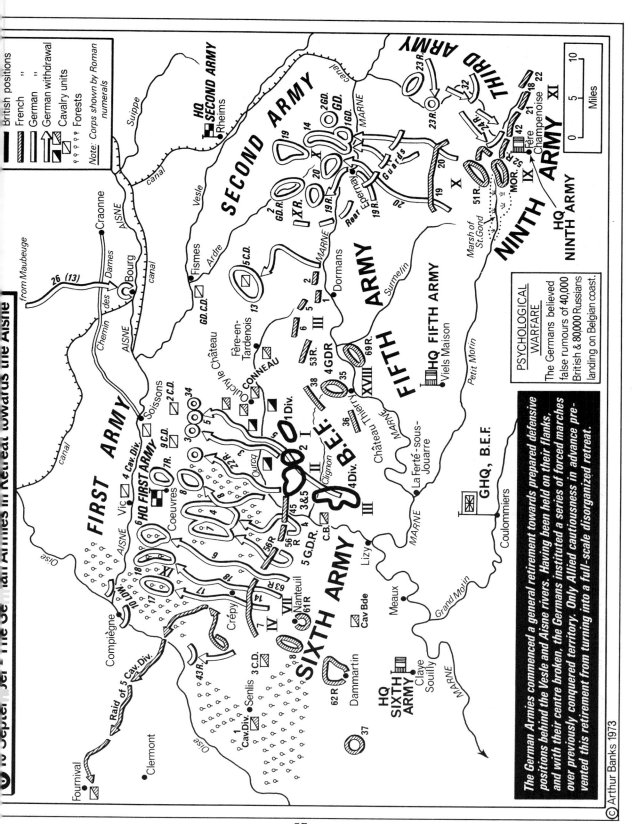

The German Armies commenced a general retirement towards prepared defensive positions behind the Vesle and Aisne rivers. Having been held on their flanks, and with their centre broken, the Germans instituted a series of forced marches over previously conquered territory. Only Allied cautiousness in advance prevented this retirement from turning into a full-scale disorganized retreat.

PSYCHOLOGICAL
WARFARE
The Germans believed
false rumours of 40,000
British & 80,000 Russians
landing on Belgian coast.

© Arthur Banks 1973

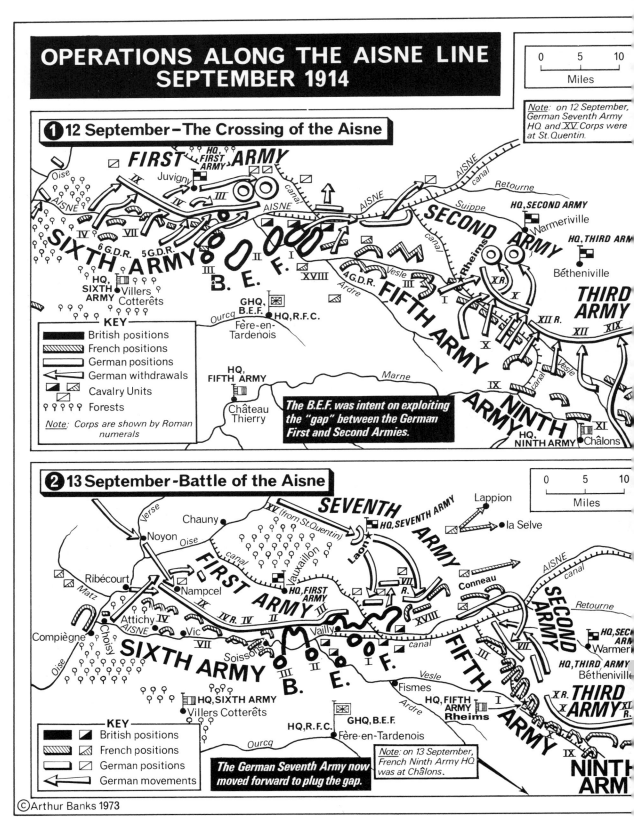

OPERATIONS ALONG THE AISNE LINE
SEPTEMBER 1914

0   5   10
Miles

Note: on 12 September, German Seventh Army HQ and XV Corps were at St.Quentin.

❶ 12 September – The Crossing of the Aisne

FIRST ARMY
HQ, FIRST ARMY
Juvigny
Oise
AISNE
AISNE canal
AISNE
Retourne
Suippe
SECOND ARMY
HQ, SECOND ARMY
Warmeriville
HQ, THIRD ARMY
Bétheniville
SIXTH ARMY
6 G.D.R. 5 G.D.R.
B. E. F.
Rheims
canal
Vesle
4 G.D.R.
Ardre
X.R.
X
THIRD ARMY
HQ, SIXTH ARMY
Villers Cotterêts
GHQ, B.E.F.
HQ, R.F.C.
Ourcq
Fère-en-Tardenois
FIFTH ARMY
XVIII
XII R.
XII XIX
X

KEY
▬ British positions
▨ French positions
▭ German positions
⬅ German withdrawals
◣ ⊠ Cavalry Units
♀♀♀♀♀ Forests

Note: Corps are shown by Roman numerals

HQ, FIFTH ARMY
Château Thierry
Marne

The B.E.F. was intent on exploiting the "gap" between the German First and Second Armies.

NINTH ARMY
HQ, NINTH ARMY
Châlons
IX
XI

0   5   10
Miles

❷ 13 September – Battle of the Aisne

SEVENTH ARMY
Lappion
HQ, SEVENTH ARMY
la Selve
Verse
Chauny
Noyon
Oise
canal
Vauxaillon
XV (from St.Quentin)
Laon
Ribécourt
Matz
Nampcel
HQ, FIRST ARMY
FIRST ARMY
VII R.
Conneau
AISNE canal
Retourne
SECOND ARMY
HQ, SECOND ARMY
Warmeri
Attichy IV
AISNE
IV.R. IV
II
III
XVIII
III
VII
HQ, THIRD ARMY
Bétheniville
Compiègne
Choisy
Oise
SIXTH ARMY
VII
Soissons
Vic
III
II
B. E. F.
I
Vailly
canal
Vesle
FIFTH ARMY
X R.
X R.
THIRD ARMY
XI
HQ, SIXTH ARMY
Villers Cotterêts
♀♀♀♀
HQ, R.F.C.
GHQ, B.E.F.
Fère-en-Tardenois
Ourcq
Fismes
Ardre
HQ, FIFTH ARMY
Rheims
I
Vesle

KEY
▬ ◣ British positions
▨ ⊠ French positions
▭ ◹ German positions
⬅ German movements

The German Seventh Army now moved forward to plug the gap.

Note: on 13 September, French Ninth Army HQ was at Châlons.

NINTH ARMY
IX

©Arthur Banks 1973

58

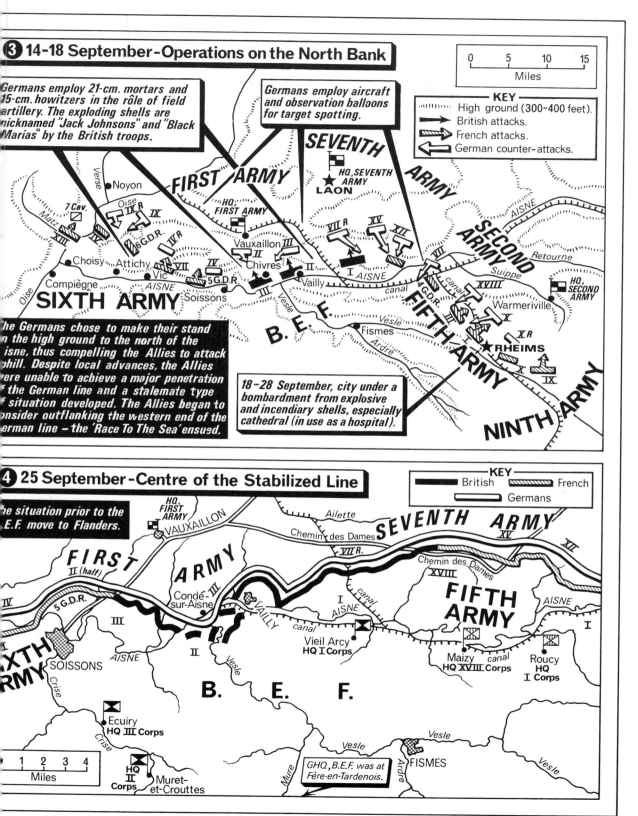

❸ 14-18 September - Operations on the North Bank

0   5   10   15
Miles

Germans employ 21-cm. mortars and 15-cm. howitzers in the rôle of field artillery. The exploding shells are nicknamed "Jack Johnsons" and "Black Marias" by the British troops.

Germans employ aircraft and observation balloons for target spotting.

KEY
- High ground (300-400 feet).
- British attacks.
- French attacks.
- German counter-attacks.

SEVENTH ARMY

FIRST ARMY

HQ, SEVENTH ARMY
LAON

HQ, FIRST ARMY

Verse

Noyon

Oise

7 Cav.

Matz

XIII

IX R

IX

6 G.D.R.

IV R

Choisy

Attichy

VII

IV

Vic

5 G.D.R.

Compiègne

Soissons

SIXTH ARMY

Oise

AISNE

Vauxaillon

Chivres

Vailly

VII R

XV

XII

I

AISNE

canal

SECOND ARMY

AISNE

Retourne

Suippe

XVIII

HQ, SECOND ARMY

Warmeriville

X

canal

4 G.D.R.

III

FIFTH ARMY

B. E. F.

Vesle

Fismes

Vesle

Ardre

RHEIMS

X R

X

IX

NINTH ARMY

The Germans chose to make their stand on the high ground to the north of the Aisne, thus compelling the Allies to attack uphill. Despite local advances, the Allies were unable to achieve a major penetration of the German line and a stalemate type of situation developed. The Allies began to consider outflanking the western end of the German line – the 'Race To The Sea' ensued.

18–28 September, city under a bombardment from explosive and incendiary shells, especially cathedral (in use as a hospital).

❹ 25 September - Centre of the Stabilized Line

KEY
British   French
Germans

The situation prior to the B.E.F. move to Flanders.

HQ, FIRST ARMY
VAUXAILLON

Ailette

Chemin des Dames

SEVENTH ARMY

XV

FIRST

ARMY

II (half)

IV

5 G.D.R.

III

Condé-sur-Aisne

III

VAILLY

II

SOISSONS

AISNE

Crise

Vesle

VII R

Chemin des Dames

XVIII

I

AISNE

canal

Vieil Arcy
HQ I Corps

Maizy
HQ XVIII Corps

canal

XII

FIFTH ARMY

AISNE

Roucy
HQ I Corps

I

B.   E.   F.

Ecuiry
HQ III Corps

Crise

Vesle

Vesle

Vesle

Mure

Ardre

FISMES

GHQ, B.E.F. was at Fère-en-Tardenois.

HQ II Corps
Muret-et-Crouttes

1 2 3 4
Miles

59

BELGIAN SORTIES FROM ANTWERP AUGUST–SEPTEMBER 1914

The main object of the sorties was to divert part of German strength from their main lines of advance into France. There was also the minor hope that some sort of breakthrough in the German rear might be won.

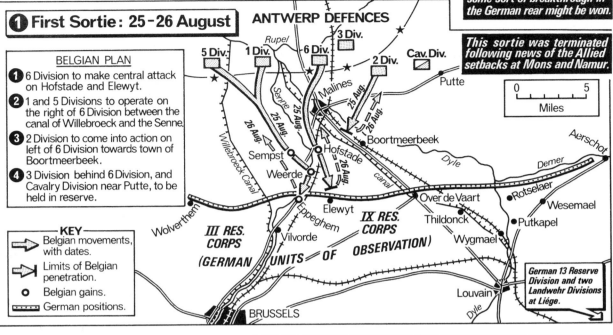

① First Sortie: 25–26 August

ANTWERP DEFENCES

This sortie was terminated following news of the Allied setbacks at Mons and Namur.

BELGIAN PLAN

❶ 6 Division to make central attack on Hofstade and Elewyt.

❷ 1 and 5 Divisions to operate on the right of 6 Division between the canal of Willebroeck and the Senne.

❸ 2 Division to come into action on left of 6 Division towards town of Boortmeerbeek.

❹ 3 Division behind 6 Division, and Cavalry Division near Putte, to be held in reserve.

—KEY—
- Belgian movements, with dates.
- Limits of Belgian penetration.
- ○ Belgian gains.
- German positions.

German 13 Reserve Division and two Landwehr Divisions at Liége.

(map labels: 5 Div., 1 Div., 6 Div., 3 Div., 2 Div., Cav. Div., Rupel, Putte, Senne, Malines, 25 Aug., 26 Aug., Boortmeerbeek, Aerschot, Sempst, Hofstade, Dyle, Demer, Weerde, Rotselaer, Wesemael, Eppeghem, Elewyt, IX RES. CORPS, Over de Vaart, Thildonck, Putkapel, Wolverthem, III RES. CORPS (GERMAN UNITS OF OBSERVATION), Vilvorde, Wygmael, Louvain, Dyle, BRUSSELS; scale 0–5 Miles)

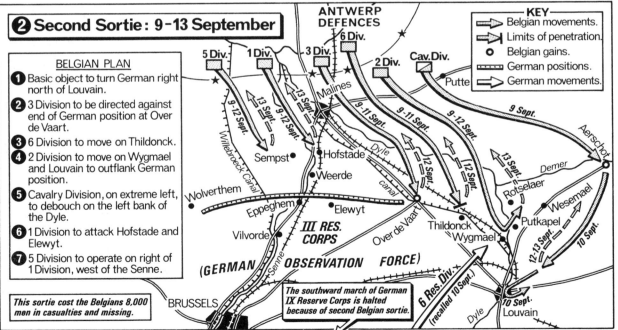

② Second Sortie: 9–13 September

ANTWERP DEFENCES

—KEY—
- Belgian movements.
- Limits of penetration.
- ○ Belgian gains.
- German positions.
- German movements.

BELGIAN PLAN

❶ Basic object to turn German right north of Louvain.

❷ 3 Division to be directed against end of German position at Over de Vaart.

❸ 6 Division to move on Thildonck.

❹ 2 Division to move on Wygmael and Louvain to outflank German position.

❺ Cavalry Division, on extreme left, to debouch on the left bank of the Dyle.

❻ 1 Division to attack Hofstade and Elewyt.

❼ 5 Division to operate on right of 1 Division, west of the Senne.

This sortie cost the Belgians 8,000 men in casualties and missing.

The southward march of German IX Reserve Corps is halted because of second Belgian sortie.

(map labels: 5 Div., 1 Div., 3 Div., 6 Div., 2 Div., Cav. Div., Putte, Malines, 9–12 Sept., 13 Sept., 9 Sept., 9–11 Sept., Aerschot, Willebroeck Canal, Sempst, Hofstade, Dyle, canal, 12 Sept., Demer, Weerde, Rotselaer, Wesemael, Wolverthem, Eppeghem, Elewyt, III RES. CORPS, Over de Vaart, Thildonck, Putkapel, Vilvorde, 13 Sept., 10 Sept., Wygmael, 12–13 Sept., (GERMAN OBSERVATION FORCE), 6 Res. Div. (recalled 10 Sept.), 10 Sept., Louvain, Dyle, BRUSSELS)

On 22 September, 700 Belgian cyclist volunteers arranged in seven detachments, left Antwerp to destroy railway lines of communication in enemy-occupied region outside the fortress. Main lines were severed in Limbourg, Brabant and Hainaut provinces, disrupting German transport. Most cyclists returned to Antwerp, but some were captured.

A third sortie, requested by Joffre on 24 September, never materialised as the Germans launched *their* offensive on Antwerp shortly after Joffre's request.

© Arthur Banks 1973

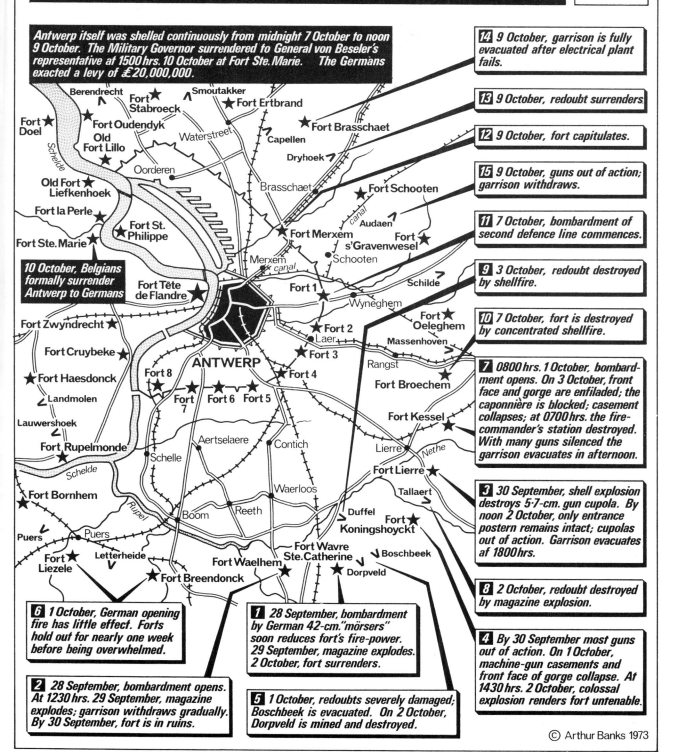

THE GERMAN VICTORY AT ANTWERP 26 SEPTEMBER – 9 OCTOBER 1914

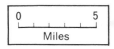

0   5
Miles

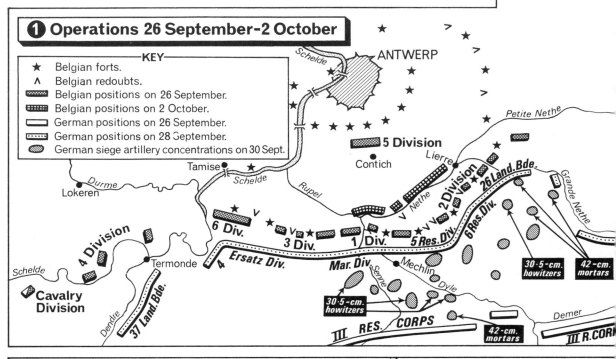

❶ Operations 26 September–2 October

KEY
- ★ Belgian forts.
- ∧ Belgian redoubts.
- Belgian positions on 26 September.
- Belgian positions on 2 October.
- German positions on 26 September.
- German positions on 28 September.
- German siege artillery concentrations on 30 Sept.

ANTWERP

Schelde

Petite Nethe

5 Division

Contich

Lierre

Tamise

Schelde

Durme

Lokeren

Rupel

Nethe

26 Land. Bde.

2 Division

Grande Nethe

6 Res. Div.

6 Div.

3 Div.

1 Div.

5 Res. Div.

30·5-cm. howitzers

42-cm. mortars

4 Division

Scheldt

Termonde

4 Ersatz Div.

Mar. Div.

Mechlin

Senne

Dyle

30·5-cm. howitzers

Cavalry Division

Dendre

37 Land. Bde.

III RES. CORPS

42-cm. mortars

Demer

III R. COR

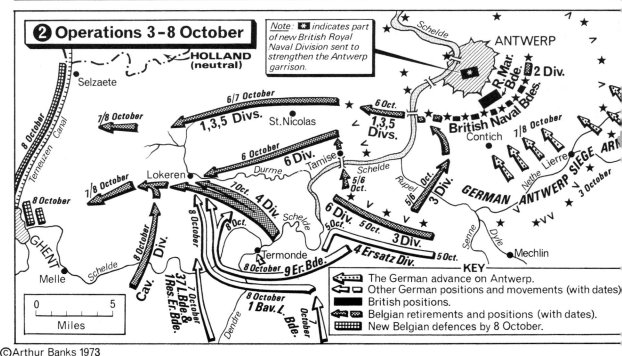

❷ Operations 3–8 October

Note: ✳ *indicates part of new British Royal Naval Division sent to strengthen the Antwerp garrison.*

HOLLAND (neutral)

Selzaete

8 October

Terneuzen Canal

7/8 October

6/7 October

1,3,5 Divs.

St. Nicolas

6 October

6 Div.

Durme

Tamise

Schelde

ANTWERP

Schelde

R. Mar. Bde.

2 Div.

British Naval Bdes.

Contich

7/8 October

6 Oct.

1,3,5 Divs.

Nethe

Lierre

GERMAN ANTWERP SIEGE ARM

3 October

8 October

7/8 October

Lokeren

7 Oct.

4 Div.

5/6 Oct.

3 Div.

Rupel

5/6 Oct.

8 October

8 October

6 Oct.

Schelde

6 Div.

5 Oct.

3 Div.

Senne

Dyle

Mechlin

GHENT

Cav. Div.

8 October

Termonde

9 Er. Bde.

4 Ersatz Div.

5 Oct.

Melle

Schelde

8 October

7 October
37 L. Bde. & 1 Res. Er. Bde.

8 October
1 Bav. L.
Bde.

7 October

Dendre

0   5
Miles

KEY
- ◁ The German advance on Antwerp.
- ◁ Other German positions and movements (with dates)
- British positions.
- ◀ Belgian retirements and positions (with dates).
- New Belgian defences by 8 October.

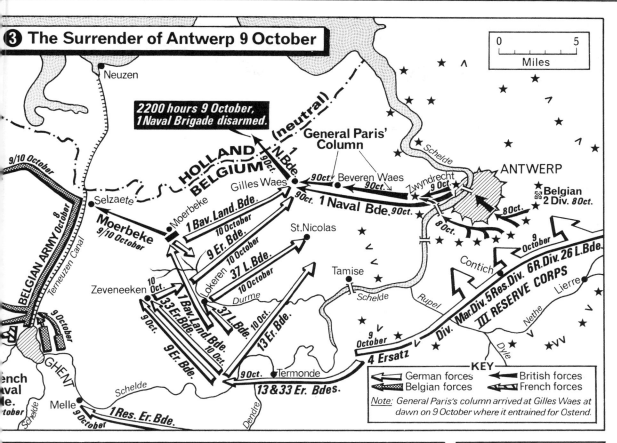

❸ The Surrender of Antwerp 9 October

2200 hours 9 October, 1 Naval Brigade disarmed.

General Paris' Column

HOLLAND (neutral)
BELGIUM

Neuzen

Selzaete

Moerbeke 9/10 October

Moerbeke

1 Bav. Land. Bde. 10 October

Gilles Waes 9 Oct.

Beveren Waes 90ct.

1 Naval Bde. 90ct.

Zwyndrecht 9 Oct.

8 Oct.

ANTWERP

★ Belgian 2 Div. 80ct.

80ct.

9 Er. Bde. 10 October

St. Nicolas

37 L. Bde. 10 October

Zeveneeken 10 Oct.

Lokeren 10 October

1 Bav. Land. Bde. 10 Oct.

33 Er. Bde.

37 L. Bde. 10 Oct.

Durme

Tamise

Schelde

13 Er. Bde. 10 Oct.

9 Er. Bde.

9 Oct.

Termonde 90ct.

13 & 33 Er. Bdes.

Contich

9 October

Div. Mar.Div. 5Res.Div. 6R.Div. 26 L.Bde.

III RESERVE CORPS

Lierre

Nethe

4 Ersatz 9 October

Dyle

Rupel

BELGIAN ARMY 8 October

Terneuzen Canal

9/10 October

9/10 October

9 October

GHENT

Schelde

French Naval Bde.

Melle

1 Res. Er. Bde. 9 October

Dendre

KEY

German forces	British forces
Belgian forces	French forces

Note: General Paris's column arrived at Gilles Waes at dawn on 9 October where it entrained for Ostend.

0 ___ 5 Miles

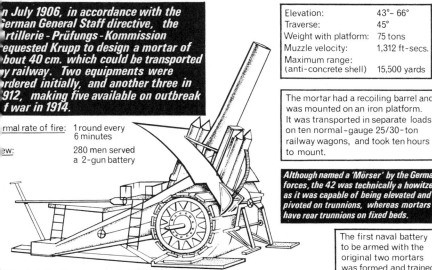

German 42-cm. (16·5-inch) L/16 Mortar "Gamma"

In July 1906, in accordance with the German General Staff directive, the Artillerie-Prüfungs-Kommission requested Krupp to design a mortar of about 40 cm. which could be transported by railway. Two equipments were ordered initially, and another three in 1912, making five available on outbreak of war in 1914.

Normal rate of fire: 1 round every 6 minutes

Crew: 280 men served a 2-gun battery

The weapon was known as "Big Bertha" or "Fat Bertha".

Elevation:	43°– 66°
Traverse:	45°
Weight with platform:	75 tons
Muzzle velocity:	1,312 ft-secs.
Maximum range: (anti-concrete shell)	15,500 yards

The mortar had a recoiling barrel and was mounted on an iron platform. It was transported in separate loads on ten normal-gauge 25/30-ton railway wagons, and took ten hours to mount.

Although named a 'Mörser' by the German forces, the 42 was technically a howitzer as it was capable of being elevated and pivoted on trunnions, whereas mortars have rear trunnions on fixed beds.

The first naval battery to be armed with the original two mortars was formed and trained in the summer of 1912.

German 42-cm. H.E. Shell

Weight (shell complete): 2,052 lb.
Bursting charge: 234 lb.

A

B

C

25mm.

1540mm.

Thickness of walls:	at A,	295mm.
	at B,	52mm.
	at C,	46mm.
Thickness of base:		95mm.
Width of driving band:		50mm.
Construction material:		Steel

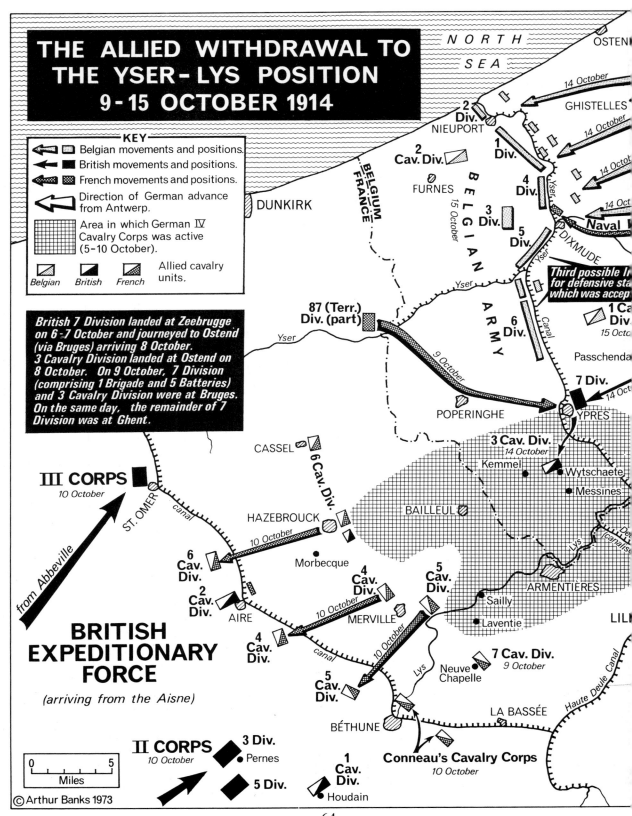

THE ALLIED WITHDRAWAL TO THE YSER-LYS POSITION
9-15 OCTOBER 1914

KEY
- Belgian movements and positions.
- British movements and positions.
- French movements and positions.
- Direction of German advance from Antwerp.
- Area in which German IV Cavalry Corps was active (5-10 October).
- Allied cavalry units. Belgian British French

British 7 Division landed at Zeebrugge on 6-7 October and journeyed to Ostend (via Bruges) arriving 8 October. 3 Cavalry Division landed at Ostend on 8 October. On 9 October, 7 Division (comprising 1 Brigade and 5 Batteries) and 3 Cavalry Division were at Bruges. On the same day, the remainder of 7 Division was at Ghent.

NORTH SEA

OSTEN

GHISTELLES

14 October

14 October

14 Oct

2 Div.

NIEUPORT

2 Cav. Div.

1 Div.

4 Div.

FURNES

BELGIAN ARMY

3 Div.

5 Div.

DIXMUDE

Naval

15 October

Yser

BELGIUM FRANCE

Third possible l... for defensive sta... which was accep...

1 Ca... Div.

15 Oct...

6 Div.

87 (Terr.) Div. (part)

Yser

9 October

Yser

Passchenda...

DUNKIRK

POPERINGHE

7 Div.

14 Oct

YPRES

3 Cav. Div.

14 October

Kemmel

Wytschaete

Messines

CASSEL

6 Cav. Div.

BAILLEUL

III CORPS
10 October

ST. OMER

HAZEBROUCK

10 October

canal

Morbecque

from Abbeville

6 Cav. Div.

2 Cav. Div.

AIRE

4 Cav. Div.

4 Cav. Div.

10 October

MERVILLE

canal

5 Cav. Div.

Lys

ARMENTIÈRES

Sailly

Laventie

LIL...

7 Cav. Div.

9 October

Neuve Chapelle

Haute Deule Canal

BRITISH EXPEDITIONARY FORCE

(arriving from the Aisne)

5 Cav. Div.

BÉTHUNE

LA BASSÉE

Conneau's Cavalry Corps

10 October

II CORPS
10 October

3 Div.
• Pernes

5 Div.

1 Cav. Div.
• Houdain

0 ____ 5
Miles

© Arthur Banks 1973

64

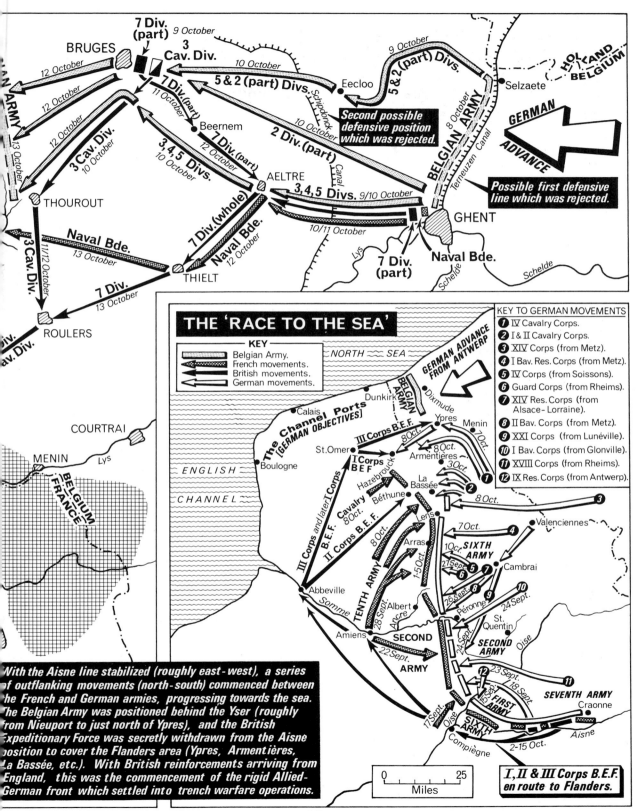

DEFENCE OF THE CHANNEL PORTS AUTUMN 1914

With Antwerp and also Ostend behind them, the German aim was to sever the sea link with England.

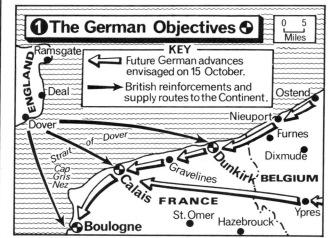

❶ The German Objectives ✛

KEY
← Future German advances envisaged on 15 October.
→ British reinforcements and supply routes to the Continent.

0 5 Miles

ENGLAND
Ramsgate
Deal
Dover
Strait of Dover
Cap Gris Nez

Ostend
Nieuport
Furnes
Dixmude
✛ Dunkirk
Gravelines
✛ Calais
BELGIUM
FRANCE
St. Omer
Hazebrouck
Ypres
✛ Boulogne

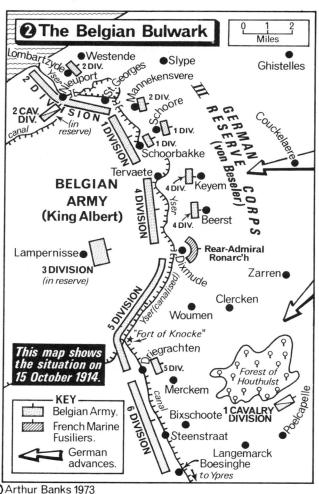

❷ The Belgian Bulwark

0 1 2 Miles

Lombartzyde
Westende 2 DIV.
Slype
Ghistelles
2 DIVISION
Yser
Nieuport
St. Georges
Mannekensvere 2 DIV.
Schoore
2 CAV. DIV. (in reserve)
canal
1 DIVISION
1 DIV.
1 DIV.
Schoorbakke
Tervaete
GERMAN RESERVE CORPS (von Beseler)
Couckelaere
4 DIVISION
4 DIV. Keyem
4 DIV. Beerst

BELGIAN ARMY (King Albert)

Lampernisse
3 DIVISION (in reserve)

Rear-Admiral Ronarc'h
Dixmude
Zarren
Clercken
Woumen
Yser (canalised)
"Fort of Knocke"
5 DIVISION
Driegrachten
5 DIV.
Merckem
6 DIVISION
Bixschoote
Steenstraat
Langemarck
Boesinghe
→ to Ypres

Forest of Houthulst
1 CAVALRY DIVISION
Poelcapelle

This map shows the situation on 15 October 1914.

KEY
▨ Belgian Army.
▤ French Marine Fusiliers.
← German advances.

❸ The Allied Line from the Sea

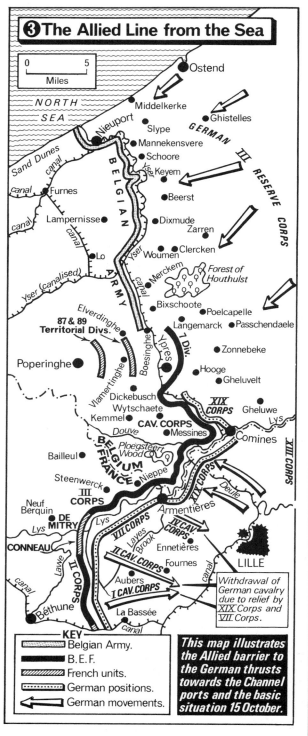

0 5 Miles

NORTH SEA

Ostend
Middelkerke
Ghistelles
Nieuport
Slype
GERMAN III RESERVE CORPS
Mannekensvere
Sand Dunes
canal
Schoore
Keyem
BELGIAN ARMY
canal
Furnes
Beerst
Lampernisse
canal
Dixmude
Zarren
Lo
Woumen
Clercken
Yser (canalised)
canal
Merckem
Forest of Houthulst
Bixschoote
Poelcapelle
Langemarck
Passchendaele

87 & 89 Territorial Divs.
Elverdinghe
Poperinghe
Boesinghe
7 DIV.
Ypres
Zonnebeke
Hooge
Gheluvelt
Vlamertinghe
Dickebusch
Wytschaete
XIX CORPS
Gheluwe
Kemmel
CAV. CORPS
Messines
Lys
Douve
Ploegsteert Wood
Comines
XIII CORPS
Bailleul
BELGIUM FRANCE
Nieppe
Steenwerck
Deule
Armentières
Neuf Berquin
III CORPS
DE MITRY
Lys
VII CORPS
IV CAV. CORPS
LILLE
CONNEAU
II CORPS
Lys
Layes Brook
II CAV. CORPS
Ennetières
Fournes
I CAV. CORPS
Aubers
canal
Béthune
La Bassée
canal

Withdrawal of German cavalry due to relief by XIX Corps and VII Corps.

KEY
▨ Belgian Army.
▬ B.E.F.
▨ French units.
┈ German positions.
← German movements.

This map illustrates the Allied barrier to the German thrusts towards the Channel ports and the basic situation 15 October.

© Arthur Banks 1973

66

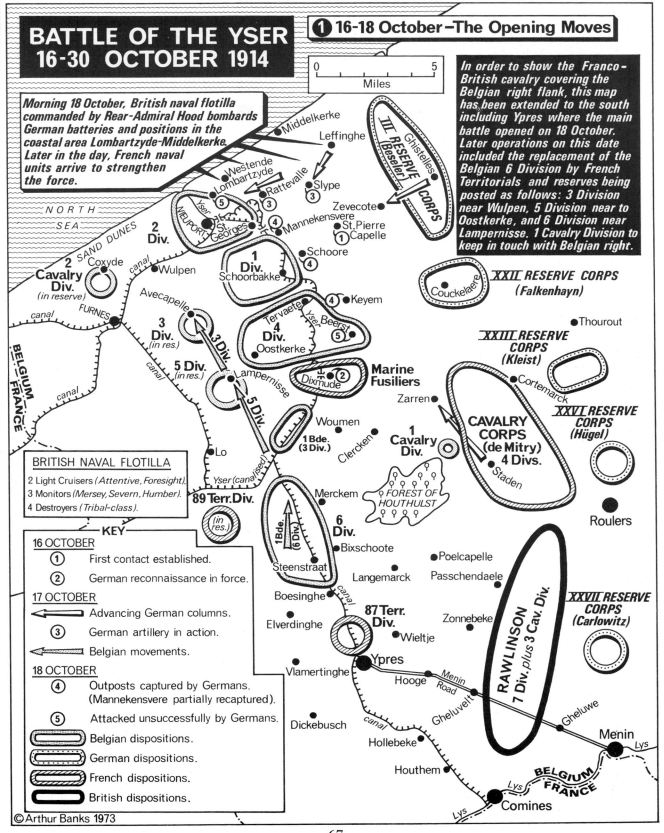

BATTLE OF THE YSER 16-30 OCTOBER 1914

1 16-18 October – The Opening Moves

0 _____ 5
Miles

In order to show the Franco-British cavalry covering the Belgian right flank, this map has been extended to the south including Ypres where the main battle opened on 18 October. Later operations on this date included the replacement of the Belgian 6 Division by French Territorials and reserves being posted as follows: 3 Division near Wulpen, 5 Division near to Oostkerke, and 6 Division near Lampernisse. 1 Cavalry Division to keep in touch with Belgian right.

Morning 18 October, British naval flotilla commanded by Rear-Admiral Hood bombards German batteries and positions in the coastal area Lombartzyde-Middelkerke. Later in the day, French naval units arrive to strengthen the force.

III RESERVE CORPS (Beseler)
Ghistelles

Middelkerke
Leffinghe
Westende
Lombartzyde
Rattevalle ③
Slype ③
Zevecote
St.Pierre ① Capelle
Mannekensvere ④
Schoore ④

NORTH SEA
SAND DUNES
NIEUPORT
St.Georges
Yser

2 Div.

2 Cavalry Div. (in reserve)
Coxyde
Wulpen
canal

1 Div.
Schoorbakke

FURNES
Avecapelle
3 Div. (in res.)
3 Div.

Tervaete
4 Div.
Oostkerke
Beerst ⑤
Keyem ④

Couckelaere

XXII RESERVE CORPS (Falkenhayn)

● Thourout

XXIII RESERVE CORPS (Kleist)
Cortemarck ●

5 Div. (in res.)
5 Div.
Lampernisse

Dixmude ②
Marine Fusiliers
Zarren ●

CAVALRY CORPS (de Mitry) 4 Divs.
Staden

XXVI RESERVE CORPS (Hügel)

BELGIUM FRANCE
canal

Lo
Yser (canalised)

Woumen
1 Bde. (3 Div.)
Clercken

1 Cavalry Div. ◉

FOREST OF HOUTHULST

● Roulers

BRITISH NAVAL FLOTILLA
2 Light Cruisers (Attentive, Foresight).
3 Monitors (Mersey, Severn, Humber).
4 Destroyers (Tribal-class).

89 Terr. Div. (in res.)

Merckem
6 Div.
Bixschoote
Langemarck
Poelcapelle ●
Passchendaele ●

——— KEY ———

16 OCTOBER
① First contact established.
② German reconnaissance in force.

17 OCTOBER
← Advancing German columns.
③ German artillery in action.
← Belgian movements.

18 OCTOBER
④ Outposts captured by Germans. (Mannekensvere partially recaptured).
⑤ Attacked unsuccessfully by Germans.

◫ Belgian dispositions.
▱ German dispositions.
▱ French dispositions.
⬭ British dispositions.

1 Bde. (6 Div.)
Steenstraat
Boesinghe
Elverdinghe
87 Terr. Div.
Vlamertinghe
Ypres
Hooge
Menin Road
Gheluvelt

Zonnebeke ●
Wieltje ●

RAWLINSON 7 Div. plus 3 Cav. Div.

XXVII RESERVE CORPS (Carlowitz)

Gheluwe ●

Dickebusch ●
Hollebeke ●
Houthem ●

Menin
Lys

BELGIUM FRANCE
Lys
Comines
Lys

© Arthur Banks 1973

67

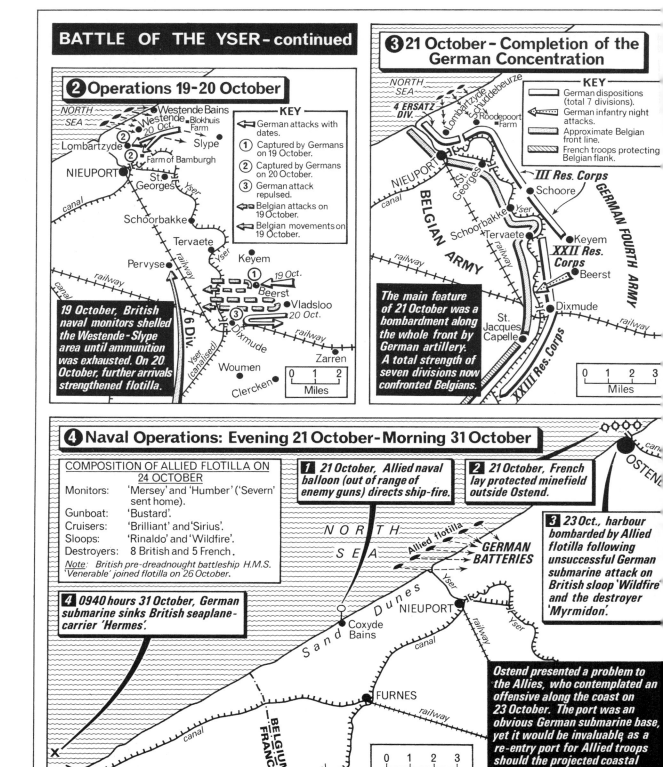

BATTLE OF THE YSER – continued

② Operations 19-20 October

NORTH SEA

Westende Bains
Westende 20 Oct.
Blokhuis Farm
Lombartzyde
Slype
Farm of Bamburgh
NIEUPORT
St. Georges
Yser
Schoorbakke
Tervaete
Keyem
Pervyse
railway
Yser
Beerst
19 Oct.
Vladsloo 20 Oct.
6 Div.
Dixmude
Yser (canalised)
Woumen
railway
Zarren
Clercken

KEY
⇐ German attacks with dates.
① Captured by Germans on 19 October.
② Captured by Germans on 20 October.
③ German attack repulsed.
⇐ Belgian attacks on 19 October.
⇐ Belgian movements on 19 October.

19 October, British naval monitors shelled the Westende - Slype area until ammunition was exhausted. On 20 October, further arrivals strengthened flotilla.

0 1 2
Miles

③ 21 October – Completion of the German Concentration

NORTH SEA
4 ERSATZ DIV.
Lombartzyde
Schuddebeurze
Roodepoort Farm
NIEUPORT
St. Georges
III Res. Corps
Schoore
Yser
Schoorbakke
Tervaete
Keyem
XXII Res. Corps
Beerst
BELGIAN ARMY
GERMAN FOURTH ARMY
Dixmude
St. Jacques Capelle
railway
XXIII Res. Corps

KEY
▭ German dispositions (total 7 divisions).
⇐ German infantry night attacks.
▨ Approximate Belgian front line.
▨ French troops protecting Belgian flank.

The main feature of 21 October was a bombardment along the whole front by German artillery. A total strength of seven divisions now confronted Belgians.

0 1 2 3
Miles

④ Naval Operations: Evening 21 October-Morning 31 October

COMPOSITION OF ALLIED FLOTILLA ON 24 OCTOBER
Monitors: 'Mersey' and 'Humber' ('Severn' sent home).
Gunboat: 'Bustard'.
Cruisers: 'Brilliant' and 'Sirius'.
Sloops: 'Rinaldo' and 'Wildfire'.
Destroyers: 8 British and 5 French.
Note: British pre-dreadnought battleship H.M.S. 'Venerable' joined flotilla on 26 October.

1 *21 October, Allied naval balloon (out of range of enemy guns) directs ship-fire.*

2 *21 October, French lay protected minefield outside Ostend.*

OSTEND

3 *23 Oct., harbour bombarded by Allied flotilla following unsuccessful German submarine attack on British sloop 'Wildfire' and the destroyer 'Myrmidon'.*

NORTH SEA

Allied flotilla
GERMAN BATTERIES
Yser

4 *0940 hours 31 October, German submarine sinks British seaplane-carrier 'Hermes'.*

Sand Dunes
Coxyde Bains
canal
NIEUPORT
railway
Yser

FURNES
railway

BELGIUM FRANCE
canal
canal

X
DUNKIRK

Ostend presented a problem to the Allies, who contemplated an offensive along the coast on 23 October. The port was an obvious German submarine base, yet it would be invaluable as a re-entry port for Allied troops should the projected coastal advance succeed.

0 1 2 3
Miles

© Arthur Banks 1973

68

An ex-Brazilian River Monitor

THE THREE MONITORS
HMS 'Humber' (ex 'Javary').
HMS 'Mersey' (ex 'Madura').
HMS 'Severn' (ex 'Solimoes').

At the outbreak of war, three "river" monitors were being built for the Brazilian Government by Vickers at Barrow. As the Royal Navy was in need of shallow-draft craft for coastal use, the British Government purchased all three on 8 August 1914.

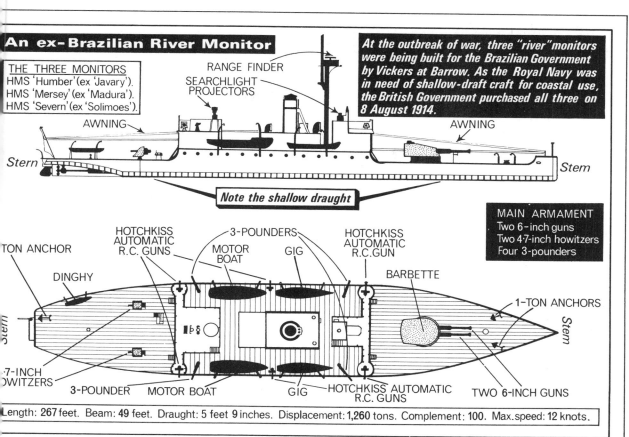

RANGE FINDER
SEARCHLIGHT PROJECTORS
AWNING
AWNING
Stern
Stem

Note the shallow draught

MAIN ARMAMENT
Two 6-inch guns
Two 4·7-inch howitzers
Four 3-pounders

TON ANCHOR
DINGHY
HOTCHKISS AUTOMATIC R.C. GUNS
MOTOR BOAT
3-POUNDERS
GIG
HOTCHKISS AUTOMATIC R.C. GUN
BARBETTE
1-TON ANCHORS
Stem
7-INCH HOWITZERS
3-POUNDER
MOTOR BOAT
GIG
HOTCHKISS AUTOMATIC R.C. GUNS
TWO 6-INCH GUNS

Length: 267 feet. Beam: 49 feet. Draught: 5 feet 9 inches. Displacement: 1,260 tons. Complement: 100. Max. speed: 12 knots.

HMS "VENERABLE" "London" Class of three ships

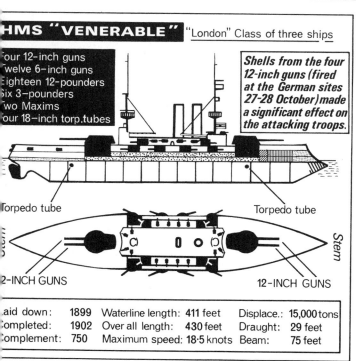

Four 12-inch guns
Twelve 6-inch guns
Eighteen 12-pounders
Six 3-pounders
Two Maxims
Four 18-inch torp.tubes

Shells from the four 12-inch guns (fired at the German sites 27-28 October) made a significant effect on the attacking troops.

Torpedo tube
Torpedo tube
Stem
12-INCH GUNS
12-INCH GUNS

		Displace.:	15,000 tons
Laid down:	1899	Waterline length: 411 feet	
Completed:	1902	Over all length: 430 feet	Draught: 29 feet
Complement:	750	Maximum speed: 18·5 knots	Beam: 75 feet

❺ Military Operations 22-23 October

4 22 October, Belgian attacks.

3 22 October, German attack repulsed by 4 Line Regiment.

Heavy fire from German artillery.

5 23 October, arrival of French 42 Division.

2 22 October, Belgian counter-attack fails to dislodge German units.

1 Night 21/22 October, Germans establish footing on west bank of Yser. They deploy infantry and guns.

Yser
Lombartzyde
Farm of Bamburgh
canal
NIEUPORT
St.Georges
canal
23 October One Bde. (French 42 Div.)
Schoorbakke
Yser
Tervaete

0 — 1
Mile

BATTLE OF THE YSER - continued

By 24 October, Belgian resistance was deteriorating due to exhaustion of troops, lack of ammunition, and only a few reinforcements arriving (French 42 Division). However, as the whole area was intersected by canals and ditches, a possibility existed of flooding the countryside to a depth sufficient to render the attacking Germans unoperational. Stated briefly, this entailed damming 22 culverts under the Nieuport - Dixmude railway embankment to contain the rising waters in the east, followed by opening the Nieuport sluices to admit the sea. This manœuvre was accomplished successfully and by 30 October the drive by the Germans along the coast was virtually at an end.

NIEUPORT'S SLUICES AND CHANNELS

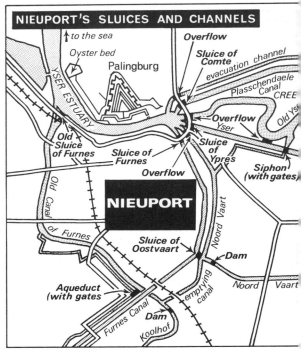

THE OLD SLUICE OF FURNES

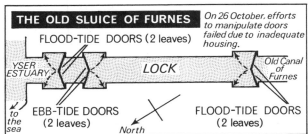

On 26 October, efforts to manipulate doors failed due to inadequate housing.

FLOOD-TIDE DOORS (2 leaves)

YSER ESTUARY

LOCK

Old Canal of Furnes

to the sea

EBB-TIDE DOORS (2 leaves)

North

FLOOD-TIDE DOORS (2 leaves)

⑥ The Irrigated Countryside

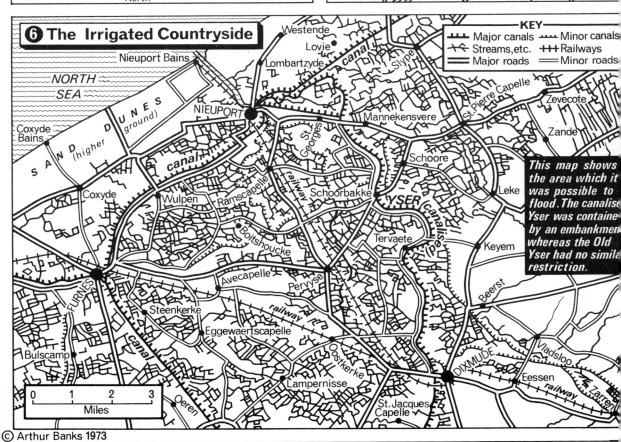

KEY
- ┥┥┥ Major canals
- ┈┈┈ Minor canals
- ✕ Streams, etc.
- +++ Railways
- ═══ Major roads
- ═══ Minor roads

This map shows the area which it was possible to flood. The canalised Yser was contained by an embankment whereas the Old Yser had no similar restriction.

❼ Military Operations 24-30 October

KEY
- Belgian retreats on 24 October.
- German attacks on 24 October.
- Franco-Belgian attack on 25 October.
- Allied withdrawals on 26 October.
- German attacks on 30 October.

NIEUPORT
St.Georges
canal
Noord Vaart
YSER
canal
Noord vaart
canal
Ramscapelle
YSER
railway
Beverdyk
canal
YSER
Pervyse
Tervaete
Oud-Stuyvekenskerke
YSER
DIXMUDE

24 October, a heavy German bombardment.

30 October, German attacks repulsed.

By 26 October, Belgian artillery ammunition was down to 100 rounds per gun.

24 October, a heavy German bombardment.

26 October, two Senegalese battalions arrive here.

15 SEPARATE ATTACKS

0   1
Mile

BELGIAN ENGINEERING OPERATIONS AT NIEUPORT

The operational procedures were extremely complex, depending for success upon tides from the North Sea being propitious, force and direction of winds being correct, plus the actual manipulation of sluice gates being feasible. At the old sluice of Furnes, the two sets of flood-tide doors needed to be held open permanently with the one set of ebb-tide doors freed from their racks so that they opened and closed according to the water pressure from rising and receding tides. At other sluices, doors and gates required to be operated manually for each manœuvre; that is, opened at high tides and closed before low tides. *(The full moon of 29 October assisted operations by causing a very high tide).*

21 October. 1100 hours, Old Yser's overflow is opened; water rapidly inundates creek; Noord Vaart-Old Yser siphon closed to avoid flooding 2 Division's established position.

25 October. Foch contemplates flooding area east of Dunkirk, but delays plan temporarily.

26 October. Attempt fails at old sluice of Furnes.

28 October. Second try succeeds; waters rise.

29 October. 1930 hours, gates of N.Vaart opened.

30 October. Manœuvre repeated; floods spread.

❽ The Inundated Countryside

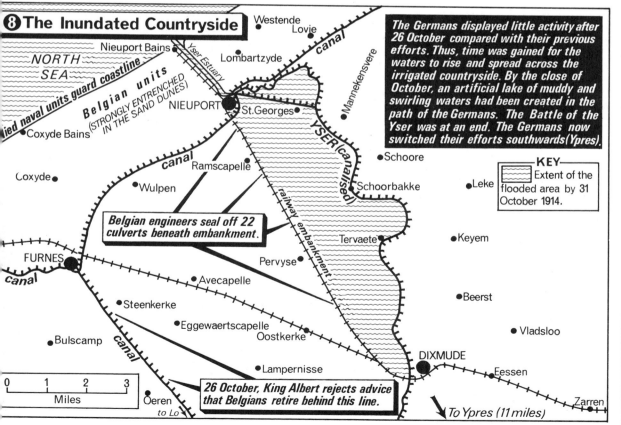

NORTH SEA

Westende
Lovie
canal
Nieuport Bains
Yser Estuary
Lombartzyde
Mannekensvere
Belgian units guard coastline
Belgian units (STRONGLY ENTRENCHED IN THE SAND DUNES)
NIEUPORT
St.Georges
Coxyde Bains
canal
Ramscapelle
Schoore
YSER (canalised)
Schoorbakke
Leke
Coxyde
Wulpen
railway embankment
Keyem
Belgian engineers seal off 22 culverts beneath embankment.
Tervaete
FURNES
Pervyse
canal
Avecapelle
Beerst
Steenkerke
Eggewaertscapelle
Oostkerke
Vladsloo
Bulscamp
canal
Lampernisse
DIXMUDE
Eessen
26 October, King Albert rejects advice that Belgians retire behind this line.
Oeren
to Lo
To Ypres (11 miles)
Zarren

0   1   2   3
Miles

The Germans displayed little activity after 26 October compared with their previous efforts. Thus, time was gained for the waters to rise and spread across the irrigated countryside. By the close of October, an artificial lake of muddy and swirling waters had been created in the path of the Germans. The Battle of the Yser was at an end. The Germans now switched their efforts southwards (Ypres).

KEY
Extent of the flooded area by 31 October 1914.

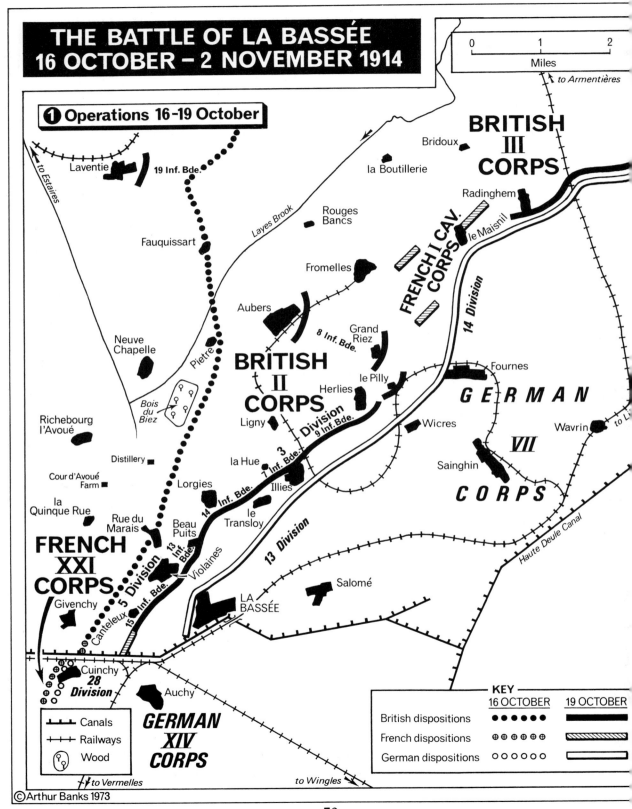

THE BATTLE OF LA BASSÉE
16 OCTOBER – 2 NOVEMBER 1914

0   1   2

Miles

to Armentières

❶ Operations 16-19 October

to Estaires

Laventie

19 Inf. Bde.

Bridoux

la Boutillerie

**BRITISH
III
CORPS**

Radinghem

le Maisnil

Layes Brook

Rouges
Bancs

Fauquissart

Fromelles

**FRENCH I CAV.
CORPS**

14 Division

Neuve
Chapelle

Aubers

Pietre

Grand
Riez

8 Inf. Bde.

**BRITISH
II
CORPS**

le Pilly

Fournes

GERMAN

Herlies

Richebourg
l'Avoué

Bois
du
Biez

Division

9 Inf. Bde.

Wicres

Wavrin

to Li

VII

Ligny

Distillery

la Hue

3
7 Inf. Bde.

Sainghin

Cour d'Avoué
Farm

Lorgies

Illies

Inf. Bde.

CORPS

la
Quinque Rue

14 Inf. Bde.

le
Transloy

Rue du
Marais

Beau
Puits

13 Division

Haute Deule Canal

**FRENCH
XXI
CORPS**

13 Inf. Bde.

5 Division

Violaines

15 Inf. Bde.

Salomé

Givenchy

Canteleux

**LA
BASSÉE**

Cuinchy

**28
Division**

Auchy

**GERMAN
XIV
CORPS**

	Canals
	Railways
	Wood

to Vermelles

to Wingles

KEY

	16 OCTOBER	19 OCTOBER
British dispositions	•••••	▬▬▬
French dispositions	⊕⊕⊕⊕⊕	▨▨▨
German dispositions	○○○○○○	▭▭▭

© Arthur Banks 1973

72

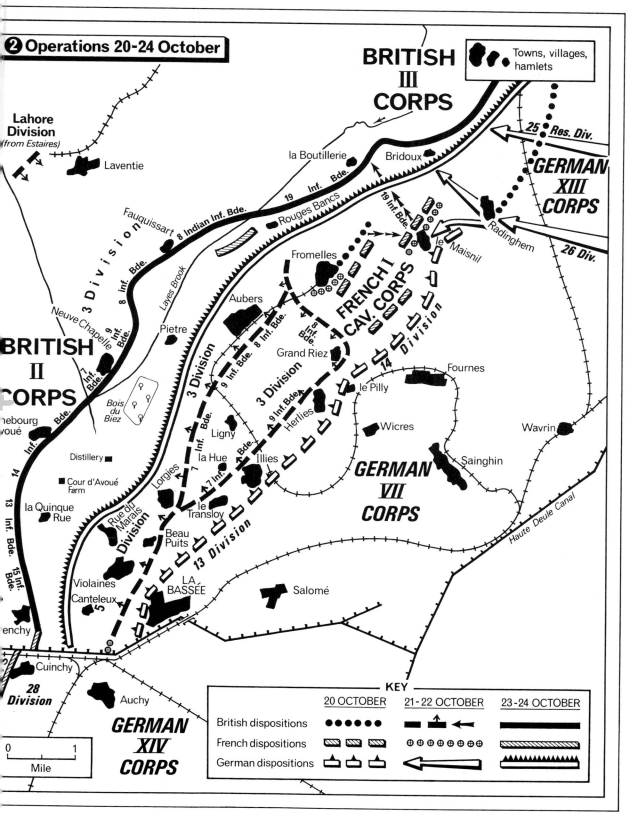

②Operations 20-24 October

Towns, villages, hamlets

BRITISH
III
CORPS

25 Res. Div.

GERMAN
XIII
CORPS

26 Div.

Lahore
Division
(from Estaires)

Laventie

la Boutillerie

Bridoux

19 Inf. Bde.

Rouges Bancs

19 Inf. Bde.

Radinghem

le Maisnil

Fauquissart

8 Indian Inf. Bde.

8 Inf. Bde.

3 Division

Layes Brook

Fromelles

FRENCH I
CAV. CORPS

Neuve Chapelle

8 Inf. Bde.

Pietre

Aubers

8 Inf. Bde.

9 Inf. Bde.

Grand Riez

Division

BRITISH
II
CORPS

7 Inf. Bde.

Bois
du
Biez

3 Division

3 Division

le Pilly

14 Division

Fournes

nebourg
oué

Distillery

Ligny

la Hue

9 Inf. Bde.

Herlies

Wicres

Wavrin

Inf.
Bde.

Cour d'Avoué
Farm

7 Inf. Bde.

Illies

Sainghin

GERMAN
VII
CORPS

la Quinque
Rue

7 Inf. Bde.

le
Transloy

13 Division

Haute Deule Canal

13
Inf.
Bde.

Rue du
Marais

Division

Beau
Puits

15 Inf.
Bde.

Violaines

LA
BASSÉE

Salomé

Canteleux

5

nchy

Cuinchy

28
Division

Auchy

GERMAN
XIV
CORPS

0   1
Mile

— KEY —

	20 OCTOBER	21-22 OCTOBER	23-24 OCTOBER
British dispositions	● ● ● ● ● ●	▬ ↑ ←	▬▬▬
French dispositions	▨ ▨ ▨	⊕⊕⊕⊕⊕⊕	▨▨▨
German dispositions	◁ ◁ ◁	◁	▲▲▲▲

73

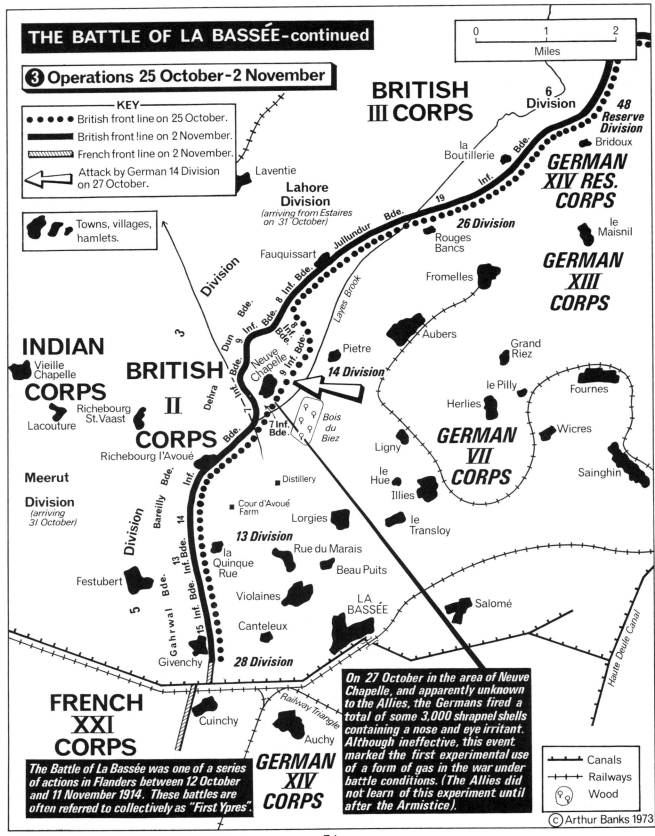

THE BATTLE OF LA BASSÉE-continued

③ Operations 25 October - 2 November

―KEY―
- **●●●●●** British front line on 25 October.
- **▬▬▬** British front line on 2 November.
- ▨▨▨ French front line on 2 November.
- ⇦ Attack by German 14 Division on 27 October.

◼◼◼ Towns, villages, hamlets.

BRITISH III CORPS

6 Division

48 Reserve Division

Bridoux

la Boutillerie

GERMAN XIV RES. CORPS

le Maisnil

26 Division

19 Inf. Bde.

Jullundur Bde.

Rouges Bancs

Laventie

Lahore Division
(arriving from Estaires on 31 October)

Fauquissart

Fromelles

GERMAN XIII CORPS

Layes Brook

8 Inf. Bde.

Pietre

Aubers

Grand Riez

Dun Bde.

9 Inf. Bde.

Neuve Chapelle

14 Division

le Pilly

Fournes

INDIAN CORPS

Vieille Chapelle

3 Division

Herlies

Wicres

BRITISH II CORPS

Dehra Bde.

9 Inf. Bde.

Bois du Biez

GERMAN VII CORPS

Richebourg St.Vaast

Lacouture

7 Inf. Bde.

Ligny

Sainghin

Richebourg l'Avoué

le Hue

Meerut Division
(arriving 31 October)

Bareilly Bde.

Inf. Bde.

Distillery

Illies

le Transloy

14 Inf. Bde.

Cour d'Avoué Farm

Lorgies

Festubert

5 Division

13 Inf. Bde.

Gahrwal Bde.

15 Inf. Bde.

la Quinque Rue

13 Division

Rue du Marais

Beau Puits

Salomé

Violaines

LA BASSÉE

Givenchy

Canteleux

28 Division

Railway Triangle

FRENCH XXI CORPS

Cuinchy

Auchy

GERMAN XIV CORPS

Haute Deule Canal

The Battle of La Bassée was one of a series of actions in Flanders between 12 October and 11 November 1914. These battles are often referred to collectively as "First Ypres".

On 27 October in the area of Neuve Chapelle, and apparently unknown to the Allies, the Germans fired a total of some 3,000 shrapnel shells containing a nose and eye irritant. Although ineffective, this event marked the first experimental use of a form of gas in the war under battle conditions. (The Allies did not learn of this experiment until after the Armistice).

0   1   2 Miles

━━ Canals
╂╂ Railways
🔵 Wood

© Arthur Banks 1973

74

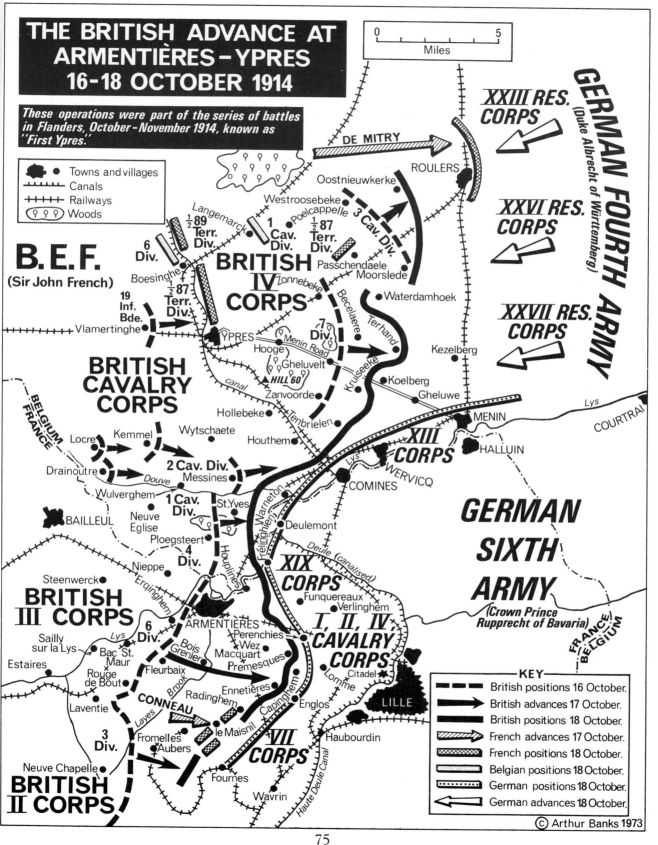

THE BRITISH ADVANCE AT ARMENTIÈRES–YPRES 16–18 OCTOBER 1914

These operations were part of the series of battles in Flanders, October – November 1914, known as "First Ypres."

Towns and villages ●
Canals
Railways
Woods ♀♀♀

0 _____ 5
Miles

B.E.F.
(Sir John French)

DE MITRY

XXIII RES. CORPS

GERMAN FOURTH ARMY
(Duke Albrecht of Württemberg)

XXVI RES. CORPS

XXVII RES. CORPS

ROULERS
Oostnieuwkerke
Westroosebeke
Poelcappelle
½ 89 Terr. Div.
Langemarck
1 Cav. Div.
½ 87 Terr. Div.
6 Div.
3 Cav. Div.
Passchendaele
Moorslede
Boesinghe
½ 87 Terr. Div.
BRITISH IV CORPS
Zonnebeke
Waterdamhoek
19 Inf. Bde.
Vlamertinghe
YPRES
7 Div.
Menin Road
Hooge
Gheluvelt
HILL 60
Zanvoorde
Becelaere
Terhand
Kezelberg
Kruiseeke
Koelberg
Gheluwe
canal
BRITISH CAVALRY CORPS
Hollebeke
Tenbrielen
MENIN
Lys
COURTRAI
BELGIUM FRANCE
Locre
Kemmel
Wytschaete
Houthem
XIII CORPS
HALLUIN
Drainoutre
2 Cav. Div.
Messines
Douve
Lys
WERVICQ
Wulverghem
1 Cav. Div.
St.Yves
Warneton
COMINES
GERMAN SIXTH ARMY
(Crown Prince Rupprecht of Bavaria)
BAILLEUL
Neuve Eglise
Ploegsteert
4 Div.
Frélinghien
Deulemont
Deule (canalised)
Nieppe
Houplines
XIX CORPS
Steenwerck
Erquinghem
Funquereaux
Verlinghem
BRITISH III CORPS
6 Div.
ARMENTIÈRES
Perenchies
Wez
Macquart
Premesques
I, II, IV, CAVALRY CORPS
FRANCE BELGIUM
Sailly sur la Lys
Bac St. Maur
Bois Grenier
Lys
Fleurbaix
Brook
Ennetières
Capinghem
Radinghem
Lomme
Englos
Citadel ★
LILLE
Estaires
Rouge de Bout
Laventie
CONNEAU
Layes
le Maisnil
Haubourdin
Neuve Chapelle
3 Div.
Fromelles
Aubers
VII CORPS
Fournes
Haute Deule Canal
BRITISH II CORPS
Wavrin

KEY
– – – British positions 16 October.
⟶ British advances 17 October.
▬▬ British positions 18 October.
⟹ French advances 17 October.
▨▨ French positions 18 October.
░░ Belgian positions 18 October.
⋯⋯ German positions 18 October.
⟵ German advances 18 October.

ⓒ Arthur Banks 1973

75

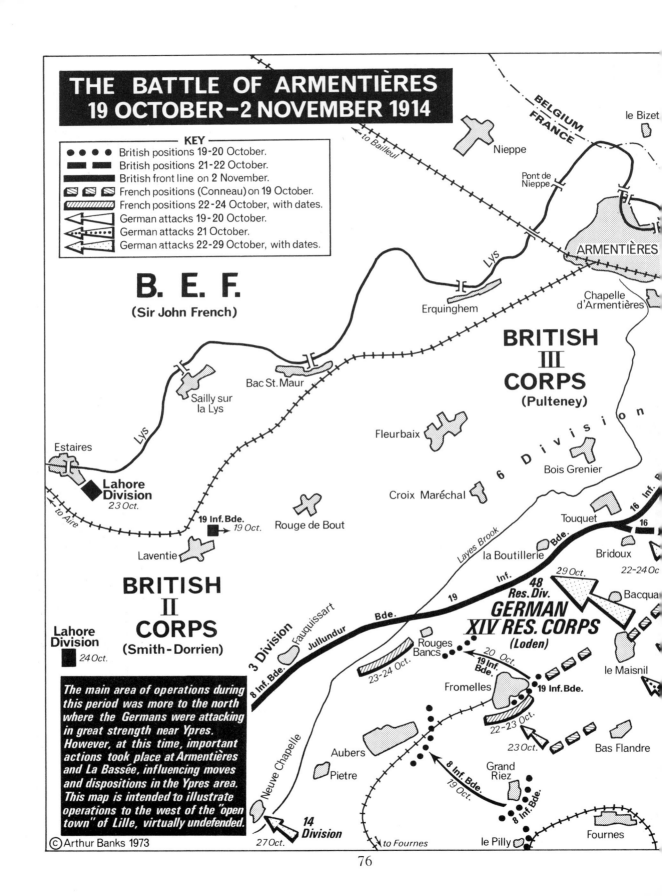

THE BATTLE OF ARMENTIÈRES
19 OCTOBER–2 NOVEMBER 1914

KEY
- ●●●● British positions 19-20 October.
- ▬▬▬ British positions 21-22 October.
- ▬▬▬ British front line on 2 November.
- ▨▨▨ French positions (Conneau) on 19 October.
- ▨▨▨ French positions 22-24 October, with dates.
- ◀ German attacks 19-20 October.
- ◀••• German attacks 21 October.
- ◀ German attacks 22-29 October, with dates.

B. E. F.
(Sir John French)

le Bizet

Nieppe

BELGIUM
FRANCE

to Bailleul

Pont de
Nieppe

ARMENTIÈRES

Lys

Erquinghem

Chapelle
d'Armentières

**BRITISH
III
CORPS
(Pulteney)**

Bac St. Maur

Sailly sur
la Lys

Fleurbaix

6 Division

Bois Grenier

Lys

Estaires

**Lahore
Division**
23 Oct.

Croix Maréchal

Touquet

16 Inf.

16 Bde.

Bridoux

22-24 Oc

Layes Brook

la Boutillerie

to Aire

19 Inf. Bde.
→ *19 Oct.*

Rouge de Bout

Laventie

Inf.

19

Bde.

48
Res. Div.

29 Oct.

Bacqua

**GERMAN
XIV RES. CORPS
(Loden)**

le Maisnil

**BRITISH
II
CORPS
(Smith-Dorrien)**

**Lahore
Division**
24 Oct.

3 Division

Fauquissart

Jullundur

8 Inf. Bde.

Rouges
Bancs

20 Oct.

19 Inf.
Bde.

19 Inf. Bde.

Fromelles

23-24 Oct.

22-23 Oct.

23 Oct.

Bas Flandre

The main area of operations during
this period was more to the north
where the Germans were attacking
in great strength near Ypres.
However, at this time, important
actions took place at Armentières
and La Bassée, influencing moves
and dispositions in the Ypres area.
This map is intended to illustrate
operations to the west of the "open
town" of Lille, virtually undefended.

Neuve Chapelle

Aubers

Pietre

Grand
Riez

8 Inf. Bde.
19 Oct.

8 Inf. Bde.

**14
Division**
27 Oct.

le Pilly

to Fournes

Fournes

© Arthur Banks 1973

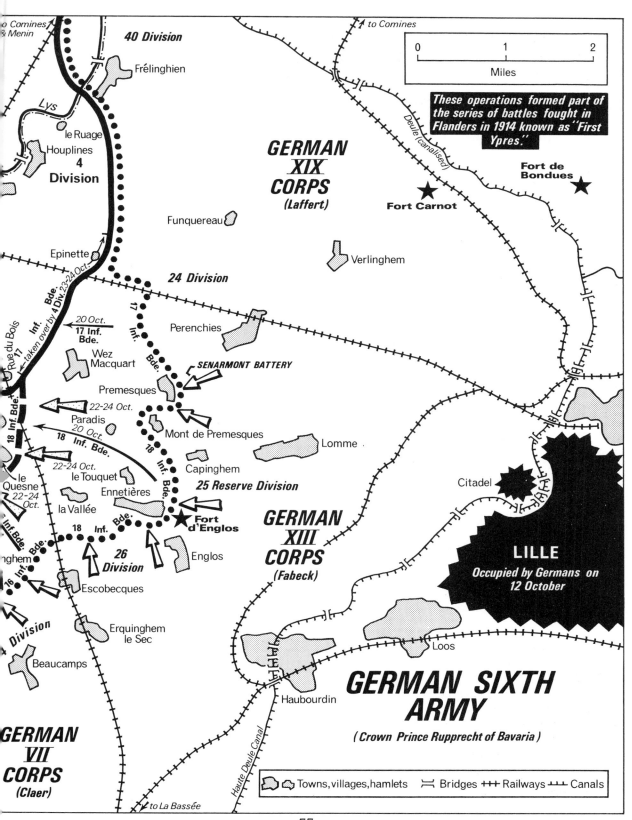

to Comines
& Menin

40 Division

Frélinghien

Lys

le Ruage

Houplines

4
Division

Epinette

GERMAN
XIX
CORPS
(Laffert)

to Comines

Deule (canalised)

0   1   2
Miles

These operations formed part of
the series of battles fought in
Flanders in 1914 known as "First
Ypres."

Fort de
Bondues

★ Fort Carnot   ★

Funquereau

Verlinghem

24 Division

taken over by 4 Div. 23-24 Oct.

Rue du Bois

17
Inf.
Bde.

17
Inf.
Bde.

20 Oct.
17 Inf.
Bde.

18 Inf. Bde.

18 Inf. Bde.

22-24 Oct.
Paradis
20 Oct.

18
Inf. Bde.

18 Inf. Bde.

22-24 Oct.
le Touquet

le
Quesne
22-24
Oct.

la Vallée

Ennetières

Inf. Bde.

18   Inf.   Bde.

nghem

Inf. Bde.

Escobecques

26
Division

Englos

Erquinghem
le Sec

Beaucamps

GERMAN
VII
CORPS
(Claer)

Wez
Macquart

Premesques

SENARMONT BATTERY

Perenchies

Mont de Premesques

Capinghem

Lomme

25 Reserve Division

Fort
d'Englos

GERMAN
XIII
CORPS
(Fabeck)

Citadel

LILLE
Occupied by Germans on
12 October

Loos

Haubourdin

Haute Deule Canal

to La Bassée

GERMAN SIXTH
ARMY
(Crown Prince Rupprecht of Bavaria)

Towns, villages, hamlets   Bridges   Railways   Canals

77

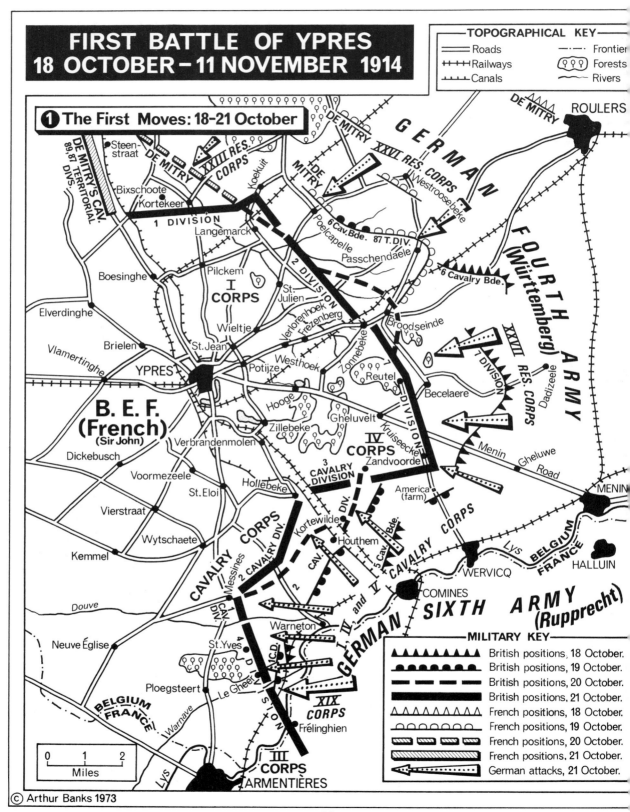

FIRST BATTLE OF YPRES
18 OCTOBER – 11 NOVEMBER 1914

TOPOGRAPHICAL KEY

Roads

Railways ++++

Canals +++

Frontier –·–·–

Forests

Rivers

❶ The First Moves: 18–21 October

DE MITRY'S CAV. 89,87 TERRITORIAL DIVS.

DE MITRY

DE MITRY

DE MITRY

ROULERS

GERMAN

XXIII RES. CORPS

XXVI RES. CORPS

FOURTH ARMY (Württemberg)

Steenstraat

Koekuit

Westroosebeke

Bixschoote

Kortekeer

1 DIVISION

Langemarck

6 Cav. Bde.

Poelcapelle

87 T. DIV.

Boesinghe

Pilckem

2 DIVISION

Passchendaele

6 Cavalry Bde.

I CORPS

St. Julien

Elverdinghe

Wieltje

Verlorenhoek

Frezenberg

Broodseinde

XXVII RES. CORPS

Dadizeele

Brielen

St. Jean

Vlamertinghe

Potijze

Westhoek

Zonnebeke

Reutel

Becelaere

YPRES

1 DIVISION

B.E.F. (French) (Sir John)

Hooge

Gheluvelt

Zillebeke

IV CORPS

Kruiseecke

Menin

Gheluwe

Road

Dickebusch

Verbrandenmolen

Zandvoorde

Voormezeele

3 CAVALRY DIVISION

America (farm)

Hollebeke

CAVALRY CORPS

MENIN

St. Eloi

Vierstraat

DIV.

Kortewilde

CAV.

5 Cav. Bde.

Lys

BELGIUM

FRANCE

HALLUIN

Wytschaete

Houthem

II. and IV. CAVALRY CORPS

WERVICQ

Kemmel

CAVALRY CORPS

Messines

2 CAVALRY DIV.

2

COMINES

Douve

1 CAV. DIV.

Warneton

GERMAN SIXTH ARMY (Rupprecht)

Neuve Église

St. Yves

6 C.D.

MILITARY KEY

Ploegsteert

Le Gheer

XIX CORPS

BELGIUM

FRANCE

Warnave

Frélinghien

▲▲▲▲▲	British positions, 18 October.
●●●●●	British positions, 19 October.
▬ ▬ ▬	British positions, 20 October.
▬▬▬	British positions, 21 October.
△△△△△	French positions, 18 October.
∩∩∩∩∩	French positions, 19 October.
▨ ▨ ▨	French positions, 20 October.
▨▨▨▨	French positions, 21 October.
◁▬▬	German attacks, 21 October.

0 1 2
Miles

III CORPS
ARMENTIÈRES

Lys

© Arthur Banks 1973

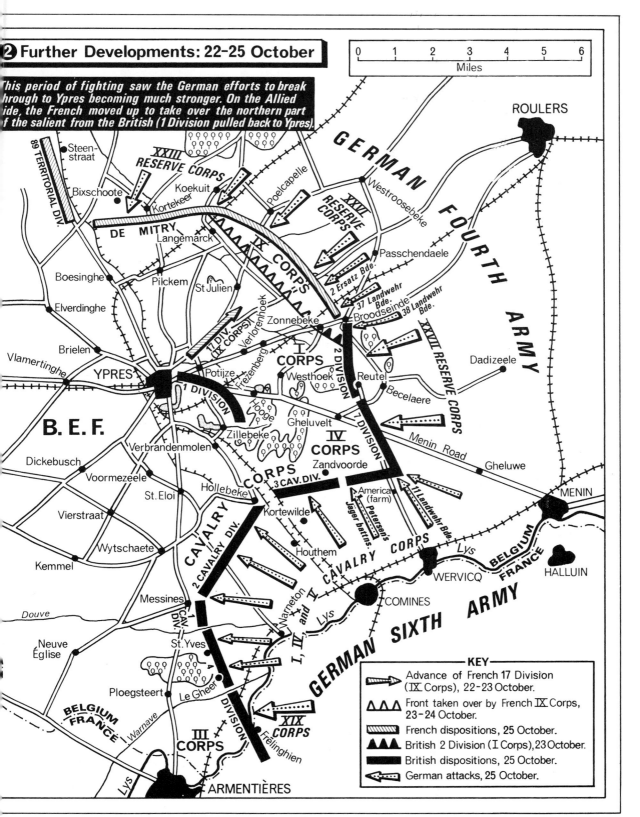

❷ Further Developments: 22–25 October

This period of fighting saw the German efforts to break through to Ypres becoming much stronger. On the Allied side, the French moved up to take over the northern part of the salient from the British (1 Division pulled back to Ypres).

Miles
0 1 2 3 4 5 6

ROULERS

GERMAN FOURTH ARMY

89 TERRITORIAL DIV.

Steen-straat

XXIII RESERVE CORPS

Bixschoote

Koekuit

Kortekeer

DE MITRY

Langemarck

Poelcapelle

Westroosebeke

XXVI RESERVE CORPS

Passchendaele

IX CORPS

Boesinghe

Pilckem

St Julien

2 Ersatz Bde.

37 Landwehr Bde.

38 Landwehr Bde.

Broodseinde

Elverdinghe

17 DIV.
IX CORPS

Verlorenhoek

Zonnebeke

XXVII RESERVE CORPS

Dadizeele

Brielen

Vlamertinghe

YPRES

Potijze

Frezenberg

I CORPS

Westhoek

2 DIVISION

Reutel

Becelaere

1 DIVISION

Hooge

Gheluvelt

7 DIVISION

B.E.F.

Zillebeke

IV CORPS

Menin Road

Gheluwe

Dickebusch

Verbrandenmolen

Zandvoorde

Voormezeele

CORPS

3 CAV. DIV.

America (farm)

11 Landwehr Bde.

MENIN

St. Eloi

Hollebeke

Kortewilde

Petersen's Jäger battns.

Vierstraat

Houthem

HALLUIN

Wytschaete

CAVALRY DIV.

CAVALRY CORPS

Lys

Kemmel

2 CAVALRY DIV.

WERVICQ

BELGIUM
FRANCE

Douve

Messines

I, IV, and V

Warneton

Lys

COMINES

GERMAN SIXTH ARMY

Neuve Église

CAV. DIV.

St. Yves

4

Ploegsteert

Le Gheer

BELGIUM
FRANCE

Warnave

III CORPS

DIVISION

XIX CORPS

Frélinghien

Lys

ARMENTIÈRES

KEY

- ▷▷ Advance of French 17 Division (IX Corps), 22–23 October.
- △△△ Front taken over by French IX Corps, 23–24 October.
- ⬚ French dispositions, 25 October.
- ▲▲▲ British 2 Division (I Corps), 23 October.
- ▬ British dispositions, 25 October.
- ◁ German attacks, 25 October.

79

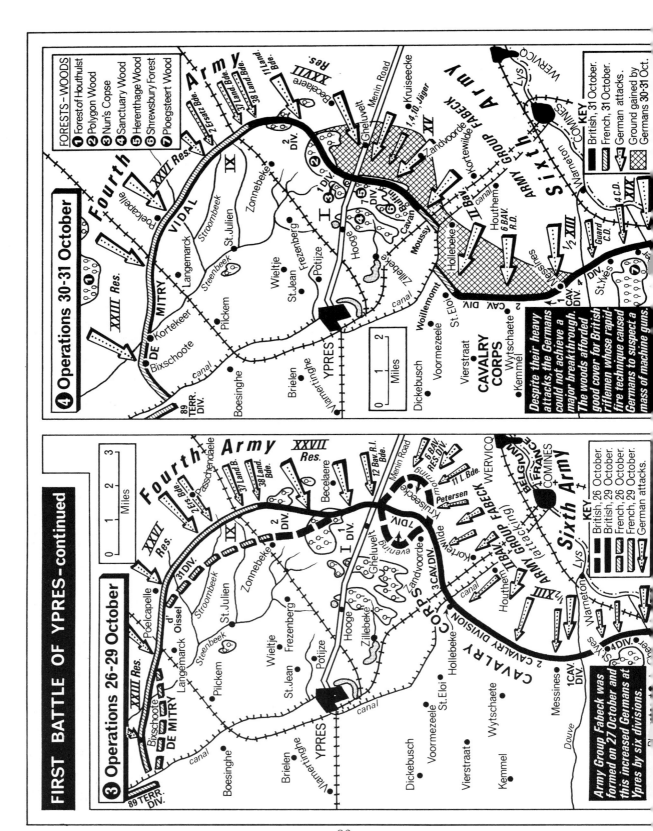

FIRST BATTLE OF YPRES—continued

④ Operations 30-31 October

FORESTS–WOODS
1 Forest of Houthulst
2 Polygon Wood
3 Nun's Copse
4 Sanctuary Wood
5 Herenthage Wood
6 Shrewsbury Forest
7 Ploegsteert Wood

Fourth Army

XXVII Res.
2 Ersatz Bde.
37 Land. Bde.
38 Land. Bde.
11 Land. Bde.
XXIII Res.
VIDAL
DE MITRY
89 TERR. DIV.

Becelaere
Peelcapelle
IX
2 DIV.
Menin Road
Gheluvelt
Kruiseecke
1,4,10. Jäger
XV
Zandvoorde
Kortewilde
canal
II Bav.
Houthem
6 BAV. R.D.
ARMY GROUP FABECK
Sixth Army
WERVICQ
COMINES
Lys
WARNETON
4 C.D.
½ XIII
XIX
Guard C.D.
St. Yves
2 CAV. DIV.
1 CAV. DIV.

Peltcapelle
1 DIV.
Zonnebeke
Langemarck
St. Julien
Stroombeek
Steenbeek
Frezenberg
Potijze
Wieltje
St. Jean
Pilckem
Kortekeer
Bixschoote
Boesinghe
Brielen
Vlamertinghe
YPRES
canal
Hooge
7 & 6 DIV.
Caran
Moussy
Zillebeke
Hollebeke
Wollemomt
St. Eloi
Dickebusch
Voormezeele
Vierstraat
Wytschaete
Kemmel
CAVALRY CORPS

Scale: 0 1 2 Miles

---

③ Operations 26-29 October

Scale: 0 1 2 3 Miles

Fourth Army
XXVII Res.
Passchendaele
2 Efs Bde.
37 Land. B.
38 Land. Bde.
12 Bav. R.I. Bde.
6 BAV. RES. DIV.
Becelaere
XXIII Res.
Bixschoote
DE MITRY
89 TERR. DIV.
d' Oissel
31 DIV.
IX
2 DIV.
I DIV.
7 DIV.
Kruiseecke
Petersen
11 L. Bde.
WERVICQ
BELGIUM
FRANCE
COMINES
Menin Road
Becelaere (evening)

Poelcapelle
Langemarck
Zonnebeke
Stroombeek
Steenbeek
St. Julien
Frezenberg
Potijze
Wieltje
St. Jean
Pilckem
Boesinghe
Brielen
Vlamertinghe
YPRES
canal
Hooge
Gheluvelt
Zillebeke
Hollebeke
Zandvoorde
Kortewilde
Houthem
3 CAV. DIV.
2 CAVALRY DIVISION
CAVALRY CORPS
II BAV. ARMY GROUP FABECK
½ XIII
½ XIX
Warneton
Lys
St. Yves
Messines
Wytschaete
St. Eloi
Voormezeele
Vierstraat
Dickebusch
Kemmel
Douve
1 CAV. DIV.
4 DIV.
Sixth Army

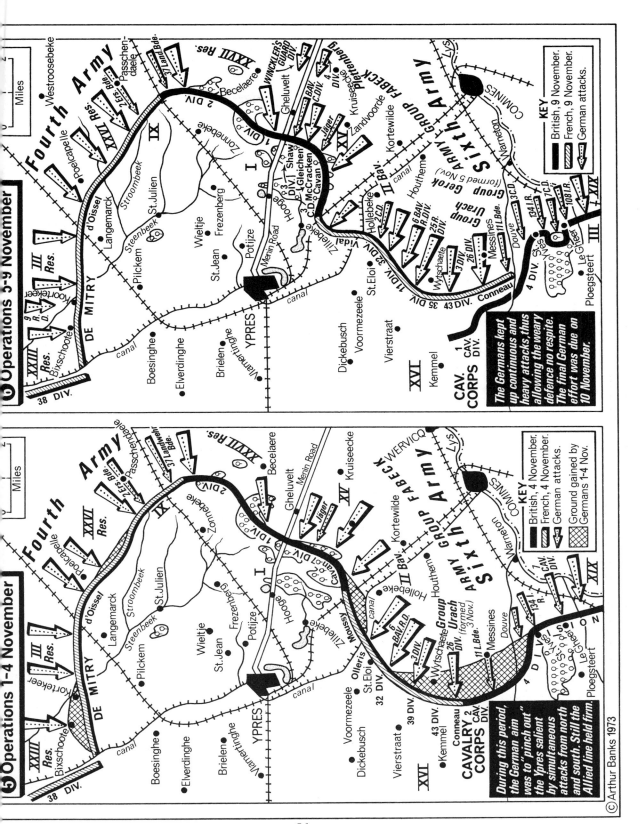

6 Operations 5-9 November

Miles

Fourth Army

Westroosebeke
Poelcapelle
Passchen-
daele

XXVII Res.
37 Land.Bde.
2 Ers.Bde.

XXVI Res.

III Res.
9 R.D.

XXIII Res.
Bixschoote
38 DIV.

DE MITRY

d'Oissel
Langemarck
Steenbeek
St.Julien
Zonnebeke
Frezenberg
Pilckem
Wieltje
St.Jean

Boesinghe
Elverdinghe
Brielen
Vlamertinghe

canal

YPRES

Potijze
Menin Road
Zillebeke
Hooge

IX

2 DIV

Becelaere

I

1 DIV

3 DIV.Shaw
L.Gleichen
C.D.McCracken
Cavan

WINCKLER'S
GUARD DIV
Gheluvelt
BAV.C.DIV. 4 DIV.

XV
Jäger

GROUP FABECK
Ploegsteeberg
Kruiseecke
Zandvoorde
Kortewilde

Sixth Army

Group Gerok (formed 5 Nov.)

Group Urach
Hollebeke
6 BAV.R.DIV.
25R.DIV.
26 DIV.

Houthem
canal
Wytschaete
Messines

XVI
Dickebusch
Voormezeele
Vierstraat
St.Eloi
Kemmel

CAV. CORPS
1 CAV. DIV.

35 DIV. 32 DIV. Vidal
11 DIV.
43 DIV. Conneau

Douve
Warneton
Lys
COMINES

134 I.R.
108 I.R.
3 C.D.
7 C.D.
11 L.Bde.
4 DIV. St.Yves
Le Gheer
Ploegsteert

III **XIX**

The Germans kept up continuous and heavy attacks, thus allowing the weary defence no respite. The final German effort was due on 10 November.

KEY
British, 9 November.
French, 9 November.
German attacks.

---

5 Operations 1-4 November

Miles

Fourth Army

Poelcapelle
Passchendaele

XXVI Res.
37 Landwehr Bde.
2 Ers.Bde.

III Res.
Moorteer

XXIII Res.
Bixschoote
38 DIV.

DE MITRY

d'Oissel
Langemarck
Steenbeek
St.Julien
Zonnebeke
Frezenberg
Pilckem
Wieltje
St.Jean

Boesinghe
Elverdinghe
Brielen
Vlamertinghe

canal

YPRES

Potijze
Hooge
Zillebeke

IX

2 DIV

Becelaere
Gheluvelt
Menin Road

I

1 DIV
Cav.1 DIV

XXVII Res.

XV
Jäger
Kruiseecke

Kortewilde
II Bav.

GROUP FABECK
WERVICQ

Sixth Army

Group Urach (formed 3 Nov.)
Hollebeke
Houthem
canal
30 DIV.
26 DIV.
11 L.Bde.
Wytschaete
Messines

XVI
Kemmel
Voormezeele
Dickebusch
Vierstraat
St.Eloi
Olleris
32 DIV.
39 DIV.
43 DIV.
Conneau

CAVALRY CORPS 2 CAV. DIV.

Warneton
Douve
Lys
COMINES

134 I.R.
4 DIV.
St.Yves
Le Gheer
Ploegsteert

XIX

During this period, the German aim was to "pinch out" the Ypres salient by simultaneous attacks from north and south. Still the Allied line held firm.

KEY
British, 4 November.
French, 4 November.
German attacks.
Ground gained by Germans 1-4 Nov.

© Arthur Banks 1973

81

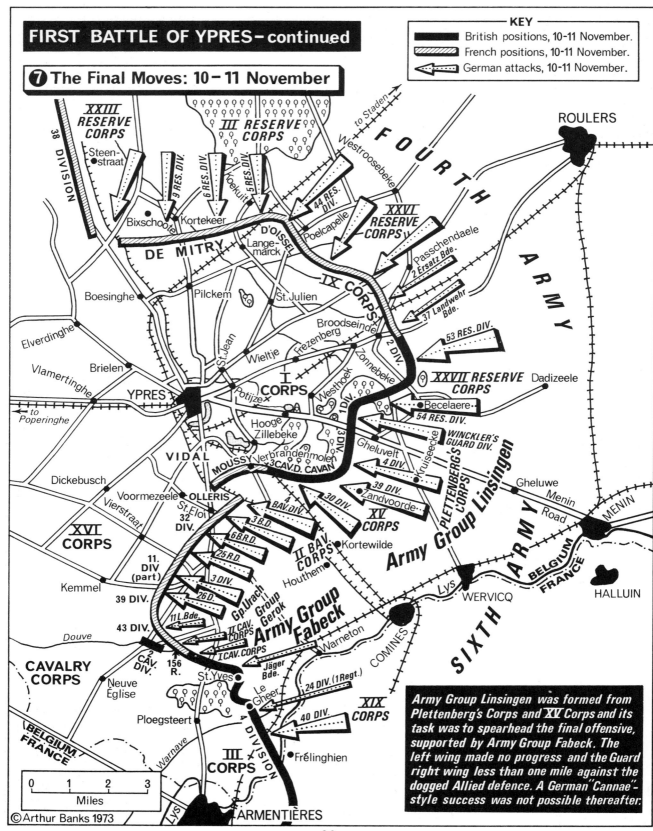

FIRST BATTLE OF YPRES – continued

7 The Final Moves: 10 – 11 November

ROULERS

XXIII RESERVE CORPS

III RESERVE CORPS

38 DIVISION

Steenstraat

9 RES. DIV.

6 RES. DIV.

5 RES. DIV.

Koekuit

44 RES. DIV.

FOURTH ARMY

to Staden

Westroosebeke

XXVI RESERVE CORPS

Bixschoote

Kortekeer

DE MITRY

D'OISSEL

Langemarck

Poelcapelle

Passchendaele

2 Ersatz Bde.

IX CORPS

Boesinghe

Pilckem

St.Julien

Broodseinde

37 Landwehr Bde.

Elverdinghe

St.Jean

Wieltje

Frezenberg

2 DIV.

53 RES. DIV.

Dadizeele

Brielen

Vlamertinghe

to Poperinghe

YPRES

Potijze

I CORPS

Westhoek

1 DIV.

Zonnebeke

XXVII RESERVE CORPS

Becelaere

54 RES. DIV.

Hooge

Zillebeke

3 DIV.

Gheluvelt

Kruiseecke

WINCKLER'S GUARD DIV.

VIDAL

Verbrandenmolen

3 CAV.D. CAVAN

4 DIV.

PLETTENBERG'S CORPS

Army Group Linsingen

Dickebusch

Voormezeele

OLLERIS

MOUSSY

30 DIV.

Zandvoorde

39 DIV.

XV CORPS

Gheluwe

Menin

Menin Road

MENIN

Vierstraat

St.Floi

32 DIV.

4 BAV. DIV.

3 B.D.

II BAV. CORPS

Kortewilde

SIXTH ARMY

HALLUIN

XVI CORPS

11. DIV. (part)

6 B.R.D.

25 R.D.

Houthem

Kemmel

3 DIV.

Gp.Urach

Group Gerok

Army Group Fabeck

Lys

WERVICQ

BELGIUM FRANCE

39 DIV.

26 D.

11 L.Bde.

II CAV. CORPS

I CAV. CORPS

Warneton

COMINES

43 DIV.

Douve

2 CAV. DIV.

1 156. R.

Jäger Bde.

CAVALRY CORPS

Neuve Église

St.Yves

24 DIV. (1 Regt.)

XIX CORPS

Ploegsteert

Le Gheer

40 DIV.

BELGIUM FRANCE

Warnave

III CORPS

4 DIVISION

Frélinghien

Lys

ARMENTIÈRES

Army Group Linsingen was formed from Plettenberg's Corps and XV Corps and its task was to spearhead the final offensive, supported by Army Group Fabeck. The left wing made no progress and the Guard right wing less than one mile against the dogged Allied defence. A German "Cannae"-style success was not possible thereafter.

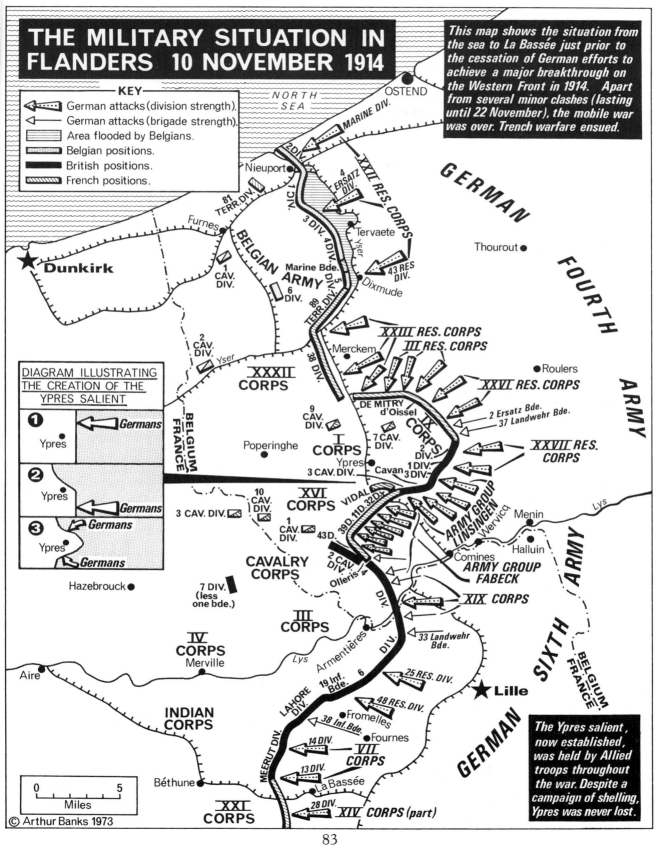

THE MILITARY SITUATION IN FLANDERS 10 NOVEMBER 1914

This map shows the situation from the sea to La Bassée just prior to the cessation of German efforts to achieve a major breakthrough on the Western Front in 1914. Apart from several minor clashes (lasting until 22 November), the mobile war was over. Trench warfare ensued.

KEY
- German attacks (division strength).
- German attacks (brigade strength).
- Area flooded by Belgians.
- Belgian positions.
- British positions.
- French positions.

NORTH SEA

OSTEND

MARINE DIV.

2 DIV.

1 DIV.

Nieuport

81 TERR. DIV.

Furnes

BELGIAN ARMY

Dunkirk

1 CAV. DIV.

Marine Bde.

6 DIV.

4 ERSATZ DIV.

XXII RES. CORPS

3 DIV. 4 DIV.

Tervaete

Yser

43 RES DIV.

Dixmude

Thourout

GERMAN FOURTH ARMY

2 CAV. DIV.

Yser

89 TERR. DIV.

38 DIV.

XXXII CORPS

Merckem

XXIII RES. CORPS

III RES. CORPS

Roulers

XXVI RES. CORPS

DIAGRAM ILLUSTRATING THE CREATION OF THE YPRES SALIENT

❶ Ypres — Germans

❷ Ypres — Germans

❸ Ypres — Germans

BELGIUM FRANCE

9 CAV. DIV.

Poperinghe

DE MITRY d'Oissel

IX CORPS

2 Ersatz Bde.

37 Landwehr Bde.

7 CAV. DIV.

I CORPS

Ypres

2 DIV.

1 DIV.

3 DIV.

XXVII RES. CORPS

3 CAV. DIV.

Cavan

3 CAV. DIV.

10 CAV. DIV.

XVI CORPS

VIDAL

39D. 11D. 32D.

43D.

ARMY GROUP LINSINGEN

Menin

Lys

1 CAV. DIV.

Wervicq

Halluin

Hazebrouck

7 DIV. (less one bde.)

CAVALRY CORPS

2 CAV. DIV.

Olleris

DIV.

Comines

ARMY GROUP FABECK

III CORPS

XIX CORPS

IV CORPS

Merville

Lys

Armentières

DIV.

33 Landwehr Bde.

GERMAN SIXTH ARMY

Aire

INDIAN CORPS

LAHORE DIV.

19 Inf. Bde.

6

25 RES. DIV.

Lille

BELGIUM FRANCE

48 RES. DIV.

Fromelles

MEERUT DIV.

38 Inf. Bde.

Fournes

VII CORPS

14 DIV.

13 DIV.

GERMAN

Béthune

La Bassée

XXI CORPS

28 DIV.

XIV CORPS (part)

The Ypres salient, now established, was held by Allied troops throughout the war. Despite a campaign of shelling, Ypres was never lost.

0 ___ 5
Miles

© Arthur Banks 1973

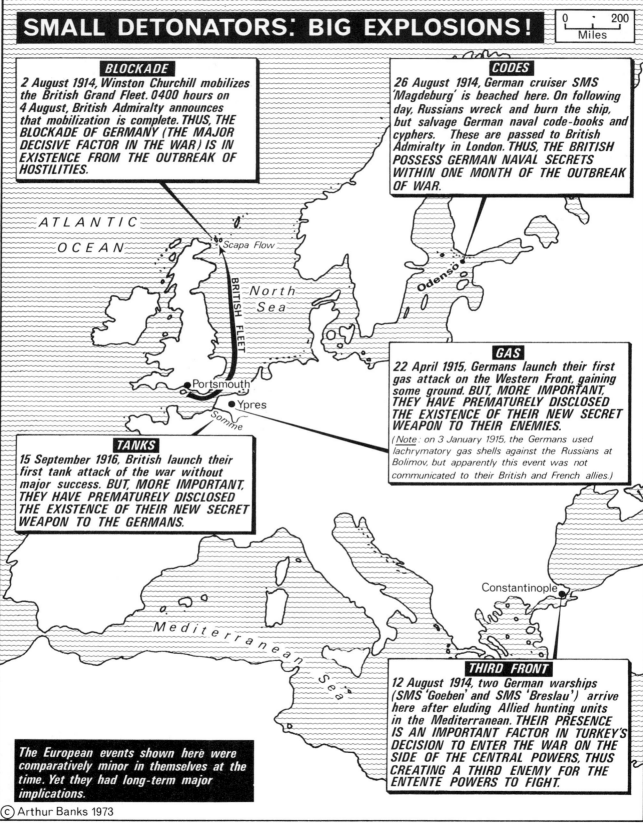

SMALL DETONATORS: BIG EXPLOSIONS!

0 · 200
Miles

BLOCKADE
2 August 1914, Winston Churchill mobilizes the British Grand Fleet. 0400 hours on 4 August, British Admiralty announces that mobilization is complete. THUS, THE BLOCKADE OF GERMANY (THE MAJOR DECISIVE FACTOR IN THE WAR) IS IN EXISTENCE FROM THE OUTBREAK OF HOSTILITIES.

CODES
26 August 1914, German cruiser SMS 'Magdeburg' is beached here. On following day, Russians wreck and burn the ship, but salvage German naval code-books and cyphers. These are passed to British Admiralty in London. THUS, THE BRITISH POSSESS GERMAN NAVAL SECRETS WITHIN ONE MONTH OF THE OUTBREAK OF WAR.

ATLANTIC OCEAN

Scapa Flow

BRITISH FLEET

North Sea

Odensö

● Portsmouth

● Ypres

Somme

GAS
22 April 1915, Germans launch their first gas attack on the Western Front, gaining some ground. BUT, MORE IMPORTANT, THEY HAVE PREMATURELY DISCLOSED THE EXISTENCE OF THEIR NEW SECRET WEAPON TO THEIR ENEMIES.
(Note: on 3 January 1915, the Germans used lachrymatory gas shells against the Russians at Bolimov, but apparently this event was not communicated to their British and French allies.)

TANKS
15 September 1916, British launch their first tank attack of the war without major success. BUT, MORE IMPORTANT, THEY HAVE PREMATURELY DISCLOSED THE EXISTENCE OF THEIR NEW SECRET WEAPON TO THE GERMANS.

Mediterranean Sea

Constantinople ●

THIRD FRONT
12 August 1914, two German warships (SMS 'Goeben' and SMS 'Breslau') arrive here after eluding Allied hunting units in the Mediterranean. THEIR PRESENCE IS AN IMPORTANT FACTOR IN TURKEY'S DECISION TO ENTER THE WAR ON THE SIDE OF THE CENTRAL POWERS, THUS CREATING A THIRD ENEMY FOR THE ENTENTE POWERS TO FIGHT.

The European events shown here were comparatively minor in themselves at the time. Yet they had long-term major implications.

© Arthur Banks 1973

84

THE WAR ON THE EASTERN FRONT

There were four other theatres of war in Europe during the autumn of 1914. Eight hundred miles to the east of the Belgian cockpit, Russian and German armies clashed in the marchlands of East Prussia while to their south other forces manoeuvred for position in the great plains of the Vistulan Basin. The principal Austrian army was concentrated at the outbreak of war in Galicia, with the well-forested range of the Carpathians in its rear, an admirable position for withstanding any Russian onslaught (compare pages 24 and 32). Farther south still, nearly four hundred miles across the Austro-Hungarian empire, another quarter of a million soldiers from Franz Josef's multinational empire were assigned the duty of 'punishing' Serbia. The commander of this Balkan Army was the former Governor of Bosnia, General Potiorek, who had been sitting in front of Archduke Franz Ferdinand on that fateful day in Sarajevo. But Potiorek, like all other Austro-Hungarian commanders, was subordinate to General Conrad von Hötzendorf, the Austrian Chief of Staff, who established his first headquarters in the reputedly impregnable Galician fortress town of Przemysl.

Although Conrad had hoped to cut off the Russians in Poland by joint Austro-German operations uniting the commands in East Prussia and Galicia, there was in fact little co-ordination between the various eastern European armies. The first shots in the whole war were fired by two monitors of the Austro-Hungarian Danube flotilla, which bombarded Belgrade on 29 July, five days before the opening of hostilities in western Europe. But thereafter all was peaceful until the middle of the second week in August when Conrad sent his First and Fourth armies northward into Russian Poland, while the first units of the Russian 1st Army invaded East Prussia, and Potiorek's troops crossed the river Sava and seized the Serbian town of Sabac.

The most dramatic of these undertakings was the Russian incursion towards the historic Prussian coronation city, Königsberg, some ninety miles from the frontier. The Schlieffen Plan had anticipated a German holding operation against Russia for some six or seven weeks, before the full weight of German arms was shifted to the West. On paper, there was no reason for

German alarm, even though the invaders had a numerical superiority of more than four to one. But on 20 August three German army corps clashed with Rennenkampf's Russian First Army at Gumbinnen and did not distinguish themselves (pages 88–89). The German commander, Prittwitz, was worried by news that the Russian Second Army, under Samsonov, was threatening his southern flank, and sent alarming messages to Moltke's headquarters in the West. The situation was saved by one of Prittwitz's staff officers, Lieutenant-Colonel Max von Hoffmann, who knew there was a deep personal vendetta between Samsonov and Rennenkampf. Hoffmann proposed that the Germans should concentrate against Samsonov, leaving the route towards Königsberg apparently open for Rennenkampf (who would not resist this bait simply to aid the rival he so detested). Thus began the deployment for the battle of Tannenberg, three days of agony for the Russians, in which the Second Army was destroyed and its commander shot himself in despair.

Tannenberg, like the Marne, became a legendary victory. The discovery of a Russian staff officer's body on the battlefield, with detailed military directives in his pocket, helped the Germans considerably; and so did the incredible folly of the three Russian headquarters in sending unciphered operations orders by wireless, with the Germans able to note down every word (see page 98). The ease of their victory made the Germans despise their Russian opponents and they therefore suffered heavy casualties in rash frontal assaults on Rennenkampf's army, which was caught at the Masurian Lakes in the first week of September. But the Masurian Lakes completed the triumph of Tannenberg: the Russians, after nibbling at the edge of East Prussia for twenty-eight days, were thrown back across the frontier, broken and demoralised. No Russian army penetrated German territory again until 1945.

The twin victories enabled the German people to find a heroic father-figure to idolise for the remainder of the War and beyond. Paul von Hindenburg was six weeks short of his sixty-seventh birthday when, on 22 August, he was summoned from obscure retirement to replace Prittwitz on the Eastern Front. Hindenburg had been decorated for bravery both in the 1866 war with Austria and the 1870 war with France and he had witnessed the proclamation of the German Empire at Versailles in 1871. No one could describe him as a strategic genius. His greatest asset was his rocklike imperturbability. The brain behind his triumphs belonged to his deputy, Ludendorff, who had already distinguished himself in reducing the Liége forts (page 41); and, at least on the Eastern Front, Ludendorff owed much to Hoffmann, who understood the Russian military mind. But, in Germany, sentiment and propaganda combined to turn Hindenburg into a colossus of victory.

Austria-Hungary discovered no such idol. Conrad's decision to send the First and Fourth armies northwards from Galicia was based upon a false assumption. He thought that the Russian commander-in-chief, Grand Duke Nicholas, had ordered the commander of the South-Western Army Group, General Ivanov, to concentrate around Lublin. In reality the Russians were farther south-east, threatening Lemberg (Lvov) where Ivanov had, in his turn, wrongly assumed the main Austrian forces to be. There was, in consequence, a curious week of shadow-boxing before Conrad turned to meet the challenge to his flank from Ivanov (see pages 100–101). Conrad made the mistake of opening up a gap in the north which was filled by the Russian Fifth Army. Fearing he might be encircled, Conrad ordered a general retreat on 11 September, and found it impossible to stabilise the Front until the Russians had penetrated over a hundred miles, reaching the Carpathian passes into Hungary. The Austrians thus sustained a humiliating defeat, with the Russians capturing two provincial capitals, Lemberg (the fourth largest city in Austria-Hungary) and Czernowitz, as well as beseiging Przemsyl. The Slav contingents in the Austro-Hungarian Army (particularly the Czechs) had little heart for a war against 'Mother Russia', but large-scale desertions did not begin until the spring of 1915, and it is clear that the disaster reflects as much on Conrad and his staff as on the quality of the troops they commanded. Eventually the Austrians were saved by an offensive mounted by Hindenburg in central Poland and threatening Warsaw. An abortive Russian counter-offensive in Poland at the end of October threatened Silesia but brought down a massive German response from the north, when Mackensen's Ninth Army fell on the Russians at Lodz and as winter set in, destroyed all prospects of avenging Tannenberg. Though the Russians had triumphed in Galicia, the first four months of fighting against the Germans had proved disastrous and left the Russian artillery desperately short of shells.

Yet the strangest development of the war was in Serbia. For Putnik, the Serbian commander-in-chief, had successfully repelled Potiorek's first incursion across the river Sava, and nipped another offensive (across the river Drina) in the bud. At the end of November Potiorek tried again and captured Belgrade on 2 December, sweeping the Serbs back into the mountain heart of the Kingdom. Yet, though short of men and munitions, the Serbs made a surprise counter-attack and within eleven days had recovered their capital. 'On the whole territory of the Serbian Government there remains not one free enemy soldier', ran a proud communiqué on 15 December. Austria's humiliation was complete. Small wonder the German High Command began privately to wonder if they were allied to a living Empire or a corpse.

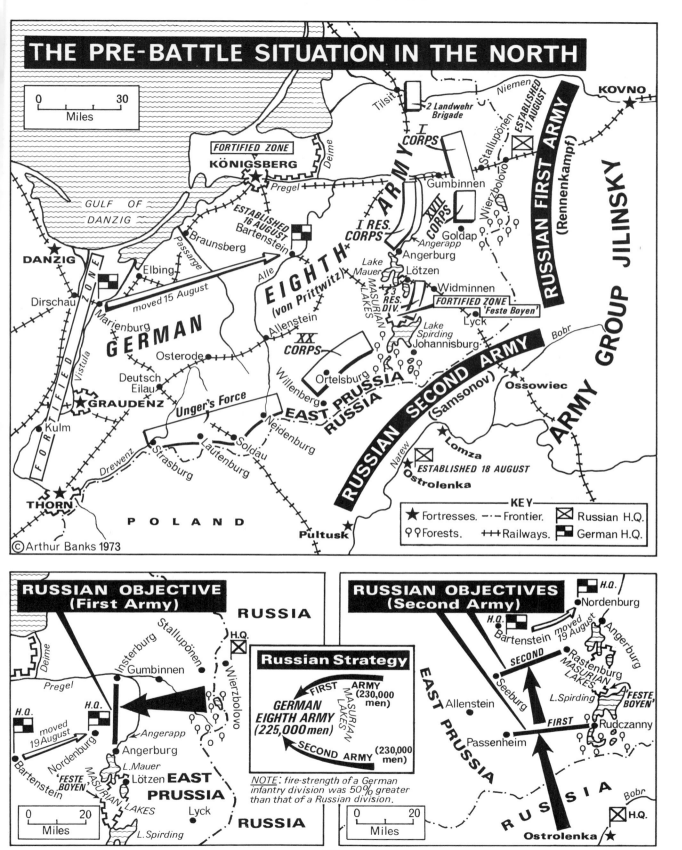

THE PRE-BATTLE SITUATION IN THE NORTH

0 — 30
Miles

KOVNO

ESTABLISHED 17 AUGUST

RUSSIAN FIRST ARMY (Rennenkampf)

Niemen

Tilsit

2 Landwehr Brigade

I ARMY CORPS

Stallupönen

Wierzbolovo

FORTIFIED ZONE
KÖNIGSBERG

Deime

Pregel

Gumbinnen

XVII CORPS

ESTABLISHED 16 AUGUST
Bartenstein

Braunsberg

Passarge

Elbing

I RES. CORPS

Angerapp

Goldap

Angerburg

Angerburg

Lötzen

GULF OF DANZIG

DANZIG

Dirschau

Marienburg

Alle

moved 15 August

Lake Mauer

3 RES. DIV.

Widminnen

FORTIFIED ZONE
'Feste Boyen'

EIGHTH ARMY
(von Prittwitz)

MASURIAN LAKES

Lyck

Lake Spirding

Johannisburg

GERMAN

Osterode

Allenstein

XX CORPS

RUSSIAN SECOND ARMY (Samsonov)

ARMY GROUP JILINSKY

Bobr

Deutsch Eilau

GRAUDENZ

Willenburg

Ortelsburg

Ossowiec

EAST PRUSSIA
RUSSIA

Unger's Force

Neidenburg

Lautenburg

Soldau

Strasburg

Drewenz

Vistula

FORTIFIED ZONE

Kulm

Narew

ESTABLISHED 18 AUGUST

Lomza

Ostrolenka

THORN

POLAND

© Arthur Banks 1973

—— KEY ——
★ Fortresses.   -·-·- Frontier.   ⊠ Russian H.Q.
♀♀ Forests.   +++ Railways.   ▦ German H.Q.

Pultusk

RUSSIAN OBJECTIVE (First Army)

RUSSIA

Deime

Insterburg

Stallupönen

H.Q.

Pregel

Gumbinnen

Wierzbolovo

H.Q.

H.Q.

moved 19 August

Nordenburg

Angerapp

Bartenstein

Angerburg

L.Mauer

'FESTE BOYEN'

Lötzen

EAST PRUSSIA

MASURIAN LAKES

Lyck

L. Spirding

RUSSIA

0 — 20
Miles

Russian Strategy

GERMAN EIGHTH ARMY (225,000 men)

FIRST ARMY (230,000 men)

SECOND ARMY (230,000 men)

MASURIAN LAKES

<u>NOTE</u>: fire-strength of a German infantry division was 50% greater than that of a Russian division.

RUSSIAN OBJECTIVES (Second Army)

H.Q.

Nordenburg

H.Q.

Bartenstein

moved 19 August

Angerburg

SECOND

Rastenburg

MASURIAN LAKES

'FESTE BOYEN'

Seeburg

L.Spirding

EAST PRUSSIA

Allenstein

FIRST

Rudczanny

Passenheim

RUSSIA

Bobr

⊠ H.Q.

Ostrolenka ★

0 — 20
Miles

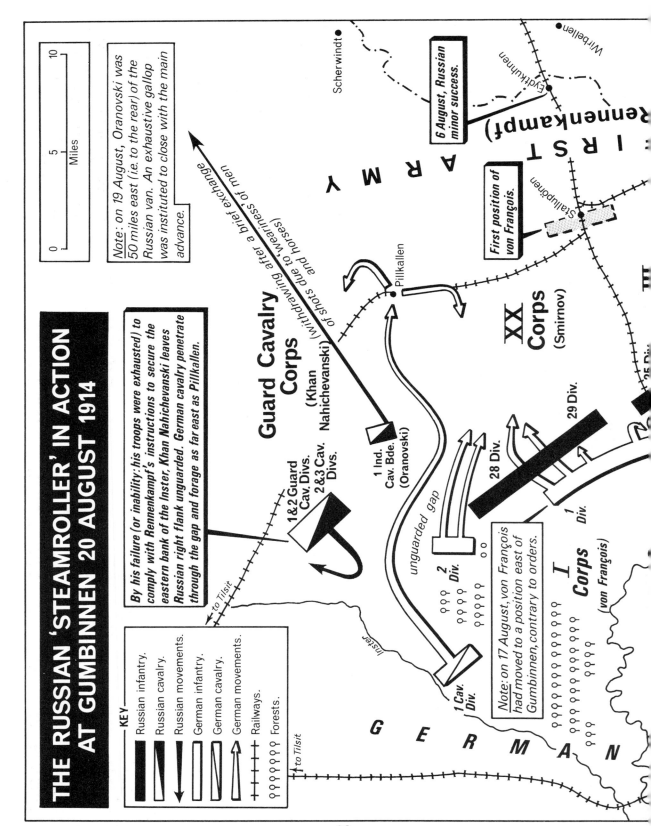

THE RUSSIAN 'STEAMROLLER' IN ACTION AT GUMBINNEN 20 AUGUST 1914

KEY

Russian infantry.
Russian cavalry.
Russian movements.
German infantry.
German cavalry.
German movements.
++++++ Railways.
ꝯꝯꝯꝯꝯ Forests.

Note: on 19 August, Oranovski was 50 miles east (i.e. to the rear) of the Russian van. An exhaustive gallop was instituted to close with the main advance.

By his failure (or inability: his troops were exhausted) to comply with Rennenkampf's instructions to secure the eastern bank of the Inster, Khan Nahichevanski leaves Russian right flank unguarded. German cavalry penetrate through the gap and forage as far east as Pillkallen.

Scherwindt ●

● Wirbellen

6 August, Russian minor success.

Eydtkuhnen ●

F I R S T   A R M Y   (Rennenkampf)

Stallupönen ●

First position of von François.

Guard Cavalry Corps
(Khan Nahichevanski) (withdrawing to 'weariness' of shots and horses)

of shots and horses)

Guard Cavalry after a brief exchange)

1&2 Guard Cav. Divs.
2&3 Cav. Divs.

1 Ind. Cav. Bde. (Oranovski)

Pillkallen

XX Corps (Smirnov)

25 Div.

29 Div.

28 Div.

unguarded gap

2 Div.

1 Div.

I Corps (von François)

Note: on 17 August, von François had moved to a position east of Gumbinnen, contrary to orders.

1 Cav. Div.

to Tilsit

Inster

G E R M A N

↑ to Tilsit

Miles
0   5   10

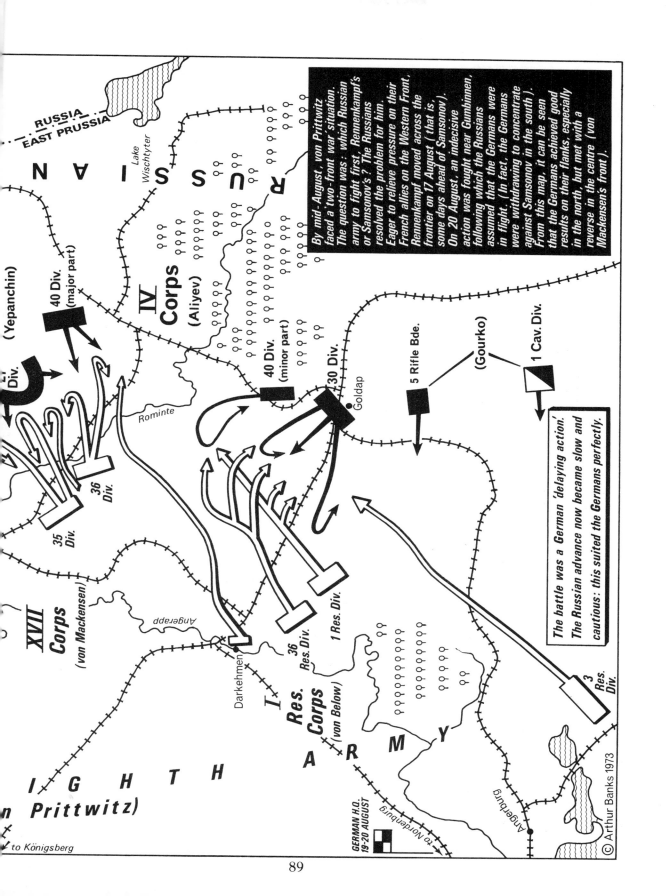

RUSSIA
EAST PRUSSIA

Lake Wischtyter

N **A** **I** **S** **S** **U** **R**

(Yepanchin)

40 Div. (major part)

Div.

IV Corps (Aliyev)

40 Div. (minor part)

Rominte

30 Div.

Goldap

5 Rifle Bde.

(Gourko)

1 Cav. Div.

35 Div.

36 Div.

XVII Corps (von Mackensen)

Angerapp

36 Res. Div.

1 Res. Div.

Darkehmen

I Res. Corps (von Below)

3 Res. Div.

E I G H T H   A R M Y

n Prittwitz)

to Königsberg

By mid-August, von Prittwitz faced a 'two-front war' situation. The question was : which Russian army to fight first, Rennenkampf's or Samsonov's ? The Russians resolved the problem for him. Eager to relieve pressure on their French allies on the Western Front, Rennenkampf moved across the frontier on 17 August (that is, some days ahead of Samsonov). On 20 August, an indecisive action was fought near Gumbinnen, following which the Russians assumed that the Germans were in flight. (In fact, the Germans were withdrawing to concentrate against Samsonov in the south). From this map, it can be seen that the Germans achieved good results on their flanks, especially in the north, but met with a reverse in the centre (von Mackensen's front).

The battle was a German 'delaying action'. The Russian advance now became slow and cautious : this suited the Germans perfectly.

GERMAN H.Q. 19-20 AUGUST

to Nordenburg

Angerburg

© Arthur Banks 1973

89

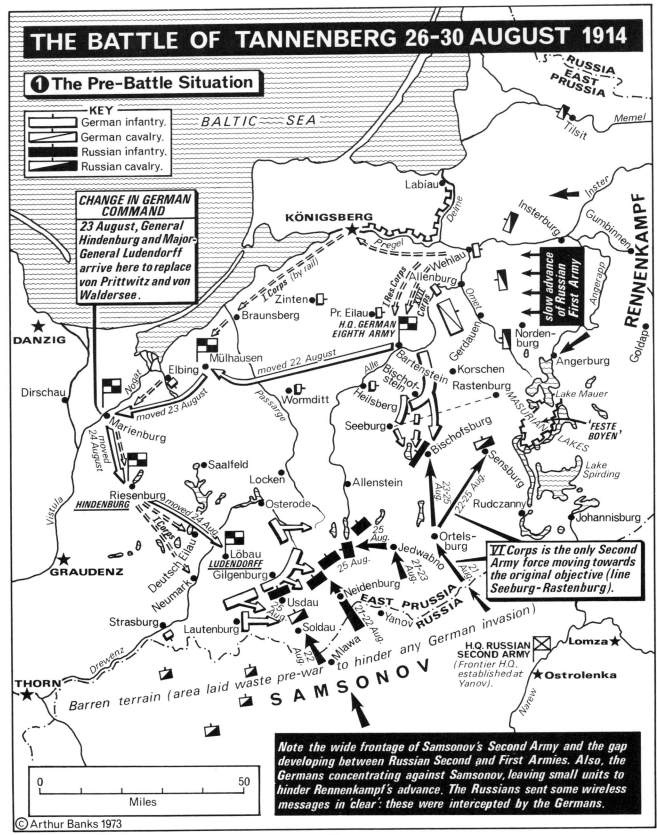

THE BATTLE OF TANNENBERG 26-30 AUGUST 1914

① The Pre-Battle Situation

KEY
- German infantry.
- German cavalry.
- Russian infantry.
- Russian cavalry.

BALTIC SEA

CHANGE IN GERMAN COMMAND
23 August, General Hindenburg and Major-General Ludendorff arrive here to replace von Prittwitz and von Waldersee.

RUSSIA
EAST
PRUSSIA

Memel

Tilsit

Labiau

Inster

RENNENKAMPF

KÖNIGSBERG

Pregel

Wehlau

Deime

Insterburg

Gumbinnen

Zinten

I Corps (by rail)

Pr. Eilau

I Res. Corps

Allenburg

XVII Corps

Omet

slow advance of Russian First Army

Braunsberg

H.Q. GERMAN EIGHTH ARMY

Nordenburg

Angerapp

Goldap

DANZIG

Elbing

Mülhausen

moved 22 August

Bartenstein

Gerdauen

Korschen

Angerburg

Lake Mauer

Alle

Bischof-stein

Rastenburg

Dirschau

Wormditt

Passarge

Heilsberg

MASURIAN LAKES

'FESTE BOYEN'

moved 23 August

Seeburg

Marienburg

Nogat

moved 24 August

Bischofsburg

Lake Spirding

Saalfeld

Locken

Allenstein

Sensburg

Rudczanny

Johannisburg

HINDENBURG

Riesenburg

moved 24 Aug.

Osterode

Vistula

I Corps

23-25 Aug.

22-25 Aug.

Ortels-burg

VI Corps is the only Second Army force moving towards the original objective (line Seeburg-Rastenburg).

GRAUDENZ

Löbau

LUDENDORFF

Gilgenburg

Deutsch Eilau

Jedwabno

21-23 Aug.

25 Aug.

Neumark

25 Aug.

Neidenburg

21 Aug.

Usdau

25 Aug.

EAST PRUSSIA

Yanov

RUSSIA

Strasburg

Lautenburg

Soldau

21-22 Aug.

Mlawa

H.Q. RUSSIAN SECOND ARMY
(Frontier H.Q. established at Yanov).

Lomza

Drewenz

Aug. 22

to hinder any German invasion)

Ostrolenka

THORN

Barren terrain (area laid waste pre-war

SAMSONOV

Narew

Note the wide frontage of Samsonov's Second Army and the gap developing between Russian Second and First Armies. Also, the Germans concentrating against Samsonov, leaving small units to hinder Rennenkampf's advance. The Russians sent some wireless messages in 'clear': these were intercepted by the Germans.

0 _____ 50

Miles

© Arthur Banks 1973

90

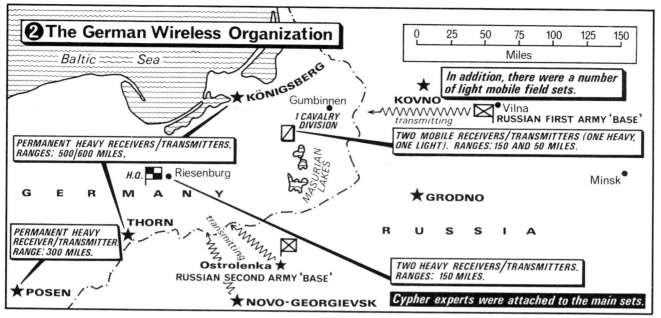

❷ The German Wireless Organization

Baltic — Sea

★ KÖNIGSBERG

Gumbinnen

1 CAVALRY DIVISION

KOVNO ★

⌇⌇⌇⌇⌇ *transmitting* ☒● Vilna
RUSSIAN FIRST ARMY 'BASE'

In addition, there were a number of light mobile field sets.

PERMANENT HEAVY RECEIVERS/TRANSMITTERS. RANGES: 500/600 MILES.

H.Q. ⚐ ● Riesenburg

TWO MOBILE RECEIVERS/TRANSMITTERS (ONE HEAVY, ONE LIGHT). RANGES: 150 AND 50 MILES.

Minsk ●

MASURIAN LAKES

G E R M A N Y

★ GRODNO

PERMANENT HEAVY RECEIVER/TRANSMITTER. RANGE: 300 MILES.

★ THORN

R U S S I A

transmitting ⌇⌇⌇⌇⌇ ☒

★ POSEN

Ostrolenka ★
RUSSIAN SECOND ARMY 'BASE'

TWO HEAVY RECEIVERS/TRANSMITTERS. RANGES: 150 MILES.

★ NOVO-GEORGIEVSK

Cypher experts were attached to the main sets.

Scale: 0 25 50 75 100 125 150 Miles

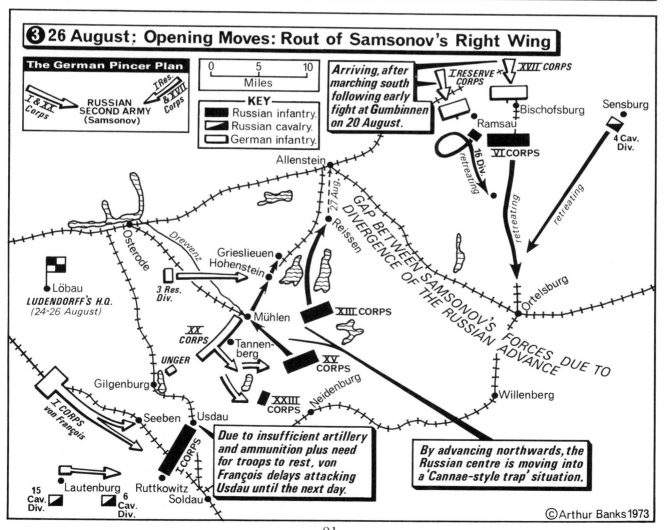

❸ 26 August: Opening Moves: Rout of Samsonov's Right Wing

The German Pincer Plan

I & XX Corps
RUSSIAN SECOND ARMY (Samsonov)
I Res. & XVII Corps

Scale: 0 5 10 Miles

KEY
- ■ Russian infantry.
- ◩ Russian cavalry.
- ▭ German infantry.

Arriving, after marching south following early fight at Gumbinnen on 20 August.

I RESERVE CORPS ✕ XVII CORPS

Sensburg

Bischofsburg

Ramsau

4 Cav. Div.

VI CORPS

16 Div *retreating*

retreating

retreating

Allenstein

27 Aug.

Reissen

GAP BETWEEN DIVERGENCE OF THE RUSSIAN ADVANCE

Osterode

Drewenz

Grieslieuen
Hohenstein

3 Res. Div.

Löbau
LUDENDORFF'S H.Q. (24-26 August)

Mühlen

XIII CORPS

Ortelsburg

SAMSONOV'S FORCES DUE TO

XX CORPS

Tannenberg

XV CORPS

UNGER

Gilgenburg

XXIII CORPS

Neidenburg

Willenberg

Seeben

Usdau

I CORPS von François

Due to insufficient artillery and ammunition plus need for troops to rest, von François delays attacking Usdau until the next day.

By advancing northwards, the Russian centre is moving into a 'Cannae-style trap' situation.

15 Cav. Div.

Lautenburg

Ruttkowitz
Soldau

6 Cav. Div.

I CORPS

© Arthur Banks 1973

91

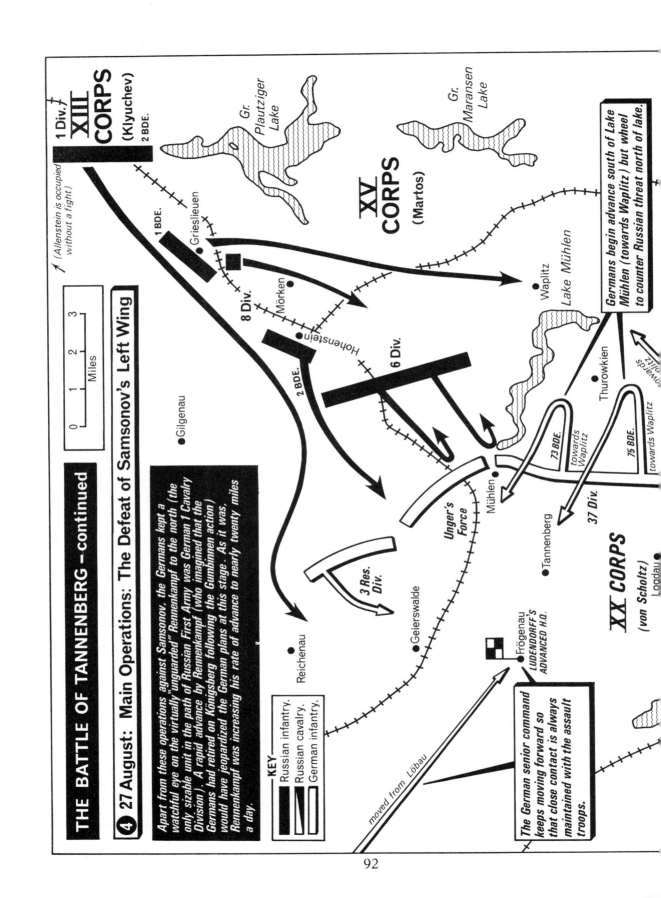

THE BATTLE OF TANNENBERG – continued

4 27 August: Main Operations: The Defeat of Samsonov's Left Wing

Apart from these operations against Samsonov, the Germans kept a watchful eye on the virtually "unguarded" Rennenkampf to the north (the only sizable unit in the path of Russian First Army was German 1 Cavalry Division). A rapid advance by Rennenkampf (who imagined that the Germans had retired on Königsberg following the Gumbinnen action) would have jeopardized the German plans at this stage. As it was, Rennenkampf was increasing his rate of advance to nearly twenty miles a day.

KEY
Russian infantry.
Russian cavalry.
German infantry.

Miles
0   1   2   3

XIII CORPS (Klyuchev)

1 Div.
2 BDE.

(Allenstein is occupied without a fight)

Gr. Plautziger Lake

Gr. Maransen Lake

XV CORPS (Martos)

1 BDE.
Grieslieuen

8 Div.
Mörken

2 BDE.
Hohenstein

6 Div.

Waplitz
Lake Mühlen

Germans begin advance south of Lake Mühlen (towards Waplitz) but wheel to counter Russian threat north of lake.

•Gilgenau

Unger's Force

Mühlen

Thurowkien

73 BDE.
towards Waplitz
75 BDE.
towards Waplitz

towards Spielberg

3 Res. Div.

•Reichenau

•Geierswalde

37 Div.

•Tannenberg

Frögenau
LUDENDORFF'S ADVANCED H.Q.

XX CORPS (von Scholtz)
Loudau

The German senior command keeps moving forward so that close contact is always maintained with the assault troops.

moved from Löbau

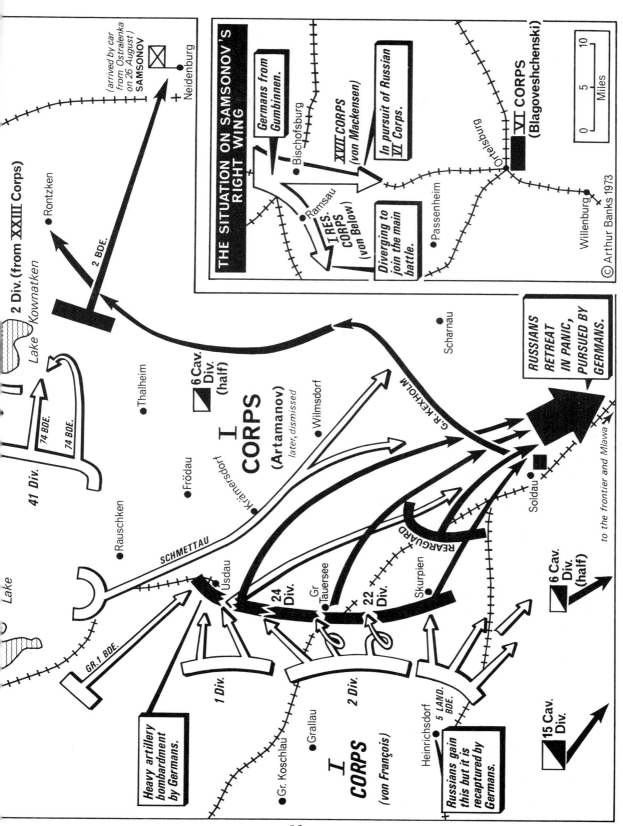

THE SITUATION ON SAMSONOV'S RIGHT WING

Germans from Gumbinnen.

XIII CORPS (von Mackensen)

In pursuit of Russian VI Corps.

VI CORPS (Blagoveshchenski)

I RES. CORPS (von Below)

Diverging to join the main battle.

• Bischofsburg

• Ramsau

• Ortelsburg

• Passenheim

• Willenburg

© Arthur Banks 1973

Miles
0   5   10

(arrived by car from Ostralenka on 26 August) **SAMSONOV**

• Neidenburg

2 Div. (from XXIII Corps)

• Rontzken

Lake Kownatken

2 BDE.

41 Div.

74 BDE.

74 BDE.

• Thalheim

6 Cav. Div. (half)

• Frödau

• Wilmsdorf

• Scharnau

I CORPS (Artamanov) *later, dismissed*

• Krämersdorf

G.R. KEXHOLM

RUSSIANS RETREAT IN PANIC, PURSUED BY GERMANS.

• Rauschken

SCHMETTAU

• Usdau

24 Div.

Gr. Tauersee

22 Div.

• Skurpien

REARGUARD

Soldau

to the frontier and Mlawa

6 Cav. Div. (half)

GR. 1. BDE.

1 Div.

• Grallau

2 Div.

• Heinrichsdorf

5 LAND. BDE.

Heavy artillery bombardment by Germans.

I CORPS (von François)

• Gr. Koschlau

Russians gain this but it is recaptured by Germans.

15 Cav. Div.

Lake

93

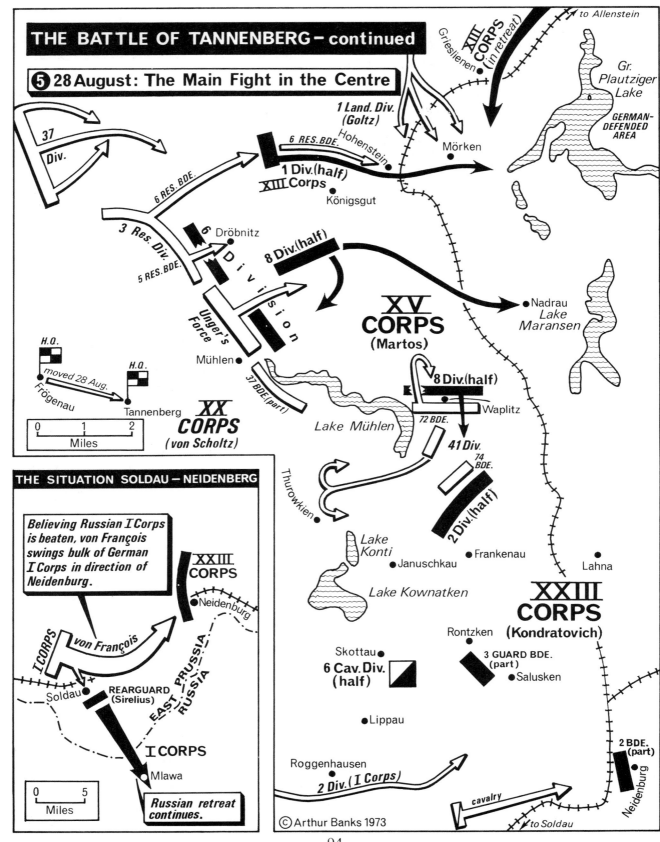

THE BATTLE OF TANNENBERG — continued

❺ 28 August: The Main Fight in the Centre

37 Div.

1 Land. Div. (Goltz)

6 RES. BDE.

Hohenstein

XIII CORPS (in retreat)

Grieslienen

to Allenstein

Gr. Plautziger Lake

GERMAN-DEFENDED AREA

Mörken

6 RES. BDE.

1 Div.(half) XIII Corps

Königsgut

3 Res. Div.

5 RES. BDE.

6 Dröbnitz

Division

8 Div.(half)

XV CORPS (Martos)

Nadrau

Lake Maransen

Unger's Force

Mühlen

37 BDE.(part)

8 Div.(half)

Waplitz

72 BDE.

41 Div.

74 BDE.

2 Div.(half)

H.Q.

moved 28 Aug.

Frögenau

H.Q.

Tannenberg

XX CORPS (von Scholtz)

0   1   2
Miles

Lake Mühlen

Thurowkien

Lake Konti

Januschkau

Frankenau

Lahna

Lake Kownatken

XXIII CORPS (Kondratovich)

Rontzken

THE SITUATION SOLDAU — NEIDENBERG

Believing Russian I Corps is beaten, von François swings bulk of German I Corps in direction of Neidenburg.

XXIII CORPS

Neidenburg

I CORPS

von François

EAST PRUSSIA

RUSSIA

Soldau

REARGUARD (Sirelius)

I CORPS

Mlawa

Russian retreat continues.

0   5
Miles

Skottau

6 Cav. Div. (half)

3 GUARD BDE. (part)

Salusken

Lippau

2 BDE. (part)

Roggenhausen

2 Div. (I Corps)

cavalry

Neidenburg

to Soldau

© Arthur Banks 1973

94

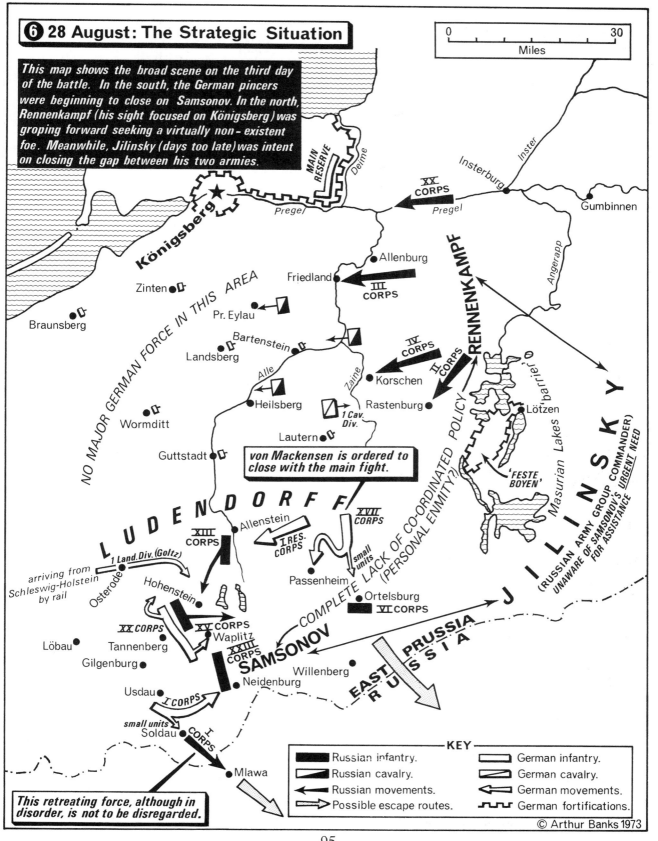

❻ 28 August: The Strategic Situation

This map shows the broad scene on the third day of the battle. In the south, the German pincers were beginning to close on Samsonov. In the north, Rennenkampf (his sight focused on Königsberg) was groping forward seeking a virtually non-existent foe. Meanwhile, Jilinsky (days too late) was intent on closing the gap between his two armies.

0   30
Miles

MAIN RESERVE

Deime

Inster

Insterburg

XX CORPS

Gumbinnen

Pregel

Pregel

Königsberg

Angerapp

RENNENKAMPF

Allenburg

Zinten

Friedland

III CORPS

Braunsberg

Pr. Eylau

NO MAJOR GERMAN FORCE IN THIS AREA

Bartenstein

IV CORPS

Landsberg

II CORPS

Korschen

'barrier'

Alle

Zaine

Heilsberg

Rastenburg

Lötzen

Wormditt

1 Cav. Div.

Lautern

Guttstadt

von Mackensen is ordered to close with the main fight.

Masurian Lakes

'FESTE BOYEN'

L U D E N D O R F F

XVII CORPS

XIII CORPS

Allenstein

I RES. CORPS

arriving from Schleswig-Holstein by rail

1 Land.Div. (Goltz)

small units

Osterode

Passenheim

Hohenstein

COMPLETE LACK OF CO-ORDINATED POLICY (PERSONAL ENMITY?)

J I L I N S K Y

(RUSSIAN ARMY GROUP COMMANDER) UNAWARE OF SAMSONOV'S URGENT NEED FOR ASSISTANCE

Ortelsburg

VI CORPS

XX CORPS

XV CORPS

Löbau

Tannenberg

Waplitz

XXIII CORPS

SAMSONOV

Gilgenburg

Willenberg

EAST PRUSSIA

R U S S I A

Usdau

I CORPS

Neidenburg

small units

Soldau

I CORPS

KEY

Mlawa

This retreating force, although in disorder, is not to be disregarded.

■ Russian infantry.	▭ German infantry.
▧ Russian cavalry.	▨ German cavalry.
← Russian movements.	⇐ German movements.
⇨ Possible escape routes.	⏛ German fortifications.

© Arthur Banks 1973

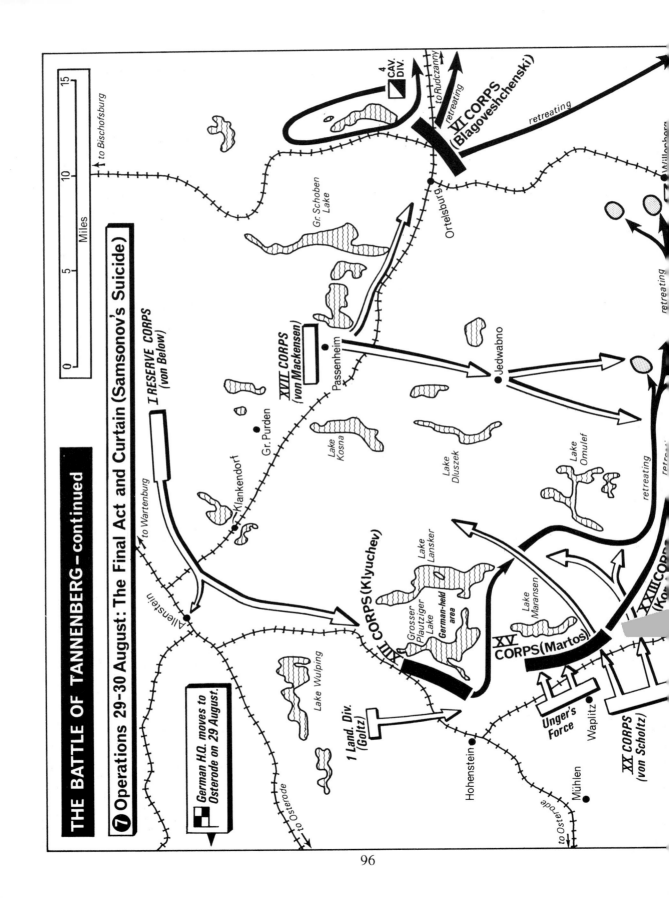

THE BATTLE OF TANNENBERG—continued

7 Operations 29–30 August: The Final Act and Curtain (Samsonov's Suicide)

German H.Q. moves to Osterode on 29 August.

to Bischofsburg

Miles

0 5 10 15

I RESERVE CORPS
(von Below)

to Wartenburg

to Osterode

Lake Wulping

1 Land. Div.
(Goltz)

Hohenstein

Mühlen

to Oster...

to Osterode

Allenstein

VI CORPS (Klyuchev)

Grosser
Plautziger
Lake

Lake
Lansker

German-held
area

XV
CORPS (Martos)

Unger's
Force

Waplitz

XX CORPS
(von Scholtz)

Lake
Maransen

XXIII CORPS
(Kon...

Klankendorf

Gr. Purden

Lake
Kosna

Lake
Dluszek

Passenheim

XVII CORPS
(von Mackensen)

Jedwabno

Lake
Omulef

retreating

retreating

Gr. Schoben
Lake

Ortelsburg

4
CAV.
DIV.

to Rudczanny

retreating

VI CORPS
(Blagoveshchenski)

retreating

Willenberg

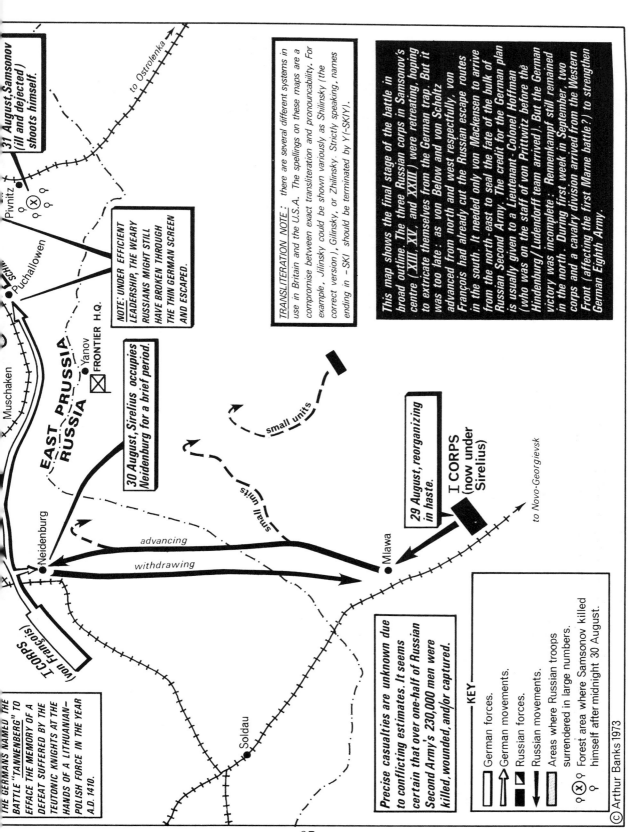

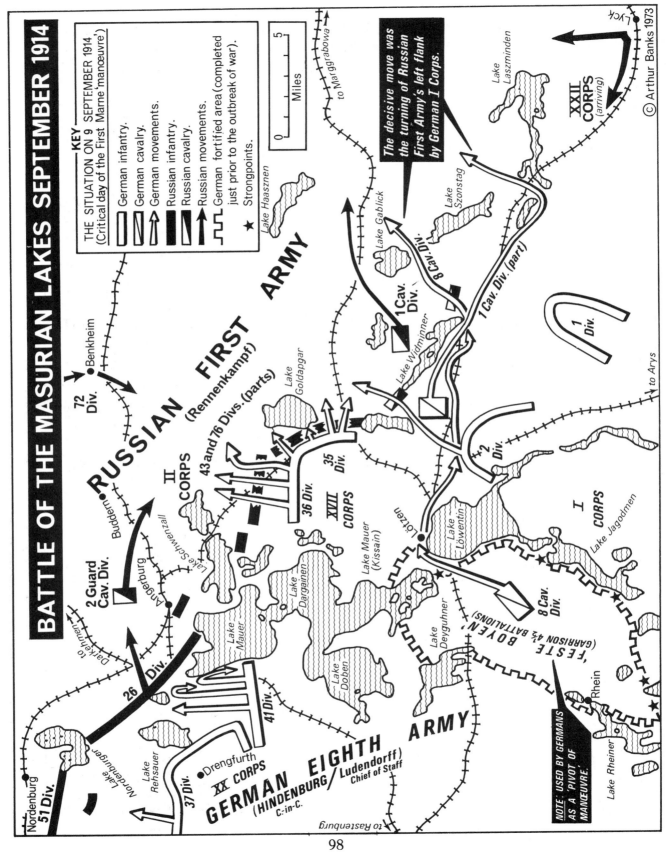

BATTLE OF THE MASURIAN LAKES SEPTEMBER 1914

KEY

THE SITUATION ON 9 SEPTEMBER 1914
(Critical day of the First Marne 'manoeuvre')

- German infantry.
- German cavalry.
- German movements.
- Russian infantry.
- Russian cavalry.
- Russian movements.
- German fortified area (completed just prior to the outbreak of war).
- ★ Strongpoints.

© Arthur Banks 1973

The decisive move was the turning of Russian First Army's left flank by German I Corps.

LYCK

XXII CORPS (arriving)

Lake Laszminden

Lake Szonstag

8 Cav. Div.

1 Cav. Div.

to Marggrabowa

Lake Gablick

1 Cav. Div. (part)

1 Div.

to Arys

Lake Haasznen

Benkheim

72 Div.

Lake Widminner

2 Div.

RUSSIAN FIRST ARMY
(Rennenkampf)

Buddern

43 and 76 Divs. (parts)

Lake Goldapgar

II CORPS

36 Div.

XVII CORPS

35 Div.

Lötzen

Lake Löwentin

I CORPS

Lake Jagodmen

2 Guard Cav. Div.

Angerburg

Lake Schwenzall

Lake Mauer (Kissain)

Lake Dargainen

Lake Deyguhner

to Dehmen

Darkehmen

26 Div.

Lake Mauer

Lake Doben

8 Cav. Div.

'FESTE BOYEN'
(GARRISON 4½ BATTALIONS)

Rhein

Lake Deyguhner

41 Div.

Nordenburg

51 Div.

Lake Nordenburg

Lake Rehsauer

Drengfurth

37 Div.

XX CORPS

GERMAN EIGHTH ARMY
(HINDENBURG / Ludendorff)
C-in-C.   Chief of Staff

to Rastenburg

Lake Rheiner

NOTE: USED BY GERMANS AS A 'PIVOT OF MANOEUVRE.

5 0 5 Miles

SERBIA IN TRAVAIL AND TRIUMPH 1914

*Punitive expedition: so-called by the Austrians after it had failed.

① Serbia's Strategic Position

Anti-Serbia: hence pro-Central Powers.

Berlin railway project

AREA OF OPERATIONS IN 1914

Railway link runs through Serbia.

Berlin • GERMANY Poland RUSSIA Vienna • AUSTRIA-HUNGARY RUMANIA ITALY SERBIA BULGARIA Constantinople GREECE TURKEY

0 100 200
Miles

② Austria's "Strafexpedition" *

12-24 AUGUST
AUSTRIAN SECOND ARMY

ONLY PART SECOND ARMY ENGAGED. (some units diverted to Galicia)

AUSTRIAN FIFTH ARMY — VIII CORPS, XIII CORPS

AUSTRIAN SIXTH ARMY

Sava — Shabatz — BELGRADE — Danube — Jadar — Drina — SERBIAN MAIN FORCE — Kolubara — Serbian units guarding Belgrade — Valjevo (Putnik's H.Q.) — Uzhitse — SERBIAN UZHITSE (UŽICE) GROUP

STRENGTHS	
Austrians:	190,000
Serbians:	180,000
CASUALTIES	
Austrians:	38,000
Serbians:	18,000

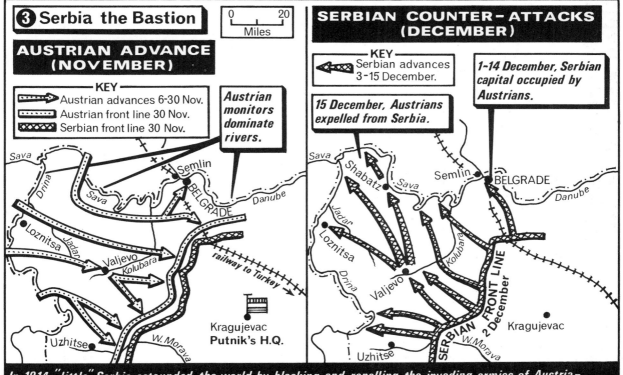

③ Serbia the Bastion

0 20
Miles

AUSTRIAN ADVANCE (NOVEMBER)

KEY
- Austrian advances 6-30 Nov.
- Austrian front line 30 Nov.
- Serbian front line 30 Nov.

Austrian monitors dominate rivers.

Sava — Drina — Sava — Semlin — BELGRADE — Danube — Loznitsa — Jadar — Valjevo — Kolubara — railway to Turkey — Uzhitse — W. Morava — Kragujevac Putnik's H.Q.

SERBIAN COUNTER-ATTACKS (DECEMBER)

KEY
Serbian advances 3-15 December.

1-14 December, Serbian capital occupied by Austrians.

15 December, Austrians expelled from Serbia.

Sava — Shabatz — Sava — Semlin — BELGRADE — Danube — Jadar — Loznitsa — Drina — Valjevo — Kolubara — SERBIAN FRONT LINE 2 December — Kragujevac — Uzhitse — W. Morava

In 1914, "little" Serbia astounded the world by blocking and repelling the invading armies of Austria-Hungary. German reaction was derisive: "Allies? We are shackled to a corpse." It is important to note that part only of Austrian Second Army was engaged in August, and these units were gradually withdrawn to fight on the Galician front. However, a Serbian Army equalled little more than an Austrian corps.

© Arthur Banks 1973

99

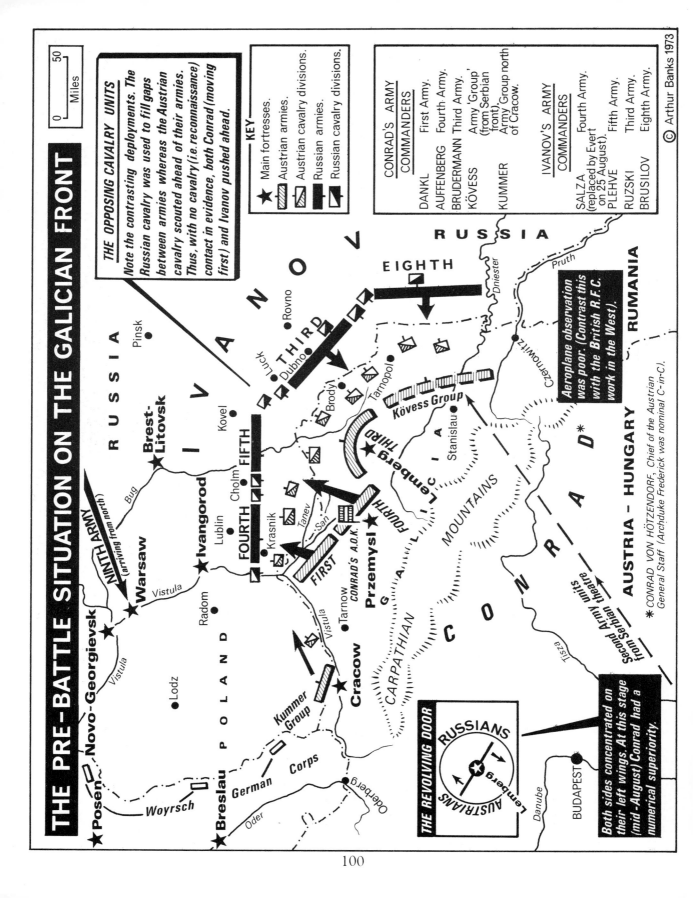

THE PRE-BATTLE SITUATION ON THE GALICIAN FRONT

© Arthur Banks 1973

THE OPPOSING CAVALRY UNITS

Note the contrasting deployments. The Russian cavalry was used to fill gaps between armies whereas the Austrian cavalry scouted ahead of their armies. Thus, with no cavalry (i.e. reconnaissance) contact in evidence, both Conrad (moving first) and Ivanov pushed ahead.

KEY

★ Main fortresses.

Austrian armies.

Austrian cavalry divisions.

Russian armies.

Russian cavalry divisions.

CONRAD'S ARMY COMMANDERS

DANKL   First Army.
AUFFENBERG   Fourth Army.
BRUDERMANN   Third Army.
KÖVESS   Army 'Group' (from Serbian front).
KUMMER   Army Group north of Cracow.

IVANOV'S ARMY COMMANDERS

SALZA (replaced by Evert on 25 August).   Fourth Army.
PLEHVE   Fifth Army.
RUZSKI   Third Army.
BRUSILOV   Eighth Army.

Aeroplane observation was poor. (Contrast this with the British R.F.C. work in the West).

* *CONRAD VON HÖTZENDORF, Chief of the Austrian General Staff (Archduke Frederick was nominal C-in-C).*

THE REVOLVING DOOR

RUSSIANS

AUSTRIANS

Lemberg

Both sides concentrated on their left wings. At this stage (mid-August) Conrad had a numerical superiority.

RUSSIA

RUMANIA

AUSTRIA – HUNGARY

POLAND

GALICIA

CARPATHIAN MOUNTAINS

I V A N O V

C O N R A D*

EIGHTH

THIRD

FIFTH

FOURTH

FIRST

FOURTH

Lemberg Third

Kövess Group

NINTH ARMY (arriving from north)

CONRAD'S A.O.K.

Kummer Group

German Corps

Woyrsch

Second Army units from Serbian theatre

Posen · Novo-Georgievsk · Warsaw · Ivangorod · Brest-Litovsk · Pinsk · Rovno · Dubno · Luck · Kovel · Lublin · Cholm · Krasnik · Tarnow · Cracow · Przemysl · Brody · Tarnopol · Stanislau · Czernowitz · BUDAPEST · Radom · Lodz · Breslau · Oderberg

Vistula · Bug · Vistula · Vistula · San · Tanev · Tisza · Danube · Pruth · Dniester · Oder

50 Miles

0

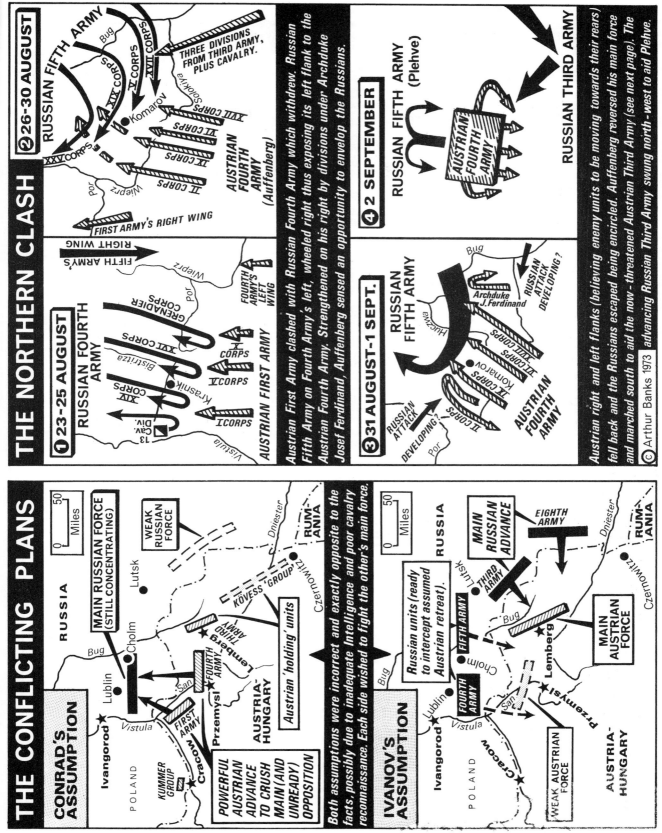

LEMBERG-PRZEMYSL OPERATIONS

The Austro-Hungarian armies were multi-racial: the graph below gives a broad guide to their heterogenous make-up.

❶ The Russian Advance on Lemberg

26-31 AUGUST

RUSSIAN THIRD ARMY (Ruzski)

AUSTRIAN THIRD ARMY (Brudermann)

Cavalry

Lemberg

Dniester

KÖVESS "GROUP" part SECOND ARMY (rest confronting Serbia)

Brzezany

Zlota Lipa

RUSSIAN EIGHTH ARMY (Brusilov)

G. Lipa

Halicz

Dniester

KEY
- ⬅ Russian attacks (corps shown).
- —x— Russian army boundary.
- ▨ Austrian line 26 August.
- ⬅ Austrian retreat (in disorder).

0 10 20 30
Miles

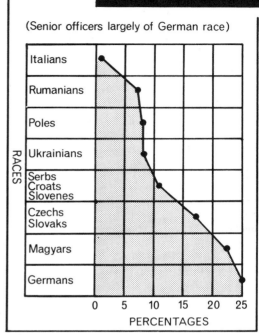

(Senior officers largely of German race)

RACES
Italians
Rumanians
Poles
Ukrainians
Serbs Croats Slovenes
Czechs Slovaks
Magyars
Germans

0 5 10 15 20 25
PERCENTAGES

❷ The Overall Scene in Outline

3-11 SEPTEMBER

Dragomirov forges ahead.

Cavalry

FIFTH

FOURTH

Plehve's army, now in good order, pursues army of Auffenberg.

Auffenberg is marching into a "trap" situation: however, intercepted Russian wireless signals alert him of the danger.

THIRD

Rava Russka

Lemberg

Ruzski, expecting to contact rear of Auffenberg's army, encounters his van.

THIRD

EIGHTH

Brusilov moves to north-west to close with Ruzski.

This repatched army tries to counter-attack but fails.

SECOND (ex-Kövess)

Böhm-Ermolli tries to turn the Russian flank but fails.

remainder of Second Army arriving from Serbian front

KEY
- ⬅ Russian armies.
- ⬅ Russian cavalry.
- ⬅ Austrian armies.

Conrad orders Austrian retirement 11 September.

❸ The Austrian Retreat

11 SEPT.- 3 OCT.

Fresh army arriving.

Vistula

Ivangorod

Lublin

NINTH

FOURTH

FIFTH

THIRD

0 20 Miles

FIRST

FIRST

Cracow

Vistula Tarnow

FOURTH

Rava Russka

Lemberg

Przemysl

Dunajetz

Gorlice

THIRD

SECOND

EIGHTH

Dniester

San

Invested by Russians 24 Sept.- 9 Oct.

KEY
- ⬅ Russian armies (attacking).
- ▨ Austrian line 11 September.
- ⬅ Austrian armies (retreating).
- ▨ Austrian line (3 October).
- ✂ Fierce clash.

THE DISCORDANT VIEWS OF CONRAD & MOLTKE

Four double-gauge railway lines running west to east across Germany form the basis of her military mobility. (Two corps west→east Sept.).

BELGIUM
WESTERN FRONT
FRANCE

E. PRUSSIA
EASTERN FRONT
POLAND

GERMANY

Berlin

"NEGLECTED" RAILWAY

RUSSIA

Vienna

AUSTRIA-HUNGARY

SERBIA

MOLTKE

This commander's attention is fixed upon the Western Front: he desires a quick victory over France so that he can switch Germany's military might against Russia. He is irritated by Conrad's exhortations for aid, regarding them as a distraction from the main task in hand.

14 September 1914, von Falkenhayn replaces Moltke (who has bungled application of amended Schlieffen Plan). The new Chief of the German General Staff recognizes Conrad's plight but is adamant that any German aid to Austria must come from East Prussia, not the Western Front.

CONRAD

This commander expects German aid from the outset (it was implied rather than promised): he feels betrayed and snubbed. (Austria's main foe is Russia, not France).

Moltke's irritation with Conrad turns to disdain when Austria fails to defeat "little" Serbia in August and the Serbs raid Hungary (Sept.).

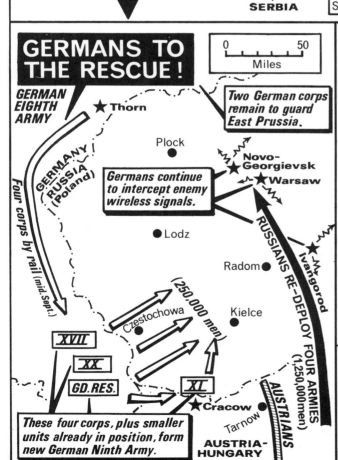

GERMANS TO THE RESCUE!

0 — 50 Miles

GERMAN EIGHTH ARMY

Thorn

Four corps by rail (mid-Sept.)

GERMANY / RUSSIA (Poland)

Plock

Two German corps remain to guard East Prussia.

Germans continue to intercept enemy wireless signals.

Novo-Georgievsk

Warsaw

Lodz

Radom

RUSSIANS RE-DEPLOY FOUR ARMIES (1,250,000 men)

Ivangorod

(250,000 men)

Czestochowa

Kielce

XVII

XX

GD. RES.

XI

Cracow

Tarnow

AUSTRIANS

AUSTRIA-HUNGARY

These four corps, plus smaller units already in position, form new German Ninth Army.

CENTRAL POWERS ON THE MOVE

0 — 20 Miles

Vistula

Plock

2 Novo-Georgievsk

Warsaw **5**

4

R U S S I A

Lodz

G E R M A N Y

P O L A N D

GERMANS

GERMANS

Radom

Ivangorod

9

Hindenburg

San

Czestochowa

AUSTRIANS

Vistula

AUSTRIA-HUNGARY

Cracow

KEY

GER. AUS.
Central Powers' line 28 September (start of advance).
Central Powers' line 17 October (limit of advance).
Central Powers' drives.
● Russian armies.

© Arthur Banks 1973

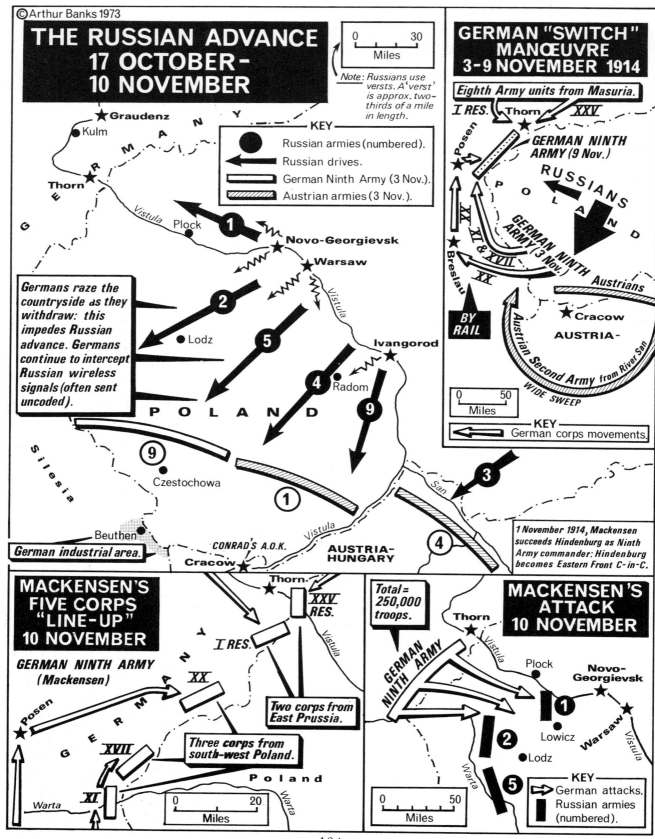

© Arthur Banks 1973

THE RUSSIAN ADVANCE 17 OCTOBER – 10 NOVEMBER

0 30
Miles

Note: Russians use versts. A 'verst' is approx. two-thirds of a mile in length.

KEY
- ● Russian armies (numbered).
- ◄ Russian drives.
- ▭ German Ninth Army (3 Nov.).
- ▨ Austrian armies (3 Nov.).

★ Graudenz
● Kulm
★ Thorn
GERMANY
Vistula
● Plock
★ Novo-Georgievsk
★ Warsaw
Vistula

1

Germans raze the countryside as they withdraw: this impedes Russian advance. Germans continue to intercept Russian wireless signals (often sent uncoded).

2
● Lodz
5
4 ● Radom
Ivangorod ★
9

P O L A N D

⑨
● Czestochowa
Silesia

① Vistula

Beuthen ●
German industrial area.

CONRAD'S A.O.K.
★ Cracow
AUSTRIA-HUNGARY
San
3

④

GERMAN "SWITCH" MANŒUVRE 3–9 NOVEMBER 1914

Eighth Army units from Masuria.
I RES. ★ Thorn XXV
Posen
GERMAN NINTH ARMY (9 Nov.)
RUSSIANS
P O L A N D
XX
GERMAN NINTH ARMY (3 Nov.)
XI & XVII
Breslau ★
XX
Austrians
BY RAIL
Austrian Second Army from River San
★ Cracow
AUSTRIA-
WIDE SWEEP

0 50
Miles

KEY
◄ German corps movements.

1 November 1914, Mackensen succeeds Hindenburg as Ninth Army commander: Hindenburg becomes Eastern Front C-in-C.

MACKENSEN'S FIVE CORPS "LINE-UP" 10 NOVEMBER

GERMAN NINTH ARMY (Mackensen)

★ Thorn
XXV RES.
I RES.
Vistula
Two corps from East Prussia.

Posen ★
GERMANY
XX
XVII
Three corps from south-west Poland.
XI
Warta
P o l a n d
Warta

0 20
Miles

MACKENSEN'S ATTACK 10 NOVEMBER

Total = 250,000 troops.

GERMAN NINTH ARMY
★ Thorn
Vistula
● Plock
Novo-Georgievsk ★
1
● Lowicz
★ Warsaw
Vistula
2
● Lodz
Warta
5

KEY
▷ German attacks.
▮ Russian armies (numbered).

0 50
Miles

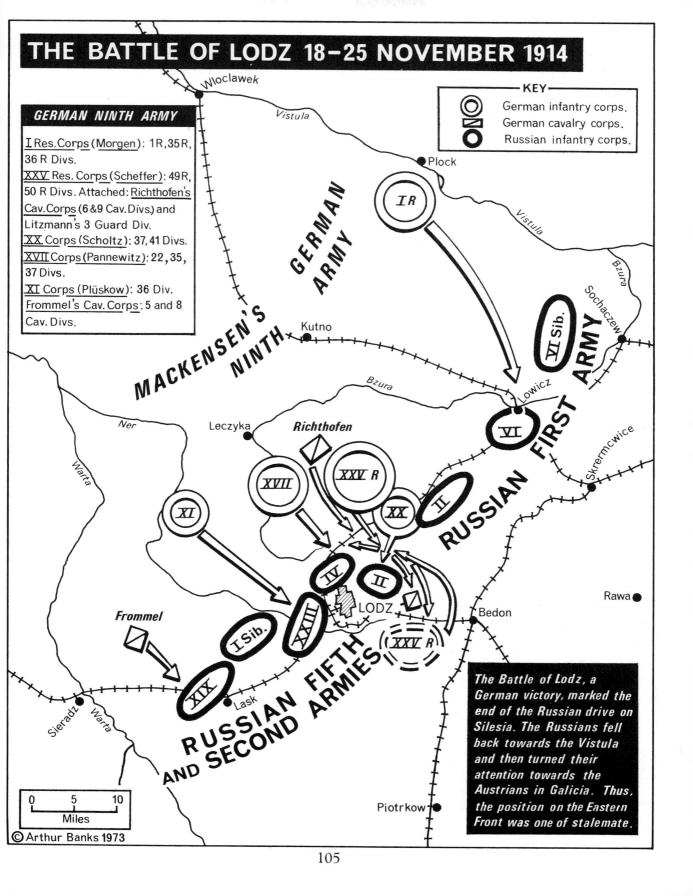

THE BATTLE OF LODZ 18–25 NOVEMBER 1914

KEY
- ◎ German infantry corps.
- ▣ German cavalry corps.
- ◯ Russian infantry corps.

GERMAN NINTH ARMY

I Res. Corps (Morgen): 1R, 35R, 36 R Divs.
XXV Res. Corps (Scheffer): 49R, 50 R Divs. Attached: Richthofen's Cav. Corps (6 & 9 Cav. Divs.) and Litzmann's 3 Guard Div.
XX Corps (Scholtz): 37, 41 Divs.
XVII Corps (Pannewitz): 22, 35, 37 Divs.
XI Corps (Plüskow): 36 Div.
Frommel's Cav. Corps: 5 and 8 Cav. Divs.

GERMAN ARMY

MACKENSEN'S NINTH

Wloclawek

Vistula

Plock

Vistula

Bzura

Sochaczew

Kutno

Ner

Bzura

Leczyka

Richthofen

Lowicz

VI Sib.

VI

RUSSIAN FIRST ARMY

Skrermcwice

Warta

XI

XVII

XXV R

XX

II

IV

II

Rawa

Frommel

I Sib.

XXIII

LODZ

Bedon

XXV R

Sieradz

Warta

XIX

Lask

RUSSIAN FIFTH AND SECOND ARMIES

Piotrkow

The Battle of Lodz, a German victory, marked the end of the Russian drive on Silesia. The Russians fell back towards the Vistula and then turned their attention towards the Austrians in Galicia. Thus, the position on the Eastern Front was one of stalemate.

```
0    5    10
     Miles
```

© Arthur Banks 1973

THE EUROPEAN MILITARY SITUATION 30 NOVEMBER 1914

0 — 200
Miles

NORWAY
CHRISTIANIA

SWEDEN

Skagerrak

Kattegat

COPEN.

DENMARK

NORTH SEA

Kiel Canal

HELIGOLAND

Kiel

Hamburg

Bremen

Elbe

BERL

G E R M A

Dresden

IRELAND

Dublin

Manchester

BRITAIN

LONDON

Southampton

THE HAGUE

Amsterdam

Antwerp

BRUSSELS

Liége

Rhine

BELGIUM

LUX.

Frankfurt

Pr

Glasgow

Edinburgh

ATLANTIC OCEAN

English Channel

Brest

Rouen

Aisne

PARIS

Marne

Seine

Munich

Dan

2 August, occupied by Germans.

Loire

Belfort

BERNE

Innsbruc

Bay of Biscay

SWITZ.

Tr

F R A N C E

Rhône

Milan

Venice

Bordeaux

Turin

Po

Genoa

A

Marseilles

Florence

I

SPAIN

CORSICA

ROM

Barcelona

BALEARIC ISLANDS

SARDINIA

TYRRHEN. SEA

Paler

M E D I T E R R A N E A N

Bizerta

Oran

ALGIERS

Bone

TUNIS

Towards the end of November 1914 the initial
energetic thrusts of the Central Powers had
exhausted themselves. After four months
of activity (the Central Powers meeting with
determined resistance on both the Eastern
and Western Fronts), the war had reached
a position of stalemate. This map depicts
the "de facto" situation that existed at this
stage of operations. As opposed to large-
scale movements, the campaign settled
into a localised trench-warfare situation,
each side testing the other, rather than
initiating a definite major advance.
Consequently the mobile war switched to
other areas (e.g. the war at sea, in the air,
the Dardanelles, Mesopotamia, etc.) in the
hope of achieving "side-show" breakthroughs
that would affect the main battle fronts.

© Arthur Banks 1973

KEY

The Entente Powers and associates on 30 November 1914.

The Central Powers on 30 November 1914. *Note:* Britain declared war on Turkey on 5 November 1914.

Neutral states on 30 November 1914.

The Western and Eastern fronts on 30 November 1914.

Gulf of Bothnia

FINLAND

PETROGRAD

STOCKHOLM

Reval

Moscow

BALTIC SEA

Riga

Libau

Smolensk

Kovno

Vilna

Gumbinnen

Königsberg

Minsk

RUSSIA

Danzig

Tannenberg

Grodno

Vistula

Brest-Litovsk

sen

Lodz

Warsaw

Kiev

Oder

POLAND

Dnieper

Lemberg

Dniester

Odessa

Pressburg

Tisza

Pruth

ENNA

Budapest

USTRIA - HUNGARY

29 November, vacated by Serbs.

Drava

RUMANIA

BLACK SEA

Sava

BUCHAREST

Frontier operations.

BELGRADE

Danube

CONSTANTINOPLE

SERBIA

BULGARIA

SOFIA

Angora

MONTE-NEGRO

ALBANIA

Salonika

Dardanelles

OTTOMAN EMPIRE [TURKEY]

Brindisi

GREECE

AEGEAN SEA

IONIAN SEA

ATHENS

Smyrna

Messina

RHODES

5 November, annexed by Britain.

CYPRUS

SICILY

SEA

CRETE

THE SITUATION AT THE END OF THE YEAR 1914

By the end of the year 1914 there was deadlock over every battlefront in Europe. From the Swiss frontier northwards fortified lines ran by way of the Vosges, the hills of the Meuse, the Argonne and the Chemin des Dames to the Aisne and up to Armentières and the Ypres Salient, reaching down to the inundated fields around Dixmude and so to the sand dunes of the North Sea. A tenth of metropolitan France, including the main French coalfields, and almost the whole of Belgium were behind the German trenches, and remained so throughout the war. The line of the Western Front did not move as much as ten miles in either direction for the following two and a half years. In the East, stalemate had come only through the onset of winter and there were no continuous systems of entrenchment to rule out a war movement. Yet there seemed little prospect of a decisive victory, and both sides had by now abandoned all hope of a short war.

Both the British and the German public were surprised by what was happening in the war at sea. After more than a decade of naval rivalry it was assumed there would be a naval battle between the great capital ships at an early date. But the Kaiser personally vetoed an engagement which might have destroyed his battle fleet until after the enemy fleet had been weakened by other means. The Germans accordingly made extensive use of their submarines (see page 246) and of minefields, although there was a sharp clash between cruisers and destroyers in Heligoland Bight at the end of August (see pages 242–245) and twice the German battle-cruisers took advantage of the long winter nights to cross the North Sea and bombard the East coast of England (see page 255). It was accepted in Britain that the days of isolation were over, a point emphasised on Christmas Eve when the first aerial bombs were dropped on English soil, at Dover.

The main clashes of sea power were, however, on the oceans. Vice-Admiral von Spee's squadron caused havoc in the Pacific and won a naval victory off Coronel before being defeated at the Falkland Islands early in December (pages 238, 240–241). The German cruiser *Emden* effectively disrupted trade in the East Indies (page 239), but by the end of the year, the British had reasserted their naval supremacy, clearing the seas of surface raiders and virtually destroying Germany's overseas commerce. Japanese, Australian and New Zealand forces mopped up Germany's island possessions in the Pacific, and British and Japanese troops occupied Kiaochow (the small German protectorate on the coast of China) in November. General von Lettow-Vorbeck retained firm control of German East Africa (pages 216–218) and the South Africans were in some difficulty in German South-West Africa but Togoland had surrendered and there was minimal resistance in the interior of the Cameroons.

The attention of the British outside Europe was from now on primarily concentrated on the Ottoman Empire. Turkey, long under the influence of Germany militarily, entered the War early in November, hoping to gain territory from Russia in the Caucasus and to recover, with German backing, her influence in the Balkans. The handing over by Germany to Turkey of the battle-cruiser *Goeben* and the cruiser *Breslau* (page 237) finally decided Turkey's course of action. Militarily Turkey was a distraction both to Britain and Russia, but her entry into the war suggested a possible alternative strategy—of toppling Germany, not on the main battlefronts, but by destroying her supports and entering Central Europe by the back door. It seemed the only way to make the war once more fluid. From such ideas developed the Dardanelles and Gallipoli campaigns, and belatedly the expedition to Salonika.

THE GALLIPOLI CAMPAIGN

The attempt to force the Dardanelles and gain control of Constantinople and the Straits was the first strategically imaginative project of the war. Its origins lie in a proposal made by Churchill to the War Council of 25 November 1914. He argued that 'the ideal method of defending Egypt' and the Suez Canal from an invading Turkish army 'was by an attack on the Gallipoli Peninsula' which, if successful, would enable the Allies to 'dictate terms at Constantinople'. Subsequently the possibilities of using British naval power to open up a new front against the enemy appealed to other members of the War Council, including Lloyd George, Admiral Sir John Fisher and the Secretary of the Council, Colonel Hankey. There was much debate over the best place for a landing, Lloyd George urging the occupation of Salonika and the transportation by rail of an army to aid Serbia against Austria-Hungary, and this plan was favoured by two leading French Generals, Gallieni and Franchet d'Espèrey. The Dardanelles project had, however, three major advantages: it appeared to be primarily a naval operation; it would rally Turkey's traditional enemies among the Balkan nations to the Allied side; and it would open up a short warm-water route for supplies to Russia. It was this third consideration which was decisive: for at the end of December gloomy reports were received from Petrograd, indicating an acute shortage of munitions and appealing for British help in relieving Turkish pressure on the Russian armies in the Caucasus. The War Council agreed on a naval expedition 'with Constantinople as its objective' on 15 January 1915.

The Gallipoli enterprise falls into four distinctive phases (which may be studied in pages 110–129, supplemented for naval and submaritime operations by pages 252–254). Naval bombardments on 19 and 26 February were followed by nearly three weeks of abortive minesweeping before the principal attempt by capital ships to force the passage of the Dardanelles on 18 March. Preparations were then made for using British, Australian and New Zealand troops for a series of landings on the Gallipoli peninsula while a French army corps temporarily occupied Kum Kale on the mainland and made a feint assault on Besika Bay. These landings were carried out on 25 April in an atmosphere of almost crusading ardour, but without proper landing craft and with no real training in amphibious operations. The Anzacs established themselves in a cove of steep cliffs and backed by a gorge covered in scrub, where it was difficult to penetrate more than half a mile inland. The British made more headway at Cape Helles, but suffered appalling casualties. Further landings in early August came near to success, but by the end of the summer the troops on the peninsula were as effectively pinned down in a network of trenches as the armies in France and Flanders; four thousand men died in seeking to secure four hundred yards on a mile front. Kitchener went out to investigate in November and accepted the inevitability of evacuation. The final phase, the withdrawal from Anzac and Suvla in December and from Helles a fortnight later, was the most successful aspect of the campaign.

The expedition failed because of confused leadership, insufficient co-ordination, inadequate planning, and sheer lack of troops and firepower; perhaps, too, it failed because the landings were made at the tip of the peninsula rather than at its neck, where there would have been greater freedom of manouvere. Failure at the Dardanelles cost Churchill his predominant position in the War Council; it deprived the Allies of a grand Balkan alliance against Berlin; above all, it completed the isolation of Russia. Gallipoli, with its high hopes twice nearly realised, was a tragic disappointment which discredited imaginative strategic thought in London for many years ahead.

TURKISH DEFENCES AT THE DARDANELLES 1915

This map depicts the Turkish defences guarding the Dardanelles prior to the Allied naval attacks during February and March 1915. Following a Russian request to the Western Allies at the end of 1914 for a "second front" to be created against Turkey to ease pressure on the Russian forces in the Caucasus, British naval authorities devised a three-point plan to force the Dardanelles passage. First, a naval bombardment of the entrance forts: secondly, a minefield-clearing operation: thirdly, a naval force to sail right through the Dardanelles to the Sea of Marmara, and thence on to the Turkish capital of Constantinople.

Vice-Admiral Carden, commander of the British squadron in the Aegean, considered that he would require the following units to successfully force the Dardanelles passage: 12 battleships, 3 battlecruisers, 3 light cruisers, 16 destroyers, 6 submarines, 4 seaplanes, 12 minesweepers, and a plentiful supply of ammunition.

— KEY TO MINEFIELDS —

- **1** 26 February 1915.
- **3** 5 November 1914 - 19 February 1915.
- **4** 5 November 1914 - 15 February 1915.
- **7** 5 November 1914 - 15 February 1915.
- **8** 5 November 1914 - 19 February 1915.
- **11** 8 March 1915 (laid by 'Nousret').

Note: The correct name for Achi Baba was Alchi Tepe: this was due to a spelling error on British maps, but Achi Baba became the accepted name.

Note: spellings are those used on British maps in 1915. For example, Chanak Kale is used instead of the Turkish name Çanakkale. The modern romanized spelling of Turkish was not introduced until 1925: prior to that, Turkish map names were shown in Arabic characters.

BULGARIA (INTERESTED OBSERVER)

Black Sea

Bosporus

Constantinople (Turkish capital)

EUROPEAN TURKEY

Sea of Marmara

ASIATIC TURKEY

DARDANELLES

Aegean Sea

REVOLUTION UPON ALLIED FLEET'S ARRIVAL? TURKEY TO MAKE PEACE?

Entrance to Sea of Marmara

Two 26-cm. L/22 Krupp
Five 24-cm. L/22 Krupp
Five 15-cm. L/26 Krupp

Nagara

Abydos Pt.

Nagara Burnu

Three 28-cm. L/22 Krupp
Four 26-cm. L/22 Krupp
Two 21-cm. L/22 Krupp
Three 15-cm. L/22 Krupp

Anodalu Mejidieh

Medjidieh Avan

Chanak Kale

Six 21-cm. mortars

One 35·5-cm. L/35 Krupp
One 35·5-cm. L/22 Krupp
One 24-cm. L/35 Krupp
One 21-cm. L/35 Krupp
Four 15-cm. howitzers

Two 25·5-cm. L/35 Krupp

THE NARROWS

Chemenlik Fort

1 53 mines
(T)
2 29 mines
3 26 mines
4 39 mines
5 M

Derma Burnu

Kilid Bahr

Namazieh II

Hamidieh II

Rumili Medjidieh

Yildiz

Hauslar

Maidos

Boghali

Koja Dere

KOJA CHEMEN TEPE (971 ft.) ▲
BESIM TEPE (900 ft.) ▲ Sari Bair Ridge
CHUNUK BAIR (850 ft.) ▲

Ari Burnu

Gaba Tepe

Six 24-cm. L/22 Krupp

One 28-cm. L/22 Krupp
One 26-cm. L/22 Krupp
Nine 24-cm. L/22 Krupp
Two 24-cm. L/35 Krupp
Three 21-cm. L/22 Krupp
Three 15-cm. howitzers

Two 35·5-cm. L/35 Krupp

Two 28-cm. L/22 Krupp
Four 24-cm. L/35 Krupp

Six 15-cm. L/26 Krupp

Four 12-cm. siege guns

Six 15-cm. howitzers

Four 7·5-cm. L/30 quick-firers

Six 4·7-cm. howitzers

Four 4·7-cm. howitzers

AEGEAN

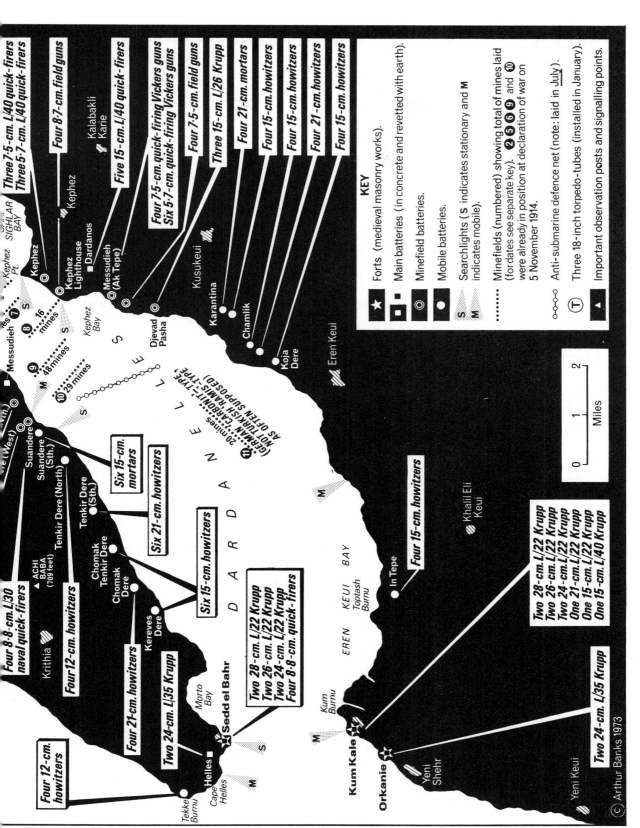

Three 7·5-cm. L/40 quick-firers
Three 5·7-cm. L/40 quick-firers

Four 8·7-cm. field guns

Kalabakli
Karie

Five 15-cm. L/40 quick-firers

Four 7·5-cm. quick-firing Vickers guns
Six 5·7-cm. quick-firing Vickers guns

Four 7·5-cm. field guns

Three 15-cm. L/26 Krupp

Four 21-cm. mortars

Four 15-cm. howitzers

Four 15-cm. howitzers

Four 21-cm. howitzers

Four 15-cm. howitzers

KEY

★ Forts (medieval masonry works).

■ Main batteries (in concrete and revetted with earth).

◎ Minefield batteries.

● Mobile batteries.

Searchlights (S indicates stationary and M indicates mobile).

⋯⋯ Minefields (numbered) showing total of mines laid (for dates see separate key). ❷❺❻❾ and ❿ were already in position at declaration of war on 5 November 1914.

○○○ Anti-submarine defence net (note: laid in July).

Ⓣ Three 18-inch torpedo-tubes (installed in January).

▲ Important observation posts and signalling points.

Kephez

Kephez

Kephez Pt.

SIGHLAR BAY

Kephez

Kephez Lighthouse
Dardanos

Messudieh (Ak Tepe)

Messudieh

Kephez Bay

Djevad Pasha

Kusukeui

Karantina

Chamlik

Koja Dere

Eren Keui

16 mines

48 mines

29 mines

(GERMAN "CARBONIT" TYPE NOT TURKISH RAMIS-TYPE AS OFTEN SUPPOSED)
20 mines

Six 15-cm. mortars

Six 21-cm. howitzers

Six 15-cm. howitzers

Four 8·8-cm. L/30 naval quick-firers

Four 12-cm. howitzers

Four 21-cm. howitzers

Two 24-cm. L/35 Krupp

Four 12-cm. howitzers

Krithia

ACHI BABA (709 feet)

Suandere (West)
Suandere (Sth.)

Tenkir Dere (North)

Tenkir Dere (Sth.)

Chomak Tenkir Dere

Chomak Dere

Kereves Dere

Morto Bay

Sedd el Bahr

Two 28-cm. L/22 Krupp
Two 26-cm. L/22 Krupp
Two 24-cm. L/22 Krupp
Four 8·8-cm. quick-firers

Helles

Cape Helles

Tekke Burnu

Four 15-cm. howitzers

Khalil Eli Keui

In Tepe

Toptash Burnu

Kum Burnu

Kum Kale

EREN KEUI BAY

Two 28-cm. L/22 Krupp
Two 26-cm. L/22 Krupp
Two 24-cm. L/22 Krupp
One 21-cm. L/22 Krupp
One 15-cm. L/22 Krupp
One 15-cm. L/40 Krupp

Yeni Shehr

Orkanie

Yeni Keui

Two 24-cm. L/35 Krupp

0 1 2
Miles

© Arthur Banks 1973

DARDANELLES

111

*FIRST NAVAL BOMBARDMENT OF THE DARDANELLES ENTRANCE WORKS 19 FEBRUARY 1915

*Note: on 3 November 1914, four Allied warships had bombarded Sedd el Bahr and Kum Kale using 12-inch guns.

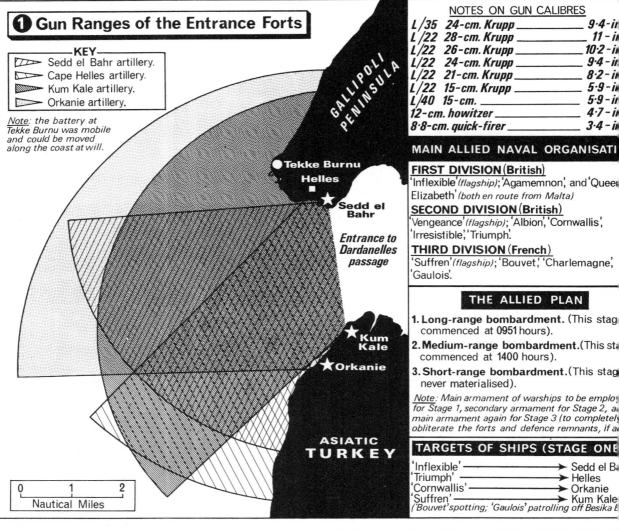

① Gun Ranges of the Entrance Forts

KEY
- ▱ Sedd el Bahr artillery.
- ◁ Cape Helles artillery.
- ◤ Kum Kale artillery.
- ▷ Orkanie artillery.

Note: the battery at Tekke Burnu was mobile and could be moved along the coast at will.

GALLIPOLI PENINSULA

● Tekke Burnu
■ Helles
★ Sedd el Bahr

Entrance to Dardanelles passage

★ Kum Kale
★ Orkanie

ASIATIC **TURKEY**

0   1   2
Nautical Miles

GUN RANGES OF TURKI[SH] ENTRANCE WORKS

Allied estimated maximu[m] ranges of the main guns:
L/35 .... 12,000 ya[rds]
L/22 .... 10,000 ya[rds]
(effective ranges rather le[ss])

NOTES ON GUN CALIBRES

L/35	24-cm. Krupp	9.4-in
L/22	28-cm. Krupp	11-in
L/22	26-cm. Krupp	10.2-in
L/22	24-cm. Krupp	9.4-in
L/22	21-cm. Krupp	8.2-in
L/22	15-cm. Krupp	5.9-in
L/40	15-cm.	5.9-in
	12-cm. howitzer	4.7-in
	8.8-cm. quick-firer	3.4-in

MAIN ALLIED NAVAL ORGANISATI[ON]

FIRST DIVISION (British)
'Inflexible' *(flagship)*; 'Agamemnon', and 'Quee[n] Elizabeth' *(both en route from Malta)*

SECOND DIVISION (British)
'Vengeance' *(flagship)*; 'Albion', 'Cornwallis', 'Irresistible', 'Triumph'.

THIRD DIVISION (French)
'Suffren' *(flagship)*; 'Bouvet', 'Charlemagne', 'Gaulois'.

THE ALLIED PLAN

1. **Long-range bombardment.** (This stag[e] commenced at 0951 hours).
2. **Medium-range bombardment.** (This sta[ge] commenced at 1400 hours).
3. **Short-range bombardment.** (This stag[e] never materialised).

Note: Main armament of warships to be employ[ed] for Stage 1, secondary armament for Stage 2, a[nd] main armament again for Stage 3 (to completel[y] obliterate the forts and defence remnants, if a[ny])

TARGETS OF SHIPS (STAGE ON[E])

'Inflexible' ⟶ Sedd el B[ahr]
'Triumph' ⟶ Helles
'Cornwallis' ⟶ Orkanie
'Suffren' ⟶ Kum Kale
('Bouvet' spotting; 'Gaulois' patrolling off Besika [Bay])

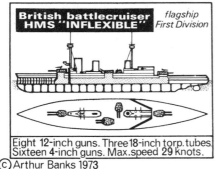

British battlecruiser HMS "INFLEXIBLE"
flagship First Division

Eight 12-inch guns. Three 18-inch torp. tubes. Sixteen 4-inch guns. Max. speed 29 knots.

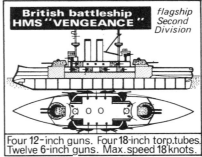

British battleship HMS "VENGEANCE"
flagship Second Division

Four 12-inch guns. Four 18-inch torp. tubes. Twelve 6-inch guns. Max. speed 18 knots.

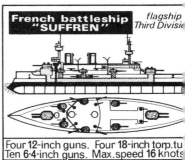

French battleship "SUFFREN"
flagship Third Divisio[n]

Four 12-inch guns. Four 18-inch torp. tu[bes] Ten 6.4-inch guns. Max. speed 16 knots[.]

© Arthur Banks 1973

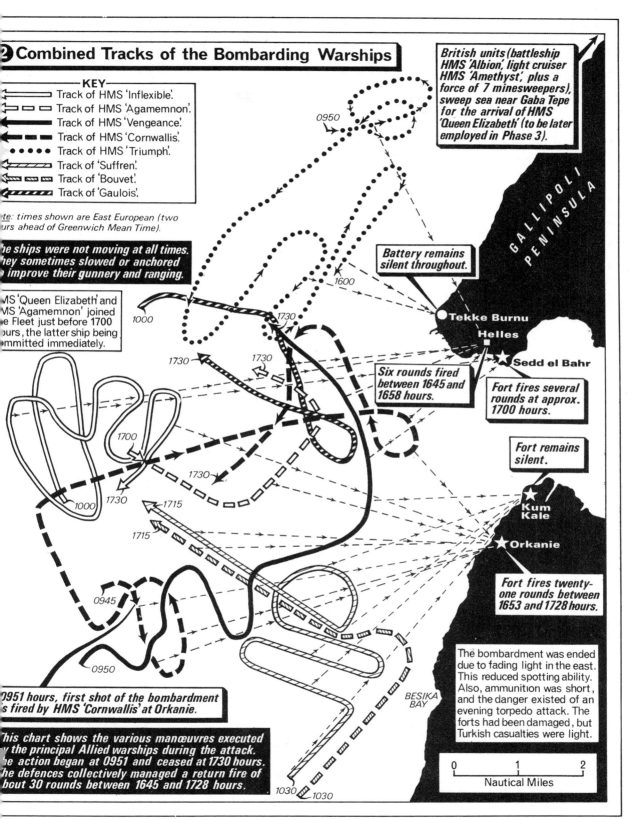

2 Combined Tracks of the Bombarding Warships

KEY

Track of HMS 'Inflexible'.
Track of HMS 'Agamemnon'.
Track of HMS 'Vengeance'.
Track of HMS 'Cornwallis'.
Track of HMS 'Triumph'.
Track of 'Suffren'.
Track of 'Bouvet'.
Track of 'Gaulois'.

Note: times shown are East European (two hours ahead of Greenwich Mean Time).

The ships were not moving at all times. They sometimes slowed or anchored to improve their gunnery and ranging.

HMS 'Queen Elizabeth' and HMS 'Agamemnon' joined the Fleet just before 1700 hours, the latter ship being committed immediately.

British units (battleship HMS 'Albion', light cruiser HMS 'Amethyst', plus a force of 7 minesweepers), sweep sea near Gaba Tepe for the arrival of HMS 'Queen Elizabeth' (to be later employed in Phase 3).

GALLIPOLI PENINSULA

Battery remains silent throughout.

Tekke Burnu
Helles
Sedd el Bahr

Six rounds fired between 1645 and 1658 hours.

Fort fires several rounds at approx. 1700 hours.

Fort remains silent.

Kum Kale

Orkanie

Fort fires twenty-one rounds between 1653 and 1728 hours.

0950

1600

1730

1000

1730

1730

1730

1700

1730

1730

1000

1715

1715

0945

0950

At 0951 hours, first shot of the bombardment was fired by HMS 'Cornwallis' at Orkanie.

This chart shows the various manœuvres executed by the principal Allied warships during the attack. The action began at 0951 and ceased at 1730 hours. The defences collectively managed a return fire of about 30 rounds between 1645 and 1728 hours.

The bombardment was ended due to fading light in the east. This reduced spotting ability. Also, ammunition was short, and the danger existed of an evening torpedo attack. The forts had been damaged, but Turkish casualties were light.

BESIKA BAY

1030 1030

0	1	2

Nautical Miles

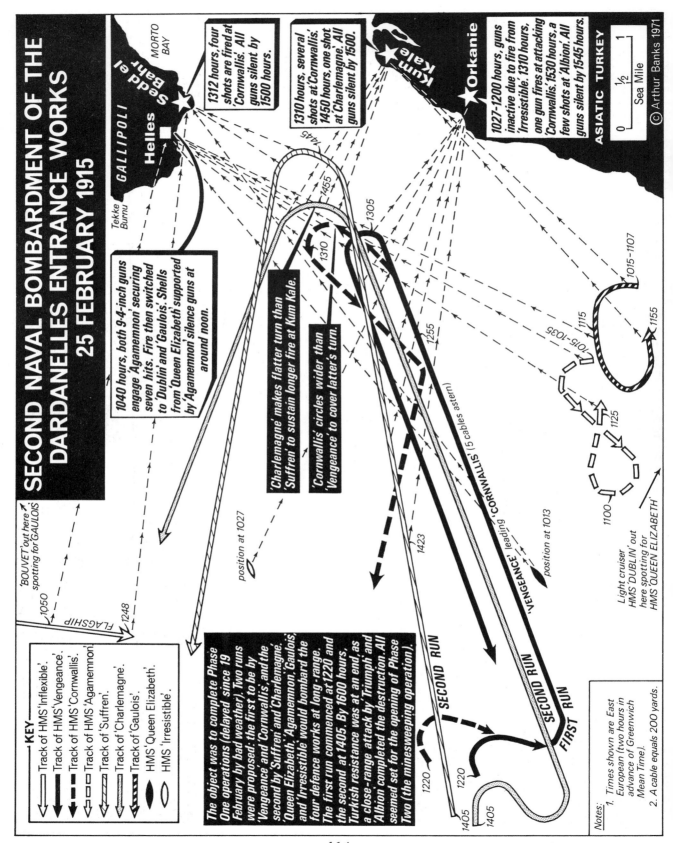

SECOND NAVAL BOMBARDMENT OF THE DARDANELLES ENTRANCE WORKS 25 FEBRUARY 1915

MORTO BAY

Sedd el Bahr

GALLIPOLI

Helles

Tekke Burnu

Kum Kale

Orkanie

ASIATIC TURKEY

0   ½   1
Sea Mile

© Arthur Banks 1971

1312 hours, four shots are fired at 'Cornwallis'. All guns silent by 1500 hours.

1310 hours, several shots at 'Cornwallis'. 1450 hours, one shot at 'Charlemagne'. All guns silent by 1500.

1027-1200 hours, guns inactive due to fire from 'Irresistible'. 1310 hours, one gun fires at attacking 'Cornwallis'. 1530 hours, a few shots at 'Albion'. All guns silent by 1545 hours.

1040 hours, both 9.4-inch guns engage 'Agamemnon' securing seven hits. Fire then switched to 'Dublin' and 'Gaulois'. Shells from 'Queen Elizabeth' silence guns at around noon.

'Charlemagne' makes flatter turn than 'Suffren' to sustain longer fire at Kum Kale.

'Cornwallis' circles wider than 'Vengeance' to cover latter's turn.

'VENGEANCE' leading 'CORNWALLIS' (5 cables astern)

position at 1013

position at 1027

'BOUVET' out here spotting for 'GAULOIS'.

FLAGSHIP

Light cruiser HMS 'DUBLIN' out here spotting for HMS 'QUEEN ELIZABETH'.

SECOND RUN

FIRST RUN

1050
1248
1220
1220
1405
1405
1423
1445
1455
1305
1310
1255
1125
1100
1115
1155
1015-1038
1015-1107

The object was to complete Phase One operations (delayed since 19 February by bad weather). Two runs were proposed: the first to be by 'Vengeance' and 'Cornwallis', and the second by 'Suffren' and 'Charlemagne'. 'Queen Elizabeth', 'Agamemnon', 'Gaulois', and 'Irresistible' would bombard the four defence works at long-range. The first run commenced at 1220 and the second at 1405. By 1600 hours, Turkish resistance was at an end, as a close-range attack by 'Triumph' and 'Albion' completed the destruction. All seemed set for the opening of Phase Two (the minesweeping operation).

KEY
⟶ Track of HMS 'Inflexible'.
⟶ Track of HMS 'Vengeance'.
⟶ Track of HMS 'Cornwallis'.
⟶ Track of HMS 'Agamemnon'.
⟶ Track of 'Suffren'.
⟶ Track of 'Charlemagne'.
⟶ Track of 'Gaulois'.
◆ HMS 'Queen Elizabeth'.
◇ HMS 'Irresistible'.

Notes:
1. Times shown are East European (two hours in advance of Greenwich Mean Time).
2. A cable equals 200 yards.

114

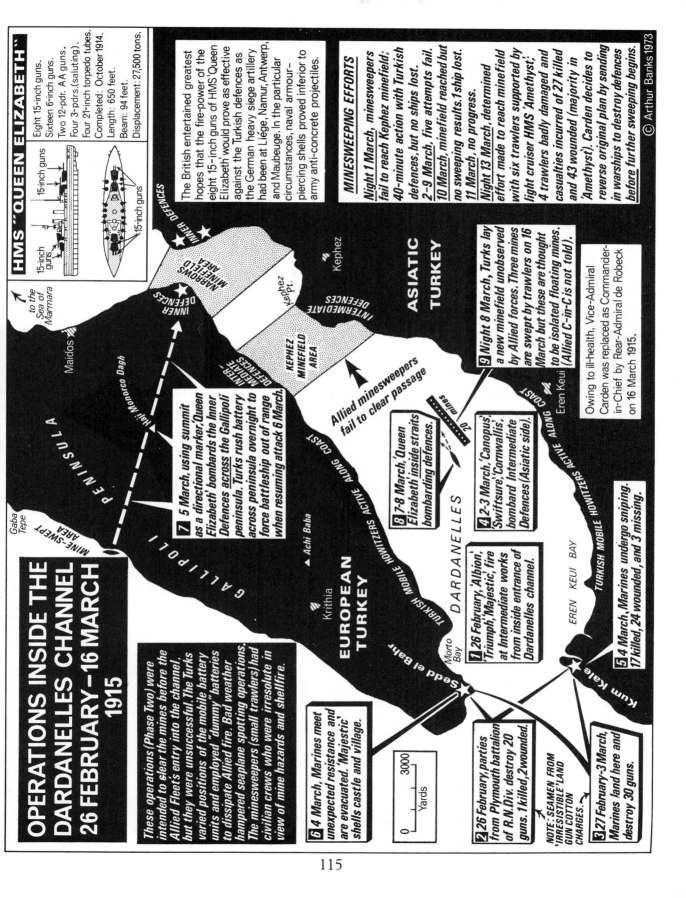

OPERATIONS INSIDE THE DARDANELLES CHANNEL 26 FEBRUARY–16 MARCH 1915

HMS "QUEEN ELIZABETH"

Eight 15-inch guns.
Sixteen 6-inch guns.
Two 12-pdr. AA guns.
Four 3-pdrs.(saluting).
Four 21-inch torpedo tubes.
Completed: October 1914.
Length: 650 feet.
Beam: 94 feet.
Displacement: 27,500 tons.

15-inch guns
15-inch guns
15-inch guns

The British entertained greatest hopes that the fire-power of the eight 15-inch guns of HMS 'Queen Elizabeth' would prove as effective against the Turkish defences as the German heavy siege artillery had been at Liège, Namur, Antwerp, and Maubeuge. In the particular circumstances, naval armour-piercing shells proved inferior to army anti-concrete projectiles.

MINESWEEPING EFFORTS

Night 1 March, minesweepers fail to reach Kephez minefield: 40-minute action with Turkish defences, but no ships lost.
2–9 March, five attempts fail.
10 March, minefield reached but no sweeping results.1 ship lost.
11 March, no progress.
Night 13 March, determined effort made to reach minefield with six trawlers supported by light cruiser HMS 'Amethyst'; 4 trawlers badly damaged and casualties incurred of 27 killed and 43 wounded (majority in 'Amethyst'). Carden decides to reverse original plan by sending in warships to destroy defences *before further sweeping begins*.

Owing to ill-health, Vice-Admiral Carden was replaced as Commander-in-Chief by Rear-Admiral de Robeck on 16 March 1915.

© Arthur Banks 1973

to the Sea of Marmara

Maidos

GALLIPOLI PENINSULA

Gaba Tepe

MINE-SWEPT AREA

Haji Monorco Dagh

INNER DEFENCES

MARROWS MINEFIELD AREA

INNER DEFENCES

INTERMEDIATE DEFENCES

Kephez Pt.

Kephez

ASIATIC TURKEY

KEPHEZ MINEFIELD AREA

INTERMEDIATE DEFENCES

Allied minesweepers fail to clear passage

Eren Keui

Kephez

0   mines

EREN KEUI BAY

Kum Kale

TURKISH MOBILE HOWITZERS ACTIVE ALONG COAST

Achi Baba

Krithia

EUROPEAN TURKEY

TURKISH MOBILE HOWITZERS ACTIVE ALONG COAST

DARDANELLES

Morto Bay

Sedd el Bahr

These operations (Phase Two) were intended to clear the mines before the Allied Fleet's entry into the channel. The Turks varied positions of the mobile battery units and employed "dummy" batteries to dissipate Allied fire. Bad weather hampered seaplane spotting operations. The minesweepers (small trawlers) had civilian crews who were irresolute in view of mine hazards and shellfire.

7 *5 March*, using summit as a directional marker,'Queen Elizabeth' bombards the Inner Defences across the Gallipoli peninsula. Turks rush battery across peninsula overnight to force battleship out of range when resuming attack 6 March.

8 *7–8 March*, 'Queen Elizabeth' inside straits bombarding defences.

9 *Night 8 March*, Turks lay a new minefield unobserved by Allied forces. Three mines are swept by trawlers on 16 March but these are thought to be isolated floating mines. (Allied C-in-C is not told).

4 *2–3 March*, 'Canopus', 'Swiftsure','Cornwallis', bombard Intermediate Defences (Asiatic side).

5 *4 March*, Marines undergo sniping. 17 killed, 24 wounded, and 3 missing.

6 *4 March*, Marines meet unexpected resistance and are evacuated. 'Majestic' shells castle and village.

1 *26 February*, 'Albion', 'Triumph','Majestic', fire at Intermediate works from inside entrance of Dardanelles channel.

2 *26 February*, parties from Plymouth battalion of R.N.Div. destroy 20 guns. 1 killed, 2 wounded.

3 *27 February–3 March*, Marines land here and destroy 30 guns.

NOTE: SEAMEN FROM 'IRRESISTIBLE' LAND GUN COTTON CHARGES.

0   3000
Yards

115

THE ALLIED FAILURE TO FORCE THE DARDANELLES PASSAGE 18 MARCH 1915

1030 hours, preceded by destroyers, the Allied fleet of 17 battleships and 1 battlecruiser entered the straits and advanced to allotted positions. Line 'A' opened fire at 1130 and Line 'B' was advanced at 1206. By 1345, the defences were inactive; consequently the minesweepers were ordered up supported by Second Division (to relieve Line 'B'). Moving out, 'Bouvet' was mined at 1355, then capsized and sank in two minutes. 1610 'Irresistible' was mined; 1614 'Inflexible' suffered a similar fate. At 1715 'Gaulois' was badly holed and had to beached. 1805 'Ocean' was mined and abandoned. Thus one-third of the capital ships were either sunk or incapacitated and the naval attempt to force the Dardanelles was called off. Prematurely? By 16 April, a British destroyer-minesweeping "fast" force was in existence ("Beagle"-class ships). This fact is not generally appreciated.

The attack of 18 March was intended to break the stalemate situation of Phase Two in which the minesweeper crews were reluctant to pursue their operations until the capital ships had silenced the Turkish main batteries. The Allied plan allowed for the trawlers to begin sweeping operations two hours after start of the long-range bombardment, whereupon they were to clear a channel 900 yards broad past Kephez Point into Sari Sighlar Bay.

(It should be noted that the Allied naval command was unaware of the full extent of the Turkish mine fields despite detailed Intelligence reports which had not been passed on).

Prior to the attack, the Allies worried over the alleged existence of torpedo-tubes on both sides of the channel. In fact, there were only three tubes in position, all at Kilid Bahr. Each tube was equipped with two torpedoes, but only one tube could fire right across the width of the Narrows, the others less than halfway across.

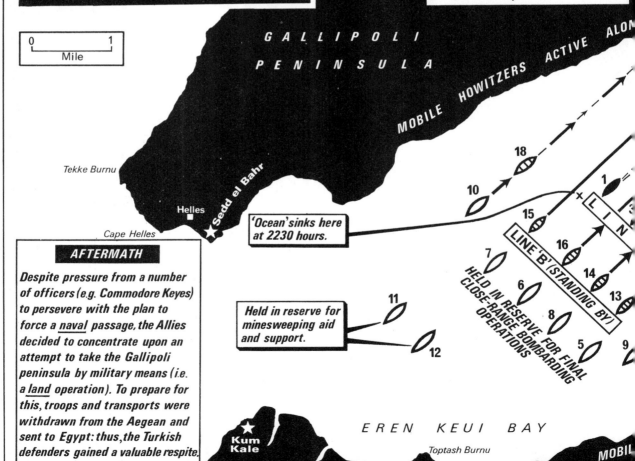

SARI TEPE

KRITHIA

0   1
Mile

GALLIPOLI PENINSULA

MOBILE HOWITZERS ACTIVE ALON

Tekke Burnu

Helles

Sedd el Bahr

Cape Helles

'Ocean' sinks here at 2230 hours.

18

10

1

LIN

15

LINE 'B' (STANDING BY)

16

14

13

7

HELD IN RESERVE FOR FINAL CLOSE-RANGE BOMBARDING OPERATIONS

6

8

5

9

11

Held in reserve for minesweeping aid and support.

12

AFTERMATH

Despite pressure from a number of officers (e.g. Commodore Keyes) to persevere with the plan to force a <u>naval</u> passage, the Allies decided to concentrate upon an attempt to take the Gallipoli peninsula by military means (i.e. a <u>land</u> operation). To prepare for this, troops and transports were withdrawn from the Aegean and sent to Egypt: thus, the Turkish defenders gained a valuable respite.

Kum Kale

EREN KEUI BAY

Toptash Burnu

MOBIL

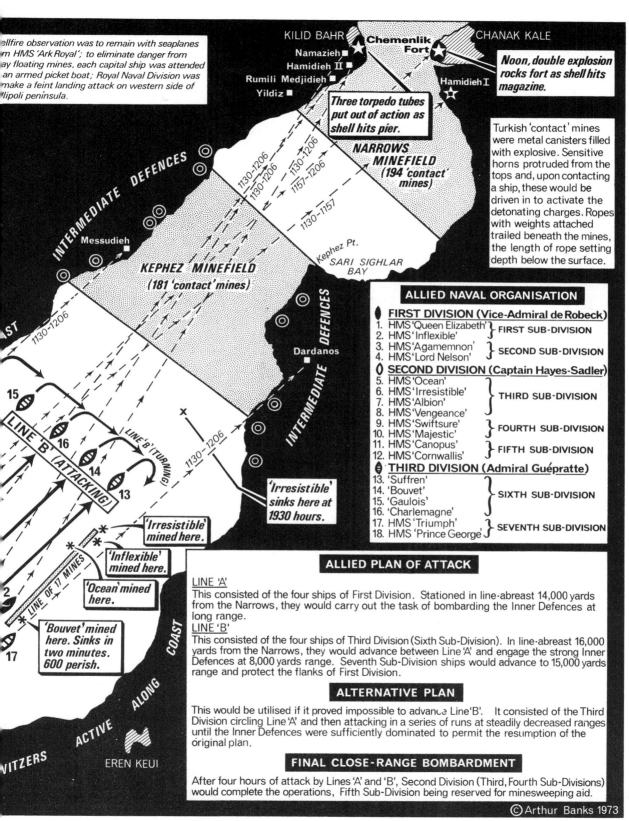

ellfire observation was to remain with seaplanes ... m HMS 'Ark Royal'; to eliminate danger from ... ay floating mines, each capital ship was attended ... an armed picket boat; Royal Naval Division was ... make a feint landing attack on western side of ... llipoli peninsula.

KILID BAHR
CHANAK KALE
Chemenlik Fort
Namazieh ■
Hamidieh II ■
Rumili Medjidieh ■
Yildiz ■
Hamidieh I ☆

Noon, double explosion rocks fort as shell hits magazine.

Three torpedo tubes put out of action as shell hits pier.

NARROWS MINEFIELD (194 'contact' mines)

Turkish 'contact' mines were metal canisters filled with explosive. Sensitive horns protruded from the tops and, upon contacting a ship, these would be driven in to activate the detonating charges. Ropes with weights attached trailed beneath the mines, the length of rope setting depth below the surface.

INTERMEDIATE DEFENCES
Messudieh ■

Kephez Pt.
SARI SIGHLAR BAY

KEPHEZ MINEFIELD (181 'contact' mines)

1130-1206 (repeated)
1157-1206
1130-1157

Dardanos ■

INTERMEDIATE DEFENCES

15
LINE 'B' (ATTACKING)
16
14
13
LINE 'B' (TURNING)

X

1130-1206

'Irresistible' sinks here at 1930 hours.

'Irresistible' mined here.

'Inflexible' mined here.

'Ocean' mined here.

LINE OF 17 MINES

'Bouvet' mined here. Sinks in two minutes. 600 perish.

2
17

ACTIVE ALONG COAST
WITZERS
EREN KEUI

ALLIED NAVAL ORGANISATION

FIRST DIVISION (Vice-Admiral de Robeck)
1. HMS 'Queen Elizabeth' ⎫ FIRST SUB-DIVISION
2. HMS 'Inflexible' ⎭
3. HMS 'Agamemnon' ⎫ SECOND SUB-DIVISION
4. HMS 'Lord Nelson' ⎭

SECOND DIVISION (Captain Hayes-Sadler)
5. HMS 'Ocean' ⎫
6. HMS 'Irresistible' ⎬ THIRD SUB-DIVISION
7. HMS 'Albion' ⎪
8. HMS 'Vengeance' ⎭
9. HMS 'Swiftsure' ⎫ FOURTH SUB-DIVISION
10. HMS 'Majestic' ⎭
11. HMS 'Canopus' ⎫ FIFTH SUB-DIVISION
12. HMS 'Cornwallis' ⎭

THIRD DIVISION (Admiral Guépratte)
13. 'Suffren' ⎫
14. 'Bouvet' ⎬ SIXTH SUB-DIVISION
15. 'Gaulois' ⎪
16. 'Charlemagne' ⎭
17. HMS 'Triumph' ⎫ SEVENTH SUB-DIVISION
18. HMS 'Prince George' ⎭

ALLIED PLAN OF ATTACK

LINE 'A'
This consisted of the four ships of First Division. Stationed in line-abreast 14,000 yards from the Narrows, they would carry out the task of bombarding the Inner Defences at long range.

LINE 'B'
This consisted of the four ships of Third Division (Sixth Sub-Division). In line-abreast 16,000 yards from the Narrows, they would advance between Line 'A' and engage the strong Inner Defences at 8,000 yards range. Seventh Sub-Division ships would advance to 15,000 yards range and protect the flanks of First Division.

ALTERNATIVE PLAN

This would be utilised if it proved impossible to advance Line 'B'. It consisted of the Third Division circling Line 'A' and then attacking in a series of runs at steadily decreased ranges until the Inner Defences were sufficiently dominated to permit the resumption of the original plan.

FINAL CLOSE-RANGE BOMBARDMENT

After four hours of attack by Lines 'A' and 'B', Second Division (Third, Fourth Sub-Divisions) would complete the operations, Fifth Sub-Division being reserved for minesweeping aid.

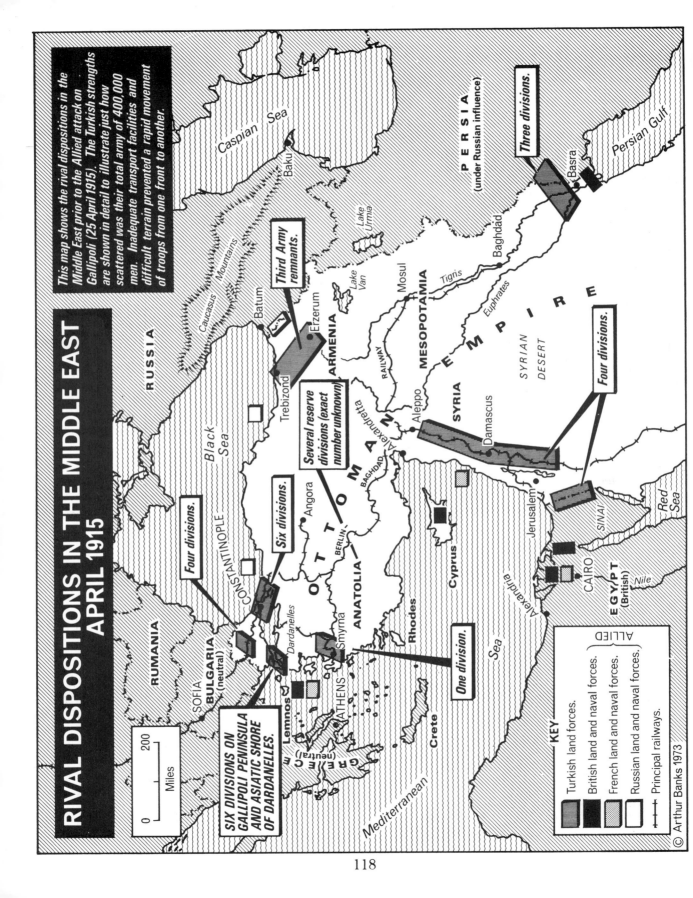

RIVAL DISPOSITIONS IN THE MIDDLE EAST APRIL 1915

This map shows the rival dispositions in the Middle East prior to the Allied attack on Gallipoli (25 April 1915). The Turkish strengths are shown in detail to illustrate just how scattered was their total army of 400,000 men. Inadequate transport facilities and difficult terrain prevented a rapid movement of troops from one front to another.

Three divisions.

Third Army remnants.

Four divisions.

Several reserve divisions (exact number unknown).

Six divisions.

Four divisions.

One division.

SIX DIVISIONS ON GALLIPOLI PENINSULA AND ASIATIC SHORE OF DARDANELLES.

Caspian Sea

Baku

PERSIA (under Russian influence)

Basra

Persian Gulf

Baghdad

Lake Urmia

Mosul

Tigris

MESOPOTAMIA

Euphrates

E M P I R E

Batum

Erzerum

ARMENIA

Lake Van

RAILWAY

SYRIAN DESERT

Trebizond

Caucasus Mountains

R U S S I A

Black Sea

O T T O M A N

Aleppo

SYRIA

Damascus

Alexandretta

BAGHDAD-

BERLIN-

RUMANIA

SOFIA

BULGARIA (neutral)

CONSTANTINOPLE

Angora

ANATOLIA

Smyrna

Dardanelles

Rhodes

Cyprus

Jerusalem

SINAI

CAIRO

Nile

EGYPT (British)

Alexandria

Red Sea

Lemnos

ATHENS

G R E E C E (neutral)

Crete

Mediterranean Sea

KEY

Turkish land forces.	
British land and naval forces.	ALLIED
French land and naval forces.	
Russian land and naval forces.	
Principal railways.	

0   200
Miles

© Arthur Banks 1973

118

GALLIPOLI PENINSULA: PHYSICAL FEATURES

Eleimer Bay

Kiretch Tepe
660'

Suvla Pt.

Suvla Bay

Nibrunesi Pt.

Salt Lake

882'
Tekke Tepe

Anafarta Sagir
Biyuk Anafarta

820'
Sari Bair
971'
850'
900'
534'
Mal Tepe

Boghali

Anafarta

Ari Burnu

Gaba Tepe

706'

Kilid Bahr
Saghir Dere

Plateau

Soghanli Dere

Achi Baba
709'

Krithia

Tenkir Tepe
490'

The Narrows

Chanak Kale
Kilid Bahr

Maidos

Sari Sighlar Bay

D A R D A N E L L E S

Erin Keui Bay

Mendere River

Cape Helles
Tekke Burnu
Sedd el Bahr

Kum Kale

Yeni Shehr

AEGEAN   SEA

Miles
0 1 2 3 4

KEY

▲ High points (in feet).

● Villages or towns.

~~~ Main watercourses (dry in summer).

TURKISH DISPOSITIONS AT THE DARDANELLES 24 APRIL 1915

A German officer, Liman von Sanders, was appointed to command the Turkish Fifth Army (six divisions totalling 84,000 men) on 24 March 1915. He set to work to improvise and strengthen defences, build supply roads, and dig trenches. By 25 April, the Turks were in a vastly superior defensive state of preparation than they had been on 18 March.

Considered by von Sanders as most critical area. If isthmus was severed, only access to Gallipoli would be across the Dardanelles.

5 DIVISION

Gulf of Saros

Sea of Marmara

Bulair

Gallipoli

1 DIVISION

ASIA MINOR

PERHAPS NOT "IMPENETRABLE" BY ALLIED WARSHIPS (16 APRIL ONWARDS)?

TURKISH MINEFIELD BARRIER

Considered by von Sanders as most vulnerable area to defend. Within range of gunfire from Allied battleships.

GALLIPOLI PENINSULA

19 DIVISION

Boghali

Maidos

Chanak Kale

Kephez

Dardanelles

Suvla Bay

3 DIVISION
11 DIVISION

9 DIVISION

Krithia

Kum Kale

Besika Bay

Miles
0   10

© Arthur Banks 1973

119

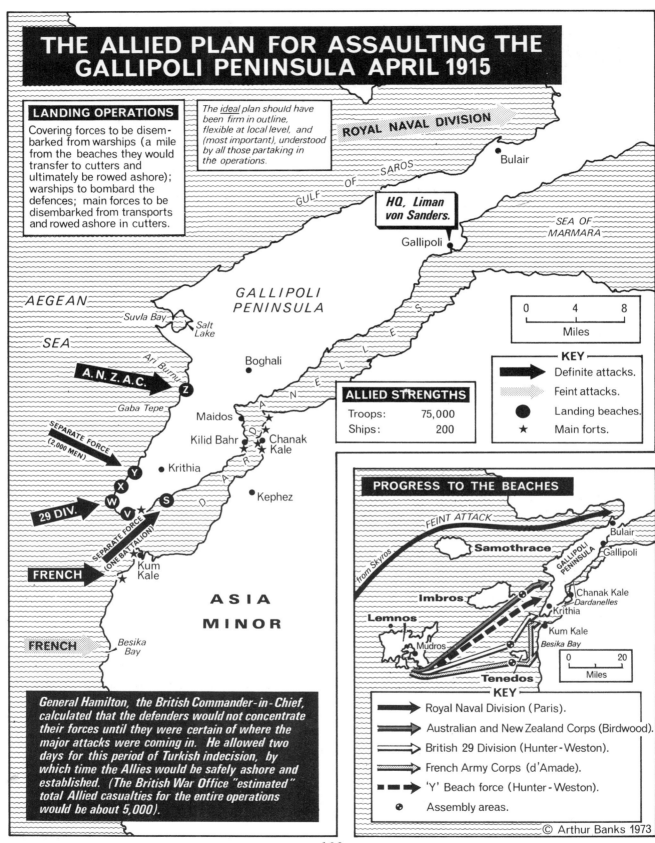

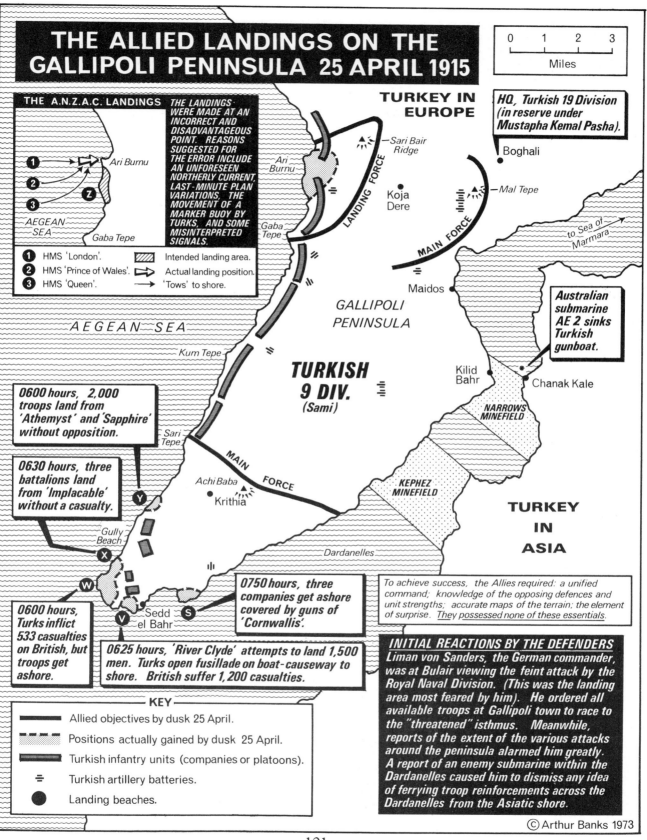

THE ALLIED LANDINGS ON THE GALLIPOLI PENINSULA 25 APRIL 1915

0 1 2 3
Miles

THE A.N.Z.A.C. LANDINGS

THE LANDINGS WERE MADE AT AN INCORRECT AND DISADVANTAGEOUS POINT. REASONS SUGGESTED FOR THE ERROR INCLUDE AN UNFORESEEN NORTHERLY CURRENT, LAST-MINUTE PLAN VARIATIONS, THE MOVEMENT OF A MARKER BUOY BY TURKS, AND SOME MISINTERPRETED SIGNALS.

Ari Burnu

AEGEAN SEA

Gaba Tepe

① HMS 'London'.   ▨ Intended landing area.
② HMS 'Prince of Wales'.   ⇨ Actual landing position.
③ HMS 'Queen'.   → 'Tows' to shore.

TURKEY IN EUROPE

HQ, Turkish 19 Division (in reserve under Mustapha Kemal Pasha).

Boghali

Sari Bair Ridge

Ari Burnu

Koja Dere

Mal Tepe

LANDING FORCE

MAIN FORCE

to Sea of Marmara

Gaba Tepe

Maidos

A E G E A N   S E A

Kum Tepe

GALLIPOLI PENINSULA

Australian submarine AE 2 sinks Turkish gunboat.

Kilid Bahr

Chanak Kale

TURKISH 9 DIV. *(Sami)*

NARROWS MINEFIELD

0600 hours, 2,000 troops land from 'Athemyst' and 'Sapphire' without opposition.

Sari Tepe

0630 hours, three battalions land from 'Implacable' without a casualty.

MAIN FORCE

Achi Baba

Krithia

KEPHEZ MINEFIELD

TURKEY IN ASIA

Gully Beach

Dardanelles

Y

X

W

V

Sedd el Bahr

S

0750 hours, three companies get ashore covered by guns of 'Cornwallis'.

To achieve success, the Allies required: a unified command; knowledge of the opposing defences and unit strengths; accurate maps of the terrain; the element of surprise. <u>They possessed none of these essentials.</u>

0600 hours, Turks inflict 533 casualties on British, but troops get ashore.

0625 hours, 'River Clyde' attempts to land 1,500 men. Turks open fusillade on boat-causeway to shore. British suffer 1,200 casualties.

INITIAL REACTIONS BY THE DEFENDERS

Liman von Sanders, the German commander, was at Bulair viewing the feint attack by the Royal Naval Division. (This was the landing area most feared by him). He ordered all available troops at Gallipoli town to race to the "threatened" isthmus. Meanwhile, reports of the extent of the various attacks around the peninsula alarmed him greatly. A report of an enemy submarine within the Dardanelles caused him to dismiss any idea of ferrying troop reinforcements across the Dardanelles from the Asiatic shore.

KEY

― Allied objectives by dusk 25 April.

▨ Positions actually gained by dusk 25 April.

▥ Turkish infantry units (companies or platoons).

≡ Turkish artillery batteries.

● Landing beaches.

© Arthur Banks 1973

121

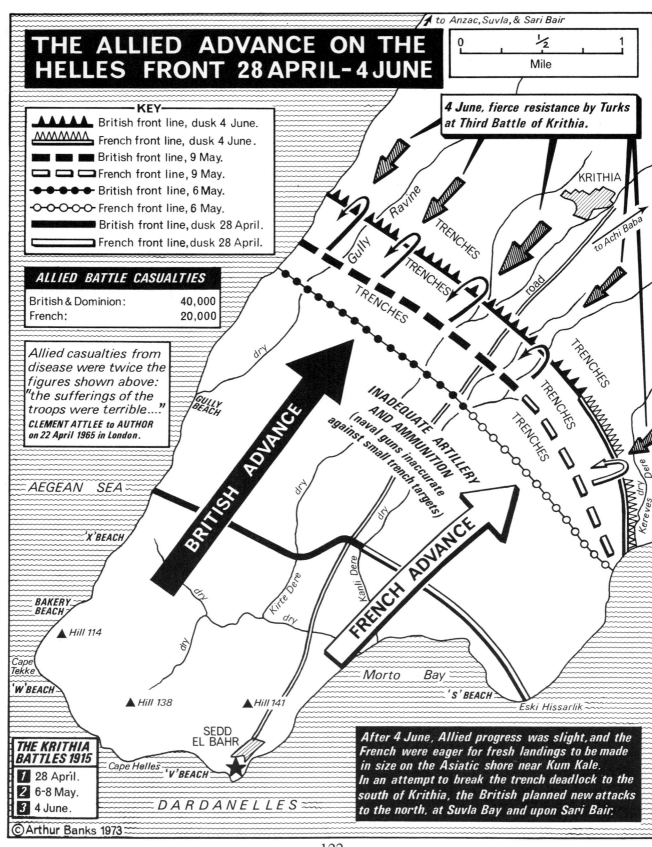

THE ALLIED ADVANCE ON THE HELLES FRONT 28 APRIL - 4 JUNE

to Anzac, Suvla, & Sari Bair

0   ½   1
Mile

KEY

- ▲▲▲▲ British front line, dusk 4 June.
- ΛΛΛΛΛ French front line, dusk 4 June.
- ▬ ▬ ▬ British front line, 9 May.
- ▭ ▭ ▭ French front line, 9 May.
- ●●●● British front line, 6 May.
- ○○○○ French front line, 6 May.
- ▬▬▬ British front line, dusk 28 April.
- ▭▭▭ French front line, dusk 28 April.

ALLIED BATTLE CASUALTIES

British & Dominion:	40,000
French:	20,000

Allied casualties from disease were twice the figures shown above: "the sufferings of the troops were terrible...."
CLEMENT ATTLEE to AUTHOR on 22 April 1965 in London.

4 June, fierce resistance by Turks at Third Battle of Krithia.

KRITHIA

to Achi Baba

Gully Ravine

TRENCHES

TRENCHES

TRENCHES

TRENCHES

TRENCHES

TRENCHES

TRENCHES

road

Gully

dry

GULLY BEACH

AEGEAN SEA

'X' BEACH

INADEQUATE ARTILLERY AND AMMUNITION (naval guns inaccurate against small trench targets)

BRITISH ADVANCE

FRENCH ADVANCE

dry

dry

Kanli Dere

Kirte Dere

dry

dry

Kereves Dere

dry

BAKERY BEACH

▲ Hill 114

Cape Tekke

'W' BEACH

▲ Hill 138

▲ Hill 141

SEDD EL BAHR

Morto Bay

'S' BEACH

Eski Hissarlik

Cape Helles

'V' BEACH

DARDANELLES

THE KRITHIA BATTLES 1915

1. 28 April.
2. 6-8 May.
3. 4 June.

*After 4 June, Allied progress was slight, and the French were eager for fresh landings to be made in size on the Asiatic shore near Kum Kale.
In an attempt to break the trench deadlock to the south of Krithia, the British planned new attacks to the north, at Suvla Bay and upon Sari Bair.*

© Arthur Banks 1973

122

FRESH BRITISH LANDINGS 1915

❶ The Suvla Plan

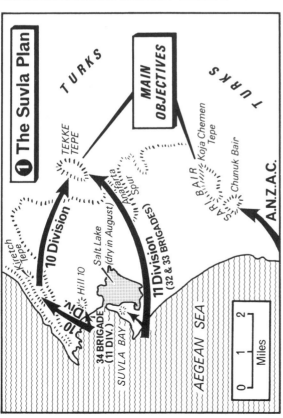

TURKS

TURKS

MAIN OBJECTIVES

TEKKE TEPE

Kireetch Tepe

Hill 10

Salt Lake (dry in August)

10 Division

11 Division (32 & 33 BRIGADES)

34 BRIGADE (11 DIV.)

ANAFARTA

Anafarta Spur

Koja Chemen Tepe

Chunuk Bair

SARI BAIR

A.N.Z.A.C.

SUVLA BAY

SUVLA PT.

KARAKOL RIDGE

AEGEAN SEA

0 1 2 Miles

❸ The Landings of 10 Division Morning 7 August

THIS MAP SHOWS MORE LANDINGS DEVIATING FROM THE ORIGINAL PLAN. THUS, THE INVADERS WERE SCATTERED AND DISORGANIZED FROM OUTSET.

British destroyer fires shell into lake to test if surface is firm for possible infantry advance. (It is not).

NOTE: AT THIS PERIOD, THE TOTAL TURKISH STRENGTH AT SUVLA WAS ONLY 1,500.

Kireetch Tepe

Ghazi Baba

KARAKOL RIDGE

Hill 10

Beach

Cut

DRY SALT LAKE

Lala Baba

Nibrunesi Pt.

Nibrunesi Beach

SUVLA BAY

Suvla Pt.

Landing area of five battalions.

Intended landing area of whole 10 Division.

Landing area of 30 and 31 Brigades.

0 ½ Mile

❷ The Landings of 11 Division Night 6/7 August

THE INCORRECT LANDFALL OF 34 BRIGADE WAS SIMILAR TO THE ERROR MADE ON 25 APRIL AT ARI BURNU.

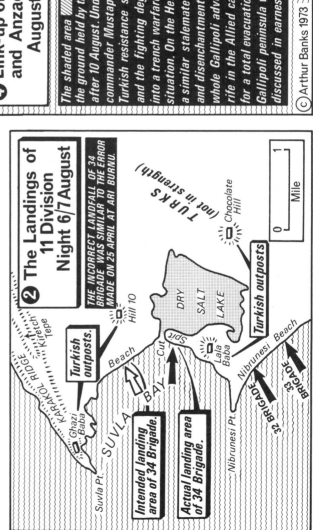

TURKS (not in strength)

Chocolate Hill

Hill 10

Kireetch Tepe

KARAKOL RIDGE

Ghazi Baba

Beach

Cut

Spit

DRY SALT LAKE

Lala Baba

Turkish outposts.

Turkish outposts.

Turkish outposts

Nibrunesi Beach

Nibrunesi Pt.

SUVLA BAY

Suvla Pt.

Intended landing area of 34 Brigade.

Actual landing area of 34 Brigade.

32 BRIGADE

33 BRIGADE

0 1 Mile

❹ Link-up of Suvla and Anzac in August

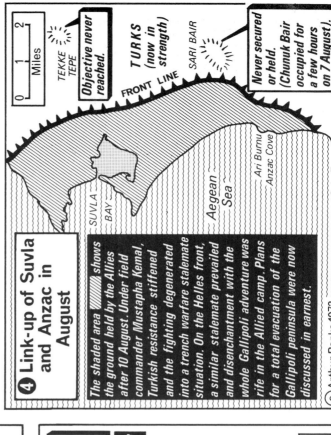

The shaded area ▨ shows the ground held by the Allies after 10 August. Under field commander Mustapha Kemal, Turkish resistance stiffened and the fighting degenerated into a trench warfare stalemate situation. On the Helles front, a similar stalemate prevailed and disenchantment with the whole Gallipoli adventure was rife in the Allied camp. Plans for a total evacuation of the Gallipoli peninsula were now discussed in earnest.

Objective never reached.

TEKKE TEPE

TURKS (now in strength)

FRONT LINE

SARI BAIR

Never secured or held. (Chunuk Bair occupied for a few hours on 7 August).

SUVLA BAY

Aegean Sea

Ari Burnu

Anzac Cove

Gaba Tepe

0 1 2 Miles

© Arthur Banks 1973

123

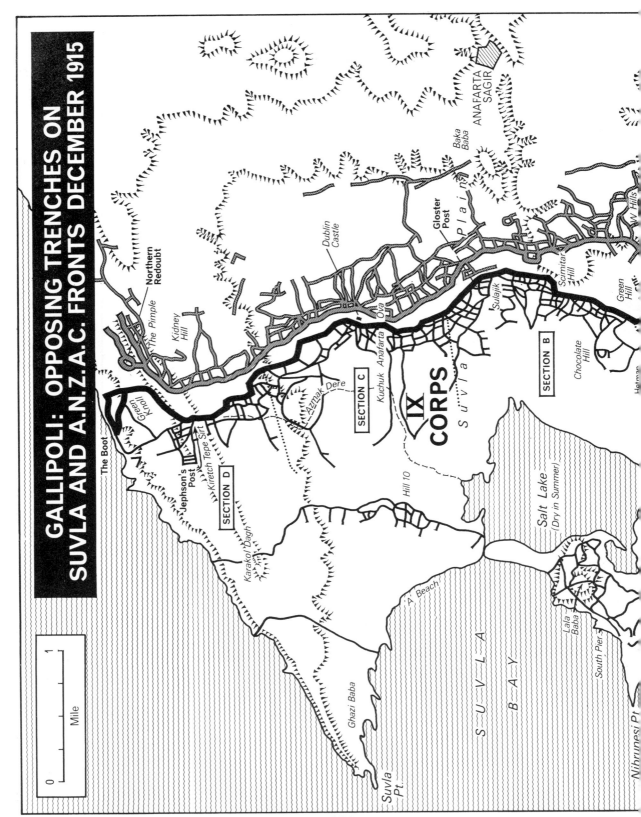

GALLIPOLI: OPPOSING TRENCHES ON
SUVLA AND A.N.Z.A.C. FRONTS DECEMBER 1915

Northern
Redoubt

The Pimple

Kidney
Hill

Green Knoll

The Boot

Jephson's
Post

Kiretch Tepe Sirt

SECTION D

Karakol Dagh

Ghazi Baba

Aznak Dere

SECTION C

Hill 10

'A' Beach

S U V L A
B A Y

Suvla
Pt.

Dublin
Castle

Gloster
Post

Kuchuk Anafarta Ova

Anafarta

IX
CORPS

S u v l a

P l a i n

Baka
Baba

ANAFARTA
SAGIR

Scimitar
Hill

'Sulajik

SECTION B

Chocolate
Hill

Green
Hill

W. Hills

Hetman

Salt Lake
(Dry in Summer)

Lala
Baba

South Pier

Nibrunesi Pt.

0   1
Mile

124

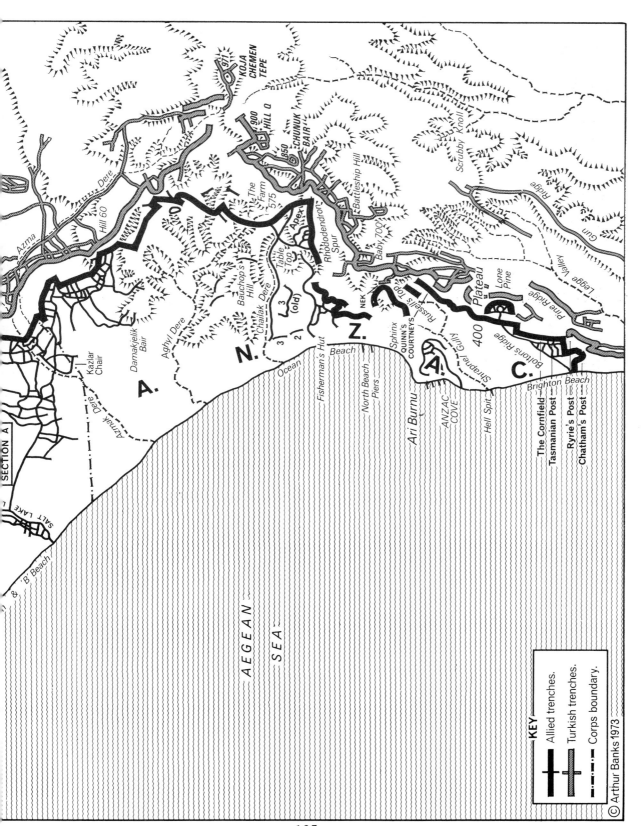

KOJA CHEMEN TEPE
971
900 HILL Q
850 CHUNUK BAIR
575
The Farm
Battleship Hill
Scrubby Knoll
Hill 60
Dere
Azma
Apex
Rhododendron Spur
Table Top
Baby 700
Gun Ridge
Legge Valley
Bauchop's Hill
3 (old)
Chailak Dere
Lone Pine
Plateau 400
Damakjelik Bair
Aghyl Dere
Kazlar Chair
Fisherman's Hut
NEK
Sphinx
QUINN'S
COURTNEY'S
Russell's Top
Shrapnel Gully
Pine Ridge
Bolton's Ridge
A.   N.   Z.   A.   C.
3   2
Beach
Ocean
North Beach
Piers
Ari Burnu
ANZAC COVE
Hell Spit
Brighton Beach

SECTION A
Azmak Dere
SALT LAKE
'B' Beach
&

AEGEAN SEA

KEY
Allied trenches.
Turkish trenches.
Corps boundary.

© Arthur Banks 1973

125

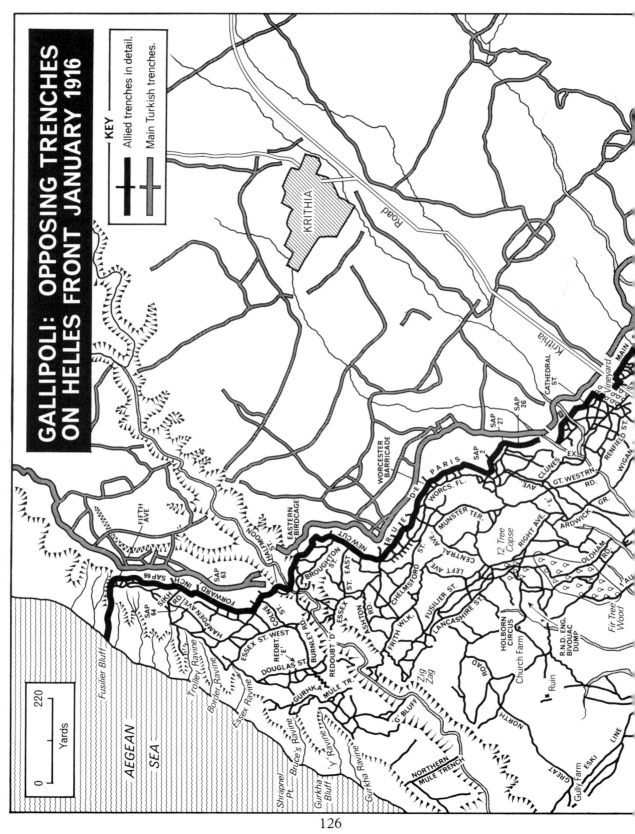

GALLIPOLI: OPPOSING TRENCHES ON HELLES FRONT JANUARY 1916

KEY

—— Allied trenches in detail.
Main Turkish trenches.

KRITHIA

Road

Krithia

CATHEDRAL ST.

SAP 27

SAP 26

SAP 2

RENFIELD ST.

EX.

CLUNES

WIGAN

GT. WESTERN

AVE.

RD.

WORCESTER BARRICADE

WORCS. FL.

RUE DE PARIS

MUNSTER TER.

GR.

ARDWICK

'E'

RIGHT AVE.

OLDHAM

12 Tree Copse

CENTRAL AVE.

LEFT AVE.

AL

RD.

EASTERN BIRDCAGE

NEW CUT

NOOLLATTAHS

ST.

FIFTH AVE

CHELMSFORD ST.

FUSILIER ST.

Fir Tree Wood

HOLBORN CIRCUS

R.N.D. ENG. BIVOUAC DUMP

Church Farm

SAP 63

BROUGHTON ST.

ESSEX ST. EAST

FRITH WLK.

LANCASHIRE ST.

SAP 66

INCH

HAMPDEN AVE. RD.

FORWARD

SAP 64

COLNE ST.

ASHTON RD.

Ruin

NORTH

ROAD

ESSEX ST. WEST

REDOUBT 'D'

BURNLEY RD.

REDBT. 'E'

DOUGLAS ST.

GURKHA

MULE TR.

Zig Zag

Fusilier Bluff

Trolley Ravine

Border Ravine

Essex Ravine

'Y' Ravine

Gurkha Ravine

GURKHA

'G' BLUFF

GREAT

ESKI

LINE

Gully Farm

220

0

Yards

AEGEAN

SEA

Shrapnel Pt.—Bruce's Ravine

Gurkha Bluff

NORTHERN MULE TRENCH

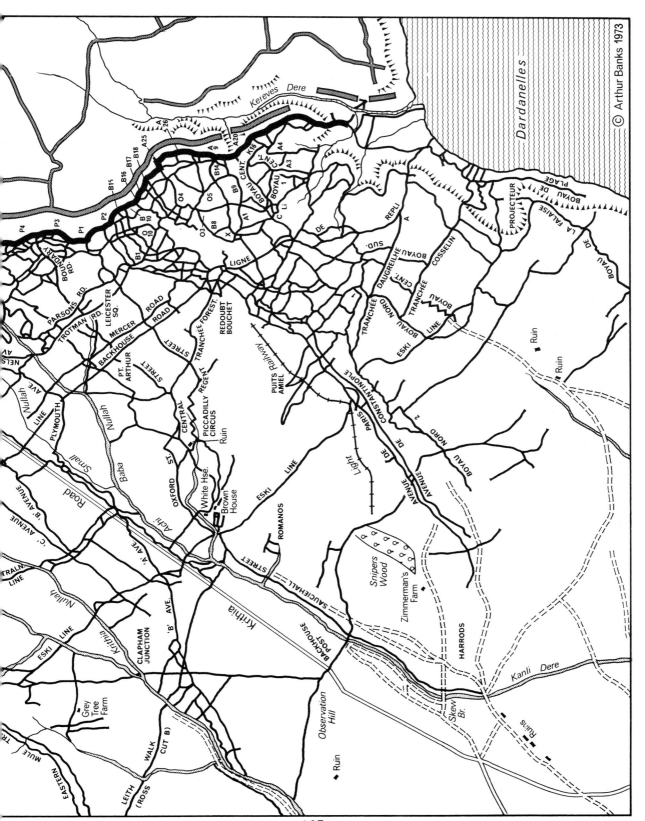

Dardanelles

© Arthur Banks 1973

Keteves Dere

A 26
A 26
A 20
B18 B17
B16
B15
B'5
A 9
9
B1M
BOYAU CENT. K16
BOYAU CENT.
C
BOYAU C 1
A4
A3
REPLI
A
P4 P3 P1
P2
O4
O5
B9
A1
C Li
DE
BOYAU DE LA FALAISE
BOYAU DE PLAGE
PROJECTEUR
BOUNDARY RD.
B'5
O3
B8
X
B 10
10
B1
LIGNE
SUD.
BOYAU NORD
TRANCHÉE DAUGREILHE
TRANCHÉE CENT.
COSSELIN
PARSONS RD.
TROTMAN RD.
LEICESTER SQ.
MERCER ROAD
ROAD
REDOUBT BOUCHET
TRANCHÉE FOREST.
PT. ARTHUR STREET
BACKHOUSE
STREET
Puits AMIEL
Railway
ESKI LINE
NELS AV
NULLAH LINE
PLYMOUTH
Baba Nullah
Small
'B' AVENUE
'C' AVENUE
CENTRAL LINE
ESKI LINE
Nullah
Achi Baba
Road
OXFORD ST.
CENTRAL ST.
PICCADILLY CIRCUS
REGENT STREET
Ruin
White Hse.
Brown House
ESKI LINE
ROMANOS
Light
DE PARIS
AVENUE DE CONSTANTINOPLE
BOYAU NORD
Ruin
Ruin
Snipers Wood
Zimmerman's Farm
HARRODS
Kanli Dere
Kirthia
'A' AVE.
'B' AVE.
CLAPHAM JUNCTION
SAUCIEHALL STREET
BACKHOUSE POST
Observation Hill
Ruin
Skew Br.
Ruins
MULE TR
EASTERN
LEITH (ROSS WALK CUT B)
Grey Tree Farm

127

THE EVACUATIONS OF THE SUVLA AND A.N.Z.A.C. POSITIONS

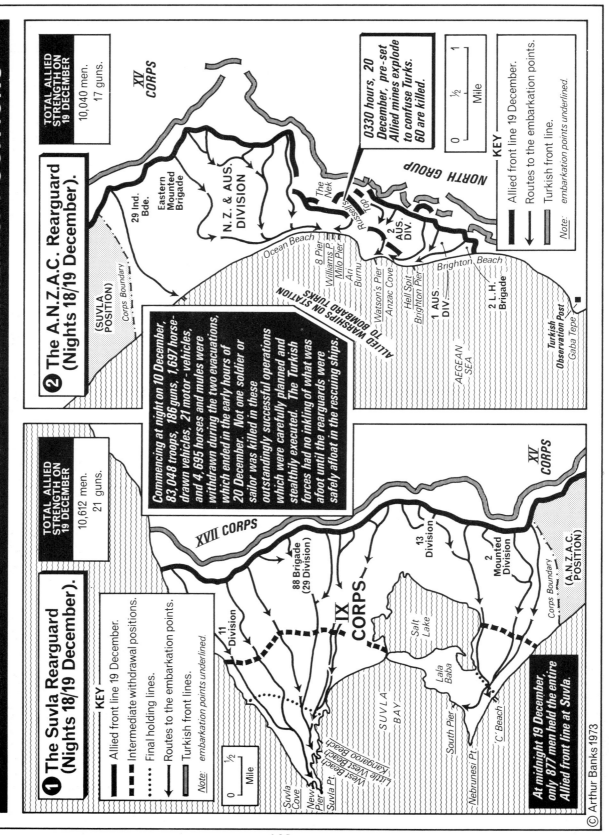

TOTAL ALLIED STRENGTH ON 19 December

10,040 men.
17 guns.

XV CORPS

Eastern Mounted Brigade

29 Ind. Bde.

N. Z. & AUS. DIVISION

❷ The A.N.Z.A.C. Rearguard (Nights 18/19 December).

(SUVLA POSITION)

Corps Boundary

0330 hours, 20 December, pre-set Allied mines explode to confuse Turks. 60 are killed.

NORTH GROUP

The Nek

Russell's Top

2 AUS. DIV.

Ocean Beach

8 Pier
Williams P.
Milo Pier
Ari Burnu
Watson's Pier
Anzac Cove
Hell Spit
Brighton Pier

Brighton Beach

1 AUS. DIV.

2 L.H. Brigade

ALLIED WARSHIPS ON STATION TO BOMBARD TURKS.

AEGEAN SEA

Turkish Observation Post

Gaba Tepe

KEY

▬▬ Allied front line 19 December.

→ Routes to the embarkation points.

〰〰 Turkish front line.

Note: embarkation points underlined.

SCALE: 0 ½ 1 Mile

Commencing at night on 10 December, 83,048 troops, 186 guns, 1,697 horse-drawn vehicles, 21 motor-vehicles, and 4,695 horses and mules were withdrawn during the two evacuations, which ended in the early hours of 20 December. Not one soldier or sailor was killed in these outstandingly successful operations which were carefully planned and stealthily executed. The Turkish forces had no inkling of what was afoot until the rearguards were safely afloat in the rescuing ships.

TOTAL ALLIED STRENGTH ON 19 December

10,612 men.
21 guns.

XVII CORPS

88 Brigade (29 Division)

11 Division

IX CORPS

13 Division

2 Mounted Division

Corps Boundary

(A.N.Z.A.C. POSITION)

XV CORPS

Salt Lake

Lala Baba

SUVLA BAY

South Pier

'C' Beach

Nebrunesi Pt.

Kangaroo Beach
Little West Beach
West Beach
Suvla Pt.
New Pier
Suvla Cove

❶ The Suvla Rearguard (Nights 18/19 December).

KEY

▬▬ Allied front line 19 December.

▬ ▬ Intermediate withdrawal positions.

···· Final holding lines.

→ Routes to the embarkation points.

〰〰 Turkish front lines.

Note: embarkation points underlined.

SCALE: 0 ½ 1 Mile

At midnight 19 December, only 877 men held the entire Allied front line at Suvla.

© Arthur Banks 1973

128

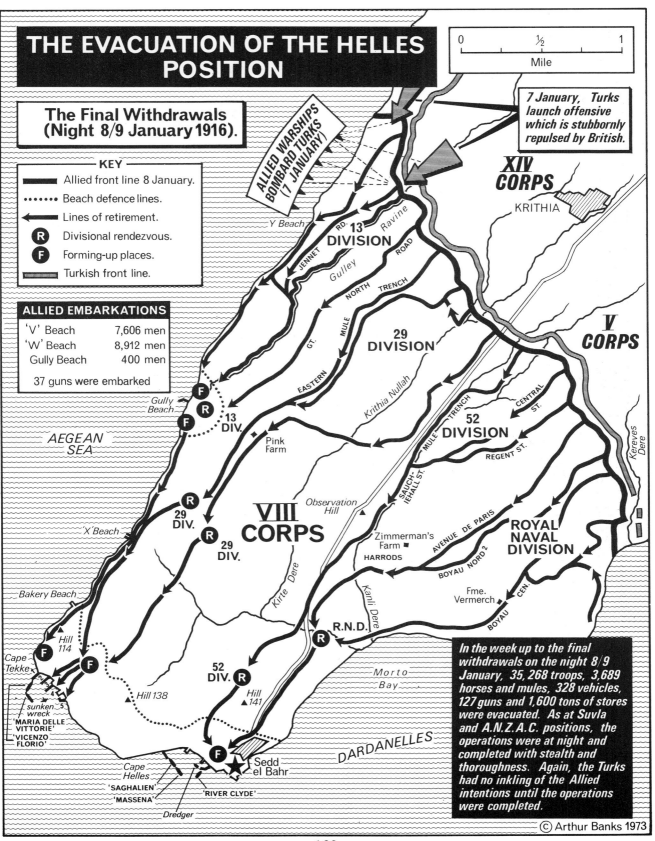

THE EVACUATION OF THE HELLES POSITION

The Final Withdrawals (Night 8/9 January 1916).

0   ½   1
Mile

KEY
— Allied front line 8 January.
••• Beach defence lines.
← Lines of retirement.
(R) Divisional rendezvous.
(F) Forming-up places.
▬▬▬ Turkish front line.

ALLIED EMBARKATIONS
'V' Beach	7,606 men
'W' Beach	8,912 men
Gully Beach	400 men

37 guns were embarked

ALLIED WARSHIPS BOMBARD TURKS (7 JANUARY)

7 January, Turks launch offensive which is stubbornly repulsed by British.

XIV CORPS

KRITHIA

V CORPS

Y Beach

RD. 13 DIVISION

Ravine

JENNET

Gulley

NORTH ROAD

MULE

TRENCH

29 DIVISION

GT.

EASTERN

Krithia Nullah

MULE TRENCH

52 DIVISION

CENTRAL ST.

REGENT ST.

Kereves Dere

Gully Beach

(F)
(R)
(F)

13 DIV.

AEGEAN SEA

Pink Farm

Observation Hill

VIII CORPS

(R)
29 DIV.

'X' Beach

(R)
29 DIV.

SAUCH-IEHALL ST.

Zimmerman's Farm

HARRODS

AVENUE DE PARIS

BOYAU NORD 2

ROYAL NAVAL DIVISION

Bakery Beach

Kirte Dere

Kanli Dere

Fme. Vermerch

BOYAU CEN.

(F)
Cape Tekke
Hill 114

(F)

sunken wreck
'MARIA DELLE VITTORIE'
'VICENZO FLORIO'

Hill 138

52 DIV. (R)

Hill 141

(R)
R.N.D.

Morto Bay

(F)

Cape Helles
'SAGHALIEN'
'MASSENA'
'RIVER CLYDE'
Dredger

Sedd el Bahr

DARDANELLES

In the week up to the final withdrawals on the night 8/9 January, 35,268 troops, 3,689 horses and mules, 328 vehicles, 127 guns and 1,600 tons of stores were evacuated. As at Suvla and A.N.Z.A.C. positions, the operations were at night and completed with stealth and thoroughness. Again, the Turks had no inkling of the Allied intentions until the operations were completed.

© Arthur Banks 1973

129

THE WAR IN 1915

The Dardanelles and Gallipoli dominated the minds of the political leaders in Whitehall during the opening months of 1915. But Sir John French and his generals across the Channel bitterly opposed any plans which might divert troops from the Western Front, and Joffre agreed with them. French and his principal subordinate, Haig, wished to attack the Germans in Belgium as soon as the weather was favourable. Joffre had hopes of a two-pronged thrust later in the spring in Artois and Champagne, intended to break through the German lines and sweep across Belgium west of the Ardennes. Reality fell short of expectation that year on every sector of the Western Front: the British gained the town of Neuve Chapelle at the cost of heavy casualties in March (pages 136–137); the German offensive in the West during April sought to eliminate the Ypres Salient, but, despite the use of poison gas, their success was limited to a few villages; and later frontal assaults by the British and the French in Artois, at Loos, and in Champagne, though shaking the vertebrae of the German defensive system, failed to crack the spinal cord. The newspapers continued to carry long casualty lists which, together with the frustrations of Gallipoli, emphasised the terrible burden of the War on families far from the battlefronts. The first Zeppelin raids (pages 286–290) brought a new terror to English homes.

The news from other fronts was no more encouraging. At first it seemed that the Russians would make some progress on the southern sector of the Eastern Front, for they at last captured the fortress of Przemysl on 22 March. But Falkenhayn, unlike Moltke in the previous year, was prepared to co-ordinate strategy with Conrad. In May a massive Austro-German offensive began in Galicia, breaking through four lines of Russian defences at Gorlice and forcing a general withdrawal from the Carpathians. The Russians were driven out of Przemysl, out of Galicia, and out of Poland as well. When the campaign ended, half a million Russians were in prisoner-of-war cages. Nor was this the limit of Falkenhayn's success. In October Mackensen, the victor of Gorlice, set up his headquarters in southern Hungary and took command of a joint Austro–Germano–Bulgarian army which overran Serbia (page 160) and gave Germany control of a continuous railway route from Berlin to Constantinople and the Middle East. The Allied response to Bulgaria's alliance with Germany was, at last, to establish a base at Salonika, but no effective aid could be given to Serbia.

Bulgaria's entry into the German camp was preceded by Italy's adhesion to the Allied cause in May 1915. But, though it was hoped in London and Paris that Italy would pose a new threat to Austria-Hungary, this Front, too, was soon paralysed by defensive trench warfare (page 200–201). Briefly it seemed possible that the German U-Boat campaign, and especially the sinking of the Cunard liner *Lusitania* with the loss of 128 American lives on 6 May, would bring the United States into the War, but the Germans gave informal assurances that passenger ships would not be sunk without warning, and America maintained her neutrality.

By the end of the year the war seemed as rapacious of lives and material as ever, and there was no prospect of peace. Among the Allies, and especially in Britain, indignation mounted at the lack of munitions. On both sides governments began to take unprecedented measures to organise their economy for a long war. The task was to prove too great for Tsarist Russia.

GERMAN CARTOGRAPHIC PROPAGANDA 1915

❶ Europe Following a Central Powers Victory

KEY
- German-dominated territory.
- Austrian-dominated territory.
- Other states.

0 — 300 Miles

NORWAY
SWEDEN
IRELAND
DENMARK
BRITAIN
HOLLAND
GREATER GERMANY
FRANCE
G
SWITZ.
GREATER AUSTRIA-HUNGARY
PORTUGAL
SPAIN
ITALY
NEUTRAL IN EARLY 1915.
RUMANIA
BULGARIA
TURKEY
RUSSIA
TURKEY

NOTE THE SMALL SIZES OF FRANCE AND RUSSIA, WITH BELGIUM (HOLLAND'S NEXT-DOOR NEIGHBOUR) WIPED OFF THE MAP. BRITAIN BECOMES A GERMAN COLONY, AND TURKEY REGAINS LOST TERRITORIES.

In early 1915, Germany was intent on wooing neutral Holland to side with her against the Entente powers. Sets of maps were sent to Holland to assist German propaganda and the basic details (anglicized) are shown here. The dominant theme would seem to be an automatic assumption that whichever side won the war would crush the losers virtually out of existence.

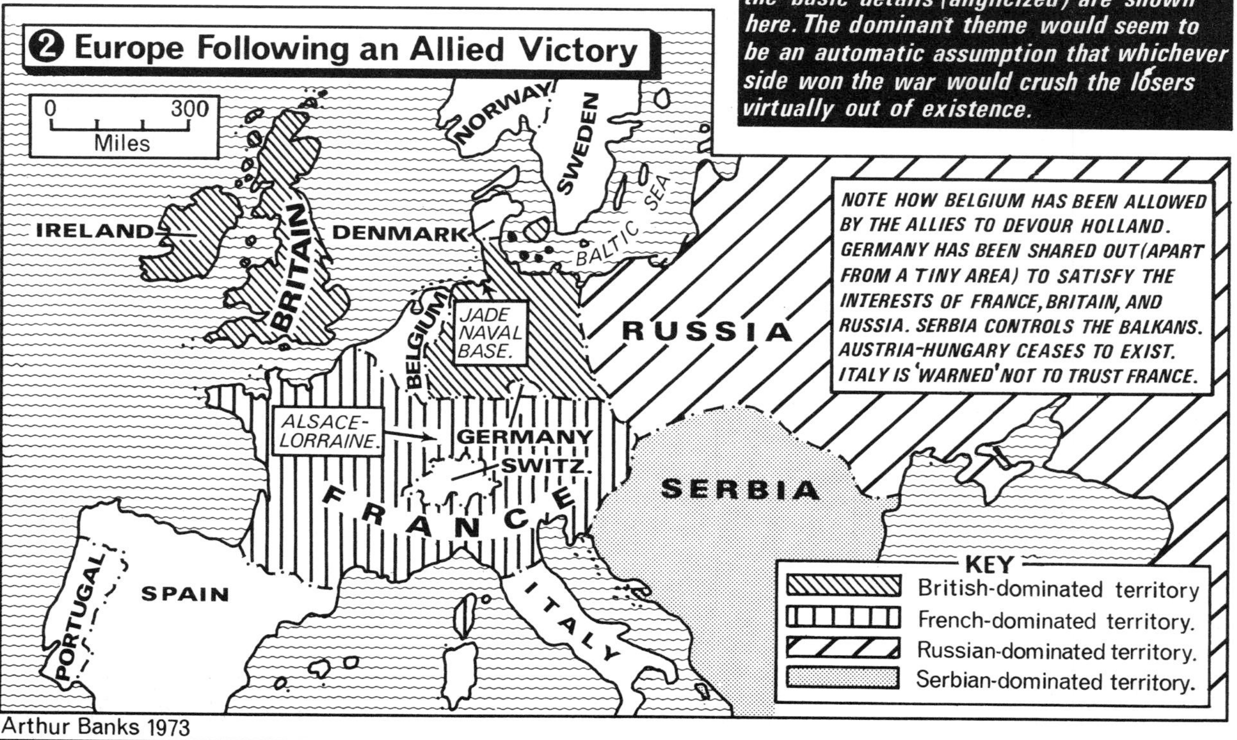

❷ Europe Following an Allied Victory

0 — 300 Miles

NORWAY
SWEDEN
IRELAND
DENMARK
BALTIC SEA
BRITAIN
RUSSIA
BELGIUM
JADE NAVAL BASE.
ALSACE-LORRAINE.
GERMANY
SWITZ.
FRANCE
SERBIA
PORTUGAL
SPAIN
ITALY

NOTE HOW BELGIUM HAS BEEN ALLOWED BY THE ALLIES TO DEVOUR HOLLAND. GERMANY HAS BEEN SHARED OUT (APART FROM A TINY AREA) TO SATISFY THE INTERESTS OF FRANCE, BRITAIN, AND RUSSIA. SERBIA CONTROLS THE BALKANS. AUSTRIA-HUNGARY CEASES TO EXIST. ITALY IS 'WARNED' NOT TO TRUST FRANCE.

KEY
- British-dominated territory
- French-dominated territory.
- Russian-dominated territory.
- Serbian-dominated territory.

© Arthur Banks 1973

132

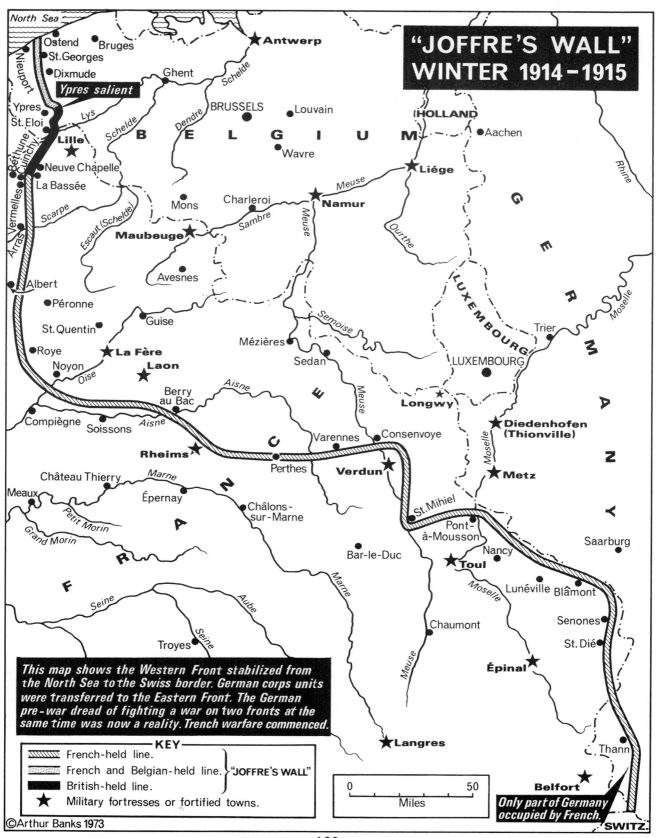

"JOFFRE'S WALL" WINTER 1914-1915

North Sea

Ostend • Bruges
St.Georges
• Dixmude
Nieuport
Ypres
St. Eloi
Lille ★
Béthune
Cuinchy • Neuve Chapelle
La Bassée
Vermelles
Arras

Antwerp ★

Ghent

Schelde
Dendre
BRUSSELS • Louvain

B E L G I U M

Lys
Schelde
• Wavre
Escaut (Schelde)
Scarpe

Mons •
Charleroi •
Sambre
Maubeuge ★

• Aachen

Meuse
★ **Liége**

★ **Namur**

Ourthe

Meuse

G E R M A N Y

L U X E M B O U R G

• Trier
Moselle

• Albert
• Péronne
St.Quentin •
• Roye
Noyon •
Oise
Compiègne •
Soissons •

Avesnes •

Guise •

La Fère ★
Laon ★

Berry au Bac
Aisne
Aisne

Méziéres •
Sedan •

Semoise

LUXEMBOURG •

Longwy ★

★ **Diedenhofen (Thionville)**

Rheims ★
Perthes •

F R A N C E

Château Thierry •
Meaux •
Petit Morin
Grand Morin

Marne
Épernay •
Châlons-sur-Marne •

Varennes •
Consenvoye •
Verdun ★

Meuse

St.Mihiel
Pont-à-Mousson •

Moselle

★ **Metz**

Saarburg •

Bar-le-Duc •
Marne

Nancy •
Toul ★

Moselle

Lunéville • Blâmont •

Seine
Troyes •
Seine
Aube

Chaumont •

Meuse
Langres ★

Épinal ★

Senones •
St.Dié •

Thann •

Belfort ★

Only part of Germany occupied by French.

SWITZ.

This map shows the Western Front stabilized from the North Sea to the Swiss border. German corps units were transferred to the Eastern Front. The German pre-war dread of fighting a war on two fronts at the same time was now a reality. Trench warfare commenced.

KEY

- ///// French-held line.
- ∴∴∴ French and Belgian-held line. } "JOFFRE'S WALL"
- ▬▬ British-held line.
- ★ Military fortresses or fortified towns.

©Arthur Banks 1973

0   50
Miles

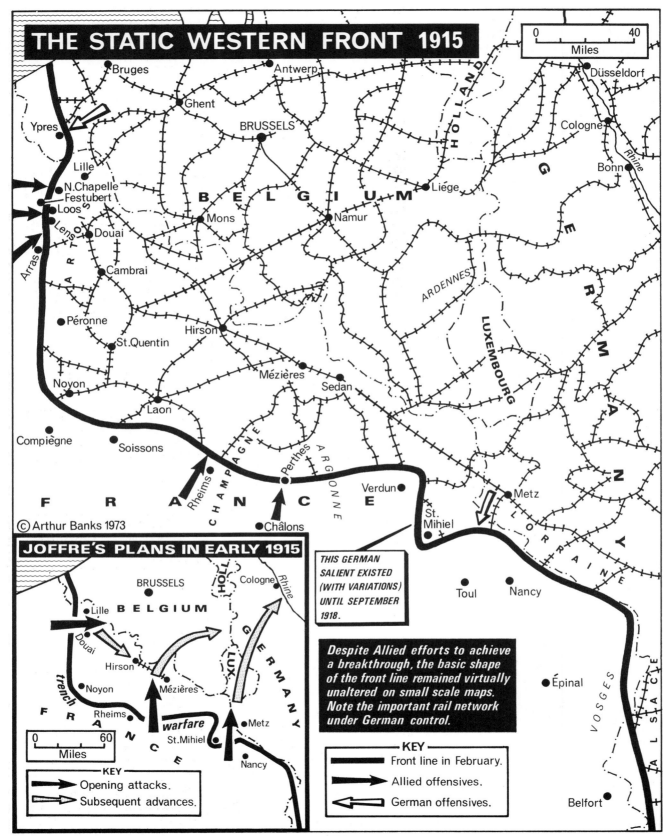

THE STATIC WESTERN FRONT 1915

0 — 40
Miles

Bruges
Antwerp
Ghent
Ypres
BRUSSELS
Lille
N.Chapelle
Festubert
Loos
Douai
Mons
Namur
Liège
Cambrai
Péronne
St.Quentin
Hirson
Noyon
Laon
Mézières
Sedan
Verdun
Compiègne
Soissons
Rheims
Perthes
St. Mihiel
Châlons
Metz
Toul
Nancy
Épinal
Belfort
Düsseldorf
Cologne
Bonn
Rhine

HOLLAND
BELGIUM
GERMANY
ARDENNES
LUXEMBOURG
LORRAINE
ALSACE
VOSGES
ARTOIS
CHAMPAGNE
ARGONNE
FRANCE

© Arthur Banks 1973

THIS GERMAN SALIENT EXISTED (WITH VARIATIONS) UNTIL SEPTEMBER 1918.

Despite Allied efforts to achieve a breakthrough, the basic shape of the front line remained virtually unaltered on small scale maps. Note the important rail network under German control.

KEY
Front line in February.
Allied offensives.
German offensives.

JOFFRE'S PLANS IN EARLY 1915

BRUSSELS
BELGIUM
Cologne
Rhine
Lille
Douai
Hirson
Noyon
Mézières
Rheims
Metz
St.Mihiel
Nancy
HOLL.
LUX.
GERMANY
FRANCE
trench
warfare

0 — 60
Miles

KEY
Opening attacks.
Subsequent advances.

134

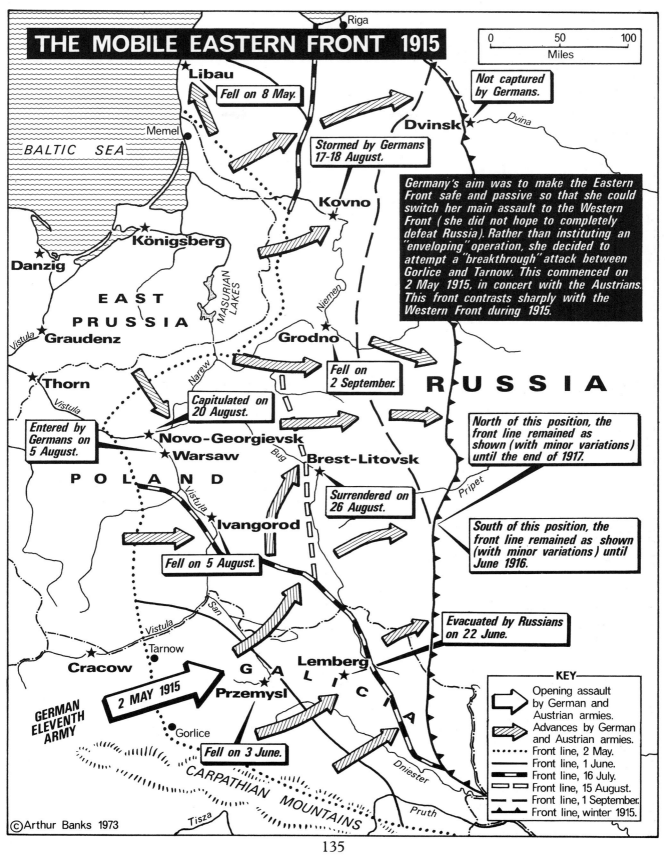

THE MOBILE EASTERN FRONT 1915

0   50   100
Miles

Not captured by Germans.

Fell on 8 May.

Stormed by Germans 17-18 August.

Germany's aim was to make the Eastern Front safe and passive so that she could switch her main assault to the Western Front (she did not hope to completely defeat Russia). Rather than instituting an "enveloping" operation, she decided to attempt a "breakthrough" attack between Gorlice and Tarnow. This commenced on 2 May 1915, in concert with the Austrians. This front contrasts sharply with the Western Front during 1915.

Fell on 2 September.

R U S S I A

North of this position, the front line remained as shown (with minor variations) until the end of 1917.

Capitulated on 20 August.

Entered by Germans on 5 August.

Surrendered on 26 August.

South of this position, the front line remained as shown (with minor variations) until June 1916.

P O L A N D

Fell on 5 August.

Evacuated by Russians on 22 June.

GERMAN ELEVENTH ARMY

2 MAY 1915

Fell on 3 June.

CARPATHIAN MOUNTAINS

© Arthur Banks 1973

BALTIC SEA

Riga
Libau
Memel
Dvinsk
Dvina
Kovno
Königsberg
Danzig
EAST PRUSSIA
MASURIAN LAKES
Niemen
Vistula
Graudenz
Grodno
Narew
Thorn
Vistula
Novo-Georgievsk
Warsaw
Bug
Brest-Litovsk
Pripet
Vistula
Ivangorod
San
Vistula
Tarnow
Cracow
Gorlice
GALICIA
Lemberg
Przemysl
Dniester
Pruth
Tisza

KEY

⟹ Opening assault by German and Austrian armies.

⟹ Advances by German and Austrian armies.

······· Front line, 2 May.

——— Front line, 1 June.

▬▬▬ Front line, 16 July.

□—□ Front line, 15 August.

– – – Front line, 1 September.

▲▲▲ Front line, winter 1915.

135

THE BATTLE OF NEUVE CHAPELLE 10-12 MARCH 1915

① 10 March–The Opening Attack

0730 hours 10 March, a British artillery bombardment commenced along the whole front. At 0805 hours the range was lengthened some 300 yards to include Neuve Chapelle, and the infantry commenced their advance which continued until dusk. The Germans began rapid consolidation of their new position, strengthening strongpoints and wiring.

The British employed some 300 guns which was thought to be a huge concentration at the time.

0   500
Yards

BRITISH IV CORPS

GERMAN VII CORPS

AUBERS

13 DIV.

Les Mottes Farm

Moulin du Pietre

Pietre

Bas Pommereau

Haut Pommereau

1 Batt. 15 Inf. Regt.

2 Companies

La Russie

Halpegarbe

14 DIV.

2 Companies 11 Jäger

Quadrilateral

Moated Grange

Orchard

Smith Dorrien Trench

NEUVE CHAPELLE

Bois du Biez

2 Companies 11 Jäger

16 INF. REGT.

Mauquissart

INF. REGT.

BRITISH FRONT LINE

GERMAN FRONT LINE

1 Battalion

Pont Logy

Port Arthur

2 Battalions

Brook

Layes

22 Inf. Bde.

23 Inf. Bde.

25 Inf. Bde.

7 DIV.

8 DIV.

BRITISH IV CORPS

Garhwal Bde.

Bareilly Bde.

Dehra Bde.

MEERUT DIV.

INDIAN CORPS

BRITISH KEY

1	2 Middlesex	**6**	2/Devon	**11**	2/3rd Gurkhas
2	2/Scottish Rifles	**7**	1/Royal Irish Rifles	**12**	2/Leics.
3	2/Lincs.	**8**	2/Rifle Brigade	**13**	3/London
4	2/Royal Berks.	**9**	13/London	**14**	1/39th. Garhwal Rifles
5	2/West Yorks.	**10**	2/39th.Garhwal Rifles		

☆ German strongpoints

② 11 March–New German Line Established

0645 hours 11 March, the offensive was resumed, but was largely ineffectual due to difficulties in concentrating a further artillery bombardment on to the new German positions. Mist impaired visibility.

Note: the Quadrilateral was a large self-contained work, strongly defended with machine-guns.

0   500
Yards

BRITISH IV CORPS

GERMAN VII CORPS

AUBERS

13 Division

DUSK ADVANCE

Les Mottes Farm

Moulin du Pietre

Pietre

Bas Pommereau

Haut Pommereau

DUSK ADVANCE

La Russie

Halpegarbe

14 Division

DUSK ADVANCE

Ligny le Petit

DUSK ADVANCE

Quadrilateral

Moated Grange

Orchard

Smith Dorrien Trench

NEUVE CHAPELLE

Bois du Biez

Brook

Layes

7 Division

8 Division

Pont Logy

Port Arthur

INDIAN CORPS

Meerut Division

KEY

━━━ New German line.
▬▬▬ German reinforcements.
▭▭▭ British front line.

136

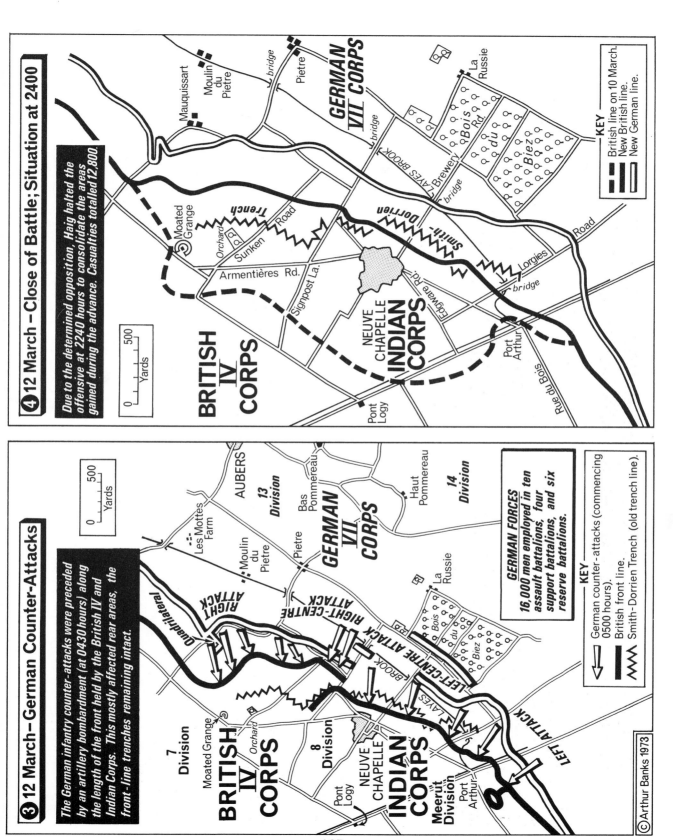

④ 12 March – Close of Battle; Situation at 2400

Due to the determined opposition, Haig halted the offensive at 2240 hours to consolidate the areas gained during the advance. Casualties totalled 12,800.

KEY

▰▰ British line on 10 March.
▭▭ New British line.
□□ New German line.

GERMAN VII CORPS

BRITISH IV CORPS

NEUVE CHAPELLE

INDIAN CORPS

Mauquissart
Moulin du Pietre
Pietre
La Russie
Bois du Biez
Brewery
LAYES BROOK
Moated Grange
Orchard
Trench
Sunken Road
Smith-Dorrien
Armentières Rd.
Signpost La.
Lorgies
bridge
Edgware Rd.
Road
Port Arthur
Pont Logy
Rue du Bois

0 500
Yards

---

③ 12 March – German Counter-Attacks

The German infantry counter-attacks were preceded by an artillery bombardment (at 0430 hours) along the length of the front held by the British IV and Indian Corps. This mostly affected rear areas, the front-line trenches remaining intact.

KEY

GERMAN FORCES
16,000 men employed in ten assault battalions, four support battalions, and six reserve battalions.

⇨ German counter-attacks (commencing 0500 hours).
▮ British front line.
ΛΛΛ Smith–Dorrien Trench (old trench line).

AUBERS
13 Division
Bas Pommereau
Haut Pommereau
14 Division

GERMAN VII CORPS

Les Mottes Farm
Moulin du Pietre
Pietre
La Russie
Bois du Biez
RIGHT ATTACK
Quadrilateral
RIGHT-CENTRE ATTACK
LEFT-CENTRE ATTACK
LAYES BROOK
LEFT ATTACK

BRITISH IV CORPS

7 Division
Moated Grange
Orchard
8 Division
NEUVE CHAPELLE
INDIAN CORPS
Meerut Division
Pont Logy
Port Arthur

0 500
Yards

© Arthur Banks 1973

137

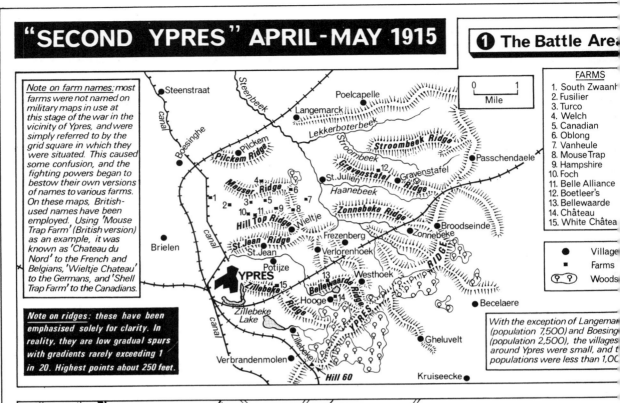

"SECOND YPRES" APRIL-MAY 1915

❶ The Battle Area

Note on farm names: most farms were not named on military maps in use at this stage of the war in the vicinity of Ypres, and were simply referred to by the grid square in which they were situated. This caused some confusion, and the fighting powers began to bestow their own versions of names to various farms. On these maps, British-used names have been employed. Using 'Mouse Trap Farm' (British version) as an example, it was known as 'Chateau du Nord' to the French and Belgians, 'Wieltje Chateau' to the Germans, and 'Shell Trap Farm' to the Canadians.

Note on ridges: these have been emphasised solely for clarity. In reality, they are low gradual spurs with gradients rarely exceeding 1 in 20. Highest points about 250 feet.

FARMS
1. South Zwaanh
2. Fusilier
3. Turco
4. Welch
5. Canadian
6. Oblong
7. Vanheule
8. Mouse Trap
9. Hampshire
10. Foch
11. Belle Alliance
12. Boetleer's
13. Bellewaarde
14. Château
15. White Château

● Village
■ Farms
♀♀ Woods

With the exception of Langemar (population 7,500) and Boesing (population 2,500), the villages around Ypres were small, and t populations were less than 1,00

Steenstraat · Poelcapelle · Langemarck · Lekkerboterbeek · Pilckem · Pilckem Ridge · Stroombeek Ridge · Passchendaele · Mauser Ridge · Gravenstafel Ridge · St. Julien · Haanebeek · Zonnebeke Ridge · Zonnebeke · Broodseinde · Hill Top Ridge · Wieltje · St. Jean Ridge · Frezenberg · Verlorenhoek · St. Jean · Potijze · YPRES · Zillebeke · Bellewaarde Ridge · Westhoek · Hooge · Becelaere · Brielen · Zillebeke Lake · Zillebeke · Verbrandenmolen · Gheluvelt · Hill 60 · Kruiseecke

0 ___ 1 Mile

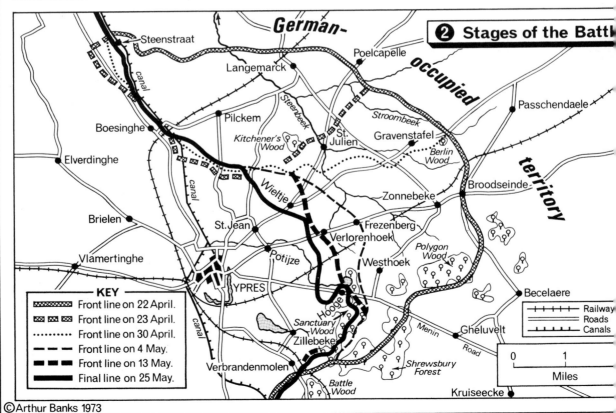

German-occupied territory

❷ Stages of the Battl

Steenstraat · Langemarck · Poelcapelle · Passchendaele · Pilckem · Boesinghe · Kitchener's Wood · St. Julien · Gravenstafel · Berlin Wood · Elverdinghe · Wieltje · Zonnebeke · Broodseinde · Brielen · St. Jean · Frezenberg · Verlorenhoek · Polygon Wood · Becelaere · Vlamertinghe · Potijze · Westhoek · YPRES · Hooge · Sanctuary Wood · Gheluvelt · Menin Road · Zillebeke · Verbrandenmolen · Shrewsbury Forest · Battle Wood · Kruiseecke

KEY
- ▨▨▨ Front line on 22 April.
- ▨ ▨ ▨ Front line on 23 April.
- ·········· Front line on 30 April.
- ─ ─ ─ Front line on 4 May.
- ▬ ▬ ▬ Front line on 13 May.
- ▬▬▬ Final line on 25 May.

- ┼┼┼ Railway
- ══ Roads
- ┴┴┴ Canals

0 ___ 1 Miles

© Arthur Banks 1973

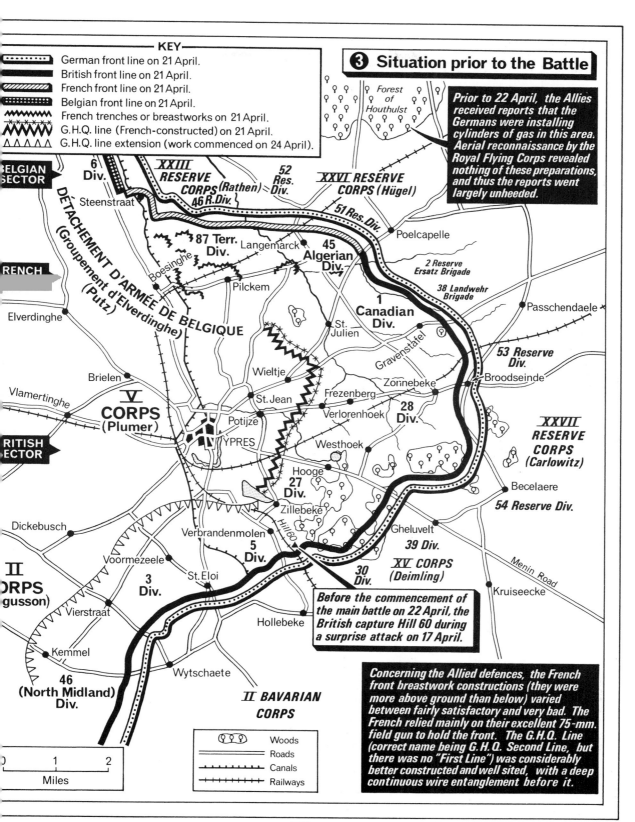

KEY
- German front line on 21 April.
- British front line on 21 April.
- French front line on 21 April.
- Belgian front line on 21 April.
- French trenches or breastworks on 21 April.
- G.H.Q. line (French-constructed) on 21 April.
- G.H.Q. line extension (work commenced on 24 April).

❸ Situation prior to the Battle

Prior to 22 April, the Allies received reports that the Germans were installing cylinders of gas in this area. Aerial reconnaissance by the Royal Flying Corps revealed nothing of these preparations, and thus the reports went largely unheeded.

Forest of Houthulst

BELGIAN SECTOR

6 Div.

XXIII RESERVE CORPS (Rathen)

46 R.Div.

Steenstraat

52 Res. Div.

XXVI RESERVE CORPS (Hügel)

51 Res. Div.

Poelcapelle

FRENCH

DÉTACHEMENT D'ARMÉE DE BELGIQUE (Groupement d'Elverdinghe) (Putz)

87 Terr. Div.

Boesinghe

Langemarck

Pilckem

45 Algerian Div.

2 Reserve Ersatz Brigade

38 Landwehr Brigade

Elverdinghe

1 Canadian Div.

Passchendaele

St. Julien

53 Reserve Div.

Brielen

Wieltje

Gravenstafel

Broodseinde

Vlamertinghe

St. Jean

Frezenberg

Zonnebeke

V CORPS (Plumer)

Potijze

Verlorenhoek

28 Div.

XXVII RESERVE CORPS (Carlowitz)

YPRES

Westhoek

BRITISH SECTOR

Hooge

27 Div.

Becelaere

Zillebeke

54 Reserve Div.

Dickebusch

Verbrandenmolen

Hill 60

Gheluvelt

39 Div.

Menin Road

Voormezeele

5 Div.

30 Div.

XV CORPS (Deimling)

Kruiseecke

II CORPS (Ferguson)

3 Div.

St. Eloi

Vierstraat

Hollebeke

Before the commencement of the main battle on 22 April, the British capture Hill 60 during a surprise attack on 17 April.

Kemmel

46 (North Midland) Div.

Wytschaete

II BAVARIAN CORPS

Concerning the Allied defences, the French front breastwork constructions (they were more above ground than below) varied between fairly satisfactory and very bad. The French relied mainly on their excellent 75-mm. field gun to hold the front. The G.H.Q. Line (correct name being G.H.Q. Second Line, but there was no "First Line") was considerably better constructed and well sited, with a deep continuous wire entanglement before it.

Woods
Roads
Canals
Railways

0   1   2
Miles

139

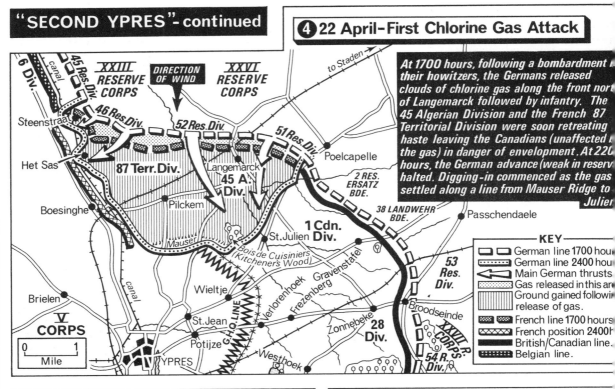

"SECOND YPRES"–continued

❹ 22 April–First Chlorine Gas Attack

6 Div. · canal · 45 Res. Div. · **XXIII RESERVE CORPS** · DIRECTION OF WIND · **XXVI RESERVE CORPS** · to Staden

46 Res. Div. · 52 Res. Div. · 51 Res. Div.

Steenstraat · Het Sas · Poelcapelle · 2 RES. ERSATZ BDE.

87 Terr. Div. · Langemarck · **45 A. Div.**

Boesinghe · Pilckem · 38 LANDWEHR BDE. · Passchendaele

Mauser · Bois de Cuisiniers (Kitchener's Wood) · St. Julien · **1 Cdn. Div.** · 53 Res. Div.

Brielen · canal · Wieltje · Verlorenhoek · Gravenstafel · Frezenberg · Broodseinde · XXVII R. CORPS

V CORPS · St. Jean · G.H.Q. LINE · Zonnebeke · **28 Div.** · 54 R. Div.

0 —— 1 Mile · Potijze · YPRES · Westhoek

At 1700 hours, following a bombardment [by] their howitzers, the Germans released clouds of chlorine gas along the front nort[h] of Langemarck followed by infantry. The 45 Algerian Division and the French 87 Territorial Division were soon retreating [in] haste leaving the Canadians (unaffected [by] the gas) in danger of envelopment. At 220[0] hours, the German advance (weak in reserve[s]) halted. Digging-in commenced as the gas settled along a line from Mauser Ridge to [St.] Julie[n].

KEY
- German line 1700 hour[s]
- German line 2400 hou[rs]
- Main German thrusts
- Gas released in this are[a]
- Ground gained followin[g] release of gas.
- French line 1700 hours
- French position 2400 h[ours]
- British/Canadian line.
- Belgian line.

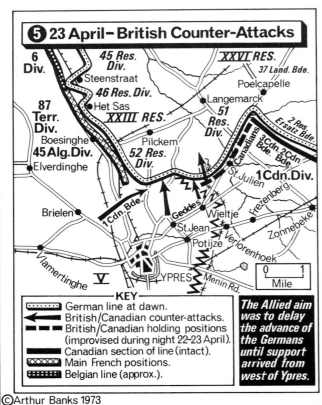

❺ 23 April–British Counter-Attacks

6 Div. · 45 Res. Div. · **XXVI RES.** · 37 Land. Bde.

Steenstraat · Poelcapelle

46 Res. Div. · Het Sas · Langemarck

87 Terr. Div. · **XXIII RES.** · 51 Res. Div. · 2 Res. Ersatz Bde.

Boesinghe · 45 Alg. Div. · Pilckem · 52 Res. Div. · Canadians · 3 Cdn. 2Cdn. Bde. Bde. · **1 Cdn. Div.**

Elverdinghe · St. Julien · Frezenberg

Brielen · 1 Cdn. Bde. · Geddes · Wieltje · Verlorenhoek · Zonnebeke

St. Jean · Potijze · 0 —— 1 Mile

Vlamertinghe · **V** · YPRES · Menin Rd.

KEY
- German line at dawn.
- British/Canadian counter-attacks.
- British/Canadian holding positions (improvised during night 22-23 April).
- Canadian section of line (intact).
- Main French positions.
- Belgian line (approx.).

The Allied aim was to delay the advance of the Germans until support arrived from west of Ypres.

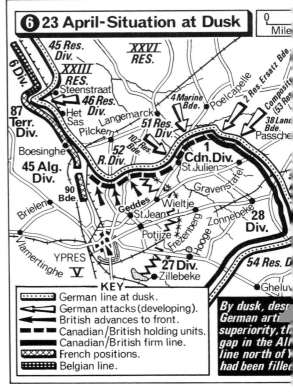

❻ 23 April–Situation at Dusk

0 —— Mile

45 Res. Div. · **XXVI RES.**

6 Div. · **XXIII RES.** · 2 Res. Ersatz Bde.

Steenstraat · 4 Marine Bde. · Poelcapelle · Composit[e] (53 Res.)

46 Res. Div. · Het Sas · Langemarck · 38 Land. Bde. · Passche[ndaele]

87 Terr. Div. · Pilckem · 51 Res. Div. · 102 Res. Bde. · **1 Cdn. Div.**

Boesinghe · 45 Alg. Div. · 52 R. Div. · St. Julien · Gravenstafel

90 Bde. · Geddes · Wieltje · 28 Div.

Brielen · St. Jean · Frezenberg · Zonnebeke

Vlamertinghe · Potijze · Hooge

YPRES · **V** · 27 Div. · 54 Res. D[iv.]

Zillebeke · Gheluv[elt]

KEY
- German line at dusk.
- German attacks (developing).
- British advances to front.
- Canadian/British holding units.
- Canadian/British firm line.
- French positions.
- Belgian line.

By dusk, des[pite] German arti[llery] superiority, th[e] gap in the All[ied] line north of Y[pres] had been fille[d]

©Arthur Banks 1973

140

⑦ 24 April-Battle of St.Julien

0—1 Mile

0130 hours, Germans occupy Lizerne. Belgians stem further progress.

37 Land. Bde.

46 Res. Div.
XXVI RES.
XXIII RES.
102 Res. Bde.
2 Res. Ersatz Bde.
Composite Bde. (53 Res. Bde.)
4 Marine Bde.
38 Land. Bde.
Passchendaele
52 R.Div.
51 R. Div.
G
Lizerne

French Attack 1330 hrs.

Fierce house-to-house fighting.

St.Julien
Zonnebeke
St.Jean
Frezenberg
Potijze
Hooge
Westhoek
53 Res. Div.
XXVII R.
54 Res.Div.
YPRES
V RPS
Zillebeke
Gheluvelt

KEY
···· German line at dawn.
▭ Main German thrusts.
▨ Ground gained by Germans.
Gas released at **G** (0400 hours).

Allied units have been omitted for clarity. German artillery batteries dominated area.

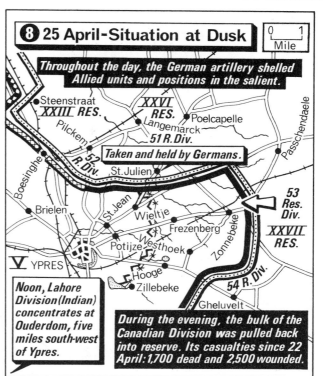

⑧ 25 April-Situation at Dusk

0—1 Mile

Throughout the day, the German artillery shelled Allied units and positions in the salient.

Steenstraat
XXIII RES.
XXVI RES.
Poelcapelle
Langemarck
Pilckem
51 R.Div.
52 R.Div.
Boesinghe

Taken and held by Germans.

St.Julien
Brielen
St.Jean
Wieltje
Frezenberg
Zonnebeke
53 Res. Div.
XXVII RES.
Potijze
Westhoek
54 R.Div.
Hooge
Zillebeke
Gheluvelt
V YPRES

Noon, Lahore Division (Indian) concentrates at Ouderdom, five miles south-west of Ypres.

During the evening, the bulk of the Canadian Division was pulled back into reserve. Its casualties since 22 April: 1,700 dead and 2,500 wounded.

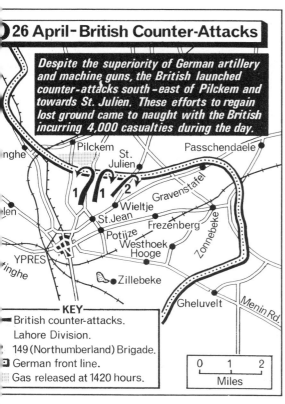

⑨ 26 April-British Counter-Attacks

Despite the superiority of German artillery and machine guns, the British launched counter-attacks south-east of Pilckem and towards St. Julien. These efforts to regain lost ground came to naught with the British incurring 4,000 casualties during the day.

Pilckem
Passchendaele
St. Julien
1 1 2
Gravenstafel
Wieltje
St.Jean
Frezenberg
Zonnebeke
Potijze
Westhoek
Hooge
YPRES
Zillebeke
Gheluvelt
Menin Rd.

KEY
▬ British counter-attacks.
Lahore Division.
1 149 (Northumberland) Brigade.
▯ German front line.
▨ Gas released at 1420 hours.

0—1—2 Miles

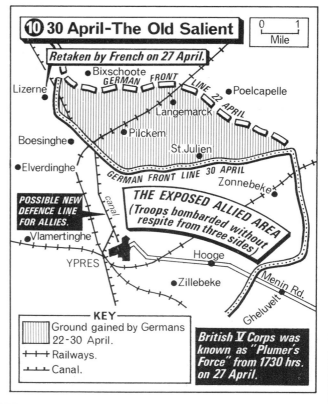

⑩ 30 April-The Old Salient

0—1 Mile

Retaken by French on 27 April.

Bixschoote
GERMAN FRONT LINE 22 APRIL
Lizerne
Poelcapelle
Langemarck
Boesinghe
Pilckem
St.Julien
Elverdinghe
GERMAN FRONT LINE 30 APRIL
Zonnebeke

POSSIBLE NEW DEFENCE LINE FOR ALLIES.

THE EXPOSED ALLIED AREA (Troops bombarded without respite from three sides)

canal
Vlamertinghe
YPRES
Hooge
Zillebeke
Menin Rd.
Gheluvelt

KEY
▨ Ground gained by Germans 22-30 April.
+++ Railways.
++++ Canal.

British V Corps was known as "Plumer's Force" from 1730 hrs. on 27 April.

141

"SECOND YPRES"-continued

⑪ 4 May-The New Salient

0 ——— 1
Mile

Between 1 and 4 May, British units retired to new positions to shorten their lines of defence.

G.H.Q. Line defences are strengthened and extended at speed.

Langemarck
Boesinghe
Pilckem
canal
Zonnebeke
Vlamertinghe
canal
YPRES
Hooge
Zillebeke
HILL 60
Menin Road
Gheluvelt

KEY
▦ Ground relinquished by British, 1-4 May.
▬▬ British front line, 1 May.
▬▬▬ British front line, 4 May.
✕✕✕✕ French front line, 4 May.

1 May, British defeat a German gas-assisted attack for first time.

⑫ 8 May-Battle of Frezenberg Ridge

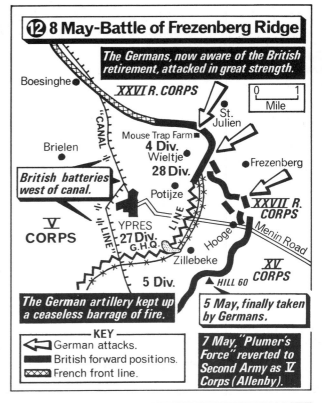

The Germans, now aware of the British retirement, attacked in great strength.

0 ——— 1
Mile

Boesinghe
XXVI R. CORPS
St. Julien
Mouse Trap Farm
4 Div.
Wieltje
28 Div.
Brielen
Frezenberg
XXVII R. CORPS
Potijze
"CANAL"
"LINE"
YPRES
27 Div.
G.H.Q.
Hooge
Menin Road
Zillebeke
XV CORPS
5 Div.
▲ HILL 60

British batteries west of canal.

V CORPS

The German artillery kept up a ceaseless barrage of fire.

5 May, finally taken by Germans.

KEY
⇐ German attacks.
▬ British forward positions.
✕✕✕✕ French front line.

7 May, "Plumer's Force" reverted to Second Army as V Corps (Allenby).

⑬ 13 May-Final Moves at Frezenberg

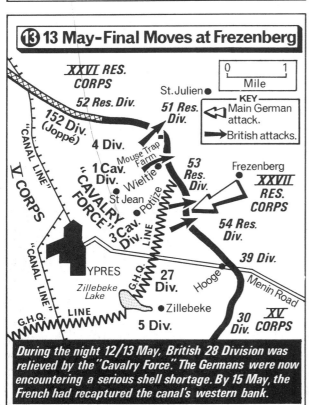

XXVI RES. CORPS
52 Res. Div.
152 Div. (Joppé)
4 Div.
St. Julien
51 Res. Div.
Mouse Trap Farm
"1 Cav. Div."
"CAVALRY FORCE"
Wieltje
St Jean
Potijze
"3 Cav. Div."
27 Div.
Zillebeke Lake
YPRES
"CANAL LINE"
G.H.Q.
"CANAL LINE"
V CORPS
53 Res. Div.
Frezenberg
XXVII RES. CORPS
54 Res. Div.
39 Div.
Hooge
Menin Road
Zillebeke
5 Div.
30 Div.
XV CORPS

0 ——— 1
Mile

KEY
⇐ Main German attack.
➡ British attacks.

During the night 12/13 May, British 28 Division was relieved by the "Cavalry Force". The Germans were now encountering a serious shell shortage. By 15 May, the French had recaptured the canal's western bank.

⑭ 24 May-Battle of Bellewaarde Ridge

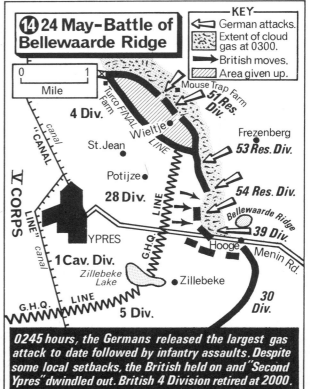

KEY
⇐ German attacks.
▦ Extent of cloud gas at 0300.
➡ British moves.
▨ Area given up.

0 ——— 1
Mile

4 Div.
canal "CANAL"
Turco Farm
FINAL LINE
Mouse Trap Farm
51 Res. Div.
Wieltje
St. Jean
Frezenberg
53 Res. Div.
Potijze
28 Div.
54 Res. Div.
Bellewaarde Ridge
39 Div.
V CORPS
"CANAL LINE"
YPRES
1 Cav. Div.
Zillebeke Lake
G.H.Q. LINE
Hooge
Menin Rd.
Zillebeke
5 Div.
30 Div.

0245 hours, the Germans released the largest gas attack to date followed by infantry assaults. Despite some local setbacks, the British held on and "Second Ypres" dwindled out. British 4 Division retired at 2000.

© Arthur Banks 1973

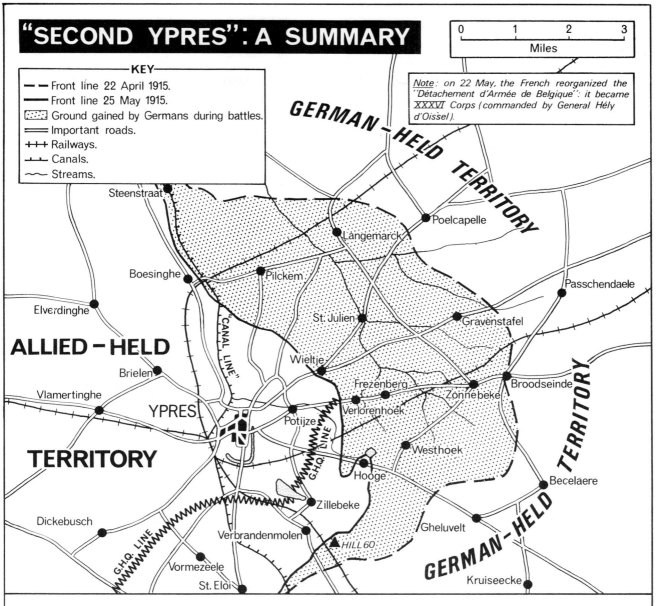

"SECOND YPRES": A SUMMARY

0 1 2 3 Miles

KEY

- ‒ ‒ Front line 22 April 1915.
- ‒‒‒ Front line 25 May 1915.
- ░░ Ground gained by Germans during battles.
- ═══ Important roads.
- +++ Railways.
- ⊥⊥⊥ Canals.
- ～ Streams.

Note: on 22 May, the French reorganized the "Détachement d'Armée de Belgique": it became XXXVI Corps (commanded by General Hély d'Oissel).

GERMAN-HELD TERRITORY

Steenstraat
Boesinghe
Elverdinghe
Poelcapelle
Langemarck
Pilckem
Passchendaele
St. Julien
Gravenstafel
ALLIED-HELD
Brielen
"CANAL LINE"
Wieltje
Vlamertinghe
Frezenberg
Broodseinde
YPRES
Verlorenhoek
Zonnebeke
TERRITORY
Potijze
G.H.Q. LINE
Westhoek
Becelaere
Hooge
Zillebeke
GERMAN-HELD
Dickebusch
Verbrandenmolen
Gheluvelt
G.H.Q. LINE
▲ HILL 60
TERRITORY
Vormezeele
Kruiseecke
St. Eloi

BRITISH CASUALTIES
(59,275)

1 Cavalry Division :	1,203
2 Cavalry Division :	244
3 Cavalry Division :	1,618
4 Division :	10,859
5 Division :	7,994
27 Division :	7,263
28 Division :	15,533
50 Division :	5,204
1 Canadian Division :	5,469
Lahore Division :	3,888

GERMAN CASUALTIES
(34,933)

XXIII Reserve Corps :	10,592
XXVI Reserve Corps :	12,845
XXVII Reserve Corps :	8,652
XV Corps :	2,844

FRENCH CASUALTIES
(10,000)

ESTIMATE *Precise figs. unknown*

BELGIAN CASUALTIES
(1,530)

BY THE CLOSE OF "SECOND YPRES", THE GERMANS HAD GAINED SOME GROUND BUT THE SALIENT STILL REMAINED, ALBEIT REDUCED IN SIZE. MORE IMPORTANT FOR THE FUTURE, THEY HAD DISCLOSED THEIR SECRET WEAPON (GAS) PREMATURELY, AS THEY WERE NOT SUFFICIENTLY EQUIPPED TO EXPLOIT THEIR INITIAL SUCCESS OF 22 APRIL. ON THE BRITISH SIDE, THE BATTLES WERE MARKED BY INDECISION AMONG THE HIGHER RANKS AS TO THE CORRECT DEFENSIVE ACTION TO EMPLOY, AND GENERAL SMITH-DORRIEN (2 ARMY COMMANDER) WAS DISMISSED ON 6 MAY AS A RESULT OF DISSENSION BETWEEN HIMSELF AND THE COMMANDER-IN-CHIEF, FIELD-MARSHAL SIR JOHN FRENCH.

© Arthur Banks 1973

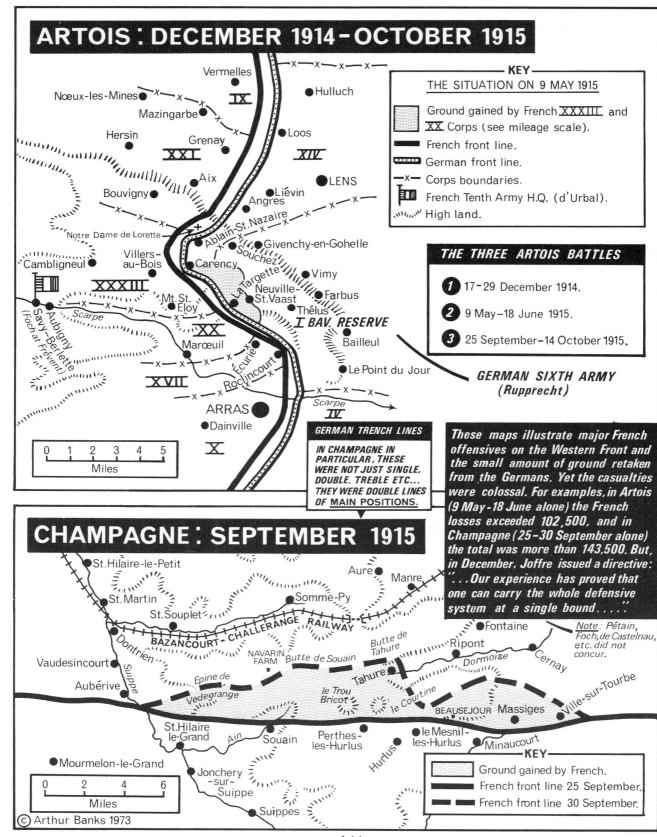

ARTOIS : DECEMBER 1914–OCTOBER 1915

Vermelles

Nœux-les-Mines

Hulluch

Mazingarbe

IX

Hersin

Loos

Grenay

XXI

XIV

Aix

LENS

Bouvigny

Liévin

Angres

Notre Dame de Lorette

Ablain-St.Nazaire

Givenchy-en-Gohelle

Villers-au-Bois

Souchez

Cambligneul

Carency

Targette

Vimy

Savy-Berlette
(Foch at Frévent)

Scarpe

XXXIII

Mt. St.
Eloy

Neuville-
St.Vaast

Farbus

Thélus

Aubigny

I BAV. RESERVE

Marœuil

XX

Bailleul

Ecurie

Roclincourt

Le Point du Jour

XVII

Scarpe

ARRAS

IV

Dainville

X

KEY

THE SITUATION ON 9 MAY 1915

Ground gained by French XXXIII and XX Corps (see mileage scale).

French front line.

German front line.

—x— Corps boundaries.

French Tenth Army H.Q. (d'Urbal).

High land.

THE THREE ARTOIS BATTLES

❶ 17–29 December 1914.

❷ 9 May–18 June 1915.

❸ 25 September–14 October 1915.

GERMAN SIXTH ARMY (Rupprecht)

0 1 2 3 4 5
Miles

GERMAN TRENCH LINES

IN CHAMPAGNE IN PARTICULAR, THESE WERE NOT JUST SINGLE, DOUBLE, TREBLE ETC... THEY WERE DOUBLE LINES OF MAIN POSITIONS.

These maps illustrate major French offensives on the Western Front and the small amount of ground retaken from the Germans. Yet the casualties were colossal. For examples, in Artois (9 May–18 June alone) the French losses exceeded 102,500, and in Champagne (25–30 September alone) the total was more than 143,500. But, in December, Joffre issued a directive: "...Our experience has proved that one can carry the whole defensive system at a single bound...."

Note: Pétain, Foch, de Castelnau, etc. did not concur.

CHAMPAGNE : SEPTEMBER 1915

St.Hilaire-le-Petit

Aure

Manre

St.Martin

Somme-Py

St.Souplet

BAZANCOURT – CHALLERANGE RAILWAY

Fontaine

Dontrien

Butte de Tahure

Ripont

Cernay

NAVARIN FARM

Butte de Souain

Vaudesincourt

Dormoise

Suippe

Epine de Vedegrange

Tahure

Aubérive

le Trou Bricot

le Courtine

Ville-sur-Tourbe

BEAUSÉJOUR

Massiges

St.Hilaire le-Grand

Ain

Souain

Perthes-
les-Hurlus

le Mesnil-
les-Hurlus

Minaucourt

Hurlus

Mourmelon-le-Grand

Jonchery-
sur-
Suippe

KEY

Ground gained by French.

French front line 25 September.

French front line 30 September.

0 2 4 6
Miles

Suippes

© Arthur Banks 1973

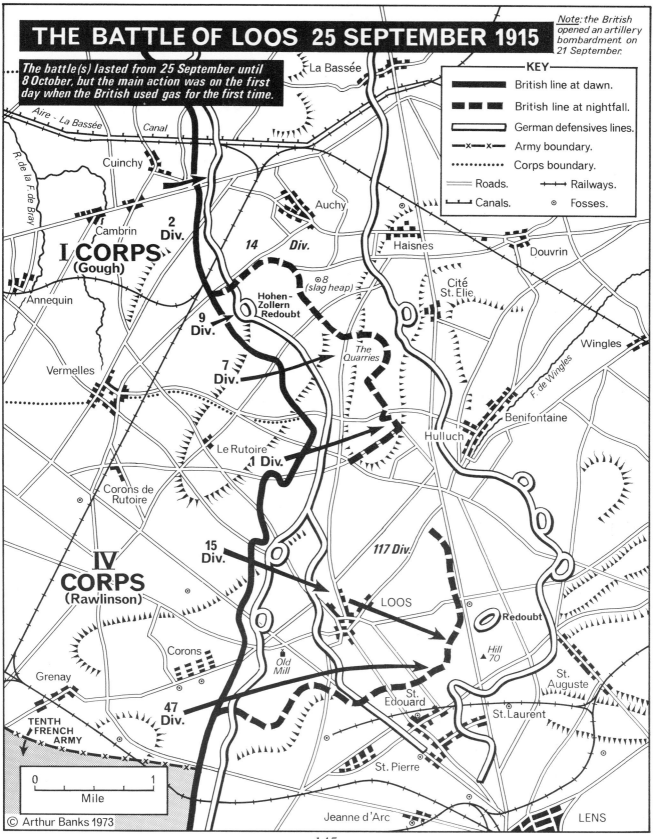

THE BATTLE OF LOOS 25 SEPTEMBER 1915

The battle(s) lasted from 25 September until 8 October, but the main action was on the first day when the British used gas for the first time.

Note: the British opened an artillery bombardment on 21 September.

KEY

▬▬▬▬	British line at dawn.
▬ ▬ ▬	British line at nightfall.
▭▭▭	German defensives lines.
—x—x—	Army boundary.
·······	Corps boundary.
——	Roads.
—+—+—	Railways.
⊢⊣	Canals.
⊙	Fosses.

La Bassée

Aire - La Bassée Canal

R. de la F. de Bray

Cuinchy

Auchy

Haisnes

Douvrin

Cambrin

2 Div.

14 Div.

I CORPS (Gough)

Annequin

⊙ 8 (slag heap)

Cité St. Elie

Hohen-Zollern Redoubt

9 Div.

The Quarries

Wingles

7 Div.

F. de Wingles

Vermelles

Benifontaine

Le Rutoire

Hulluch

1 Div.

Corons de Rutoire

15 Div.

117 Div.

IV CORPS (Rawlinson)

LOOS

Redoubt

Corons

Hill 70

Old Mill

Grenay

St. Auguste

47 Div.

St. Edouard

St. Laurent

TENTH FRENCH ARMY

St. Pierre

0 — 1
Mile

© Arthur Banks 1973

Jeanne d'Arc

LENS

THE WAR IN 1916

The costly failures of 1915 had led to changes in command before the end of the year. In the autumn, against the advice of his ministers, Tsar Nicholas II assumed command on the Eastern Front, sending Grand Duke Nicholas to hold the Caucasus against the Turks (page 163). The heavy casualties at Loos discredited Sir John French who, in December, was replaced as British commander-in-chief by Sir Douglas Haig. At the same time Kitchener, though remaining War Minister, surrendered responsibility for operations to a new Chief of the Imperial General Staff, Sir William Robertson, an ex-footman who had enlisted as a private thirty-nine years before. Only in France did Joffre's supremacy pass unchallenged.

Haig and Robertson were a formidable partnership. They insisted that, after the frustrations of Gallipoli, the Western Front was to have priority over all other Fronts. This decision was endorsed by the Cabinet on 28 December 1915; it was welcomed by Joffre. His own plans for 1916 looked for wearing-down operations by his allies preparatory to a major offensive by the French later in the spring. But the initiative on the Western Front was seized by the Germans. Falkenhayn won the Kaiser's consent for a different concept of military operations: he proposed massive attack on a narrow sector where reasons of national sentiment would 'compel the French General Staff to throw in every man they have'. The sector he recommended for this attempt 'to bleed France white' (Falkenhayn's own expression) was Verdun, the historic city on the Meuse whose fall in 1792 precipitated the panic September massacres in revolutionary Paris.

The battle of Verdun, which began with a concentrated artillery barrage on 21 February 1916 and continued for 300 days, overshadowed—and to some extent predetermined—all other military events of the year. Verdun, like Ypres, never fell to the Germans; it consumed Joffre's reserves; it left the French Army permanently shell-shocked; but it also brought disillusionment to the Germans, who sustained a third of a million casualties in occupying a crater filled wasteland one-sixth the size of the Isle of Wight. Never again was morale steady, either in France or Germany.

Ultimately the defenders of Verdun were relieved by actions elsewhere. By midsummer Haig, supported by Foch's Sixth Army, was ready to attack on the Somme. 20,000 British soldiers perished on the first day of the battle, more than were killed in action during the five years of Wellington's Peninsular Campaign. Yet, despite the terrible losses, Haig continued to pound the German lines on the Somme, employing in September, for the first time, tanks to cross trenches and destroy machine gun nests. The Somme was a traumatic as Verdun.

Success in 1916 came on the south-west sector of the Eastern Front where General Brusilov convinced the Tsar that it was possible to break through the Austrian defences and, if assisted by an enveloping movement farther north, to knock Austria-Hungary out of the war. Brusilov forced the Austrians to fall back sixty or seventy miles in confusion: the Germans rushed divisions from the Western Front to plug the gap, the Austrians relaxed pressure on Italy, and even a Turkish Corps was hurried to Galicia. The northern attack never materialised, but Brusilov gained a remarkable triumph, sufficient to tempt Rumania into the war as an ally, although the Rumanians were speedily defeated (page 162). The victory over Rumania was won by Mackensen and Falkenhayn, who had been replaced as Chief of the German General Staff by Hindenburg when the Kaiser despaired of his Verdun policy at the end of August.

At sea, 1916 was the year of Jutland (pages 256–261), of intensified measures by the British to blockade Germany, and of a fifty per cent increase over the 1915 figures for the tonnage of Allied shipping sunk by U-boats. The outlook for 1917 was ominous.

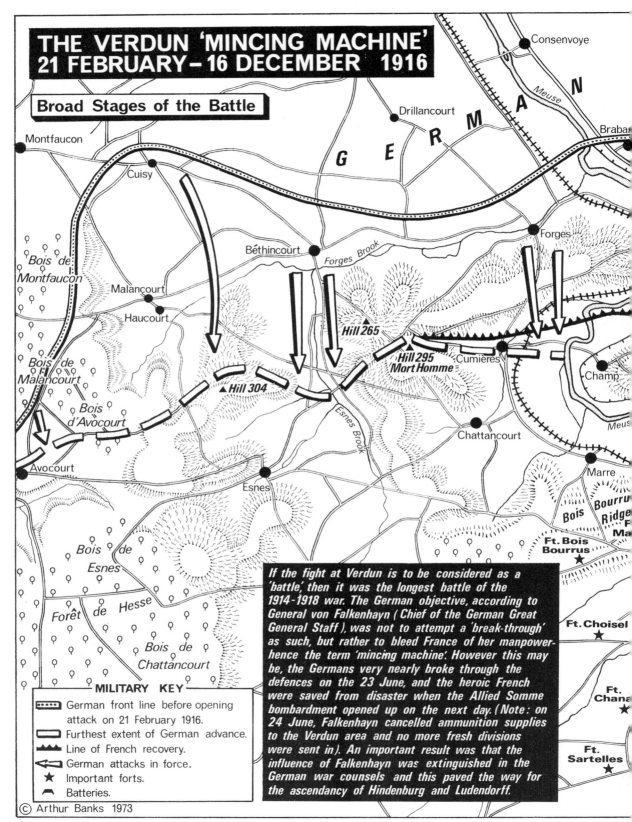

THE VERDUN 'MINCING MACHINE' 21 FEBRUARY – 16 DECEMBER 1916

Broad Stages of the Battle

Consenvoye

Drillancourt

Brabai

GERMAN

Meuse

Montfaucon

Cuisy

Bois de Montfaucon

Béthincourt

Forges Brook

Forges

Malancourt

Haucourt

Hill 265

Bois de Malancourt

Hill 295
'Mort Homme'

Cumières

Champ

Bois d'Avocourt

Hill 304

Esnes Brook

Chattancourt

Meus

Avocourt

Esnes

Marre

Bois Bourru

Bois Ridge
F
Ma

Bois de Esnes

Ft. Bois Bourrus ★

Forêt de Hesse

Ft. Choisel ★

Bois de Chattancourt

Ft. Chana ★

MILITARY KEY

- ∙∙∙∙∙ German front line before opening attack on 21 February 1916.
- ▭ Furthest extent of German advance.
- ▲▲▲ Line of French recovery.
- ⬅ German attacks in force.
- ★ Important forts.
- ⌐ Batteries.

Ft. Sartelles ★

© Arthur Banks 1973

If the fight at Verdun is to be considered as a 'battle', then it was the longest battle of the 1914-1918 war. The German objective, according to General von Falkenhayn (Chief of the German Great General Staff), was not to attempt a 'break-through' as such, but rather to bleed France of her manpower—hence the term 'mincing machine'. However this may be, the Germans very nearly broke through the defences on the 23 June, and the heroic French were saved from disaster when the Allied Somme bombardment opened up on the next day. (Note: on 24 June, Falkenhayn cancelled ammunition supplies to the Verdun area and no more fresh divisions were sent in). An important result was that the influence of Falkenhayn was extinguished in the German war counsels and this paved the way for the ascendancy of Hindenburg and Ludendorff.

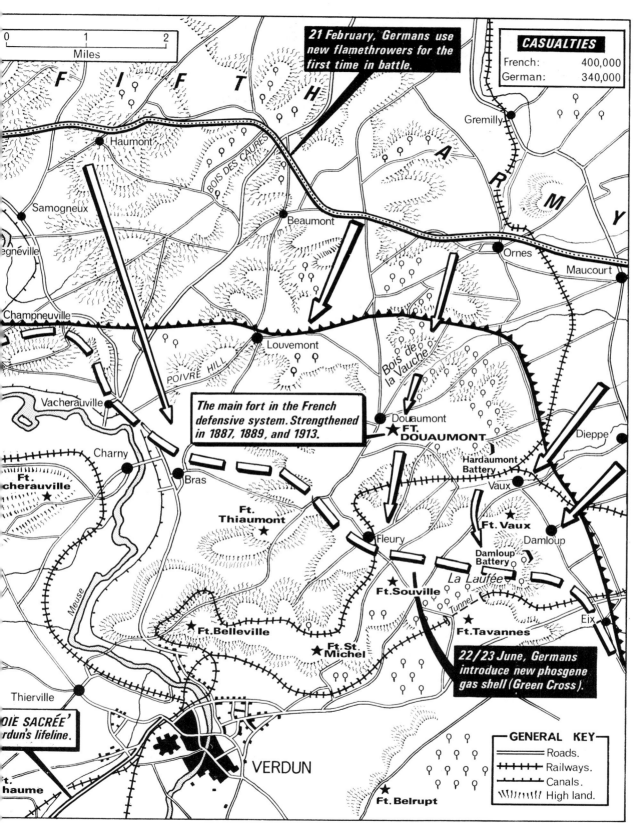

0   **1**   **2**
Miles

21 February, Germans use new flamethrowers for the first time in battle.

CASUALTIES
French: 400,000
German: 340,000

F I F T H   A R M Y

Gremilly

Haumont

BOIS DES CAURES

Samogneux

Beaumont

Ornes

egnéville

Maucourt

Champneuville

The main fort in the French defensive system. Strengthened in 1887, 1889, and 1913.

Louvemont

POIVRE HILL

Bois de la Vauche

Douaumont

Dieppe

★ **FT. DOUAUMONT**

Vacherauville

Hardaumont Battery

Vaux

Charny

cherauville

Bras

★ **Ft. Vaux**

★

Damloup

Ft. Thiaumont ★

Fleury

Damloup Battery

Meuse

La Laufée

★ **Ft.Souville**

Tunnel

Eix

★ **Ft.Belleville**

Ft.St. Michel ★

★ **Ft.Tavannes**

Thierville

22/23 June, Germans introduce new phosgene gas shell (Green Cross).

OIE SACRÉE' rdun's lifeline.

t. haume

VERDUN

GENERAL KEY
Roads.
Railways.
Canals.
High land.

★ **Ft.Belrupt**

149

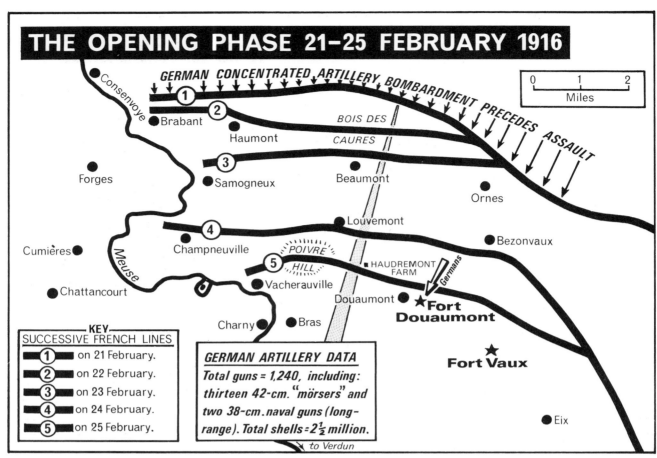

THE OPENING PHASE 21–25 FEBRUARY 1916

GERMAN CONCENTRATED ARTILLERY BOMBARDMENT PRECEDES ASSAULT

0   1   2
Miles

Consenvoye

Brabant

Haumont

BOIS DES
CAURES

Forges

Samogneux

Beaumont

Ornes

Cumières

Meuse

Champneuville

Louvemont

POIVRE
HILL

Bezonvaux

Chattancourt

Vacherauville

■ HAUDREMONT
FARM

Germans

Charny

Bras

Douaumont

★ **Fort**
Douaumont

★ **Fort Vaux**

Eix

KEY
SUCCESSIVE FRENCH LINES

① on 21 February.
② on 22 February.
③ on 23 February.
④ on 24 February.
⑤ on 25 February.

GERMAN ARTILLERY DATA
Total guns = 1,240, including:
thirteen 42-cm. "mörsers" and
two 38-cm. naval guns (long-
range). Total shells = 2½ million.

↓ *to Verdun*

WEST OF THE MEUSE 6 MARCH - 10 APRIL 1916

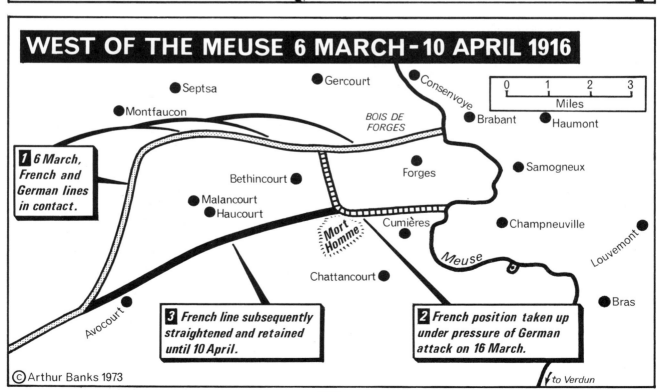

Septsa

Gercourt

Consenvoye

0   1   2   3
Miles

Montfaucon

BOIS DE
FORGES

Brabant

Haumont

1 *6 March,*
French and
German lines
in contact.

Bethincourt

Forges

Samogneux

Malancourt
Haucourt

Mort
Homme

Cumières

Champneuville

Louvemont

Meuse

Avocourt

Chattancourt

Bras

3 *French line subsequently*
straightened and retained
until 10 April.

2 *French position taken up*
under pressure of German
attack on 16 March.

↓ *to Verdun*

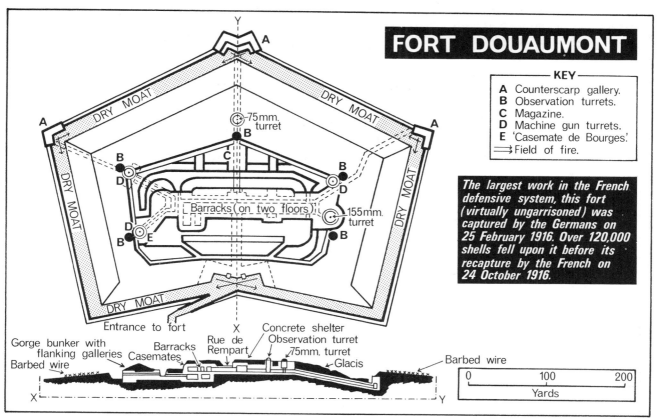

FORT DOUAUMONT

KEY
A Counterscarp gallery.
B Observation turrets.
C Magazine.
D Machine gun turrets.
E 'Casemate de Bourges'.
⟹ Field of fire.

75mm. turret

155mm. turret

Barracks (on two floors)

The largest work in the French defensive system, this fort (virtually ungarrisoned) was captured by the Germans on 25 February 1916. Over 120,000 shells fell upon it before its recapture by the French on 24 October 1916.

DRY MOAT

Entrance to fort

Gorge bunker with flanking galleries
Barbed wire
Barracks
Casemates
Rue de Rempart
Concrete shelter
Observation turret
75mm. turret
Glacis
Barbed wire

X ..... Y

0	100	200

Yards

FORT VAUX

KEY
A Counterscarp gallery.
B Observation turrets.
C Magazines.
D Exit to superstructure.
E 'Casemate de Bourges'.
⟹ Field of fire.

0	25

Yards

The smallest work in the French defensive system, this fort (after a stubborn and heroic resistance) was captured by the Germans on 7 June 1916. It was retaken by the French on 2 November 1916.

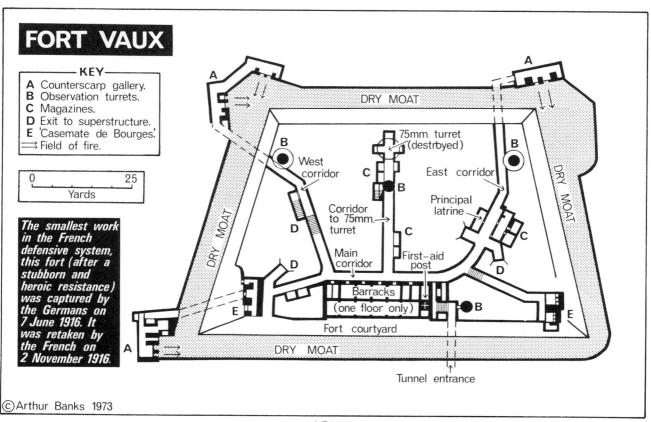

DRY MOAT

75mm. turret (destroyed)

West corridor

East corridor

Principal latrine

Corridor to 75mm. turret

Main corridor

First-aid post

Barracks (one floor only)

Fort courtyard

DRY MOAT

Tunnel entrance

© Arthur Banks 1973

151

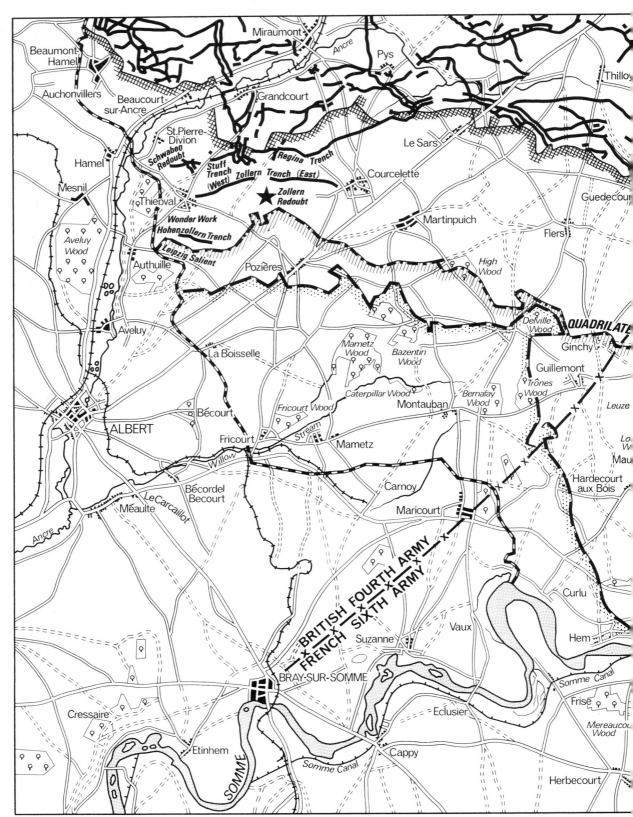

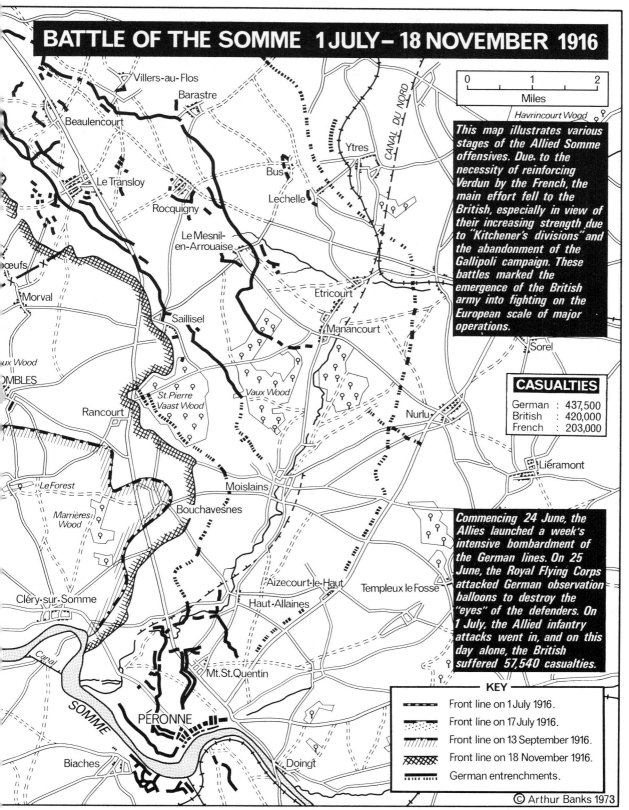

BATTLE OF THE SOMME 1 JULY – 18 NOVEMBER 1916

Villers-au-Flos

Barastre

Beaulencourt

Le Transloy

Rocquigny

Le Mesnil-
en-Arrouaise

œufs

Morval

Saillisel

Vaux Wood

ux Wood

St.Pierre
Vaast Wood

OMBLES

Rancourt

Le Forest

Marrières
Wood

Clery-sur-Somme

Bouchavesnes

Moislains

Aizecourt-le-Haut

Haut-Allaines

Mt.St.Quentin

SOMME

Canal

PÉRONNE

Biaches

Doingt

Bus

Lechelle

Ytres

CANAL DU NORD

Havrincourt Wood

Etricourt

Manancourt

Sorel

Nurlu

Lieramont

Templeux le Fosse

0	1	2

Miles

This map illustrates various stages of the Allied Somme offensives. Due to the necessity of reinforcing Verdun by the French, the main effort fell to the British, especially in view of their increasing strength due to "Kitchener's divisions" and the abandonment of the Gallipoli campaign. These battles marked the emergence of the British army into fighting on the European scale of major operations.

CASUALTIES

German : 437,500
British : 420,000
French : 203,000

Commencing 24 June, the Allies launched a week's intensive bombardment of the German lines. On 25 June, the Royal Flying Corps attacked German observation balloons to destroy the "eyes" of the defenders. On 1 July, the Allied infantry attacks went in, and on this day alone, the British suffered 57,540 casualties.

KEY

- Front line on 1 July 1916.
- Front line on 17 July 1916.
- Front line on 13 September 1916.
- Front line on 18 November 1916.
- German entrenchments.

© Arthur Banks 1973

153

Thiepval Wood

Thiepval

Moquet Farm

Pozières

Authuille Wood

Contalmaison Villa

Ovillers la Boisselle

Contalmaison Wood

Lower Wood

Pearl Wood

Mash Valley

Bailiff Wood

Contalmaison

Mametz Wood

Peake Woods

Acid Drop Copse

la Boisselle

Birch Tree Wood

The Quadrangle

Willow Stream

Sausage Valley

Shelter Wood

Bottom Wood

Lozenge Wood

Railway Copse

Bécourt

Fricourt Farm

Bécourt Wood

Fricourt Wood

FRICOURT

MAMETZ

Willow Stream

0   1000
Yards

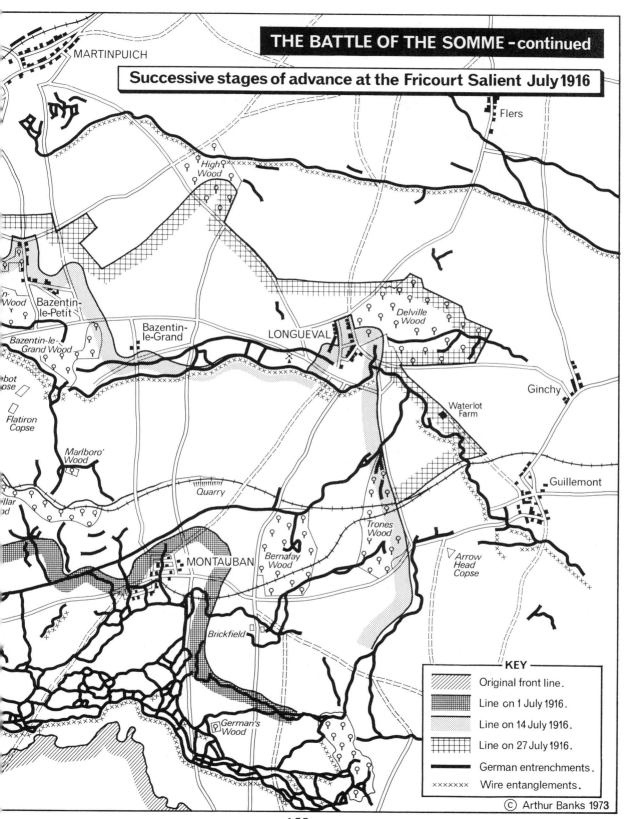

THE BATTLE OF THE SOMME - continued

Successive stages of advance at the Fricourt Salient July 1916

MARTINPUICH

Flers

High Wood

Bazentin-le-Petit

Bazentin-le-Grand Wood

Bazentin-le-Grand

LONGUEVAL

Delville Wood

Ginchy

Flatiron Copse

Waterlot Farm

Marlboro' Wood

Quarry

Guillemont

Trones Wood

Bernafay Wood

MONTAUBAN

Arrow Head Copse

Brickfield

German's Wood

KEY

Original front line.

Line on 1 July 1916.

Line on 14 July 1916.

Line on 27 July 1916.

German entrenchments.

×××××× Wire entanglements.

© Arthur Banks 1973

155

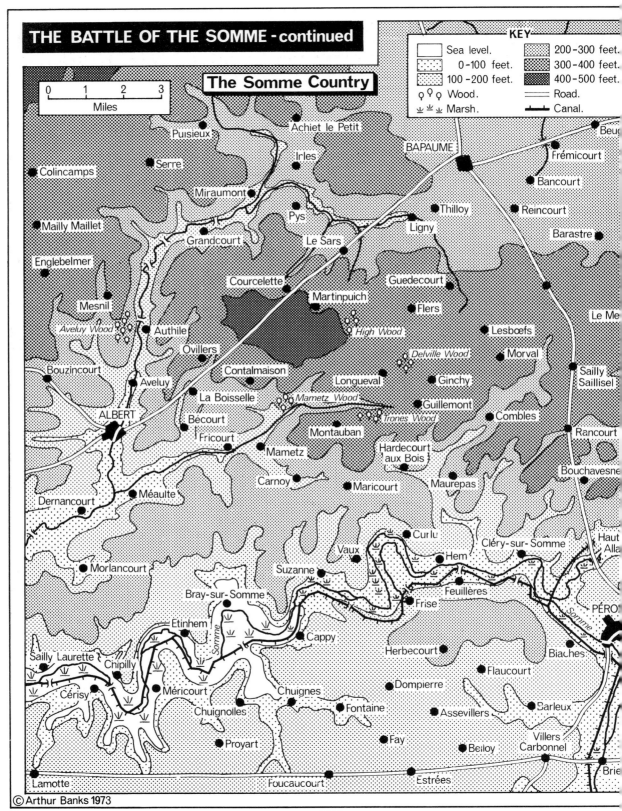

THE BATTLE OF THE SOMME - continued

The Somme Country

KEY

Sea level.
0-100 feet.
100-200 feet.
200-300 feet.
300-400 feet.
400-500 feet.
♀ ♀ ♀ Wood.
⚓ ⚓ ⚓ Marsh.
Road.
Canal.

Miles
0   1   2   3

Puisieux

Achiet le Petit

Irles

BAPAUME

Beug

Frémicourt

Serre

Colincamps

Miraumont

Pys

Thilloy

Reincourt

Bancourt

Mailly Maillet

Grandcourt

Ligny

Barastre

Englebelmer

Le Sars

Courcelette

Guedecourt

Martinpuich

Le Me

Mesnil

Flers

Aveluy Wood

Authile

High Wood

Lesbœufs

Ovillers

Delville Wood

Morval

Bouzincourt

Contalmaison

Longueval

Ginchy

Sailly
Saillisel

Aveluy

La Boisselle

Mametz Wood

Guillemont

Combles

ALBERT

Bécourt

Trones Wood

Rancourt

Fricourt

Montauban

Bouchavesne

Mametz

Hardecourt
aux Bois

Carnoy

Maricourt

Maurepas

Dernancourt

Méaulte

Curlu

Cléry-sur-Somme

Haut
Alla

Vaux

Hem

Morlancourt

Suzanne

Feuillères

Bray-sur-Somme

Frise

PÉRO

Etinhem

Cappy

Somme

Herbecourt

Biaches

Sailly Laurette

Chipilly

Flaucourt

Cérisy

Méricourt

Chuignes

Dompierre

Barleux

Chuignolles

Fontaine

Assevillers

Proyart

Fay

Beiloy

Villers
Carbonnel

Lamotte

Foucaucourt

Estrées

Brie

© Arthur Banks 1973

156

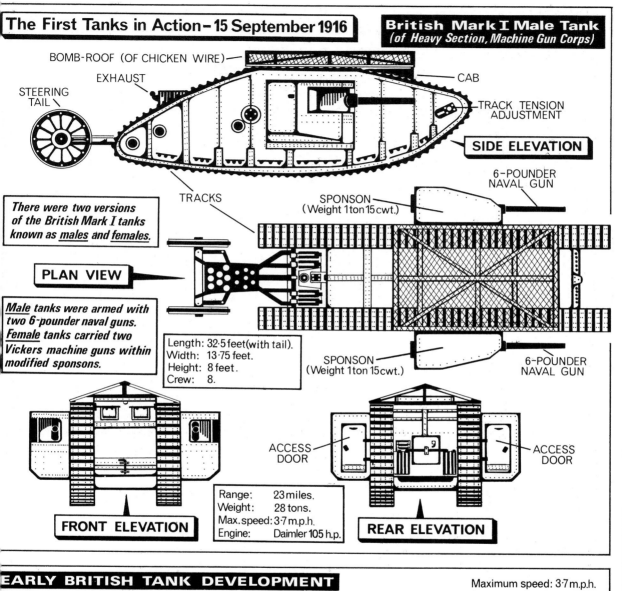

The First Tanks in Action – 15 September 1916

British Mark I Male Tank
(of Heavy Section, Machine Gun Corps)

BOMB-ROOF (OF CHICKEN WIRE)

EXHAUST

CAB

STEERING TAIL

TRACK TENSION ADJUSTMENT

SIDE ELEVATION

TRACKS

There were two versions of the British Mark I tanks known as <u>males</u> and <u>females</u>.

PLAN VIEW

SPONSON (Weight 1 ton 15 cwt.)

6-POUNDER NAVAL GUN

<u>Male</u> tanks were armed with two 6-pounder naval guns. <u>Female</u> tanks carried two Vickers machine guns within modified sponsons.

Length: 32·5 feet (with tail).
Width: 13·75 feet.
Height: 8 feet.
Crew: 8.

SPONSON (Weight 1 ton 15 cwt.)

6-POUNDER NAVAL GUN

ACCESS DOOR

ACCESS DOOR

FRONT ELEVATION

Range: 23 miles.
Weight: 28 tons.
Max. speed: 3·7 m.p.h.
Engine: Daimler 105 h.p.

REAR ELEVATION

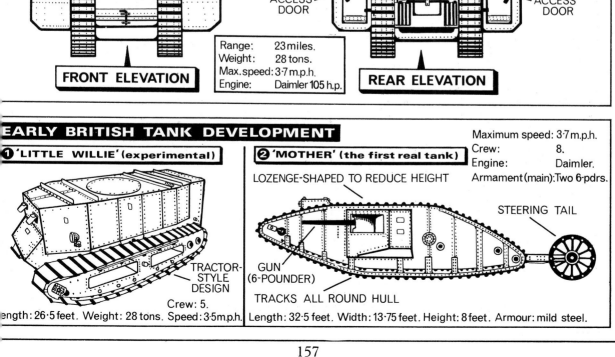

EARLY BRITISH TANK DEVELOPMENT

Maximum speed: 3·7 m.p.h.
Crew: 8.
Engine: Daimler.
Armament (main): Two 6-pdrs.

❶ 'LITTLE WILLIE' (experimental)

TRACTOR-STYLE DESIGN

Crew: 5.
Length: 26·5 feet. Weight: 28 tons. Speed: 3·5 m.p.h.

❷ 'MOTHER' (the first real tank)

LOZENGE-SHAPED TO REDUCE HEIGHT

STEERING TAIL

GUN (6-POUNDER)

TRACKS ALL ROUND HULL

Length: 32·5 feet. Width: 13·75 feet. Height: 8 feet. Armour: mild steel.

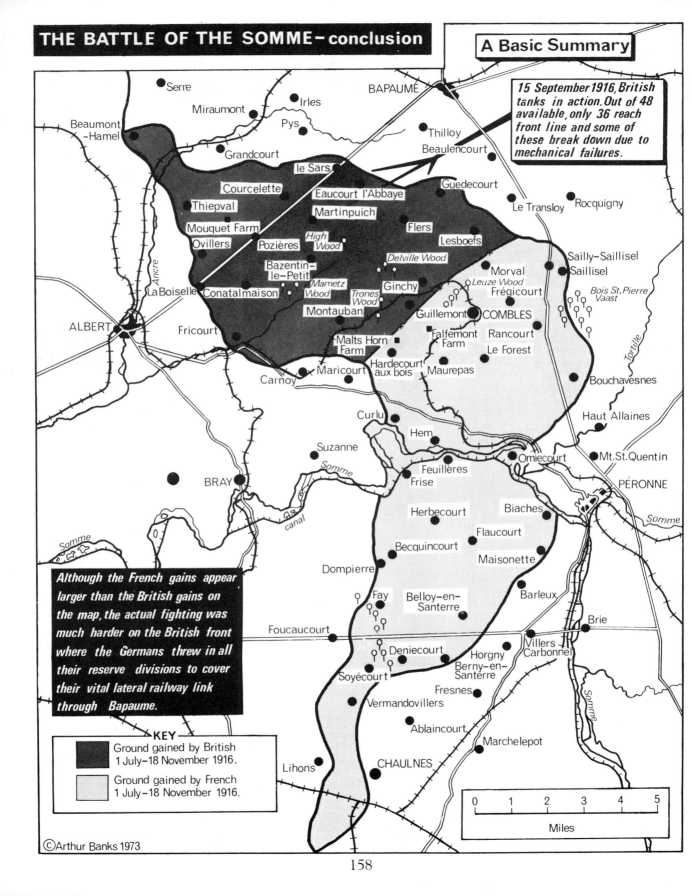

THE BATTLE OF THE SOMME – conclusion

A Basic Summary

15 September 1916, British tanks in action. Out of 48 available, only 36 reach front line and some of these break down due to mechanical failures.

Although the French gains appear larger than the British gains on the map, the actual fighting was much harder on the British front where the Germans threw in all their reserve divisions to cover their vital lateral railway link through Bapaume.

KEY

Ground gained by British 1 July–18 November 1916.

Ground gained by French 1 July–18 November 1916.

Serre
Miraumont
Irles
Pys
BAPAUME
Beaumont-Hamel
Grandcourt
Thilloy
Beaulencourt
le Sars
Guedecourt
Courcelette
Eaucourt l'Abbaye
Le Transloy
Rocquigny
Thiepval
Martinpuich
Mouquet Farm
Flers
Ovillers
Pozières
High Wood
Lesboefs
Sailly-Saillisel
Saillisel
Bazentin-le-Petit
Delville Wood
Morval
Bois St. Pierre Vaast
Mametz Wood
Ginchy
Leuze Wood
Frégicourt
La Boiselle
Conatalmaison
Trones Wood
Montauban
Guillemont
COMBLES
ALBERT
Fricourt
Malts Horn Farm
Falfemont Farm
Rancourt
Le Forest
Bouchavesnes
Maricourt
Hardecourt aux bois
Maurepas
Carnoy
Haut Allaines
Curlu
Hem
Suzanne
Omiecourt
Mt. St. Quentin
Somme
BRAY
Feuillères
Frise
PÉRONNE
Somme
canal
Herbecourt
Biaches
Somme
Flaucourt
Becquincourt
Maisonette
Dompierre
Barleux
Fay
Belloy-en-Santerre
Brie
Foucaucourt
Villers Carbonnel
Deniecourt
Horgny
Berny-en-Santerre
Soyécourt
Fresnes
Somme
Vermandovillers
Lihons
Ablaincourt
Marchelepot
CHAULNES

0 1 2 3 4 5
Miles

©Arthur Banks 1973

158

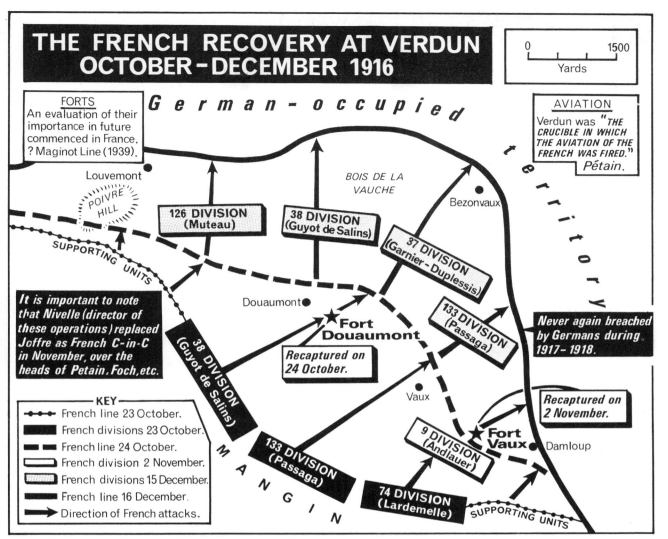

THE FRENCH RECOVERY AT VERDUN OCTOBER – DECEMBER 1916

0 — 1500
Yards

G e r m a n - o c c u p i e d

FORTS
An evaluation of their importance in future commenced in France. ? Maginot Line (1939).

AVIATION
Verdun was *"THE CRUCIBLE IN WHICH THE AVIATION OF THE FRENCH WAS FIRED."*
Pétain.

t e r r i t o r y

Louvemont

POIVRE HILL

BOIS DE LA VAUCHE

Bezonvaux

SUPPORTING UNITS

126 DIVISION (Muteau)

38 DIVISION (Guyot de Salins)

37 DIVISION (Garnier - Duplessis)

It is important to note that Nivelle (director of these operations) replaced Joffre as French C-in-C in November, over the heads of Petain, Foch, etc.

Douaumont

★ **Fort Douaumont**

133 DIVISION (Passaga)

38 DIVISION (Guyot de Salins)

Recaptured on 24 October.

Never again breached by Germans during 1917 – 1918.

Vaux

Recaptured on 2 November.

9 DIVISION (Andlauer)

★ **Fort Vaux**

Damloup

― KEY ―
- •―•―• French line 23 October.
- ▮ French divisions 23 October.
- ▬ ▬ French line 24 October.
- ▭ French division 2 November.
- ▒ French divisions 15 December.
- ▬ French line 16 December.
- → Direction of French attacks.

133 DIVISION (Passaga)

74 DIVISION (Lardemelle)

SUPPORTING UNITS

M A N G I N

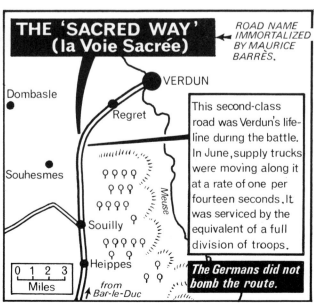

THE 'SACRED WAY' (la Voie Sacrée)

ROAD NAME IMMORTALIZED BY MAURICE BARRÈS.

Dombasle

VERDUN

Regret

Souhesmes

Meuse

Souilly

Heippes

This second-class road was Verdun's lifeline during the battle. In June, supply trucks were moving along it at a rate of one per fourteen seconds. It was serviced by the equivalent of a full division of troops.

The Germans did not bomb the route.

0 1 2 3
Miles

from Bar-le-Duc

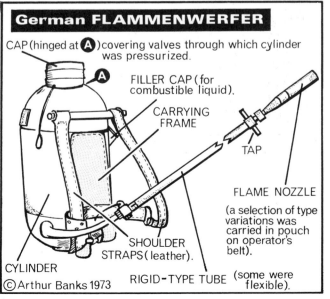

German FLAMMENWERFER

CAP (hinged at Ⓐ) covering valves through which cylinder was pressurized.

FILLER CAP (for combustible liquid).

CARRYING FRAME

TAP

FLAME NOZZLE
(a selection of type variations was carried in pouch on operator's belt).

SHOULDER STRAPS (leather).

RIGID-TYPE TUBE (some were flexible).

CYLINDER

© Arthur Banks 1973

159

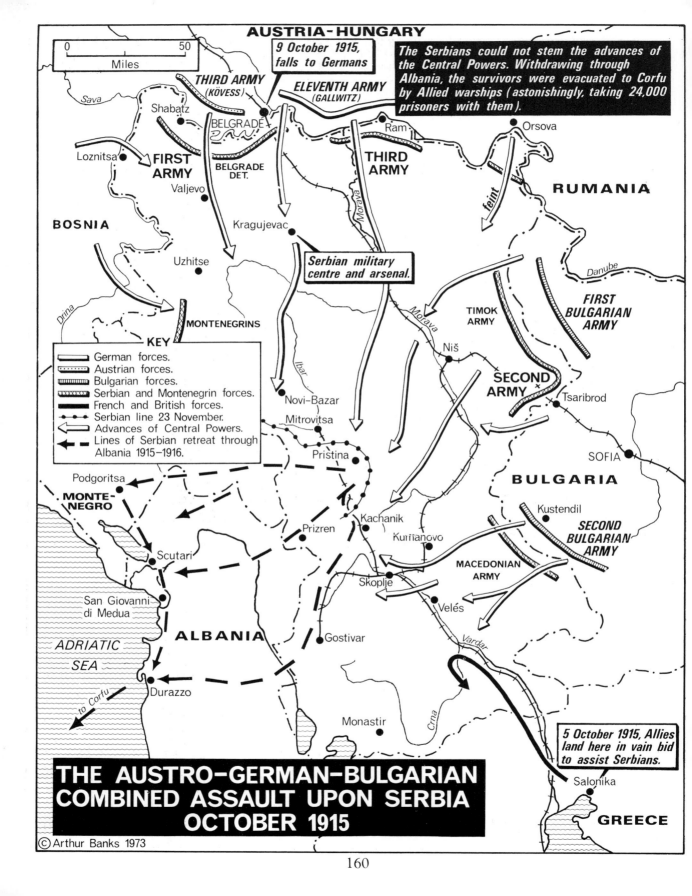

AUSTRIA-HUNGARY

0 ____ 50
Miles

9 October 1915, falls to Germans

The Serbians could not stem the advances of the Central Powers. Withdrawing through Albania, the survivors were evacuated to Corfu by Allied warships (astonishingly, taking 24,000 prisoners with them).

Sava

THIRD ARMY (KÖVESS)

ELEVENTH ARMY (GALLWITZ)

Shabatz

BELGRADE

Ram

Orsova

Loznitsa

FIRST ARMY

BELGRADE DET.

THIRD ARMY

RUMANIA

Valjevo

feint

BOSNIA

Kragujevac

Morava

Uzhitse

Serbian military centre and arsenal.

Danube

TIMOK ARMY

FIRST BULGARIAN ARMY

Drina

MONTENEGRINS

Ibar

Morava

Niš

SECOND ARMY

Tsaribrod

KEY
▭ German forces.
▭ Austrian forces.
▭ Bulgarian forces.
▭ Serbian and Montenegrin forces.
▬ French and British forces.
•••• Serbian line 23 November.
⇦ Advances of Central Powers.
◄-- Lines of Serbian retreat through Albania 1915–1916.

SOFIA

Novi-Bazar

BULGARIA

Mitrovitsa

Pristina

Podgoritsa

Kustendil

MONTE-NEGRO

Kachanik

SECOND BULGARIAN ARMY

Prizren

Kurfianovo

Scutari

MACEDONIAN ARMY

San Giovanni di Medua

Skoplje

Velés

ALBANIA

Gostivar

Vardar

ADRIATIC SEA

to Corfu

Durazzo

Monastir

Crna

5 October 1915, Allies land here in vain bid to assist Serbians.

Salonika

GREECE

THE AUSTRO-GERMAN-BULGARIAN COMBINED ASSAULT UPON SERBIA OCTOBER 1915

© Arthur Banks 1973

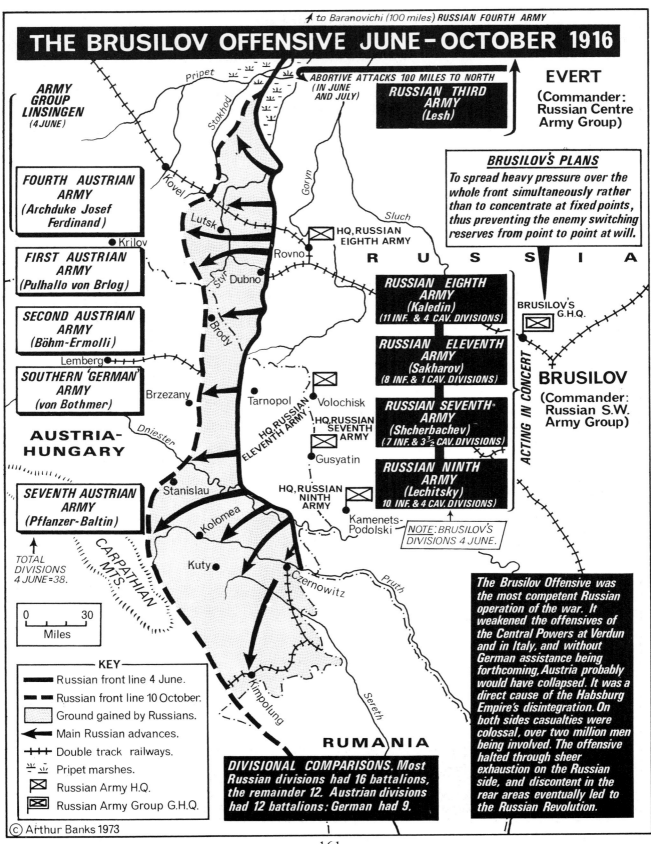

THE BRUSILOV OFFENSIVE JUNE–OCTOBER 1916

to Baranovichi (100 miles) RUSSIAN FOURTH ARMY

ABORTIVE ATTACKS 100 MILES TO NORTH (IN JUNE AND JULY)

EVERT (Commander: Russian Centre Army Group)

RUSSIAN THIRD ARMY (Lesh)

ARMY GROUP LINSINGEN (4 JUNE)

FOURTH AUSTRIAN ARMY (Archduke Josef Ferdinand)

FIRST AUSTRIAN ARMY (Pulhallo von Brlog)

SECOND AUSTRIAN ARMY (Böhm-Ermolli)

SOUTHERN 'GERMAN' ARMY (von Bothmer)

AUSTRIA-HUNGARY

SEVENTH AUSTRIAN ARMY (Pflanzer-Baltin)

TOTAL DIVISIONS 4 JUNE = 38.

CARPATHIAN MTS.

BRUSILOV'S PLANS
To spread heavy pressure over the whole front simultaneously rather than to concentrate at fixed points, thus preventing the enemy switching reserves from point to point at will.

R U S S I A

HQ, RUSSIAN EIGHTH ARMY

RUSSIAN EIGHTH ARMY (Kaledin) (11 INF. & 4 CAV. DIVISIONS)

RUSSIAN ELEVENTH ARMY (Sakharov) (8 INF. & 1 CAV. DIVISIONS)

RUSSIAN SEVENTH ARMY (Shcherbachev) (7 INF. & 3½ CAV. DIVISIONS)

RUSSIAN NINTH ARMY (Lechitsky) (10 INF. & 4 CAV. DIVISIONS)

HQ, RUSSIAN ELEVENTH ARMY

HQ, RUSSIAN SEVENTH ARMY

HQ, RUSSIAN NINTH ARMY

BRUSILOV'S G.H.Q.

ACTING IN CONCERT

BRUSILOV (Commander: Russian S.W. Army Group)

NOTE: BRUSILOV'S DIVISIONS 4 JUNE.

Kovel
Lutsk
Krilov
Rovno
Dubno
Brody
Lemberg
Brzezany
Tarnopol
Volochisk
Gusyatin
Stanislau
Kamenets-Podolski
Kolomea
Kuty
Czernowitz
Kimpolung

Pripet
Stokhod
Goryn
Sluch
Styr
Dniester
Pruth
Sereth

The Brusilov Offensive was the most competent Russian operation of the war. It weakened the offensives of the Central Powers at Verdun and in Italy, and without German assistance being forthcoming, Austria probably would have collapsed. It was a direct cause of the Habsburg Empire's disintegration. On both sides casualties were colossal, over two million men being involved. The offensive halted through sheer exhaustion on the Russian side, and discontent in the rear areas eventually led to the Russian Revolution.

RUMANIA

0   30
Miles

— KEY —
——— Russian front line 4 June.
- - - Russian front line 10 October.
░░░ Ground gained by Russians.
◀ Main Russian advances.
+++ Double track railways.
〜 Pripet marshes.
⊠ Russian Army H.Q.
⊠ Russian Army Group G.H.Q.

© Arthur Banks 1973

DIVISIONAL COMPARISONS. Most Russian divisions had 16 battalions, the remainder 12. Austrian divisions had 12 battalions: German had 9.

THE RUMANIAN CAMPAIGN 1916

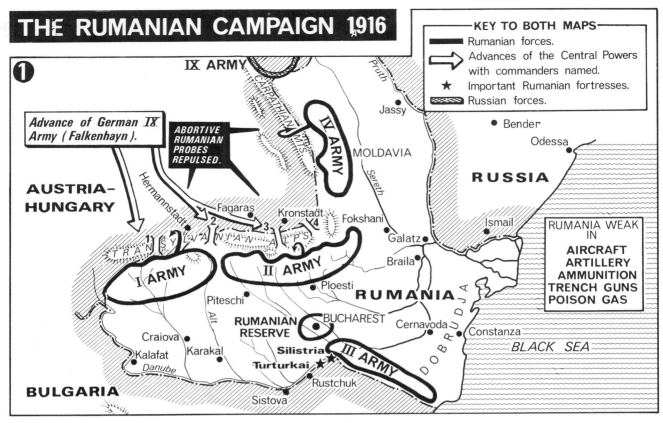

KEY TO BOTH MAPS
- ▬▬ Rumanian forces.
- ⇨ Advances of the Central Powers with commanders named.
- ★ Important Rumanian fortresses.
- ▨ Russian forces.

❶

IX ARMY

Advance of German IX. Army (Falkenhayn).

ABORTIVE RUMANIAN PROBES REPULSED.

IV ARMY

MOLDAVIA

Jassy

Bender

Odessa

RUSSIA

AUSTRIA-HUNGARY

Hermannstadt

Fagaras

2

Kronstadt

3

4

Fokshani

Galatz

Braila

Ismail

RUMANIA WEAK IN AIRCRAFT ARTILLERY AMMUNITION TRENCH GUNS POISON GAS

1

TRANSYLVANIAN ALPS

I ARMY

II ARMY

Piteschi

Ploesti

Craiova

RUMANIAN RESERVE

BUCHAREST

Cernavoda

Constanza

Karakal

Silistria
Turturkai

III ARMY

DOBRUDJA

BLACK SEA

Kalafat

Danube

Rustchuk

BULGARIA

Sistova

---

❷

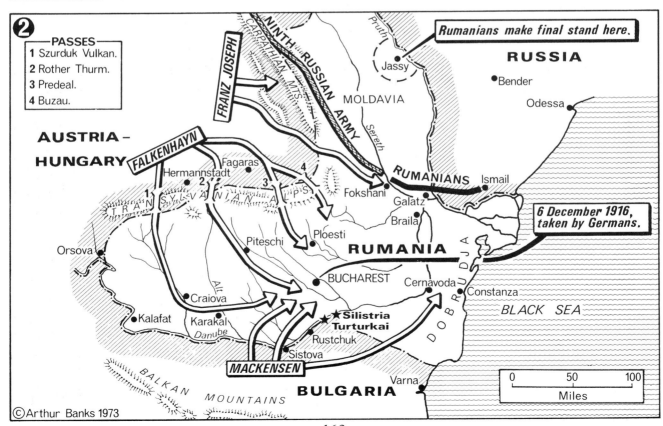

PASSES
1 Szurduk Vulkan.
2 Rother Thurm.
3 Predeal.
4 Buzau.

FRANZ JOSEPH

NINTH RUSSIAN ARMY

Pruth

Rumanians make final stand here.

Jassy

RUSSIA

Bender

Odessa

MOLDAVIA

AUSTRIA-HUNGARY

FALKENHAYN

Hermannstadt

Fagaras

2

3

4

Sereth

Fokshani

RUMANIANS

Ismail

1

TRANSYLVANIAN ALPS

Galatz

Braila

Ploesti

Piteschi

RUMANIA

6 December 1916, taken by Germans.

Orsova

BUCHAREST

Cernavoda

Constanza

Craiova

Karakal

Kalafat

Danube

★ **Silistria Turturkai**

DOBRUDJA

BLACK SEA

Rustchuk

Sistova

MACKENSEN

BALKAN MOUNTAINS

BULGARIA

Varna

0   50   100
Miles

© Arthur Banks 1973

162

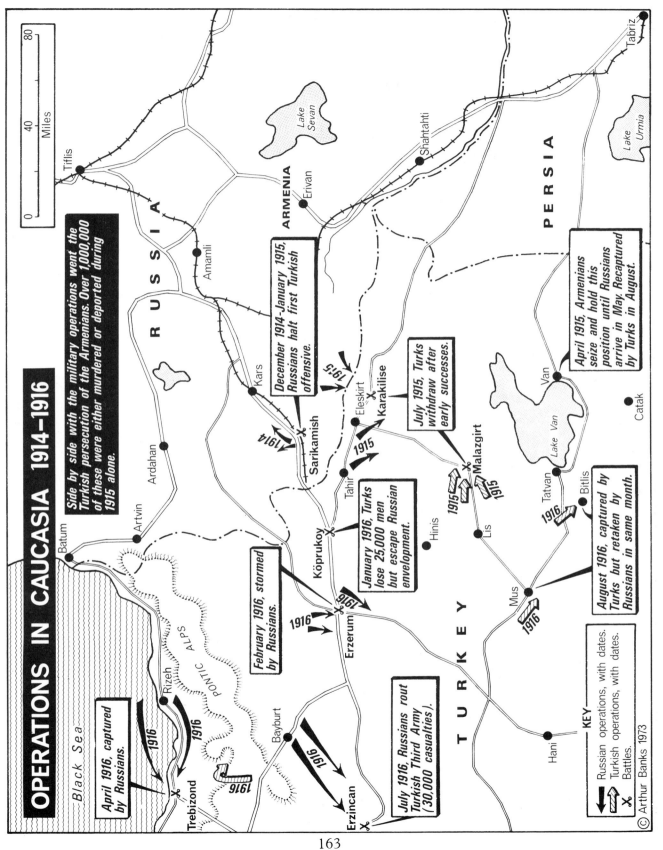

OPERATIONS IN CAUCASIA 1914–1916

Side by side with the military operations went the Turkish persecution of the Armenians. Over 1,000,000 of these were either murdered or deported during 1915 alone.

80
40
0
Miles

Black Sea

RUSSIA

ARMENIA

PERSIA

TURKEY

PONTIC ALPS

Lake Sevan

Lake Van

Lake Urmia

Tiflis
Amamli
Kars
Ardahan
Artvin
Batum
Rizeh
Trebizond
Bayburt
Erzincan
Erzerum
Köprukoy
Tahir
Sarikamish
Eleskirt
Karakilise
Erivan
Shantahti
Malazgirt
Hinis
Lis
Tatvan
Van
Bitlis
Mus
Catak
Hani
Tabriz

December 1914–January 1915, Russians halt first Turkish offensive.

July 1915, Turks withdraw after early successes.

April 1915, Armenians seize and hold this position until Russians arrive in May. Recaptured by Turks in August.

January 1916, Turks lose 25,000 men but escape Russian envelopment.

February 1916, stormed by Russians.

August 1916, captured by Turks but retaken by Russians in same month.

July 1916, Russians rout Turkish Third Army (30,000 casualties).

April 1916, captured by Russians.

1914
1915
1916

KEY
Russian operations, with dates.
Turkish operations, with dates.
Battles.

© Arthur Banks 1973

163

THE WAR IN 1917

The wasteful slaughter of 1916 was followed by a year of astonishing political change and upheaval. When, on 1 February 1917, the Germans announced a resumption of unrestricted U-Boat warfare, they knew that they ran the risk of bringing America into the conflict, but they calculated that they could eliminate Russia and France on land and starve the British into surrender before the effects of American belligerency were felt in Europe. In the event, the United States was finally brought to declare war on Germany in April 1917 as much by evidence of German intrigues in Mexico (the Zimmermann telegram) as by the submarine (see page 214). The fall of the Tsarist autocracy and the establishment of a democratic Provisional Government in Russia (page 177) made it easier for Congress to accept the idea of war; but British and French hopes that the Provisional Government would purge corruption and make Russia again an efficient military partner proved ill-founded. The so-called Kerensky Offensive of July 1917 soon petered out (page 176); the Russian people were apathetic and anxious only for 'peace and bread'. When in the first week of November Lenin's Bolsheviks seized power in Petrograd, Russia virtually withdrew from the war, opened negotiations with Germany and her allies, and concluded a separate peace (the Treaty of Brest-Litovsk, March 1918) by which Russia surrendered Poland, the Ukraine, the Baltic provinces, Finland and much of the Caucasus (see page 178).

Bolshevik propaganda contributed to unrest elsewhere in the Allied camp, notably among the French and Russians in Macedonia (page 204) and among mutinous French units on the Western Front (page 168). Although there was disaffection among the Austro-Hungarian forces, their morale was strengthened by the combined Austro-German victory over the Italians at Caporetto (page 202), in which the rout was only halted by the arrival of British and French reinforcements. The principal successes of the Allies during 1917 were in Asia. The Tigris port of Kut (where the first British expedition of Mesopotamia had been forced to surrender to the Turks in the spring of 1916) was retaken in February and Baghdad captured a fortnight later. The most dramatic victory was won by Allenby in Palestine, enabling the British to enter Jerusalem at the beginning of December. (For Mesopotamia see pages 206–210 and for Palestine see pages 211–213.)

On the Western Front Nivelle had succeeded Joffre in the second week of December 1916. The new commander-in-chief planned an offensive towards Laon, and persisted in his project even when the Germans withdrew to stronger defensive positions. The offensive was a disaster; Nivelle was replaced by Pétain, who with great skill gradually restored the confidence of the French soldiery. But there was little the French Army could do for the remainder of the year. Haig hoped to defeat the Germans in Flanders, a policy which appealed to the British naval chiefs, since it would have eliminated the U-boat bases on the Belgian coast. Heavy bombardments and rain made the ground impassable, and the 'third battle of Ypres' came to a disastrous halt in the mud of Passchendaele. Earlier in the year the Canadians gained a striking success at Vimy Ridge, north-east of Arras, and the British Second Army (which included an Australian and New Zealand Corps) won a comprehensive local victory at Messines, south of Ypres. Potentially the most significant military development of the year was the breakthrough by massed British tanks at Cambrai in November, but Haig by now did not have sufficient reserves to consolidate the gains made by the tanks, and the Germans recovered much of the land they had lost in a counter-attack ten days later.

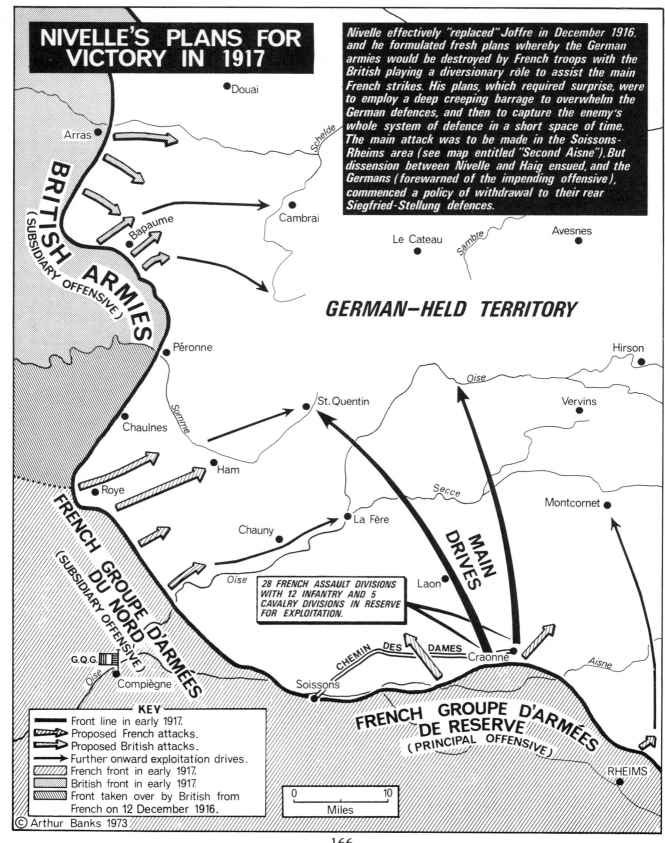

NIVELLE'S PLANS FOR VICTORY IN 1917

Nivelle effectively "replaced" Joffre in December 1916, and he formulated fresh plans whereby the German armies would be destroyed by French troops with the British playing a diversionary rôle to assist the main French strikes. His plans, which required surprise, were to employ a deep creeping barrage to overwhelm the German defences, and then to capture the enemy's whole system of defence in a short space of time. The main attack was to be made in the Soissons-Rheims area (see map entitled "Second Aisne"). But dissension between Nivelle and Haig ensued, and the Germans (forewarned of the impending offensive), commenced a policy of withdrawal to their rear Siegfried-Stellung defences.

Douai

Arras

Schelde

BRITISH ARMIES (SUBSIDIARY OFFENSIVE)

Bapaume

Cambrai

GERMAN–HELD TERRITORY

Le Cateau

Sambre

Avesnes

Péronne

Hirson

Oise

St. Quentin

Vervins

Chaulnes

Somme

Ham

Secce

Montcornet

Roye

FRENCH GROUPE D'ARMÉES DU NORD (SUBSIDIARY OFFENSIVE)

Chauny

La Fère

Oise

MAIN DRIVES

Laon

28 FRENCH ASSAULT DIVISIONS WITH 12 INFANTRY AND 5 CAVALRY DIVISIONS IN RESERVE FOR EXPLOITATION.

G.Q.G.

Oise

Compiègne

CHEMIN DES DAMES

Craonne

Aisne

Soissons

FRENCH GROUPE D'ARMÉES DE RESERVE (PRINCIPAL OFFENSIVE)

KEY
— Front line in early 1917.
⬎ Proposed French attacks.
⬎ Proposed British attacks.
→ Further onward exploitation drives.
▨ French front in early 1917.
▨ British front in early 1917.
▨ Front taken over by British from French on 12 December 1916.

© Arthur Banks 1973

RHEIMS

0   10
Miles

THE GERMAN WITHDRAWAL FEBRUARY–APRIL 1917

0 — 10
Miles

In early 1917, German strategy on the Western Front was defensive (in contrast to her U-boat naval offensive), and she decided to shorten her line by a planned withdrawal to a new prepared position (Siegfried-Stellung). The area evacuated was devastated, towns and villages razed, roads destroyed, woods levelled, and water sources poisoned.

THE GERMAN CODE-NAME FOR THIS OPERATION WAS "ALBERICH" (THE DECEITFUL DWARF OF THE NIBELUNG LEGEND).

Note: through a misunderstanding of a German deserter's statement by Allied Intelligence, the Siegfried-Stellung was misnamed "The Hindenburg Line".

Scarpe
Ancre
Somme
Avre
Schelde
Omignon
Oise
Serre
Oise
Aisne

• Arras
• Neuville Vitasse
• Cambrai
• Bapaume
• Le Catelet
• Péronne
• Vermand
• St. Quentin
• Ham
• Roye
• La Fère
• Chauny
• Noyon
• Laon
• Allemant
• Filain
• Cerny
• Laffaux
• Vailly
• Missy
• Soissons

KEY
- - - German front line 25 February 1917.
▲▲▲ German front line 5 April 1917.
▒▒ Area evacuated by Germans.

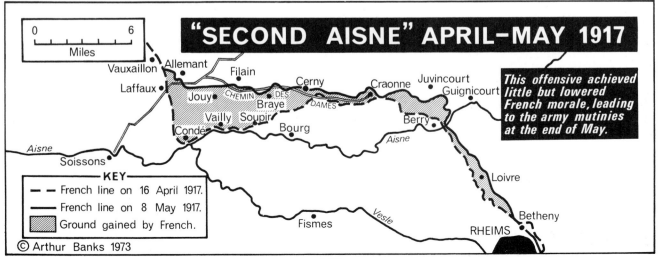

"SECOND AISNE" APRIL–MAY 1917

0 — 6
Miles

This offensive achieved little but lowered French morale, leading to the army mutinies at the end of May.

Aisne
Aisne
Vesle

• Vauxaillon
• Allemant
• Filain
• Cerny
• Craonne
• Juvincourt
• Guignicourt
• Laffaux
• Jouy
CHEMIN DES DAMES
• Braye
• Vailly Soupir
• Condé
• Bourg
• Berry
• Soissons
• Loivre
• Betheny
• Fismes
RHEIMS

KEY
- - - French line on 16 April 1917.
—— French line on 8 May 1917.
▨▨ Ground gained by French.

© Arthur Banks 1973

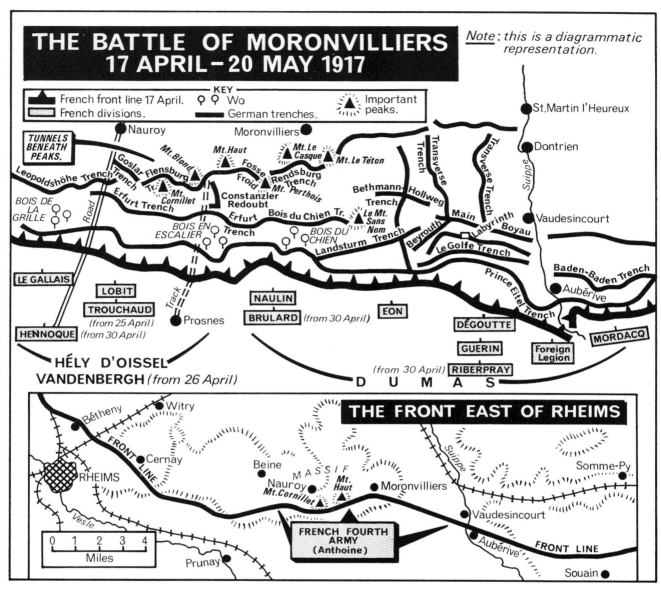

THE BATTLE OF MORONVILLIERS
17 APRIL – 20 MAY 1917

Note: this is a diagrammatic representation.

KEY

▲ French front line 17 April. ⚲⚲ Wo ▲ Important peaks.
▨ French divisions. ▬ German trenches.

St.Martin l'Heureux

Nauroy

Moronvilliers

Dontrien

TUNNELS BENEATH PEAKS.

Mt.Blond Mt.Haut Mt.Le Casque Mt.Le Téton

Goslar Trench Flensburg Trench Fosse Froid Rendsburg Trench Mt.Perthois

Leopoldshöhe Trench

Transverse Trench Transverse Trench

Suippe

Erfurt Trench Mt.Cornillet Constanzler Redoubt Bethmann-Hollweg Trench

Vaudesincourt

BOIS DE LA GRILLE Road Erfurt Trench Bois du Chien Tr. Le Mt. Sans Nom Main

BOIS EN ESCALIER *BOIS DU CHIEN* Beyrouth Labyrinth Boyau

Landsturm Trench Le Golfe Trench

Baden-Baden Trench

LE GALLAIS Track Prince Eitel Trench Aubérive

LOBIT **NAULIN** **EON**

TROUCHAUD **BRULARD** *(from 30 April)* **DÉGOUTTE** **MORDACQ**

(from 25 April) *(from 30 April)* Prosnes

HENNOQUE **GUERIN** **Foreign Legion**

HÉLY D'OISSEL **RIBERPRAY**
VANDENBERGH *(from 26 April)* *(from 30 April)* D U M A S

THE FRONT EAST OF RHEIMS

Bétheny Witry

Cernay **FRONT LINE**

RHEIMS Beine

Somme-Py

M A S S I F Nauroy Mt.Haut Moronvilliers

Mt.Cornillet

Vesle Suippe

Vaudesincourt

FRENCH FOURTH ARMY (Anthoine) Aubérive **FRONT LINE**

0 1 2 3 4
Miles

Prunay Souain

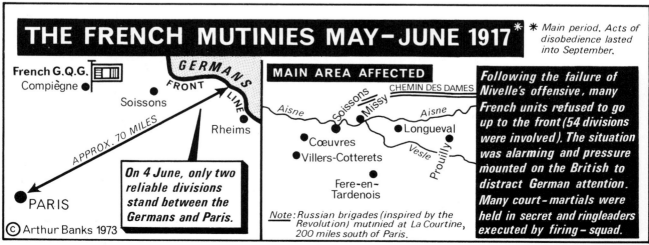

THE FRENCH MUTINIES MAY – JUNE 1917

* *Main period. Acts of disobedience lasted into September.*

French G.Q.G.
Compiègne

GERMANS FRONT LINE

Soissons

APPROX. 70 MILES

Rheims

On 4 June, only two reliable divisions stand between the Germans and Paris.

PARIS

© Arthur Banks 1973

MAIN AREA AFFECTED

CHEMIN DES DAMES

Aisne Soissons Missy Aisne

Cœuvres Longueval

Villers-Cotterets Vesle Prouilly

Fere-en-Tardenois

Note: Russian brigades (inspired by the Revolution) mutinied at La Courtine, 200 miles south of Paris.

Following the failure of Nivelle's offensive, many French units refused to go up to the front (54 divisions were involved). The situation was alarming and pressure mounted on the British to distract German attention. Many court-martials were held in secret and ringleaders executed by firing-squad.

168

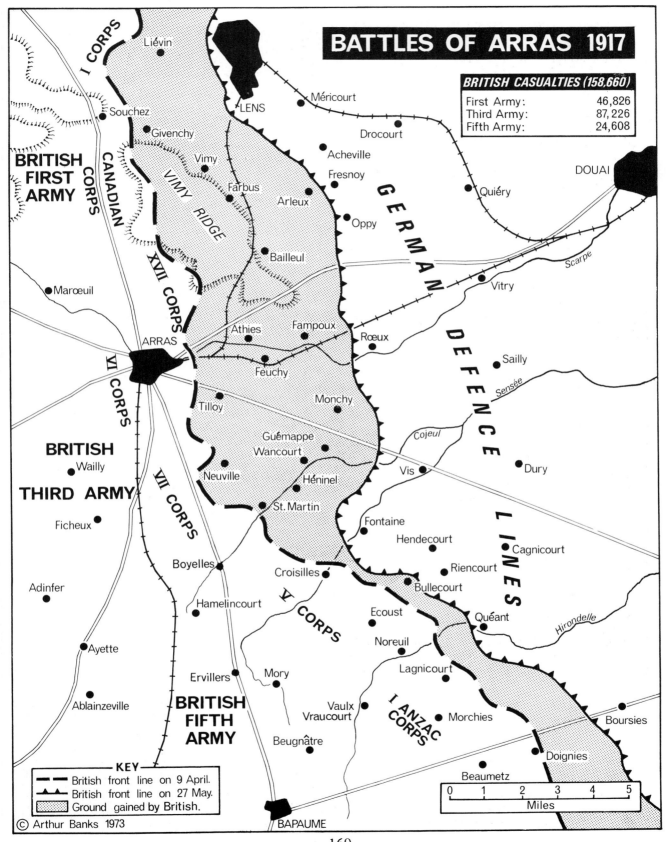

BATTLES OF ARRAS 1917

BRITISH CASUALTIES (158,660)

First Army:	46,826
Third Army:	87,226
Fifth Army:	24,608

I CORPS

Liévin

Méricourt

LENS

Drocourt

BRITISH FIRST ARMY

CANADIAN CORPS

Souchez

Givenchy

Vimy

VIMY RIDGE

Farbus

Arleux

Acheville

Fresnoy

DOUAI

Quiéry

XVII CORPS

Maroeuil

Bailleul

Oppy

GERMAN

Scarpe

Vitry

Athies

Fampoux

Roeux

DEFENCE

Sailly

ARRAS

VI CORPS

Feuchy

Sensée

Tilloy

Monchy

Cojeul

BRITISH

Wailly

Guémappe
Wancourt

Vis

Dury

THIRD ARMY

VII CORPS

Neuville

Héninel

LINES

Ficheux

St. Martin

Fontaine

Hendecourt

Cagnicourt

Adinfer

Boyelles

Croisilles

Riencourt

Bullecourt

Hirondelle

Hamelincourt

Ecoust

Quéant

Ayette

V CORPS

Noreuil

Ervillers

Mory

Lagnicourt

Ablainzeville

BRITISH FIFTH ARMY

Vaulx
Vraucourt

I ANZAC CORPS

Morchies

Boursies

Beugnâtre

Doignies

KEY

- – – British front line on 9 April.
- ▲▲▲ British front line on 27 May.
- ▓ Ground gained by British.

Beaumetz

0	1	2	3	4	5
Miles

© Arthur Banks 1973

BAPAUME

169

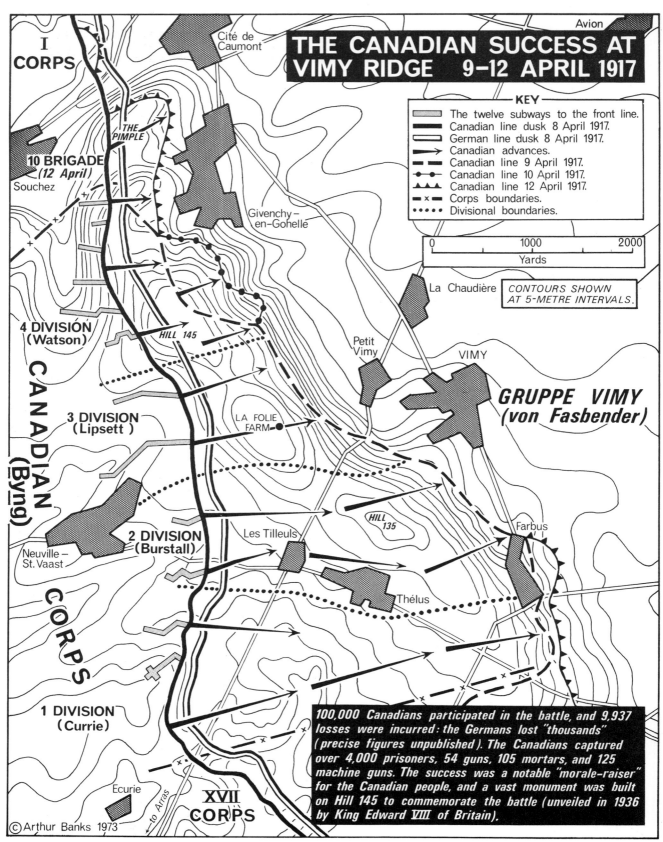

THE CANADIAN SUCCESS AT VIMY RIDGE 9–12 APRIL 1917

I CORPS

Cité de Caumont

Avion

KEY
- The twelve subways to the front line.
- Canadian line dusk 8 April 1917.
- German line dusk 8 April 1917.
- Canadian advances.
- Canadian line 9 April 1917.
- Canadian line 10 April 1917.
- Canadian line 12 April 1917.
- Corps boundaries.
- Divisional boundaries.

0   1000   2000
Yards

CONTOURS SHOWN AT 5-METRE INTERVALS.

THE PIMPLE

10 BRIGADE *(12 April)*

Souchez

Givenchy–en-Gohelle

La Chaudière

4 DIVISION (Watson)

HILL 145

Petit Vimy

VIMY

GRUPPE VIMY (von Fasbender)

3 DIVISION (Lipsett)

LA FOLIE FARM

CANADIAN (Byng)

2 DIVISION (Burstall)

Les Tilleuls

HILL 135

Farbus

Neuville–St. Vaast

Thélus

CORPS

1 DIVISION (Currie)

Ecurie

to Aras

XVII CORPS

100,000 Canadians participated in the battle, and 9,937 losses were incurred: the Germans lost "thousands" (precise figures unpublished). The Canadians captured over 4,000 prisoners, 54 guns, 105 mortars, and 125 machine guns. The success was a notable "morale-raiser" for the Canadian people, and a vast monument was built on Hill 145 to commemorate the battle (unveiled in 1936 by King Edward VIII of Britain).

© Arthur Banks 1973

170

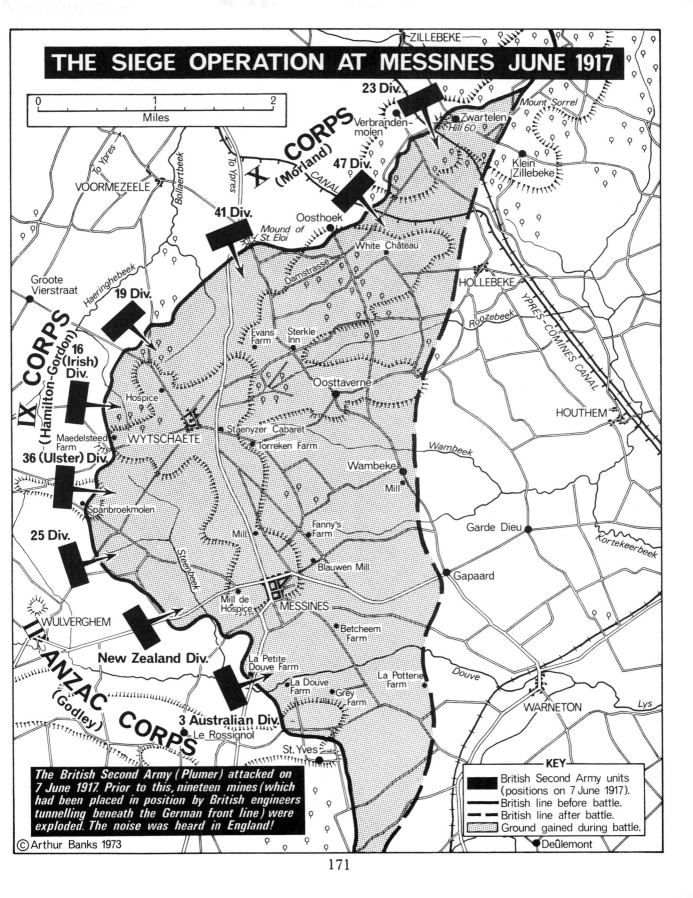

THE SIEGE OPERATION AT MESSINES JUNE 1917

ZILLEBEKE

0   1   2
Miles

X CORPS (Morland)

23 Div.

Mount Sorrel

Zwartelen
Hill 60

47 Div.

Verbranden-molen

Klein Zillebeke

To Ypres

VOORMEZEELE

CANAL

41 Div.

Oosthoek

Mound of St. Eloi

White Château

Damstrasse

HOLLEBEKE

Groote Vierstraat

Haeringhebeek

19 Div.

Evans Farm

Sterkle Inn

Roozebeek

YPRES-COMINES CANAL

HOUTHEM

IX CORPS (Hamilton-Gordon)

16 (Irish) Div.

Hospice

Oosttaverne

Maedelsteed Farm

WYTSCHAETE

Staenyzer Cabaret

Torreken Farm

Wambeek

Wambeke

36 (Ulster) Div.

Mill

Spanbroekmolen

Garde Dieu

Kortekeerbeek

25 Div.

Mill

Fanny's Farm

Steenbeek

Blauwen Mill

Gapaard

WULVERGHEM

Mill de Hospice

MESSINES

Betcheem Farm

La Petite Douve Farm

Douve

II ANZAC CORPS (Godley)

New Zealand Div.

La Douve Farm

Grey Farm

La Potterie Farm

WARNETON

Lys

3 Australian Div.

Le Rossignol

St. Yves

The British Second Army (Plumer) attacked on 7 June 1917. Prior to this, nineteen mines (which had been placed in position by British engineers tunnelling beneath the German front line) were exploded. The noise was heard in England!

© Arthur Banks 1973

KEY

■ British Second Army units (positions on 7 June 1917).
— British line before battle.
--- British line after battle.
░ Ground gained during battle.

• Deûlemont

171

BRITISH PLANS FOR "WIPERS THREE" 1917

© Arthur Banks 1973

ALLIED DISPOSITIONS

- **N** Allied naval forces.
- **4** British Fourth Army.
- **B** Belgians.
- **F** French.
- **5** British Fifth Army.
- **2** British Second Army.

Haig (secretly under intense French pressure to distract German attention from their mutinous sectors) outlined these plans to a meeting of the Cabinet Committee on War Policy in London on 21 June. Jellicoe stressed the German U-boat threat: Haig stated that Bruges was his main objective.

NORTH SEA

NOTE: IN FACT, THESE WERE SHORT-RANGE CRAFT.

U-BOATS

ZEEBRUGGE

DUNES

OSTEND

U-BOATS

GERMAN FLANDERS SUBMARINE BASE.

U-BOATS

Middelkerke

FEN COUNTRY

3 BRUGES

Nieuport

DUNES

Yser (canalised)

Couckelaere

STRATEGIC

Dixmude

2

Thourout
Cortemarck

RAILWAY

To Ghent (possible Fourth Objective).

Aeltre

Yser

Staden

ROULERS

Thielt

LINE

Lys

Passchendaele

RIDGE

YPRES

1

Gheluvelt

STIRLING CASTLE (chateau)

Menin

COURTRAI

Hooge

Known to British troops as "Wipers."

Wytschaete

Messines

Comines

Warneton

TOURCOING

ROUBAIX

Lys

Armentières

LILLE

0	5	10

Miles

KEY

- ▬▬ Allied front line 21 June.
- ▓ Allied-held territory.
- **1**➤ Opening assault.
- ▬ ▬ Haig's First Objective.
- **2**➤ "Follow-up" assault.
- ▥▥▥ Haig's Second Objective.
- **3**➤ Main concentrated attack.
- ▒ Haig's Third (Main) Objective.
- ⟹ Flankguards along River Lys.
- ⟸ German U-boat routes to sea.
- ┴┴┴ Canals (note Bruges area).

"THIRD YPRES" (PASSCHENDAELE): JULY – NOVEMBER 1917

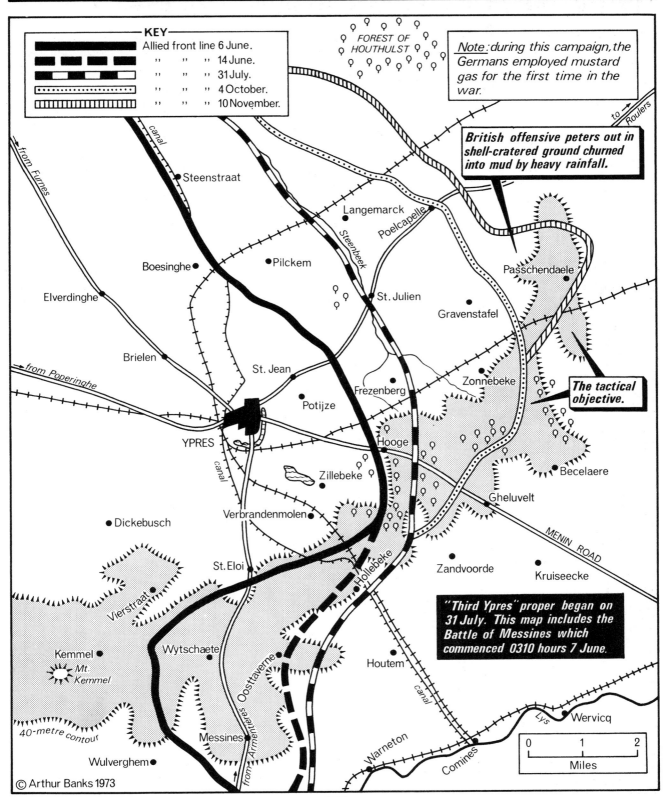

KEY

▬▬▬▬	Allied front line 6 June.
▬ ▬ ▬ ▬	,, ,, ,, 14 June.
▬ □ ▬ □ ▬	,, ,, ,, 31 July.
·····•·····	,, ,, ,, 4 October.
▥▥▥▥▥	,, ,, ,, 10 November.

FOREST OF HOUTHULST

Note: during this campaign, the Germans employed mustard gas for the first time in the war.

to Roulers

British offensive peters out in shell-cratered ground churned into mud by heavy rainfall.

from Furnes

canal

Steenstraat

Langemarck

Poelcapelle

Passchendaele

Boesinghe

Pilckem

Steenbeek

St. Julien

Gravenstafel

Elverdinghe

Brielen

from Poperinghe

St. Jean

Zonnebeke

The tactical objective.

Potijze

Frezenberg

YPRES

Hooge

Zillebeke

Becelaere

canal

Verbrandenmolen

Gheluvelt

Dickebusch

MENIN ROAD

St. Eloi

Hollebeke

Zandvoorde

Kruiseecke

Vierstraat

Oostaverne

"Third Ypres" proper began on 31 July. This map includes the Battle of Messines which commenced 0310 hours 7 June.

Kemmel

Mt. Kemmel

Wytschaete

Houtem

canal

Warneton

Lys

Wervicq

40-metre contour

Messines

Comines

from Armentières

Wulverghem

© Arthur Banks 1973

0	1	2

Miles

THE BRITISH TANK-SPEARHEADED OFFENSIVE AT CAMBRAI 1917

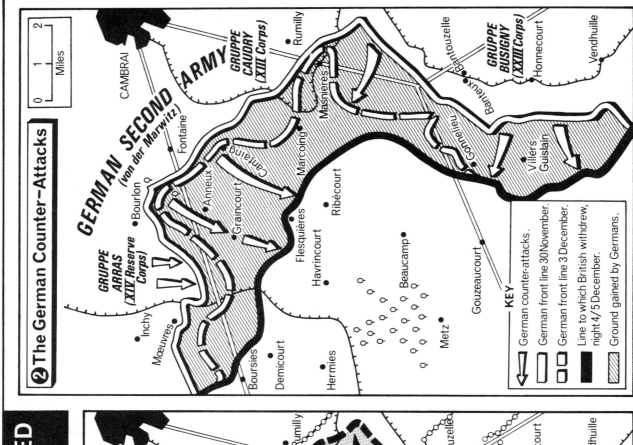

② The German Counter-Attacks

GERMAN SECOND ARMY (von der Marwitz)

GRUPPE CAUDRY (XIII Corps)

GRUPPE BUSIGNY (XXIII Corps)

GRUPPE ARRAS (XIV Reserve Corps)

CAMBRAI

Rumilly · Bantouzelle · Honnecourt · Vendhuille

Masnières · Gonnelieu · Villers Guislain

Fontaine · Marcoing · Cantaing · Ribécourt · Flesquières · Havrincourt · Beaucamp · Gouzeaucourt · Metz

Bourlon · Anneux · Graincourt

Inchy · Mœuvres · Boursies · Demicourt · Hermies

KEY
- German counter-attacks.
- German front line 30 November.
- German front line 3 December.
- Line to which British withdrew, night 4/5 December.
- Ground gained by Germans.

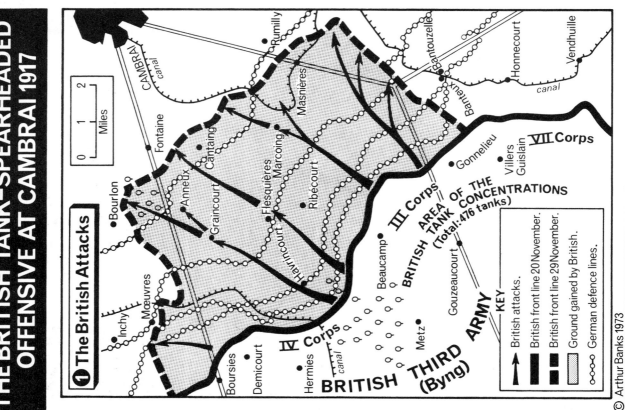

① The British Attacks

CAMBRAI · canal

Rumilly · Bantouzelle · Honnecourt · Vendhuille · canal

Masnières · Banteux

VII Corps

Fontaine · Cantaing · Marcoing · Gonnelieu · Villers Guislain

Bourlon · Anneux · Graincourt · Flesquières · Ribécourt · Havrincourt

III Corps

AREA OF THE BRITISH TANK CONCENTRATIONS (Total: 476 tanks)

IV Corps

Inchy · Mœuvres · Boursies · Demicourt · Hermies · Beaucamp · Gouzeaucourt · Metz · canal

BRITISH THIRD ARMY (Byng)

KEY
- British attacks.
- British front line 20 November.
- British front line 29 November.
- Ground gained by British.
- German defence lines.

© Arthur Banks 1973

TRENCH WARFARE: A TYPICAL SECTION OF FRONT SOUTH-EAST OF ARRAS   FEBRUARY 1917

KEY
- German trenches.
- British trenches.
- Barbed wire entanglements.
- Railway.
- Road.

ARRAS

BRITISH LINES

GERMAN LINES

NO MAN'S LAND

to Douai

to Cambrai

Gosport Trench
Gloucester Terrace
Gosford Terrace
Gourock Trench
Glenarm Lane
Glenelg Lane
Hermes Trench
Guildford Trench
Hertford Trench
Henley Lane
Glengarry Trench
Hove Trench
Havant Lane
Hornsea Lane
Gillingham Trench
Glasgow Trench
Hastings Lane
Harfleur Trench
Gairloch Trench
Gateshead Trench
Galway Trench

Iron St.
Income Tax
Inns of Court
Ivory St.
Interpreter St.
Islington St.
Islington St.
Cemetery Tr.
Ivy St.
Ivy St.
Ings Ave.
Ink Trench
Imp St.
Infantry
Road
Idiot St.
Italy Trench
Idiot St.
India Lane
Ink Trench
Idle St.
Inverness Lane
Iris St.
India Lane
Imperial St.
Iodine
Twenty St.
Nineteen St.
Eighteen St.
Hunter St.
Iceland St.
Ice St.
Hooge St.
Halifax St.
Horace St.
Hunter St.
Hazebrouck St.
Halstead St.
Hooge St.

Note the consecutive lines of defence on the German side with "switch" trenches incorporated to compartment any Allied intrusion. By comparison, the British system was simpler and somewhat haphazard. British names for German trenches are utilized on this map.

© Arthur Banks 1973

175

② Central Powers' Backlash 19 July – 4 August

Despite some early success the Russian offensive petered-out by 16 July. The troops were war-weary and supplies failed to arrive. The Germans brought reinforcements (via their railways) from the west and began a counter-offensive on 19 July. The Russians collapsed under the onslaught and fled back to the River Zbrucz. Only insufficient reserves and logistical factors halted the German advance.

RUSSIANS

Khotin

Zbrucz

Sereth

Pruth

Tarnopol

Dniester

Czernowitz

Zloczow

Strypa

Brzezany

Zlota

Lipa

Kolomea

Pruth

Halicz

Stanislau

Dniester

Kalusz

Lemberg

CENTRAL POWERS

GERMAN RIGA OFFENSIVE 1–5 SEPTEMBER 1917

KEY

0 5 10 15 Miles

German advances.

Russian defences.

German tactics: assault troops by-pass strongpoint which is reduced by the "follow-up" units.

RUSSIAN ESCAPE ROUTE.

road

Dvina

GULF OF RIGA

RIGA

marsh

GERMAN EIGHTH ARMY (von Hutier)

① The Kerensky Offensive 1–16 July

OR "SECOND BRUSILOV"

RUSSIAN UNUSED ARMY

R U S S I A

Zbrucz

ELEVENTH ARMY (Erdelli)

BRUSILOV'S H.Q.

Tarnopol

SEVENTH ARMY (Belkovitch)

Sereth

1 July

AUSTRIA–HUNGARY

Strypa

Dniester

EIGHTH ARMY (Kornilov)

Czernowitz

RUMANIA

Brody

Zloczow

Brzezany

Zlota

Lipa

Jezupol

Kolomea

6 July

Pruth

SÜDARMEE (4 German, 3 Austrian, 1 Turkish div.)

Halicz

Stanislau

KEY

0 30 Miles

GALICIA

AUSTRIAN SECOND ARMY

Lemberg

Russian objective.

Dniester

Kalusz

AUSTRIA THIRD ARMY

AUSTRIAN SEVENTH ARMY

Turning flank move.

Russian armies.

Russian advances.

Extent of main Russian advance 16 July.

Extent of Russian retreat 4 August.

Armies of Central Powers.

Counter-drives of Central Powers.

© Arthur Banks 1973

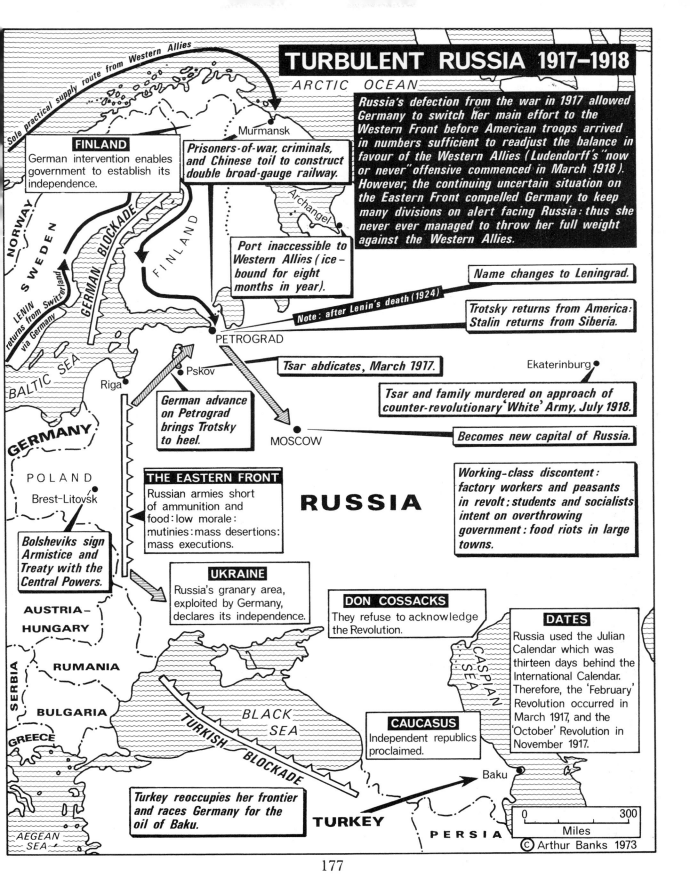

TURBULENT RUSSIA 1917–1918

ARCTIC OCEAN

Russia's defection from the war in 1917 allowed Germany to switch her main effort to the Western Front before American troops arrived in numbers sufficient to readjust the balance in favour of the Western Allies (Ludendorff's "now or never" offensive commenced in March 1918). However, the continuing uncertain situation on the Eastern Front compelled Germany to keep many divisions on alert facing Russia: thus she never ever managed to throw her full weight against the Western Allies.

Sole practical supply route from Western Allies

Murmansk

FINLAND
German intervention enables government to establish its independence.

Prisoners-of-war, criminals, and Chinese toil to construct double broad-gauge railway.

Archangel

Port inaccessible to Western Allies (ice-bound for eight months in year).

NORWAY

SWEDEN

GERMAN BLOCKADE

FINLAND

LENIN returns from Switzerland via Germany

Name changes to Leningrad.

Trotsky returns from America: Stalin returns from Siberia.

Note: after Lenin's death (1924)

PETROGRAD

Tsar abdicates, March 1917.

Ekaterinburg

BALTIC SEA

Riga

Pskov

German advance on Petrograd brings Trotsky to heel.

Tsar and family murdered on approach of counter-revolutionary 'White' Army, July 1918.

MOSCOW

Becomes new capital of Russia.

GERMANY

RUSSIA

POLAND

Brest-Litovsk

THE EASTERN FRONT
Russian armies short of ammunition and food: low morale: mutinies: mass desertions: mass executions.

Working-class discontent: factory workers and peasants in revolt: students and socialists intent on overthrowing government: food riots in large towns.

Bolsheviks sign Armistice and Treaty with the Central Powers.

AUSTRIA–HUNGARY

UKRAINE
Russia's granary area, exploited by Germany, declares its independence.

DON COSSACKS
They refuse to acknowledge the Revolution.

DATES
Russia used the Julian Calendar which was thirteen days behind the International Calendar. Therefore, the 'February' Revolution occurred in March 1917, and the 'October' Revolution in November 1917.

SERBIA

RUMANIA

CASPIAN SEA

BULGARIA

BLACK SEA

CAUCASUS
Independent republics proclaimed.

GREECE

TURKISH BLOCKADE

Baku

Turkey reoccupies her frontier and races Germany for the oil of Baku.

TURKEY

PERSIA

AEGEAN SEA

0	300

Miles

© Arthur Banks 1973

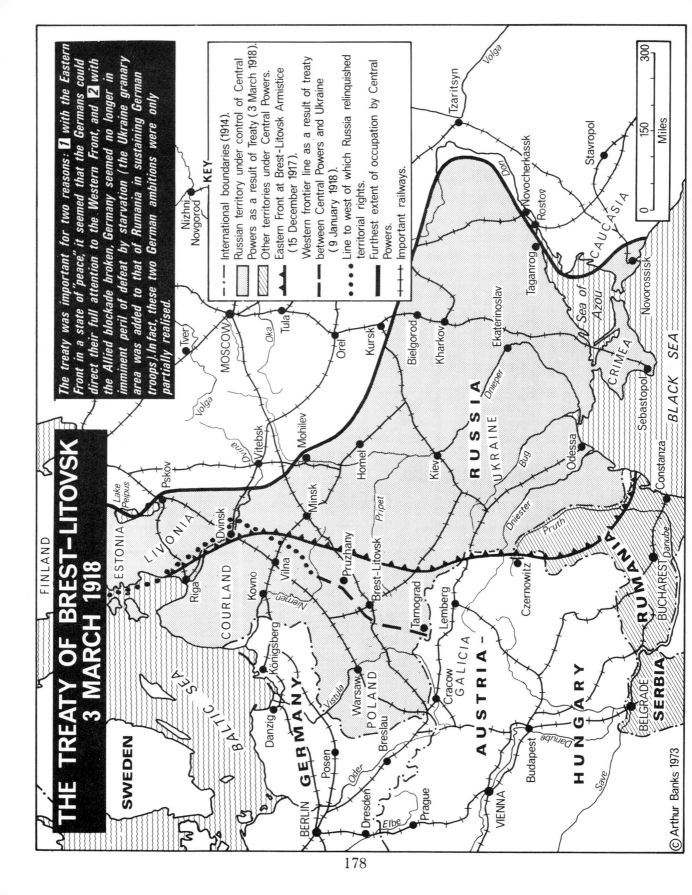

THE TREATY OF BREST–LITOVSK 3 MARCH 1918

SWEDEN

FINLAND

The treaty was important for two reasons: **1** with the Eastern Front in a state of "peace," it seemed that the Germans could direct their full attention to the Western Front, and **2** with the Allied blockade broken, Germany seemed no longer in imminent peril of defeat by starvation (the Ukraine granary area was added to that of Rumania in sustaining German troops). In fact, these two German ambitions were only partially realised.

KEY

- – · – International boundaries (1914).
- Russian territory under control of Central Powers as a result of Treaty (3 March 1918).
- Other territories under Central Powers.
- Eastern Front at Brest-Litovsk Armistice (15 December 1917).
- – · – Western frontier line as a result of treaty between Central Powers and Ukraine (9 January 1918).
- · · · · · Line to west of which Russia relinquished territorial rights.
- Furthest extent of occupation by Central Powers.
- +—+ Important railways.

300
150
0
Miles

Nizhni Novgorod
Volga
Tver
MOSCOW
Oka
Tula
Volga
Tzaritsyn
Stavropol
Novocherkassk
Don
Rostov
CAUCASIA
Taganrog
Sea of Azou
Novorossisk

Orel
Kursk
Bielgorod
Kharkov
Ekaterinoslav
Dnieper
CRIMEA
Sebastopol

Vitebsk
Mohilev
Duina
Homel
Kiev
RUSSIA
UKRAINE
Bug
Odessa
BLACK SEA

Pskov
Lake Peipus
ESTONIA
LIVONIA
Dvinsk
Minsk
Pripet
Dniester
Pruth
Constanza
Danube
BUCHAREST

BALTIC SEA
Riga
COURLAND
Kovno
Vilna
Niemen
Pruzhany
Brest-Litovsk
Tarnograd
Lemberg
Czernowitz
RUMANIA
BELGRADE
SERBIA

Danzig
Königsberg
Vistula
Warsaw
POLAND
Cracow
GALICIA
AUSTRIA –
HUNGARY
Danube
Budapest
Save

BERLIN
GERMANY
Posen
Breslau
Oder
Prague
Dresden
Elbe
VIENNA

© Arthur Banks 1973

178

THE WAR IN 1918

The war weariness which had assailed the Russian people at the start of winter in 1917–1918 threatened to spread to other countries which had been subjected to many years of heavy casualties and short rations. The German home front was hard-pressed by the British blockade while the British themselves had come close to disaster during the worst month of sinkings by U-boat, April 1917. There was widespread disaffection in Austria-Hungary, accentuated by conflicts between the nationalities within the Empire, and an extensive peace movement in Bulgaria, while desertions from the Turkish army in Palestine began to increase sharply. It was therefore essential for Hindenburg and Ludendorff to achieve a rapid military victory on the Western Front, using reinforcements from the East to defeat the British and French armies in the field before the Americans flooded in. In March 1917 there were three Allied soldiers to every two Germans in France and Belgium: a year later, the troop trains from Russia had changed the balance to four Germans to every three Allies.

The French and British prime ministers, Clemenceau and Lloyd George, anticipated a hard thrust by Germany; but no one believed it possible for Ludendorff to have achieved such concentration of firepower as the Germans mounted in March 1918. Within a week the Germans penetrated the Allied line to a depth of forty miles, although the Germans caused problems to themselves by outrunning their supplies. In April they struck farther north, penetrating a section of the Flanders Front held by inexperienced Portuguese troops; and in May Ludendorff succeeded in bringing the campaign back to the Marne and threatening Paris. His last great stroke, around Rheims on 15 July, was checked by astute defensive positioning on the part of Pétain. The German drive was brought to a standstill, with an exhausted army exposing the flanks of a series of salients to counter-attack.

The Allies had at last accepted the principle of unified command, entrusting Foch with the task of throwing back the Germans. American troops, disembarking in France at the rate of a quarter of a million each month, replenished the Allied armies. On 18 July tanks (as at Cambrai) provided the spearhead for Foch's counter-offensive although it was the German break in morale on 8 August which convinced Ludendorff Germany could not win the War. In September the Allied attacks seemed to lose impetus, but the British at last penetrated the Hindenburg Line on 29 September. At the same time news reached Supreme German Headquarters of collapse elsewhere: Bulgaria capitulated, after Franchet d'Espèrey's Salonika armies broke through on the Macedonian Front (page 204); Allenby and Lawrence's Arab Legion entered Damascus (3 October), and the Turks began to seek peace; at the end of October the Italians, with British and French support, launched a furious offensive on the Piave and induced Austria-Hungary to seek terms (page 203). Lloyd George, who had long believed in 'knocking away the props from under Germany', found his policy vindicated.

Hindenburg accepted the need for peace on 3 October, but he became more optimistic once he saw the Allies were themselves tiring. It was, in the end, bread riots, revolution and a mutiny of the fleet which convinced the German High Command the war was over. The tightening grip of the blockade prevented any hopes of further resistance, while a mass influenza epidemic lowered the morale of the civilian population. A German armistice delegation set out from Berlin on 6 November. The Armistice became effective five days later.

179

THE GERMAN OFFENSIVES 21 MARCH - 17 JULY 1918

0 — 25
Miles

KEY
⭕ GERMAN ARMIES

German troop strengths in the west had increased by 30% between November 1917 and 21 March 1918, primarily due to transfer of troops from the east following the Treaty of Brest-Litovsk. British strengths had decreased by 25% since "Third Ypres" (Passchendaele) 1917 as they were content to wait upon the arrival of the fresh American troops.

NORTH SEA

Flushing

HOLLAND

ANTWERP

Zeebrugge

Ostend

Bruges

Ghent

Schelde

Nieuport
Furnes
Dunkirk
Hondschoote
Calais **BELGIAN ARMY**

Thourout
Dixmude
Thielt
④
Roulers
Lys
Menin
Courtrai
Oudenarde
Tourcoing
Roubaix
⑥
LILLE
Tournai

BRUSSELS

B E L G I U M

Boulogne

Ypres
Cassel
St.Omer
Hazebrouck
Aire

BRITISH SECOND ARMY

Armentières

Georgette

Béthune
La Bassée
Lens
Douai
Scarpe
St. Amand
RUPPRECHT A.G.H.Q.
Mons
Charleroi

G.H.Q.
Montreuil
St.Pol

BRITISH FIRST ARMY

⑰
Michael I
Valenciennes
Maubeuge
Sambre

Frévent
Arras
Cambrai
②
Michael II
Le Cateau
O.H.L.
Avesnes

Doullens
BRITISH THIRD ARMY
Bapaume
Albert

Abbeville
Somme
Amiens

Peronne
BRITISH FIFTH ARMY
Gneisenau
Ham
St.Quentin
Michael III
⑱
Guise
Hirson
Vervins
⑦

Aumale
Nesle
Roye
La Fère
Marle
Bärisis
Yorck
Blücher
Laon
Crâonne
Rethel

Montdidier
Noyon
Matz
CHEMIN DES DAMES
Aisne
①

Beauvais
Compiègne
G.Q.G.
Aisne
Vailly
Fismes
RHEIMS
Rheims

Clermont
Soissons
Marne

Creil
Oise
Villers Cotterêts
FRENCH SECOND ARMY
FRENCH FOURTH ARMY

Senlis
F R E N C H   S I X T H   A R M Y
Épernay
Châlons -sur-Marne

Chantilly
Dormans
Marne

KEY
▨ 'MICHAEL' 21 March-5 April.
▦ 'GEORGETTE' 9-11 April.
▥ 'BLÜCHER-YORCK' 27 May.
▩ 'GNEISENAU' 9 June.
▤ 'MARNE-RHEIMS' 15-17 July.
····· Army boundaries.
▭ Army General Headquarters.
▯ Army Headquarters.

Meaux
La Ferté
PARIS

© Arthur Banks 1973

180

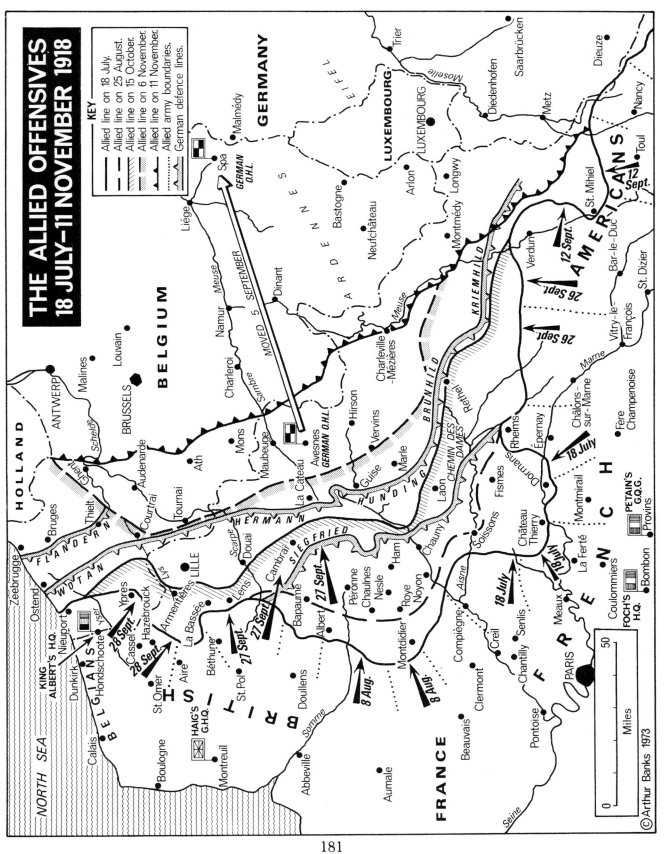

THE ALLIED OFFENSIVES 18 JULY–11 NOVEMBER 1918

KEY

- Allied line on 18 July.
- Allied line on 25 August.
- Allied line on 15 October.
- Allied line on 6 November.
- Allied line on 11 November.
- Allied army boundaries.
- German defence lines.

© Arthur Banks 1973

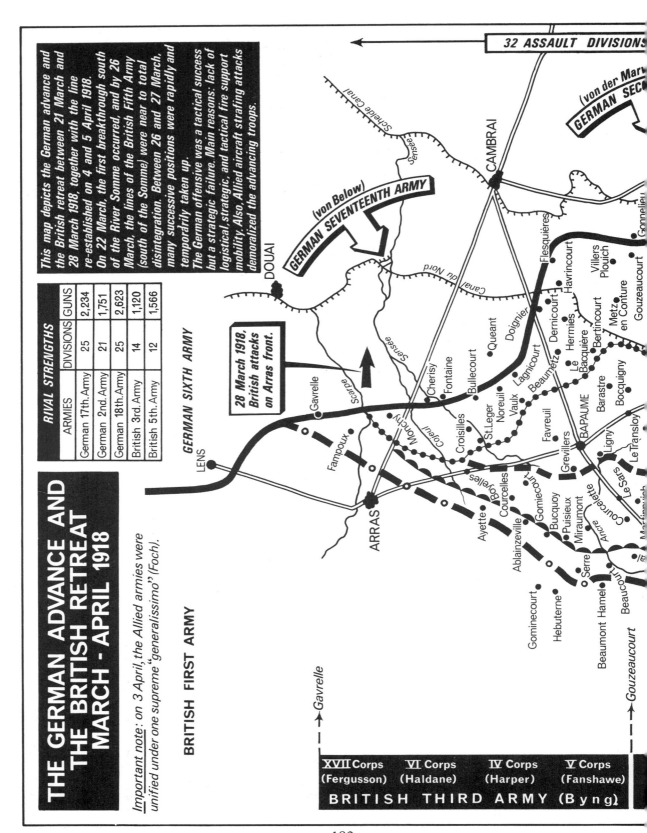

THE GERMAN ADVANCE AND THE BRITISH RETREAT MARCH – APRIL 1918

Important note: on 3 April, the Allied armies were unified under one supreme "generalissimo" (Foch).

This map depicts the German advance and the British retreat between 21 March and 28 March 1918, together with the line re-established on 4 and 5 April 1918. On 22 March, the first breakthrough south of the River Somme occurred, and by 26 March, the lines of the British Fifth Army (south of the Somme) were near to total disintegration. Between 26 and 27 March, many successive positions were rapidly and temporarily taken up.

The German offensive was a tactical success but a strategic failure. Main reasons: lack of logistical, strategic, and tactical fire support mobility. Also, Allied aircraft strafing attacks demoralized the advancing troops.

RIVAL STRENGTHS		
ARMIES	DIVISIONS	GUNS
German 17th. Army	25	2,234
German 2nd. Army	21	1,751
German 18th. Army	25	2,623
British 3rd. Army	14	1,120
British 5th. Army	12	1,566

28 March 1918, British attacks on Arras front.

32 ASSAULT DIVISIONS

(von der Marwitz) GERMAN SECOND ARMY

(von Below) GERMAN SEVENTEENTH ARMY

GERMAN SIXTH ARMY

BRITISH FIRST ARMY

| XVII Corps (Fergusson) | VI Corps (Haldane) | IV Corps (Harper) | V Corps (Fanshawe) |

BRITISH THIRD ARMY (Byng)

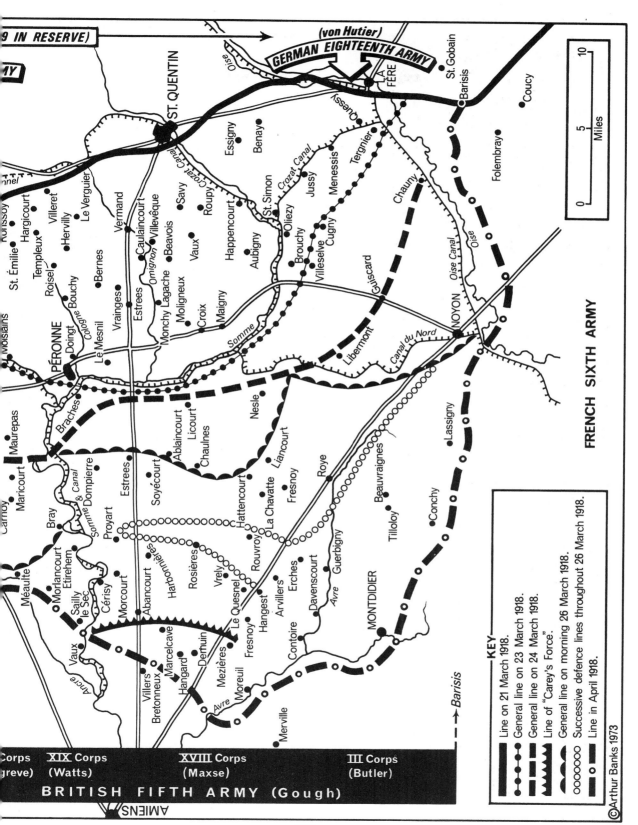

AMIENS

BRITISH FIFTH ARMY (Gough)

... Corps	XIX Corps	XVIII Corps	III Corps
(...greve)	(Watts)	(Maxse)	(Butler)

(von Hutier)

GERMAN EIGHTEENTH ARMY

(...9 IN RESERVE)

...MY

St. Quentin

La Fère

St. Gobain

Barisis

Coucy

Essigny

Benay

Folembray

St. Émile

Roisel

Hargicourt

Villeret

Hervilly

Le Verguier

Templeux

Bernes

Roisel

Bouchy

Cologne

Vermand

Caulaincourt

Villevêque

Estrees

Omignon

Beavois

Savy

Roupy

Happencourt

St. Simon

Oliezy

Brouchy

Jussy

Cugny

Menessis

Tergnier

Chauny

Vaux

Aubigny

Villeselve

Guiscard

Noyon

Le Mesnil

Vrainges

Monchy Lagache

Croix

Maigny

Molineux

Somme

Libermont

Canal du Nord

Oise Canal

Péronne

Doingt

Maurepas

Braches

Ablaincourt

Licourt

Chaulnes

Nesle

Roye

Lassigny

Carnoy

Maricourt

Bray

Somme & Canal

Dompierre

Proyart

Estrees

Soyécourt

Hattencourt

Liancourt

Fresnoy

La Chavatte

Rouvroy

Beauvraignes

Conchy

Tilloloy

Méaulte

Morlancourt

Etirehem

Sailly le Sec

Cérisy

Morcourt

Abancourt

Harbonnières

Rosières

Vrely

Le Quesnel

Hangest

Arvillers

Erches

Guerbigny

Davenscourt

Contoire

MONTDIDIER

Vaux

Villers Bretonneux

Marcelcave

Hangard

Demuin

Mezières

Moreuil

Fresnoy

Avre

Ancre

Merville

→ Barisis

FRENCH SIXTH ARMY

Oise

Crozat Canal

Quessy

Miles

0   5   10

KEY

▬▬▬	Line on 21 March 1918.
•–•–•	General line on 23 March 1918.
┴┴┴┴	General line on 24 March 1918.
▲▲▲▲	Line of "Carey's Force."
•••••	General line on morning 26 March 1918.
ooooo	Successive defence lines throughout 26 March 1918.
▬o▬o▬	Line in April 1918.

183

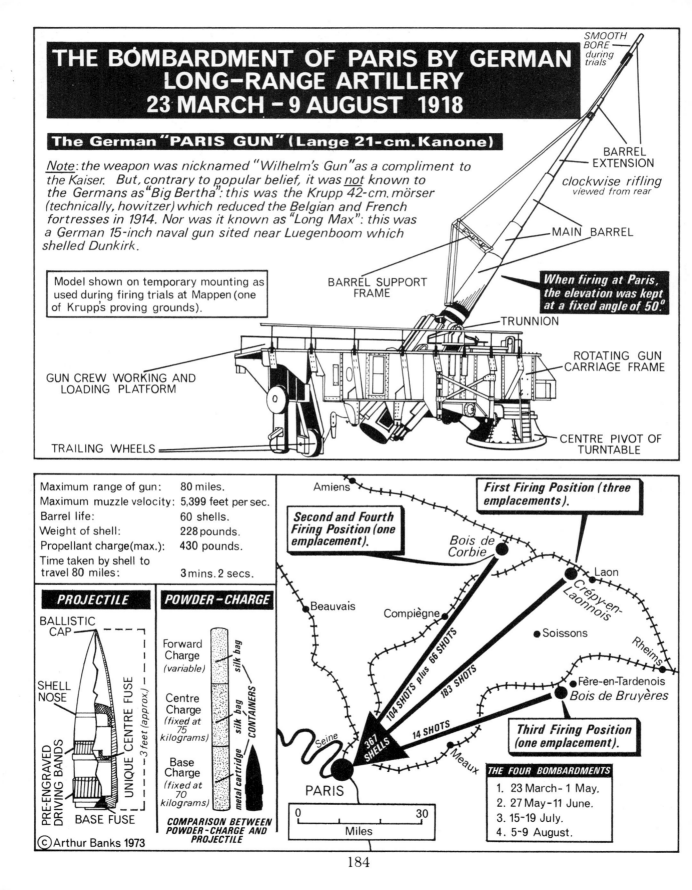

THE BOMBARDMENT OF PARIS BY GERMAN LONG-RANGE ARTILLERY 23 MARCH – 9 AUGUST 1918

The German "PARIS GUN" (Lange 21-cm. Kanone)

Note: the weapon was nicknamed "Wilhelm's Gun" as a compliment to the Kaiser. But, contrary to popular belief, it was *not* known to the Germans as "Big Bertha": this was the Krupp 42-cm. mörser (technically, howitzer) which reduced the Belgian and French fortresses in 1914. Nor was it known as "Long Max": this was a German 15-inch naval gun sited near Luegenboom which shelled Dunkirk.

Model shown on temporary mounting as used during firing trials at Mappen (one of Krupp's proving grounds).

SMOOTH BORE *during trials*

BARREL EXTENSION

clockwise rifling viewed from rear

MAIN BARREL

When firing at Paris, the elevation was kept at a fixed angle of 50°.

BARREL SUPPORT FRAME

TRUNNION

ROTATING GUN CARRIAGE FRAME

GUN CREW WORKING AND LOADING PLATFORM

CENTRE PIVOT OF TURNTABLE

TRAILING WHEELS

Maximum range of gun: 80 miles.
Maximum muzzle velocity: 5,399 feet per sec.
Barrel life: 60 shells.
Weight of shell: 228 pounds.
Propellant charge (max.): 430 pounds.
Time taken by shell to travel 80 miles: 3 mins. 2 secs.

PROJECTILE

BALLISTIC CAP

SHELL NOSE

UNIQUE CENTRE FUSE

PRE-ENGRAVED DRIVING BANDS

BASE FUSE

~3 feet (approx.)

POWDER-CHARGE

Forward Charge *(variable)* — silk bag

Centre Charge *(fixed at 75 kilograms)* — silk bag

Base Charge *(fixed at 70 kilograms)* — metal cartridge

CONTAINERS

COMPARISON BETWEEN POWDER-CHARGE AND PROJECTILE

© Arthur Banks 1973

Amiens

First Firing Position (three emplacements).

Second and Fourth Firing Position (one emplacement).

Bois de Corbie

Laon

Crépy-en-Laonnois

Beauvais

Compiègne

Soissons

Rheims

Fère-en-Tardenois

Bois de Bruyères

Third Firing Position (one emplacement).

104 SHOTS plus 66 SHOTS

183 SHOTS

14 SHOTS

Seine

367 SHELLS

Meaux

PARIS

0 — 30
Miles

THE FOUR BOMBARDMENTS
1. 23 March – 1 May.
2. 27 May – 11 June.
3. 15 – 19 July.
4. 5 – 9 August.

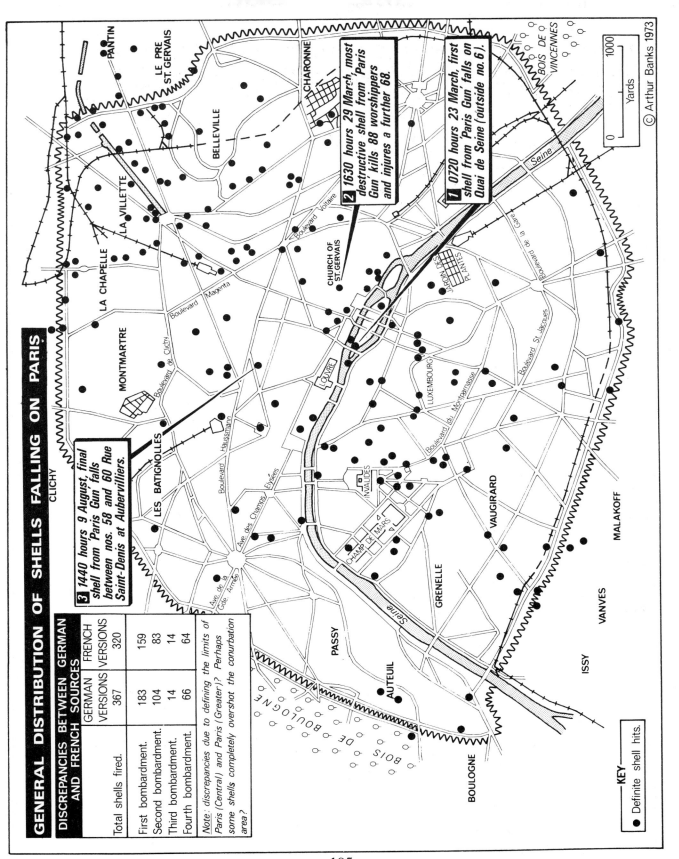

GENERAL DISTRIBUTION OF SHELLS FALLING ON PARIS

© Arthur Banks 1973

2 1630 hours 29 March, most destructive shell from 'Paris Gun' kills 88 worshippers and injures a further 68.

1 0720 hours 23 March, first shell from 'Paris Gun' falls on Quai de Seine (outside no. 6).

3 1440 hours 9 August, final shell from 'Paris Gun' falls between nos. 58 and 60 Rue Saint-Denis at Aubervilliers.

DISCREPANCIES BETWEEN GERMAN AND FRENCH SOURCES

	GERMAN VERSIONS	FRENCH VERSIONS
Total shells fired.	367	320
First bombardment.	183	159
Second bombardment.	104	83
Third bombardment.	14	14
Fourth bombardment.	66	64

Note: discrepancies due to defining the limits of Paris (Central) and Paris (Greater)? Perhaps some shells completely overshot the conurbation area?

KEY
● Definite shell hits.

185

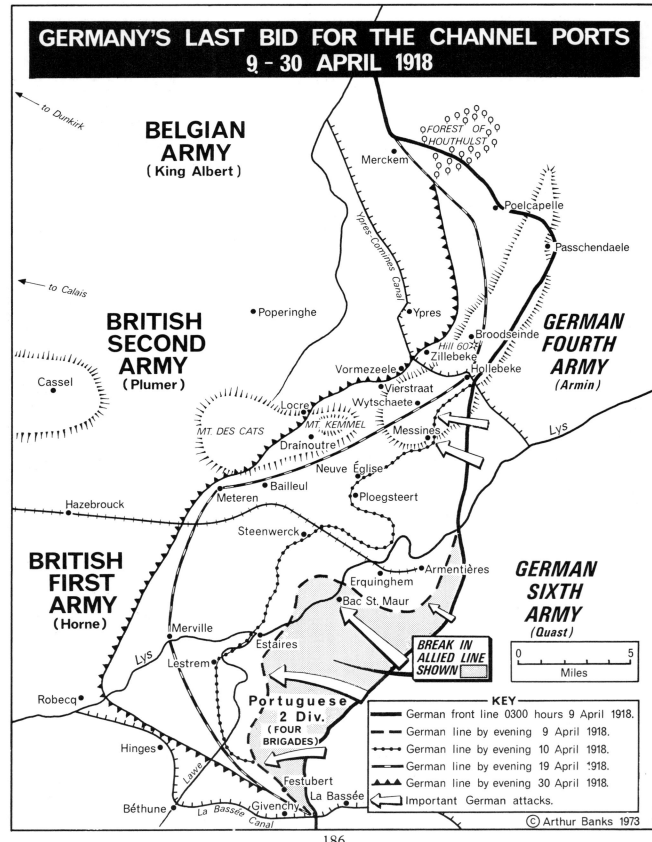

GERMANY'S LAST BID FOR THE CHANNEL PORTS 9 - 30 APRIL 1918

to Dunkirk

BELGIAN ARMY
(King Albert)

FOREST OF HOUTHULST

Merckem

Poelcapelle

Passchendaele

to Calais

BRITISH SECOND ARMY
(Plumer)

Poperinghe

Ypres

Ypres-Comines Canal

Broodseinde

Hill 60

Zillebeke

GERMAN FOURTH ARMY
(Armin)

Cassel

Vormezeele

Hollebeke

Vierstraat

Lys

Locre

Wytschaete

MT. DES CATS

MT. KEMMEL

Messines

Drainoutre

Neuve Église

Bailleul

Ploegsteert

Meteren

Hazebrouck

Steenwerck

BRITISH FIRST ARMY
(Horne)

Armentières

Erquinghem

Bac St. Maur

GERMAN SIXTH ARMY
(Quast)

Merville

Estaires

Lys

Lestrem

BREAK IN ALLIED LINE SHOWN

| 0 | | | | | 5 |
Miles

Robecq

Portuguese 2 Div. (FOUR BRIGADES)

Hinges

Lawe

Festubert

La Bassée

KEY
━━━ German front line 0300 hours 9 April 1918.
╺ ╺ German line by evening 9 April 1918.
•••• German line by evening 10 April 1918.
━┄━ German line by evening 19 April 1918.
▲▲▲ German line by evening 30 April 1918.
⬅ Important German attacks.

Béthune

Givenchy

La Bassée Canal

© Arthur Banks 1973

186

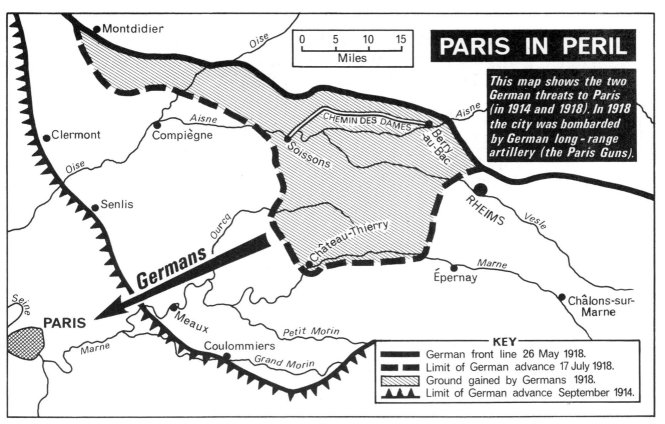

PARIS IN PERIL

This map shows the two German threats to Paris (in 1914 and 1918). In 1918 the city was bombarded by German long-range artillery (the Paris Guns).

Montdidier

Oise

0 5 10 15
Miles

Clermont

Compiègne

Aisne

CHEMIN DES DAMES

Berry-au-Bac

Soissons

Aisne

RHEIMS

Oise

Senlis

Ourcq

Vesle

Château-Thierry

Seine

Marne

Épernay

Châlons-sur-Marne

PARIS

Germans

Meaux

Marne

Petit Morin

Coulommiers

Grand Morin

KEY
— German front line 26 May 1918.
– – Limit of German advance 17 July 1918.
▨ Ground gained by Germans 1918.
▲▲ Limit of German advance September 1914.

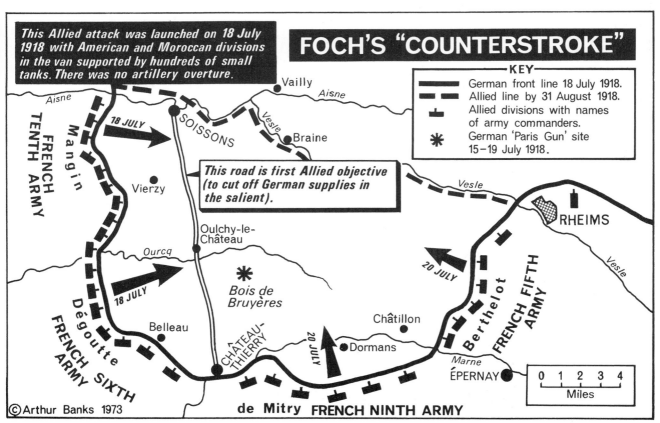

FOCH'S "COUNTERSTROKE"

This Allied attack was launched on 18 July 1918 with American and Moroccan divisions in the van supported by hundreds of small tanks. There was no artillery overture.

KEY
— German front line 18 July 1918.
– – Allied line by 31 August 1918.
⊥ Allied divisions with names of army commanders.
✳ German 'Paris Gun' site 15–19 July 1918.

Aisne

FRENCH TENTH ARMY

Mangin

18 JULY

Vailly

Aisne

SOISSONS

Vesle

Braine

Vierzy

This road is first Allied objective (to cut off German supplies in the salient).

Vesle

Oulchy-le-Château

Ourcq

RHEIMS

Vesle

Dégoutte FRENCH SIXTH ARMY

18 JULY

✳ Bois de Bruyères

20 JULY

Berthelot FRENCH FIFTH ARMY

Belleau

CHÂTEAU-THIERRY

Châtillon

20 JULY

Dormans

Marne

ÉPERNAY

© Arthur Banks 1973

de Mitry FRENCH NINTH ARMY

0 1 2 3 4
Miles

187

THE AMERICAN EXPEDITIONARY FORCE IN EUROPE 1918

The United States declared war on Germany on 6 April 1917, and against Austria-Hungary on 7 December 1917. General John Joseph Pershing was appointed commander of the American Expeditionary Force to Europe, and a vast training and camp-building programme was commenced. By May 1918, there were over 500,000 U.S. troops in France, and by mid-July, over 1,000,000 men had arrived in Europe.

NUMBERS OF UNITED STATES TROOPS

EMBARKED FOR EUROPE AT:		DISEMBARKED IN EUROPE AT:	
New York	1,656,000 men	Liverpool (including 4,000at Manchester)	848,000 men
Newport News	288,000 men	Brest	791,000 men
Boston	46,000 men	St. Nazaire	198,000 men
Philadelphia	35,000 men	London	62,000 men
Portland	6,000 men	Southampton	57,000 men
Baltimore	4,000 men	Bassens (including Bordeaux)	50,000 men
		Glasgow	45,000 men
PLUS 45,000 TROOPS EMBARKED AT CANADIAN PORTS		Le Havre	13,000 men
		Bristol	11,000 men
		La Pallice (including La Rochelle)	4,000 men
Montreal	32,000 men	Cherbourg	2,000 men
Quebec	11,000 men	Marseilles	1,000 men
Halifax	5,000 men	Plymouth	1,000 men
St. John's	1,000 men	Falmouth	1,000 men
	2,084,000 men		2,08 ,000 men

Precise figs. 71 men were lost in Atlantic crossings.

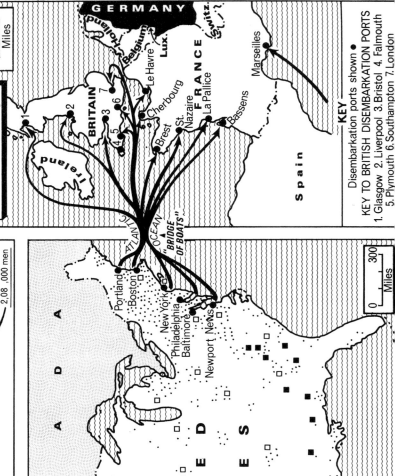

Arrival in Europe

"BRIDGE OF BOATS"

ATLANTIC OCEAN

Portland, Boston, New York, Philadelphia, Baltimore, Newport News

BRITAIN, Ireland, Glasgow (1), (2), (3), (4), (5), (6), (7)

Brest, Cherbourg, Le Havre, St. Nazaire, La Pallice, Bassens

FRANCE, Marseilles, Spain, GERMANY, Belgium, Lux., Switz.

0 ——— 150 Miles

KEY
Disembarkation ports shown ●

KEY TO BRITISH DISEMBARKATION PORTS
1. Glasgow 2. Liverpool 3. Bristol 4. Falmouth
5. Plymouth 6. Southampton 7. London

Mobilization

CANADA

UNITED STATES

MEXICO

0 ——— 300 Miles

KEY
■ National Guard camps.
□ National Army camps.
∴ Construction projects.
● Embarkation ports.

Lines of Communication to the Front

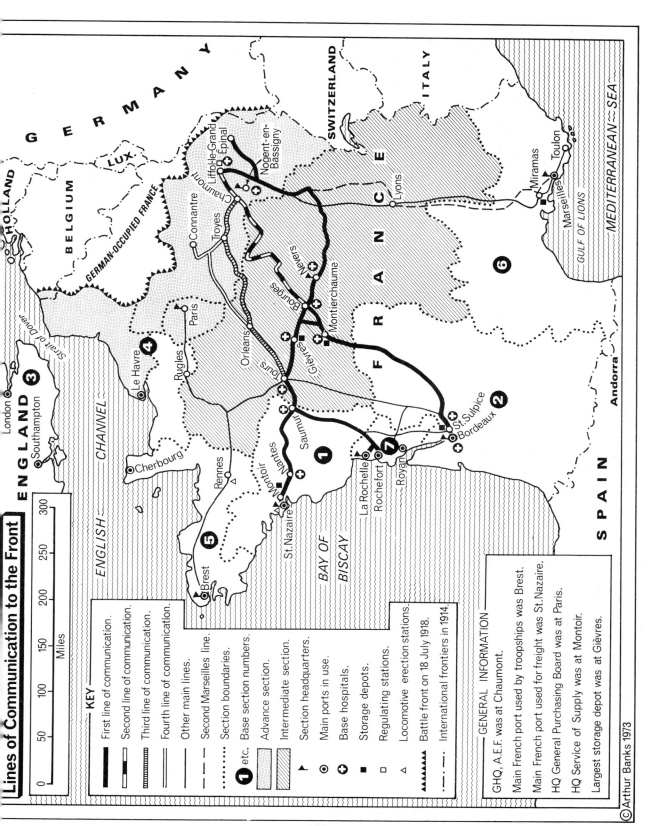

KEY

▬▬▬	First line of communication.
▬■▬	Second line of communication.
▦▦▦	Third line of communication.
────	Fourth line of communication.
─·─·─	Other main lines.
········	Second Marseilles line.
··········	Section boundaries.
①etc.	Base section numbers.
▒▒	Advance section.
▨▨	Intermediate section.
▲	Section headquarters.
◉	Main ports in use.
✚	Base hospitals.
■	Storage depots.
□	Regulating stations.
△	Locomotive erection stations.
▲▲▲▲▲	Battle front on 18 July 1918.
─·─·─	International frontiers in 1914.

GENERAL INFORMATION

GHQ, A.E.F. was at Chaumont.
Main French port used by troopships was Brest.
Main French port used for freight was St.Nazaire.
HQ General Purchasing Board was at Paris.
HQ Service of Supply was at Montoir.
Largest storage depot was at Gièvres.

© Arthur Banks 1973

Miles

0 50 100 150 200 250 300

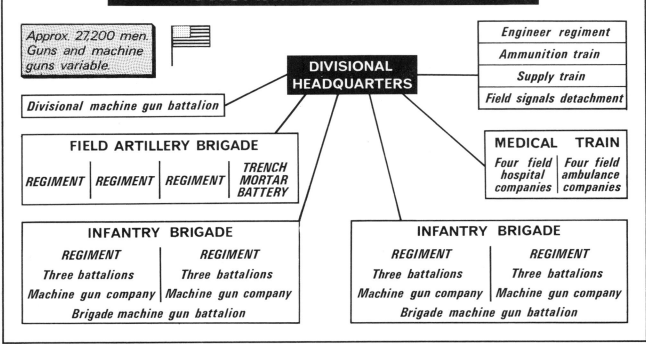

AMERICAN INFANTRY DIVISIONAL ORGANIZATION 1918

Approx 27,200 men. Guns and machine guns variable.

DIVISIONAL HEADQUARTERS

Engineer regiment
Ammunition train
Supply train
Field signals detachment

Divisional machine gun battalion

MEDICAL TRAIN

Four field hospital companies	Four field ambulance companies

FIELD ARTILLERY BRIGADE

REGIMENT	REGIMENT	REGIMENT	TRENCH MORTAR BATTERY

INFANTRY BRIGADE

REGIMENT	REGIMENT
Three battalions	Three battalions
Machine gun company	Machine gun company
Brigade machine gun battalion	

INFANTRY BRIGADE

REGIMENT	REGIMENT
Three battalions	Three battalions
Machine gun company	Machine gun company
Brigade machine gun battalion	

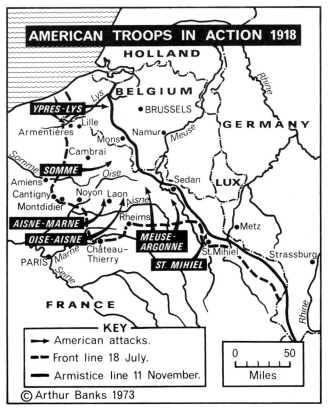

AMERICAN TROOPS IN ACTION 1918

HOLLAND
BELGIUM
BRUSSELS
GERMANY
YPRES-LYS
Lille
Armentières
Namur
Meuse
Rhine
Mons
Cambrai
Somme
SOMME
Oise
Amiens
Cantigny
Noyon
Laon
Sedan
LUX.
Montdidier
Aisne
AISNE-MARNE
Rheims
Metz
OISE-AISNE
Château-Thierry
MEUSE-ARGONNE
St. Mihiel
PARIS
Marne
ST. MIHIEL
Strassburg
Seine
Rhine
FRANCE

KEY
→ American attacks.
--- Front line 18 July.
— Armistice line 11 November.

0   50
Miles

© Arthur Banks 1973

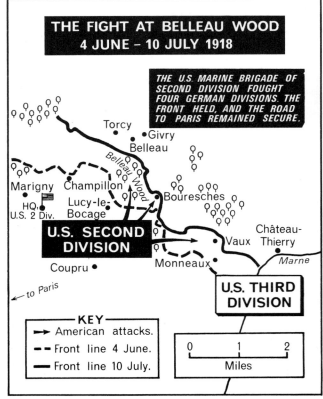

THE FIGHT AT BELLEAU WOOD
4 JUNE – 10 JULY 1918

THE U.S. MARINE BRIGADE OF SECOND DIVISION FOUGHT FOUR GERMAN DIVISIONS. THE FRONT HELD, AND THE ROAD TO PARIS REMAINED SECURE.

Torcy
Givry
Belleau
Belleau Wood
Marigny
Champillon
Bouresches
HQ
U.S. 2 Div.
Lucy-le-Bocage
U.S. SECOND DIVISION
Vaux
Château-Thierry
Monneaux
Marne
to Paris
Coupru
U.S. THIRD DIVISION

KEY
→ American attacks.
--- Front line 4 June.
— Front line 10 July.

0   1   2
Miles

"BLACK DAY OF THE GERMAN ARMY" 8 AUGUST 1918

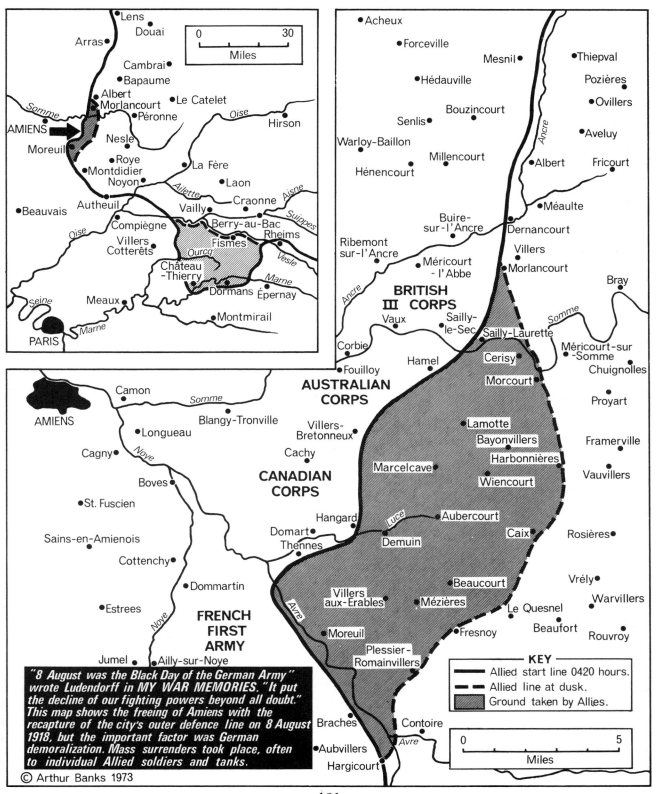

Miles 0 — 30

Lens
Douai
Arras
Cambrai
Bapaume
Albert
Morlancourt
Le Catelet
Péronne
Somme
Oise
Hirson
AMIENS
Nesle
Moreuil
Roye
Montdidier
Noyon
La Fère
Laon
Ailette
Autheuil
Craonne
Vailly
Aisne
Beauvais
Oise
Compiègne
Villers
Cotterêts
Berry-au-Bac
Fismes
Rheims
Suippes
Ourcq
Château
-Thierry
Vesle
Marne
Dormans
Épernay
Seine
Meaux
Marne
Montmirail
PARIS

Acheux
Forceville
Mesnil
Thiepval
Hédauville
Pozières
Bouzincourt
Ovillers
Senlis
Aveluy
Warloy-Baillon
Millencourt
Albert
Fricourt
Hénencourt
Ancre
Méaulte
Buire-
sur-l'Ancre
Dernancourt
Villers
Ribemont
sur-l'Ancre
Morlancourt
Méricourt
- l'Abbe
Bray
BRITISH
III CORPS
Ancre
Vaux
Sailly-
le-Sec
Somme
Sailly-Laurette
Méricourt-sur
-Somme
Corbie
Cerisy
Chuignolles
Hamel
Morcourt
Fouilloy
Proyart
AUSTRALIAN
CORPS
Lamotte
Bayonvillers
Framerville
Marcelcave
Harbonnières
Villers-
Bretonneux
Wiencourt
Vauvillers
Cachy
CANADIAN
CORPS
Aubercourt
Hangard
Luce
Caix
Rosières
Domart
Demuin
Thennes
Avre
Beaucourt
Vrély
Villers
aux-Erables
Mézières
Warvillers
Le Quesnel
Beaufort
Moreuil
Rouvroy
Fresnoy
Plessier-
Romainvillers

Camon
Somme
Blangy-Tronville
AMIENS
Longueau
Cagny
Noye
Boves
St. Fuscien
Sains-en-Amienois
Cottenchy
Dommartin
FRENCH
FIRST
ARMY
Estrees
Noye
Jumel
Ailly-sur-Noye
Braches
Contoire
Avre
Aubvillers
Hargicourt

"8 August was the Black Day of the German Army"
wrote Ludendorff in MY WAR MEMORIES. "It put
the decline of our fighting powers beyond all doubt."
This map shows the freeing of Amiens with the
recapture of the city's outer defence line on 8 August
1918, but the important factor was German
demoralization. Mass surrenders took place, often
to individual Allied soldiers and tanks.

© Arthur Banks 1973

— KEY —
—— Allied start line 0420 hours.
– – – Allied line at dusk.
▨ Ground taken by Allies.

Miles 0 — 5

191

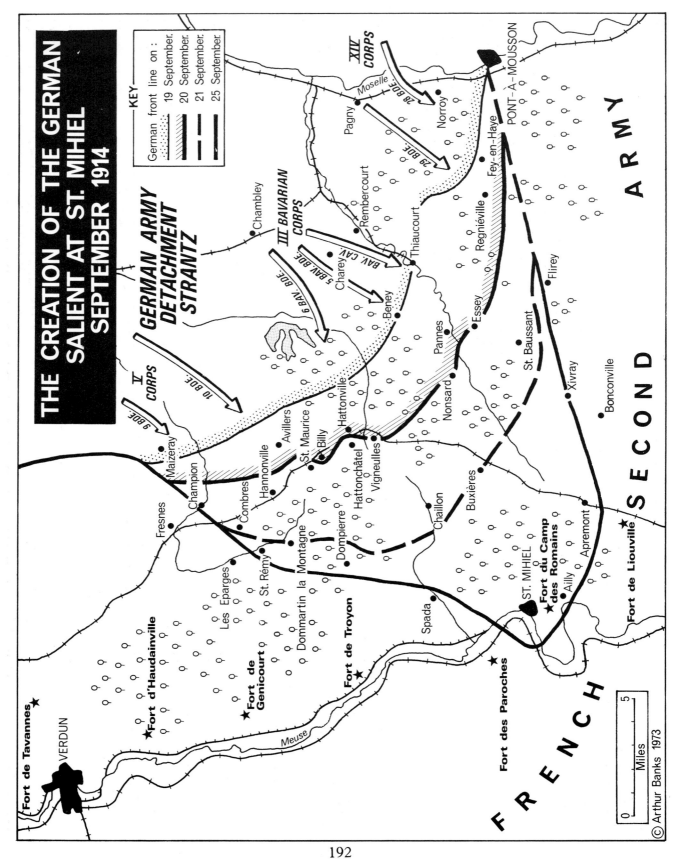

THE CREATION OF THE GERMAN
SALIENT AT ST. MIHIEL
SEPTEMBER 1914

KEY

German front line on:
19 September.
20 September.
21 September.
25 September.

GERMAN ARMY
DETACHMENT
STRANTZ

XIII CORPS

III BAVARIAN CORPS

V CORPS

© Arthur Banks 1973

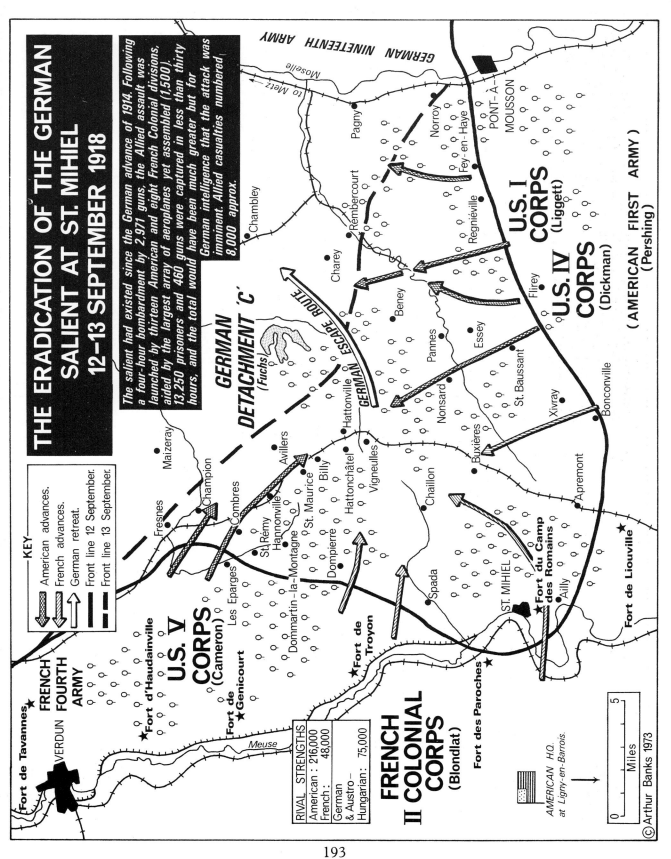

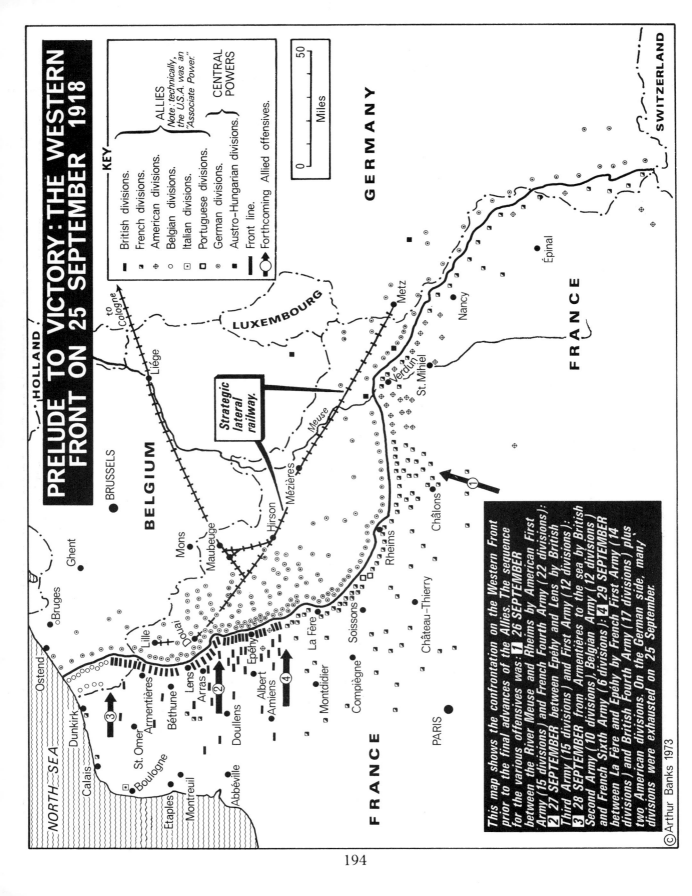

PRELUDE TO VICTORY: THE WESTERN FRONT ON 25 SEPTEMBER 1918

KEY

ALLIES
Note: technically, the U.S.A. was an "Associate Power."

- British divisions.
- French divisions.
- American divisions.
- Belgian divisions.
- Italian divisions.
- Portuguese divisions.

CENTRAL POWERS
- German divisions.
- Austro-Hungarian divisions.
- Front line.
- Forthcoming Allied offensives.

Miles
0 — 50

Strategic lateral railway.

HOLLAND

BELGIUM

LUXEMBOURG

GERMANY

FRANCE

SWITZERLAND

NORTH SEA

to Cologne

Brussels
Ghent
Bruges
Ostend
Dunkirk
Calais
Boulogne
St. Omer
Montreuil
Etaples
Abbéville
Armentières
Béthune
Lens
Arras
Lille
Douai
Liége
Mons
Maubeuge
Hirson
Mézières
Meuse
Metz
Nancy
Épinal
Verdun
St. Mihiel
Châlons
Rheims
Soissons
Compiègne
Château-Thierry
Montdidier
Amiens
Albert
Doullens
La Fère
Epéhy
PARIS

This map shows the confrontation on the Western Front prior to the final advances of the Allies. The sequence for the various offensives was: ① 26 SEPTEMBER between the River Meuse and Rheims by American First Army (15 divisions) and French Fourth Army (22 divisions): ② 27 SEPTEMBER between Epéhy and Lens by British Third Army (15 divisions) and First Army (12 divisions): ③ 28 SEPTEMBER from Armentières to the sea by British Second Army (10 divisions), Belgian Army (12 divisions) and French Sixth Army (6 divisions): ④ 29 SEPTEMBER between La Fère and Epéhy by French First Army (14 divisions) and British Fourth Army (17 divisions) plus two American divisions. On the German side, many divisions were exhausted on 25 September.

© Arthur Banks 1973

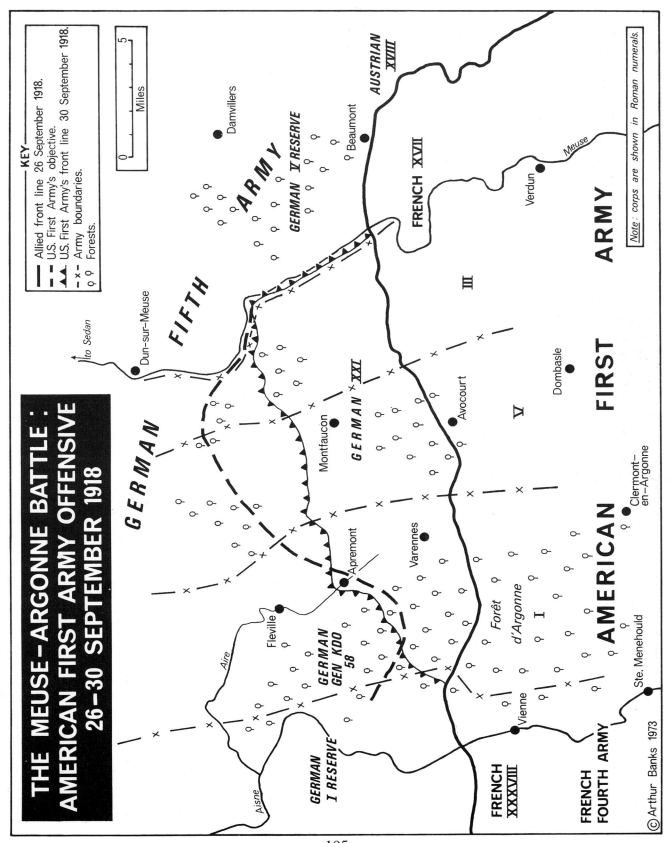

THE MEUSE–ARGONNE BATTLE:
AMERICAN FIRST ARMY OFFENSIVE
26–30 SEPTEMBER 1918

KEY

Allied front line 26 September 1918.
U.S. First Army's objective.
U.S. First Army's front line 30 September 1918.
Army boundaries.
Forests.

Miles
0   5

Note: corps are shown in Roman numerals.

AUSTRIAN XVIII

Damvillers

GERMAN V RESERVE

Beaumont

FRENCH XVII

Meuse

Verdun

FIFTH ARMY

Dun-sur-Meuse

to Sedan

GERMAN

III

GERMAN XXI

Montfaucon

Avocourt

V

Dombasle

FIRST ARMY

Varennes

Apremont

Clermont–en–Argonne

Fleville

Aire

GERMAN GEN KDO 58

Forêt d'Argonne

I

AMERICAN

Ste. Menehould

GERMAN I RESERVE

Vienne

Aisne

FRENCH XXXVIII

FRENCH FOURTH ARMY

© Arthur Banks 1973

195

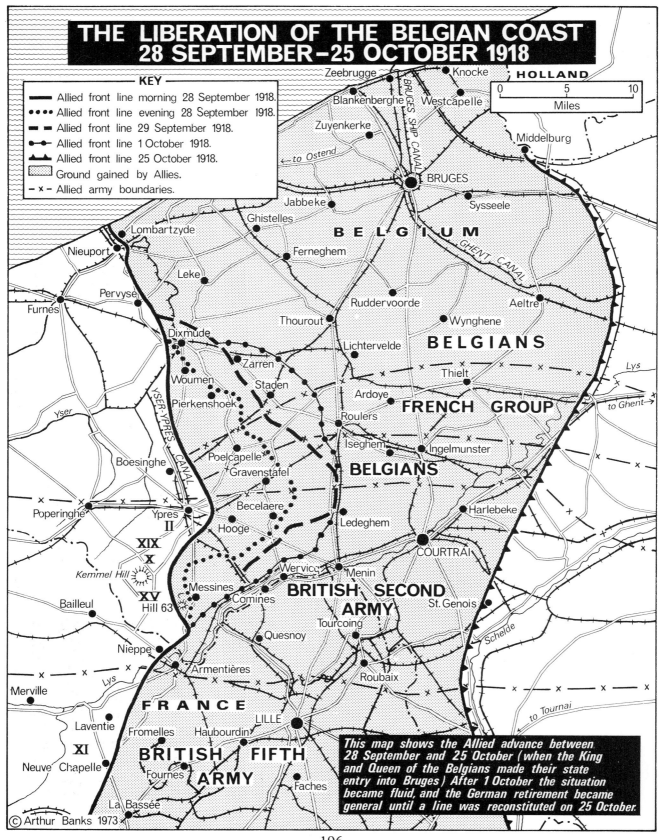

THE LIBERATION OF THE BELGIAN COAST 28 SEPTEMBER–25 OCTOBER 1918

KEY
— Allied front line morning 28 September 1918.
•••• Allied front line evening 28 September 1918.
– – – Allied front line 29 September 1918.
•–•– Allied front line 1 October 1918.
▲▲▲ Allied front line 25 October 1918.
▒▒▒ Ground gained by Allies.
–×– Allied army boundaries.

HOLLAND

0   5   10
Miles

Zeebrugge
Knocke
Westcapelle
Blankenberghe
Middelburg
BRUGES SHIP CANAL
Zuyenkerke
to Ostend
BRUGES
Jabbeke
Sysseele
Ghistelles
BELGIUM
Lombartzyde
GHENT CANAL
Nieuport
Leke
Ferneghem
Ruddervoorde
Aeltre
Furnes
Pervyse
Wynghene
Thourout
Lys
Dixmude
BELGIANS
YSER
Zarren
Lichtervelde
Thielt
Woumen
Staden
Ardoye
to Ghent
YSER-YPRES CANAL
Pierkenshoek
Roulers
FRENCH GROUP
Boesinghe
Poelcapelle
Iseghem
Ingelmunster
Gravenstafel
BELGIANS
Poperinghe
Ypres
Becelaere
II
XIX
Hooge
Harlebeke
X
Ledeghem
Kemmel Hill
COURTRAI
XV
Messines
Wervicq
Menin
Bailleul
Hill 63
Comines
BRITISH SECOND
ARMY
St. Genois
Nieppe
Quesnoy
Tourcoing
Schelde
Armentières
Merville
Roubaix
Lys
to Tournai
FRANCE
LILLE
Laventie
Fromelles
Haubourdin
XI
BRITISH FIFTH
Neuve Chapelle
Fournes
ARMY
Faches
La Bassée
© Arthur Banks 1973

This map shows the Allied advance between 28 September and 25 October (when the King and Queen of the Belgians made their state entry into Bruges) After 1 October the situation became fluid, and the German retirement became general until a line was reconstituted on 25 October.

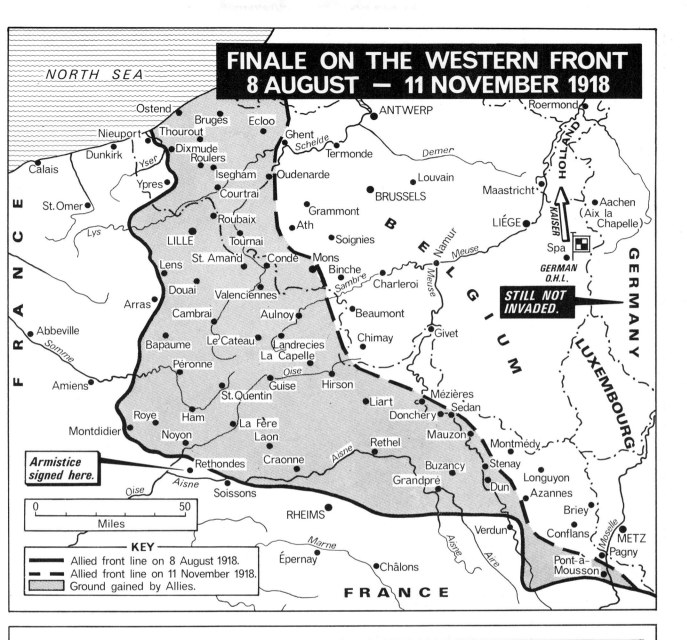

FINALE ON THE WESTERN FRONT
8 AUGUST — 11 NOVEMBER 1918

NORTH SEA

Ostend
Bruges
Ecloo
Nieuport
Thourout
Ghent
Dixmude
Roulers
Schelde
Demer
Termonde
ANTWERP
Roermond
HOLLAND
Calais
Dunkirk
Yser
Isegham
Oudenarde
Louvain
Maastricht
Aachen
(Aix la Chapelle)
Ypres
Courtrai
BRUSSELS
KAISER
St.Omer
Lys
Roubaix
Grammont
LIÉGE
Ath
Soignies
LILLE
Tournai
Spa
Lens
St. Amand
Condé
Mons
Binche
Namur
Meuse
GERMANY
GERMAN O.H.L.
Douai
Valenciennes
Sambre
Charleroi
Arras
Cambrai
Aulnoy
Beaumont
Meuse
Givet
STILL NOT INVADED.
Abbeville
Bapaume
Le Cateau
Landrecies
Chimay
Somme
Péronne
La Capelle
Oise
Amiens
Guise
Hirson
Mézières
Roye
Ham
St.Quentin
Liart
Sedan
LUXEMBOURG
Montdidier
Noyon
La Fère
Donchery
Laon
Rethel
Mauzon
Montmédy
Armistice signed here.
Rethondes
Craonne
Aisne
Buzancy
Stenay
Longuyon
Oise
Aisne
Soissons
Grandpré
Dun
Azannes
0   50
Miles
RHEIMS
Marne
Épernay
Verdun
Conflans
Briey
Moselle
METZ
Pagny
Châlons
Aisne
Aire
Pont-à-Mousson
KEY
Allied front line on 8 August 1918.
Allied front line on 11 November 1918.
Ground gained by Allies.
FRANCE

© Arthur Banks 1973

Since 18 July, when Foch sent Mangin and Dégoutte to open the Allied attack, the following prisoners had been taken: 188,000 (by the British), 140,000 (by the French), 44,000, (by the Americans), and 14,000 (by the Belgians). Plus some 7,000 guns captured. If German killed and wounded are added, it is plain that the German armies could not continue to fight on effectively.

On 10 November, the Kaiser fled to Holland, followed by the Crown Prince. The basic Armistice terms signed at 1100 hours on 11 November were: immediate cessation of hostilities: German evacuation of invaded territory and of Alsace–Lorraine: repatriation of Allied citizens and prisoners of war: surrender of war materials and weapons: evacuation of the Rhine's left bank and bridgeheads: surrender of U–boats: internment of German surface warships: a declaration that the Treaties of Bucharest and Brest–Litovsk were null and void.

NOTE: MONS (FROM WHICH THE BRITISH RETREAT HAD BEGUN IN 1914) WAS RETAKEN BY THE CANADIANS A FEW HOURS PRIOR TO THE ARMISTICE.

197

THE PERIPHERAL CAMPAIGNS

Throughout the War most military leaders in Britain and France were 'Westerners'; they believed the principal task of their armies was to defeat the enemy in the theatre of operations which the Germans had themselves selected for their main effort. All other campaigns were dangerous 'sideshows', eating up men and munitions; and it was not until the final months of the war that a resolute effort was made to gain victories against Germany's allies in northern Italy, the Balkans, and the Middle East.

In practice these peripheral campaigns fall strategically into three categories. Some were intended, at least originally, as offensive thrusts against the central bloc from new points of the compass: the Italian and Macedonian Fronts, for example. Others were forced on the allies by Turkey's adhesion to the Germano-Austrian side: the need to defend the Suez lifeline by a campaign in Palestine, and to secure Anglo-Persian oil supplies by an offensive up the Shatt-el-Arab. Finally there was the fighting in Africa, and notably in German East Africa, where General von Lettow-Vorbeck waged colonial warfare throughout the four years of the European conflict, eventually surrendering a fortnight after the Armistice in France.

The character of several of these campaigns changed as the war dragged on: thus operations to safeguard oil refineries and counter intrigues in the Middle East developed into a lengthy campaign in Mesopotamia, with the possibility of a strike against the interior of Turkey. Conversely, the Italian Front, where it was hoped in 1915 that Austria-Hungary would drain away her last resources, became a burden for Italy's allies, although the Italian troops fought at first with fiercely whipped-up patriotic courage. They suffered from inadequate supplies of munitions and artillery, from poor training, and from the assumption that frontal assaults were the sole method of achieving victory. The Italians sustained 600,000 casualties in eleven offensives along the river Isonzo from mid-June 1915 to mid-September 1917; and after all this terrible fighting, they succeeded in advancing the front line only seven miles. The twelfth Isonzo battle, the combined German and Austrian offensive at Caporetto in October 1917, pushed the Italians back fifty miles to the river Piave. Eventually, on the first anniversary of Caporetto, the Italians launched an attack on the Austrian positions which cost them 25,000 casualties in sixty hours of grim combat, before the Austrians lost their headquarters at Vittorio Veneto and sued for peace.

The Salonika Front, originating with the Austro-German-Bulgarian offensive against Serbia (page 160) was for long quiescent, although joint operations by Serbs, Italians, Russians and French liberated Serbian Monastir in November 1916 and the British were heavily engaged with the Bulgarians around Lake Doiran and the River Struma in the spring of 1917. Disease, especially malaria, caused the heaviest casualties in Macedonia. The final offensive of 1918 involved an initial assault by the French and the Serbs on a formless ridge known as the Dobropolje, more than 7,000 feet above sea-level. Subsequently Franchet d'Espèrey's army made the swiftest long advance of the war, sweeping up to the Danube and the plains of Hungary, and preparing to march on Berlin by way of Budapest and Dresden.

In Palestine General Allenby, with elaborate deception and imaginative use of cavalry pushed the Turks (and the German 'Asia Corps') rapidly northwards into the Lebanon and Syria in the autumn of 1918. His advanced cavalry reached Aleppo before Turkish delegates concluded an armistice at Mudros on 30 October, with the commander-in-chief of the British Mediterranean Fleet. Both Allenby in Palestine and Franchet d'Espèrey in Salonika had shown the need for unconventional commanders filled with offensive spirit in the fringe theatres of war. So, indeed, did Lettow-Vorbeck in East Africa.

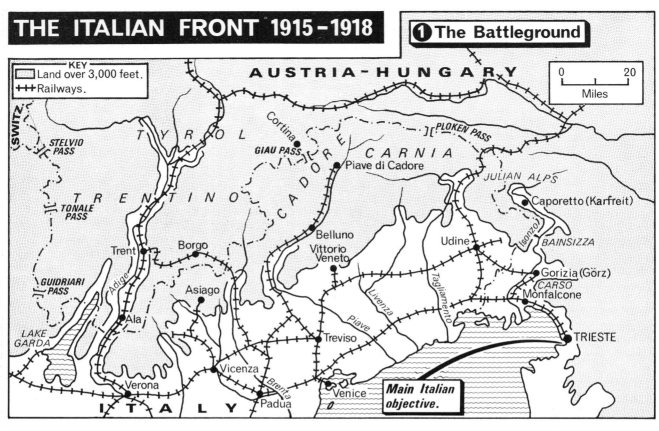

THE ITALIAN FRONT 1915-1918

① The Battleground

KEY
- ☐ Land over 3,000 feet.
- ╫╫╫ Railways.

0 — 20 Miles

AUSTRIA-HUNGARY

SWITZ.

STELVIO PASS

TYROL

Cortina

GIAU PASS
Piave di Cadore

CADORE

PLOKEN PASS

CARNIA

JULIAN ALPS

Caporetto (Karfreit)

BAINSIZZA

TRENTINO

TONALE PASS

Belluno
Vittorio Veneto

Udine

Isonzo

Trent   Borgo

Adige

GUIDRIARI PASS

Asiago

Ala

Livenza

Tagliamento

Gorizia (Görz)
CARSO
Monfalcone

LAKE GARDA

Treviso

Piave

TRIESTE

Verona

Vicenza

Brenta

Padua

Venice

Main Italian objective.

ITALY

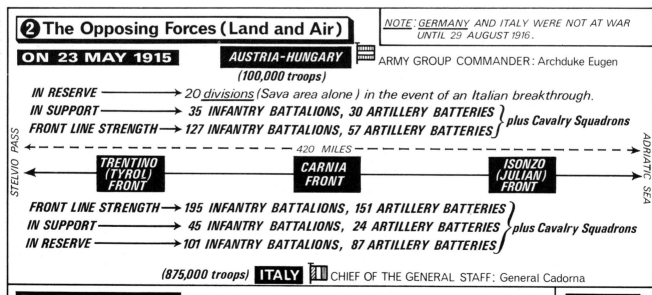

② The Opposing Forces (Land and Air)

NOTE: GERMANY AND ITALY WERE NOT AT WAR UNTIL 29 AUGUST 1916.

ON 23 MAY 1915

AUSTRIA-HUNGARY
(100,000 troops)

ARMY GROUP COMMANDER: Archduke Eugen

IN RESERVE ——→ 20 <u>divisions</u> (Sava area alone) in the event of an Italian breakthrough.

IN SUPPORT ——→ 35 INFANTRY BATTALIONS, 30 ARTILLERY BATTERIES ⎱ plus Cavalry Squadrons

FRONT LINE STRENGTH ——→ 127 INFANTRY BATTALIONS, 57 ARTILLERY BATTERIES ⎰

STELVIO PASS

←— — — — — — — — — — 420 MILES — — — — — — — — —→

ADRIATIC SEA

TRENTINO (TYROL) FRONT   **CARNIA FRONT**   **ISONZO (JULIAN) FRONT**

FRONT LINE STRENGTH ——→ 195 INFANTRY BATTALIONS, 151 ARTILLERY BATTERIES ⎫

IN SUPPORT ——→ 45 INFANTRY BATTALIONS, 24 ARTILLERY BATTERIES ⎬ plus Cavalry Squadrons

IN RESERVE ——→ 101 INFANTRY BATTALIONS, 87 ARTILLERY BATTERIES ⎭

(875,000 troops) **ITALY** CHIEF OF THE GENERAL STAFF: General Cadorna

BY 15 JUNE 1915

	ITALY	AUSTRIA-HUNGARY
INFANTRY BATTALIONS	415	234
ARTILLERY BATTERIES	326	155
CAVALRY SQUADRONS	116	21

<u>Note</u>: figures are deceptive.

Austria was stronger in heavy artillery and machine guns and many of her troops were already battle-experienced.

IN THE AIR
ITALY
77 Aircraft
including seaplanes
7 Airships
AUSTRIA-HUNGARY
136 Aircraft
including seaplanes
1 Airship

© Arthur Banks 1973

200

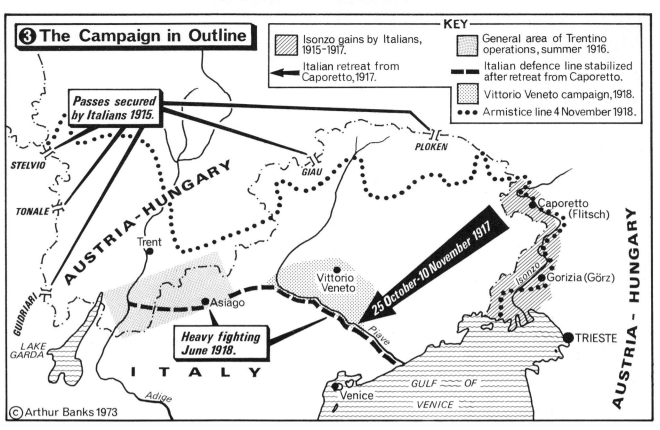

❸ The Campaign in Outline

— KEY —

Isonzo gains by Italians, 1915–1917.

Italian retreat from Caporetto, 1917.

General area of Trentino operations, summer 1916.

Italian defence line stabilized after retreat from Caporetto.

Vittorio Veneto campaign, 1918.

Armistice line 4 November 1918.

Passes secured by Italians 1915.

STELVIO

TONALE

GUIDRIARI

LAKE GARDA

AUSTRIA–HUNGARY

Trent

GIAU

PLOKEN

Caporetto (Flitsch)

Isonzo

Gorizia (Görz)

AUSTRIA – HUNGARY

25 October-10 November 1917

Vittorio Veneto

Asiago

Heavy fighting June 1918.

Plave

ITALY

Adige

Venice

TRIESTE

GULF — OF — VENICE

ⓒ Arthur Banks 1973

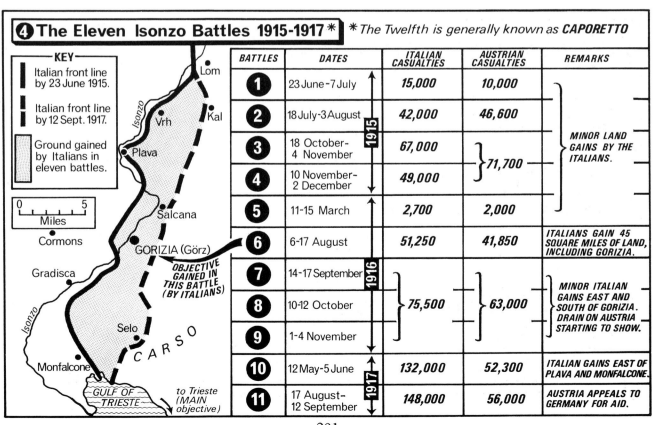

❹ The Eleven Isonzo Battles 1915-1917 *

* The Twelfth is generally known as CAPORETTO

— KEY —

Italian front line by 23 June 1915.

Italian front line by 12 Sept. 1917.

Ground gained by Italians in eleven battles.

0 ———— 5
Miles

Lom

Isonzo

Vrh

Kal

Plava

Cormons

Salcana

GORIZIA (Görz)

OBJECTIVE GAINED IN THIS BATTLE (BY ITALIANS)

Gradisca

Selo

CARSO

Monfalcone

GULF OF TRIESTE

to Trieste (MAIN objective)

BATTLES	DATES	ITALIAN CASUALTIES	AUSTRIAN CASUALTIES	REMARKS
❶	23 June-7 July	15,000	10,000	MINOR LAND GAINS BY THE ITALIANS.
❷	18 July-3 August	42,000	46,600	
❸	18 October-4 November	67,000	} 71,700	
❹	10 November-2 December	49,000		
❺	11-15 March	2,700	2,000	
❻	6-17 August	51,250	41,850	ITALIANS GAIN 45 SQUARE MILES OF LAND, INCLUDING GORIZIA.
❼	14-17 September	} 75,500	} 63,000	MINOR ITALIAN GAINS EAST AND SOUTH OF GORIZIA. DRAIN ON AUSTRIA STARTING TO SHOW.
❽	10-12 October			
❾	1-4 November			
❿	12 May-5 June	132,000	52,300	ITALIAN GAINS EAST OF PLAVA AND MONFALCONE.
⓫	17 August-12 September	148,000	56,000	AUSTRIA APPEALS TO GERMANY FOR AID.

(1915 spanning battles ❶–❹; 1916 spanning battles ❺–❾; 1917 spanning battles ❿–⓫)

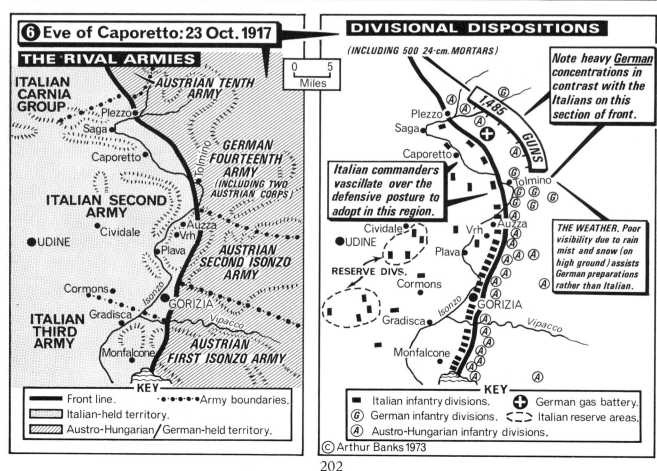

THE ITALIAN FRONT – continued

⑤ Austrian Trentino Offensive 1916

STAGE 1. AUSTRIAN ADVANCE

0 — 30
Miles

Bolzano

T R E N T I N O

Adige

AUSTRIAN ELEVENTH and THIRD ARMIES

Trent

Arco

ITALIAN

Arsiero

Asiago

FIRST ARMY

Feltre

Mt. Grappa

LAKE GARDA

Adige

KEY
- ——— Austrian front line 14 May.
- ⟹ Austrian drives.
- ▬ ▬ ▬ Austrian front line 16 June.
- ▨ Ground gained.

STAGE 2. ITALIAN COUNTER-OFFENSIVE

0 — 5
Miles

AUSTRIA-HUNGARY

pass

Roama

Asiago

pass

Arsiero

ITALY

KEY
- ——— Italian front line 17 June.
- ◀━━ Italian counter-attacks.
- ▬ ▬ ▬ Italian front line 1 July.
- ⣿ Ground regained by Italians.
- —·—·— Frontier.

CASUALTIES
AUSTRIAN
180,000
(estimate)
ITALIAN
286,000

⑥ Eve of Caporetto: 23 Oct. 1917

THE RIVAL ARMIES

0 — 5
Miles

ITALIAN CARNIA GROUP

AUSTRIAN TENTH ARMY

Plezzo

Saga

Caporetto

Tolmino

GERMAN FOURTEENTH ARMY (INCLUDING TWO AUSTRIAN CORPS)

ITALIAN SECOND ARMY

Cividale

Vrh

Auzza

Plava

AUSTRIAN SECOND ISONZO ARMY

UDINE

Cormons

Isonzo

GORIZIA

Vipacco

Gradisca

ITALIAN THIRD ARMY

Monfalcone

AUSTRIAN FIRST ISONZO ARMY

KEY
- ▬▬▬ Front line.
- ·•·•·• Army boundaries.
- ░ Italian-held territory.
- ▨ Austro-Hungarian / German-held territory.

DIVISIONAL DISPOSITIONS

(INCLUDING 500 24-cm. MORTARS)

Note heavy __German__ concentrations in contrast with the Italians on this section of front.

1,485 GUNS

Plezzo

Saga

Caporetto

Tolmino

Auzza

Italian commanders vascillate over the defensive posture to adopt in this region.

Cividale

Vrh

Plava

UDINE

RESERVE DIVS.

Cormons

Isonzo

GORIZIA

Vipacco

Gradisca

Monfalcone

THE WEATHER. Poor visibility due to rain mist and snow (on high ground) assists German preparations rather than Italian.

KEY
- ■ Italian infantry divisions.
- Ⓖ German infantry divisions.
- Ⓐ Austro-Hungarian infantry divisions.
- ✛ German gas battery.
- ⊂⊃ Italian reserve areas.

© Arthur Banks 1973

202

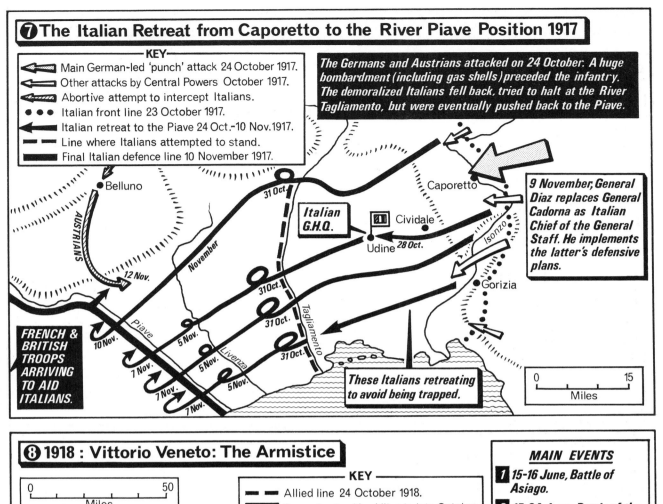

⑦ The Italian Retreat from Caporetto to the River Piave Position 1917

KEY

- ⬅ Main German-led 'punch' attack 24 October 1917.
- ⬅ Other attacks by Central Powers October 1917.
- ⬅ Abortive attempt to intercept Italians.
- ••• Italian front line 23 October 1917.
- ⬅ Italian retreat to the Piave 24 Oct.-10 Nov.1917.
- – – Line where Italians attempted to stand.
- ▬ Final Italian defence line 10 November 1917.

The Germans and Austrians attacked on 24 October. A huge bombardment (including gas shells) preceded the infantry. The demoralized Italians fell back, tried to halt at the River Tagliamento, but were eventually pushed back to the Piave.

9 November, General Diaz replaces General Cadorna as Italian Chief of the General Staff. He implements the latter's defensive plans.

Italian G.H.Q.

These Italians retreating to avoid being trapped.

FRENCH & BRITISH TROOPS ARRIVING TO AID ITALIANS.

Belluno · AUSTRIANS · 31 Oct. · November · 12 Nov. · Piave · 10 Nov. · 5 Nov. · 7 Nov. · 7 Nov. · 7 Nov. · 5 Nov. · Livenza · 5 Nov. · 31 Oct. · 31 Oct. · 31 Oct. · Tagliamento · Udine · 28 Oct. · Cividale · Caporetto · Isonzo · Gorizia

0 — 15 Miles

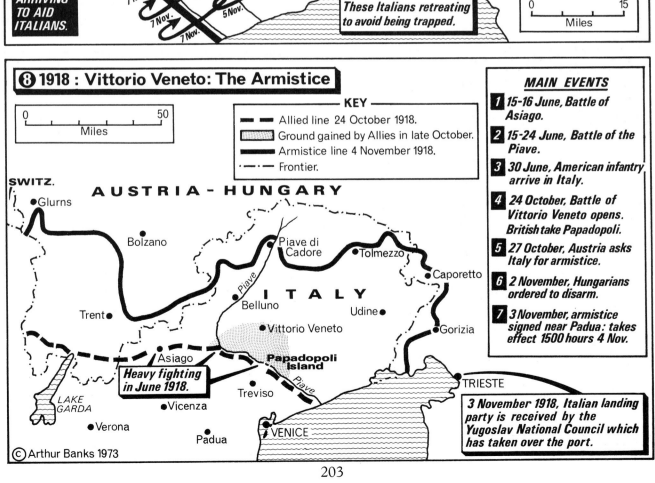

⑧ 1918 : Vittorio Veneto: The Armistice

0 — 50 Miles

KEY

- – – Allied line 24 October 1918.
- ▒ Ground gained by Allies in late October.
- ▬ Armistice line 4 November 1918.
- –·–· Frontier.

MAIN EVENTS

1 15-16 June, Battle of Asiago.

2 15-24 June, Battle of the Piave.

3 30 June, American infantry arrive in Italy.

4 24 October, Battle of Vittorio Veneto opens. British take Papadopoli.

5 27 October, Austria asks Italy for armistice.

6 2 November, Hungarians ordered to disarm.

7 3 November, armistice signed near Padua: takes effect 1500 hours 4 Nov.

SWITZ. · Glurns · AUSTRIA - HUNGARY · Bolzano · Piave di Cadore · Tolmezzo · Caporetto · Trent · I T A L Y · Piave · Belluno · Udine · Vittorio Veneto · Gorizia · Asiago · Papadopoli Island · TRIESTE · LAKE GARDA · Vicenza · Treviso · Piave · Verona · Padua · VENICE

Heavy fighting in June 1918.

3 November 1918, Italian landing party is received by the Yugoslav National Council which has taken over the port.

© Arthur Banks 1973

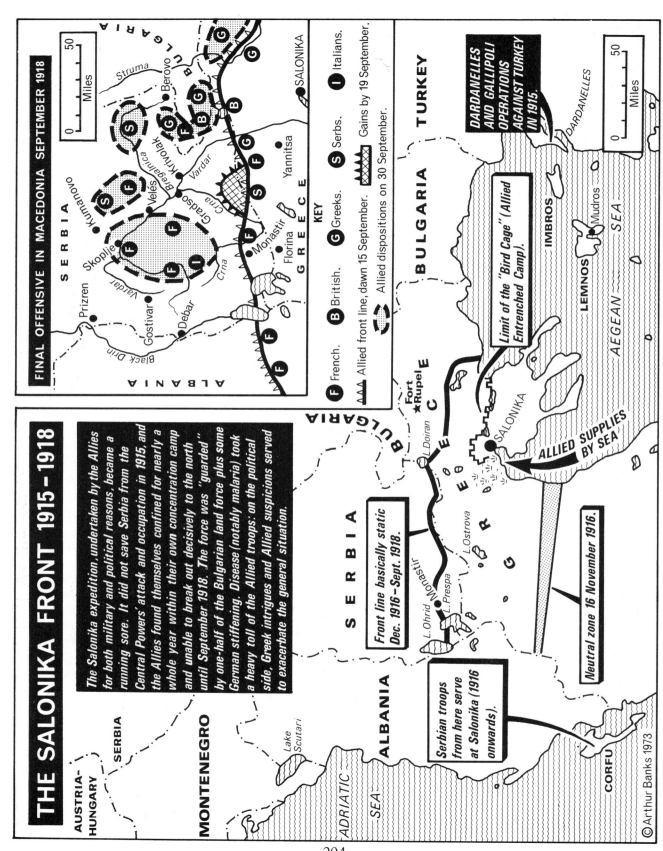

THE SALONIKA FRONT 1915–1918

The Salonika expedition, undertaken by the Allies for both military and political reasons, became a running sore. It did not save Serbia from the Central Powers' attack and occupation in 1915, and the Allies found themselves confined for nearly a whole year within their own concentration camp and unable to break out decisively to the north until September 1918. The force was "guarded" by one-half of the Bulgarian land force plus some German stiffening. Disease (notably malaria) took a heavy toll of the Allied troops: on the political side, Greek intrigues and Allied suspicions served to exacerbate the general situation.

AUSTRIA-HUNGARY

SERBIA

MONTENEGRO

Lake Scutari

ADRIATIC SEA

ALBANIA

SERBIA

Serbian troops from here serve at Salonika (1916 onwards).

Front line basically static Dec. 1916 – Sept. 1918.

L.Ohrid
Monastir
L.Prespa

Neutral zone 16 November 1916.

L.Ostrova

G R E E C E

BULGARIA

Fort Rupel
L.Doiran

SALONIKA

ALLIED SUPPLIES BY SEA

CORFU

ADRIATIC SEA

FINAL OFFENSIVE IN MACEDONIA SEPTEMBER 1918

Miles 0 ... 50

BULGARIA

Struma
Berovo

SERBIA

Kumanovo
Skopje
Prizren
Gostivar
Debar

Black Drin
Vardar

Krivolak
Gradsko
Veles
Bregalnica
Crna

Yannitsa
SALONIKA

Monastir
Florina
Crna

G R E E C E

ALBANIA

KEY

- **I** Italians.
- **S** Serbs.
- **G** Greeks.
- **B** British.
- **F** French.

Gains by 19 September.

Allied dispositions on 30 September.

Allied front line, dawn 15 September.

Allied dispositions on 30 September.

TURKEY

BULGARIA

DARDANELLES AND GALLIPOLI OPERATIONS AGAINST TURKEY IN 1915.

DARDANELLES

Limit of the "Bird Cage" (Allied Entrenched Camp).

IMBROS

LEMNOS
Mudros

AEGEAN SEA

Miles 0 ... 50

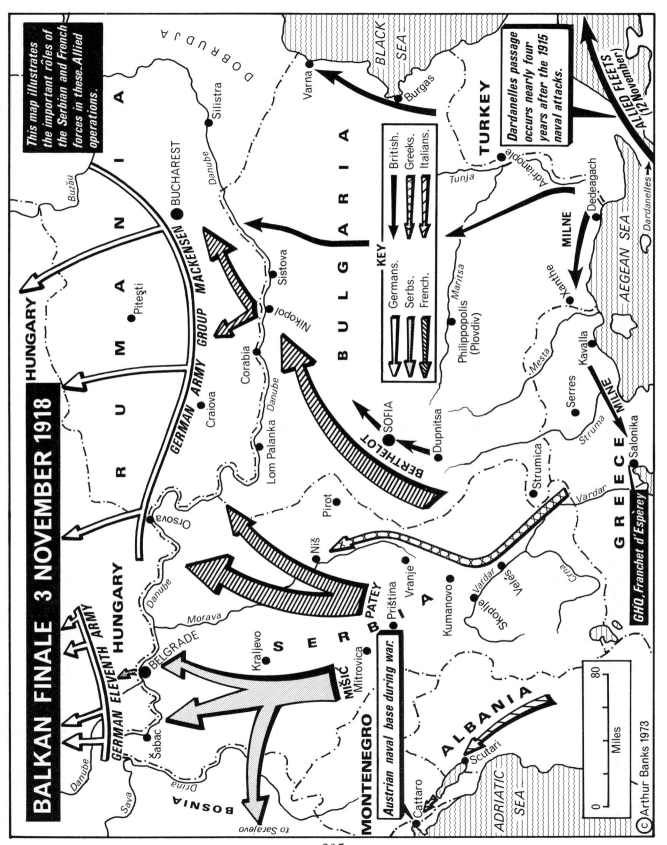

BALKAN FINALE 3 NOVEMBER 1918

This map illustrates the important rôles of the Serbian and French forces in these Allied operations.

Dardanelles passage occurs nearly four years after the 1915 naval attacks.

Austrian naval base during war.

KEY

British.	Greeks.	Italians.
Germans.	Serbs.	French.

GHQ, Franchet d'Esperey

ALLIED FLEETS (12 November)

DOBRUDJA

BLACK SEA

Varna
Burgas
Silistra

R U M A N I A

Buzău
BUCHAREST
Piteşti
Craiova
Danube
Sistova
Nikopol
Corabia
Lom Palanka
Danube
Orsova

HUNGARY

GERMAN ARMY GROUP MACKENSEN

TURKEY
Adrianople
Tunja

MILNE
Dedeagach
AEGEAN SEA
Dardanelles

B U L G A R I A

Maritsa
Philippopolis (Plovdiv)
SOFIA
Dupnitsa
BERTHELOT
Mesta
Serres
Kavalla
Struma
Strumica
MILNE
Salonika

Pirot
Niš
PATEY
Vranje
Priština
Kumanovo
Vardar
Veles
Skopje
Crna
Vardar

S E R B I A

Kraljevo
MIŠIĆ
Mitrovica
BELGRADE

GERMAN ELEVENTH ARMY

HUNGARY
Danube
Morava
Danube
Sava
Drina
Šabac

BOSNIA

MONTENEGRO

ALBANIA
Scutari
Cattaro

G R E E C E

ADRIATIC SEA

to Sarajevo

| 0 | Miles | 80 |

© Arthur Banks 1973

205

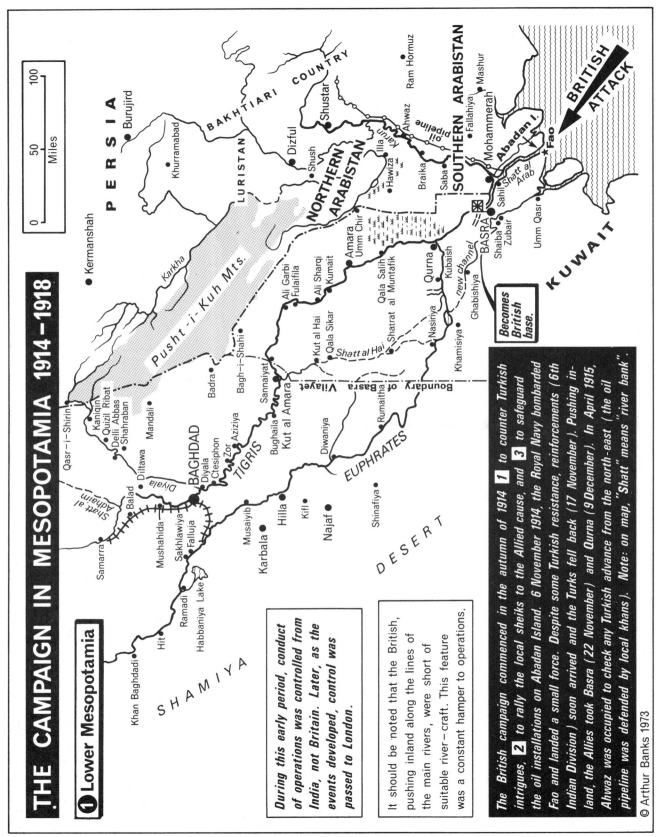

THE CAMPAIGN IN MESOPOTAMIA 1914–1918

1 Lower Mesopotamia

During this early period, conduct of operations was controlled from India, not Britain. Later, as the events developed, control was passed to London.

It should be noted that the British, pushing inland along the lines of the main rivers, were short of suitable river-craft. This feature was a constant hamper to operations.

The British campaign commenced in the autumn of 1914 ① to counter Turkish intrigues, ② to rally the local sheiks to the Allied cause, and ③ to safeguard the oil installations on Abadan Island. 6 November 1914, the Royal Navy bombarded Fao and landed a small force. Despite some Turkish resistance, reinforcements (6th Indian Division) soon arrived and the Turks fell back (17 November). Pushing in-land, the Allies took Basra (22 November) and Qurna (9 December). In April 1915, Ahwaz was occupied to check any Turkish advance from the north-east (the oil pipeline was defended by local khans). Note: on map, "Shatt" means "river bank".

© Arthur Banks 1973

PERSIA

BAKHTIARI COUNTRY

LURISTAN

NORTHERN ARABISTAN

SOUTHERN ARABISTAN

BRITISH ATTACK

Pusht-i-Kuh Mts.

Boundary of Basra Vilayet

TIGRIS

EUPHRATES

DESERT

SHAMIYA

KUWAIT

BAGHDAD

BASRA

Becomes British base.

• Kermanshah
• Burujird
• Khurramabad
Dizful •
Shush •
Shustar •
• Ram Hormuz
Illa •
Hawiza •
Karun
oil pipeline
Ahwaz •
Mashur •
• Fallahiya
• Mohammerah
Abadan I.
★ Fao
Sahil
Shatt al Arab
Braika •
Saba •
Zubair •
Shaiba •
Umm Qasr •
new channel
Ghabishiya •
Kubaish •
Qurna •
Amara
Umm Chir
Ali Sharqi
Kumait •
Qala Salih •
Shatrat al Muntafik •
Nasiriya •
Khamisiya •
Ali Garbi •
Fulaifila •
Kut al Hai •
Qala Sikar •
Shatt al Hai
Rumaitha •
Diwaniya •
Shinafiya •
Najaf •
Kifl •
Hilla •
Karbala •
Musaiyib •
Habbaniya Lake
Falluja •
Sakhlawiya •
Mushahida •
Balad •
Samarra •
Shatt al Adhaim
Ramadi •
Hit •
Khan Baghdadi •
Qasr-i-Shirin •
Kaniqin •
Quizil Ribat •
Delli Abbas •
Shahraban •
Mandali •
Dilltawa •
Diyala
Ctesiphon •
Zor •
Aziziya •
Sannaiyat •
Bughaila
Kut al Amara
Badra •
Bagh-i-Shahi •
Khaninghela
Kharkha
Karkha

Miles
0 50 100

206

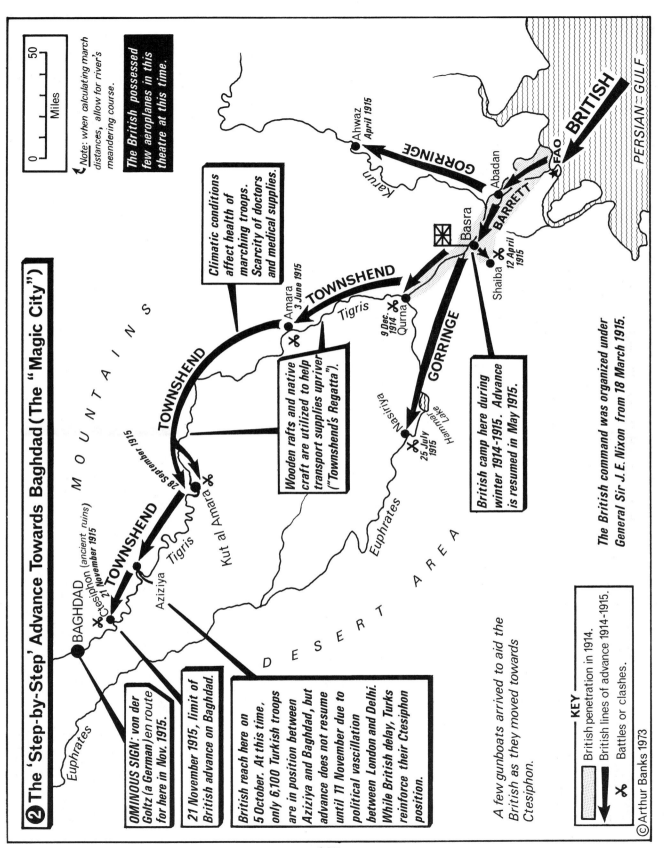

② The 'Step-by-Step' Advance Towards Baghdad (The "Magic City")

Note: when calculating march distances, allow for river's meandering course.

The British possessed few aeroplanes in this theatre at this time.

Climatic conditions affect health of marching troops. Scarcity of doctors and medical supplies.

Wooden rafts and native craft are utilized to help transport supplies upriver ("Townshend's Regatta").

British camp here during winter 1914-1915. Advance is resumed in May 1915.

A few gunboats arrived to aid the British as they moved towards Ctesiphon.

OMINOUS SIGN': von der Goltz (a German) en route for here in Nov. 1915.

21 November 1915, limit of British advance on Baghdad.

British reach here on 5 October. At this time, only 6,100 Turkish troops are in position between Aziziya and Baghdad, but advance does not resume until 11 November due to political vascillation between London and Delhi. While British delay, Turks reinforce their Ctesiphon position.

The British command was organized under General Sir J. E. Nixon from 18 March 1915.

BRITISH

GORRINGE

BARRETT

TOWNSHEND

TOWNSHEND

TOWNSHEND

GORRINGE

PERSIAN GULF

Ahwaz *April 1915*

Karun

FAO

Abadan

Basra

Shaiba
12 April 1915

9 Dec. 1914 Qurna

Tigris

Amara *3 June 1915*

M O U N T A I N S

Kut al Amara

Tigris

Aziziya

Ctesiphon *21 November 1915*

BAGHDAD *(ancient ruins)*

28 September 1915

Euphrates

Euphrates

Nasiriya

Hammar Lake

25 July 1915

D E S E R T   A R E A

50

Miles

0

KEY
British penetration in 1914.
British lines of advance 1914-1915.
Battles or clashes.

© Arthur Banks 1973

207

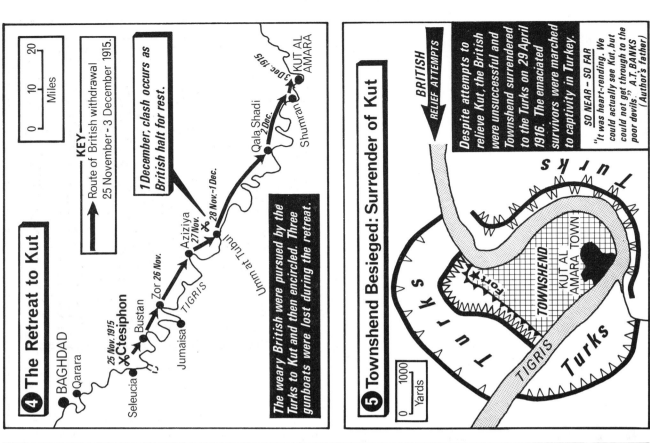

4 The Retreat to Kut

BAGHDAD
Qarara

Seleucia
Ctesiphon 25 Nov. 1915
Jumaisa
Bustan
Zor 26 Nov.
TIGRIS
Aziziya 27 Nov.
28 Nov.–1 Dec.
Umm at Tubul
Qala Shadi 2 Dec.
Shumran
KUT AL AMARA
3 Dec. 1915

KEY
→ Route of British withdrawal 25 November – 3 December 1915.

0 10 20
Miles

1 December, clash occurs as British halt for rest.

The weary British were pursued by the Turks to Kut and then encircled. Three gunboats were lost during the retreat.

5 Townshend Besieged: Surrender of Kut

Despite attempts to relieve Kut, the British were unsuccessful and Townshend surrendered to the Turks on 29 April 1916. The emaciated survivors were marched into captivity in Turkey.

BRITISH RELIEF ATTEMPTS

SO NEAR – SO FAR
"It was heart-rending. We could actually see Kut, but could not get through to the poor devils." A.T. BANKS (Author's father)

Turks
FORT
TOWNSHEND
KUT AL AMARA TOWN
TIGRIS
Turks
Turks

0 1000
Yards

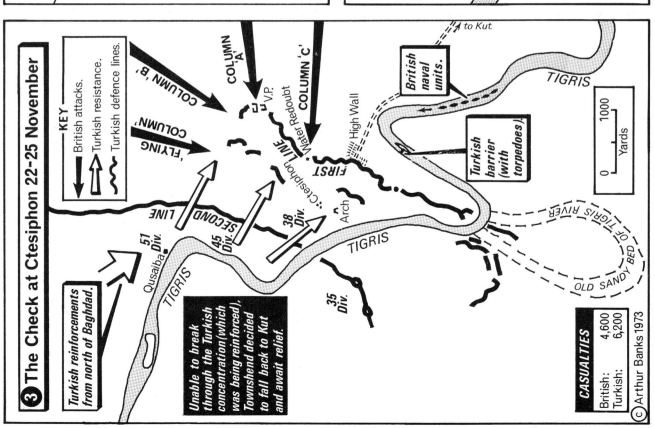

3 The Check at Ctesiphon 22–25 November

Turkish reinforcements from north of Baghdad.

KEY
→ British attacks.
⇧ Turkish resistance.
∿ Turkish defence lines.

COLUMN 'A'
COLUMN 'B'
COLUMN 'C'
'FLYING' COLUMN
V.P.
Water Redoubt
High Wall
FIRST LINE
SECOND LINE
Ctesiphon
Arch
51 Div.
Qusaiba
45 Div.
38 Div.
35 Div.
TIGRIS
TIGRIS
TIGRIS
OLD SANDY BED OF TIGRIS RIVER
to Kut
British naval units.
Turkish barrier (with torpedoes).

0 1000
Yards

Unable to break through the Turkish concentration (which was being reinforced), Townshend decided to fall back to Kut and await relief.

CASUALTIES
British: 4,600
Turkish: 6,200

© Arthur Banks 1973

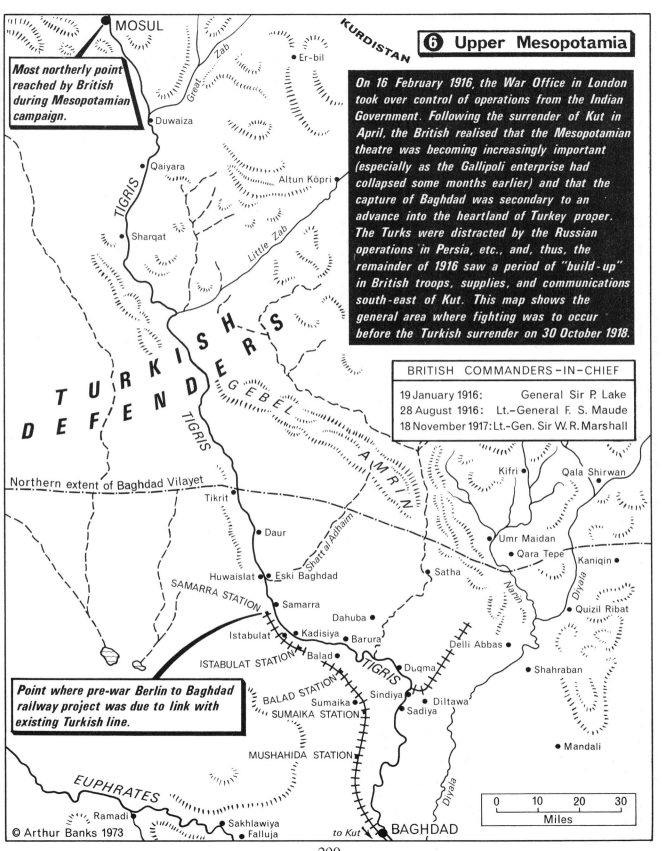

MOSUL

KURDISTAN

6 Upper Mesopotamia

Great Zab

• Er-bil

Most northerly point reached by British during Mesopotamian campaign.

• Duwaiza

• Qaiyara

Altun Köpri •

TIGRIS

Little Zab

• Sharqat

On 16 February 1916, the War Office in London took over control of operations from the Indian Government. Following the surrender of Kut in April, the British realised that the Mesopotamian theatre was becoming increasingly important (especially as the Gallipoli enterprise had collapsed some months earlier) and that the capture of Baghdad was secondary to an advance into the heartland of Turkey proper. The Turks were distracted by the Russian operations in Persia, etc., and, thus, the remainder of 1916 saw a period of "build-up" in British troops, supplies, and communications south-east of Kut. This map shows the general area where fighting was to occur before the Turkish surrender on 30 October 1918.

BRITISH COMMANDERS – IN – CHIEF

19 January 1916:   General Sir P. Lake
28 August 1916:   Lt.-General F. S. Maude
18 November 1917: Lt.-Gen. Sir W. R. Marshall

T U R K I S H

D E F E N D E R S

GEBEL

TIGRIS

HAMRIN

Kifri •

Qala Shirwan •

Northern extent of Baghdad Vilayet

• Tikrit

• Daur

Umr Maidan •

Qara Tepe •

Kaniqin •

Shatt al Adhaim

Huwaislat • Eski Baghdad

SAMARRA STATION

• Satha

Narin

Diyala

• Quizil Ribat

• Samarra

Dahuba •

Istabulat

• Kadisiya

• Barura

Delli Abbas •

ISTABULAT STATION

Balad •

TIGRIS

Duqma •

• Shahraban

BALAD STATION

Sumaika •

Sindiya •

Sadiya •

• Diltawa

Point where pre-war Berlin to Baghdad railway project was due to link with existing Turkish line.

SUMAIKA STATION

• Mandali

MUSHAHIDA STATION

EUPHRATES

Diyala

| 0 | 10 | 20 | 30 |

Miles

• Ramadi

© Arthur Banks 1973

Sakhlawiya •
• Falluja

to Kut

BAGHDAD

209

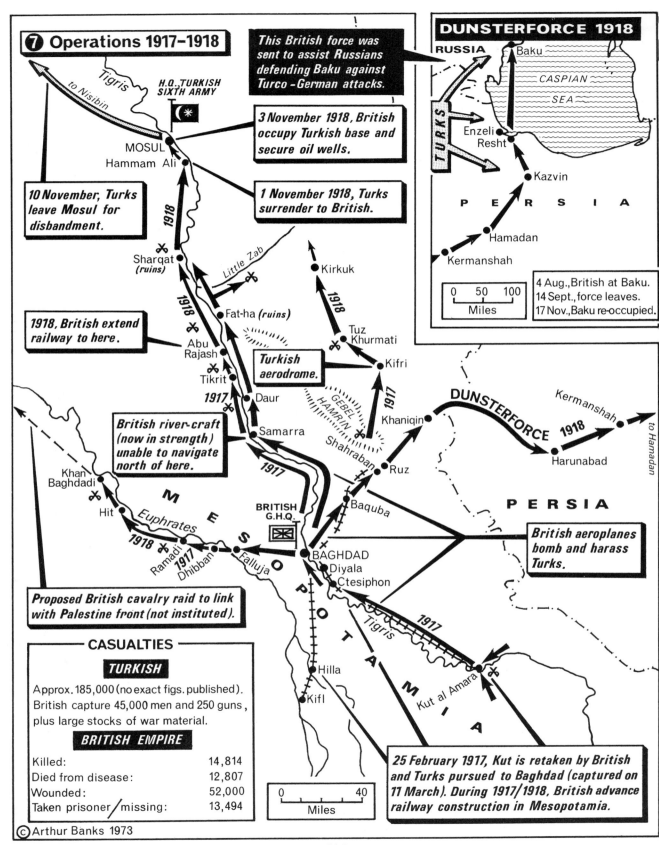

7 Operations 1917–1918

This British force was sent to assist Russians defending Baku against Turco-German attacks.

DUNSTERFORCE 1918

RUSSIA

Baku

CASPIAN SEA

TURKS

Enzeli
Resht

Kazvin

PERSIA

Hamadan

Kermanshah

4 Aug., British at Baku.
14 Sept., force leaves.
17 Nov., Baku re-occupied.

0   50   100
Miles

Tigris

to Nisibin

H.Q., TURKISH SIXTH ARMY

3 November 1918, British occupy Turkish base and secure oil wells.

MOSUL
Hammam Ali

10 November, Turks leave Mosul for disbandment.

1 November 1918, Turks surrender to British.

1918

Sharqat (ruins)

Little Zab

Kirkuk

1918, British extend railway to here.

1918

Fat-ha (ruins)

Tuz Khurmati

Abu Rajash

Turkish aerodrome.

Kifri

1918

Tikrit

1917

Daur

GEBEL HAMRIN

Khaniqin

DUNSTERFORCE

Kermanshah

1918

Samarra

British river-craft (now in strength) unable to navigate north of here.

Shahraban

1917

Ruz

Harunabad

to Hamadan

Khan Baghdadi

Hit

Euphrates

M E S

1917

Baquba

PERSIA

1918

Ramadi

1917

Dhibban

Falluja

O

BRITISH G.H.Q.

BAGHDAD

Diyala

British aeroplanes bomb and harass Turks.

Proposed British cavalry raid to link with Palestine front (not instituted).

P

Ctesiphon

O

T

Tigris

1917

CASUALTIES

TURKISH

Approx. 185,000 (no exact figs. published). British capture 45,000 men and 250 guns, plus large stocks of war material.

BRITISH EMPIRE

Killed:	14,814
Died from disease:	12,807
Wounded:	52,000
Taken prisoner/missing:	13,494

A

Hilla

M

Kut al Amara

I

Kifl

A

0   40
Miles

25 February 1917, Kut is retaken by British and Turks pursued to Baghdad (captured on 11 March). During 1917/1918, British advance railway construction in Mesopotamia.

© Arthur Banks 1973

210

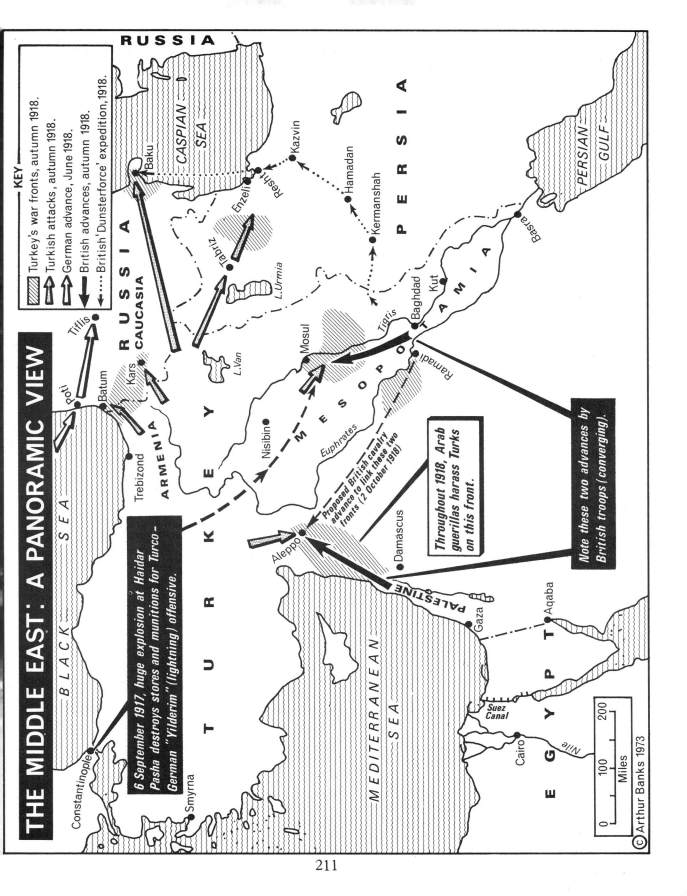

THE MIDDLE EAST: A PANORAMIC VIEW

KEY

Turkey's war fronts, autumn 1918.
Turkish attacks, autumn 1918.
German advance, June 1918.
British advances, autumn 1918.
British 'Dunsterforce' expedition, 1918.

RUSSIA

CASPIAN SEA

PERSIA

PERSIAN GULF

Baku

Kazvin

Enzeli

Resht

Hamadan

Tabriz

Kermanshah

L. Urmia

Basra

Tiflis

RUSSIA
CAUCASIA

Mosul

Baghdad

Kut

Tigris

Ramadi

poti

Batum

Kars

L. Van

MESOPOTAMIA

Trebizond

ARMENIA

Nisibin

Euphrates

Proposed British cavalry advance to link these two fronts (2 October 1918)

Throughout 1918, Arab guerillas harass Turks on this front.

Damascus

Note these two advances by British troops (converging).

T U R K E Y

Aleppo

PALESTINE

Gaza

Aqaba

6 September 1917, huge explosion at Haidar Pasha destroys stores and munitions for Turco–German "Yilderim" (lightning) offensive.

BLACK SEA

Constantinople

Smyrna

MEDITERRANEAN SEA

Suez Canal

Nile

Cairo

E G Y P T

0   100   200

Miles

© Arthur Banks 1973

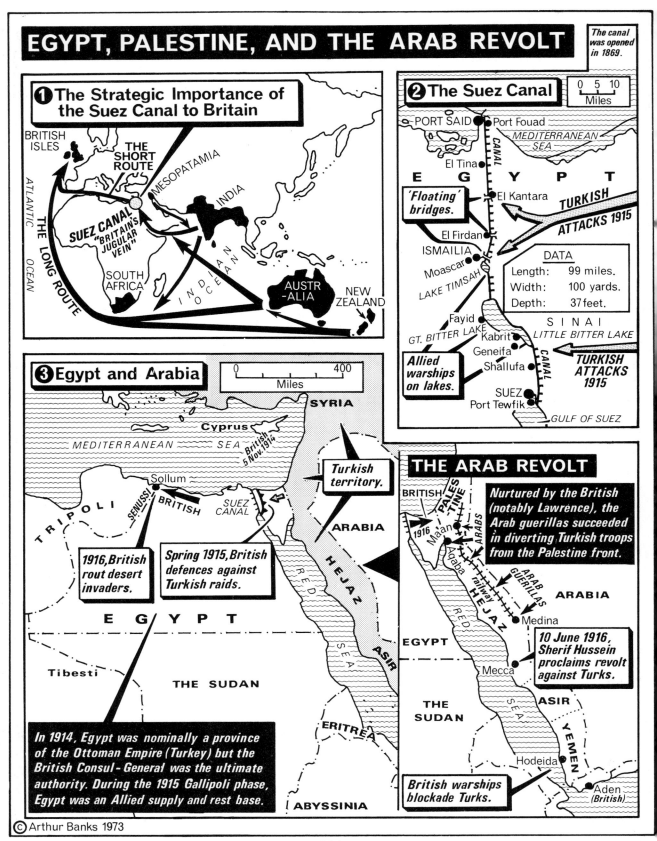

EGYPT, PALESTINE, AND THE ARAB REVOLT

The canal was opened in 1869.

❶ The Strategic Importance of the Suez Canal to Britain

BRITISH ISLES

THE SHORT ROUTE

ATLANTIC OCEAN

THE LONG ROUTE

MESOPATAMIA

INDIA

SUEZ CANAL "BRITAIN'S JUGULAR VEIN"

SOUTH AFRICA

INDIAN OCEAN

AUSTR-ALIA

NEW ZEALAND

❷ The Suez Canal

0 5 10 Miles

PORT SAID — Port Fouad

MEDITERRANEAN SEA

El Tina

E G Y P T

El Kantara

CANAL

TURKISH ATTACKS 1915

'Floating' bridges.

El Firdan

ISMAILIA

Moascar

LAKE TIMSAH

DATA	
Length:	99 miles.
Width:	100 yards.
Depth:	37 feet.

Fayid

GT. BITTER LAKE

Kabrit

Geneifa

Shallufa

S I N A I

LITTLE BITTER LAKE

Allied warships on lakes.

SUEZ

Port Tewfik

CANAL

TURKISH ATTACKS 1915

GULF OF SUEZ

❸ Egypt and Arabia

0 400 Miles

SYRIA

Cyprus

MEDITERRANEAN SEA

British 5 Nov. 1914

Sollum

SENUSSI

BRITISH

SUEZ CANAL

TRIPOLI

Turkish territory.

ARABIA

1916, British rout desert invaders.

Spring 1915, British defences against Turkish raids.

E G Y P T

HEJAZ

RED SEA

ASIR

Tibesti

THE SUDAN

ERITREA

In 1914, Egypt was nominally a province of the Ottoman Empire (Turkey) but the British Consul-General was the ultimate authority. During the 1915 Gallipoli phase, Egypt was an Allied supply and rest base.

ABYSSINIA

THE ARAB REVOLT

Nurtured by the British (notably Lawrence), the Arab guerillas succeeded in diverting Turkish troops from the Palestine front.

BRITISH

PALESTINE

1916

Ma'an

ARABS

Aqaba

ARAB railway

ARAB GUERILLAS

ARABIA

HEJAZ

RED SEA

Medina

EGYPT

10 June 1916, Sherif Hussein proclaims revolt against Turks.

Mecca

ASIR

THE SUDAN

YEMEN

Hodeida

British warships blockade Turks.

Aden (British)

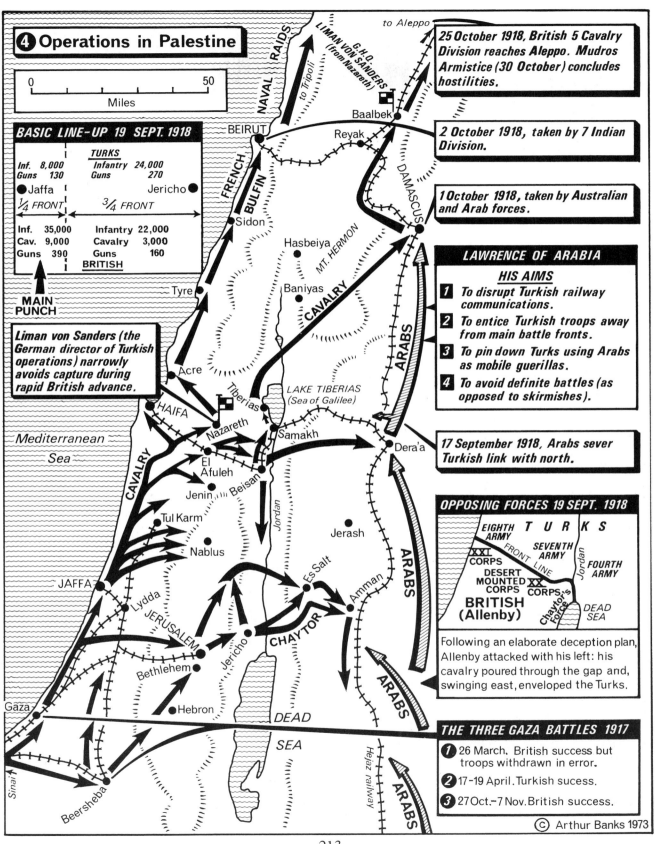

④ Operations in Palestine

0 _____ 50
Miles

BASIC LINE-UP 19 SEPT. 1918

	TURKS
Inf. 8,000	Infantry 24,000
Guns 130	Guns 270
● Jaffa	Jericho ●
¼ FRONT	¾ FRONT
Inf. 35,000	Infantry 22,000
Cav. 9,000	Cavalry 3,000
Guns 390	Guns 160
	BRITISH

MAIN PUNCH

Liman von Sanders (the German director of Turkish operations) narrowly avoids capture during rapid British advance.

NAVAL RAIDS

to Tripoli

G.H.Q. LIMAN VON SANDERS (from Nazareth)

to Aleppo

25 October 1918, British 5 Cavalry Division reaches Aleppo. Mudros Armistice (30 October) concludes hostilities.

Baalbek

Reyak

2 October 1918, taken by 7 Indian Division.

1 October 1918, taken by Australian and Arab forces.

FRENCH

BULFIN

BEIRUT

Sidon

Hasbeiya

MT. HERMON

Baniyas

DAMASCUS

CAVALRY

ARABS

LAWRENCE OF ARABIA

HIS AIMS

1 To disrupt Turkish railway communications.

2 To entice Turkish troops away from main battle fronts.

3 To pin down Turks using Arabs as mobile guerillas.

4 To avoid definite battles (as opposed to skirmishes).

Tyre

Acre

Mediterranean Sea

HAIFA

Tiberias

LAKE TIBERIAS (Sea of Galilee)

Nazareth

Samakh

Dera'a

17 September 1918, Arabs sever Turkish link with north.

CAVALRY

El Afuleh

Jenin

Beisan

Jordan

Tul Karm

Nablus

Jerash

ARABS

OPPOSING FORCES 19 SEPT. 1918

T U R K S

EIGHTH ARMY

XXI CORPS

FRONT LINE

SEVENTH ARMY

Jordan

FOURTH ARMY

DESERT MOUNTED CORPS

XX CORPS

Chaytor's Force

BRITISH (Allenby)

DEAD SEA

Following an elaborate deception plan, Allenby attacked with his left: his cavalry poured through the gap and, swinging east, enveloped the Turks.

JAFFA

Lydda

JERUSALEM

Jericho

Bethlehem

Es Salt

Amman

CHAYTOR

ARABS

Gaza

Hebron

DEAD SEA

Hejaz railway

ARABS

THE THREE GAZA BATTLES 1917

❶ 26 March. British success but troops withdrawn in error.

❷ 17-19 April. Turkish sucess.

❸ 27 Oct.-7 Nov. British success.

Sinai

Beersheba

© Arthur Banks 1973

213

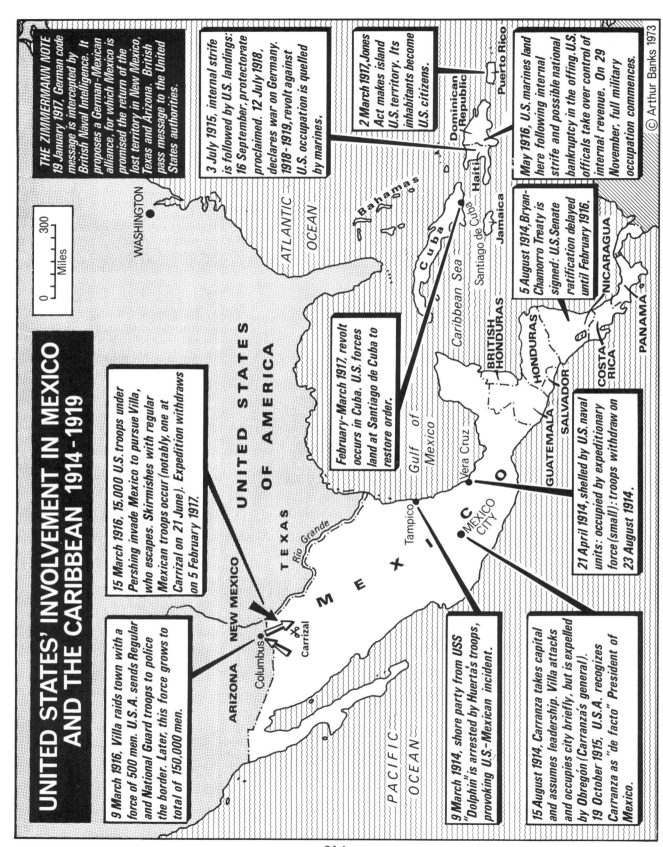

UNITED STATES' INVOLVEMENT IN MEXICO AND THE CARIBBEAN 1914-1919

© Arthur Banks 1973

THE ZIMMERMANN NOTE 19 January 1917, German code message is intercepted by British Naval Intelligence. It proposes a German-Mexican alliance, for which Mexico is promised the return of the lost territory in New Mexico, Texas and Arizona. British pass message to the United States authorities.

3 July 1915, internal strife is followed by U.S. landings: 16 September, protectorate proclaimed. 12 July 1918, declares war on Germany. 1918-1919, revolt against U.S. occupation is quelled by marines.

2 March 1917, Jones Act makes island U.S. territory. Its inhabitants become U.S. citizens.

May 1916, U.S. marines land here following internal strife and possible national bankruptcy in the offing. U.S. officials take over control of internal revenue. On 29 November, full military occupation commences.

5 August 1914, Bryan-Chamorro Treaty is signed: U.S. Senate ratification delayed until February 1916.

9 March 1916, Villa raids town with a force of 500 men. U.S.A. sends Regular and National Guard troops to police the border. Later, this force grows to total of 150,000 men.

15 March 1916, 15,000 U.S. troops under Pershing invade Mexico to pursue Villa, who escapes. Skirmishes with regular Mexican troops occur (notably, one at Carrizal on 21 June). Expedition withdraws on 5 February 1917.

February-March 1917, revolt occurs in Cuba. U.S. forces land at Santiago de Cuba to restore order.

21 April 1914, shelled by U.S. naval units: occupied by expeditionary force (small): troops withdraw on 23 August 1914.

9 March 1914, shore party from USS "Dolphin" is arrested by Huerta's troops, provoking U.S.-Mexican incident.

15 August 1914, Carranza takes capital and assumes leadership. Villa attacks and occupies city briefly, but is expelled by Obregón (Carranza's general). 19 October 1915, U.S.A. recognizes Carranza as "de facto" President of Mexico.

WASHINGTON

ATLANTIC OCEAN

Bahamas

Cuba

Santiago de Cuba

Jamaica

Haiti

Dominican Republic

Puerto Rico

Caribbean Sea

BRITISH HONDURAS

HONDURAS

NICARAGUA

SALVADOR

GUATEMALA

COSTA RICA

PANAMA

UNITED STATES OF AMERICA

ARIZONA

NEW MEXICO

TEXAS

Rio Grande

Columbus

Carrizal

Gulf of Mexico

Vera Cruz

Tampico

MEXICO CITY

MEXICO

PACIFIC OCEAN

0   300
Miles

214

SOUTH AMERICA 1914-1918

KEY

■ At war against the Central Powers 1917-1918.

☐ Neutral states.

▨ British territory.

▨ French territory.

➜ Track of SMS 'Dresden' from 8 December 1914 to 14 March 1915.

0 — 500 Miles

Panama Canal

VENEZUELA

DUTCH GUIANA

BRITISH GUIANA

FRENCH GUIANA

COLOMBIA

ECUADOR

PERU

B R A Z I L

BOLIVIA

PARAGUAY

ATLANTIC OCEAN

PACIFIC OCEAN

CHILE

ARGENTINA

URUGUAY

Buenos Aires

Coronel

April 1917, the 'Paraná' is sunk by a German submarine.
11 April 1917, Brazil severs her relations with Germany and on 1 June 1917, revokes neutrality in favour of the Allies.
26 October 1917, Brazil declares war upon the Central Powers.

1914, revolt led by Benavides ends in the overthrow of President Billinghurst. Pardo is president from 1914 to 1919; breaks off diplomatic relations with Germany in 1917.

14 March 1915, SMS 'Dresden' is destroyed following action with HMS 'Glasgow' and 'Kent'.

Juan Fernandez Islands

1 November 1914, naval battle.

HUNTED BY BRITISH WARSHIPS

1917, three Argentinian ships are sunk by German submarines. After secret diplomatic exchanges, the German minister is withdrawn from Buenos Aires.

German cruiser SMS 'Dresden' is the sole survivor from the Falkland Islands naval battle.

Brazil was the sole Latin American state at war with the Central Powers. In 1918, a Brazilian squadron served for nine months with the Allies off the African coast, and on 10 November 1918, Brazilian warships entered the Mediterranean Sea for further duty with the Allies.

'Dresden' hides in this area from 11 December 1914 to 8 February 1915.

Falkland Islands

8 December 1914, naval battle.

© Arthur Banks 1973

215

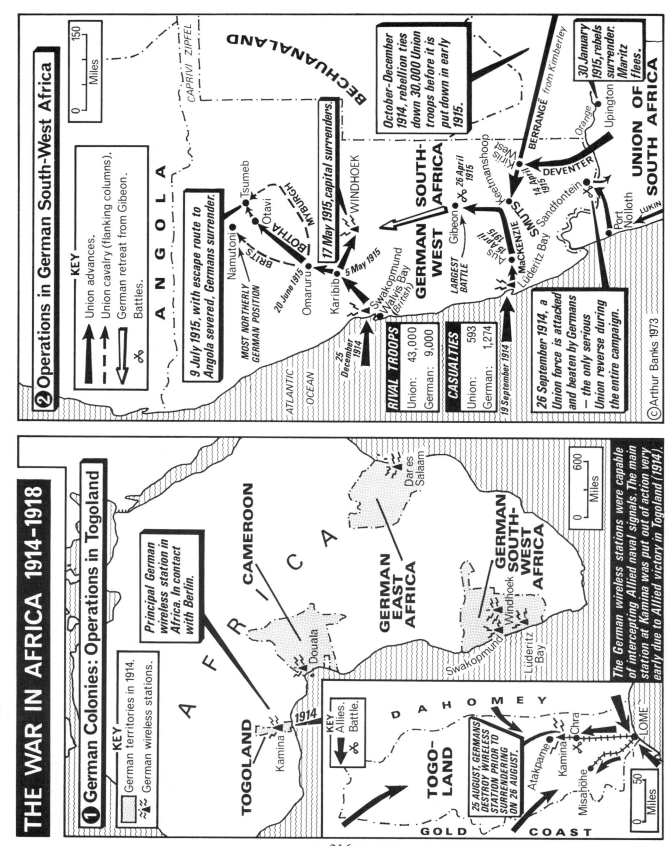

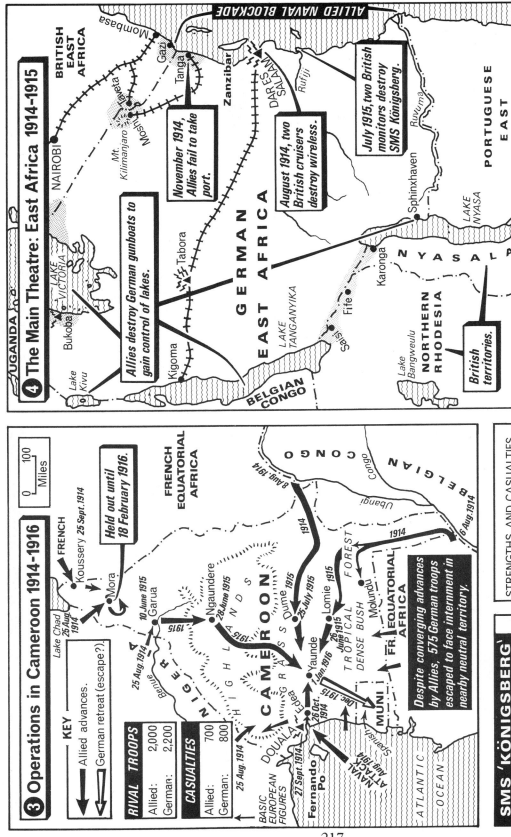

④ The Main Theatre: East Africa 1914-1915

BRITISH EAST AFRICA

Mombasa

Gazi

Tanga

Zanzibar

DAR ES SALAAM

Rufiji

INDIAN OCEAN

MOZAMBIQUE

November 1914, Allies fail to take port.

August 1914, two British cruisers destroy wireless.

July 1915, two British monitors destroy SMS Königsberg.

NAIROBI

Mt. Kilimanjaro

Moshi

Taveta

UGANDA

LAKE VICTORIA

Bukoba

Allies destroy German gunboats to gain control of lakes.

Tabora

G E R M A N   E A S T   A F R I C A

Kigoma

LAKE TANGANYIKA

BELGIAN CONGO

Lake Kivu

Saisi

Fife

Karonga

Sphinxhaven

LAKE NYASA

PORTUGUESE EAST AFRICA

Ruvuma

ZOMBA

Lake Chilwa

Blantyre

N Y A S A L A N D

NORTHERN RHODESIA

Lake Bangweulu

British territories.

KEY

0   150
Miles

Areas where fighting occurred.

Wireless stations.

© Arthur Banks 1973

③ Operations in Cameroon 1914-1916

0   100
Miles

FRENCH

Koussery 25 Sept. 1914

Held out until 18 February 1916.

FRENCH EQUATORIAL AFRICA

Lake Chad

26 Aug. 1914

Mora

25 Aug. 1914

10 June 1915

Garua

1915

N I G E R I A

Benue

25 Aug. 1914

H I G H L A N D S

G R A S S

Ngaundere

28 June 1915

Dume

25 July 1915

Lomie

June 1915

26 June 1915

1915

Yaunde

Jan. 1916

C A M E R O O N

Edea

DOUALA

26 Oct. 1914

Dec. 1915

Oct. 1915

Spanish

27 Sept. 1914

NAVAL ATTACK Aug. 1914

Fernando Po

25 Aug. 1914

ATLANTIC OCEAN

C O N G O

8 Aug. 1914

1914

6 Aug. 1914

1914

Ubangi

Congo

B E L G I A N

Molundu

T R O P I C A L   D E N S E   B U S H

FR. EQUATORIAL AFRICA

E Q U A T O R I A L   F O R E S T

MUNI

Despite converging advances by Allies, 575 German troops escaped to face internment in nearby neutral territory.

KEY

Allied advances.

German retreat (escape?).

RIVAL TROOPS
BASIC EUROPEAN FIGURES

Allied: 2,000
German: 2,200

CASUALTIES

Allied: 700
German: 800

SMS 'KÖNIGSBERG'

The German light cruiser 'Königsberg' sank HMS 'Pegasus' in Zanzibar harbour in September 1914 but later was blockaded in the Rufiji river. She was destroyed on 11 July 1915 after an action with British monitors and two aircraft, but her guns were salvaged and used by the Germans in east Africa.

STRENGTHS AND CASUALTIES

These cannot be given precisely on maps as a detailed analysis of each total is necessary. For example, the German force which surrendered at Abercorn on 25 November 1918, included 30 German officers, 125 other Europeans, Askari, porters, headmen, natives, and women.

217

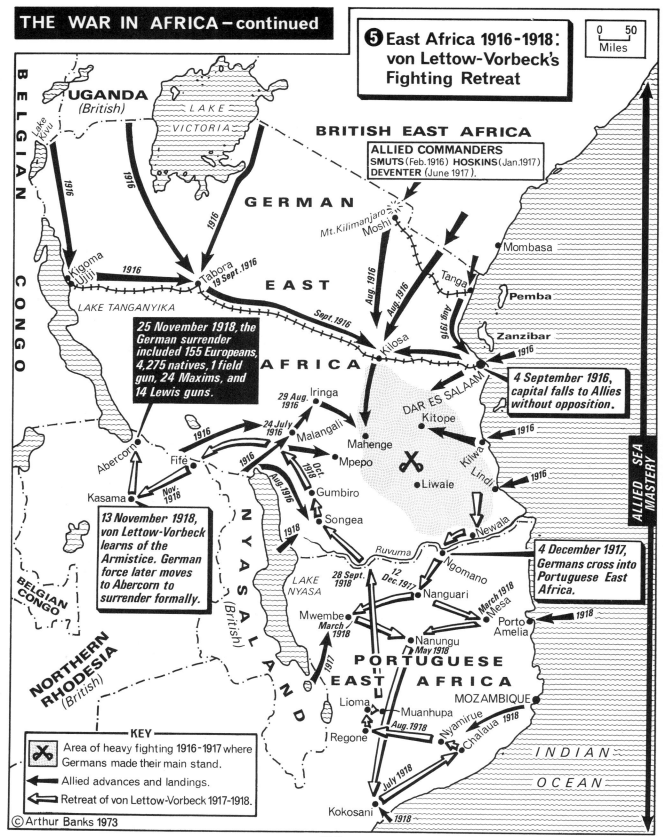

THE WAR IN AFRICA – continued

⑤ East Africa 1916-1918: von Lettow-Vorbeck's Fighting Retreat

0 50 Miles

BELGIAN CONGO

UGANDA *(British)*

LAKE VICTORIA

Lake Kivu

GERMAN

EAST

AFRICA

BRITISH EAST AFRICA

ALLIED COMMANDERS
SMUTS (Feb.1916) HOSKINS (Jan.1917)
DEVENTER (June 1917).

Mt.Kilimanjaro
Moshi

Mombasa

Tanga

Pemba

Zanzibar

Aug.1916

1916

1916

1916

Kigoma Ujiji

1916

Tabora *19 Sept.1916*

LAKE TANGANYIKA

Sept.1916

Kilosa

DAR ES SALAAM

Kitope

4 September 1916, capital falls to Allies without opposition.

25 November 1918, the German surrender included 155 Europeans, 4,275 natives, 1 field gun, 24 Maxims, and 14 Lewis guns.

29 Aug. 1916 Iringa

24 July 1916 Malangali

Mahenge

Kilwa

1916

Lindi

1916

Abercorn

1916

Fife

1916

Aug.1916

Oct. 1918

Mpepo

Liwale

Newala

Kasama

Nov. 1918

Gumbiro

1918

Songea

Ruvuma

Ngomano

4 December 1917, Germans cross into Portuguese East Africa.

13 November 1918, von Lettow-Vorbeck learns of the Armistice. German force later moves to Abercorn to surrender formally.

BELGIAN CONGO

NORTHERN RHODESIA *(British)*

LAKE NYASA

N Y A S A L A N D *(British)*

28 Sept. 1918

12 Dec.1917

Nanguari

March 1918 Mesa

Mwembe *March 1918*

1917

Nanungu *May 1918*

Porto Amelia

1918

PORTUGUESE EAST AFRICA

MOZAMBIQUE

Lioma

Muanhupa

Nyamirue

Chalaua 1918

Aug.1918

Regone

July 1918

Kokosani

1918

INDIAN OCEAN

ALLIED SEA MASTERY

KEY
✕ Area of heavy fighting 1916-1917 where Germans made their main stand.
← Allied advances and landings.
⇐ Retreat of von Lettow-Vorbeck 1917-1918.

© Arthur Banks 1973

218

WEAPONS

During the half century preceding the First World War military science had taken note of technological developments but had not appreciated the extent to which they revolutionised traditional concepts of warfare. French infantrymen armed with the *chassepot* breech-loading rifle had wrought havoc with the German attackers in 1870 and convinced military authorities that rifles would henceforth strengthen the defensive position of troops, especially if they were also supported by artillery. But because the original French machine guns —the *mitrailleuses*—of 1870 had proved ineffectual, the potentialities of this weapon were ignored. The trench fighting of the Russo-Japanese War (1905–1905) should have awakened an interest in the machine gun, for Maxim's water-cooled weapon of 1884, firing 2,000 rounds in three minutes, was very different from the prototypes of the Franco-Prussian campaign; and it was eventually the German Maxim which proved so terribly effective on the first day of the Somme (compare pages 152–153 and page 224). Without well-sited machine guns and barbed-wire entanglements, there would have been no war of stalemate on the Western Front.

At first it was assumed that mobility could be restored to warfare by artillery power. This, at least, had been a lesson of the Russo-Japanese War, and in the ten years before Sarajevo much attention was given to the development of howitzers, the heaviest models being used to reduce the Belgian fortifications in 1914 (pages 33 and 62). The most effective field gun was the French 75-mm (page 33), with a buffer recoil system which allowed a fire rate of 20/30 rounds a minute. By contrast, the British 18-pounder had a rate of fire of only 8 rounds a minute, and this was faster than the best German and Austrian guns. During the First World War three-quarters of the wounds caused by guns came from shells, high explosive or shrapnel, rather from bullets.

The experience of the long barrages used as preparation for offensives in 1915 showed that artillery was a less decisive weapon in the field than the experts had anticipated. Concrete pill-boxes stood up against most normal field artillery, while the barrages ruled out all element of surprise and made soft ground impassable to heavily encumbered infantry. It was partly to overcome these problems that petrol driven armoured vehicles with caterpillar tracks were introduced, first as 'tanks' in the British army and then into the armies of other countries. No commander, however, felt sufficiently confident to develop the tank as a revolutionary weapon in its own right. On the Somme in 1916 tanks suffered as much as infantry from shell craters, and at Cambrai in 1917 (page 174) no attempt was made to follow penetration by exploitation with vehicles mounted on caterpillar tracks. Moreover, although use was made of armoured cars, lorries (notably at Verdun), and the famous Paris taxis (page 55), the value of the internal combustion engine was only slowly perceived.

This hardly is surprising: military minds did not rapidly assimilate the changed patterns of daily life. Thus, although the transport of armies by rail from one war zone to another dates from 1862–1863 (both Confederate and Union forces in the American Civil War), it was not until the outbreak of the First World War that the smooth running of a railway transport system was recognised as an essential prerequisite for offensive operations. General Groener, who succeeded Ludendorff as virtual field commander in the last days of the War, was the first military leader to have 'graduated' as a railway specialist.

By contrast, trench warfare brought new forms of old weapons: clubs, knives, canisters of burning oil, pistols and revolvers. The greatest innovations of all, however, were in the skies and under the waves.

219

British 4·5-inch howitzer

Length of gun (overall):	13 feet, 6 inches.
Weight of gun in action:	3,004 pounds.
Range:	7,000 yards.
Elevation:	−5 to +45 degs.
Barrel length:	13·33 calibres.
Weight of shell:	35 pounds.
Muzzle velocity:	1,010 ft./sec.
Rate of fire:	4 rds. per min.

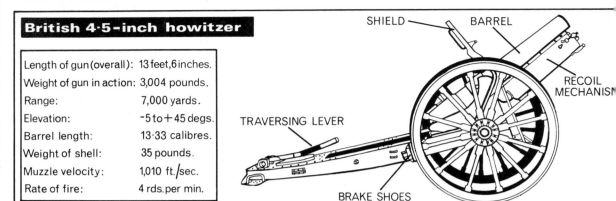

SHIELD BARREL

RECOIL
MECHANISM

TRAVERSING LEVER

BRAKE SHOES

British 60-pounder field gun

Length of gun (overall):	21 feet, 7 inches.
Weight of gun in action:	11,705 pounds.
Range:	10,300 yards.
Elevation:	$21°30'$
Barrel length:	33·61 calibres.
Weight of shell:	60 pounds.
Muzzle velocity:	2,149 ft./sec.
Rate of fire:	2 rds. per min.
Traverse:	4° left / 4° right.
Calibre:	5 inches.

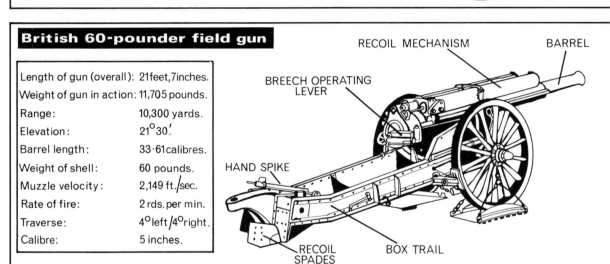

RECOIL MECHANISM BARREL

BREECH OPERATING
LEVER

HAND SPIKE

RECOIL
SPADES BOX TRAIL

British 9·2-inch (Mark I) howitzer

Length of gun (overall):	11 feet, 1·5 inches.
Weight of gun in action:	25,906 pounds.
Range:	10,000 yards.
Elevation:	55.°
Barrel length:	14·5 calibres.
Weight of shell:	290 pounds.
Muzzle velocity:	1,187 ft./sec.
Rate of fire:	2 rds. per min.
Traverse:	30° left / 30° right.
Height:	8 feet, 6 inches.

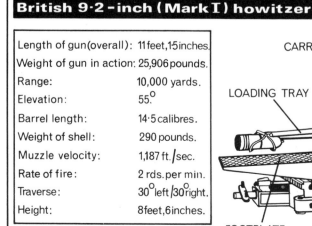
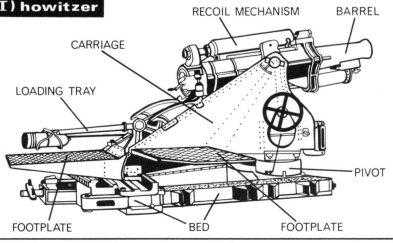

RECOIL MECHANISM BARREL

CARRIAGE

LOADING TRAY

PIVOT

FOOTPLATE BED FOOTPLATE

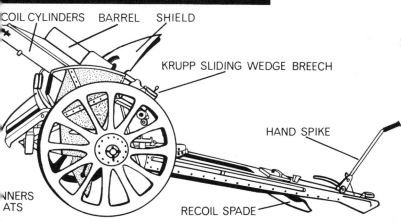

German 10·5-cm. howitzer 1916

COIL CYLINDERS   BARREL   SHIELD

KRUPP SLIDING WEDGE BREECH

HAND SPIKE

NNERS
ATS

RECOIL SPADE

Length of gun (overall):	12 feet.
Weight of gun in action:	3,036 pounds.
Range:	6,250 yards.
Elevation:	40°.
Barrel length:	22 calibres.
Weight of shell:	34·5 pounds.
Muzzle velocity:	1,400 ft./sec.
Rate of fire:	4 rds. per min.
Traverse:	4° left/4° right.

(note: unusual nine increment cartridge).

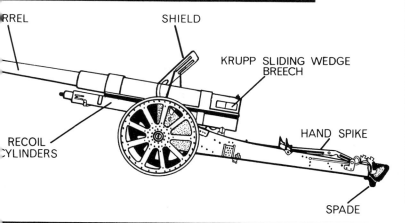

German 13-cm. (Model 1913) field gun

RREL   SHIELD

KRUPP SLIDING WEDGE
BREECH

RECOIL
CYLINDERS

HAND SPIKE

SPADE

Length of gun (overall):	22 feet.
Weight of gun in action:	12,768 pounds.
Range:	15,750 yards.
Elevation:	26°.
Barrel length:	35 calibres.
Weight of shell:	89 pounds.
Muzzle velocity:	2,280 ft./sec.
Rate of fire:	2 rds. per min.
Traverse:	2° left/2° right.

(note: shrapnel shell contains 1,170 lead bullets).

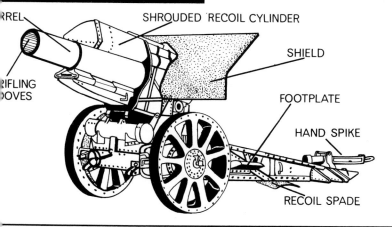

German 21-cm. "mörser"

RREL   SHROUDED RECOIL CYLINDER

SHIELD

RIFLING
OVES

FOOTPLATE

HAND SPIKE

RECOIL SPADE

Length of gun (overall):	20 feet.
Weight of gun in action:	9,828 pounds.
Range:	10,280 yards.
Elevation:	70°.
Barrel length:	12 calibres.
Weight of shell:	184 pounds.
Muzzle velocity:	1,203 ft./sec.
Rate of fire:	2 rds. per min.
Traverse:	2° left/2° right.

(note: H.E. shell contains 17 pounds of amatol).

French 155-mm. Grande Puissance Filloux gun

Length of gun (overall):	29 feet, 7 inches.
Weight of gun in action:	24,640 pounds.
Range:	19,650 yards.
Elevation:	35°.
Barrel length:	38·2 calibres.
Weight of shell:	97 pounds.
Muzzle velocity:	2,339 ft./sec.
Rate of fire:	2 rds. per min.

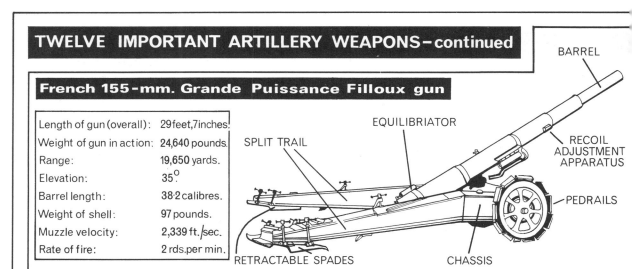

BARREL

EQUILIBRIATOR

SPLIT TRAIL

RECOIL ADJUSTMENT APPARATUS

PEDRAILS

RETRACTABLE SPADES

CHASSIS

British 18-pounder (Mark I) field gun

Length of gun (overall):	13 feet, 8 inches.
Weight of gun in action:	2,904 pounds.
Range:	7,000 yards.
Calibre:	3·3 inches.
Elevation:	−5 to +6 degs.
Barrel length:	28 calibres.
Weight of shell:	18 pounds.
Muzzle velocity:	1,614 ft./sec.
Rate of fire:	8 rds. per min.

(note: developed from the lessons of the Boer War).

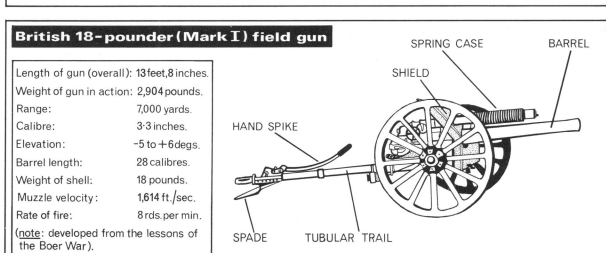

SPRING CASE

BARREL

SHIELD

HAND SPIKE

SPADE

TUBULAR TRAIL

British 12-inch (Mark III) railway howitzer

Length of mounting:	41 feet, 3 inches.
Weight of gun in action:	76 tons.
Range:	14,300 yards.
Elevation:	40°.
Barrel length:	17·3 calibres.
Weight of shell:	750 pounds.
Muzzle velocity:	1,474 ft./sec.
Rate of fire:	1 rd. per min.
Traverse:	5° left/5° right.

(note: most used British railway howitzer).

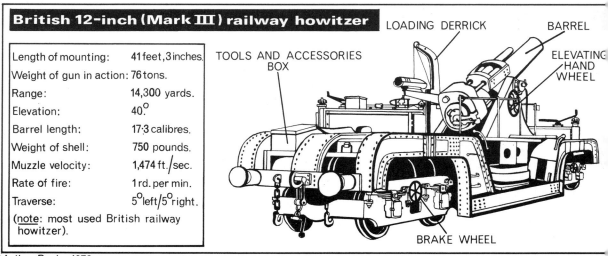

LOADING DERRICK

BARREL

TOOLS AND ACCESSORIES BOX

ELEVATING HAND WHEEL

BRAKE WHEEL

German 10-cm. (Model 1917) field gun

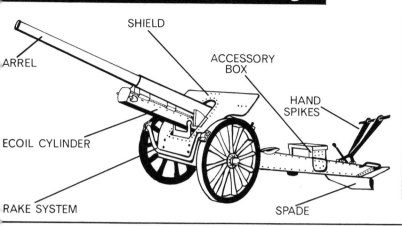

SHIELD

BARREL

ACCESSORY BOX

HAND SPIKES

RECOIL CYLINDER

BRAKE SYSTEM

SPADE

Length of gun(overall):	20 feet.
Weight of gun in action:	6,104 pounds.
Range:	12,085 yards.
Elevation:	-5 to +30 degs.
Barrel length:	35 calibres.
Weight of shell:	39·5 pounds.
Muzzle velocity:	1,923 ft./sec.
Rate of fire:	2 rds. per min.
Traverse:	2^{O} left/2^{O} right.

(note: smallest high-velocity gun in field use during 1914–1918 war).

Austrian 10·4-cm. field gun M.14

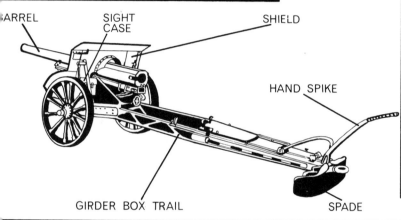

BARREL

SIGHT CASE

SHIELD

HAND SPIKE

GIRDER BOX TRAIL

SPADE

Length of gun(overall):	14 feet.
Weight of gun in action:	5,040 pounds.
Range:	13,670 yards.
Elevation:	-10 to +30 degs.
Barrel length:	35 calibres.
Weight of shell:	38·5 pounds.
Muzzle velocity:	2,230 ft./sec.
Rate of fire:	4 rds. per min.
Traverse:	3° left/3° right.

(note: first Austrian steel field gun: previous guns were bronze).

French 370-mm. mortar

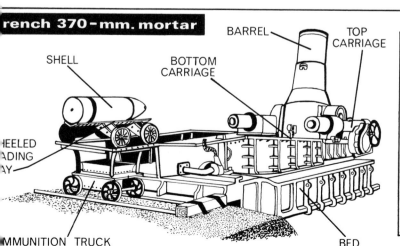

BARREL

TOP CARRIAGE

SHELL

BOTTOM CARRIAGE

WHEELED LOADING TRAY

AMMUNITION TRUCK

BED

Length of gun:	13 feet.
Weight of gun in action:	30 tons.
Range:	8,820 yards.
Elevation:	60°
Barrel length:	8 calibres.
Weight of shell:	1,076 pounds.
Muzzle velocity:	1,230 ft./sec.
Rate of fire:	1 rd. per 2 mins.
Traverse:	Nil.

(note: shell contains 262 pounds of high explosive).

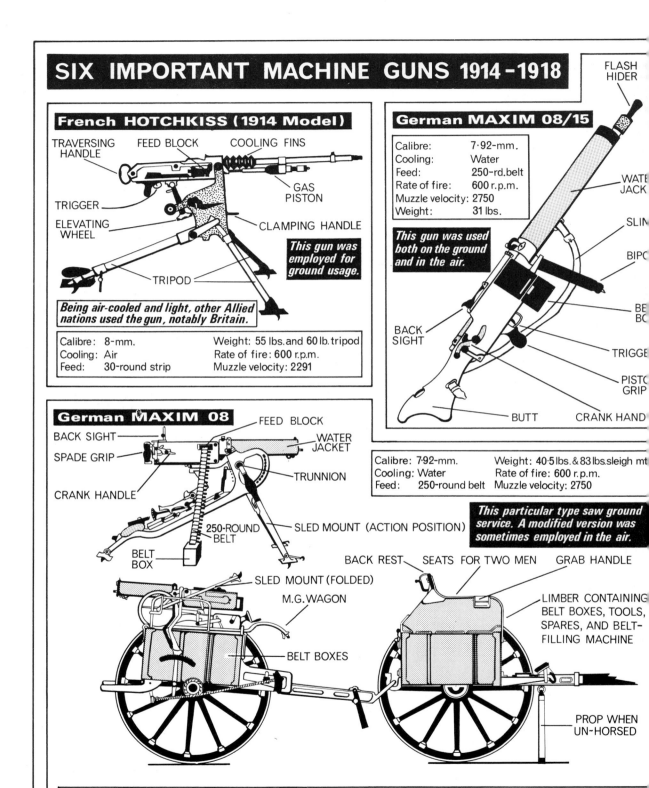

SIX IMPORTANT MACHINE GUNS 1914-1918

French HOTCHKISS (1914 Model)

TRAVERSING HANDLE
FEED BLOCK
COOLING FINS
GAS PISTON
TRIGGER
ELEVATING WHEEL
CLAMPING HANDLE
TRIPOD

This gun was employed for ground usage.

Being air-cooled and light, other Allied nations used the gun, notably Britain.

Calibre:	8-mm.	Weight: 55 lbs. and 60 lb. tripod
Cooling:	Air	Rate of fire: 600 r.p.m.
Feed:	30-round strip	Muzzle velocity: 2291

German MAXIM 08/15

Calibre:	7·92-mm.
Cooling:	Water
Feed:	250-rd. belt
Rate of fire:	600 r.p.m.
Muzzle velocity:	2750
Weight:	31 lbs.

This gun was used both on the ground and in the air.

FLASH HIDER
WATER JACKET
SLING
BIPOD
BELT BOX
TRIGGER
PISTOL GRIP
BACK SIGHT
BUTT
CRANK HANDLE

German MAXIM 08

BACK SIGHT
FEED BLOCK
WATER JACKET
SPADE GRIP
TRUNNION
CRANK HANDLE
250-ROUND BELT
SLED MOUNT (ACTION POSITION)
BELT BOX

Calibre:	7·92-mm.	Weight: 40·5 lbs. & 83 lbs. sleigh mt
Cooling:	Water	Rate of fire: 600 r.p.m.
Feed:	250-round belt	Muzzle velocity: 2750

This particular type saw ground service. A modified version was sometimes employed in the air.

BACK REST
SEATS FOR TWO MEN
GRAB HANDLE
SLED MOUNT (FOLDED)
M.G. WAGON
LIMBER CONTAINING BELT BOXES, TOOLS, SPARES, AND BELT-FILLING MACHINE
BELT BOXES
PROP WHEN UN-HORSED

This gun was the "slayer" of 1 July 1916, the opening day of the Allied infantry offensive at the Battle of the Somme. Its devastating fire-power accounted for 90% of the 60,000 Allied casualties (mainly British) incurred on that one day.

American-designed LEWIS

Although somewhat prone to jamming in damp conditions, this gun was used by the Allies both on the ground and in the air.

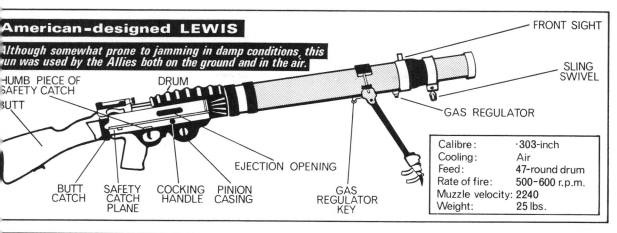

FRONT SIGHT

SLING SWIVEL

GAS REGULATOR

THUMB PIECE OF SAFETY CATCH

BUTT

DRUM

EJECTION OPENING

GAS REGULATOR KEY

BUTT CATCH

SAFETY CATCH PLANE

COCKING HANDLE

PINION CASING

Calibre:	·303-inch
Cooling:	Air
Feed:	47-round drum
Rate of fire:	500-600 r.p.m.
Muzzle velocity:	2240
Weight:	25 lbs.

Russian MAXIM "Sokolov" (1910 Model)

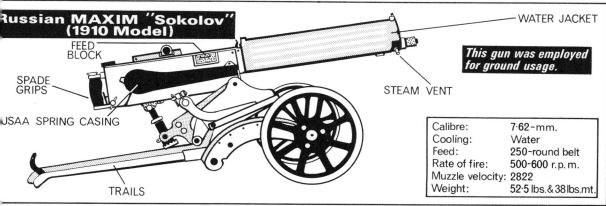

WATER JACKET

This gun was employed for ground usage.

FEED BLOCK

SPADE GRIPS

STEAM VENT

USAA SPRING CASING

TRAILS

Calibre:	7·62-mm.
Cooling:	Water
Feed:	250-round belt
Rate of fire:	500-600 r.p.m.
Muzzle velocity:	2822
Weight:	52·5 lbs. & 38 lbs.mt.

British VICKERS

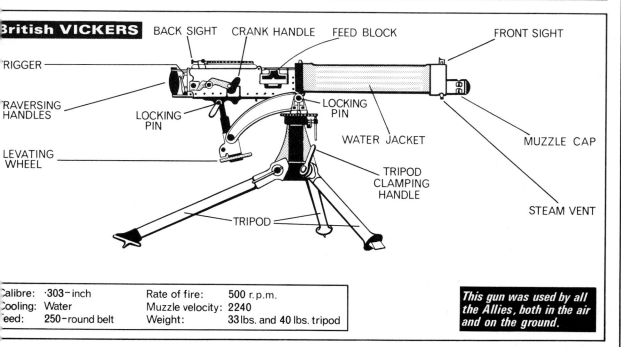

BACK SIGHT   CRANK HANDLE   FEED BLOCK   FRONT SIGHT

TRIGGER

TRAVERSING HANDLES

LOCKING PIN

LOCKING PIN

MUZZLE CAP

ELEVATING WHEEL

WATER JACKET

TRIPOD CLAMPING HANDLE

STEAM VENT

TRIPOD

Calibre:	·303-inch	Rate of fire:	500 r.p.m.	
Cooling:	Water	Muzzle velocity:	2240	
Feed:	250-round belt	Weight:	33 lbs. and 40 lbs. tripod	

This gun was used by all the Allies, both in the air and on the ground.

FOUR IMPORTANT TANKS 1916-1918

Weight:	14 tons.
Speed:	8·3 m.p.h.
Range:	80 miles.
Crew:	3.
Engines:	2 Tylor (total: 90 h.p.).

British Medium Mark A "Whippet"

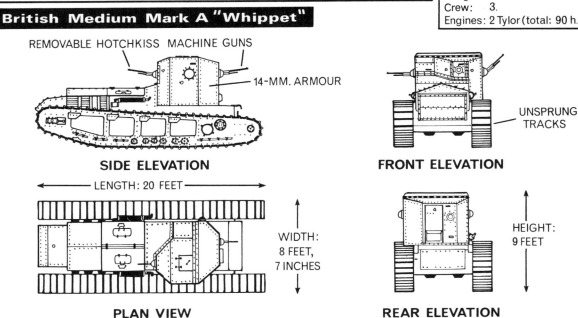

REMOVABLE HOTCHKISS MACHINE GUNS

14-MM. ARMOUR

SIDE ELEVATION

UNSPRUNG TRACKS

FRONT ELEVATION

LENGTH: 20 FEET

WIDTH: 8 FEET, 7 INCHES

PLAN VIEW

HEIGHT: 9 FEET

REAR ELEVATION

German A7V Sturmpanzerwagen

Weight: 30 tons.	Speed: 8 m.p.h.	Crew: 18.
Engines: 2 Daimler four-cylinder (total: 200 h.p.).		

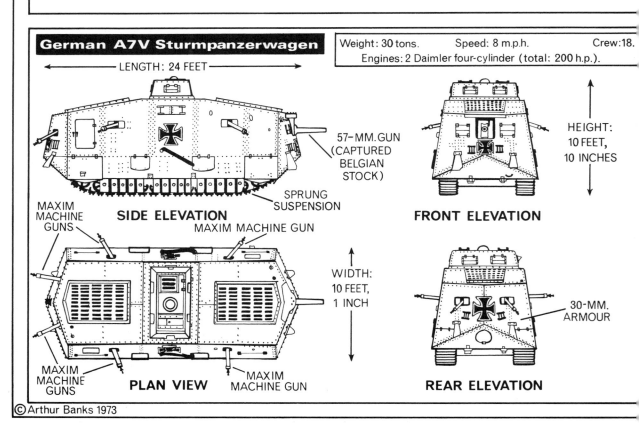

LENGTH: 24 FEET

57-MM. GUN (CAPTURED BELGIAN STOCK)

SPRUNG SUSPENSION

MAXIM MACHINE GUNS

SIDE ELEVATION

MAXIM MACHINE GUN

HEIGHT: 10 FEET, 10 INCHES

FRONT ELEVATION

WIDTH: 10 FEET, 1 INCH

MAXIM MACHINE GUNS

PLAN VIEW

MAXIM MACHINE GUN

30-MM. ARMOUR

REAR ELEVATION

© Arthur Banks 1973

French Schneider M.16 CA1

Weight:	13·5 tons.
Speed:	4·5 m.p.h.
Range:	25 miles.
Crew:	6/7.
Engine:	Schneider, four-cylinder, watercooled, 55 h.p.

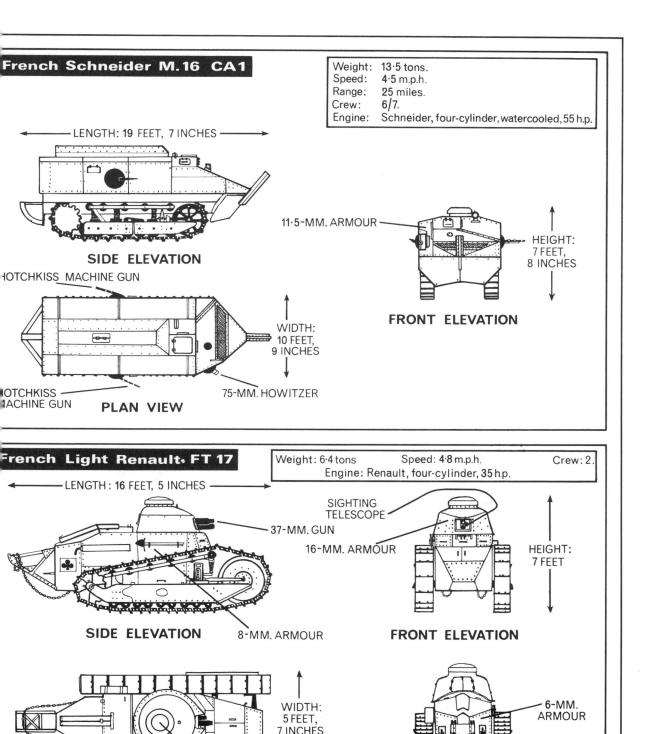

LENGTH: 19 FEET, 7 INCHES

SIDE ELEVATION

11·5-MM. ARMOUR

HEIGHT: 7 FEET, 8 INCHES

FRONT ELEVATION

HOTCHKISS MACHINE GUN

WIDTH: 10 FEET, 9 INCHES

HOTCHKISS MACHINE GUN

PLAN VIEW

75-MM. HOWITZER

French Light Renault· FT 17

Weight: 6·4 tons	Speed: 4·8 m.p.h.	Crew: 2.
Engine: Renault, four-cylinder, 35 h.p.		

LENGTH : 16 FEET, 5 INCHES

37-MM. GUN

SIGHTING TELESCOPE

16-MM. ARMOUR

HEIGHT: 7 FEET

SIDE ELEVATION

8-MM. ARMOUR

FRONT ELEVATION

WIDTH: 5 FEET, 7 INCHES

6-MM. ARMOUR

ROUND TURRET

PLAN VIEW

REAR ELEVATION

NINE IMPORTANT RIFLES 1914-1918

The rifles of the 1914—1918 war were basically similar in performance. All incorporated hand-operated bolt actions, some straight pull, others turn-bolt. Reliability varied somewhat, but no single rifle had any outstanding advantage over the others. In 1918, efforts were made to produce rifles of a self-loading nature, but only one type saw some limited service. The vast majority of rifles used were of the basic types shown on these pages.

THE BRITISH REGULAR ARMY

Prior to the war, the British Regular Army paid particular attention to training its infantry in marksmanship and "rapid fire" techniques and by the outbreak in August 1914, regiments contained riflemen with ability to fire at rates of 15-20 rounds per minute with great accuracy.

German "MAUSER" (Model 1898)

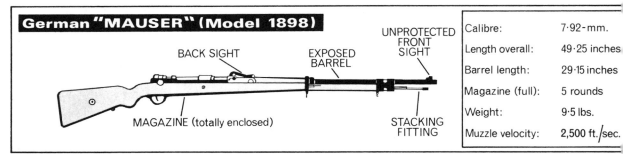

BACK SIGHT — EXPOSED BARREL — UNPROTECTED FRONT SIGHT — MAGAZINE (totally enclosed) — STACKING FITTING

Calibre:	7·92-mm.
Length overall:	49·25 inches
Barrel length:	29·15 inches
Magazine (full):	5 rounds
Weight:	9·5 lbs.
Muzzle velocity:	2,500 ft./sec.

French "LEBEL" (Model 1916)

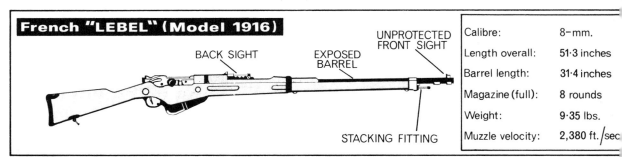

BACK SIGHT — EXPOSED BARREL — UNPROTECTED FRONT SIGHT — STACKING FITTING

Calibre:	8-mm.
Length overall:	51·3 inches
Barrel length:	31·4 inches
Magazine (full):	8 rounds
Weight:	9·35 lbs.
Muzzle velocity:	2,380 ft./sec

United States "SPRINGFIELD" (Model 1903)

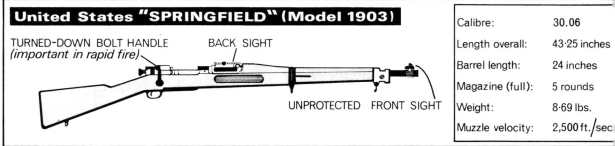

TURNED-DOWN BOLT HANDLE *(important in rapid fire)* — BACK SIGHT — UNPROTECTED FRONT SIGHT

Calibre:	30.06
Length overall:	43·25 inches
Barrel length:	24 inches
Magazine (full):	5 rounds
Weight:	8·69 lbs.
Muzzle velocity:	2,500 ft./sec

United States (Model 1917)

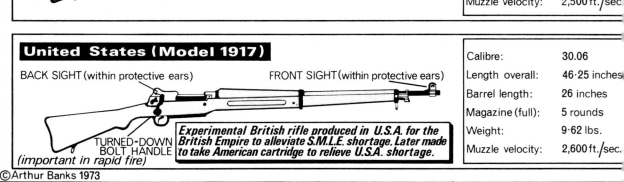

BACK SIGHT (within protective ears) — FRONT SIGHT (within protective ears) — TURNED-DOWN BOLT HANDLE *(important in rapid fire)*

Experimental British rifle produced in U.S.A. for the British Empire to alleviate S.M.L.E. shortage. Later made to take American cartridge to relieve U.S.A. shortage.

Calibre:	30.06
Length overall:	46·25 inches
Barrel length:	26 inches
Magazine (full):	5 rounds
Weight:	9·62 lbs.
Muzzle velocity:	2,600 ft./sec.

© Arthur Banks 1973

British SHORT MAGAZINE "LEE-ENFIELD" Mark III

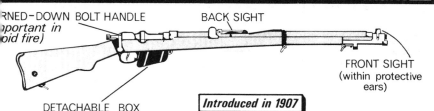

TURNED-DOWN BOLT HANDLE
(important in
rapid fire)

BACK SIGHT

FRONT SIGHT
(within protective
ears)

DETACHABLE BOX

Introduced in 1907

Calibre:	·303-inch
Length overall:	44·5 inches
Barrel length:	25·19 inches
Magazine (full):	10 rounds
Weight:	8·12 lbs.
Muzzle velocity:	2,060 ft./sec.

Canadian "ROSS" Mark III B

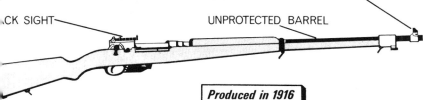

UNPROTECTED FRONT SIGHT

UNPROTECTED BARREL

BACK SIGHT

Produced in 1916

Calibre:	·303-inch
Length overall:	50·5 inches
Barrel length:	30·5 inches
Magazine (full):	5 rounds
Weight:	9·75 lbs.
Muzzle velocity:	2,060 ft./sec.

Russian "MOISIN-NAGANT" (Model 1891)

BACK SIGHT

UNPROTECTED FRONT SIGHT

STACKING FITTING

Calibre:	7·62-mm.
Length overall:	51·37 inches
Barrel length:	31·6 inches
Magazine (full):	5 rounds
Weight:	9·62 lbs.
Muzzle velocity:	2,660 ft./sec.

Austrian "MÄNNLICHER" (Model 1895)

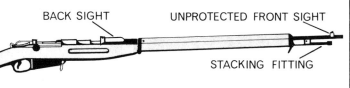

UNPROTECTED
FRONT SIGHT

Diagram and main details refer
to the long version.

BACK SIGHT

SHORT VERSION (variations)
Length overall: 40 inches
Barrel length: 19 inches
Weight: 7·8 lbs.

Calibre:	8-mm.
Length overall:	50 inches
Barrel length:	30 inches
Magazine (full):	5 rounds
Weight:	8·4 lbs.
Muzzle velocity:	2,030 ft./sec.

Italian "MÄNNLICHER-CARCANO" (Model 1891)

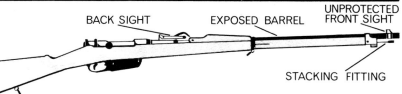

BACK SIGHT

EXPOSED BARREL

UNPROTECTED
FRONT SIGHT

STACKING FITTING

Calibre:	6·5-mm.
Length overall:	50·75 inches
Barrel length:	30·7 inches
Magazine (full):	6 rounds
Weight:	9 lbs.
Muzzle velocity:	2,200 ft./sec.

TWENTY TRENCH WEAPONS AND MUNITIONS

German 240-mm. old style Minenwerfer "Iko"

BARREL
ELEVATING GEAR
SECTIONAL PLATFORM
EARTH

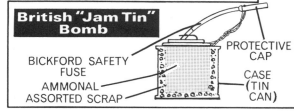

British "Jam Tin" Bomb

BICKFORD SAFETY FUSE
AMMONAL
ASSORTED SCRAP
PROTECTIVE CAP
CASE (TIN CAN)

German 75-mm. new style Minenwerfer

RECOIL CYLINDER
REAR SIGHT
ELEVATING LEVER
TRAVERSING LEVER
BARREL
RECOIL SPADE
EARTH

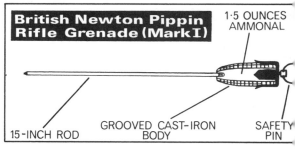

British Newton Pippin Rifle Grenade (Mark I)

1·5 OUNCES AMMONAL
15-INCH ROD
GROOVED CAST-IRON BODY
SAFETY PIN

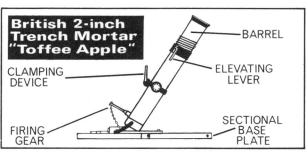

British 2-inch Trench Mortar "Toffee Apple"

BARREL
ELEVATING LEVER
CLAMPING DEVICE
FIRING GEAR
SECTIONAL BASE PLATE

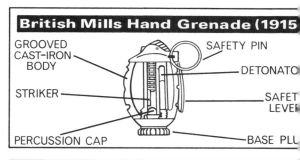

British Mills Hand Grenade (1915)

GROOVED CAST-IRON BODY
SAFETY PIN
DETONATOR
STRIKER
SAFETY LEVER
PERCUSSION CAP
BASE PLUG

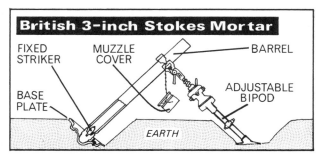

British 3-inch Stokes Mortar

FIXED STRIKER
MUZZLE COVER
BARREL
BASE PLATE
ADJUSTABLE BIPOD
EARTH

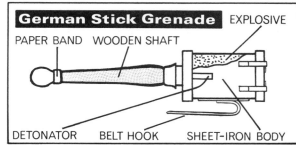

German Stick Grenade

EXPLOSIVE
PAPER BAND
WOODEN SHAFT
DETONATOR
BELT HOOK
SHEET-IRON BODY

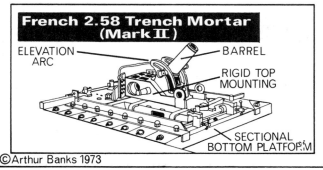

French 2.58 Trench Mortar (Mark II)

ELEVATION ARC
BARREL
RIGID TOP MOUNTING
SECTIONAL BOTTOM PLATFORM

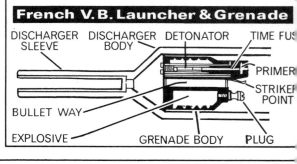

French V.B. Launcher & Grenade

DISCHARGER SLEEVE
DISCHARGER BODY
DETONATOR
TIME FUSE
PRIMER
STRIKER POINT
BULLET WAY
EXPLOSIVE
GRENADE BODY
PLUG

©Arthur Banks 1973

230

...ypical High Explosive Shell

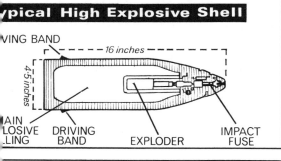

VING BAND

4·5 inches

← 16 inches →

AIN
LOSIVE
LING

DRIVING
BAND

EXPLODER

IMPACT
FUSE

German 76-mm. Minenwerfer Message Shell

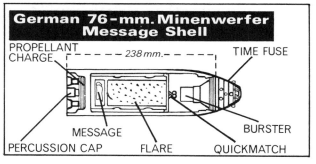

PROPELLANT
CHARGE

← 238 mm. →

TIME FUSE

MESSAGE

BURSTER

PERCUSSION CAP

FLARE

QUICKMATCH

...ypical Shrapnel Shell

TRANSIT PLUG
INSTEAD OF
TIME FUSE

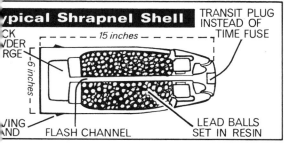

CK
WDER
RGE

← 15 inches →

·6 inches

VING
AND

FLASH CHANNEL

LEAD BALLS
SET IN RESIN

Trench Club

**IMPROVISED IN
THE TRENCHES**

SCRAP LEAD

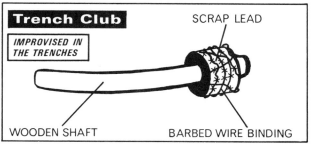

WOODEN SHAFT

BARBED WIRE BINDING

...ypical Gas Shell

TRANSIT PLUG

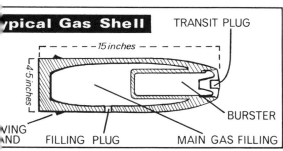

VING
AND

← 15 inches →

4·5 inches

BURSTER

FILLING PLUG

MAIN GAS FILLING

Old Welsh Knife

**TRADITIONAL FROM DAYS
OF THE LONGBOW**

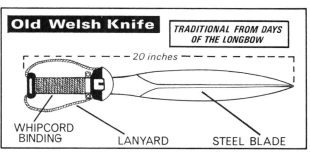

← 20 inches →

WHIPCORD
BINDING

LANYARD

STEEL BLADE

...ypical Semi Armour-Piercing Shell

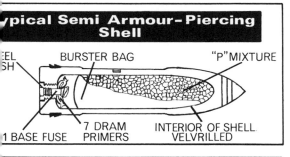

EL
SH

BURSTER BAG

"P" MIXTURE

1 BASE FUSE

7 DRAM
PRIMERS

INTERIOR OF SHELL
VELVRILLED

Knuckleduster Knife

HILT

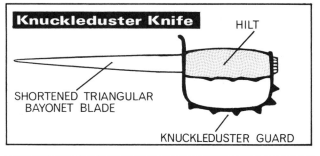

SHORTENED TRIANGULAR
BAYONET BLADE

KNUCKLEDUSTER GUARD

...ypical Incendiary (Thermite) Shell

EET-STEEL BODY

SAFETY PINS

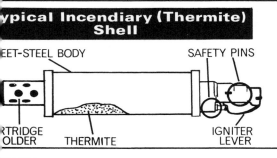

RTRIDGE
OLDER

THERMITE

IGNITER
LEVER

British Webley (Mark VI) Stock & Bayonet

MODIFIED FRENCH BAYONET

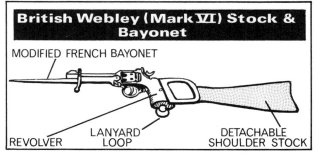

REVOLVER

LANYARD
LOOP

DETACHABLE
SHOULDER STOCK

EIGHT IMPORTANT PISTOLS AND REVOLVERS 1914 – 1918

United States COLT M 1917

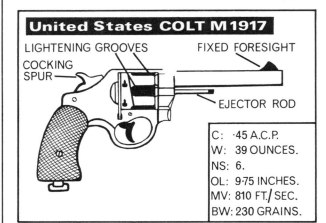

LIGHTENING GROOVES   FIXED FORESIGHT
COCKING SPUR
EJECTOR ROD

C: ·45 A.C.P.
W: 39 OUNCES.
NS: 6.
OL: 9·75 INCHES.
MV: 810 FT./SEC.
BW: 230 GRAINS.

British WEBLEY Mark VI

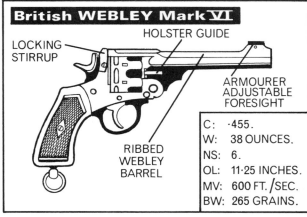

LOCKING STIRRUP   HOLSTER GUIDE
ARMOURER ADJUSTABLE FORESIGHT
RIBBED WEBLEY BARREL

C: ·455.
W: 38 OUNCES.
NS: 6.
OL: 11·25 INCHES.
MV: 600 FT./SEC.
BW: 265 GRAINS.

British COLT

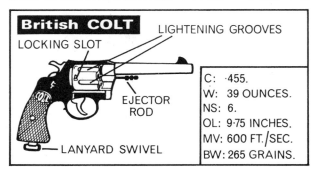

LOCKING SLOT   LIGHTENING GROOVES
EJECTOR ROD
LANYARD SWIVEL

C: ·455.
W: 39 OUNCES.
NS: 6.
OL: 9·75 INCHES.
MV: 600 FT./SEC.
BW: 265 GRAINS.

British WEBLEY-FOSBERY

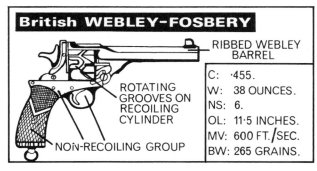

RIBBED WEBLEY BARREL
ROTATING GROOVES ON RECOILING CYLINDER
NON-RECOILING GROUP

C: ·455.
W: 38 OUNCES.
NS: 6.
OL: 11·5 INCHES.
MV: 600 FT./SEC.
BW: 265 GRAINS.

German MAUSER

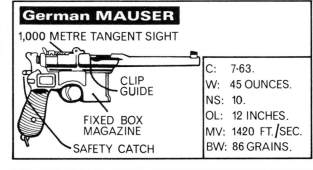

1,000 METRE TANGENT SIGHT
CLIP GUIDE
FIXED BOX MAGAZINE
SAFETY CATCH

C: 7·63.
W: 45 OUNCES.
NS: 10.
OL: 12 INCHES.
MV: 1420 FT./SEC.
BW: 86 GRAINS.

German LUGER (Parabellum)

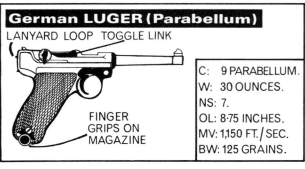

LANYARD LOOP   TOGGLE LINK
FINGER GRIPS ON MAGAZINE

C: 9 PARABELLUM.
W: 30 OUNCES.
NS: 7.
OL: 8·75 INCHES.
MV: 1,150 FT./SEC.
BW: 125 GRAINS.

Italian GLISENTI

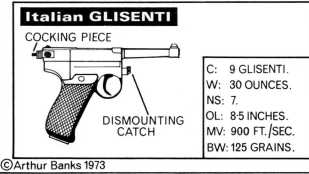

COCKING PIECE
DISMOUNTING CATCH

C: 9 GLISENTI.
W: 30 OUNCES.
NS: 7.
OL: 8·5 INCHES.
MV: 900 FT./SEC.
BW: 125 GRAINS.

Japanese NAMBU

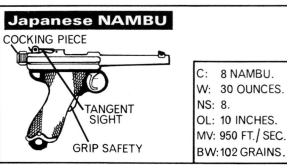

COCKING PIECE
TANGENT SIGHT
GRIP SAFETY

C: 8 NAMBU.
W: 30 OUNCES.
NS: 8.
OL: 10 INCHES.
MV: 950 FT./SEC.
BW: 102 GRAINS.

FIVE IMPORTANT ANTI-AIRCRAFT GUNS 1914-1918

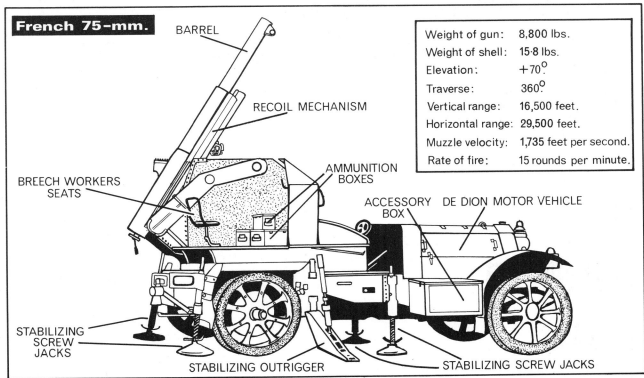

French 75-mm.

BARREL

RECOIL MECHANISM

Weight of gun:	8,800 lbs.
Weight of shell:	15·8 lbs.
Elevation:	+70°.
Traverse:	360°.
Vertical range:	16,500 feet.
Horizontal range:	29,500 feet.
Muzzle velocity:	1,735 feet per second.
Rate of fire:	15 rounds per minute.

BREECH WORKERS SEATS

AMMUNITION BOXES

ACCESSORY BOX   DE DION MOTOR VEHICLE

STABILIZING SCREW JACKS

STABILIZING OUTRIGGER

STABILIZING SCREW JACKS

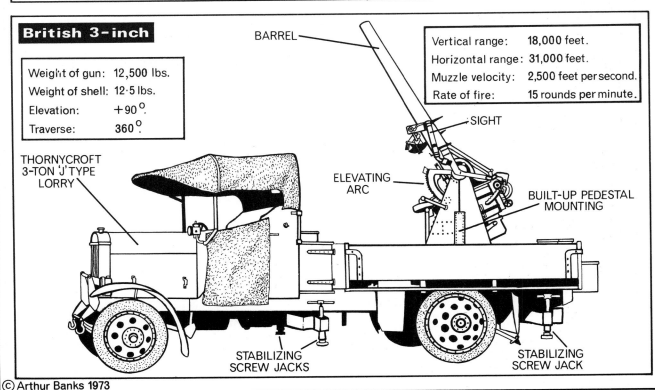

British 3-inch

BARREL

Weight of gun:	12,500 lbs.
Weight of shell:	12·5 lbs.
Elevation:	+90°.
Traverse:	360°.

Vertical range:	18,000 feet.
Horizontal range:	31,000 feet.
Muzzle velocity:	2,500 feet per second.
Rate of fire:	15 rounds per minute.

SIGHT

THORNYCROFT 3-TON 'J' TYPE LORRY

ELEVATING ARC

BUILT-UP PEDESTAL MOUNTING

STABILIZING SCREW JACKS

STABILIZING SCREW JACK

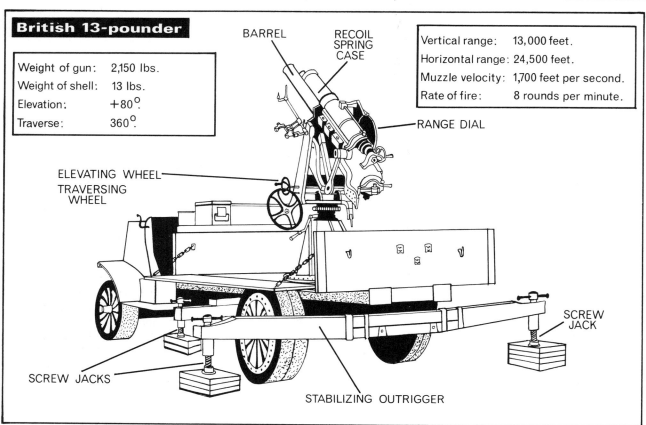

British 13-pounder

Weight of gun:	2,150 lbs.
Weight of shell:	13 lbs.
Elevation:	+80°.
Traverse:	360°.

Vertical range:	13,000 feet.
Horizontal range:	24,500 feet.
Muzzle velocity:	1,700 feet per second.
Rate of fire:	8 rounds per minute.

BARREL

RECOIL SPRING CASE

RANGE DIAL

ELEVATING WHEEL
TRAVERSING WHEEL

SCREW JACK

SCREW JACKS

STABILIZING OUTRIGGER

German 8·8-cm.

Weight of gun:	6,700 lbs.
Weight of shell:	21 lbs.
Elevation:	+70°.
Traverse:	360°.
Vert. range:	12,500 feet.
Horiz. range:	35,500 feet.

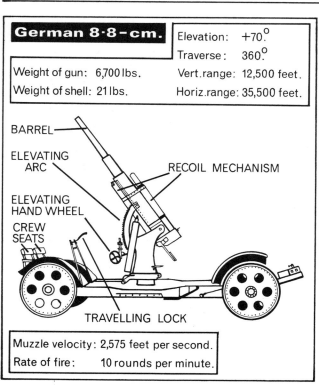

BARREL

ELEVATING ARC

ELEVATING HAND WHEEL

CREW SEATS

RECOIL MECHANISM

TRAVELLING LOCK

Muzzle velocity:	2,575 feet per second.
Rate of fire:	10 rounds per minute.

German 7·7-cm.

Weight of shell:	15 lbs.
Vertical range:	14,000 ft.
Weight of gun:	3,675 lbs.
Horiz. range:	26,000 ft.

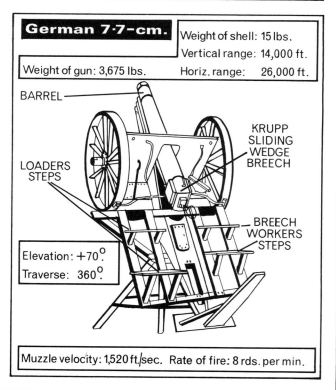

BARREL

LOADERS STEPS

KRUPP SLIDING WEDGE BREECH

BREECH WORKERS STEPS

Elevation:	+70°.
Traverse:	360°.

Muzzle velocity: 1,520 ft./sec.	Rate of fire: 8 rds. per min.

THE WAR AT SEA

During the first decade of the century a radical change in warship construction led to the development of 'all big gun' battleships. The first British vessel of this type was H.M.S. *Dreadnought* (ten 12-inch guns and a speed of 21 knots), laid down in October 1905, launched February 1906, at sea by October 1906. The Dreadnoughts could outrange and outpace all previous battleships, which were soon made obsolete. Other countries followed Britain's lead: a German dreadnought, the *Nassau*, was launched in 1907. The Royal Navy in 1914 had twenty dreadnoughts or 'super-dreadnoughts' based in home waters: Germany, the second largest naval power in Europe, had fifteen. Everyone awaited a dreadnought Trafalgar. A difference in concepts of naval strategy postponed the clash. The Germans hoped to offset their numerical inferiority by splitting the British Grand Fleet by a feint, enabling their battle squadrons to fall on the enemy a portion at a time; the British, on the other hand, were content to use dreadnoughts as a distant deterrent, exercising naval supremacy in home waters from Scapa Flow, in the Orkneys. The prospect of a great naval battle receded.

Meanwhile, the British, French, Russian and Japanese navies were confronted with the problem of German cruisers in distant seas. The battle-cruiser *Goeben* and the cruiser *Breslau* succeeded in evading pursuit in the Mediterranean and took refuge at Constantinople, where their transference to the Turkish fleet played a considerable part in inducing the Turks to enter the war. The German Pacific Squadron (Spee) inflicted, off Coronel, the first defeat sustained by the Royal Navy since the 1812 War with America, sinking an outdated armoured cruiser and a light cruiser. Coronel was avenged at the Falkland Islands five weeks later, while the lone raider *Emden* was tracked down by the Australian cruiser *Sydney* in the Indian Ocean. The chivalrous seamanship of the commanders of the German surface vessels won high regard; but the development by the Germans of submarine warfare, and especially the increasing number of underwater attacks on merchantmen and passenger liners, aroused anger and resentment in Britain and the United States. On the other hand, the Americans also resented the British imposition of a naval blockade on Germany and her allies. British submarine activity was especially effective in the Sea of Marmara, off Constantinople, and in the Baltic.

In January 1915 the battle-cruisers of the Grand Fleet, under Beatty, intercepted Admiral Hipper's 'scouting group' off the Dogger Bank and pursued the Germans but lost contact after Beatty's flagship was immobilised. The German armoured cruiser *Blücher* was sunk, and the Germans concentrated for the remainder of the year on U-boat activity. In February 1916 Admiral Scheer took command of the High Seas Fleet at Wilhelmshaven, and planned to tempt Beatty into another battle-cruiser engagement, with a pack of U-boats waiting to intercept the dreadnoughts of the Grand Fleet (Jellicoe) as they moved south. Surface, submarine and Zeppelin activity was, however, not as co-ordinated as Scheer wished. The British were remarkably well-informed of German movements (by wireless interception), and were prepared for a major battle in May 1916.

Jutland, the largest naval action in world history, was essentially a battle of feints and manoeuvres. It involved 151 British warships and 99 German vessels although the dreadnoughts themselves (28 British, 16 German) were in action against each other for only twenty minutes during the evening of 31 May. Beatty, realising the German cruisers were seeking to draw his squadron towards the heavy guns of the High Seas Fleet, himself tried to lure the Germans towards Jellicoe's squadron. The British battle-cruisers suffered heavily from accurate German fire, but tactically trapped Scheer into allowing the Grand Fleet to get between his vessels and his home port. Jellicoe hoped to bring Scheer to battle next morning, but the Germans evaded him at night, partly through sheer speed and partly through better training for a running battle by night. British casualties and losses were far higher than those of the Germans at Jutland; but it was harder for the Germans to fill the gaps in their fleet. Strategically Jutland was a British victory, for it reinforced the Kaiser's inclination to preserve his navy intact, rather than risk another encounter with the Grand Fleet.

After Jutland there was little surface conflict between rival warships. The Austro-Hungarian fleet made a number of sorties on the barrage which the Allies sought to establish across the Strait of Otranto, so as to seal off the Adriatic from the Mediterranean; and there were occasional alarms in the Black Sea, where the Russian and Turkish fleets had already clashed briefly off the southern tip of the Crimea in November 1914. It is often said that the German High Seas Fleet remained inactive off Heligoland and Kiel for the remainder of the War until a break in morale led to mutiny in 1918. Yet, though the Kaiser was opposed to offensive action, Scheer took the Fleet to sea again in the third week of August 1916 and, for the last time, in April 1918. These sweeps seem, however, to have been intended as diversions rather than as preliminaries to another battle, and no contact was made with British surface vessels. It should, of course, be noted (page 276) that the rival fleets were increasingly hemmed in by minefields.

Both the British and German Admiralties had anticipated that attempts would be made in any war to strangle the economy of a country, and cut off its food supply, by means of a blockade. The British system (for which a separate Government department, the Ministry of Blockade, was eventually established early in 1916) was basically an extension of the controversial rights exercised during the Napoleonic Wars: an Order in Council of March 1915 authorising the seizure by British warships of goods destined for Germany by way of a neutral port provoked similar hostility to the notorious Orders in Council of 1807, although German submarine ruthlessness assuaged the wrath of some neutral countries. Neither the British nor the Germans had worked out the implications of using the submarine as a destroyer of commerce; but by the spring of 1916 the U-boat was recognised in Berlin as the most effective of all naval weapons. Attempts were made later that summer to counter the U-boat menace with new minefields, increased defensive nets and disguised 'mystery ships' (Q-ships). Yet the tonnage of merchant shipping sunk by U-boat averaged 300,000 a month in the last quarter of 1916 and rose dramatically in February when the Germans began unrestricted submarine warfare. Over half a million tons of British merchant shipping was lost in April 1917, one in four vessels leaving British ports never returning there again. Corn supplies in England were down to six weeks.

The U-boat menace was mastered by a return to the eighteenth century concept of convoys, imposed on a reluctant Admiralty by the Prime Minister Lloyd George, in May 1917 (see page 266). The addition of American naval strength to Atlantic patrols helped ensure the effectiveness of convoying. At the same time, new anti-submarine techniques were perfected, notably the depth-charge. The Admiralty remained concerned over the use which the Germans made of the Belgian ports as U-boat bases. In April 1918 a raid was made on Zeebrugge—the prototype of amphibious commando raids in the Second World War—which sought to block the canal to Bruges, where there were docking facilities for destroyers and as many as 30 U-boats. An attempt was also made on the Bruges–Ostend Canal. The Zeebrugge Raid (for which eight Victoria Crosses were awarded) was only partially successful and the accompanying raid on Ostend (which won another three Victoria Crosses) was so disappointing that a second assault had to be made a fortnight later. It, too, proved largely abortive. But the Zeebrugge–Ostend operations sealed off the U-boats and destroyers at Bruges, even if the shallow-draught boats were soon able to move again out to sea. The chief effect of the raids was as a fillip to lagging morale in Britain.

A final plan to challenge the Grand Fleet in the hopes of securing better Armistice terms in 1918 came to nothing when the German naval ratings mutinied, first at the fleet anchorage off Wilhelmshaven on 29 October and later at Kiel. It was the beginning of the revolution which, within a fortnight, turned Germany from an autocracy to a republic.

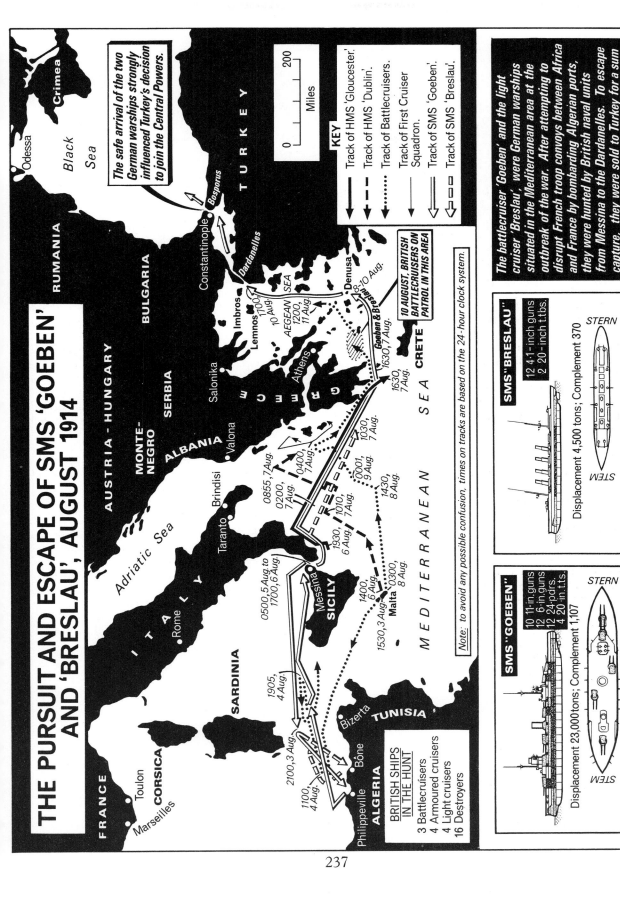

THE PURSUIT AND ESCAPE OF SMS 'GOEBEN' AND 'BRESLAU', AUGUST 1914

The safe arrival of the two German warships strongly influenced Turkey's decision to join the Central Powers.

Black Sea

Crimea
Odessa

T U R K E Y

Bosporus

Constantinople

Dardanelles

RUMANIA

BULGARIA

AUSTRIA - HUNGARY

SERBIA

MONTE-NEGRO

ALBANIA
Valona

SALONIKA
Athens
G R E E C E

AEGEAN SEA

Imbros
Lemnos
Denusa

8-10 Aug.

1700, 10 Aug.
1200, 11 Aug.

Goeben & Breslau
1630, 7 Aug.

10 AUGUST, BRITISH BATTLECRUISERS ON PATROL IN THIS AREA

C R E T E

1630, 7 Aug.

M E D I T E R R A N E A N   S E A

Adriatic Sea

Brindisi
Taranto

I T A L Y
Rome

Messina
SICILY

0855, 7 Aug.
0200, 7 Aug.
0400, 7 Aug.
1030, 7 Aug.
1010, 7 Aug.
1930, 6 Aug.
0001, 9 Aug.
1430, 8 Aug.
0300, 8 Aug.
Malta
1400, 6 Aug.
1530, 3 Aug.

0500, 5 Aug. to 1700, 6 Aug.

1905, 4 Aug.

SARDINIA

CORSICA

FRANCE
Toulon
Marseilles

Bizerta
Bône
TUNISIA

ALGERIA
Philippeville

2100, 3 Aug.

1100, 4 Aug.

KEY

→ Track of HMS 'Gloucester'.
–→ Track of HMS 'Dublin'.
⋯→ Track of Battlecruisers.
↓ Track of First Cruiser Squadron.
⇨ Track of SMS 'Goeben'.
⇢ Track of SMS 'Breslau'.

0   200
Miles

Note: to avoid any possible confusion, times on tracks are based on the 24-hour clock system.

BRITISH SHIPS IN THE HUNT

3 Battlecruisers
4 Armoured cruisers
4 Light cruisers
16 Destroyers

The battlecruiser 'Goeben' and the light cruiser 'Breslau', were German warships situated in the Mediterranean area at the outbreak of the war. After attempting to disrupt French troop convoys between Africa and France by bombarding Algerian ports, they were hunted by British naval units from Messina to the Dardanelles. To escape capture, they were sold to Turkey for a sum of £3,800,000, and then used against Russia.

SMS "BRESLAU"

12 4.1-inch guns
2 20-inch t.tbs.

STERN
STEM

Displacement 4,500 tons; Complement 370

Laid down 1910; Completed 1912; Maximum speed 30 knots

SMS "GOEBEN"

10 11-in. guns
12 6-in. guns
12 24-pdrs.
4 20-in. t.tbs.

STERN
STEM

Displacement 23,000 tons; Complement 1,107

Laid down 1909; Completed 1912; Maximum speed 28 knots

© Arthur Banks 1973

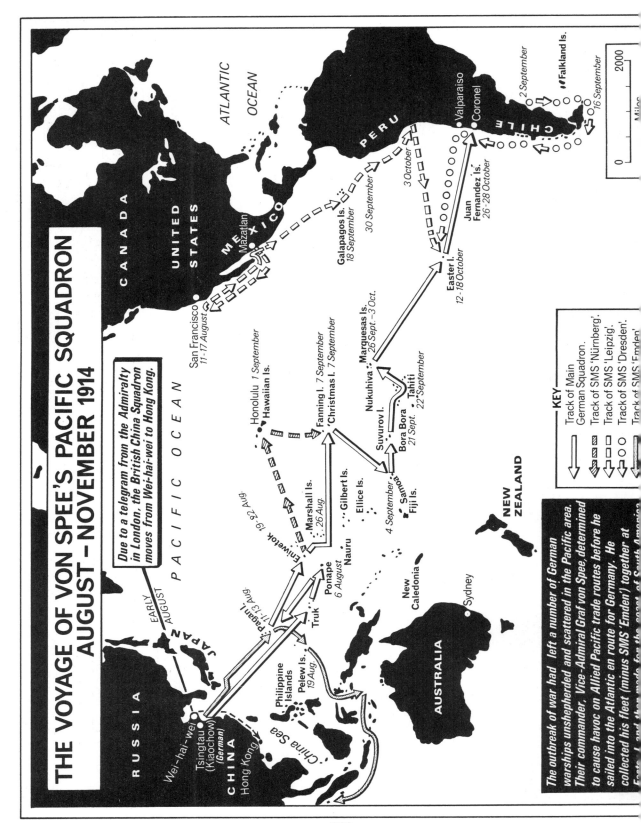

THE VOYAGE OF VON SPEE'S PACIFIC SQUADRON
AUGUST – NOVEMBER 1914

Due to a telegram from the Admiralty
in London, the British China Squadron
moves from Wei-hai-wei to Hong Kong.

ATLANTIC

OCEAN

CANADA

UNITED
STATES

MEXICO

PERU

CHILE

Valparaiso
Coronel

2 September

Falkland Is.

16 September

2000

Miles

0

San Francisco
11-17 August

Mazatlan

Galapagos Is.
18 September

30 September

3 October

Juan
Fernandez Is.
26–28 October

Easter I.
12 - 18 October

Honolulu 1 September
Hawaiian Is.

Fanning I. 7 September
Christmas I. 7 September

Nukuhiva
Marquesas Is.
26 Sept.–3 Oct.

Suvurov I.

Bora Bora
21 Sept.

Tahiti
22 September

PACIFIC   OCEAN

EARLY
AUGUST

JAPAN

Eniwetok 19-22 Aug.

Pagan I. 11-13 Aug.

Marshall Is.
26 Aug.

Gilbert Is.

Ellice Is.

4 September
Samoa
Fiji Is.

Ponape
6 August

Nauru

Truk

Philippine
Islands

Pelew Is.
19 Aug.

China Sea

RUSSIA

Wei-hai-wei
Tsingtau (Kiaochow)
(German)

CHINA
Hong Kong

NEW
ZEALAND

New
Caledonia

Sydney

AUSTRALIA

— KEY —

Track of Main
German Squadron.

Track of SMS 'Nürnberg'.

Track of SMS 'Leipzig'.

Track of SMS 'Dresden'.

Track of SMS 'Emden'

The outbreak of war had left a number of German
warships unshepherded and scattered in the Pacific area.
Their commander, Vice-Admiral Graf von Spee, determined
to cause havoc on Allied Pacific trade routes before he
sailed into the Atlantic en route for Germany. He
collected his fleet (minus SMS 'Emden') together at
Easter I. and then made for the coast of South America.

238

THE FINAL CRUISE OF SMS 'EMDEN' AUGUST–NOVEMBER 1914

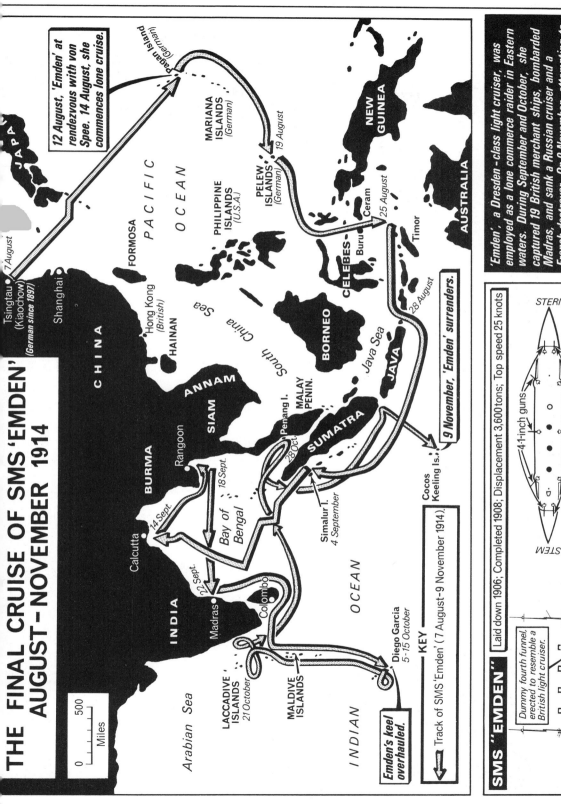

12 August, 'Emden' at rendezvous with von Spee. 14 August, she commences lone cruise.

JAPAN

Tsingtau (Kiaochow) (German since 1897) 7 August

Shanghai

CHINA

FORMOSA

Hong Kong (British)

HAINAN

South China Sea

ANNAM

SIAM

BURMA

Rangoon

14 Sept.

18 Sept.

Calcutta

22 Sept.

Bay of Bengal

INDIA

Madras

Colombo

LACCADIVE ISLANDS 21 October

MALDIVE ISLANDS

Diego Garcia 5–15 October

Emden's keel overhauled.

INDIAN OCEAN

Arabian Sea

0   500
Miles

PACIFIC OCEAN

Pagan Island (German)

MARIANA ISLANDS (German)

PHILIPPINE ISLANDS (U.S.A.)

PELEW ISLANDS (German) 19 August

Buru

Ceram 25 August

CELEBES

Timor

28 August

NEW GUINEA

AUSTRALIA

BORNEO

Java Sea

JAVA

SUMATRA

Penang I. 28 Oct.

MALAY PENIN.

Simalur I. 4 September

Cocos Keeling Is.

9 November, 'Emden' surrenders.

KEY
→ Track of SMS 'Emden' (7 August–9 November 1914).

'Emden', a Dresden -class light cruiser, was employed as a lone commerce raider in Eastern waters. During September and October, she captured 19 British merchant ships, bombarded Madras, and sank a Russian cruiser and a French destroyer. On 9 November, attempting to destroy the Cocos Keeling wireless station, she was engaged by HMAS 'Sydney'. Forced ashore half-sunk, 'Emden' surrendered after losing 111 men.

SMS "EMDEN"

Laid down 1906; Completed 1908; Displacement 3,600 tons; Top speed 25 knots

STERN

4·1-inch guns

4·1-inch guns

STEM

'Emden', complement 321, carried an armament of ten 4·1-inch guns, eight 5-pounders & two 17·7-in. t.tbs.

Dummy fourth funnel, erected to resemble a British light cruiser.

© Arthur Banks 1973

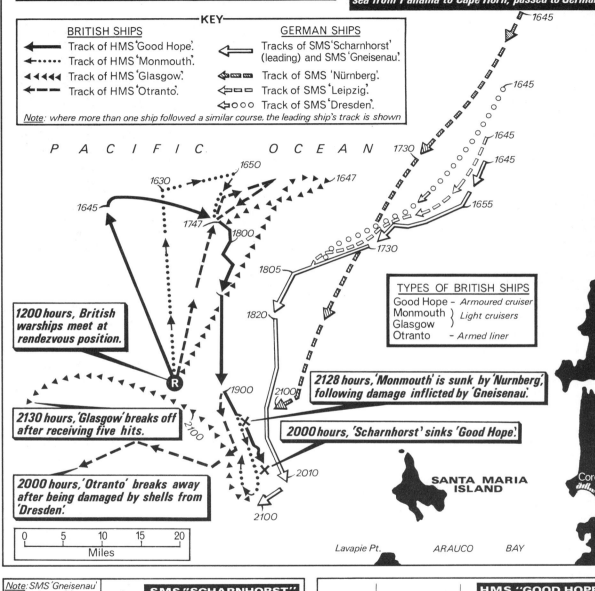

THE BATTLE OF CORONEL 1 NOVEMBER 1914

The Battle of Coronel resulted in a German victory. It was the first major British naval reverse for over a century, and command of th[e] sea from Panama to Cape Horn, passed to German

─────────────────KEY─────────────────

BRITISH SHIPS
- ◀━━━━ Track of HMS 'Good Hope'.
- ◀•••• Track of HMS 'Monmouth'.
- ◀◀◀◀◀ Track of HMS 'Glasgow'.
- ◀━━ Track of HMS 'Otranto'.

GERMAN SHIPS
- ⇐══ Tracks of SMS 'Scharnhorst' (leading) and SMS 'Gneisenau'.
- ⇐▭▭ Track of SMS 'Nürnberg'.
- ⇐▭▭ Track of SMS 'Leipzig'.
- ⇐ooo Track of SMS 'Dresden'.

Note: where more than one ship followed a similar course, the leading ship's track is shown

P A C I F I C   O C E A N

1645

1650

1630

1647

1645

1747

1800

1805

1730

1820

1200 hours, British warships meet at rendezvous position.

TYPES OF BRITISH SHIPS
Good Hope – Armoured cruiser
Monmouth } Light cruisers
Glasgow }
Otranto – Armed liner

R

1900

2100

2130 hours, 'Glasgow' breaks off after receiving five hits.

2128 hours, 'Monmouth' is sunk by 'Nurnberg', following damage inflicted by 'Gneisenau'.

2000 hours, 'Scharnhorst' sinks 'Good Hope'.

2010

2100

2000 hours, 'Otranto' breaks away after being damaged by shells from 'Dresden'.

2100

SANTA MARIA ISLAND

0   5   10   15   20
Miles

Lavapie Pt.   ARAUCO   BAY

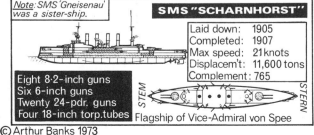

Note: SMS 'Gneisenau' was a sister-ship.

SMS "SCHARNHORST"

Laid down: 1905
Completed: 1907
Max speed: 21 knots
Displacem't: 11,600 tons
Complement: 765

Eight 8·2-inch guns
Six 6-inch guns
Twenty 24-pdr. guns
Four 18-inch torp.tubes

Flagship of Vice-Admiral von Spee

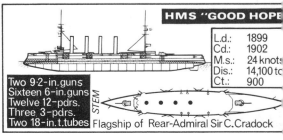

HMS "GOOD HOPE"

L.d.: 1899
Cd.: 1902
M.s.: 24 knots
Dis.: 14,100 to[ns]
Ct.: 900

Two 9·2-in.guns
Sixteen 6-in.guns
Twelve 12-pdrs.
Three 3-pdrs.
Two 18-in.t.tubes

Flagship of Rear-Admiral Sir C.Cradock

240

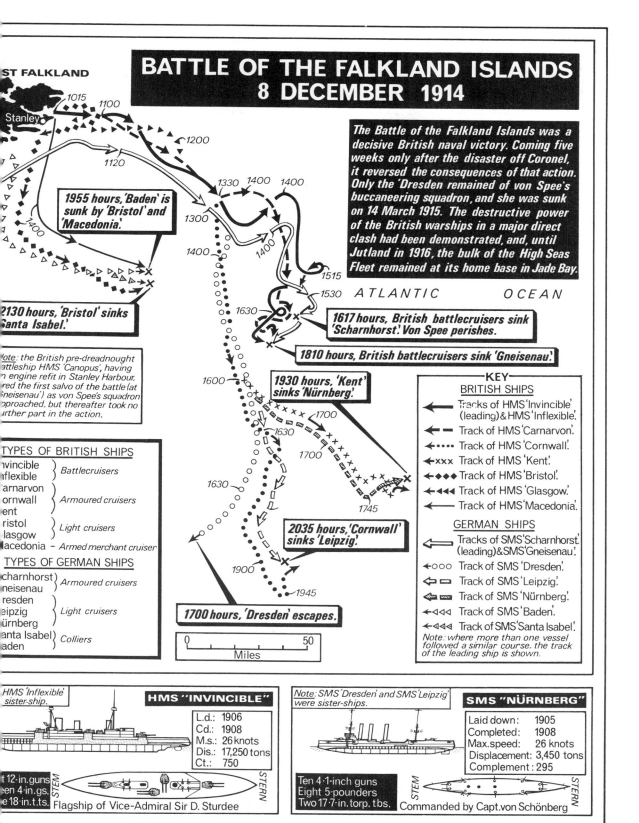

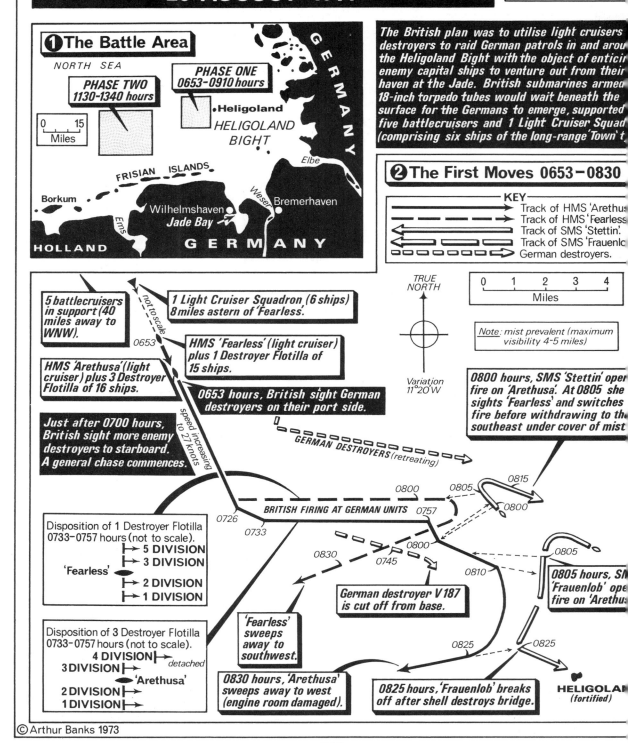

THE BATTLE OF HELIGOLAND BIGHT 28 AUGUST 1914

① The Battle Area

NORTH SEA

PHASE TWO 1130-1340 hours

PHASE ONE 0653-0910 hours

• Heligoland

HELIGOLAND BIGHT

0 — 15
Miles

FRISIAN ISLANDS

Elbe

Borkum

Weser

Bremerhaven

Wilhelmshaven
Jade Bay

Ems

HOLLAND   G E R M A N Y

The British plan was to utilise light cruisers destroyers to raid German patrols in and arou the Heligoland Bight with the object of entici enemy capital ships to venture out from their haven at the Jade. British submarines armed 18-inch torpedo tubes would wait beneath the surface for the Germans to emerge, supported five battlecruisers and 1 Light Cruiser Squad (comprising six ships of the long-range 'Town' t

② The First Moves 0653−0830

KEY
Track of HMS 'Arethus
Track of HMS 'Fearless
Track of SMS 'Stettin'.
Track of SMS 'Frauenlo
German destroyers.

TRUE NORTH

0 1 2 3 4
Miles

Note: mist prevalent (maximum visibility 4-5 miles)

Variation 11°20'W

5 battlecruisers in support (40 miles away to WNW).

1 Light Cruiser Squadron (6 ships) 8 miles astern of 'Fearless'.

not to scale

0653

HMS 'Fearless' (light cruiser) plus 1 Destroyer Flotilla of 15 ships.

HMS 'Arethusa' (light cruiser) plus 3 Destroyer Flotilla of 16 ships.

0653 hours, British sight German destroyers on their port side.

Just after 0700 hours, British sight more enemy destroyers to starboard. A general chase commences.

speed increasing to 27 knots

0800 hours, SMS 'Stettin' ope fire on 'Arethusa'. At 0805 she sights 'Fearless' and switches fire before withdrawing to th southeast under cover of mist

GERMAN DESTROYERS (retreating)

0800   0805   0815
0757   0800

BRITISH FIRING AT GERMAN UNITS

0726
0733

0830   0800   0810
0745   0805

Disposition of 1 Destroyer Flotilla 0733-0757 hours (not to scale).
→ 5 DIVISION
→ 3 DIVISION
'Fearless'
→ 2 DIVISION
→ 1 DIVISION

German destroyer V 187 is cut off from base.

0805 hours, SM 'Frauenlob' ope fire on 'Arethus

'Fearless' sweeps away to southwest.

Disposition of 3 Destroyer Flotilla 0733-0757 hours (not to scale).
4 DIVISION → detached
3 DIVISION →
'Arethusa'
2 DIVISION →
1 DIVISION →

0825   0825

0830 hours, 'Arethusa' sweeps away to west (engine room damaged).

0825 hours, 'Frauenlob' breaks off after shell destroys bridge.

HELIGOLAN (fortified)

242

The Sinking of German Destroyer V187

0910 hours, V187 sinks here.

0900

0835

0915 *(reappearing)*

SMS 'Stettin' fires on British warships rescuing survivors.

3 DIV. (1 FLOTILLA)

0910

0835

HMS 'Ferret'

0838

Destroyers of 5 Division, 1 Destroyer Flotilla.

0838

0930

00 hours, E4 rfaces to scue German rvivors.

The German heavy destroyer V187 had been headed off from her base and she became a prey for several British warships. Following severe damage, she sank at 0910 hours. SMS 'Stettin' now reappeared on the scene and fired at British craft rescuing survivors from V187. Later, E4 surfaced to pick up men.

TRUE NORTH

tion 11°25'W

1000   2000
Yards

0830

0838

KEY
GERMAN
⇦▭▭ Track of German destroyer V187.
⇦ Track of SMS 'Stettin'.
BRITISH
← Tracks of British destroyers *(from 1 Flotilla)*.
← Tracks of HMS 'Nottingham' *leading* and HMS 'Lowestoft' *(both detached from 1 Light Cruiser Squadron)*.
←••• Track of British sub. E4 *(submerged)*.

SMS 'STETTIN'

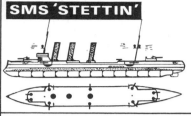

Ten 4·1-in. guns.   Laid down: 1905.
Eight 5-pdrs.   Completed: 1908.
Length: 360 feet. Complement: 320.
Beam: 44 feet.   Displacement: 3,450 tons.

SMS 'FRAUENLOB'

Ten 4·1-in guns.   Laid down: 1900.
Ten 1-pdrs.   Completed: 1903.
Length: 330 feet. Complement: 265.
Beam: 40 feet.   Displacement: 2,715 tons.

V 187

Note: the letter 'V' referred to the Vulkan construction yard at Stettin.

Two 24-pdr. guns. Complement: 84.
Three 18-in. torp. tbs. Max. speed: 35 knots.

E 4

Built by Vickers at Chatham, the 'E' referred to the class. The serial no. was 84.

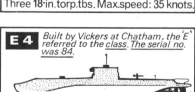

Five 18-in. torp. tubes.   One 12-pdr. gun.
Displacement: 700 tons.   Length: 181 feet.
Complement: 30.   Beam: 22·5 feet.

The German battlecruisers were "trapped" behind the sand bar at the Jade and could not move out until high tide. Meanwhile, several cruisers were despatched at full speed to engage the enemy (unaware of the British battlecruisers being near at hand). SMS 'Strassburg' and SMS 'Mainz' were the first arrivals.

MS 'ARETHUSA'

Light cruiser of 'Arethusa' class.

Laid down:	1912.	Two 6-inch guns *(as built: later a third was added, replacing part of 4-inch armament)*.
Completed:	1914.	
Length:	450 feet.	
Beam:	39 feet.	Six 4-inch guns.
Complement:	319.	Two 3-inch guns.
Displacement:	3,512 tons.	Eight 21-inch torp. tbs *(four above water)*.
Max. speed:	29 knots.	

MS 'FEARLESS'

Scout light cruiser of 'Active' class.

Laid down:	1911.	Ten 4-inch guns.
Completed:	1913.	Four 3-pounder guns.
Length:	385 feet.	Two 21-inch torp. tbs.
Beam:	41·5 feet.	Armour: nil. *(double skin amidships)*.
Complement:	320.	
Displacement:	3,440 tons.	Mean draught: 14 feet.
Max. speed:	26 knots.	H.P. 18,000.

THE BATTLE OF HELIGOLAND BIGHT – continued

0 _____ 10,0[?]
Yards

④ Start of Phase Two: Operations 1130–1200 hours

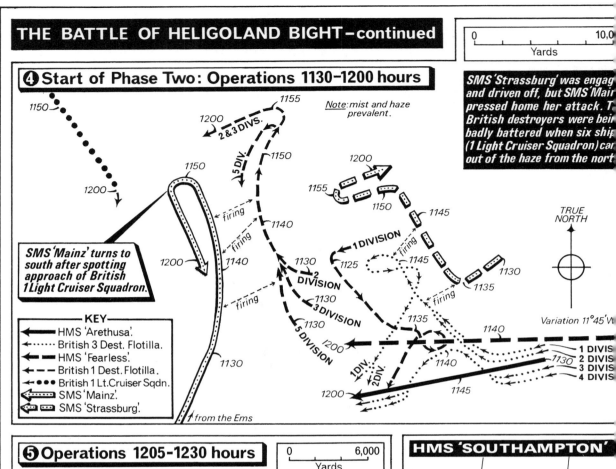

Note: mist and haze prevalent.

SMS 'Mainz' turns to south after spotting approach of British 1 Light Cruiser Squadron.

1150
1200
1155
2 & 3 DIVS.
5 DIV.
1150
1150
1200
1155
1150
1145
1 DIVISION
1130
2 DIVISION
3 DIVISION
5 DIVISION
1130
1135
1130
1125
1145
1135
1130
1140
1200
1140
1200
1140
1145
1130
firing
TRUE NORTH
Variation 11°45′W
1 DIVS
2 DIVS
3 DIVS
4 DIVS
1DIV
2DIV

SMS 'Strassburg' was engag[?] and driven off, but SMS 'Mair[?] pressed home her attack. T[?] British destroyers were bei[?] badly battered when six ship[?] (1 Light Cruiser Squadron) car[?] out of the haze from the nort[?]

KEY
◀━━	HMS 'Arethusa'.
◀·····	British 3 Dest. Flotilla.
◀━ ━	HMS 'Fearless'.
◀━ ─	British 1 Dest. Flotilla.
◀━ •••	British 1 Lt.Cruiser Sqdn.
⟨▭▭	SMS 'Mainz'.
⟨▭ ▭	SMS 'Strassburg'.

↑ from the Ems

⑤ Operations 1205–1230 hours

0 _____ 6,000
Yards

TRUE NORTH
Variation 11°50′W

1205
1210
5 DIV.
1230
1220
Arriving on scene.
'Fearless' turns to miss torpedo.
1225
Arriving on scene.
1205
1205
1230
1230
1DIV.
2DIV.
1DIV. 1205
3 DIV.
4 DIV.
1230
1220
firing
1220
firing
1220
firing
firing
1230

'Mainz' damaged and sinking.

SMS 'Mainz' was engaged by the new arrivals and rapidly reduced to a blazing inferno.

KEY
⟨▭▭	SMS 'Mainz'.
⟨▭	SMS 'Stettin'.
⟨▭▭	SMS 'Köln'.
◀━•⊙⊙	SMS 'Stralsund'.
◀━━	HMS 'Arethusa'.
◀·····	British 3 D.Flotilla.
◀━ ━	HMS 'Fearless'.
◀━ ─	British 1 D.Flotilla.
◀━ ••	British 1 L.C.Sqdn.

© Arthur Banks 1973

HMS 'SOUTHAMPTON'

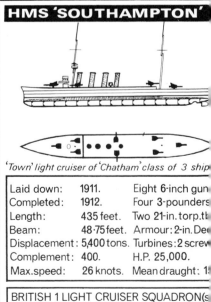

'Town' light cruiser of 'Chatham' class of 3 ship[?]

Laid down:	1911.	Eight 6-inch gun[?]
Completed:	1912.	Four 3-pounders[?]
Length:	435 feet.	Two 21-in. torp.t[?]
Beam:	48·75 feet.	Armour: 2-in. De[?]
Displacement:	5,400 tons.	Turbines: 2 screw[?]
Complement:	400.	H.P. 25,000.
Max. speed:	26 knots.	Mean draught: 1[?]

BRITISH 1 LIGHT CRUISER SQUADRON(s[?]
HMS 'Southampton'.	HMS 'Lowesto[?]
HMS 'Birmingham'.	HMS 'Falmouth[?]
HMS 'Nottingham'.	HMS 'Liverpoo[?]

The Final Moves: 1230-1340 hours

...alizing that sizable German reinforcements were arriving on ...e scene, the British battlecruisers were called into action. ...eir fire-power proved decisive: SMS 'Köln' was sunk and SMS ...riadne' severely damaged (sinking later). Only the mist shroud ...evented the remaining German ships from suffering like fates.

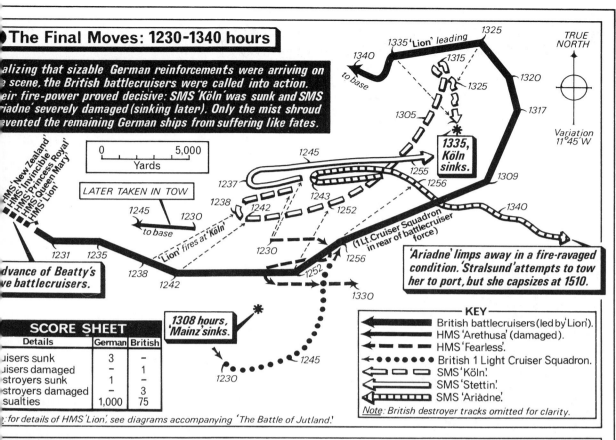

TRUE NORTH

Variation 11°45'W

1335 'Lion' leading
1340
to base
1325
1315
1325
1320
1317
1305
1309
1335, Köln sinks.
1245
1237
1238
1242
1243
1252
1255
1256
1256
1340
1245
1230
to base
'Lion' fires at 'Köln'
1230
1252
1330
(1 Lt.Cruiser Squadron in rear of battlecruiser force)

HMS 'New Zealand'
HMS 'Invincible'
HMS 'Princess Royal'
HMS 'Queen Mary'
HMS 'Lion'

0 — 5,000 Yards

LATER TAKEN IN TOW

1231 1235
1238
1242

...dvance of Beatty's ...e battlecruisers.

'Ariadne' limps away in a fire-ravaged condition. 'Stralsund' attempts to tow her to port, but she capsizes at 1510.

1308 hours, 'Mainz' sinks.

SCORE SHEET

Details	German	British
...uisers sunk	3	–
...uisers damaged	–	1
...stroyers sunk	1	–
...stroyers damaged	–	3
...sualties	1,000	75

...: for details of HMS 'Lion', see diagrams accompanying 'The Battle of Jutland.'

KEY

⬅	British battlecruisers (led by 'Lion').
⬅	HMS 'Arethusa' (damaged).
⬅ - -	HMS 'Fearless'.
⬅ ••••	British 1 Light Cruiser Squadron.
⬅ ☐ ☐	SMS 'Köln'.
⬅	SMS 'Stettin'.
⬅ ▥▥▥	SMS 'Ariadne'.

<u>Note</u>: British destroyer tracks omitted for clarity.

...MS 'MAINZ' & SMS 'KÖLN'

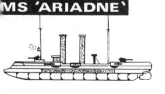

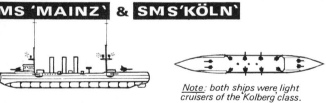

<u>Note</u>: both ships were light cruisers of the 'Kolberg' class.

Laid down: 1907	⎫ 'Mainz'	Twelve 4.1-inch guns.
Completed: 1909	⎭	Four 5-pounder guns.
Laid down: 1908	⎫ 'Köln'	Four machine guns.
Completed: 1910	⎭	Two 18-inch torpedo tubes.
Length:	428 feet.	Complement: 375.
Beam:	46 feet.	Max.speed: 27 knots.
Displacement:	4,350 tons.	Max.draught: 18 feet.

...MS 'ARIADNE'

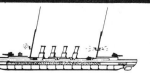

Protected cruiser of 'Nymphe' class.

Laid down:	1899.	Ten 4.1-inch guns.
Completed:	1901.	Fourteen 1-pounder guns.
Length:	328 feet.	Four machine guns.
Beam:	40 feet.	Two 17.7-inch torp.tubes.
Complement:	265.	Max.draught:17.25 feet.
Displacement:	2,670 tons.	Armour: 2-in.Deck (amid.).
Max.speed:	21 knots.	" 1-in.Deck (ends).

...MS 'STRASSBURG'

<u>Note</u>: SMS 'Stralsund' was a sister-ship. (Similar details, including later armament alterations).

Light cruiser of 'Breslau' class.

Laid down:	1910.	Twelve 4.1-inch guns.
Completed:	1912.	(<u>Note</u>: later altered to seven 5.9-inch and two 3.4-inch A.A.guns).
Length:	445 feet.	
Beam:	43 feet.	
Complement:	370.	Two 20-inch torp.tubes.
Displacement:	4,550 tons.	Mean draught:16.5 feet.
Max.speed:	28 knots.	Armour: 2-in.Deck (amid.).

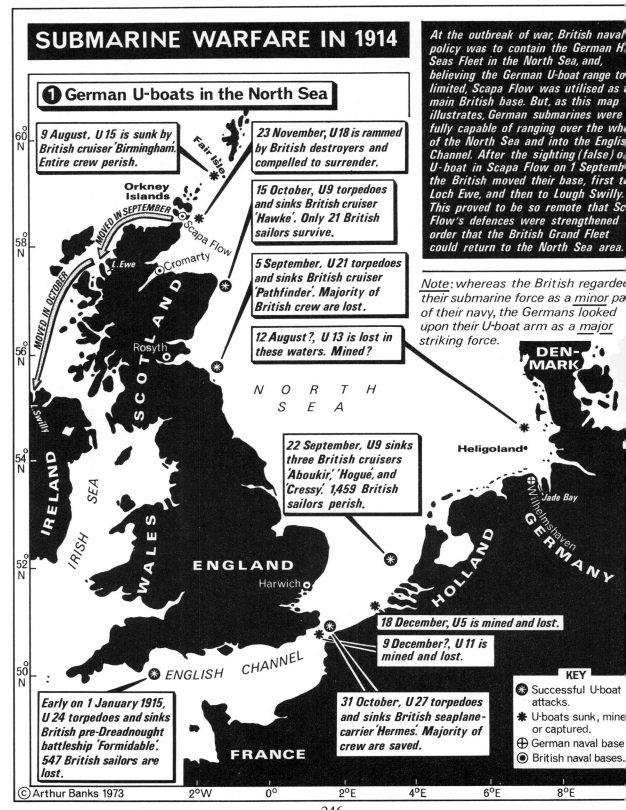

SUBMARINE WARFARE IN 1914

① German U-boats in the North Sea

9 August, U 15 is sunk by British cruiser 'Birmingham'. Entire crew perish.

23 November, U 18 is rammed by British destroyers and compelled to surrender.

15 October, U 9 torpedoes and sinks British cruiser 'Hawke'. Only 21 British sailors survive.

5 September, U 21 torpedoes and sinks British cruiser 'Pathfinder'. Majority of British crew are lost.

12 August?, U 13 is lost in these waters. Mined?

22 September, U 9 sinks three British cruisers 'Aboukir', 'Hogue', and 'Cressy'. 1,459 British sailors perish.

18 December, U 5 is mined and lost.

9 December?, U 11 is mined and lost.

Early on 1 January 1915, U 24 torpedoes and sinks British pre-Dreadnought battleship 'Formidable'. 547 British sailors are lost.

31 October, U 27 torpedoes and sinks British seaplane-carrier 'Hermes'. Majority of crew are saved.

At the outbreak of war, British naval policy was to contain the German High Seas Fleet in the North Sea, and, believing the German U-boat range to be limited, Scapa Flow was utilised as the main British base. But, as this map illustrates, German submarines were fully capable of ranging over the whole of the North Sea and into the English Channel. After the sighting (false) of a U-boat in Scapa Flow on 1 September, the British moved their base, first to Loch Ewe, and then to Lough Swilly. This proved to be so remote that Scapa Flow's defences were strengthened in order that the British Grand Fleet could return to the North Sea area.

Note: whereas the British regarded their submarine force as a <u>minor part</u> of their navy, the Germans looked upon their U-boat arm as a <u>major</u> striking force.

DEN-MARK

Heligoland

Jade Bay

Wilhelmshaven

GERMANY

HOLLAND

N O R T H S E A

Fair Isle

Orkney Islands

Scapa Flow

MOVED IN SEPTEMBER

L. Ewe **Cromarty**

MOVED IN OCTOBER

L. Swilly

Rosyth

SCOTLAND

IRELAND

IRISH SEA

WALES

ENGLAND

Harwich

ENGLISH CHANNEL

FRANCE

KEY
⊛ Successful U-boat attacks.
✳ U-boats sunk, mined or captured.
⊕ German naval base
◉ British naval bases.

60° N
58° N
56° N
54° N
52° N
50° N

2°W   0°   2°E   4°E   6°E   8°E

© Arthur Banks 1973

246

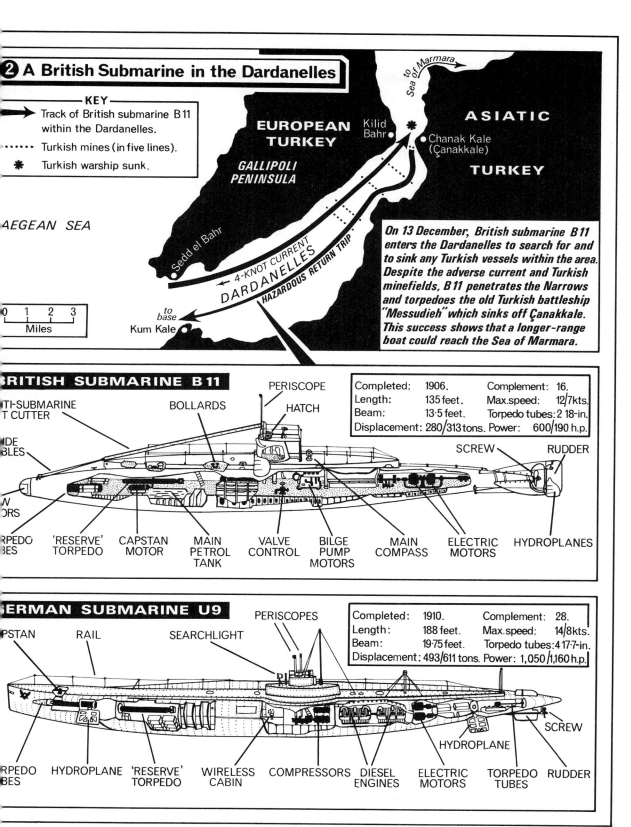

② A British Submarine in the Dardanelles

KEY
→ Track of British submarine B 11 within the Dardanelles.

····· Turkish mines (in five lines).

✳ Turkish warship sunk.

EUROPEAN TURKEY

GALLIPOLI PENINSULA

AEGEAN SEA

Sedd el Bahr

4-KNOT CURRENT

DARDANELLES

HAZARDOUS RETURN TRIP

to base
Kum Kale

to Sea of Marmara

Kilid Bahr

Chanak Kale (Çanakkale)

ASIATIC TURKEY

0 1 2 3
Miles

On 13 December, British submarine B 11 enters the Dardanelles to search for and to sink any Turkish vessels within the area. Despite the adverse current and Turkish minefields, B 11 penetrates the Narrows and torpedoes the old Turkish battleship "Messudieh" which sinks off Çanakkale. This success shows that a longer-range boat could reach the Sea of Marmara.

BRITISH SUBMARINE B 11

Completed:	1906.	Complement:	16.
Length:	135 feet.	Max. speed:	12/7 kts.
Beam:	13·5 feet.	Torpedo tubes:	2 18-in.
Displacement:	280/313 tons.	Power:	600/190 h.p.

PERISCOPE
BOLLARDS
HATCH
ANTI-SUBMARINE NET CUTTER
GUIDE CABLES
SCREW
RUDDER
BOW PLANES
TORPEDO TUBES
'RESERVE' TORPEDO
CAPSTAN MOTOR
MAIN PETROL TANK
VALVE CONTROL
BILGE PUMP MOTORS
MAIN COMPASS
ELECTRIC MOTORS
HYDROPLANES

GERMAN SUBMARINE U9

Completed:	1910.	Complement:	28.
Length:	188 feet.	Max. speed:	14/8 kts.
Beam:	19·75 feet.	Torpedo tubes:	4 17·7-in.
Displacement:	493/611 tons.	Power:	1,050/1,160 h.p.

PERISCOPES
SEARCHLIGHT
CAPSTAN
RAIL
SCREW
HYDROPLANE
TORPEDO TUBES
HYDROPLANE
'RESERVE' TORPEDO
WIRELESS CABIN
COMPRESSORS
DIESEL ENGINES
ELECTRIC MOTORS
TORPEDO TUBES
RUDDER

247

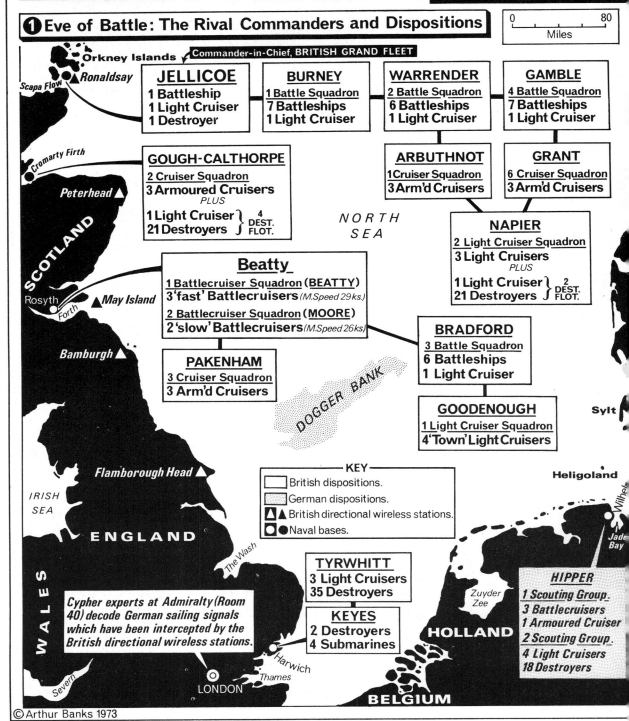

BATTLE OF THE DOGGER BANK
24 JANUARY 1915

Note: in August 1914, SMS 'Magdeburg' (a German light cruiser of the 'Breslau' class) was lost in the Baltic. The Russians recovered its signal code book and passed them to the Admiralty in London. British cypher experts utilised these for decoding purposes.

① Eve of Battle: The Rival Commanders and Dispositions

```
0                    80
        Miles
```

Orkney Islands

Ronaldsay

Scapa Flow

Commander-in-Chief, BRITISH GRAND FLEET

JELLICOE
1 Battleship
1 Light Cruiser
1 Destroyer

BURNEY
1 Battle Squadron
7 Battleships
1 Light Cruiser

WARRENDER
2 Battle Squadron
6 Battleships
1 Light Cruiser

GAMBLE
4 Battle Squadron
7 Battleships
1 Light Cruiser

Cromarty Firth

GOUGH-CALTHORPE
2 Cruiser Squadron
3 Armoured Cruisers
PLUS
1 Light Cruiser ⎱ 4
21 Destroyers ⎰ DEST. FLOT.

ARBUTHNOT
1 Cruiser Squadron
3 Arm'd Cruisers

GRANT
6 Cruiser Squadron
3 Arm'd Cruisers

Peterhead ▲

SCOTLAND

NORTH SEA

NAPIER
2 Light Cruiser Squadron
3 Light Cruisers
PLUS
1 Light Cruiser ⎱ 2
21 Destroyers ⎰ DEST. FLOT.

Rosyth

May Island ▲

Forth

Beatty
1 Battlecruiser Squadron (BEATTY)
3 'fast' Battlecruisers *(M.Speed 29 ks.)*
2 Battlecruiser Squadron (MOORE)
2 'slow' Battlecruisers *(M.Speed 26 ks.)*

Bamburgh ▲

PAKENHAM
3 Cruiser Squadron
3 Arm'd Cruisers

BRADFORD
3 Battle Squadron
6 Battleships
1 Light Cruiser

GOODENOUGH
1 Light Cruiser Squadron
4 'Town' Light Cruisers

Sylt

DOGGER BANK

Flamborough Head ▲

IRISH SEA

ENGLAND

WALES

---KEY---
☐ British dispositions.
▨ German dispositions.
▲△ British directional wireless stations.
◉● Naval bases.

Heligoland

Wilhelmshaven

Jade Bay

The Wash

TYRWHITT
3 Light Cruisers
35 Destroyers

Zuyder Zee

HIPPER
1 Scouting Group.
3 Battlecruisers
1 Armoured Cruiser
2 Scouting Group.
4 Light Cruisers
18 Destroyers

Cypher experts at Admiralty (Room 40) decode German sailing signals which have been intercepted by the British directional wireless stations.

KEYES
2 Destroyers
4 Submarines

HOLLAND

Harwich

Thames

Severn

◎ **LONDON**

BELGIUM

© Arthur Banks 1973

248

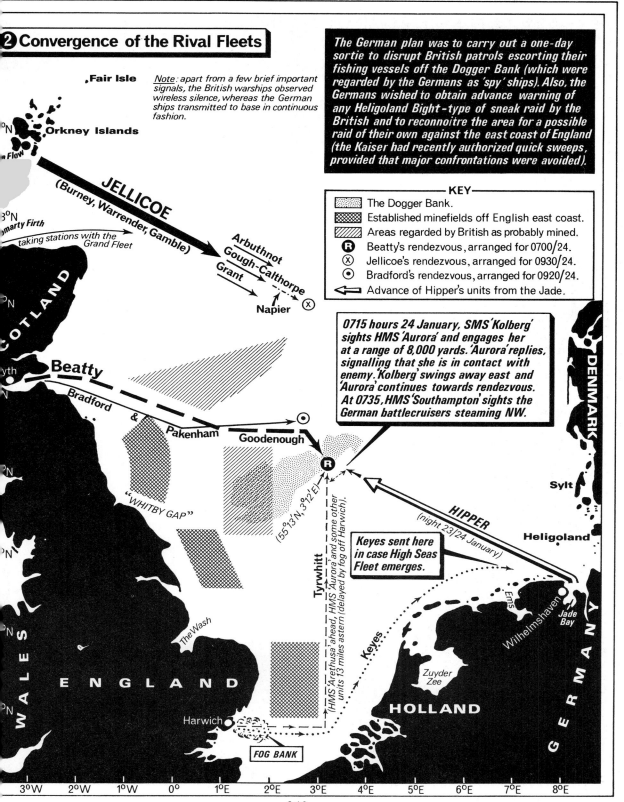

② Convergence of the Rival Fleets

Fair Isle

Note: apart from a few brief important signals, the British warships observed wireless silence, whereas the German ships transmitted to base in continuous fashion.

Orkney Islands

Flow

JELLICOE

(Burney, Warrender, Gamble)

marty Firth

taking stations with the Grand Fleet

Arbuthnot
Gough-Calthorpe
Grant

Napier Ⓧ

COTLAND

yth

Beatty

Bradford

&

Pakenham

Goodenough

⊙

Ⓡ

(55°13'N, 3°12'E)

Tyrwhitt

(HMS 'Arethusa' ahead, HMS 'Aurora' and some other units 13 miles astern (delayed by fog off Harwich).

"WHITBY GAP"

Keyes

The Wash

ENGLAND

W A L E S

Harwich

FOG BANK

The German plan was to carry out a one-day sortie to disrupt British patrols escorting their fishing vessels off the Dogger Bank (which were regarded by the Germans as 'spy' ships). Also, the Germans wished to obtain advance warning of any Heligoland Bight-type of sneak raid by the British and to reconnoitre the area for a possible raid of their own against the east coast of England (the Kaiser had recently authorized quick sweeps, provided that major confrontations were avoided).

KEY

- ▨ The Dogger Bank.
- ▨ Established minefields off English east coast.
- ▨ Areas regarded by British as probably mined.
- Ⓡ Beatty's rendezvous, arranged for 0700/24.
- Ⓧ Jellicoe's rendezvous, arranged for 0930/24.
- ⊙ Bradford's rendezvous, arranged for 0920/24.
- ⇐ Advance of Hipper's units from the Jade.

0715 hours 24 January, SMS 'Kolberg' sights HMS 'Aurora' and engages her at a range of 8,000 yards. 'Aurora' replies, signalling that she is in contact with enemy. 'Kolberg' swings away east and 'Aurora' continues towards rendezvous. At 0735, HMS 'Southampton' sights the German battlecruisers steaming NW.

DENMARK

Sylt

Heligoland

HIPPER

(night 23/24 January)

Keyes sent here in case High Seas Fleet emerges.

Ems

Wilhelmshaven

Jade Bay

Zuyder Zee

HOLLAND

G E R M A N Y

3°W 2°W 1°W 0° 1°E 2°E 3°E 4°E 5°E 6°E 7°E 8°E

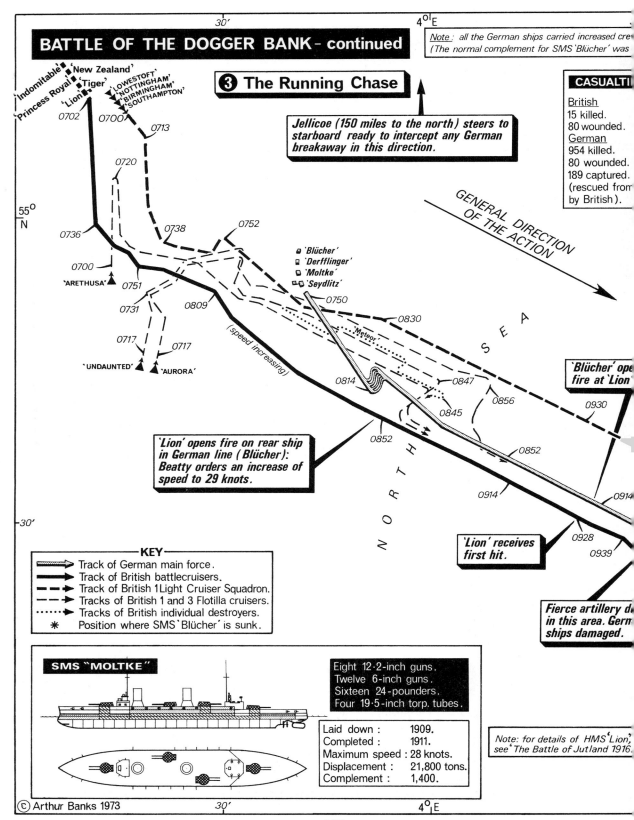

BATTLE OF THE DOGGER BANK - continued

Note: all the German ships carried increased cre
(The normal complement for SMS 'Blücher' was

③ The Running Chase

Jellicoe (150 miles to the north) steers to starboard ready to intercept any German breakaway in this direction.

CASUALTI

British
15 killed.
80 wounded.
German
954 killed.
80 wounded.
189 captured.
(rescued from
by British).

'Indomitable' 'New Zealand'
'Princess Royal' 'Tiger'
'Lion'
LOWESTOFT'
'NOTTINGHAM'
'BIRMINGHAM'
'SOUTHAMPTON'

0702   0700   0713
0720
0736
0700   0738   0752
'ARETHUSA'   0751
0731   0809
0717   0717
'UNDAUNTED'   'AURORA'

55°
N

-30'

GENERAL DIRECTION OF THE ACTION

'Blücher'
'Derfflinger'
'Moltke'
'Seydlitz'

0750
0830
Meteor
0814   0847
0845   0856
0852   0852
0914   0914
0928
0939
0930

(speed increasing)

NORTH   SEA

*'Blücher' ope
fire at 'Lion'*

'Lion' opens fire on rear ship in German line (Blücher): Beatty orders an increase of speed to 29 knots.

'Lion' receives first hit.

*Fierce artillery d
in this area. Germ
ships damaged.*

KEY
- ∿∿▶ Track of German main force.
- ▬▶ Track of British battlecruisers.
- ▬ ▬▶ Track of British 1 Light Cruiser Squadron.
- — · —▶ Tracks of British 1 and 3 Flotilla cruisers.
- · · · ·▶ Tracks of British individual destroyers.
- ＊ Position where SMS 'Blücher' is sunk.

SMS "MOLTKE"

Eight 12·2-inch guns.
Twelve 6-inch guns.
Sixteen 24-pounders.
Four 19·5-inch torp. tubes.

Laid down : 1909.
Completed : 1911.
Maximum speed : 28 knots.
Displacement : 21,800 tons.
Complement : 1,400.

Note: for details of HMS 'Lion',
see 'The Battle of Jutland 1916.

30'   4°E

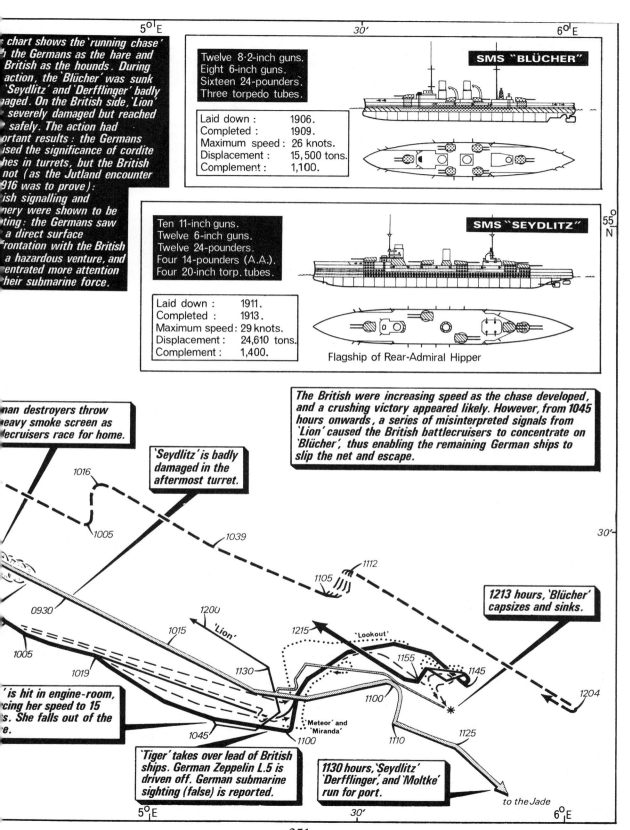

...e chart shows the 'running chase' ...h the Germans as the hare and ...British as the hounds. During ...action, the 'Blücher' was sunk ...'Seydlitz' and 'Derfflinger' badly ...aged. On the British side, 'Lion' ...severely damaged but reached ...safely. The action had ...ortant results: the Germans ...ised the significance of cordite ...hes in turrets, but the British ...not (as the Jutland encounter ...916 was to prove): ...ish signalling and ...nery were shown to be ...ting: the Germans saw ...a direct surface ...rontation with the British ...a hazardous venture, and ...entrated more attention ...heir submarine force.

Twelve 8·2-inch guns.
Eight 6-inch guns.
Sixteen 24-pounders.
Three torpedo tubes.

SMS "BLÜCHER"

Laid down :	1906.
Completed :	1909.
Maximum speed :	26 knots.
Displacement :	15,500 tons.
Complement :	1,100.

Ten 11-inch guns.
Twelve 6-inch guns.
Twelve 24-pounders.
Four 14-pounders (A.A.).
Four 20-inch torp. tubes.

SMS "SEYDLITZ"

Laid down :	1911.
Completed :	1913.
Maximum speed :	29 knots.
Displacement :	24,610 tons.
Complement :	1,400.

Flagship of Rear-Admiral Hipper

55⁰N

The British were increasing speed as the chase developed, and a crushing victory appeared likely. However, from 1045 hours onwards, a series of misinterpreted signals from 'Lion' caused the British battlecruisers to concentrate on 'Blücher', thus enabling the remaining German ships to slip the net and escape.

...man destroyers throw ...eavy smoke screen as ...ecruisers race for home.

'Seydlitz' is badly damaged in the aftermost turret.

1016
1005
1039

30'

1105   1112

1213 hours, 'Blücher' capsizes and sinks.

0930
1200
'Lion'
1015
1215
'Lookout'
1130
1155
1145
1204
1005
1019
1100
1100
1110
1125

...' is hit in engine-room, ...cing her speed to 15 ...s. She falls out of the ...e.

'Meteor' and 'Miranda'

1045

'Tiger' takes over lead of British ships. German Zeppelin L.5 is driven off. German submarine sighting (false) is reported.

1130 hours, 'Seydlitz' 'Derfflinger', and 'Moltke' run for port.

to the Jade

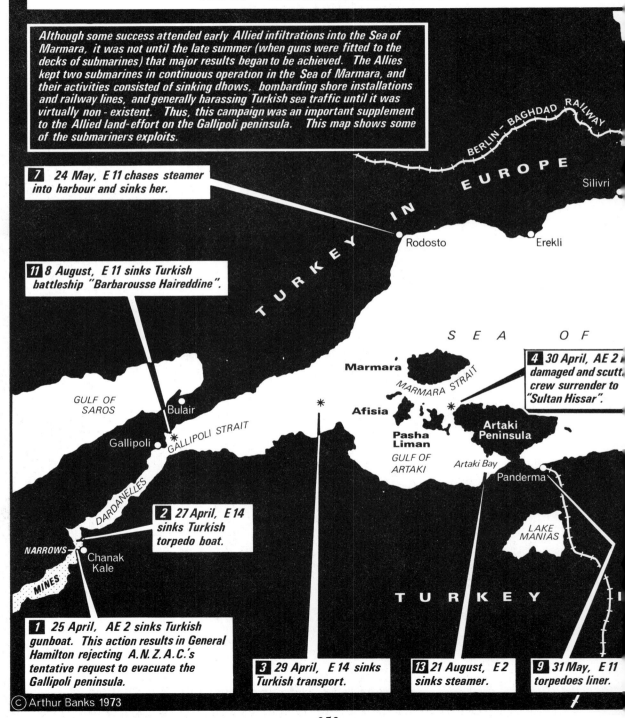

THE SUCCESSFUL ALLIED SUBMARINE CAMPAIGN AT THE TIME OF THE GALLIPOLI EXPEDITION MAY-DECEMBER 1915

Although some success attended early Allied infiltrations into the Sea of Marmara, it was not until the late summer (when guns were fitted to the decks of submarines) that major results began to be achieved. The Allies kept two submarines in continuous operation in the Sea of Marmara, and their activities consisted of sinking dhows, bombarding shore installations and railway lines, and generally harassing Turkish sea traffic until it was virtually non-existent. Thus, this campaign was an important supplement to the Allied land-effort on the Gallipoli peninsula. This map shows some of the submariners exploits.

7 *24 May, E 11 chases steamer into harbour and sinks her.*

11 *8 August, E 11 sinks Turkish battleship "Barbarousse Haireddine".*

4 *30 April, AE 2 [damaged and scutt... crew surrender to "Sultan Hissar".*

2 *27 April, E 14 sinks Turkish torpedo boat.*

1 *25 April, AE 2 sinks Turkish gunboat. This action results in General Hamilton rejecting A.N.Z.A.C.'s tentative request to evacuate the Gallipoli peninsula.*

3 *29 April, E 14 sinks Turkish transport.*

13 *21 August, E 2 sinks steamer.*

9 *31 May, E 11 torpedoes liner.*

BERLIN - BAGHDAD RAILWAY

TURKEY IN EUROPE

Silivri

Rodosto

Erekli

GULF OF SAROS

Bulair

Gallipoli

GALLIPOLI STRAIT

DARDANELLES

NARROWS

Chanak Kale

MINES

SEA OF

Marmara

MARMARA STRAIT

Afisia

Pasha Liman

GULF OF ARTAKI

Artaki Peninsula

Artaki Bay

Panderma

LAKE MANIAS

TURKEY

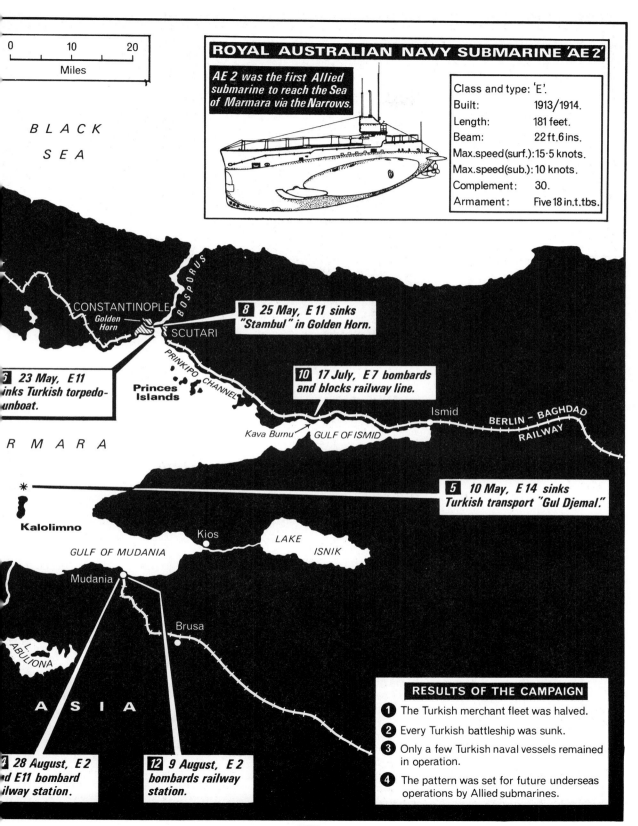

BLACK
SEA

ROYAL AUSTRALIAN NAVY SUBMARINE 'AE 2'

AE 2 was the first Allied submarine to reach the Sea of Marmara via the Narrows.

Class and type:	'E'.
Built:	1913/1914.
Length:	181 feet.
Beam:	22 ft. 6 ins.
Max. speed (surf.):	15·5 knots.
Max. speed (sub.):	10 knots.
Complement:	30.
Armament:	Five 18 in. t. tbs.

CONSTANTINOPLE
Golden Horn
SCUTARI

BOSPORUS

8 25 May, E 11 sinks "Stambul" in Golden Horn.

6 23 May, E 11 sinks Turkish torpedo-gunboat.

PRINKIPO CHANNEL

Princes Islands

10 17 July, E 7 bombards and blocks railway line.

Ismid

BERLIN – BAGHDAD RAILWAY

Kava Burnu   GULF OF ISMID

M A R A

5 10 May, E 14 sinks Turkish transport "Gul Djemal."

*✱
Kalolimno*

Kios

LAKE
ISNIK

GULF OF MUDANIA

Mudania

Brusa

L. ABULIONA

A S I A

28 August, E 2 and E 11 bombard railway station.

12 9 August, E 2 bombards railway station.

RESULTS OF THE CAMPAIGN

1 The Turkish merchant fleet was halved.

2 Every Turkish battleship was sunk.

3 Only a few Turkish naval vessels remained in operation.

4 The pattern was set for future underseas operations by Allied submarines.

0   10   20
Miles

BRITISH BATTLESHIP LOSSES DURING THE GALLIPOLI CAMPAIGN MAY 1915

KEY

✳ Positions of the three British battleships when sunk during May.

★ Main forts.

On 12 May, HMS "Queen Elizabeth" was ordered home from the Aegean area to strengthen the British Grand Fleet. On 13 May, the British battleship HMS "Goliath" was sunk by a Turkish destroyer, and later in the month the U21 sank two more British battleships. The Allied heavy warships were withdrawn from the Gallipoli operations leaving the land troops with no large naval guns to support them until the new monitors arrived in August.

Boghali ●

Gaba Tepe ✳

2 1225 hours 25 May, U 21 torpedoes HMS"Triumph" in full view of A.N.Z.A.C. troops. 3 British officers and 70 men are lost. De Robeck promptly recalls all large warships to Mudros: this causes a demoralizing effect upon the Allied troops on land. HMS "Majestic" is ordered to 'W' Beach on 26 May.

Maidos ●

GALLIPOLI PENINSULA

Kilid Bahr ●★

★ Chanak Kale

DARDANELLES

| 0 | 1 | 2 | 3 |

Miles

AEGEAN SEA

● Krithia

'W.' Beach ○

Cape Helles ★

Morto Bay ✳

Eski Hissarlik Pt.

1 0116 hours 13 May, HMS"Goliath" is sunk by Turkish destroyer "Muavenet-i-Miliet." Operating under cover of a thick mist, the destroyer fires three torpedoes. 570 British officers and men are lost. This is the largest single disaster suffered by the Royal Navy throughout the entire Dardanelles and Gallipoli campaign.

3 0645 hours 27 May, U 21 fires two torpedoes at HMS "Majestic". The "fish" penetrate the protecting torpedo-nets and British battleship sinks with the loss of 40 men.

ROUTE OF U 21 TO THE AEGEAN

U 21 DEPARTS 25 APRIL.

U 21 ARRIVES HERE ON 13 MAY. CREW RESTS FOR ONE WEEK WHILE SUBMARINE IS REFUELLED AND STORES REPLENISHED.

Wilhelmshaven ○

Cattaro ○

Cape Helles

| 0 | 600 |

Miles

25 MAY, U 21 ARRIVES OFF CAPE HELLES.

NORTH SEA RIVAL STRATEGIES

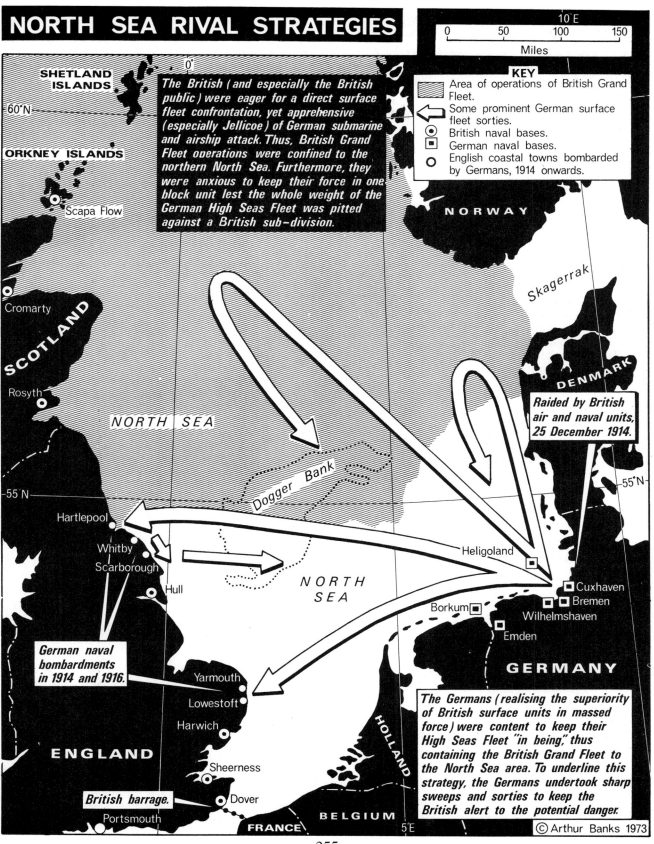

KEY

- Area of operations of British Grand Fleet.
- Some prominent German surface fleet sorties.
- ⊙ British naval bases.
- ▣ German naval bases.
- ○ English coastal towns bombarded by Germans, 1914 onwards.

0   50   100   150
Miles

SHETLAND ISLANDS

60°N

ORKNEY ISLANDS

Scapa Flow

NORWAY

The British (and especially the British public) were eager for a direct surface fleet confrontation, yet apprehensive (especially Jellicoe) of German submarine and airship attack. Thus, British Grand Fleet operations were confined to the northern North Sea. Furthermore, they were anxious to keep their force in one block unit lest the whole weight of the German High Seas Fleet was pitted against a British sub-division.

Cromarty

SCOTLAND

Rosyth

NORTH SEA

Skagerrak

DENMARK

Raided by British air and naval units, 25 December 1914.

55°N

Dogger Bank

Hartlepool

Whitby

Scarborough

Hull

NORTH SEA

Heligoland

□ Cuxhaven
▣ □ Bremen
Wilhelmshaven

Borkum ▣

Emden

GERMANY

German naval bombardments in 1914 and 1916.

Yarmouth

Lowestoft

Harwich

HOLLAND

ENGLAND

Sheerness

The Germans (realising the superiority of British surface units in massed force) were content to keep their High Seas Fleet "in being," thus containing the British Grand Fleet to the North Sea area. To underline this strategy, the Germans undertook sharp sweeps and sorties to keep the British alert to the potential danger.

British barrage.

Dover

Portsmouth

FRANCE

BELGIUM

© Arthur Banks 1973

THE BATTLE OF JUTLAND 31 MAY 1916

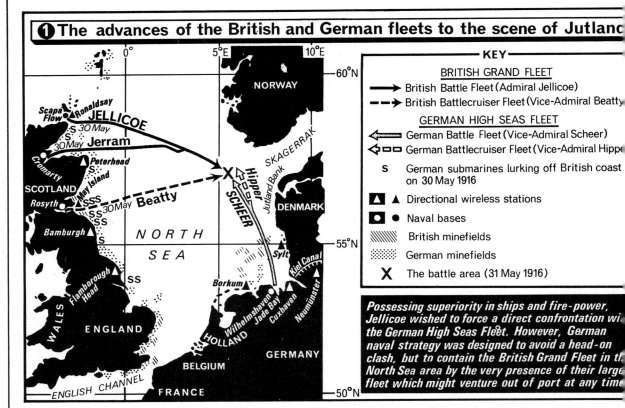

❶ The advances of the British and German fleets to the scene of Jutland

KEY

BRITISH GRAND FLEET
→ British Battle Fleet (Admiral Jellicoe)
--→ British Battlecruiser Fleet (Vice-Admiral Beatty_

GERMAN HIGH SEAS FLEET
⇐□□□ German Battle Fleet (Vice-Admiral Scheer)
⇐□□ German Battlecruiser Fleet (Vice-Admiral Hippe_

S   German submarines lurking off British coast on 30 May 1916

▲ ▲   Directional wireless stations

⬛ ●   Naval bases

▨   British minefields

▦   German minefields

X   The battle area (31 May 1916)

*Possessing superiority in ships and fire-power, Jellicoe wished to force a direct confrontation wi_ the German High Seas Fleet. However, German naval strategy was designed to avoid a head-on clash, but to contain the British Grand Fleet in th_ North Sea area by the very presence of their large_ fleet which might venture out of port at any time_*

❷ The Opening Action – clash of the battlecruisers

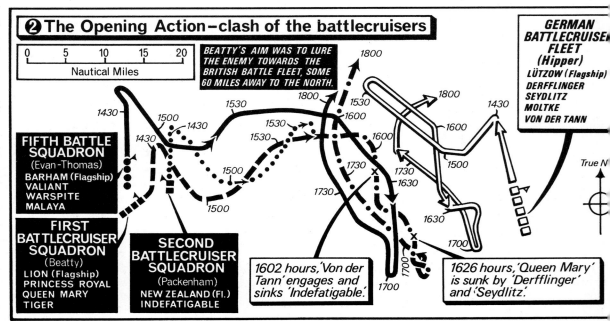

0 5 10 15 20
Nautical Miles

BEATTY'S AIM WAS TO LURE THE ENEMY TOWARDS THE BRITISH BATTLE FLEET, SOME 60 MILES AWAY TO THE NORTH.

GERMAN BATTLECRUISE_ FLEET (Hipper)
LÜTZOW (Flagship)
DERFFLINGER
SEYDLITZ
MOLTKE
VON DER TANN

*True N_*

FIFTH BATTLE SQUADRON
(Evan-Thomas)
BARHAM (Flagship)
VALIANT
WARSPITE
MALAYA

FIRST BATTLECRUISER SQUADRON
(Beatty)
LION (Flagship)
PRINCESS ROYAL
QUEEN MARY
TIGER

SECOND BATTLECRUISER SQUADRON
(Packenham)
NEW ZEALAND (Fl.)
INDEFATIGABLE

1602 hours,'Von der Tann' engages and sinks 'Indefatigable'.

1626 hours,'Queen Mary' is sunk by 'Derfflinger' and 'Seydlitz'.

© Arthur Banks 1973

256

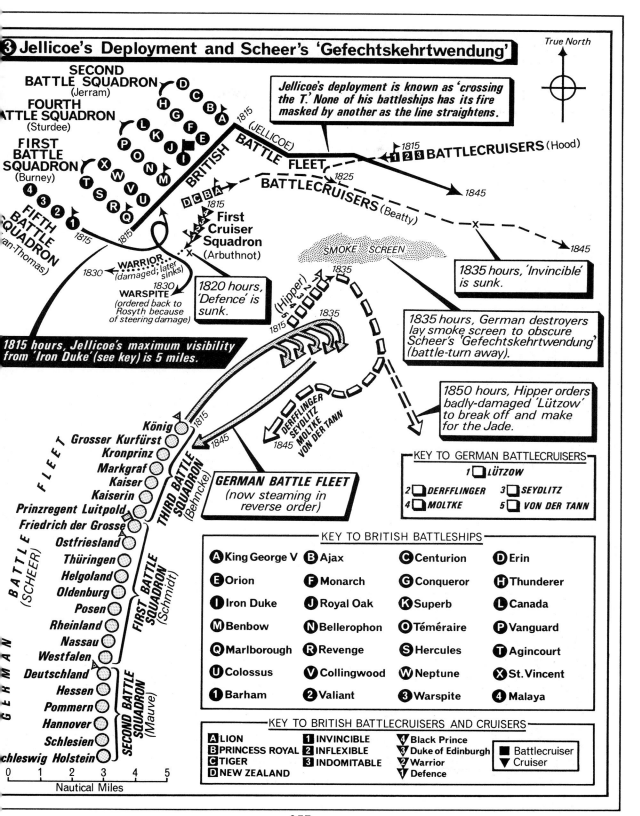

3 Jellicoe's Deployment and Scheer's 'Gefechtskehrtwendung'

True North

SECOND BATTLE SQUADRON (Jerram)

FOURTH BATTLE SQUADRON (Sturdee)

FIRST BATTLE SQUADRON (Burney)

FIFTH BATTLE SQUADRON (Evan-Thomas)

Jellicoe's deployment is known as 'crossing the T.' None of his battleships has its fire masked by another as the line straightens.

1815 (JELLICOE)

BRITISH BATTLE FLEET

1815 BATTLECRUISERS (Hood)

1825 BATTLECRUISERS (Beatty)

1845

First Cruiser Squadron (Arbuthnot)

1845

X

1845

SMOKE SCREEN

1835

1835 hours, 'Invincible' is sunk.

WARRIOR (damaged; later sinks)

1830

WARSPITE (ordered back to Rosyth because of steering damage)

1830

1820 hours, 'Defence' is sunk.

(Hipper)

1815

1835

1835 hours, German destroyers lay smoke screen to obscure Scheer's 'Gefechtskehrtwendung' (battle-turn away).

1815 hours, Jellicoe's maximum visibility from 'Iron Duke' (see key) is 5 miles.

1850 hours, Hipper orders badly-damaged 'Lützow' to break off and make for the Jade.

König
Grosser Kurfürst
Kronprinz
Markgraf
Kaiser
Kaiserin
Prinzregent Luitpold
Friedrich der Grosse
Ostfriesland
Thüringen
Helgoland
Oldenburg
Posen
Rheinland
Nassau
Westfalen
Deutschland
Hessen
Pommern
Hannover
Schlesien
Schleswig Holstein

THIRD BATTLE SQUADRON (Behncke)

FIRST BATTLE SQUADRON (Schmidt)

SECOND BATTLE SQUADRON (Mauve)

BATTLE FLEET (Scheer)

GERMAN

1815

1845

DERFFLINGER SEYDLITZ MOLTKE VON DER TANN

1845

GERMAN BATTLE FLEET (now steaming in reverse order)

KEY TO GERMAN BATTLECRUISERS
1 Lützow
2 DERFFLINGER   3 SEYDLITZ
4 MOLTKE   5 VON DER TANN

KEY TO BRITISH BATTLESHIPS

Ⓐ King George V	Ⓑ Ajax	Ⓒ Centurion	Ⓓ Erin
Ⓔ Orion	Ⓕ Monarch	Ⓖ Conqueror	Ⓗ Thunderer
Ⓘ Iron Duke	Ⓙ Royal Oak	Ⓚ Superb	Ⓛ Canada
Ⓜ Benbow	Ⓝ Bellerophon	Ⓞ Téméraire	Ⓟ Vanguard
Ⓠ Marlborough	Ⓡ Revenge	Ⓢ Hercules	Ⓣ Agincourt
Ⓤ Colossus	Ⓥ Collingwood	Ⓦ Neptune	Ⓧ St. Vincent
❶ Barham	❷ Valiant	❸ Warspite	❹ Malaya

KEY TO BRITISH BATTLECRUISERS AND CRUISERS

Ⓐ LION	1 INVINCIBLE	4 Black Prince	
Ⓑ PRINCESS ROYAL	2 INFLEXIBLE	3 Duke of Edinburgh	■ Battlecruiser
Ⓒ TIGER	3 INDOMITABLE	2 Warrior	▼ Cruiser
Ⓓ NEW ZEALAND		1 Defence	

0 1 2 3 4 5
Nautical Miles

THE BATTLE OF JUTLAND - continued

True North

❹ The Battle Fleets in action for the second time

Following its battle-turn away at 1835 hours, the German Fleet was steering west, away from its home base at the Jade. Realising his situation, Scheer turned east to head for home, noting that the advantageous hours of darkness were in the offing. Again the two fleets came into contact, whereupon the Germans executed a further battle-turn away from the British.

BRITISH BATTLE FLEET

- Ⓐ Ⓑ 1st. Battle Squadron
- Ⓒ Ⓓ 2nd. Battle Squadron
- Ⓔ Ⓕ 4th. Battle Squadron
- Ⓖ 5th. Battle Squadron

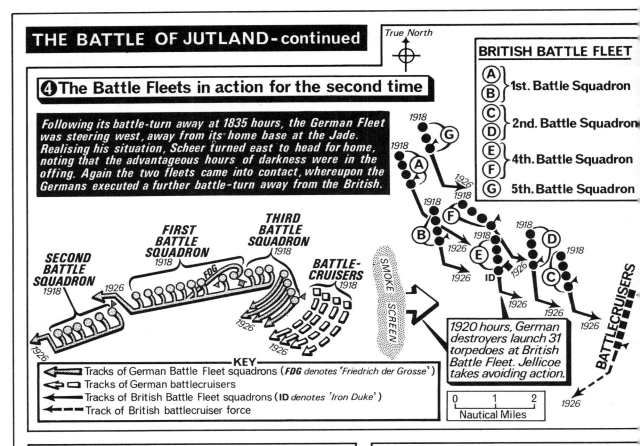

SECOND BATTLE SQUADRON 1918

FIRST BATTLE SQUADRON 1918

THIRD BATTLE SQUADRON 1918

BATTLE-CRUISERS 1918

SMOKE SCREEN

FDG

BATTLECRUISERS

1920 hours, German destroyers launch 31 torpedoes at British Battle Fleet. Jellicoe takes avoiding action.

KEY

- Tracks of German Battle Fleet squadrons (*FDG* denotes *'Friedrich der Grosse'*)
- Tracks of German battlecruisers
- Tracks of British Battle Fleet squadrons (*ID* denotes *'Iron Duke'*)
- Track of British battlecruiser force

0   1   2
Nautical Miles

A BRITISH BATTLECRUISER GUN TURRET

The loss of three British battlecruisers at Jutland was attributed to lack of adequate anti-flash screening between magazine and handling-room.

GUN HOUSE
GUN
RAMMER
MOUNTING
WORKING CHAMBER
RAMMERS
MAIN TRUNK
HANDLING ROOM
HANDLING ROOM
CORDITE CHARGES
CAGE
MAGAZINE
SHELL ROOM
SHELL ROOM

A shell exploding in the gun house of a turret could ignite a chain of charges down to the magazine section.

© Arthur Banks 1973

BRITISH AND GERMAN LOSSES AT JUTLAND

DETAILS	BRITISH	GERMAN
Total of ships engaged	151	99
Total of men employed	60,000	36,000
Battleships sunk	0	1
Battlecruisers sunk	3	1
Armoured cruisers sunk	3	0
Light cruisers sunk	0	4
Destroyers sunk	8	5
Casualties	6,097	2,551

The Battle of Jutland (known to the Germans as the 'Skagerrak') was a German success in terms of ships sunk and men lost, and contributed to Russia's exit from the war. Allied supplies to the hard-pressed Russian armies could not be guaranteed, as the Baltic approaches remained in possession of the High Seas Fleet. A controversy commenced in Britain to apportion the blame for the result, and a Jellicoe versus Beatty campaign ensued. Nevertheless, the German Fleet had been badly mauled, and U-boat warfare against British commerce was a consequence

5 The escape of the German Fleet–the night chase

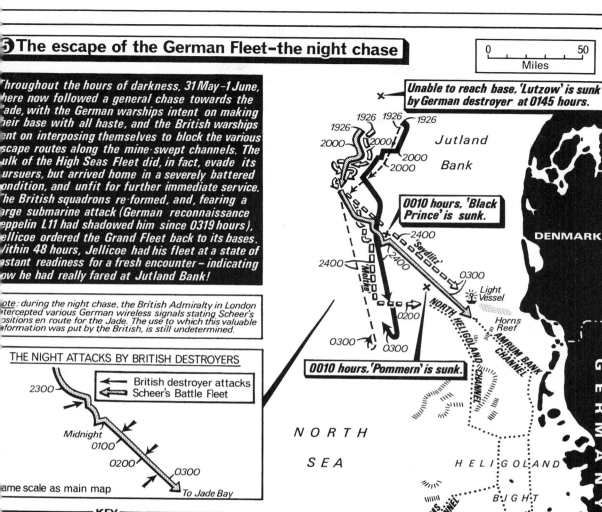

Throughout the hours of darkness, 31 May–1 June, there now followed a general chase towards the Jade, with the German warships intent on making their base with all haste, and the British warships bent on interposing themselves to block the various escape routes along the mine-swept channels. The bulk of the High Seas Fleet did, in fact, evade its pursuers, but arrived home in a severely battered condition, and unfit for further immediate service. The British squadrons re-formed, and, fearing a large submarine attack (German reconnaissance Zeppelin L11 had shadowed him since 0319 hours), Jellicoe ordered the Grand Fleet back to its bases. Within 48 hours, Jellicoe had his fleet at a state of instant readiness for a fresh encounter – indicating how he had really fared at Jutland Bank!

Note: during the night chase, the British Admiralty in London intercepted various German wireless signals stating Scheer's positions en route for the Jade. The use to which this valuable information was put by the British, is still undetermined.

THE NIGHT ATTACKS BY BRITISH DESTROYERS

2300

Midnight
0100

0200

0300

To Jade Bay

→ British destroyer attacks
⇐ Scheer's Battle Fleet

same scale as main map

KEY
- Track of Jellicoe's Battle Fleet
- Track of Beatty's Battlecruisers
- Track of Scheer's Battle Fleet
- Tracks of Hipper's Battlecruisers
- British-laid minefields by 1 June, 1916
- German-swept channels 1 June 1916

Map labels:

Unable to reach base, 'Lutzow' is sunk by German destroyer at 0145 hours.

Jutland Bank

1926 1926 1926
2000 2000
2000 2000

0010 hours, 'Black Prince' is sunk.

DENMARK

2400 'Seydlitz'

2400 'Moltke' 2400

0300

Light Vessel

Horns Reef

AMRUM BANK CHANNEL

NORTH HELIGOLAND CHANNEL

0200

0300 0300

0010 hours, 'Pommern' is sunk.

N O R T H
S E A

H E L I G O L A N D

B I G H T

EMS CHANNEL

Frisian Islands

HOLLAND

Elbe
Cuxhaven
Bremer-haven

Weser

Wilhelmshaven
Emden   Jade Bay

G E R M A N Y

Smaller units were operating with the British and German Battle and Battlecruiser Fleets – these are listed below
Abbreviations:– S = Squadron, F = Flotilla, AC = Armoured Cruiser, LC = Light Cruiser, D = Destroyer, SG = Scouting Group

BRITISH BATTLE FLEET		BRITISH BATTLECRUISER FLEET		GERMAN BATTLE FLEET		GERMAN BATTLECRUISER FLEET	
. ACS	4 ships	1st. LCS	4 ships	4th. SG (LC)	5 ships	2nd. SG (LC)	4 ships
d. ACS	4 ships	2nd. LCS	4 ships	LC	1 ship	LC	1 ship
. LCS	5 ships	3rd. LCS	4 ships	1st. DF (half)	4 ships	2nd. DF	10 ships
. LCS (attached)	6 ships	1st. DF	10 ships	3rd. DF	7 ships	6th. DF	9 ships
. DF	19 ships	9th. & 10th. DF (comb.)	8 ships	5th. DF	11 ships	9th. DF	11 ships
n. DF	16 ships	13th. DF	11 ships	7th. DF	9 ships		
h. DF	16 ships						
plus		plus					
elayers	1 ship	Seaplane Carriers	1 ship				
enders	1 ship						

259

THE BATTLE OF JUTLAND – continued

HMS "IRON DUKE" (Flagship of Admiral Jellicoe)

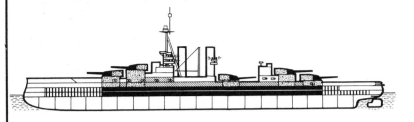

The 'Iron Duke' was a Dreadnought battleship, and the class was named after her. Sister-ships were 'Benbow', 'Emperor of India', and 'Marlboroug[h]'

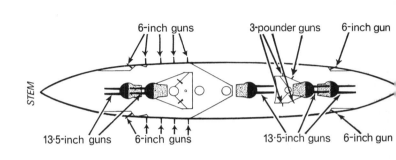

6-inch guns   3-pounder guns   6-inch gun

STEM

13·5-inch guns   6-inch guns   13·5-inch guns   6-inch gun

Laid down:	1912
Completed:	1914
Displacement:	25,000 tons
Waterline length:	620 feet
Maximum speed:	23 knots
Complement:	900

HMS "LION" (Flagship of Vice-Admiral Beatty)

ARMAMENT
Eight 13·5-inch guns
Sixteen 4-inch guns
Three 21-inch torpedo tube[s]

The 'Lion' was a battle-cruiser, and the class wa[s] named after her. There was one sister-ship, 'Princess Royal'.

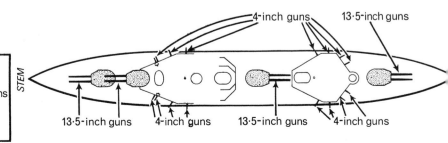

4-inch guns   13·5-inch guns

STEM

13·5-inch guns   4-inch guns   13·5-inch guns   4-inch guns

Laid down:	1909
Completed:	1912
Displacement:	26,350 tons
Waterline length:	675 feet
Maximum speed:	29 knots
Complement:	1,000

SMS "FRIEDRICH DER GROSSE" (Flagship of Vice-Admiral Scheer)

ARMAMENT
Ten 12-inch guns
Fourteen 6-inch guns
Twelve 24-pounder guns
Four 14-pounder anti-aerial guns
Five 20-inch torpedo tubes

The 'Friedrich der Grosse' was a Dreadnought battleship of the 'Kaiser' class. Sister-ships were 'Kaiser', 'Kaiserin', 'Prinzregent Luitpold', and 'König Albert'.

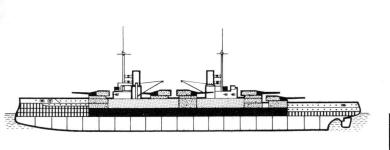

12-inch guns   6-inch guns   24-pounder guns

STEM   STERN

24-pounder guns   6-inch guns   12-inch guns   6-inch guns   12-inch guns

Laid down:	1909
Completed:	1912
Displacement:	24,700 tons
Waterline length:	564 feet
Maximum speed:	23 knots
Complement:	1,088

SMS "LÜTZOW" (Flagship of Vice-Admiral Hipper)

ARMAMENT
Eight 12-inch guns
Twelve 6-inch guns
Twelve 24-pounder guns
Five 22-inch torpedo tubes

Note: during the battle, Hipper transferred his flag from the badly-damaged 'Lützow' to the 'Moltke'.

The 'Lützow' was a battle-cruiser, and sister-ships were 'Derfflinger' and 'Ersatz Hertha'.

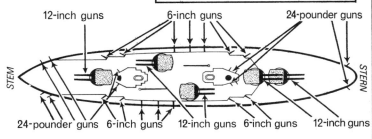

6-inch guns

STEM   STERN

12-inch guns   6-inch guns   12-inch guns

Laid down:	1912
Completed:	1915
Displacement:	28,000 tons
Waterline length:	590 feet
Maximum speed:	29 knots
Complement:	1,100

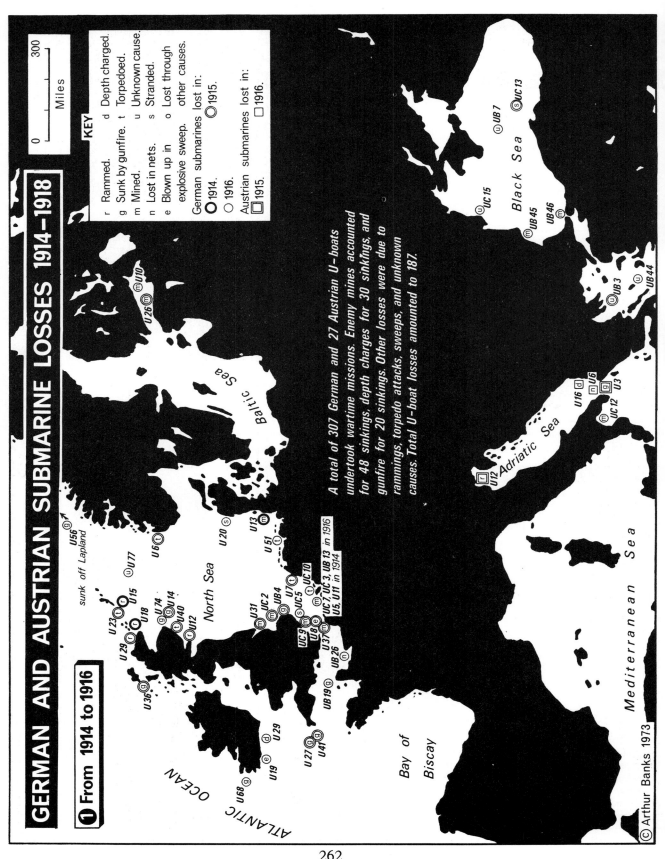

GERMAN AND AUSTRIAN SUBMARINE LOSSES 1914–1918

1 From 1914 to 1916

KEY

r Rammed.   d Depth charged.
g Sunk by gunfire.   t Torpedoed.
m Mined.   u Unknown cause.
n Lost in nets.   s Stranded.
e Blown up in   o Lost through
   explosive sweep.   other causes.

German submarines lost in:
● 1914. ◎ 1915.
○ 1916.
Austrian submarines lost in:
□ 1915. □ 1916.

A total of 307 German and 27 Austrian U–boats undertook wartime missions. Enemy mines accounted for 48 sinkings, depth charges for 30 sinkings, and gunfire for 20 sinkings. Other losses were due to rammings, torpedo attacks, sweeps, and unknown causes. Total U–boat losses amounted to 187.

ATLANTIC OCEAN

North Sea

Baltic Sea

Bay of Biscay

Mediterranean Sea

Adriatic Sea

Black Sea

sunk off Lapland

© Arthur Banks 1973

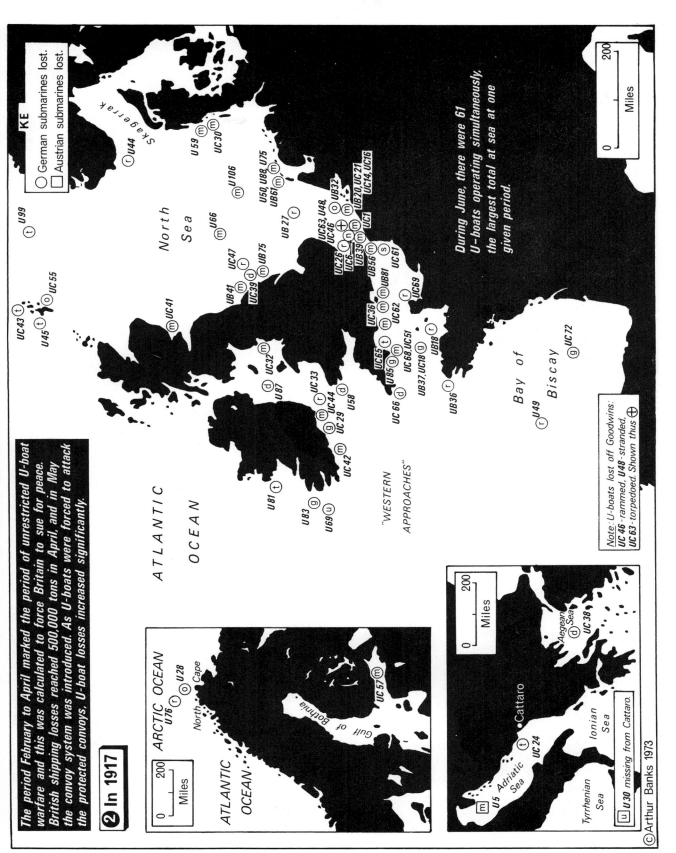

KE
○ German submarines lost.
□ Austrian submarines lost.

The period February to April marked the period of unrestricted U-boat warfare and this was calculated to force Britain to sue for peace. British shipping losses reached 500,000 tons in April, and in May the convoy system was introduced. As U-boats were forced to attack the protected convoys, U-boat losses increased significantly.

② In 1917

During June, there were 61 U-boats operating simultaneously, the largest total at sea at one given period.

Note: U-boats lost off Goodwins: UC 46 - rammed. U48 - stranded. UC 63 - torpedoed. Shown thus ⊕

North Sea

ATLANTIC OCEAN

"WESTERN APPROACHES"

Bay of Biscay

Skagerrak

0   200
Miles

ARCTIC OCEAN
North Cape
Gulf of Bothnia
ATLANTIC OCEAN..

0   200
Miles

Adriatic Sea
Cattaro
Ionian Sea
Aegean Sea
Tyrrhenian Sea

m U5
U30 missing from Cattaro.

0   200
Miles

© Arthur Banks 1973

263

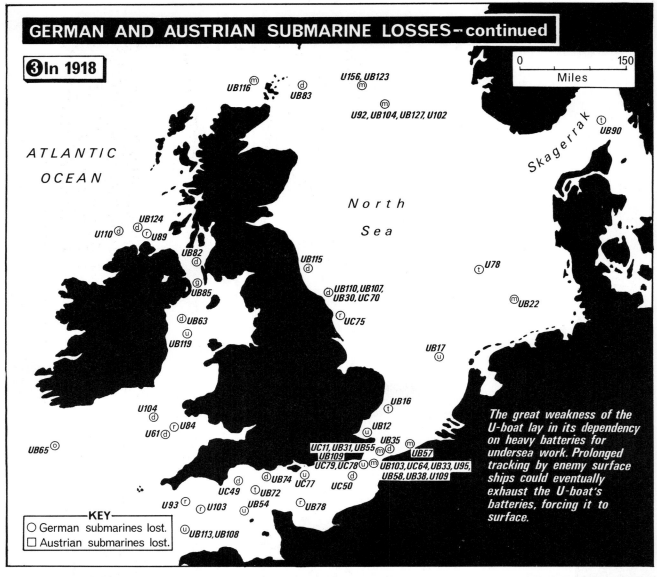

3 In 1918

0 ——— 150
Miles

ATLANTIC OCEAN

UB116 (m)

(d) UB83

U156, UB123 (m)

(m)
U92, UB104, UB127, U102

Skagerrak (t) UB90

North Sea

UB124
U110 (d) (d) (r) U89
UB82 (d)

(t) U78

UB115 (d)

(m) UB22

UB110, UB107, UB30, UC70
(r) UC75

UB17 (u)

(g) UB85
(d) UB63
(u) UB119

U104 (d)
U61 (d) (r) U84

UB16 (t)

UB12 (u)
UB35 (m) UB57
UC11, UB31, UB55 (m) (u)
UB109
UC79, UC78 (u) (m)
UB103, UC64, UB33, U95, UB58, UB38, U109

UB65 (○)

(d) UB74
(d) UC77
UC49
(d) UC50

(r) UB72

U93 (r) (r) U103 (u) UB54 (r) UB78

The great weakness of the U-boat lay in its dependency on heavy batteries for undersea work. Prolonged tracking by enemy surface ships could eventually exhaust the U-boat's batteries, forcing it to surface.

KEY
○ German submarines lost.
□ Austrian submarines lost.

(u) UB113, UB108

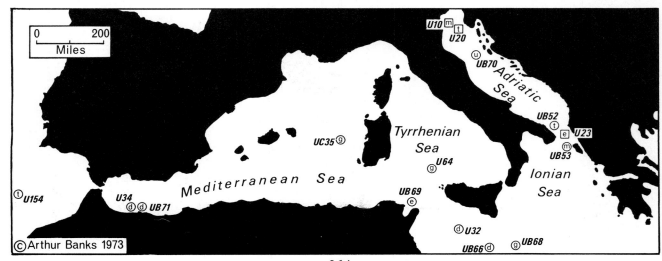

0 ——— 200
Miles

U10 (m) (t)
U20

(u) UB70 *Adriatic Sea*

UB52 (t)
(e) U23
(m)
UB53

UC35 (g)

Tyrrhenian Sea

U64 (g)

Ionian Sea

Mediterranean Sea

UB69 (e)

(t) U154

U34 (d)(d) UB71

(d) U32

UB66 (d) (g) UB68

© Arthur Banks 1973

A SPECIALLY-CONSTRUCTED BRITISH 'Q'-SHIP: HMS "HYDERABAD"

Built by John I. Thorneycroft & Co. Ltd., in four months during 1917.

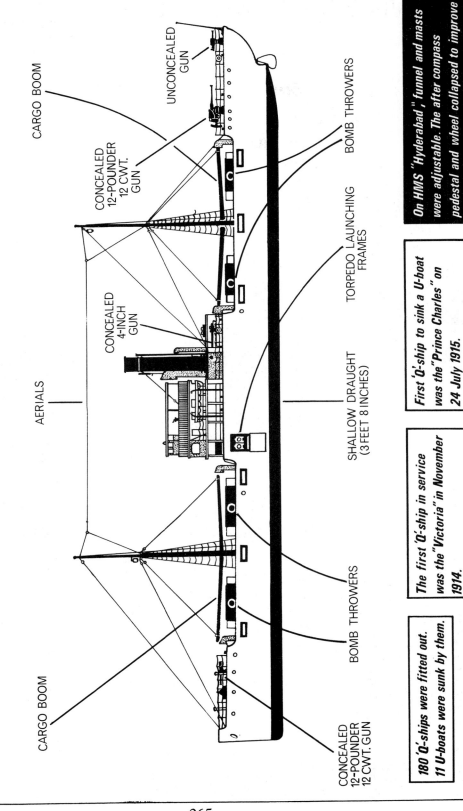

AERIALS

CARGO BOOM

CONCEALED 12-POUNDER 12 CWT. GUN

UNCONCEALED GUN

CONCEALED 4-INCH GUN

BOMB THROWERS

TORPEDO LAUNCHING FRAMES

SHALLOW DRAUGHT (3 FEET 8 INCHES)

BOMB THROWERS

CARGO BOOM

CONCEALED 12-POUNDER 12 CWT. GUN

The first 'Q'-ship in service was the "Victoria" in November 1914.

First 'Q'-ship to sink a U-boat was the "Prince Charles" on 24 July 1915.

On HMS "Hyderabad", funnel and masts were adjustable. The after compass pedestal and wheel collapsed to improve field of fire.

180 'Q'-ships were fitted out. 11 U-boats were sunk by them.

© Arthur Banks 1973

265

THE U-BOAT WAR AGAINST ALLIED MERCHANT SHIPPING IN 1917

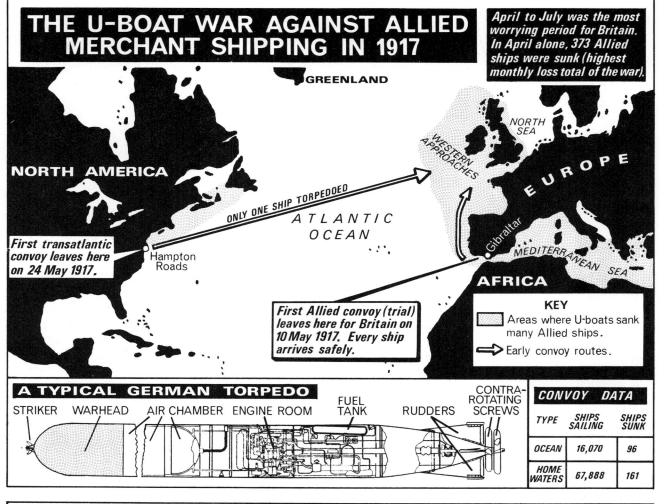

April to July was the most worrying period for Britain. In April alone, 373 Allied ships were sunk (highest monthly loss total of the war).

GREENLAND

NORTH AMERICA

ONLY ONE SHIP TORPEDOED

ATLANTIC OCEAN

NORTH SEA

WESTERN APPROACHES

EUROPE

Gibraltar

MEDITERRANEAN SEA

AFRICA

First transatlantic convoy leaves here on 24 May 1917.

Hampton Roads

First Allied convoy (trial) leaves here for Britain on 10 May 1917. Every ship arrives safely.

KEY
- Areas where U-boats sank many Allied ships.
- ⇨ Early convoy routes.

A TYPICAL GERMAN TORPEDO

STRIKER   WARHEAD   AIR CHAMBER   ENGINE ROOM   FUEL TANK   RUDDERS   CONTRA-ROTATING SCREWS

CONVOY DATA

TYPE	SHIPS SAILING	SHIPS SUNK
OCEAN	16,070	96
HOME WATERS	67,888	161

THE INTRODUCTION OF CONVOYS MAY 1917

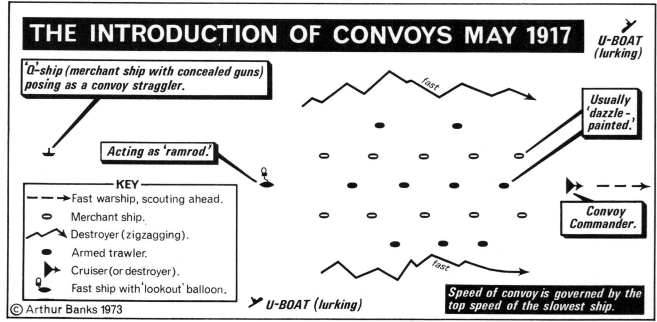

U-BOAT (lurking)

'Q'-ship (merchant ship with concealed guns) posing as a convoy straggler.

fast

Usually 'dazzle-painted.'

Acting as 'ramrod.'

Convoy Commander.

KEY
- – –→ Fast warship, scouting ahead.
- ⊖ Merchant ship.
- ∿ Destroyer (zigzagging).
- ● Armed trawler.
- ▶ Cruiser (or destroyer).
- ⚲ Fast ship with 'lookout' balloon.

fast

U-BOAT (lurking)

Speed of convoy is governed by the top speed of the slowest ship.

© Arthur Banks 1973

266

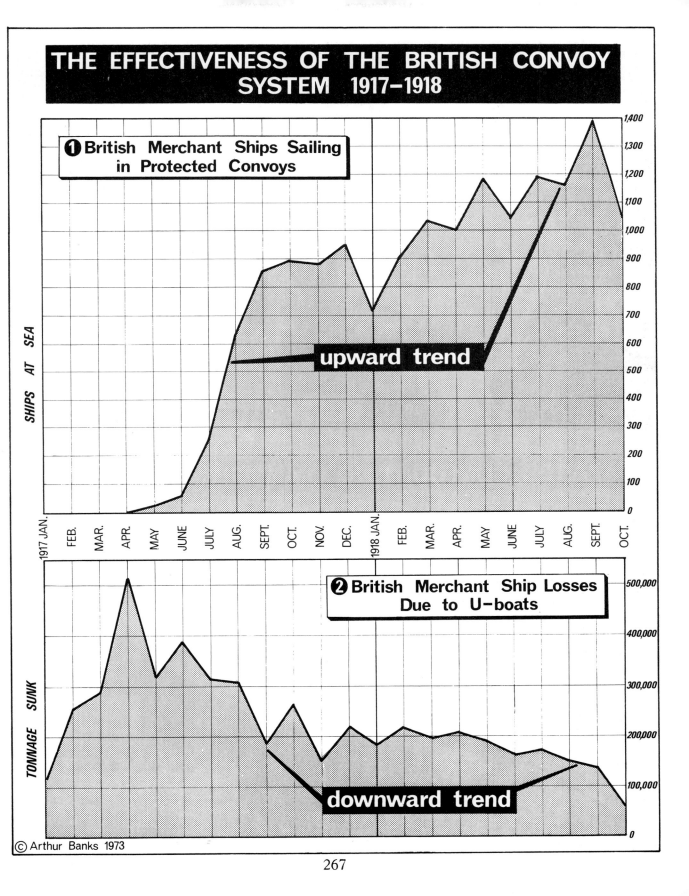

THE EFFECTIVENESS OF THE BRITISH CONVOY SYSTEM 1917–1918

❶ British Merchant Ships Sailing in Protected Convoys

upward trend

SHIPS AT SEA

1,400
1,300
1,200
1,100
1,000
900
800
700
600
500
400
300
200
100
0

1917 JAN. FEB. MAR. APR. MAY JUNE JULY AUG. SEPT. OCT. NOV. DEC. 1918 JAN. FEB. MAR. APR. MAY JUNE JULY AUG. SEPT. OCT.

❷ British Merchant Ship Losses Due to U-boats

downward trend

TONNAGE SUNK

500,000
400,000
300,000
200,000
100,000
0

© Arthur Banks 1973

267

HAZARDS CONFRONTING GERMAN-BASED U-BOATS

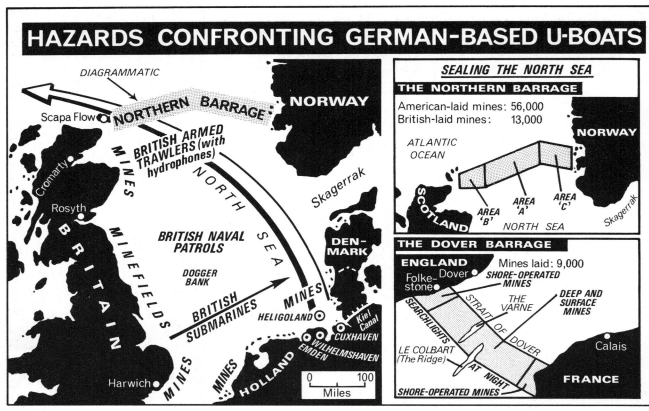

DIAGRAMMATIC

NORTHERN BARRAGE

NORWAY

Scapa Flow

BRITISH ARMED TRAWLERS (with hydrophones)

Cromarty

Rosyth

MINES

NORTH SEA

Skagerrak

BRITISH NAVAL PATROLS

DEN-MARK

BRITAIN

MINEFIELDS

DOGGER BANK

BRITISH SUBMARINES

MINES

HELIGOLAND

Kiel Canal

CUXHAVEN

WILHELMSHAVEN

EMDEN

MINES

MINES

HOLLAND

Harwich

MINES

0 — 100 Miles

SEALING THE NORTH SEA
THE NORTHERN BARRAGE
American-laid mines: 56,000
British-laid mines: 13,000

ATLANTIC OCEAN

NORWAY

SCOTLAND

AREA 'B'

AREA 'A'

AREA 'C'

NORTH SEA

Skagerrak

THE DOVER BARRAGE
ENGLAND   Mines laid: 9,000

Folke-stone   Dover   SHORE-OPERATED MINES

THE VARNE

DEEP AND SURFACE MINES

SEARCHLIGHTS

STRAIT OF DOVER

Calais

LE COLBART (The Ridge)

AT NIGHT

FRANCE

SHORE-OPERATED MINES

HAZARDS CONFRONTING FLANDERS-BASED U·BOATS

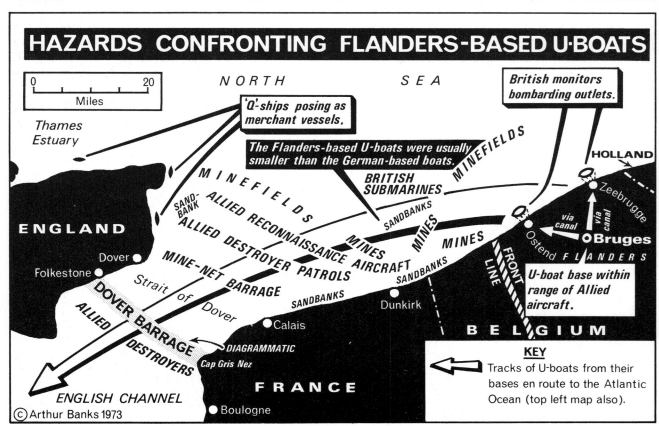

0 — 20 Miles

NORTH   SEA

Thames Estuary

'Q'-ships posing as merchant vessels.

British monitors bombarding outlets.

The Flanders-based U-boats were usually smaller than the German-based boats.

BRITISH SUBMARINES

MINEFIELDS

HOLLAND

ENGLAND

MINEFIELDS

SAND-BANK

ALLIED RECONNAISSANCE AIRCRAFT

SANDBANKS

MINES

MINES

MINES

Zeebrugge

via canal

via canal

Bruges

Dover

ALLIED DESTROYER PATROLS

MINES

FLANDERS

Folkestone

MINE-NET BARRAGE

SANDBANKS

Ostend

FRONT LINE

U-boat base within range of Allied aircraft.

Strait of Dover

Dunkirk

DOVER BARRAGE

ALLIED DESTROYERS

SANDBANKS

Calais

DIAGRAMMATIC

Cap Gris Nez

BELGIUM

ENGLISH CHANNEL

FRANCE

© Arthur Banks 1973

Boulogne

KEY
Tracks of U-boats from their bases en route to the Atlantic Ocean (top left map also).

BRITISH SUBMARINES IN THE BALTIC

© Arthur Banks 1973

0 — 100 Miles

THE TWO SEA ROUTES TO RUSSIA FROM BRITAIN

BAD WEATHER AND ICE

Four 'C'-class boats 1917

North Sea

A

P

Via lakes rivers and canals.

'E'-class boats 1914-1915.

0 — 500 Miles

KEY
P = Petrograd.
A = Archangel.

Swedish iron ore exports to Germany from here.

IRON ORE MINES

Luleå

RUSSIA (Finland)

Gulf of Bothnia

March 1918, British submarines are scuttled in approaches to prevent their capture by Germans (arriving to aid Finns against Reds).

German cargo-ships

'E'-class base 1917-1918.

Russian capital.

Helsingfors

Gulf of Finland

PETROGRAD (St. Petersburg) (later, Leningrad)

NORWAY

CHRISTIANIA

SWEDEN

STOCKHOLM

British attacks

Hangö

Reval

RUSSIA

1914, E1 and E9 both penetrate The Sound and reach Reval. 1915, E8, E18, and E19 duplicate the feat but E13 runs aground on Saltholm (19 August).

British base after 7 May 1915.

Dagö

Ösel

GULF OF RIGA

19 August 1915, E1 torpedoes and disables SMS 'Moltke.'

Skagerrak

Kattegat

THE SOUND

B A L T I C   S E A (mined)

Gotland

Öland

Libau

'C'-class base in 1917.

Riga

DENMARK

Saltholm

Russian base in 1914. Later moves to Reval.

The British were keen to have some submarines operating in the Baltic for three basic reasons: **1** to demonstrate to the world that the Baltic was not an exclusive German "lake" **2** to assist the Russians in opposing German operations in the Gulfs of Finland and Riga **3** to disrupt the export of iron ore from Luleå in Sweden to Germany. The journey from the North Sea to Russia was extremely hazardous at all times.

Kiel Canal

Kiel

1915, E19 torpedoes SMS 'Udine'.

Lübeck

GERMANY

Main German Baltic base.

Low salinity makes continuous depth maintenance difficult for submarines. Short summer hours of darkness curtail battery recharging time on surface.

THE MEDITERRANEAN SEA 1914-1918

During 1917 alone, nearly 900 Allied merchant ships were sunk.

①The U-boat Offensive Against Allied Merchant Shipping

FROM GERMANY

E U R O P E

Main bases of Mediterranean U-boats.

Cattaro

Constantinople

A S I A

M E D I T E R R A N E A N   S E A

A F R I C A

KEY

➭ U-boat routes into the Mediterranean Sea.
⊗ Minefields laid by U-boats.
⠿ Areas where heavy Allied losses occurred.

0   400
Miles

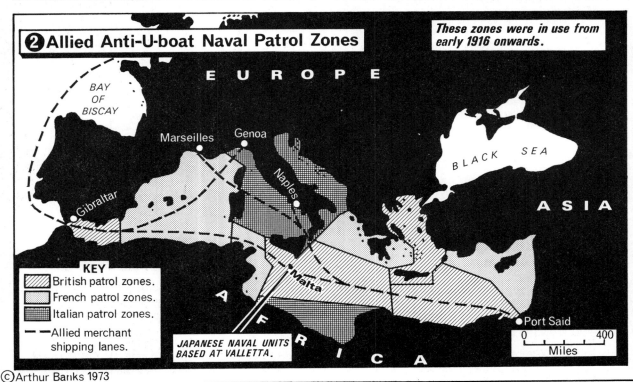

②Allied Anti-U-boat Naval Patrol Zones

These zones were in use from early 1916 onwards.

E U R O P E

BAY OF BISCAY

Marseilles   Genoa

Naples

BLACK   SEA

Gibraltar

A S I A

Malta

KEY
▨ British patrol zones.
▥ French patrol zones.
▦ Italian patrol zones.
- - Allied merchant shipping lanes.

JAPANESE NAVAL UNITS BASED AT VALLETTA.

A F R I C A

Port Said

0   400
Miles

© Arthur Banks 1973

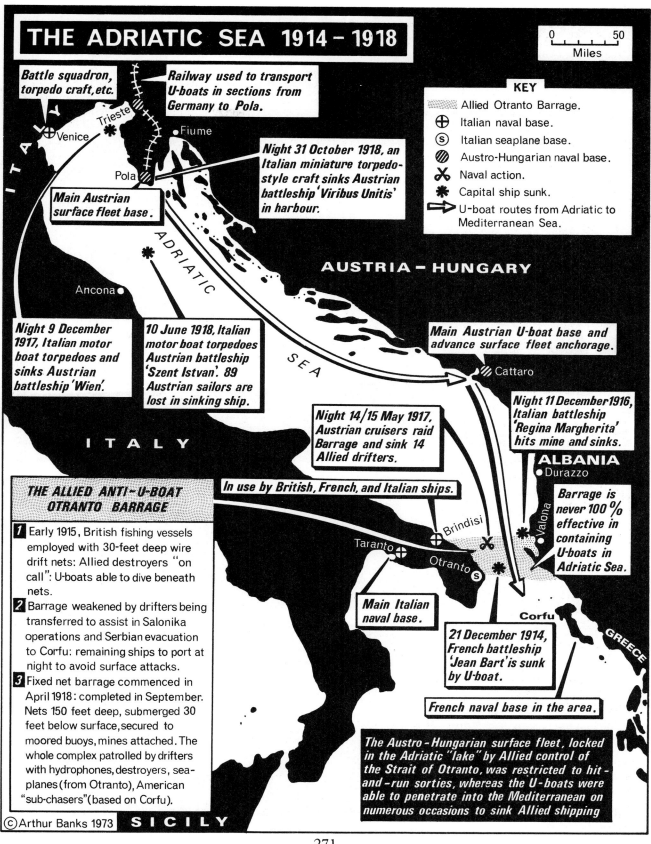

THE ADRIATIC SEA 1914 – 1918

0   50
Miles

KEY
- Allied Otranto Barrage.
- ⊕ Italian naval base.
- Ⓢ Italian seaplane base.
- ◍ Austro-Hungarian naval base.
- ✕ Naval action.
- ✳ Capital ship sunk.
- ⇨ U-boat routes from Adriatic to Mediterranean Sea.

Battle squadron, torpedo craft, etc.

Railway used to transport U-boats in sections from Germany to Pola.

Night 31 October 1918, an Italian miniature torpedo-style craft sinks Austrian battleship 'Viribus Unitis' in harbour.

Trieste
Venice
Fiume
Pola

Main Austrian surface fleet base.

ITALY

ADRIATIC

SEA

AUSTRIA – HUNGARY

Ancona

Night 9 December 1917, Italian motor boat torpedoes and sinks Austrian battleship 'Wien'.

10 June 1918, Italian motor boat torpedoes Austrian battleship 'Szent Istvan'. 89 Austrian sailors are lost in sinking ship.

Main Austrian U-boat base and advance surface fleet anchorage.

Cattaro

Night 11 December 1916, Italian battleship 'Regina Margherita' hits mine and sinks.

Night 14/15 May 1917, Austrian cruisers raid Barrage and sink 14 Allied drifters.

ITALY

ALBANIA
Durazzo

In use by British, French, and Italian ships.

THE ALLIED ANTI-U-BOAT OTRANTO BARRAGE

1 Early 1915, British fishing vessels employed with 30-feet deep wire drift nets: Allied destroyers "on call": U-boats able to dive beneath nets.

2 Barrage weakened by drifters being transferred to assist in Salonika operations and Serbian evacuation to Corfu: remaining ships to port at night to avoid surface attacks.

3 Fixed net barrage commenced in April 1918: completed in September. Nets 150 feet deep, submerged 30 feet below surface, secured to moored buoys, mines attached. The whole complex patrolled by drifters with hydrophones, destroyers, sea-planes (from Otranto), American "sub-chasers" (based on Corfu).

Valona

Barrage is never 100% effective in containing U-boats in Adriatic Sea.

Brindisi
Taranto ⊕
Otranto Ⓢ

Main Italian naval base.

Corfu

21 December 1914, French battleship 'Jean Bart' is sunk by U-boat.

French naval base in the area.

GREECE

The Austro-Hungarian surface fleet, locked in the Adriatic "lake" by Allied control of the Strait of Otranto, was restricted to hit-and-run sorties, whereas the U-boats were able to penetrate into the Mediterranean on numerous occasions to sink Allied shipping

© Arthur Banks 1973   SICILY

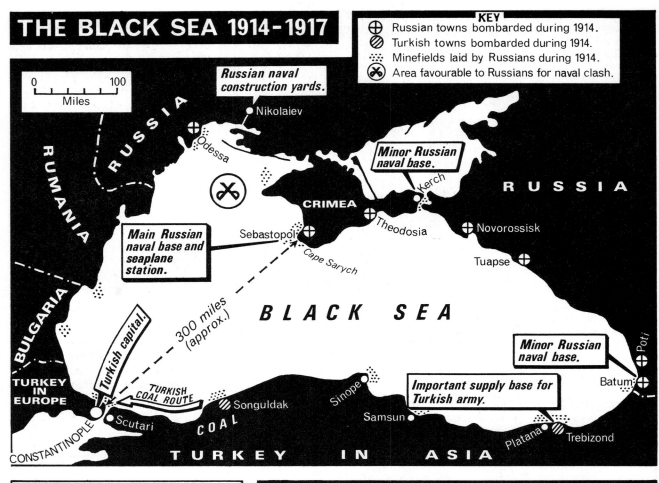

THE BLACK SEA 1914-1917

0   100
Miles

Russian naval construction yards.
● Nikolaiev

RUSSIA

RUMANIA

⊕ Odessa

Minor Russian naval base.
Kerch

RUSSIA

CRIMEA

● Novorossisk

Main Russian naval base and seaplane station.
Sebastopol ⊕ ⊗ Theodosia

● Tuapse

Cape Sarych

BLACK SEA

Minor Russian naval base.
⊕ Poti

BULGARIA

300 miles (approx.)

Turkish capital.

Important supply base for Turkish army.

Batum ⊕

TURKEY IN EUROPE

TURKISH COAL ROUTE

Sinope

CONSTANTINOPLE

Scutari

COAL

⊘ Songuldak

Samsun ●

Platana ⠿ ⊘ Trebizond

TURKEY   IN   ASIA

RIVAL NAVAL STRENGTHS IN 1914

RUSSIAN FLEET

5 Pre-Dreadnought Battleships.
2 Cruisers.
4 Destroyers.
4 Submarines.
(3 Dreadnought Battleships and 2 Cruisers under construction)

TURKISH/GERMAN FLEET

1 Battlecruiser (SMS 'Goeben').
3 Pre-Dreadnought Battleships.
3 Cruisers (including SMS 'Breslau').
2 Destroyers.

The importance of the German warships must be stressed. SMS 'Goeben' was the most powerful warship in the area in 1914.

© Arthur Banks 1973

In 1914, the Black Sea naval scene was basically as follows : the Turkish/ German fleet was intent on sorties from Constantinople to bombard Russian ports (spearheaded by SMS 'Goeben', the most powerful warship in the area). The Russians, eager to disrupt Turkish coal supplies by sea from Songuldak to Constantinople (there was no land railway link), yearned for a supply base on the Bulgarian coastline to shorten the distance between Sebastopol and Constantinople. They laid minefields off Turkish ports to impede enemy sorties, and entertained hopes that if a major naval confrontation occurred, it would take place between Odessa and Sebastopol, within range of Russian seaplanes.

THE NAVAL CLASH OFF CAPE SARYCH 18 NOVEMBER 1914

MIST

CLEAR WEATHER

◌ SMS 'Breslau'
◌ SMS 'GOEBEN'

firing

1221 hours
▼▼▼ Russian cruisers
RUSSIAN BATTLE FLEET

This 14-minute action marked the first encounter between 'Goeben' and Russian capital ships. The old pre-dreadnoughts equalled the 'Goeben's' hit-rate of 10% from salvoes fired before the Germans broke off. There were 14 hits on 'Goeben' causing casualties of 115 killed and 59 wounded.

272

During 1915, two new dreadnoughts came into service with the Russian Black Sea fleet. These battleships, "Imperatritsa Maria" and "Ekaterina II," altered the naval balance of power, although the former was sunk at Sebastopol in the following year (27 October 1916): SMS "Goeben" made her final Black Sea sortie on 8 January 1916. In September 1915, U-boats appeared in the Black Sea, and in that year Bulgaria joined the Central Powers. Rumania became involved in 1916. There was no all-out naval clash, but several fights took place, sometimes involving Russian seaplanes. Russian troops were transported across the sea to fight on the Turkish shore. Trebizond was captured in April 1916 and used as a military port.

1915. BOMBARDED BY TURKISH/GERMAN FLEET AT TIME OF ALLIED OPERATIONS AT DARDANELLES AND GALLIPOLI TO DISTRACT AND DISRUPT RUSSIAN SUPPORT.

RUSSIAN EMBARKATION PORT FOR TROOPS. SAFE FROM ENEMY ATTACKS.

Odessa — Mariapol

RUMANIA

RUSSIA

CRIMEA

Sebastopol

RUSSIAN TROOPS BY SEA 1916

BLACK SEA

BULG.

Varna

1915. BOMBARDED BY RUSSIANS.

TURKISH COAST

Bosporus — Erigli — Songuldak

MAY 1915, RUSSIANS LAND AND DESTROY POWER STATION.

Trebizond — Rizeh

THE UNSUCCESSFUL BRITISH AERIAL BID TO SINK SMS "GOEBEN" MAY-JULY 1916

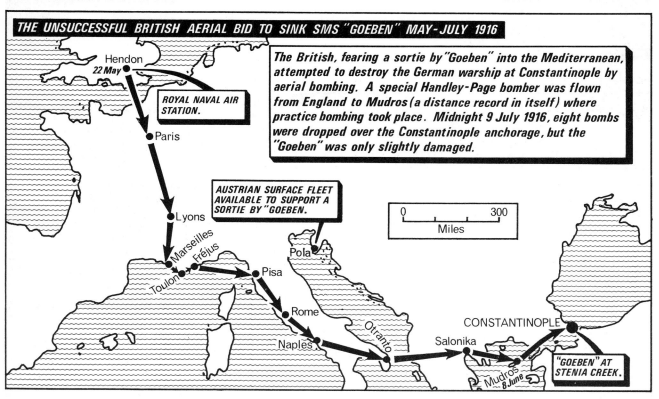

The British, fearing a sortie by "Goeben" into the Mediterranean, attempted to destroy the German warship at Constantinople by aerial bombing. A special Handley-Page bomber was flown from England to Mudros (a distance record in itself) where practice bombing took place. Midnight 9 July 1916, eight bombs were dropped over the Constantinople anchorage, but the "Goeben" was only slightly damaged.

Hendon 22 May

ROYAL NAVAL AIR STATION.

Paris

AUSTRIAN SURFACE FLEET AVAILABLE TO SUPPORT A SORTIE BY "GOEBEN."

0 — 300 Miles

Lyons

Marseilles — Fréjus

Pola

Toulon

Pisa

Rome

Naples

Otranto

CONSTANTINOPLE

Salonika

Mudros 8 June

"GOEBEN" AT STENIA CREEK.

"GOEBEN" AND "BRESLAU" IN THE AEGEAN 20 JANUARY 1918

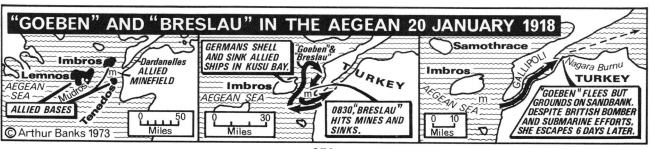

Imbros

Lemnos

AEGEAN SEA

Mudros

Tenedos

ALLIED BASES

Dardanelles ALLIED MINEFIELD

m

© Arthur Banks 1973

0 — 50 Miles

GERMANS SHELL AND SINK ALLIED SHIPS IN KUSU BAY.

"Goeben" & "Breslau"

TURKEY

Imbros

AEGEAN SEA

m

0830, "BRESLAU" HITS MINES AND SINKS.

0 — 30 Miles

Samothrace

Imbros

AEGEAN SEA

m

GALLIPOLI

Nagara Burnu

TURKEY

"GOEBEN" FLEES BUT GROUNDS ON SANDBANK. DESPITE BRITISH BOMBER AND SUBMARINE EFFORTS, SHE ESCAPES 6 DAYS LATER.

0 — 10 Miles

273

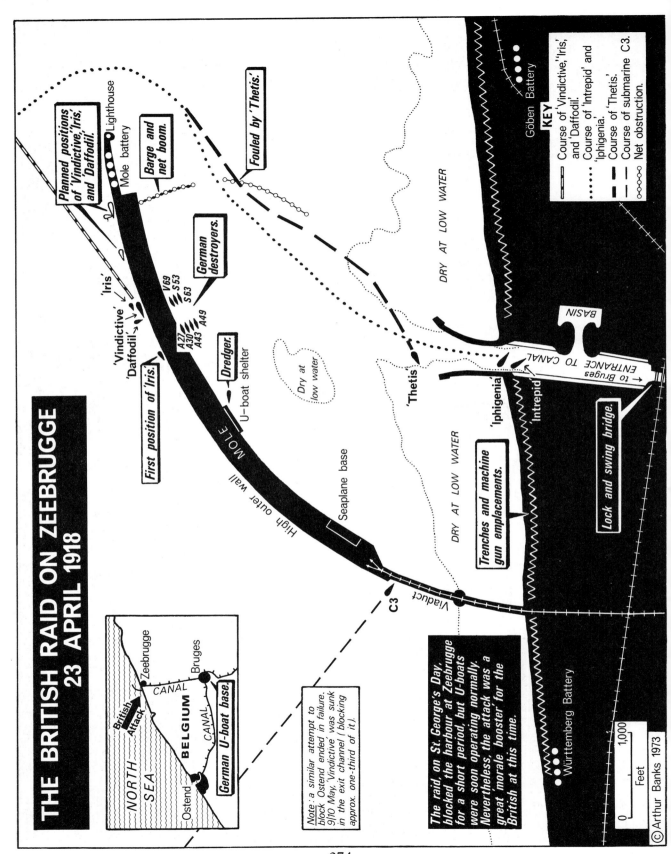

THE BRITISH RAID ON ZEEBRUGGE 23 APRIL 1918

Göben Battery

KEY
- Course of 'Vindictive,' 'Iris,' and 'Daffodil.'
- Course of 'Intrepid' and 'Iphigenia.'
- Course of 'Thetis.'
- Course of submarine C.3.
- Net obstruction.

Planned positions of 'Vindictive,' 'Iris,' and 'Daffodil.'

Lighthouse

Mole battery

Barge and net boom.

Fouled by 'Thetis.'

DRY AT LOW WATER

German destroyers.

V 69
S 53
S 63

A 49
A 43
A 30
A 27

'Iris'

'Vindictive'
'Daffodil'

First position of 'Iris.'

Dredger.

U-boat shelter

MOLE

Dry at low water

'Thetis'

Seaplane base

High outer wall

DRY AT LOW WATER

'Iphigenia'

'Intrepid'

to Bruges   ENTRANCE TO CANAL

BASIN

Trenches and machine gun emplacements.

Lock and swing bridge.

C.3.

Viaduct

Wurttemberg Battery

Note: a similar attempt to block Ostend ended in failure. 9/10 May, 'Vindictive' was sunk in the exit channel (blocking approx. one-third of it).

The raid, on St. George's Day, blocked the harbour at Zeebrugge for a short period, but U-boats were soon operating normally. Nevertheless, the attack was a great morale 'booster' for the British at this time.

NORTH SEA

Zeebrugge

Bruges

CANAL

BELGIUM

CANAL

British Attack

Ostend

German U-boat base.

0   Feet   1,000

© Arthur Banks 1973

GERMAN PLANS FOR A FINAL NAVAL CONFRONTATION OCTOBER 1918

0   100
Miles

Note: the Germans appeared to consider Scapa Flow as the main British naval base. In fact, this had been moved to Rosyth in April 1918.

Night 28 October, UB 116 is destroyed by electrically-detonated loop-style minefield in Hoxa Sound.

Shetland Islands

Fair Isle

ATLANTIC OCEAN

Orkney Islands

UB116   Scapa Flow

NORWAY

seven Zeppelins to be sent to report Grand Fleet's movements

Skagerrak

U-boats to patrol this area.

SCOTLAND

28 October, U 78 is torpedoed and sunk by the British sub. G2.

DENMARK

British naval base.

Rosyth

assumed British line of approach

N O R T H

S E A

U78

Germans hope to bring about the action in this area (favourable for them).

Jade Bay

IRELAND

IRISH SEA

German light cruisers to lay mines in British path.

Frisian Islands

Wilhelmshaven

German naval base.

WALES

ENGLAND

Harwich

HOLLAND

GERMANY

Light cruiser sorties to entice the British south from Scapa.

BELGIUM

English Channel

In an attempt to influence the Armistice negotiations,* the German naval authorities formulated plans to bring about the long-awaited clash between the German and British battle fleets. It came to naught due to mutinies and demoralization among the German crews. However, twenty-five U-boats actually set sail on 25 October, and two were destroyed by the British.

Historical note: In June 1667, de Ruyter's Dutch raid on the Medway influenced the peace negotiations for the Treaty of Breda in July 1667.

FRANCE

© Arthur Banks 1973

275

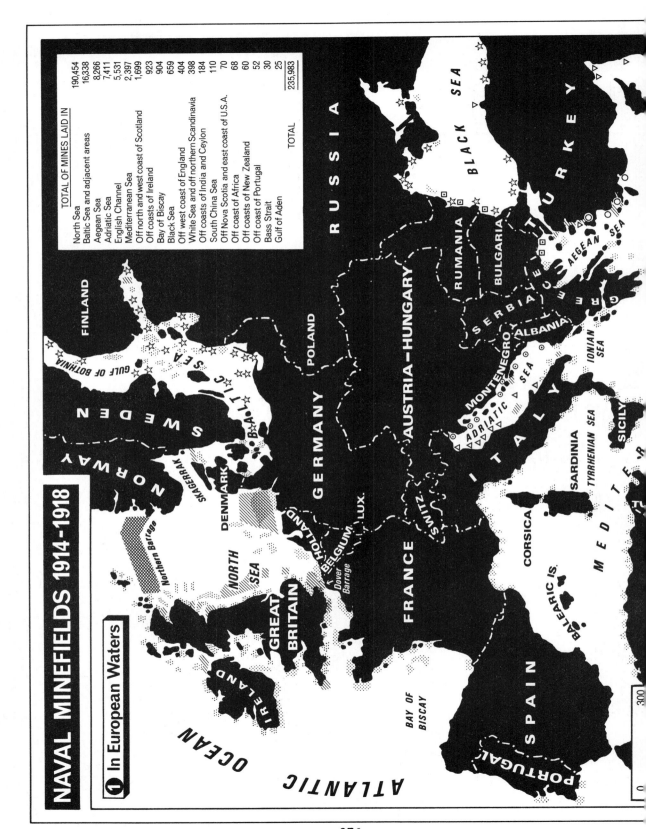

NAVAL MINEFIELDS 1914–1918

1 In European Waters

TOTAL OF MINES LAID IN	
North Sea	190,454
Baltic Sea and adjacent areas	16,338
Aegean Sea	8,266
Adriatic Sea	7,411
English Channel	5,531
Mediterranean Sea	2,397
Off north and west coast of Scotland	1,699
Off coasts of Ireland	923
Bay of Biscay	904
Black Sea	659
Off west coast of England	404
White Sea and off northern Scandinavia	398
Off coasts of India and Ceylon	184
South China Sea	110
Off Nova Scotia and east coast of U.S.A.	70
Off coast of Africa	68
Off coasts of New Zealand	60
Off coast of Portugal	52
Bass Strait	30
Gulf of Aden	25
TOTAL	235,983

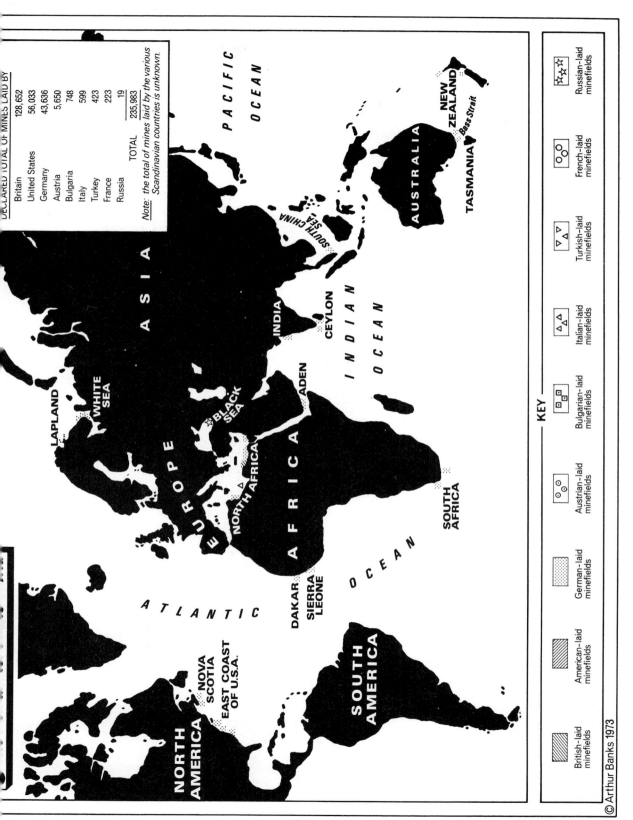

DECLARED TOTAL OF MINES LAID BY

Country	Mines
Britain	128,652
United States	56,033
Germany	43,636
Austria	5,650
Bulgaria	748
Italy	599
Turkey	423
France	223
Russia	19
TOTAL	235,983

Note: the total of mines laid by the various Scandinavian countries is unknown.

KEY

British-laid minefields
American-laid minefields
German-laid minefields
Austrian-laid minefields
Bulgarian-laid minefields
Italian-laid minefields
Turkish-laid minefields
French-laid minefields
Russian-laid minefields

© Arthur Banks 1973

NAVAL MINING

German contact mine

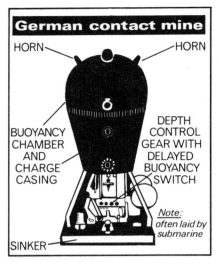

HORN — HORN

BUOYANCY CHAMBER AND CHARGE CASING

DEPTH CONTROL GEAR WITH DELAYED BUOYANCY SWITCH

SINKER

Note: often laid by submarine

An Observation Minefield

TELESCOPE FOR OBSERVING VESSELS

MINES IN POSITION JUST BELOW SURFACE

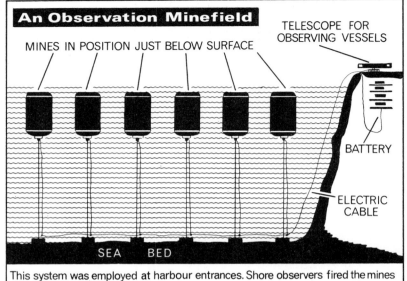

BATTERY

ELECTRIC CABLE

SEA BED

This system was employed at harbour entrances. Shore observers fired the mines by electrical methods at the moment when a hostile ship passed over the line.

The Antenna Mine

Note: the salt water acts as an electrolyte.

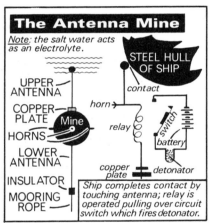

STEEL HULL OF SHIP

UPPER ANTENNA

COPPER PLATE

HORNS

LOWER ANTENNA

INSULATOR

MOORING ROPE

Mine

contact

horn

relay

switch

battery

copper plate

detonator

Ship completes contact by touching antenna; relay is operated pulling over circuit switch which fires detonator.

Hydrostatic depth-taking

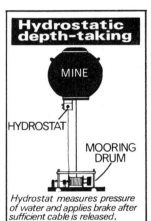

MINE

HYDROSTAT

MOORING DRUM

Hydrostat measures pressure of water and applies brake after sufficient cable is released.

The "HERZ" Horn

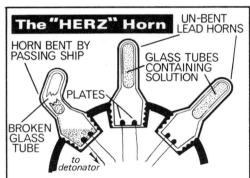

UN-BENT LEAD HORNS

HORN BENT BY PASSING SHIP

GLASS TUBES CONTAINING SOLUTION

PLATES

BROKEN GLASS TUBE

to detonator

The inside of the horn is similar to an electrical battery. A bichromate solution comes in contact with zinc and carbon plates, thus making voltage.

Plummet system of automatic depth-taking (non-buoyant unit)

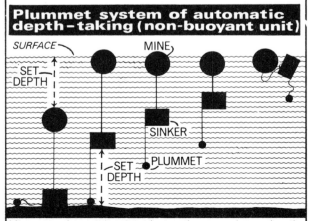

SURFACE

MINE

SET DEPTH

SINKER

SET DEPTH

PLUMMET

Mine parts from sinker upon laying; thus, an unknown length of wire spins out before unit settles, making laying haphazard.

Plummet system of automatic depth-taking (buoyant unit)

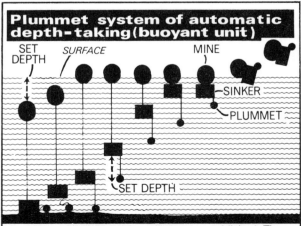

SET DEPTH

SURFACE

MINE

SINKER

PLUMMET

SET DEPTH

Mine stays with sinker until equilibrium is established. Thus, depth-taking with this system is more accurate and precise.

© Arthur Banks 1973

278

SEVEN IMPORTANT NAVAL MINES 1914–1918

TYPES OF MINE

CONTROLLED MINES (employed defensively, e.g. placed at harbour entrances). Fired from shore via electric wire.

INDEPENDENT MINES (employed both offensively and defensively in open sea, off coasts, etc. Types included moored, sea-bed, drifting, creeping, and oscillating.

British "SERVICE"

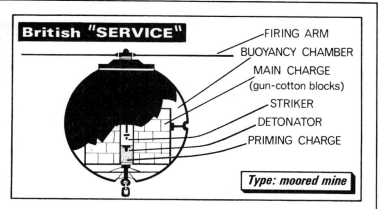

- FIRING ARM
- BUOYANCY CHAMBER
- MAIN CHARGE (gun-cotton blocks)
- STRIKER
- DETONATOR
- PRIMING CHARGE

Type: moored mine

British "H.2"

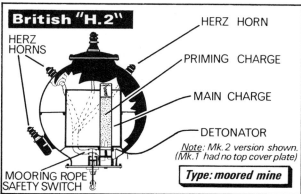

- HERZ HORNS
- HERZ HORN
- PRIMING CHARGE
- MAIN CHARGE
- DETONATOR
- MOORING ROPE
- SAFETY SWITCH

Note: Mk.2 version shown. (Mk.1 had no top cover plate)

Type: moored mine

British "ELIA"

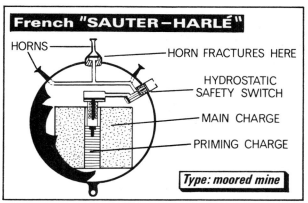

- PRIMING CHARGE
- MAIN CHARGE
- FIRING ARM

Type: moored mine

French "BREGUET"

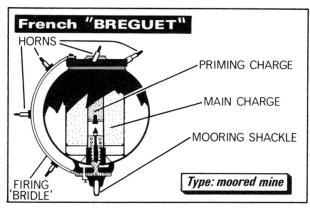

- HORNS
- PRIMING CHARGE
- MAIN CHARGE
- MOORING SHACKLE
- FIRING 'BRIDLE'

Type: moored mine

French "SAUTER–HARLÉ"

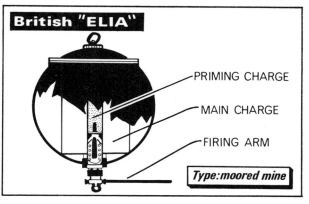

- HORNS
- HORN FRACTURES HERE
- HYDROSTATIC SAFETY SWITCH
- MAIN CHARGE
- PRIMING CHARGE

Type: moored mine

German "CARBONIT"

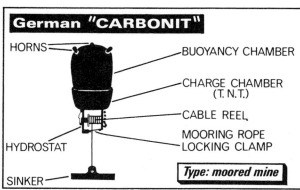

- HORNS
- BUOYANCY CHAMBER
- CHARGE CHAMBER (T.N.T.)
- CABLE REEL
- MOORING ROPE LOCKING CLAMP
- HYDROSTAT
- SINKER

Type: moored mine

Swedish–designed "LÉON"

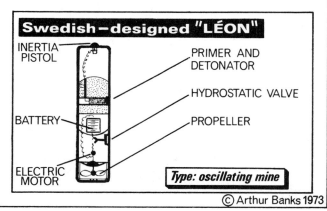

- INERTIA PISTOL
- PRIMER AND DETONATOR
- HYDROSTATIC VALVE
- PROPELLER
- BATTERY
- ELECTRIC MOTOR

Type: oscillating mine

SUBMARINE DEVELOPMENT DURING THE WAR

'DEUTSCHLAND' – first commercial boat

PLAIN MAST

PERISCOPES

CARGO DERRICK AND MAST

Surface displm't:	1512 tons.
Length:	213 feet.
Beam:	29 feet.
Maximum surface speed:	12·4 knots.
Maximum submerged speed:	5·2 knots.
Complement:	56.

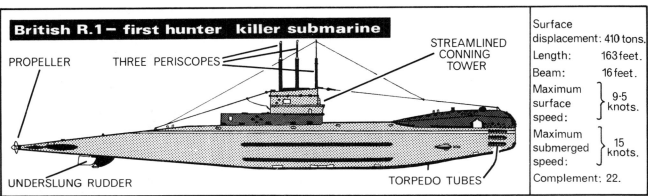

British R.1 – first hunter killer submarine

PROPELLER

THREE PERISCOPES

STREAMLINED CONNING TOWER

UNDERSLUNG RUDDER

TORPEDO TUBES

Surface displacement:	410 tons.
Length:	163 feet.
Beam:	16 feet.
Maximum surface speed:	9·5 knots.
Maximum submerged speed:	15 knots.
Complement:	22.

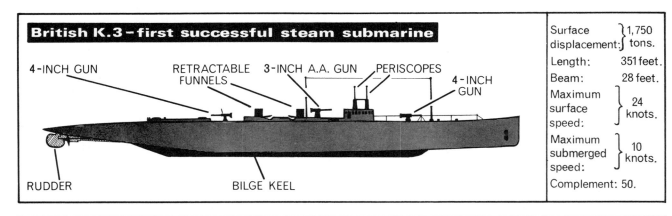

British K.3 – first successful steam submarine

4-INCH GUN

RETRACTABLE FUNNELS

3-INCH A.A. GUN

PERISCOPES

4-INCH GUN

RUDDER

BILGE KEEL

Surface displacement:	1,750 tons.
Length:	351 feet.
Beam:	28 feet.
Maximum surface speed:	24 knots.
Maximum submerged speed:	10 knots.
Complement:	50.

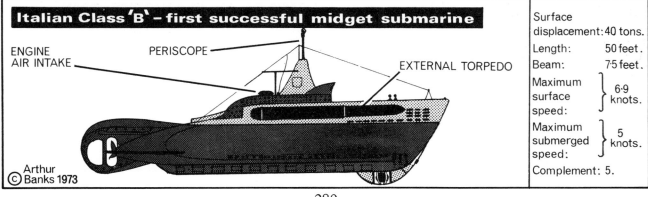

Italian Class 'B' – first successful midget submarine

ENGINE AIR INTAKE

PERISCOPE

EXTERNAL TORPEDO

Arthur
© Banks 1973

Surface displacement:	40 tons.
Length:	50 feet.
Beam:	7·5 feet.
Maximum surface speed:	6·9 knots.
Maximum submerged speed:	5 knots.
Complement:	5.

THE WAR IN THE AIR

On 1 November 1911 a primitive Italian aeroplane, supporting military operations in Libya, dropped four specially modified grenades on Turkish troops near Zuwarah. The pilot of the aircraft, Lieutenant Cavotti, was thus inaugurating a new and terrible phase of warfare, less than eight years since the first heavier-than-air machine had lifted off the ground. The French, German and American armies were already, in 1911, experimenting with aircraft, though they were uncertain how to use them. The British War Secretary, Haldane, took the lead in establishing a Royal Flying Corps in 1912, while at the Admiralty Churchill warmly supported the aeronautical enterprises (and himself took flying lessons). But by 1914 military and naval leaders, if not actively hostile to 'an air arm', saw in planes and airships little more than reconnaissance machines and gunnery spotters.

The only combatant possessing an aerial fleet of any significance was Germany, with eleven rigid airships, all except one manufactured by Count Zeppelin. During the early months of the war these craft bombed Liége, Antwerp and Warsaw. They proved, however, vulnerable to gunfire when used in close support of the army, and, at the beginning of 1915, it was decided that they would be most effective against targets in England, bringing 'terror to the people of London'. Navigational difficulties saved London from raids on several occasions (and similarly ruled out projected attacks on Petrograd), but the British capital was attacked by Zeppelins twelve times between May 1915 and October 1917. There were forty other raids on Britain, with bombs dropped in the Midlands, Liverpool, Newcastle and Hull as well as East Anglia and the Home Counties. Night bombing by Zeppelins interfered with efficiency in vital factories. Subsequently this role was assumed by aircraft, and the ten night raids of September–October 1917 (see page 296) had a particularly bad effect on civilian morale.

The Zeppelins which raided England in August 1915 were faster and bigger than the craft of a year earlier: they carried twice the weight of bombs. Without these technological improvements, it would have been impossible to mount what was, in effect, a strategic air offensive against civilian and military targets. But improvements to airships were equalled by developments in aeroplane construction. The most revolutionary of these was Anthony Fokker's invention of an interrupter, a cam which could stop a machine gun firing when the propeller blade swept across the muzzle. This device made the fighter aircraft a weapon in itself. German Fokkers were able to check the mounting pressure by the French bombing planes, an arm in which Joffre himself had long been interested. The British developed DH 4s and DH 9s as light bombers to attack front line troops, and depended on the manoeuvrable Sopwith Camel and S.E. 5a as the principal fighters. The Royal Naval Air Service used seaplane carriers during the Dardanelles Operations and experimented with dropping torpedoes from aircraft, a technique which could be perfected only with more powerful engines, giving a greater impetus.

The 'dog fight', a new form of combat creating its own tactics, gave the opportunity for individualists to make themselves reputations as 'aces'. Yet by the spring of 1917 the most famous of these German aces, Richthofen, was himself perfecting a 'circus', a squadron which was standardising at a rate technical level the accumulated skills of air fighting. Nor were these developments limited to the German side.

By the last winter in the war the British Government had so far accepted the significance of air power that on 1 April 1918, it created a third military service, a Royal Air Force with an 'Air Staff', totally independent of army and navy. The light bombers of the R.A.F. played a prominent part in the final defeat of the Bulgarians in the Balkan mountains and of the Turks in the coastal plain of Palestine; but the authorities were more interested in the effects of strategic bombing on Germany's factories.

GERMAN AIRSHIPS

GERMAN AIRSHIP RAIDS ON BRITAIN 1915-1918

YEAR	NUMBER OF RAIDS	BOMBS DROPPED (All types)	CIVILIANS KILLED	CIVILIANS INJURED
1915	20	1,525	207	533
1916	22	3,458	293	691
1917	7	580	40	75
1918	4	188	16	59
TOTALS	53*	5,751	556	1,358

*Note: London was attacked on twelve occasions

NORTH-WEST GERMAN AIRSHIP BASES

NORTH SEA
Tondern
BALTIC SEA
HQ Naval Airship Division
14 Oct. 1914 - 25 July. 1917
10 Jan. 1918 - 9 Nov. 1918
Kiel
GERMANY
Nordholz
Fuhlsbüttel
Hage
HQ Naval Airship Division
25 July 1917 - 10 Jan. 1918
Wittmundhaven
HOLLAND
Alhorn Wildeshausen

L.3 – First Zeppelin to raid Britain

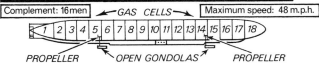

Complement: 16 men ← GAS CELLS → Maximum speed: 48 m.p.h.

PROPELLER   OPEN GONDOLAS   PROPELLER

Completed: 11 May 1914	Gas volume: 794,500 cubic ft.
Commissioned: 23 May 1914	Height: 60 ft. 3 ins.
Length: 518 ft. 2 ins.	Diameter: 48 ft. 6 ins.

Zeppelin "P" Type

Length: 536 ft. 5 ins.   Maximum speed: 59 m.p.h.   Gas volume: 1,126,400 cubic ft.
Diameter: 61 ft. 4 ins.   Complement: 16 men   Height: 79 ft. 4 ins.

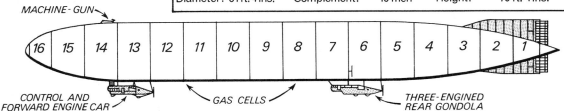

MACHINE-GUN

CONTROL AND FORWARD ENGINE CAR   GAS CELLS   THREE-ENGINED REAR GONDOLA

NAVAL NUMBER	COMMISSIONED	ACTUAL RAIDS	TOTAL FLIGHTS	TERMINATION OF SERVICE
L.10	17 May 1915	5	28	3 September 1915: destroyed off Neuwerk I.
L.11	8 June 1915	18	118	24 November 1917: dismantled at Hage.
L.12	22 June 1915	1	14	10 August 1915: burned at Ostend.
L.13	25 July 1915	17	159	11 December 1917: dismantled at Hage.
L.14	10 August 1915	17	127	23 June 1919: wrecked at Nordholz.
L.15	12 September 1915	3	36	1 April 1916: sank in sea at Knock Deep.
L.16	24 September 1915	16	132	19 October 1917: wrecked at Nordholz.
L.17	22 October 1915	11	73	28 December 1916: burned at Tondern.
L.18	6 November 1915	0	4	17 November 1915: burned at Tondern.
L.19	22 November 1915	1	14	2 February 1916: sank in North Sea.

MAIN RING BRACING

THE THREE BASIC TYPES OF AIRSHIP

1 Non-rigid
A balloon, the shape of which was held by internal pressure.

2 Semi-rigid
A shaped balloon with a rigid girder to which the main weights were slung.

3 Rigid
A group of balloons inside a rigid frame with, usually, a fabric cover.

During the war, the Germans manufactured two main types of rigid airships, the Schütte-Lanz and the Zeppelin. The early S.L.'s were wooden-framed, and the Zeppelins metal-framed (the metal used was duralumin). Hydrogen was the gas employed, and Germany paid particular attention to purity to avoid explosions.

© Arthur Banks 1973

Zeppelin "R" Type

Length: 644 ft. 8 ins.	Maximum speed: 64 m.p.h.	Gas volume: 1,949,600 cubic ft.
Diameter: 78 ft. 5 ins.	Complement: 19 men	Height: 90 ft. 10 ins.

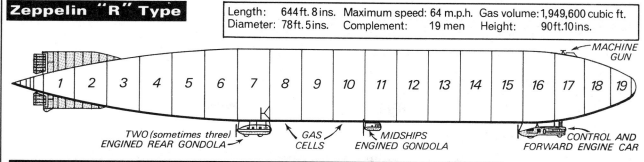

MACHINE GUN

1 2 3 4 5 6 7 8 9 10 11 12 13 14 15 16 17 18 19

TWO (sometimes three) ENGINED REAR GONDOLA →
GAS CELLS
MIDSHIPS ENGINED GONDOLA
CONTROL AND FORWARD ENGINE CAR

NAVAL NUMBER	COMMISSIONED	ACTUAL RAIDS	TOTAL FLIGHTS	TERMINATION OF SERVICE
L.30	30 May 1916	9	115	Broken up in 1920: parts to Belgium.
L.31	14 July 1916	8	19	2 October 1916: destroyed at Potters Bar.
L.32	7 August 1916	3	13	24 September 1916: destroyed at Gt. Burstead.
L.33	2 September 1916	1	10	24 Sept. 1916: captured at Little Wigborough.
L.34	22 September 1916	2	11	27 November 1916: destroyed off Hartlepool.
L.35	12 October 1916	5	54	September 1918: broken up at Jüterbog.
L.36	7 November 1916	1	20	7 February 1917: crashed on frozen River Aller.
L.37	27 November 1916	4	50 ?	Broken up in 1920: parts to Japan.
L.38	26 November 1916	1	10	29 December 1916: captured at Seemuppen.
L.39	18 December 1916	1	24	17 March 1917: destroyed at Compiègne.
L.40	7 January 1917	2	30	17 June 1917: dismantled at Nevenwald.
L.41	30 January 1917	4	36	23 June 1919: destroyed at Nordholz.
L.45	7 April 1917	3	27	20 October 1917: captured at Sisteron.
L.47	3 May 1917	4	44	5 January 1918: destroyed at Alhorn.
L.50	12 June 1917	2	19	20 October 1917: lost in Mediterranean.

MAIN RING BRACING

Note: there were minor design variations in certain of the 'R'-type airships. Gondolas were altered here and there to improve the performance of engines and propellers.

GERMAN AIRSHIP BASES IN THE EASTERN BALTIC

On 26 January 1915, the German Naval Airship Division lost its first airship of the war when the Parseval PL.19 set out from the Army shed near Königsberg to raid the Russian naval base at Libau. It crashed in the Baltic seven miles from the coast after severe icing which jammed a propellor and fractured an engine. Finally, the envelope buckled due to loss of pressure.

Wainoden (from 1916)
X Libau
Baltic Sea
RUSSIA
Memel
Telshi
Tilsit
GULF OF DANZIG
Königsberg
Seddin
Seerappen
Danzig
EAST PRUSSIA
Elbing
0   50 Miles
GERMANY   Bases shown thus ◯

During the night of 21-22 March 1915, three German army airships attempted to raid Paris. The ZX and the LZ.35 dropped seven high explosive and 45 incendiaries on Paris and its suburbs, killing one civilian and injuring a further eight. Hit by ground fire, the ZX was destroyed at St. Quentin on the return trip. Damaged by gunfire, the third airship (Schütte-Lanz SL.2) never reached the French capital, but distributed her bombs over Compiègne.

During the war, both the naval and the army airship services made unsuccessful attempts to raid the Russian capital of St. Petersburg (Petrograd). Distance alone prevented success during the early period, but the main problem throughout was bad weather. Ice and snow fouled engines and propellors, congealed oil, and made airships top-heavy and unstable.

Airships worked as scouts with the German navy and were present at a number of sea battles, such as Jutland and Dogger Bank. However, they were never used in conjunction with the U-boat offensive in the Atlantic.

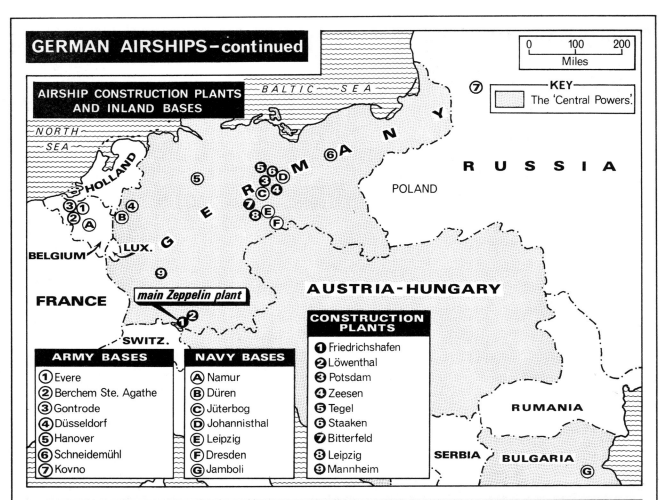

GERMAN AIRSHIPS – continued

AIRSHIP CONSTRUCTION PLANTS AND INLAND BASES

⑦ **KEY** — The 'Central Powers'.

BALTIC SEA

NORTH SEA

HOLLAND

G E R M A N Y

RUSSIA

POLAND

BELGIUM

LUX.

FRANCE

AUSTRIA-HUNGARY

main Zeppelin plant

SWITZ.

RUMANIA

SERBIA | BULGARIA

ARMY BASES

① Evere
② Berchem Ste. Agathe
③ Gontrode
④ Düsseldorf
⑤ Hanover
⑥ Schneidemühl
⑦ Kovno

NAVY BASES

Ⓐ Namur
Ⓑ Düren
Ⓒ Jüterbog
Ⓓ Johannisthal
Ⓔ Leipzig
Ⓕ Dresden
Ⓖ Jamboli

CONSTRUCTION PLANTS

① Friedrichshafen
② Löwenthal
③ Potsdam
④ Zeesen
⑤ Tegel
⑥ Staaken
⑦ Bitterfeld
⑧ Leipzig
⑨ Mannheim

On 5 January 1918, five German airships were destroyed in a sudden and still-unexplained fire at Alhorn. Zeppelins L.46, L.47, L.51, and L.58, plus the Schütte-Lanz SL.20, were involved and the German Naval Airship Division lost 10 men dead, 30 seriously injured, and 104 slightly injured. A further 4 civilian technicians were killed. The most widely held theory is that the blaze originated in the rear gondola of L.51 through the use of petroleum as a cleaning agent by civilian workmen. The German airship service never properly recovered from this disaster.

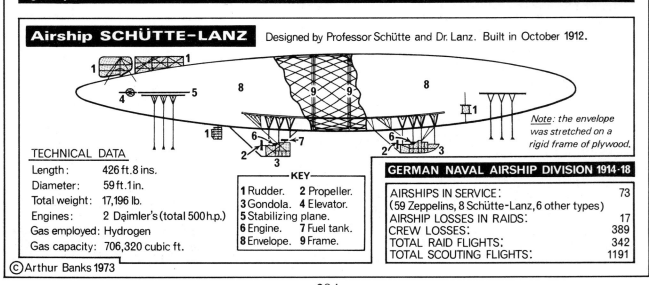

Airship SCHÜTTE-LANZ

Designed by Professor Schütte and Dr. Lanz. Built in October 1912.

Note: the envelope was stretched on a rigid frame of plywood.

TECHNICAL DATA

Length: 426 ft. 8 ins.
Diameter: 59 ft. 1 in.
Total weight: 17,196 lb.
Engines: 2 Daimler's (total 500 h.p.)
Gas employed: Hydrogen
Gas capacity: 706,320 cubic ft.

KEY

1 Rudder.   2 Propeller.
3 Gondola.   4 Elevator.
5 Stabilizing plane.
6 Engine.   7 Fuel tank.
8 Envelope.   9 Frame.

GERMAN NAVAL AIRSHIP DIVISION 1914-18

AIRSHIPS IN SERVICE:	73
(59 Zeppelins, 8 Schütte-Lanz, 6 other types)	
AIRSHIP LOSSES IN RAIDS:	17
CREW LOSSES:	389
TOTAL RAID FLIGHTS:	342
TOTAL SCOUTING FLIGHTS:	1191

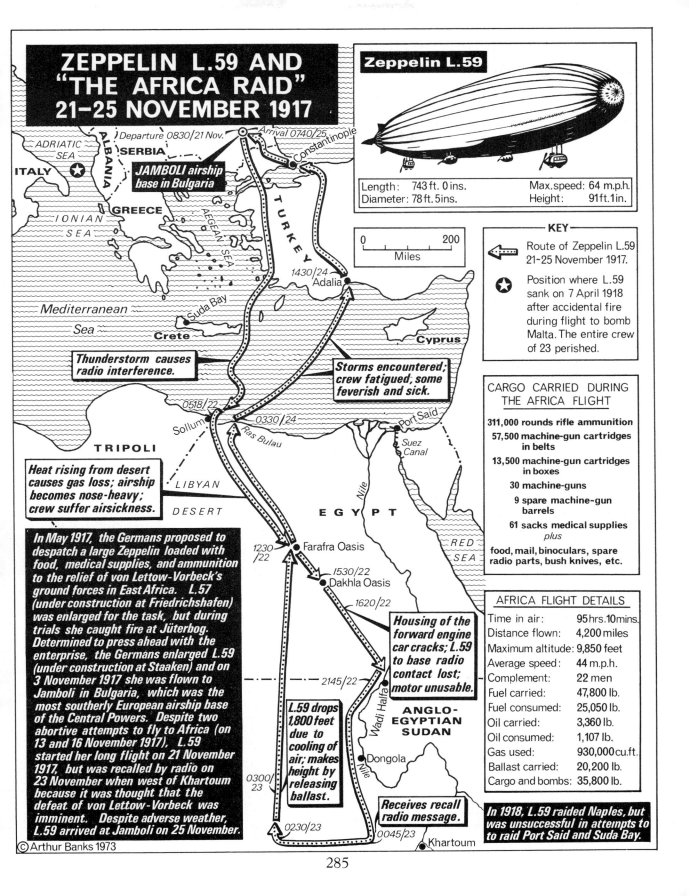

ZEPPELIN L.59 AND "THE AFRICA RAID" 21–25 NOVEMBER 1917

Zeppelin L.59

| Length: | 743 ft. 0 ins. | Max. speed: | 64 m.p.h. |
| Diameter: | 78 ft. 5 ins. | Height: | 91 ft. 1 in. |

Departure 0830/21 Nov.

Arrival 0740/25

ADRIATIC SEA

ITALY

ALBANIA

SERBIA

Constantinople

TURKEY

JAMBOLI airship base in Bulgaria

GREECE

IONIAN SEA

AEGEAN SEA

0   200
Miles

KEY

← Route of Zeppelin L.59 21–25 November 1917.

★ Position where L.59 sank on 7 April 1918 after accidental fire during flight to bomb Malta. The entire crew of 23 perished.

Suda Bay

Crete

Mediterranean Sea

1430/24
Adalia

Cyprus

Thunderstorm causes radio interference.

Storms encountered; crew fatigued; some feverish and sick.

CARGO CARRIED DURING THE AFRICA FLIGHT

311,000 rounds rifle ammunition
57,500 machine-gun cartridges in belts
13,500 machine-gun cartridges in boxes
30 machine-guns
9 spare machine-gun barrels
61 sacks medical supplies
plus
food, mail, binoculars, spare radio parts, bush knives, etc.

0518/22
Sollum

0330/24

Ras Bulau

Port Said

Suez Canal

TRIPOLI

Heat rising from desert causes gas loss; airship becomes nose-heavy; crew suffer airsickness.

LIBYAN DESERT

Nile

E G Y P T

RED SEA

In May 1917, the Germans proposed to despatch a large Zeppelin loaded with food, medical supplies, and ammunition to the relief of von Lettow-Vorbeck's ground forces in East Africa. L.57 (under construction at Friedrichshafen) was enlarged for the task, but during trials she caught fire at Jüterbog. Determined to press ahead with the enterprise, the Germans enlarged L.59 (under construction at Staaken) and on 3 November 1917 she was flown to Jamboli in Bulgaria, which was the most southerly European airship base of the Central Powers. Despite two abortive attempts to fly to Africa (on 13 and 16 November 1917), L.59 started her long flight on 21 November 1917, but was recalled by radio on 23 November when west of Khartoum because it was thought that the defeat of von Lettow-Vorbeck was imminent. Despite adverse weather, L.59 arrived at Jamboli on 25 November.

1230/22
Farafra Oasis

1530/22
Dakhla Oasis

1620/22

AFRICA FLIGHT DETAILS

Time in air:	95 hrs. 10 mins.
Distance flown:	4,200 miles
Maximum altitude:	9,850 feet
Average speed:	44 m.p.h.
Complement:	22 men
Fuel carried:	47,800 lb.
Fuel consumed:	25,050 lb.
Oil carried:	3,360 lb.
Oil consumed:	1,107 lb.
Gas used:	930,000 cu. ft.
Ballast carried:	20,200 lb.
Cargo and bombs:	35,800 lb.

Housing of the forward engine car cracks; L.59 to base radio contact lost; motor unusable.

2145/22

L.59 drops 1,800 feet due to cooling of air; makes height by releasing ballast.

ANGLO-EGYPTIAN SUDAN

Wadi Halfa

Dongola

Nile

0300/23

0230/23

0045/23

Receives recall radio message.

Khartoum

In 1918, L.59 raided Naples, but was unsuccessful in attempts to to raid Port Said and Suda Bay.

© Arthur Banks 1973

285

GERMAN AIRSHIP RAIDS ON BRITAIN 1915–1918

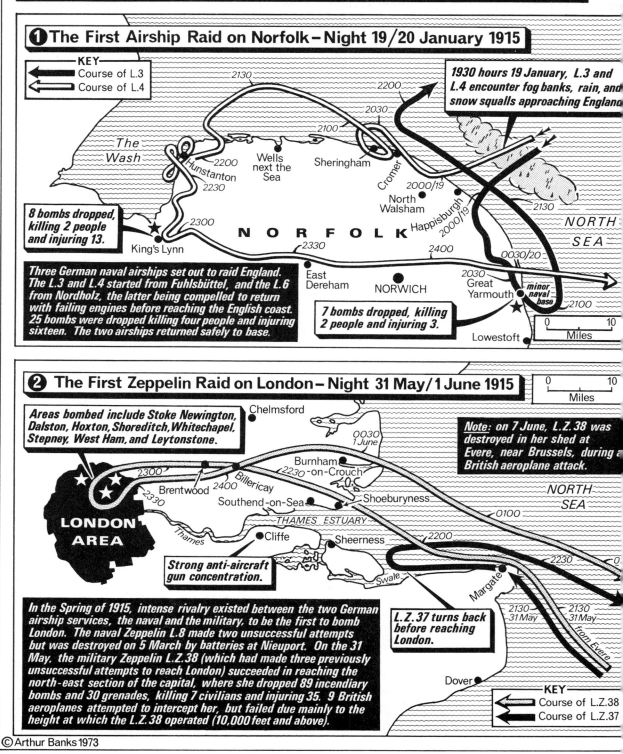

① The First Airship Raid on Norfolk – Night 19/20 January 1915

KEY
Course of L.3
Course of L.4

1930 hours 19 January, L.3 and L.4 encounter fog banks, rain, and snow squalls approaching England

2130
2200
2030
2100

The Wash

Wells next the Sea
Sheringham
Cromer
2000/19
North Walsham
Happisburgh 2000/19
2130

Hunstanton
2200
2230

8 bombs dropped, killing 2 people and injuring 13.

2300

King's Lynn

N O R F O L K
2330
2400

East Dereham
NORWICH
Great Yarmouth
2030
0030/20
minor naval base
2100

NORTH SEA

Three German naval airships set out to raid England. The L.3 and L.4 started from Fuhlsbüttel, and the L.6 from Nordholz, the latter being compelled to return with failing engines before reaching the English coast. 25 bombs were dropped killing four people and injuring sixteen. The two airships returned safely to base.

7 bombs dropped, killing 2 people and injuring 3.

Lowestoft

0   10
Miles

---

② The First Zeppelin Raid on London – Night 31 May/1 June 1915

0   10
Miles

Areas bombed include Stoke Newington, Dalston, Hoxton, Shoreditch, Whitechapel, Stepney, West Ham, and Leytonstone.

Chelmsford

0030 1 June

Burnham -on-Crouch
2230

Billericay
2400
Brentwood
2300
2330

LONDON AREA

Southend-on-Sea
Shoeburyness

THAMES ESTUARY

0100

Thames
Cliffe
Sheerness
2200

Strong anti-aircraft gun concentration.

Swale
Margate

Note: *on 7 June, L.Z.38 was destroyed in her shed at Evere, near Brussels, during a British aeroplane attack.*

NORTH SEA

2230

L.Z.37 turns back before reaching London.

2130 31 May
2130 31 May

from Evere

Dover

In the Spring of 1915, intense rivalry existed between the two German airship services, the naval and the military, to be the first to bomb London. The naval Zeppelin L.8 made two unsuccessful attempts but was destroyed on 5 March by batteries at Nieuport. On the 31 May, the military Zeppelin L.Z.38 (which had made three previously unsuccessful attempts to reach London) succeeded in reaching the north-east section of the capital, where she dropped 89 incendiary bombs and 30 grenades, killing 7 civilians and injuring 35. 9 British aeroplanes attempted to intercept her, but failed due mainly to the height at which the L.Z.38 operated (10,000 feet and above).

KEY
Course of L.Z.38
Course of L.Z.37

© Arthur Banks 1973

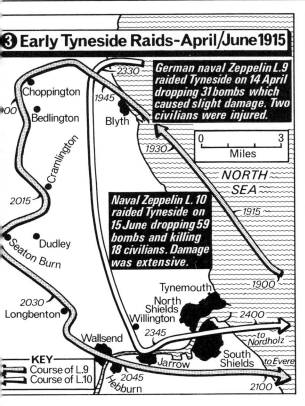

❸ Early Tyneside Raids–April/June 1915

German naval Zeppelin L.9 raided Tyneside on 14 April dropping 31 bombs which caused slight damage. Two civilians were injured.

Naval Zeppelin L.10 raided Tyneside on 15 June dropping 59 bombs and killing 18 civilians. Damage was extensive.

0 — 3 Miles

NORTH SEA

2330
1945
1930
2015
1915
1900
2030
2400
2345
2100
2045

Choppington
Bedlington
Blyth
Cramlington
Dudley
Seaton Burn
Longbenton
Wallsend
Jarrow
Hebburn
Tynemouth
North Shields
Willington
South Shields
to Nordholz
to Evere

KEY
Course of L.9
Course of L.10

❹ First Humber Raid–6/7 June 1915

0 — 10 Miles

2330

KEY
← Course of L.9

L.9 stays over Hull for twenty minutes, bombing docks, shipping, houses and shops.

24 killed 40 injured

Pom-pom guns fire at L.9 but no hits result from action.

The German naval Zeppelin L.9 which attacked Hull at midnight on 6 June 1915, dropped 13 high explosive and 39 incendiary bombs. Going on to Grimsby she dropped 7 incendiaries.

Flamborough Head
NORTH SEA
2300
2400
HULL
HUMBER
Immingham
Grimsby
0030/7
Waltham
2230
0100
from Hage
2200/6

❺ The First Sizable Raid on the Midlands–Night 31 January/1 February 1916

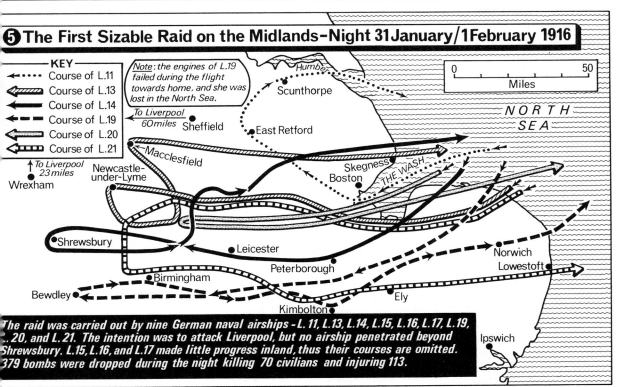

KEY
•••• Course of L.11
Course of L.13
← Course of L.14
-- Course of L.19
⇐ Course of L.20
⇐ Course of L.21

Note: the engines of L.19 failed during the flight towards home, and she was lost in the North Sea.

0 — 50 Miles

NORTH SEA

To Liverpool 60 miles
To Liverpool 23 miles

Humber
Scunthorpe
East Retford
Sheffield
Macclesfield
Newcastle-under-Lyme
Wrexham
Skegness
Boston
THE WASH
Shrewsbury
Leicester
Peterborough
Norwich
Lowestoft
Bewdley
Birmingham
Kimbolton
Ely
Ipswich

The raid was carried out by nine German naval airships – L.11, L.13, L.14, L.15, L.16, L.17, L.19, L.20, and L.21. The intention was to attack Liverpool, but no airship penetrated beyond Shrewsbury. L.15, L.16, and L.17 made little progress inland, thus their courses are omitted. 379 bombs were dropped during the night killing 70 civilians and injuring 113.

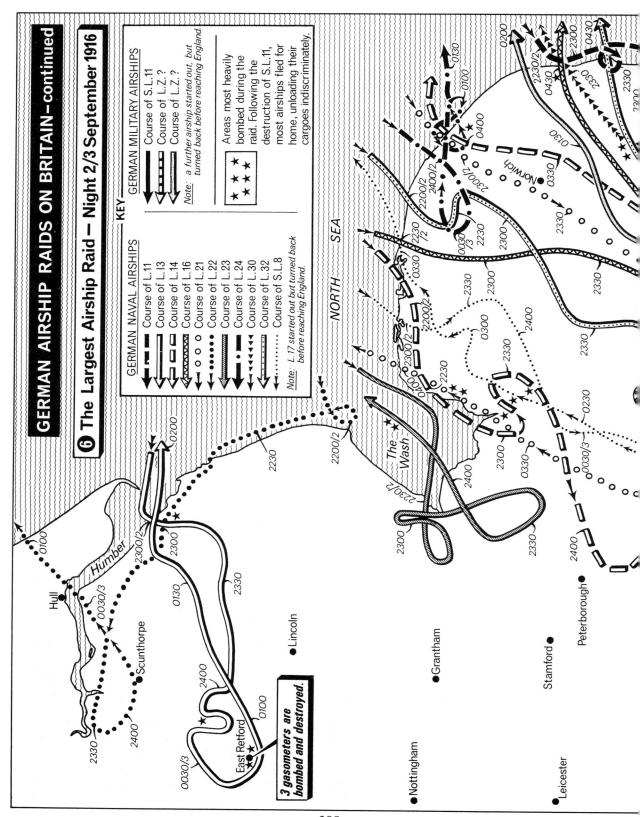

GERMAN AIRSHIP RAIDS ON BRITAIN—continued

❻ The Largest Airship Raid – Night 2/3 September 1916

KEY

GERMAN NAVAL AIRSHIPS

- Course of L.11
- Course of L.13
- Course of L.14
- Course of L.16
- Course of L.21
- Course of L.22
- Course of L.23
- Course of L.24
- Course of L.30
- Course of L.32
- Course of S.L.8

Note: L.17 started out but turned back before reaching England.

GERMAN MILITARY AIRSHIPS

- Course of S.L.11
- Course of L.Z.?
- Course of L.Z.?

Note: a further airship started out, but turned back before reaching England.

★★★
★★★

Areas most heavily bombed during the raid. Following the destruction of S.L.11, most airships fled for home, unloading their cargoes indiscriminately.

3 gasometers are bombed and destroyed.

NORTH SEA

The Wash

Humber

Hull
Scunthorpe
East Retford
Lincoln
Grantham
Stamford
Peterborough
Nottingham
Leicester
Norwich

0100
0200
2230
2300
2330
2400
0130
0030/3
0100
2300/2
2200/2
2230/2
2300
2230
2300/3
2230/2
2400/2
2300
2330
0300
0330
0230
0030/3
0400
0130
2300/2
2400/2
0100
0030
0200
0130
0430
2300
2330
2230/2

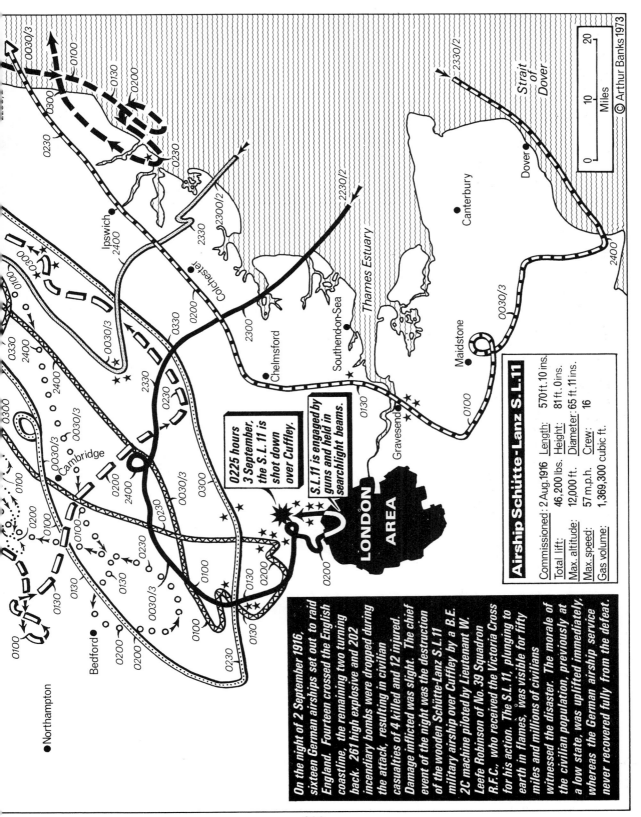

Airship Schütte-Lanz S.L.11

Commissioned:	2 Aug.1916	Length:	570 ft. 10 ins.
Total lift:	46,200 lbs.	Height:	81 ft. 0 ins.
Max. altitude:	12,000 ft.	Diameter:	65 ft. 11 ins.
Max. speed:	57 m.p.h.	Crew:	16
Gas volume:	1,369,300 cubic ft.		

0225 hours 3 September, the S.L.11 is shot down over Cuffley.

S.L.11 is engaged by guns and held in searchlight beams.

LONDON AREA

On the night of 2 September 1916, sixteen German airships set out to raid England. Fourteen crossed the English coastline, the remaining two turning back. 261 high explosive and 202 incendiary bombs were dropped during the attack, resulting in civilian casualties of 4 killed and 12 injured. Damage inflicted was slight. The chief event of the night was the destruction of the wooden Schütte-Lanz S.L.11 military airship over Cuffley by a B.E. 2C machine piloted by Lieutenant W. Leefe Robinson of No. 39 Squadron R.F.C., who received the Victoria Cross for his action. The S.L.11, plunging to earth in flames, was visible for fifty miles and millions of civilians witnessed the disaster. The morale of the civilian population, previously at a low state, was uplifted immediately, whereas the German airship service never recovered fully from the defeat.

© Arthur Banks 1973

Miles

289

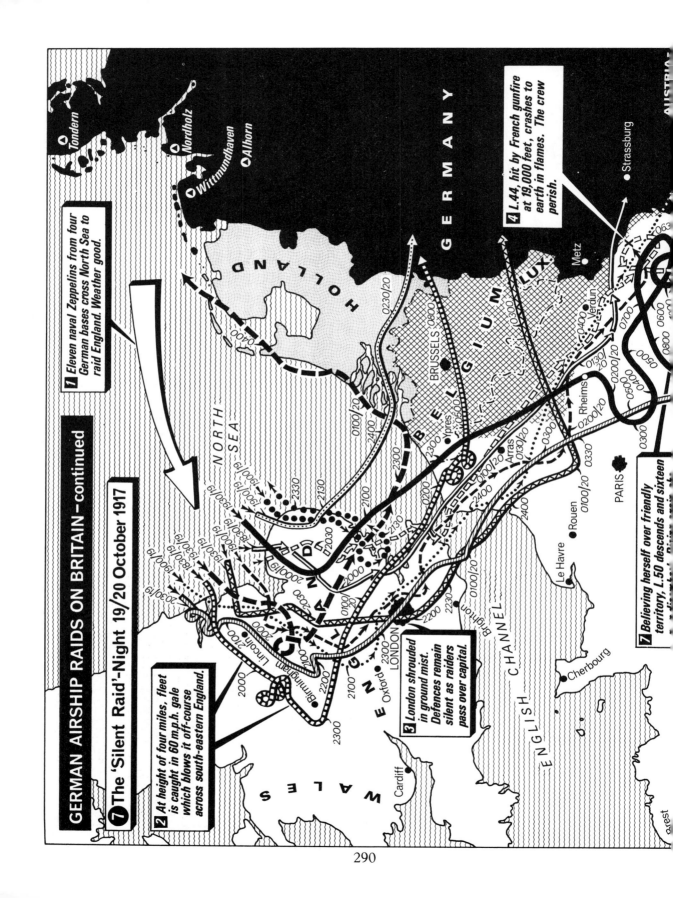

GERMAN AIRSHIP RAIDS ON BRITAIN – continued

7 The 'Silent Raid'–Night 19/20 October 1917

1 Eleven naval Zeppelins from four German bases cross North Sea to raid England. Weather good.

2 At height of four miles, fleet is caught in 60 m.p.h. gale which blows it off-course across south-eastern England.

3 London shrouded in ground mist. Defences remain silent as raiders pass over capital.

4 L.44, hit by French gunfire at 19,000 feet, crashes to earth in flames. The crew perish.

7 Believing herself over friendly territory, L.50 descends and sixteen

NORTH SEA

HOLLAND

GERMANY

BELGIUM

LUX

ENGLAND

WALES

ENGLISH CHANNEL

Tondern
Nordholz
Alhorn
Wittmundhaven

Strassburg
Metz
Verdun
Rheims
Arras
Ypres
BRUSSELS

Lincoln
Birmingham
Oxford
LONDON
Brighton

Cardiff

Le Havre
Rouen
PARIS
Cherbourg

AUSTRIA

2330 2130 2030 2100 2200 2300 2400 2000 2100 2030
1800/19 1830/19 1900/19 1930/19 2000/19 2030/19
0100/20 0230/20 0800 0500 0200/20 0300 0130/20 0200/20 0400 0500 0600 0700 0800

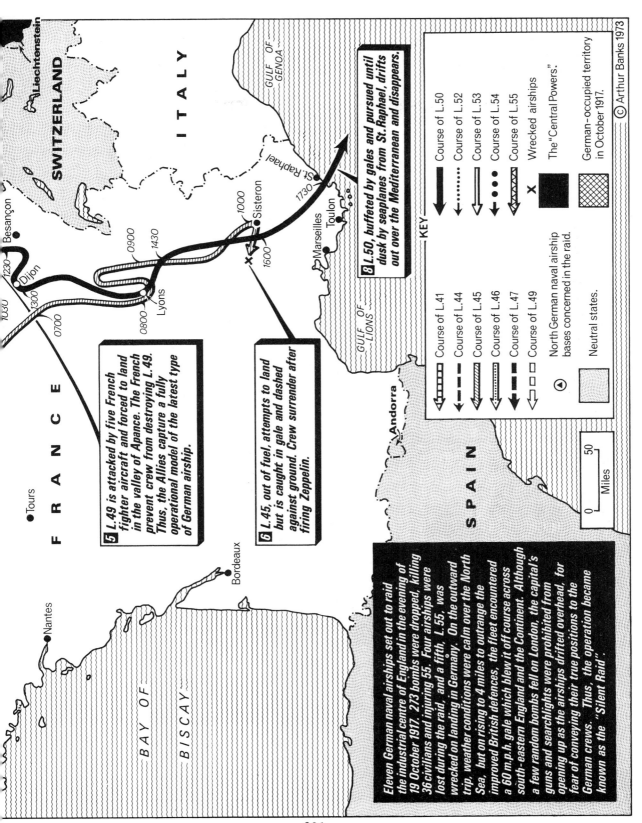

SWITZERLAND

ITALY

GULF OF GENOA

8 *L.50, buffeted by gales and pursued until dusk by seaplanes from St. Raphael, drifts out over the Mediterranean and disappears.*

St. Raphael

1730

Marseilles
Toulon

GULF OF LIONS

Besançon

1230
Dijon
1300

1030

0700

0900
1430

0800
Lyons

1000
Sisteron

1600

×

Tours

5 *L.49 is attacked by five French fighter aircraft and forced to land in the valley of Apance. The French prevent crew from destroying L.49. Thus, the Allies capture a fully operational model of the latest type of German airship.*

6 *L.45, out of fuel, attempts to land but is caught in gale and dashed against ground. Crew surrender after firing Zeppelin.*

F R A N C E

Bordeaux

Nantes

BAY OF

BISCAY

Andorra

S P A I N

0   50
Miles

KEY

Course of L.50	
Course of L.52	
Course of L.53	
Course of L.54	
Course of L.55	

Course of L.41
Course of L.44
Course of L.45
Course of L.46
Course of L.47
Course of L.49

×   Wrecked airships

The "Central Powers".

German-occupied territory in October 1917.

North German naval airship bases concerned in the raid.

Neutral states.

© Arthur Banks 1973

Eleven German naval airships set out to raid the industrial centre of England in the evening of 19 October 1917. 273 bombs were dropped, killing 36 civilians and injuring 55. Four airships were lost during the raid, and a fifth, L.55, was wrecked on landing in Germany. On the outward trip, weather conditions were calm over the North Sea, but on rising to 4 miles to outrange the improved British defences, the fleet encountered a 60 m.p.h. gale which blew it off course across south-eastern England and the Continent. Although a few random bombs fell on London, the capital's guns and searchlights were prohibited from opening up as the airships drifted overhead, for fear of conveying their true positions to the German crews. Thus, the operation became known as the "Silent Raid".

291

GERMAN BOMBER RAIDS ON ENGLAND 1917–1918

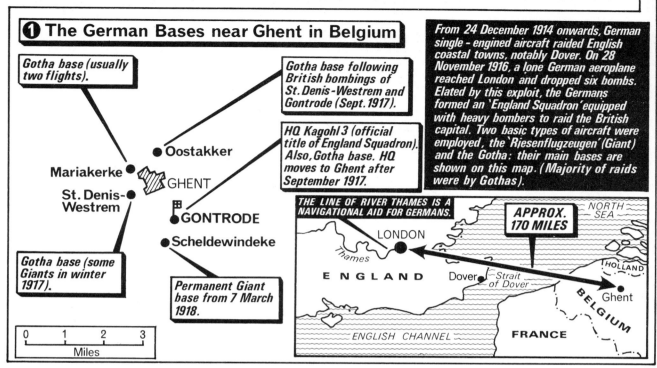

① The German Bases near Ghent in Belgium

Gotha base (usually two flights).

Gotha base following British bombings of St. Denis-Westrem and Gontrode (Sept. 1917).

HQ Kagohl 3 (official title of England Squadron). Also, Gotha base. HQ moves to Ghent after September 1917.

From 24 December 1914 onwards, German single-engined aircraft raided English coastal towns, notably Dover. On 28 November 1916, a lone German aeroplane reached London and dropped six bombs. Elated by this exploit, the Germans formed an 'England Squadron' equipped with heavy bombers to raid the British capital. Two basic types of aircraft were employed, the 'Riesenflugzeugen' (Giant) and the Gotha: their main bases are shown on this map. (Majority of raids were by Gothas).

Oostakker

Mariakerke

St. Denis-Westrem

GHENT

GONTRODE

Scheldewindeke

Gotha base (some Giants in winter 1917).

Permanent Giant base from 7 March 1918.

THE LINE OF RIVER THAMES IS A NAVIGATIONAL AID FOR GERMANS.

APPROX. 170 MILES

NORTH SEA

LONDON

Thames

ENGLAND

Dover — Strait of Dover

HOLLAND

Ghent

BELGIUM

ENGLISH CHANNEL

FRANCE

0 1 2 3
Miles

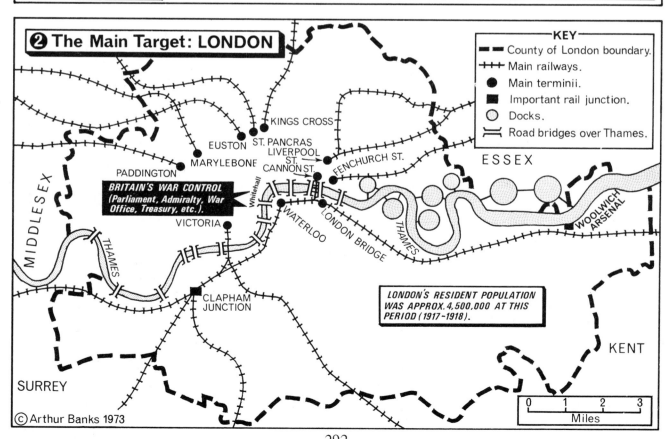

② The Main Target: LONDON

KEY
- — — County of London boundary.
- ┼┼┼ Main railways.
- ● Main terminii.
- ■ Important rail junction.
- ○ Docks.
- ⌒ Road bridges over Thames.

KINGS CROSS

EUSTON

ST. PANCRAS

MARYLEBONE

PADDINGTON

LIVERPOOL ST.

CANNON ST.

FENCHURCH ST.

ESSEX

MIDDLESEX

BRITAIN'S WAR CONTROL (Parliament, Admiralty, War Office, Treasury, etc.).

Whitehall

VICTORIA

WATERLOO

LONDON BRIDGE

THAMES

THAMES

WOOLWICH ARSENAL

CLAPHAM JUNCTION

LONDON'S RESIDENT POPULATION WAS APPROX. 4,500,000 AT THIS PERIOD (1917–1918).

KENT

SURREY

© Arthur Banks 1973

0 1 2 3
Miles

Employing Gotha bombers, the Germans made eight mass-attacks in daylight against England in 1917. 165 aircraft flights were involved and nearly 73,000 lbs. of bombs were dropped, killing or injuring 1,364 English civilians. Seventeen Gothas were destroyed during the period 25 May – 22 August 1917. Four of the attacks are shown below.

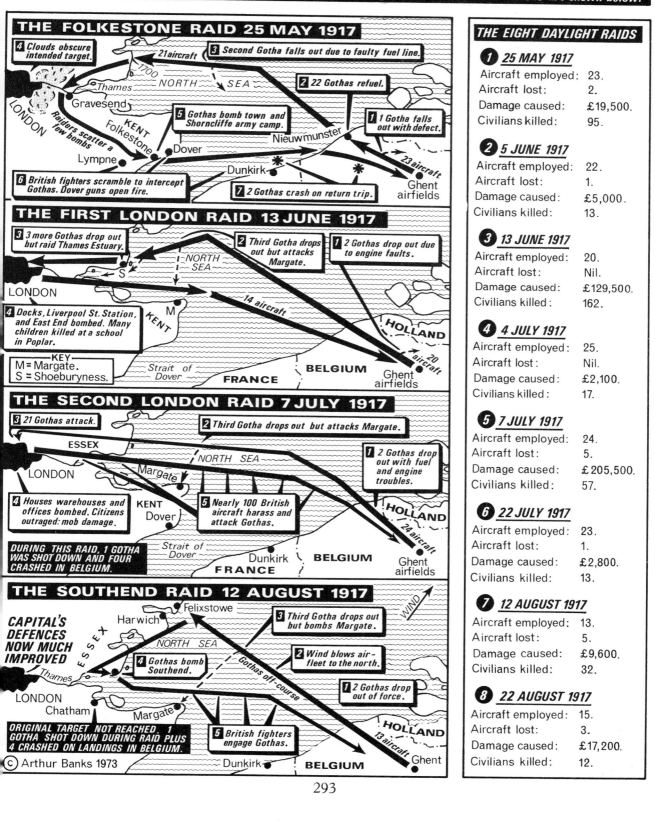

THE FOLKESTONE RAID 25 MAY 1917

4 Clouds obscure intended target.

21 aircraft

1700 NORTH SEA

3 Second Gotha falls out due to faulty fuel line.

2 22 Gothas refuel.

Thames
Gravesend

5 Gothas bomb town and Shorncliffe army camp.

1 1 Gotha falls out with defect.

LONDON

KENT
Folkestone

Raiders scatter a few bombs

Dover

Nieuwmunster

23 aircraft

Lympne

Dunkirk

Ghent airfields

6 British fighters scramble to intercept Gothas. Dover guns open fire.

7 2 Gothas crash on return trip.

THE FIRST LONDON RAID 13 JUNE 1917

3 3 more Gothas drop out but raid Thames Estuary.

2 Third Gotha drops out but attacks Margate.

1 2 Gothas drop out due to engine faults.

NORTH SEA

S

LONDON

14 aircraft

M

KENT

HOLLAND

4 Docks, Liverpool St. Station, and East End bombed. Many children killed at a school in Poplar.

20 aircraft

7 aircraft

KEY
M = Margate.
S = Shoeburyness.

Strait of Dover

BELGIUM

FRANCE

Ghent airfields

THE SECOND LONDON RAID 7 JULY 1917

3 21 Gothas attack.

2 Third Gotha drops out but attacks Margate.

ESSEX

1 2 Gothas drop out with fuel and engine troubles.

LONDON

Margate

NORTH SEA

4 Houses warehouses and offices bombed. Citizens outraged: mob damage.

KENT
Dover

5 Nearly 100 British aircraft harass and attack Gothas.

HOLLAND

24 aircraft

Strait of Dover

Dunkirk

BELGIUM

DURING THIS RAID, 1 GOTHA WAS SHOT DOWN AND FOUR CRASHED IN BELGIUM.

FRANCE

Ghent airfields

THE SOUTHEND RAID 12 AUGUST 1917

CAPITAL'S DEFENCES NOW MUCH IMPROVED

Felixstowe
Harwich

3 Third Gotha drops out but bombs Margate.

WIND

E S S E X

NORTH SEA

Gothas off-course

2 Wind blows air-fleet to the north.

Thames

4 Gothas bomb Southend.

1 2 Gothas drop out of force.

LONDON
Chatham

Margate

HOLLAND

ORIGINAL TARGET NOT REACHED. 1 GOTHA SHOT DOWN DURING RAID PLUS 4 CRASHED ON LANDINGS IN BELGIUM.

5 British fighters engage Gothas.

13 aircraft

© Arthur Banks 1973

Dunkirk

BELGIUM

Ghent

THE EIGHT DAYLIGHT RAIDS

1 25 MAY 1917
Aircraft employed: 23.
Aircraft lost: 2.
Damage caused: £19,500.
Civilians killed: 95.

2 5 JUNE 1917
Aircraft employed: 22.
Aircraft lost: 1.
Damage caused: £5,000.
Civilians killed: 13.

3 13 JUNE 1917
Aircraft employed: 20.
Aircraft lost: Nil.
Damage caused: £129,500.
Civilians killed: 162.

4 4 JULY 1917
Aircraft employed: 25.
Aircraft lost: Nil.
Damage caused: £2,100.
Civilians killed: 17.

5 7 JULY 1917
Aircraft employed: 24.
Aircraft lost: 5.
Damage caused: £205,500.
Civilians killed: 57.

6 22 JULY 1917
Aircraft employed: 23.
Aircraft lost: 1.
Damage caused: £2,800.
Civilians killed: 13.

7 12 AUGUST 1917
Aircraft employed: 13.
Aircraft lost: 5.
Damage caused: £9,600.
Civilians killed: 32.

8 22 AUGUST 1917
Aircraft employed: 15.
Aircraft lost: 3.
Damage caused: £17,200.
Civilians killed: 12.

GERMAN BOMBER RAIDS ON ENGLAND*-continued

Because of the increasing efficiency of Britain's defences, the Germans switched from daylight to darkness for their attacks. 19 raids were carried out between 3 September 1917 and 20 May 1918 and often several towns were bombed during a single raid. At one period, 300,000 Londoners sought refuge at Underground stations.

❸ Main Targets of the Night Raiders

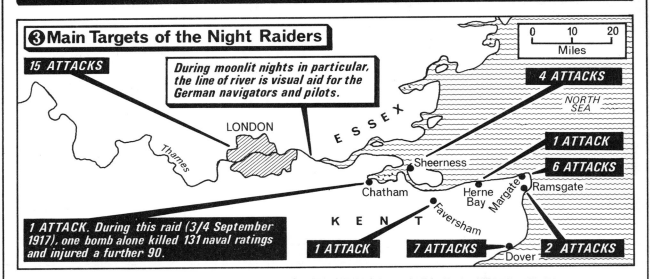

0   10   20
Miles

15 ATTACKS

During moonlit nights in particular, the line of river is visual aid for the German navigators and pilots.

4 ATTACKS

NORTH SEA

LONDON

Thames

E S S E X

1 ATTACK

6 ATTACKS

Sheerness

Chatham

Herne Bay   Margate   Ramsgate

K E N T   Faversham

1 ATTACK. During this raid (3/4 September 1917), one bomb alone killed 131 naval ratings and injured a further 90.

1 ATTACK   **7 ATTACKS**   Dover   **2 ATTACKS**

THE 19 DARKNESS RAIDS

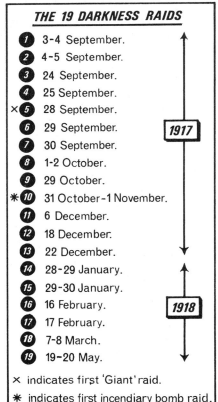

① 3-4 September.
② 4-5 September.
③ 24 September.
④ 25 September.
×⑤ 28 September.
⑥ 29 September.
⑦ 30 September.
⑧ 1-2 October.
⑨ 29 October.
✳⑩ 31 October-1 November.
⑪ 6 December.
⑫ 18 December.
⑬ 22 December.
⑭ 28-29 January.
⑮ 29-30 January.
⑯ 16 February.
⑰ 17 February.
⑱ 7-8 March.
⑲ 19-20 May.

1917

1918

× indicates first 'Giant' raid.
✳ indicates first incendiary bomb raid.

THE GERMAN 'ELEKTRON' BOMB (AUGUST 1918)

Weighing approx. one kilogram, this incendiary device ignited upon contact. Constructed of magnesium, its main feature was that when sprayed with water, the existing fire became even fiercer. The Germans planned to drop large numbers on London (and Paris), but the Allied offensives in the autumn of 1918 frustrated this idea.

GERMAN BOMBER LOSSES

43 Gothas (from 383 flights) ⎫ ALL ATTACKS, ⎧ shot down, crashed,
2 Giants (from 30 flights) ⎭ NIGHT AND DAY ⎩ missing, etc.

SOUTH-EAST ENGLAND'S DEFENCES AUTUMN 1918

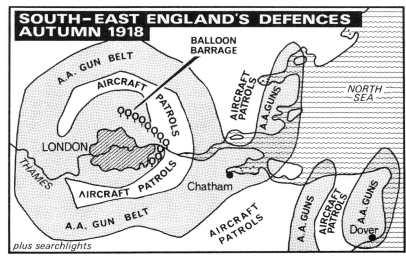

BALLOON BARRAGE

A.A. GUN BELT

AIRCRAFT PATROLS

AIRCRAFT PATROLS

A.A. GUNS

NORTH SEA

LONDON

THAMES

AIRCRAFT PATROLS

Chatham

A.A. GUN BELT

AIRCRAFT PATROLS

A.A. GUNS   AIRCRAFT PATROLS   A.A. GUNS

Dover

plus searchlights

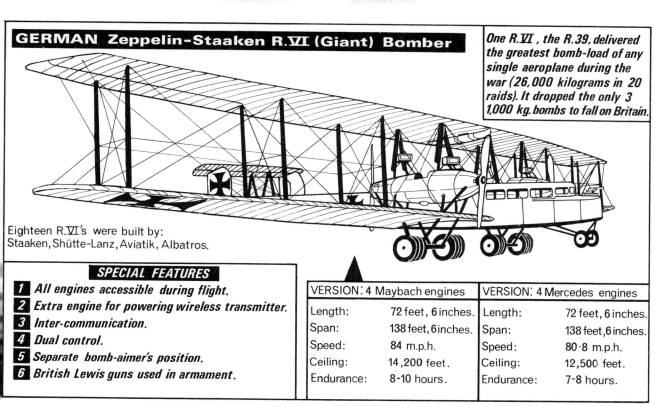

GERMAN Zeppelin-Staaken R.Ⅵ (Giant) Bomber

One R.Ⅵ, the R.39, delivered the greatest bomb-load of any single aeroplane during the war (26,000 kilograms in 20 raids). It dropped the only 3 1,000 kg. bombs to fall on Britain.

Eighteen R.Ⅵ's were built by:
Staaken, Shütte-Lanz, Aviatik, Albatros.

SPECIAL FEATURES

1 All engines accessible during flight.
2 Extra engine for powering wireless transmitter.
3 Inter-communication.
4 Dual control.
5 Separate bomb-aimer's position.
6 British Lewis guns used in armament.

VERSION: 4 Maybach engines		VERSION: 4 Mercedes engines	
Length:	72 feet, 6 inches.	Length:	72 feet, 6 inches.
Span:	138 feet, 6 inches.	Span:	138 feet, 6 inches.
Speed:	84 m.p.h.	Speed:	80·8 m.p.h.
Ceiling:	14,200 feet.	Ceiling:	12,500 feet.
Endurance:	8-10 hours.	Endurance:	7-8 hours.

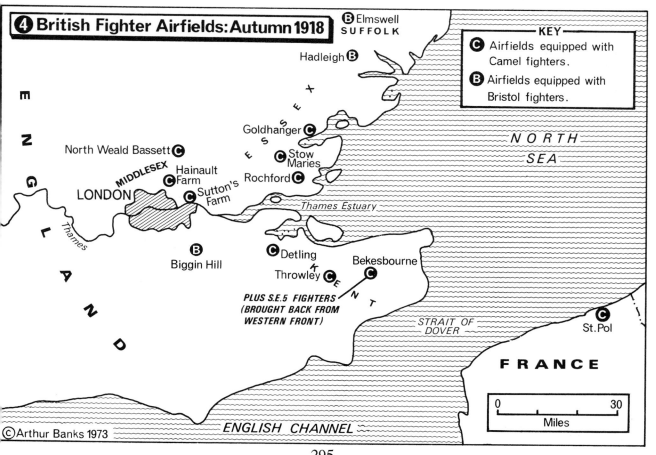

④ British Fighter Airfields: Autumn 1918

Ⓑ Elmswell
SUFFOLK

Hadleigh Ⓑ

— KEY —
Ⓒ Airfields equipped with Camel fighters.
Ⓑ Airfields equipped with Bristol fighters.

ESSEX

Goldhanger Ⓒ

North Weald Bassett Ⓒ

Stow Ⓒ Maries

MIDDLESEX

Hainault Ⓒ Farm

Rochford Ⓒ

LONDON

Ⓒ Sutton's Farm

NORTH SEA

Thames

Thames Estuary

Ⓑ
Biggin Hill

Ⓒ Detling

Throwley Ⓒ

Bekesbourne Ⓒ

KENT

PLUS S.E.5 FIGHTERS
(BROUGHT BACK FROM WESTERN FRONT)

STRAIT OF DOVER

Ⓒ St. Pol

FRANCE

ENGLAND

0	30
Miles	

ENGLISH CHANNEL

© Arthur Banks 1973

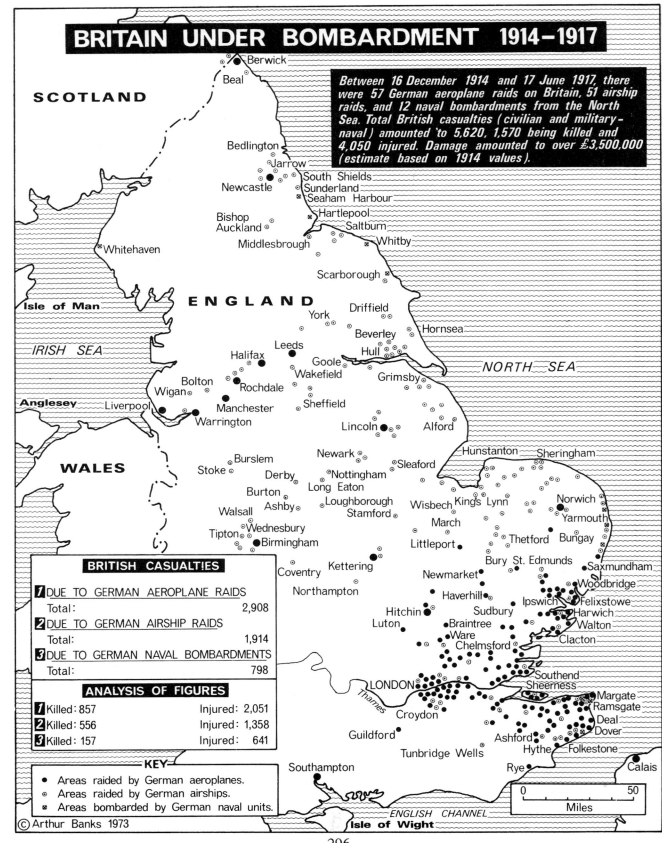

BRITAIN UNDER BOMBARDMENT 1914–1917

SCOTLAND

Between 16 December 1914 and 17 June 1917, there were 57 German aeroplane raids on Britain, 51 airship raids, and 12 naval bombardments from the North Sea. Total British casualties (civilian and military-naval) amounted to 5,620, 1,570 being killed and 4,050 injured. Damage amounted to over £3,500,000 (estimate based on 1914 values).

Berwick
Beal

Bedlington
Jarrow
South Shields
Newcastle
Sunderland
Seaham Harbour
Bishop Auckland
Hartlepool
Saltburn
Middlesbrough
Whitby

Whitehaven

Scarborough

ENGLAND

Driffield
York
Beverley
Hornsea
Hull

Isle of Man

Halifax
Leeds
Goole
Wakefield
Grimsby

IRISH SEA

NORTH SEA

Bolton
Wigan
Rochdale
Sheffield

Anglesey
Liverpool
Manchester
Warrington
Lincoln
Alford

Burslem
Newark
Hunstanton
Sheringham

WALES
Stoke
Derby
Nottingham
Sleaford

Burton
Long Eaton
Norwich

Walsall
Ashby
Loughborough
Wisbech
Kings Lynn
Yarmouth
Stamford
Bungay

Tipton
Wednesbury
March
Thetford

Birmingham
Littleport
Bury St. Edmunds
Saxmundham

Coventry
Kettering
Newmarket
Woodbridge

Northampton
Haverhill
Ipswich
Felixstowe
Harwich

Hitchin
Sudbury
Walton

Luton
Braintree
Clacton

Ware
Chelmsford

LONDON
Southend
Sheerness

Thames
Margate
Croydon
Ramsgate
Deal
Dover

Guildford
Ashford
Hythe
Folkestone

Tunbridge Wells
Rye
Calais

Southampton

BRITISH CASUALTIES

1 DUE TO GERMAN AEROPLANE RAIDS
Total: 2,908

2 DUE TO GERMAN AIRSHIP RAIDS
Total: 1,914

3 DUE TO GERMAN NAVAL BOMBARDMENTS
Total: 798

ANALYSIS OF FIGURES

1 Killed: 857	Injured: 2,051
2 Killed: 556	Injured: 1,358
3 Killed: 157	Injured: 641

KEY
- • Areas raided by German aeroplanes.
- ⊙ Areas raided by German airships.
- ⊠ Areas bombarded by German naval units.

0 ——— 50
Miles

ENGLISH CHANNEL
Isle of Wight

© Arthur Banks 1973

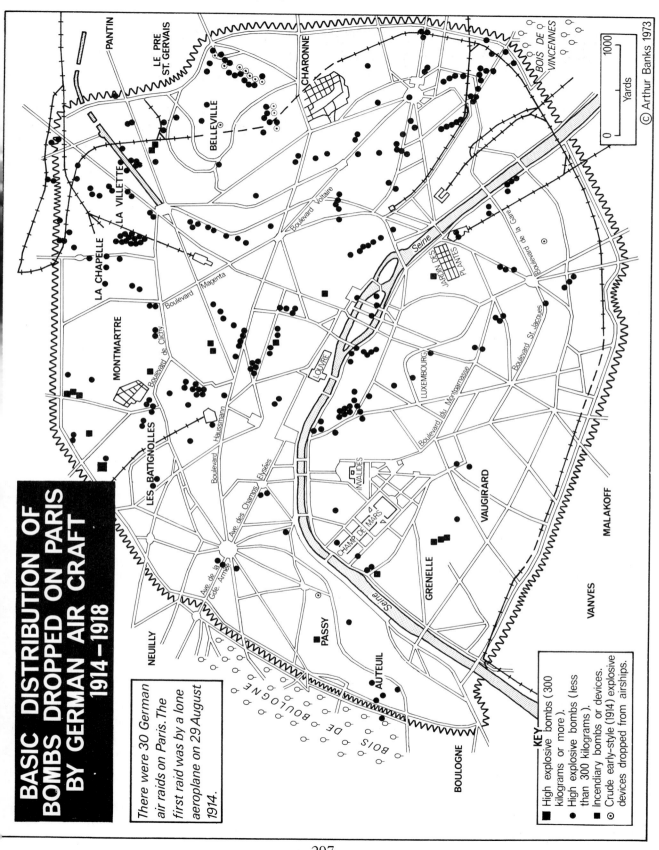

BASIC DISTRIBUTION OF
BOMBS DROPPED ON PARIS
BY GERMAN AIR CRAFT
1914 – 1918

There were 30 German air raids on Paris. The first raid was by a lone aeroplane on 29 August 1914.

© Arthur Banks 1973

0 ___ 1000

Yards

KEY

■ High explosive bombs (300 kilograms or more).

● High explosive bombs (less than 300 kilograms).

■ Incendiary bombs or devices.

⊙ Crude early-style (1914) explosive devices dropped from airships.

PANTIN

LE PRE ST. GERVAIS

CHARONNE

BOIS DE VINCENNES

BELLEVILLE

LA VILLETTE

LA CHAPELLE

Boulevard Voltaire

Seine

JARDIN DES PLANTES

Boulevard de la Gare

MONTMARTRE

Boulevard Magenta

Boulevard de Clichy

Boulevard Haussmann

LOUVRE

LUXEMBOURG

Boulevard St. Jacques

Boulevard du Montparnasse

LES BATIGNOLLES

Boulevard des Champs Elysées

INVALIDES

VAUGIRARD

Ave. des Champs Elysées

CHAMP DE MARS

GRENELLE

MALAKOFF

NEUILLY

Ave. de la Gde. Armée

Seine

AUTEUIL

PASSY

VANVES

BOIS DE BOULOGNE

BOULOGNE

297

THE BRITISH STRATEGIC BOMBING OFFENSIVE OF 1918

The Independent Air Force was formed to conduct operations against the heartland of Germany (rather than as a tactical support force) and to destroy the weapons in their factories before they reached the battlefield.

0 — 30
Miles

KEY
● Towns bombed by the British.
⊕ German aerodromes.
○—○—○ German balloon barrages.
– – – German fighter patrol lines.

Cologne ● ● Deutz ↖ to Leverkusen

to Düren ← Bonn ⊕ Hangelar

Steel works.

Rhine

⊕ Coblenz

Moselle

BELGIUM

Frankfurt

Wiesbaden ●

Mainz ⊕

Dormstadt ⊕

Wittlich ●

Kreuznach ●

Ehrang ●

LUXEMBOURG

Trier ●

Conz ●

GERMANY

Worms ●

Frankenthal ●

Saarburg ●

Luxembourg ●

to Ecouviez ←

Bettembourg ●

Volperweiler ⊕

Kaiserslautern ●

Ludwigshaven ● ● Mannheim

Schütte-Lanz works.

Esch ●

Speyer ⊕

Merzig ●

Longuyon ●

Audan le Roman ●

Steel works.

Saar

Dillingen ●

Saarlouis ●

Wadgassen ⊕ ● Bous

Völkingen ●

Zweibrücken ●

Kreuzwald ●

Saarbrücken ●

Pirmasens ●

Boulay ⊕

Forbach ●

Metz ⊕

Frescaty ⊕

Bitche ●

Karlsruhe ●

Arnaville ●

Verny ●

Han ●

Saaralbe ●

Bayonet firms.

Champey ●

Morhange ⊕

Rastaff ●

Dieuze ●

Haguenau ⊕

Sollingen ●

to Pforzheim →

Bühl ⊕

Baden Baden ●

Réchicourt ●

Saarburg ●

to Stuttgart →

Avricourt ●

Lorquin ●

Hattigny ⊕

Barbas ●

Offenburg ●

Azelot ⊕

Xaffévillers ⊕

to Oberndorf

Autreville ⊕

Lahr ●

Mauser factory. →

Roville ●

Bettoncourt ⊕

Powder factory.

Meurthe

to Rottweil

Moselle

Meuse

FRANCE

to Friedrichshafen

Freiburg ⊕

Main Zeppelin plant. →

© Arthur Banks 1973

298

DEVELOPMENTS IN AERIAL SURVEYING 1914-1918

❶ Balloon Photography

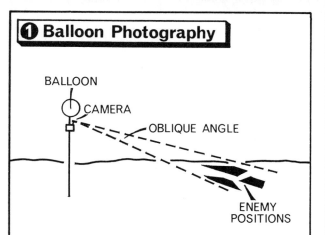

From the cartographic viewpoint, this method was unsatisfactory due to distortion of scale. What was required was overhead 'plan view' photography.

❷ Overhead Photography

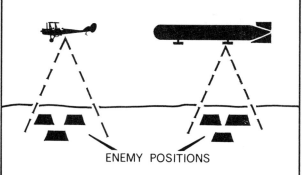

By utilising aeroplanes and airships, overhead views could be obtained. Battle maps improved both in scale accuracy and in detail shown.

❸ The Mosaic Map

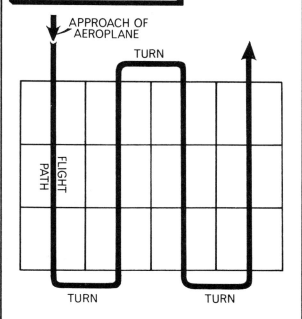

To cover large areas, photographs were butt-jointed together to form one vast panoramic spread.

❹ The Overlap Refinement

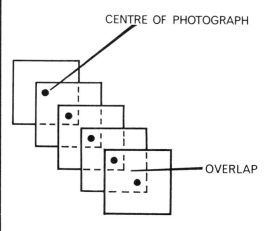

The mosaic map left much to be desired as only the centres of photographs were true to scale, and these varied individually. By regulating camera shutters at fixed intervals while aircraft maintained a consistent height, resulting prints could be overlapped to register uniformly.

THE FIGHTER 'ACES'

Note: main decorations only shown.

THE INTERNATIONAL TOP TEN SCORERS

POSITION	NAME	COUNTRY	'KILLS'
1	RICHTHOFEN	GERMANY	80
2	FONCK	FRANCE	75 ?
3	MANNOCK	BRITAIN	73 ?
4	BISHOP	CANADA	72
5	UDET	GERMANY	62
6	COLLISHAW	CANADA	60
7	McCUDDEN	BRITAIN	57
8	BEAUCHAMP-PROCTOR	SOUTH AFRICA	54
8	MacLAREN	CANADA	54
8	GUYNEMER	FRANCE	54

GERMAN TOP SCORERS

1	Rittmeister Manfred von Richthofen		80 kills
2	Oberleutnant Ernst Udet		62 kills
3	Oberleutnant Erich Loewenhardt	All six aces won *Pour le Mérite* (in Germany an 'ace' implied 10 or more victories).	53 kills
4	Leutnant Werner Voss		48 kills
5	Hauptmann Rudolf Berthold		44 kills
6	Leutnant Paul Bäumer		43 kills

FRENCH TOP SCORERS

1	Capitaine Rene Paul Fonck, L d'H, C de G with 28 Palms, MC, CK	75 kills
2	Capitaine Georges M.L.J. Guynemer, L d'H, MM, C de G (26 Palms)	54 kills
3	Lieutenant Charles E J M Nungesser, L d'H, MM, C de G	45 kills
4	Capitaine Georges Felix Madon, L d'H, MM, C de G	41 kills
5	Lieutenant Maurice Bayau, L d'H, MM, C de G	35 kills
6	Lieutenant Michel Coifford, L d'H, MM, C de G	34 kills

BRITISH EMPIRE TOP SCORERS

1	Major Edward Mannock, VC, DSO and 2 bars, MC and bar	73 kills
2	Lt. Colonel William A. Bishop, VC, DSO and bar, MC, DFC, L d H	72 kills
3	Lt. Colonel Raymond Collishaw, DSO and bar, DSC, DFC, C de G	60 kills
4	Major James T.B. McCudden, VC, DSO and bar, MC and bar, MM	57 kills
5	Captain Anthony W. Beauchamp-Proctor, VC, DSO, MC and bar	54 kills
6	Major Donald R. MacLaren, DSO, MC and bar, DFC, L d'H, C de G	54 kills

RUSSIAN TOP SCORERS

1	Staff Captain Alexander A. Kazakov, (13 Russian), DSO, MC, DFC	17 kills
2	Captain d'Argüeeff (Argeyev ?), Order of St. George	15 kills
3	Lt. Commander Alexander Prokofieff de Seversky, (all high Russian)	13 kills

© Arthur Banks 1973

THE RED BARON

Manfred von Richthofen was the highest scoring German fighter pilot 'ace' of the 1914-1918 war. He was credited with 80 enemy aircraft destroyed, and although the majority of these were reconnaissance machines, this total made him the top individual scorer of any country involved in the war.

He began flying as an active fighter pilot in March 1916, and was associated with the red Fokker triplane, the machine gun of which was synchronised to fire through the propeller.

He formed the group of squadrons known by the British as Richthofen's "circus", and was awarded the Pour le Mérite (the Blue Max) in February 1917. He was finally shot down on 21 April 1918, and was buried by the British with full military honours at Bertangles in France.

After the war he was reburied with much pomp and ceremony in Berlin.

AUSTRO-HUNGARIAN TOP SCORER

Hauptmann Godwin Brumowski	40 kills

BELGIAN TOP SCORER

Second Lieutenant Willy Coppens de Houthulst, DSO	37 kills

ITALIAN TOP SCORER

Maggiore Francesco Baracca	34 kills

UNITED STATES' TOP SCORER

Captain Edward V. Rickenbacker, CMH	26 kills

DECORATIONS: abbreviations employed here

VC = Victoria Cross.
DSO = Distinguished Service Order.
DSC = Distinguished Service Cross.
DFC = Distinguished Flying Cross.
MC = Military Cross.
MM = Military Medal.
L d'H = Légion d'Honneur.
C de G = Croix de Guerre.
CK = Cross of Karageorgevitch.
CMH = Congressional Medal of Honor.

EUROPEAN RANKINGS: Approx. equivalents

note: army ranks

Rittmeister	=	Cavalry captain.
Hauptmann	=	Captain.
Oberleutnant	=	Lieutenant.
Leutnant	=	Second Lieutenant.
Maggiore	=	Major.
Capitaine	=	Captain.

THE LOOP

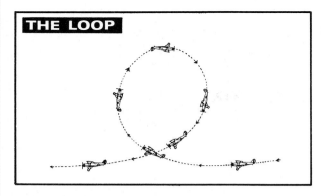

HALF ROLL ON TOP OF LOOP

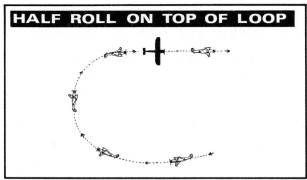

SLOW ROLL

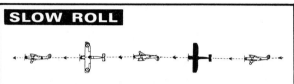

THE TOP SCORER: AN ANALYSIS

MANFRED VON RICHTHOFEN: THE RED BARON

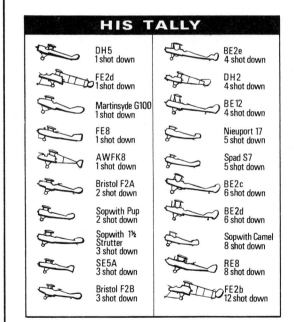

HIS TALLY

	DH5 1 shot down		BE2e 4 shot down
	FE2d 1 shot down		DH2 4 shot down
	Martinsyde G100 1 shot down		BE12 4 shot down
	FE8 1 shot down		Nieuport 17 5 shot down
	AWFK8 1 shot down		Spad S7 5 shot down
	Bristol F2A 2 shot down		BE2c 6 shot down
	Sopwith Pup 2 shot down		BE2d 6 shot down
	Sopwith 1½ Strutter 3 shot down		Sopwith Camel 8 shot down
	SE5A 3 shot down		RE8 8 shot down
	Bristol F2B 3 shot down		FE2b 12 shot down

ATTACK FROM ASTERN ①

FIXED MACHINE GUN FIRING FORWARD.

LINE OF ATTACK

HEIGHT ADVANTAGE (CLEAR VIEW).

This position was advantageous to the rear aircraft when the front machine carried only one occupant.

ATTACK FROM ASTERN ②

OWN FUSELAGE IMPEDES REAR MACHINE GUNNER'S LINE OF FIRE.

LINE OF ATTACK

This position was advantageous to the rear aircraft when the front machine carried two occupants.

THE DECEPTIVE SIDE TURN PLAN VIEW

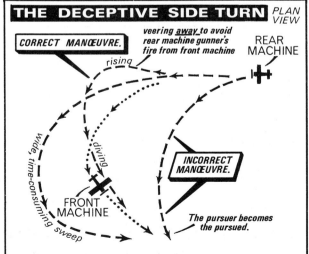

This diagram illustrates problems confronting a pilot when his quarry turned or banked to escape attack.

SOME OTHER FAMOUS 'ACES'	KILLS
AUSTRALIAN Captain Robert A. Little, DSO and bar, DSC, C de G	47
BRITISH Captain Albert Ball, VC, DSO and 2 bars, MC	44
GERMAN Hauptmann Oswald Boelcke, Pour le Mérite	40
GERMAN Oberleutnant Max Immelmann, Pour le Mérite	15

TWELVE IMPORTANT AIRCRAFT 1914-1918

BRITISH B.E. 2C

FRONT ELEVATION

SIDE ELEVATION

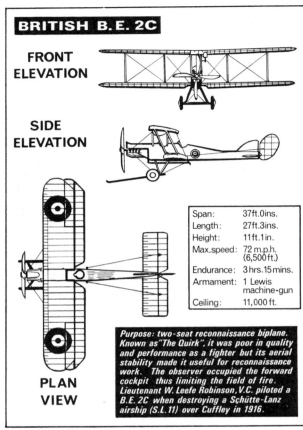

Span:	37ft.0ins.
Length:	27ft.3ins.
Height:	11ft.1in.
Max.speed:	72 m.p.h. (6,500 ft.)
Endurance:	3 hrs.15 mins.
Armament:	1 Lewis machine-gun
Ceiling:	11,000 ft.

Purpose: two-seat reconnaissance biplane. Known as "The Quirk", it was poor in quality and performance as a fighter but its aerial stability made it useful for reconnaissance work. The observer occupied the forward cockpit thus limiting the field of fire. Lieutenant W. Leefe Robinson, V.C. piloted a B.E. 2C when destroying a Schütte-Lanz airship (S.L. 11) over Cuffley in 1916.

PLAN VIEW

FRENCH Nieuport 17 C.1

FRONT ELEVATION

SIDE ELEVATION

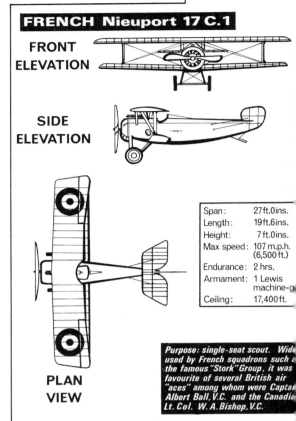

Span:	27ft.0ins.
Length:	19ft.6ins.
Height:	7ft.0ins.
Max speed:	107 m.p.h. (6,500 ft.)
Endurance:	2 hrs.
Armament:	1 Lewis machine-g
Ceiling:	17,400 ft.

Purpose: single-seat scout. Wide used by French squadrons such the famous "Stork" Group, it was favourite of several British air "aces" among whom were Captai Albert Ball, V.C. and the Canadia Lt. Col. W. A. Bishop, V.C.

PLAN VIEW

GERMAN Albatros D-1

SIDE ELEVATION

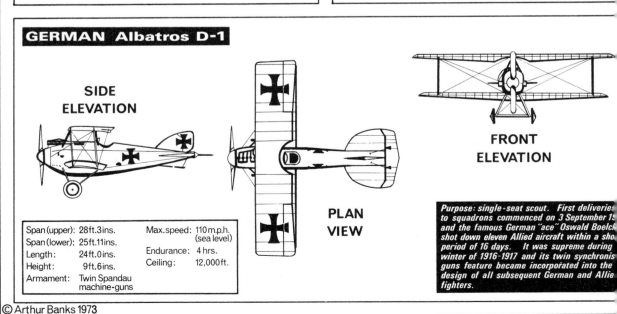

PLAN VIEW

FRONT ELEVATION

Span (upper):	28ft.3ins.
Span (lower):	25ft.11ins.
Length:	24ft.0ins.
Height:	9ft.6ins.
Armament:	Twin Spandau machine-guns

Max.speed:	110 m.p.h. (sea level)
Endurance:	4 hrs.
Ceiling:	12,000 ft.

Purpose: single-seat scout. First deliverie to squadrons commenced on 3 September 1 and the famous German "ace" Oswald Boelck shot down eleven Allied aircraft within a sho period of 16 days. It was supreme during winter of 1916-1917 and its twin synchronis guns feature became incorporated into the design of all subsequent German and Allie fighters.

BRITISH Bristol F.2B

SIDE ELEVATION

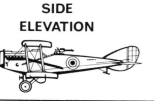

FRONT ELEVATION

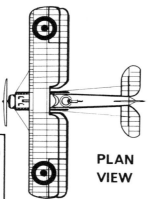

PLAN VIEW

Span:	39ft.4ins.	Armament:	1 Vickers machine-gun for the pilot
Length:	26ft.2ins.		
Height:	10ft.1in.		1 or 2 Lewis guns for the observer
Max.speed:	125 m.p.h. (sea level)		
Endurance:	3 hrs.		Racks for light bombs
Ceiling:	20,000 ft.		

Purpose: two-seat fighter/reconnaissance aircraft. Possibly the finest all-round fighter of the Allies in the war, it was extremely manœuvrable and carried the advantage of a "sting in the tail". Known as the "Brisfit" or "Biff", it was a favourite of British "ace" Captain McKeever who won most of his thirty victories with this type.

FRENCH Spad S-7 C.1

SIDE ELEVATION

FRONT ELEVATION

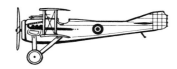

PLAN VIEW

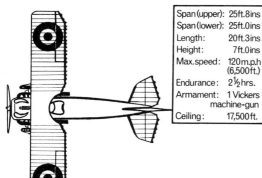

Span (upper):	25ft.8ins
Span (lower):	25ft.0ins
Length:	20ft.3ins
Height:	7ft.0ins
Max.speed:	120m.p.h (6,500ft.)
Endurance:	2½hrs.
Armament:	1 Vickers machine-gun
Ceiling:	17,500ft.

Purpose: single-seat scout. First flown in July 1916, over 5,000 Spad S-7's were built in France, and 400 in England. The famous French "Stork" Group, of which the "ace" Georges Guynemer was a member, flew this type.

GERMAN Fokker Dr-1 Triplane

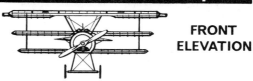

FRONT ELEVATION

SIDE ELEVATION

Span (upper):	23ft.7ins.
Span (centre):	20ft.6ins.
Span (lower):	18ft.9ins.
Length:	19ft.0ins.
Height:	9ft.0ins.
Max.speed:	122 m.p.h. at 8,000 ft.
Endurance:	2hrs.30mins.
Armament:	Twin Spandau machine-guns
Ceiling:	20,000 ft.

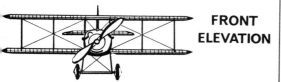

PLAN VIEW

Purpose: single-seat scout. First employed in August 1917, it was a favourite of German "aces" such as Manfred von Richthofen and Werner Voss and was the supreme German "dogfighter" of the war.

TWELVE IMPORTANT AIRCRAFT-continued

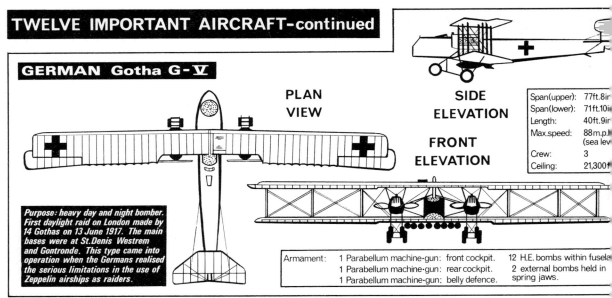

GERMAN Gotha G-Ⅴ

PLAN VIEW

SIDE ELEVATION

FRONT ELEVATION

Span(upper):	77ft.8in
Span(lower):	71ft.10in
Length:	40ft.9in
Max.speed:	88 m.p.h (sea lev
Crew:	3
Ceiling:	21,300f

Purpose: *heavy day and night bomber. First daylight raid on London made by 14 Gothas on 13 June 1917. The main bases were at St.Denis Westrem and Gontronde. This type came into operation when the Germans realised the serious limitations in the use of Zeppelin airships as raiders.*

Armament:	1 Parabellum machine-gun: front cockpit.	12 H.E. bombs within fusela
	1 Parabellum machine-gun: rear cockpit.	2 external bombs held in
	1 Parabellum machine-gun: belly defence.	spring jaws.

BRITISH Sopwith F.1 "Camel"

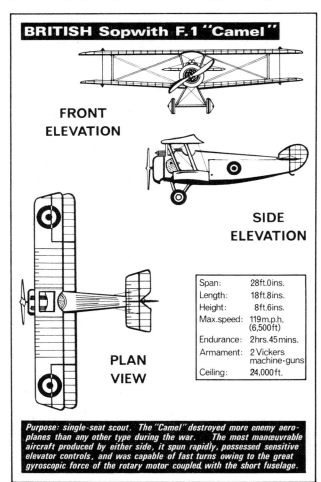

FRONT ELEVATION

SIDE ELEVATION

PLAN VIEW

Span:	28ft.0ins.
Length:	18ft.8ins.
Height:	8ft.6ins.
Max.speed:	119m.p.h. (6,500ft)
Endurance:	2hrs.45mins.
Armament:	2 Vickers machine-guns
Ceiling:	24,000ft.

Purpose: *single-seat scout. The "Camel" destroyed more enemy aeroplanes than any other type during the war. The most manœuvrable aircraft produced by either side, it spun rapidly, possessed sensitive elevator controls, and was capable of fast turns owing to the great gyroscopic force of the rotary motor coupled with the short fuselage.*

BRITISH S.E.5a

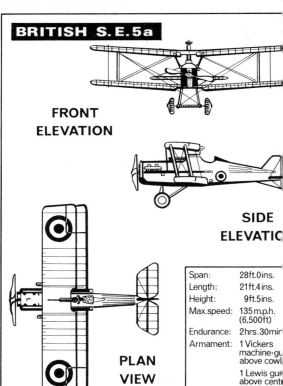

FRONT ELEVATION

SIDE ELEVATIO

PLAN VIEW

Span:	28ft.0ins.
Length:	21ft.4ins.
Height:	9ft.5ins.
Max.speed:	135 m.p.h. (6,500ft)
Endurance:	2hrs.30mir
Armament:	1 Vickers machine-gu above cowl
	1 Lewis gu above cent section
Ceiling:	20,000ft.

Purpose: *single-seat scout. The S.E.5a was remarkable for its "do fighting" qualities. Although less manœuvrable than the Sopwith "Camel", it was notable for its marked stability as a gun-platform. It is to be noted that the famous "aces" Major E. Mannock,V.C. and Major J.T.B.McCudden,V.C. scored most of their victories in this sc*

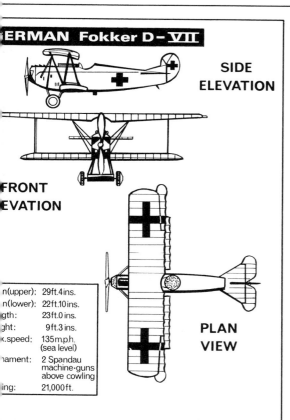

GERMAN Fokker D–VII

SIDE ELEVATION

FRONT ELEVATION

PLAN VIEW

n(upper):	29ft.4ins.
n(lower):	22ft.10ins.
gth:	23ft.0 ins.
ght:	9ft.3 ins.
x.speed:	135m.p.h. (sea level)
nament:	2 Spandau machine-guns above cowling
ing:	21,000ft.

ose: single-seat scout. Possibly the finest of all German fighters
duced during the 1914-1918 war, it was credited with 565 victims in
ust 1918 alone. Hermann Goering (also of 1939-1945 war fame)
w this type. By the autumn of 1918 every German scout squadron on
Western Front was equipped with this aircraft.

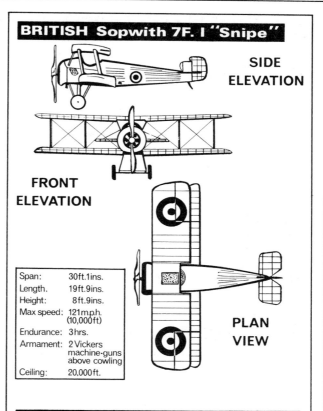

BRITISH Sopwith 7F. I "Snipe"

SIDE ELEVATION

FRONT ELEVATION

PLAN VIEW

Span:	30ft.1ins.
Length.	19ft.9ins.
Height:	8ft.9ins.
Max speed:	121m.p.h. (10,000ft)
Endurance:	3hrs.
Armament:	2 Vickers machine-guns above cowling
Ceiling:	20,000ft.

Purpose: single-seat scout. Although operational during only the final three months of the war, it showed itself to be a first-class fighter. Among those who piloted this type was the famous Canadian "ace" Major W.G. Barker, V.C. In all 264 "Snipes" were built, 97 being used on the Western Front. The plan was to fully replace the "Camel" with this newest scout, but the Armistice closed its brief military career.

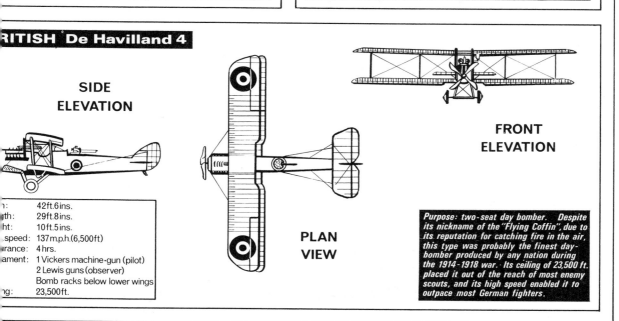

RITISH De Havilland 4

SIDE ELEVATION

FRONT ELEVATION

PLAN VIEW

n:	42ft.6ins.
gth:	29ft.8ins.
ht:	10ft.5ins.
speed:	137m.p.h.(6,500ft)
urance:	4hrs.
ament:	1 Vickers machine-gun (pilot) 2 Lewis guns (observer) Bomb racks below lower wings
ng:	23,500ft.

Purpose: two-seat day bomber. Despite its nickname of the "Flying Coffin", due to its reputation for catching fire in the air, this type was probably the finest day-bomber produced by any nation during the 1914-1918 war. Its ceiling of 23,500 ft. placed it out of the reach of most enemy scouts, and its high speed enabled it to outpace most German fighters.

General Index *

* Prepared by Mrs Brenda Hall, Society of Indexers.

Belkovitch, General, 176
Belle Alliance Farm, Ypres, 138
Belleau, 187
Belleau Wood, 190
Bellewaarde Farm, Ypres, 138
Bellewaarde Ridge, Ypres, 142
Belloy-en-Santerre, 156, 158
Belluno, 200, 203
Below, General Otto von, 88–9, 92–3, 96–7, 182–3
Benavides, 215
Beney, 192, 193
Berchem Ste Agathe, airship base, 284
Bergues, 38–9
Berlin, 18
Berlin-Baghdad Railway, 5, 118, 209, 252–3
Berlin, Treaty of, 1878, 7
Berlin Wood, Ypres, 138
Bernafay Wood, 154–5
Bernay, 182–3
Bernes, 182–3
Berny-en-Santerre, 158
Berrangé, General, 216
Berry-au-Bac, 187
Berthelot, General, 187, 205
Berthold, Hauptmann Rudoph, 300
Bertincourt, 182–3
Bertry, 50
Berwick, air raid on, 296
Besançon, 31
Beseler, General von, 13–15, 61, 66, 67
Besika Bay, Gallipoli, 109
Besim Tepe, Gallipoli, 110–11
Bétheniville, 58
Bétheny, 168
Béthincourt, 148–50
Bethlehem, 213
Bethmann-Hollweg Trench, Moron-villiers, 168
Bethune, 180
Bettembourg, bombing of, 298
Bettoncourt, German air base at, 298
Betz, 47
Beverley, air raid on, 296
Bewdley, air raid on, 287
Beyrouth Main Boyau, Moron-villiers, 168
Bézonvaux, 148–50, 159
Biaches, 156
Big Bertha, see Howitzers, German 42-cm.
Biggin Hill, fighter airfield, 295
Billinghurst, President, 215
Billy, 192, 193
Binche, 38–9, 48–9
Birdwood, Lieutenant-General W. R., 120
Birmingham, air raid on, 287, 296
Bischofsburg, 90–1
Bishop, Lieutenant-Colonel William A., 300, 302

Bishop Auckland, air raid on, 296
Bismarck, Otto, Prince von, 3, 5
Bitche, 298
Bitlis, 163
Bitsch, 26
Bitterfeld, airship construction plant, 284
Bixschoote, 78–82
Biyuk Anafarta, Gallipoli, 119
'Black Day' of German army, 191
Black Hand, 10
'Black Marias', 59
Black Sea
minefields, 272, 276; naval war in, 235–6, 272–3; Turkish blockade in, 177
Blagoveschchenski, General, 92–3, 96–7
Blâmont, 45
Blankenberghe, 196
Blockades see Naval blockades
Blondlat, General, 193
Blücher, German offensive, 1918, 180
Blue Max award, 300
Boelcke, Hauptmann Oswald, 301, 302
Boesinghe, 75, 138, 173
Boetleer's Farm, Ypres, 138
Boghali, Gallipoli, 119, 121
Bohain, 48–9
Böhm-Ermoli, General, 102, 161
Bois Blancs, 76–7
Bois de Bruyères, bombardment of Paris from, 184, 187
Bois de Corbie, bombardment of Paris from, 184
Bois des Cusiniers see Kitchener's Wood
Bois du Chien Trench, Moron-villiers, 168
Bois Grenier, 75, 76–7
Bolimov, first use of gas near, 33
Bolsheviks, propaganda campaign, 165
Bolton, air raid on, 296
Bombers see Air, War in, Aircraft, and individual types of plane
Bombon, 181
Bombs
British 'Jam Tin', 230; numbers dropped on Britain, 282, 286–96; numbers, types, dropped on Paris, 297
Bonconville, 193
Bonn, bombing of, 298
Bous, German air base, 298
Bordeaux, 53, 188–9
Borgo, 200
Borkum, 255
Boschbeek, 61
Bosnia
annexation by Austria-Hungary, 7; Serbian advance through, 1918, 205

Bosphorus, bombardment of, 273
Boston, U.S.A., embarkation point, 188
Botha, Louis, 216
Bothmer, General von, 161
Bouchy, 182–3
Boulay, German air base, 298
Bouleaux Wood, 152–3
Boulogne, 17, 66
Bouresches, 190
Bourlon, 174
Boyelles, 182–3
Brabant, 60, 148–50
Braches, 182–3
Bradford, Vice-Admiral E. E., 248–51
Braine, 16
Braintree, air raid on, 296
Bras, 148–50
Bray, 182–3
Braye, 167
Brazil, alignment with Allies, 215
Brazilian Navy, service off Africa, in Mediterranean, 215
Bread riots in Germany, 179
Breech-loading rifles see Rifles
'Breguet' mines, French, 279
Bremen, 255
Brenta River, 200
Breslau, 18, 100
'Breslau' class of light cruisers, 245, 248; see also Armed Forces Index
Brest, U.S. troops passing through, 188–9
Brest-Litovsk, 18, 100, 135
Brest-Litovsk, Treaty of, 165, 177, 178, 197
Breteuil, 16, 48–9
Bretonnaux, 182–3
Brialmont, Henri, 28, 29
Bridging trains, in German divisional organization, 34
Bridoux, General, 48–9
Bridoux (place), 76–7
Brie, 47
Briey, 16
Brigades, in divisional organization, 34–7, 190; see also Armed Forces Index
Brindisi, Italian naval base at, 271
Briog, Pulhallo von, 161
Bristol, U.S. troops passing through, 188
Bristol F. 2B aircraft, 295, 303
Britain
alliances, treaty obligations, 1, 2, 3, 11; armistice with Turkey, 199, 213; declarations of war, 11, 106–7; extent, resources of empire, 4, 6; German bombing raids on, 281, 282, 283, 286–96; impact of submarine warfare, 179; indignation at lack of munitions, 131; military strength in 1914, 4;

Condé-sur-Aisne, 59
Congreve, General, 182–3
Conneau, General, 48–9; *see also* Armed Forces Index *under* French army
Conrad von Hötzendorf *see* Hötzendorf
Consenvoye, 148–50
Constantinople
Allied desire for control of, 109, 110–11; attempt to bomb S.M.S. Goeben at, 273; transfer of S.M.S. Goeben, Breslau to Turkish fleet at, 237; U-boat base at, 270
Constanzier Redoubt, Moronvilliers, 168
Contact mines, 117, 278
Contalmaison, 154–5, 156, 158
Contoire, 182–3
Convoy system, 236, 263, 266–7
Conz, bombing of, 298
Coppens de Houthulst, Second Lieutenant Willy, 300
Cordite flashes, in gun turrets, 250–1, 258
Corfu
French naval base, 271; Serbian troops from, at Salonika, 204
Cormons, 202
Coronel, battle of, 108, 215, 235, 240
Corps, in divisional organization, 34–5
Cortina, Tyrol, 200
Cossacks, Don, refusal to recognize revolution, 177
Coulommiers, 16, 47, 48–9, 54–7, 187
Courcelette, 152–3, 156, 158, 182–3
Courcelles, 182–3
Courland, 178
Courtrai, 17, 172, 181, 196, 197
Coventry, air raid on, 296
Cracow, 18, 100, 104
Craddock, Rear Admiral Sir C., 240
Craonne, 27, 166, 167, 197
Crécy, 54–6
Creeping mines, 279
Crépy-en-Laonnois, 27, 54–7, 184
Crete
union with Greece, 7; unsuccessful Zeppelin raid on, 285
Crèvecoeur, 48–9
Croatians
minority group in Austria-Hungary, 5; percentage of soldiers from, in Austro-Hungarian army, 102
Croisilles, 182–3
Croix, 182–3
Cromarty, naval base at, 246, 255
Croutoy, 47
Croydon, air raids on, 296
Cruisers
British, at Jutland, 257–9; in

flotilla bombarding coast in battle of the Yser, 68; 'Nymphe' class, 245; Russian, Turkish strength in, 272; transfer of S.M.S. Goeben, Breslau to Turkey, 108
Cruisers, Light
at battle of Dogger Bank, 248–51; at battle of Heligoland Bight, 242–5; at Coronel, 240; at Falkland Islands, 241; in flotilla bombarding coast in battle of the Yser, 67; in pursuit of S.M.S. Goeben, Breslau, 237; 'Kohlberg' class, 245; *see also* Battlecruisers
Ctesiphon, 207, 208, 210
Cuba, revolt in, 214
Čubrilović, Vaso, 10
Cuffley, destruction of SL 11 over, 288–9, 302
Cugny, 182–3
Cumières, 148–50
Curlu, 152–3, 156, 158
Currie, 170
Cuxhaven, naval base at, 255
Cyprus
British dispositions in, 118; British territory from 1914, 212
Czechoslovakians
minority group in Austria-Hungary, 5; percentage of soldiers in Austro-Hungarian army, 102
Czernowitz, 85–6, 161, 176

d'Amade, General, 46, 120
d'Argueeff (? D'Argeyev), Captain, 300
d'Esperey, Franchet, 13–15, 47–8, 54–7, 109, 179, 199
d'Oissel, General Hély, 80–2, 83, 143, 168
d'Urbal, General, 144
Dagö, naval base at, 269
Dahomey, Allied advance on Togoland from, 216
Dalston, air raid on, 286
Damascus, 118, 179, 213
Damloup Battery, Verdun, 148–9
Dammartin, 54–7
Dankl, General, 100
Danube, River, region
Austro-Hungarian flotilla on, 85–6; German retreat through, 199, 205
Danzig, 18, 87
Dar es Salaam, 216, 217, 218
Dardanelles
Allied attempt to force passage, 109, 110–11, 115–17; Allied fleets' passage of, 205; Allied strategic concepts, 106–7, 109; Allied submarine campaign, 252–3; escape of S.M.S. Goeben, Breslau through, 237; minefields, 109, 110–11, 113, 115, 116–17; naval

bombardments, 112–17; penetration by British submarine B 11, 247; Turkish dispositions, defences, 110–11, 115, 116–17, 118, 119; use of seaplanes, seaplane carriers in, 281; *see also* Gallipoli campaign
Dardanos, 110–11
Daur, 210
Davenscourt, 182–3
de Castelnau, General, 30–1, 44, 144
De Dion motor vehicles, 233
De Havilland 4, British aircraft, 305
de Mitry, General, 66, 67, 75
Deal, air raids on, 296
Decorations, awarded to fighter aces, 300–1
Degoutte, General, 168, 187, 197
Deimling, General, 139
Delville Wood, 152–3, 154–5, 156, 158
Demuin, 182–3, 191
Dendre, River, 52
Deniecourt, 158
Depthcharges, submarines sunk by, 236, 262–4
Dera'a, 213
Derby, air raid on, 296
Derma Burnu, Gallipoli, 110–11
Dernicourt, 182–3
Destroyers
anti-submarine patrols, 268; at battle of Dogger Bank, 248–51; contestants' strength in, in Black Sea area, 272; function in convoys, 266; German, at Zeebrugge, 274; in battle of Heligoland Bight, 242–5; in flotilla bombarding coast in battle of the Yser, 67, 68; in pursuit of S.M.S. Goeben, Breslau, 237; 'Tribal' class, 67, 68; Turkish, during Gallipoli campaign, 254
Detling, fighter airfield at, 295
Deulemont, 75
'Deutschland', commercial submarine, 280
Deutz, bombing of, 298
Deventer, General, 216, 218
Dhibban, 210
Diaz, General, 203
Dickman, Major General, G.I., 203
Diedenhofen (Thionville), 16, 22, 26, 30–1
Diekirch, 16
Dienze, bombing of, 298
Dieppe, 17
Dijon, 31
Dillingen, bombing of, 298
Dinant, 16, 23, 33, 38–9, 48–9
Disease, casualties caused by, 122, 204, 210
Divisions, in contestants' military organization, 34–7

Ghistelles, 196
'Giant' bombers, German, 292, 294
Giau Pass, 200, 201
Gibeon, 216
Gièvres, U.S. storage depot, 189
Ginchy, 152–3, 154–5, 156, 158
Givenchy, 17, 169
Givet (Fort de Charlemont), 16, 26, 38–9, 52
Glasgow, U.S. troops disembarkation point, 188
Glisenti pistols, Italian, 232
Gneisenau, German offensive, 1918, 180
Godley, General, 171
Goering, Hermann, 30?
Gold Coast, advance on Togoland from, 216
Golden Horn, submarine attack on 'Stambul' in, 252–3
Goldhanger, Essex, airfield at, 295
Goltz, General von der, 94, 95, 96–7, 207
Gomiecourt, 182–3
Gonnelieu, 174
Gontrode, air base at, 284, 292
Goodenough, Rear-Admiral W. E., 248–51
Goole, air raid on, 296
Gorizia (Görz), 200, 201, 202–3
Gorlice, 131, 135
Gorringe, Lieutenant-General, 207
Goslar Trench, Moronvilliers, 168
Gotha G-V aircraft, German, 292, 293, 294, 304
Gough, General Sir H., 145, 182–3
Gough-Calthorpe, Rear-Admiral, 248–51
Gourko, General Basil, 88–9
Gouzeaucourt, 182–3
Grabez, Trifko, 10
Gradisca, 202
Graincourt, 174
Grand Morin, River, 16, 17, 52, 54–7
Grande Puissance Filloux gun, French, 222
Grant, Captain H. W., 248–51
Graudenz, 18, 87
Gravelines, 66
Gravenstafel, 138–41, 143, 173, 196
Gravenstafel Ridge, Ypres, 138
Great Bitter Lake, defence of, 212
Great Yarmouth, air raid on, 286, 296
Greece
    involvement in, repercussions of Balkan Wars, 8, 9; Salonika front, 199, 204; union with Crete, 7
Greek army, 204, 205
Green cross gas see Gas warfare
Grenades, 230
Grevillers, 182–3
Grimsby, air raid on, 287, 296
Grodno, 18, 135

Groener, General, 219
Guémappe, 169
Guépratte, Vice-Admiral, 116–17
Guerbigny, 182–3
Guérin, General, 168
Guidriari Pass, 200, 201
Guildford, air raid on, 296
Guillemont, 152–3, 154–5, 156, 158
Guiscard, 182–3
Guise, 16, 23, 47, 48–9, 51, 180, 181, 197
Gulf of Aden, minefields, 276–7
Gulf of Saros, strategic significance, 119
Gully Beach, Gallipoli, 121
Gumbinnen, action at, 1914, 85–6, 88–9
Gumbiro, German East Africa, 218
Gun turrets, structural defects in British battlecruisers, 250–1, 258
Gunboats
    British, in flotilla bombarding coast in battle of the Yser, 68; use on Tigris, 207, 208; German destruction on African lakes, 217
Gunfire, submarines sunk by, 262–4
Guns see Artillery and under individual weapons, types of weapon
Gusyatin, 161
Guynemer, Capitaine Georges, 300, 303
Guyot de Salins, General, 159

Hadleigh, fighter airfield at, 295
Hage, airship base, 282
Haguenau, air base, 298
Haidar Pasha, explosion at, 211
Haifa, 213
Haig, Field Marshal Sir Douglas, 46, 131, 137, 147, 166, 172
Hainault, 60
Hainault Farm, fighter airfield, 295
Haiti
    declaration of war on Germany, 214; United States' involvement in, 214
Haldane, General J. A. L., 182–3
Haldane, Lord, 281
Halicz, 176
Halifax, Nova Scotia, U.S. embarkation port, 188
Halifax, Yorks, air raid on, 296
Halluin, 75
Ham, 47, 166, 167, 180, 181, 197
Ham-sur-Sambre, 43
Hamadan, 210, 211
Hamidieh, Dardanelles, 110–11
Hamidieh II, Gallipoli, 110–11
Hamilton, General, 120, 252–3
Hamilton, Lieutenant-General Gordon, 171
Hamman Ali, 210
Hampshire Farm, Ypres, 138
Han, bombing of, 298

Hand grenades, British, 230
Handley-Page bombers, 273
Hangard, 182–3
Hangelar, air base, 298
Hangest, 182–3
Hankey, Lord, 109
Hannonville, 192, 193
Hanover, airship base, 284
Happencourt, 182–3
Harbonnières, 182–3, 191
Harbour entrances, mining of, 178, 179
Hardaumont Battery, Verdun, 148–9
Hardecourt au Bois, 152–3, 156, 158
Hargicourt, 182–3
Harlebeke, 196
Harper, Lieutenant-General, 182–3
Hartlepool, bombardment of, 255, 296
Harunabad, 210
Harwich
    air raid on, 296; naval base at, 246, 255
Hasselt, 30
Hastière, 38–9
Hattencourt, 182–3
Hattigny, air base at, 298
Hattonchâtel, 192, 193
Hattonville, 192, 193
Haubourdin, 196
Haucourt, 50, 148–50
Haumont, 148–50
Hauptmann, rank of, British equivalents, 300
Hausen, 30, 38–9, 48–9, 51, 54
Hauslar, Gallipoli, 110–11
Haussner, Konrad, 33
Haverhill, air raid on, 296
Havrincourt, 174, 182–3
Hayes-Sadler, Rear-Admiral A., 116–17
Hebburn, Tyneside, air raid on, 287
Hebron, 213
Heeringen, 30–1, 45
Heinrichsdorf, 92–3
Hejaz, 212
Hejaz Railway, 213
Heligoland, naval base at, 255
Heligoland Bight, battle of, 108, 242–3
Helles
    Allied bombardment of, 112–14; contestants' trench lines, 123, 126–7; defences, 110–11, 112–14; evacuation, 129
Hellimer, 44
Hem, 152–3, 156, 158
Hendon, Royal Naval Air Station, 273
Héninel, 169
Hennoque, 168
Herbecourt, 156, 158
Herenthage Wood, Ypres, 80
Hermann defence line, 181

Lvov *see* Lemberg
Lympne, fighter base, 293
Lys, River, region, 17, 52, 64–5, 172, 190

Macclesfield, air raid on, 287
McCudden, Major James T. B., 300, 304
Macedonia
course of campaign in, 179, 199; Greek acquisitions in, 8, 9; losses through disease, 199
Machine guns
Austro-Hungarian strength, on Italian front, 200; Canadian captures of, at Vimy, 170; differing reliance placed on, in 1914, 4; in contestants' divisional organization, 34–7, 190; in Jäger battalions, 36; mounted batteries, German, 36; synchronization with aircraft propellers, 281, 300, 302; types in use, 219, 224–5, 226–7; use in tanks, 157, 226–7
McKeever, Captain, 303
Mackensen, General von, 85–6, 88–9, 92–3, 95, 96–7, 104–5, 131, 147, 162, 205
MacKenzie, General, 216
MacLaren, Major Donald R., 300
Madon, Capitaine Georges Felix, 300
Madura *see* Armed Forces Index, British Navy, H.M.S. Mersey
Maggiore, rank of, British equivalent, 300
Maginot Line, 159
Magyars
minority group in Austria-Hungary, 4, 5; percentage in Austro-Hungarian army, 102
Mahenge, German East Africa, 218
Mai Tepe, Gallipoli, 119
Maidos, Gallipoli, 119
Maigny, 182–3
Mainz, air base at, 298
Maisonette, 158
Maizeray, 192
Maizy, 59
Malancourt, 148–50
Malangali, German East Africa, 218
Malaria, casualties caused by, 199, 204
Malazgirt, 163
Malta
Japanese naval units based at, 270; unsuccessful attempt to bomb, 285
Malts Horn Farm, Somme, 158
Mametz, 152–3, 154–5, 156
Mametz Wood, 152–3, 154–5, 156, 158
Manchester, air raid on, 296
Mangin, 159, 187, 197
Mannekensvere, 67

Mannheim
airship construction plant, 284; bombing of, 298
Mannlicher rifles, Austrian, 229
Mannlicher-Carcano rifles, Italian, 229
Mannock, Major Edward, 300, 304
Manoary *see* Maunoury
Marcelcave, 182–3, 191
March, air raid on, 296
Marche, 16, 38–9
Marchiennes, 38–9
Marcoing, 174
Mareuil, 56
Margate, air raids on, 293, 294, 296
Mariakerke, air base at, 292
Mariapol, Russian embarkation port, 273
Maricourt, 156, 182–3
Marienbourg, 42, 87, 90
Maritz, 216
Marle, 16, 27, 48–9, 180, 181
Marne, battle of the, 13–15, 16, 17, 33, 53, 54–7, 96–7
Marne, River, region, 16, 17, 52, 53, 190
Marolles, 47
Marrières Wood, 152–3
Marseilles, number of U.S. troops passing through, 188–9
Marshall, Lieutenant-General Sir W. R., 209
Martinpuich, 152–3, 154–5, 156, 158, 182–3
Martos, General, 92–3, 94, 96–7
Marwitz, 38–9, 174, 182–3
Marwitz Cavalry Corps, 50
Masnières, 174
Massiges, 144
Masurian Lakes, battle of, 85–6, 87, 98
Maubeuge
base for R.F.C., 1914, 38, 46; battles for, 23, 46, 48–9, 52, 115, 181; B.E.F. concentration area, 30; fortifications, 26, 46; relation to static Western Front lines, 17
Maude, Lieutenant-General F. S., 209
Maunoury, General Michel-Joseph, 13–15, 47–8, 54, 56
Maurepas, 152–3, 156, 158, 182–3
Mauser pistols, revolvers, German, 232
Mauser Ridge, Ypres, 138, 140
Mauser rifles, German, 228
Mauve, Rear-Admiral F., 257–9
Mauzon, 197
Maxim weapons
machine guns, 219, 224, 225, 226; naval guns, 69
Maximilian, Emperor of Mexico, 10
Maxse, Lieutenant-General, 182–3
May Island, wireless station on, 248

Méaulte, 182–3
Meaux, 16, 17, 47, 48–9, 54–7, 187
Mecca, Arab revolt in, 212
Medical sections, in divisional organization, 34, 190
Medina, severance of Hijaz railway link, 212, 213
Mediterranean Sea
Allied anti-U-boat patrols, 270; Franco-British agreement on domination of, 2, 3; minefields, 270, 276; pursuit of S.M.S. Goeben, Breslau through, 235, 237; submarine warfare in, 270
Medjidieh Avan, Dardanelles, 110–11
Mehmedbašić, Mohammed, 10
Mellet, 48–9
Melun, 54
Menessis, 182–3
Menin, 75, 196
Menin Road, battles at, 13–15, 75, 78–82
Merckem, 186
Merville, 186
Merzig, bombing of, 298
Mesa, Portuguese East Africa, 218
Mesopotamia, campaign in
British commanders in chief, 209; casualties, 210; climatic problems, 207; contestants' dispositions, 1915, 118; direction of campaign from India, London, 106, 207, 209; prisoners taken, 208, 210; proposed cavalry link with Palestine, 210, 211; railways improved by British, 210; strategic significance, 106–7, 199, 206, 209, 210, 211; terrain, communications, 206, 209, 210; Turkish attacks, 211; *see also individual towns*
Message shells, 231
Messines, 17, 64–5, 75, 78–81, 165, 171, 173, 186, 196
Messudieh (Ak Tepe), Dardanelles, 110–11
Meteren, 186
Metz
contestants' dispositions round, 1914, 22, 53; fortifications, 16, 26; German air base at, 298; German attack from, 1914, 30–1; relation to static Western Front lines, 17, 134; strategic significance of railway link with Lille, 194
Metz en Conture, 182–3
Meuse, River, region, 16, 17, 52, 53, 190, 194, 195; *see also* Verdun, battle of
Mexico
German intrigues in, 1917, 165; struggles for power in, 214; United States' involvement in, 214
Mézières, 16, 17, 22, 134, 182–3, 191, 194, 197

321

Michael I, German offensive, 1918, 180

Michael II, German offensive, 1918, 180

Michael III, German offensive, 1918, 180

Middelburg, 196

Middelkerke, bombardment of, 67

Middle East, dispositions in, 1915, 118

Middlesbrough, air raid on, 296

Midget submarines, Italian, 271, 280

Midlands, airship raids over, 281, 287, 296

Mills hand grenades, 230

Milne, General, 205

Minefields

destruction of submarines in, 236, 246, 262–4, 268, 275; European, 236, 276; German use of, 108; in Baltic, 269; in Mediterranean, 270, 276; in North Sea, 236, 246, 249, 256, 259, 268, 276; land, use in Gallipoli, 128; outside Ostend, 68; systems, 278; Turkish, in Dardanelles, Black Sea, 110–17, 119, 246, 272; world-wide distribution, 277; see also Mines

Minenwerfers, German, 230, 231

Mines

systems for laying, 278; totals laid, 276–7; types, construction, 117, 275, 278–9

Minesweepers, in Dardanelles, 113, 115, 116–17

Mining, of German lines at Messines, 171

Miraumont, 156, 182–3

Misahohe, Togoland, 216

Misic, General, 205

Missy, 167, 168

Mitrailleuses, French, 219

Mlawa, 90, 94–7

Mobilization, critical nature of speed of, 11, 13–15, 20, 22, 24, 25

Moeuvres, 174

'Moisin-Nagant' rifles, Russian, 219

Moislains, 182–3

Moligneux, 182–3

Moltke, Helmuth von (Elder), 20, 21

Moltke, Helmuth von (Younger), 13–15, 20, 22, 24, 30, 103

Molundu, Cameroon, 217

Monastir, battle of, 1912, 8

Monchy, 169, 182–3

Monfalcone, 200, 201, 202

Monitors, British naval, 67, 68, 69, 268

Monneaux, 190

Mons

battle for, 1914, 33, 38–9, 46; battle for, 1918, 180, 181, 197; Belgian strategy following Allied defeat at, 60; physical geography,

16; relation to static Western Front lines, 17, 134; target in Schlieffen Plan, 22

Mont Blond, Moronvilliers, 168

Mont Cornilet, Moronvilliers, 168

Mont des Cats, 186

Mont Haut, Moronvilliers, 168

Mont Kemmel, 186

Mont le Casque, Moronvilliers, 168

Mont le Téton, Moronvilliers, 168

Mont Porthois, Moronvilliers, 168

Montauban, 152–3, 154–5, 156, 158, 182–3

Montcornet, 48–9, 166

Montdidier, 16, 17, 48–9, 180, 181, 182–3, 197

Montenegro

army in retreat, 1915, 160; declaration of war on Austria, 11; involvement in repercussions of Balkan Wars, 8, 9; physical, regional geography, 18; troop concentrations, 1914, 32

Montfaucon, 195

Montignies-le-Tilleul, 43

Montmédy, 16, 26, 52, 53

Montmirail, 16, 48–9, 54–5

Montmort, 56

Montoir, 189

Montois, 47

Montreal, U.S. embarkation point, 188

Montreuil, 180

Mont-Ste. Aldegonde, 43

Moore, Rear-Admiral Sir Archibald, 248–51

Moored mines, 279

Moorslede, 75

Mora, Cameroon, 217

Morcourt, 182–3, 191

Mordacq, General, 168

Moreuil, 48–9, 182–3, 191

Morgen, General von, 105

Morhange

air base at, 298; troop concentrations, 1914, 22

Morlancourt, 182–3, 191

Morland, Lieutenant-General, 171

Morocco, crises in, 1905–12, 1, 7; see also Armed Forces Index, French Armed Forces

Moronvilliers, 168

Mörsers see Howitzers, Mortars

Mortars

appreciation of importance by Germany, 4; for trench warfare, 190, 230; French, 223; German, 202; howitzers distinguished, 63; see also Howitzers

Mortier, 41

Morto Bay, Gallipoli, 110–11

Morval, 152–3, 156, 158, 182–3

Mosaic maps, techniques for making, 299

Moscow, adoption as Russian capital city, 177

Moselle, River, 16, 17, 52, 53

Moshi, German East Africa, 218

Moslem Slavs, minority groups in Austria-Hungary, 5

Mosul, 209, 210, 211

Mouquet (Moquet) Farm, 154–5, 158

Mouse Trap Farm, Ypres, 138

Moussy, General, 80–2

Mozambique, Portuguese East Africa, 218

Mpepo, German East Africa, 218

Muanhupa, Portuguese East Africa, 218

Mud, halt of offensive at Passchendaele by, 173

Mudania, submarine attacks on, 252–3

Mudros, Turkish signature of armistice at, 199, 213

Mülhausen, 31, 45, 90

Mun-i-Zaffer, Gallipoli, 110–11

Muni, West Africa, 217

Munitions

amounts used, in battle of Verdun, 150, 151; German shortage of shells at 2 Ypres, 142; in use by various types of artillery, 220–3; indignation at lack of, in Britain, 131; loss of Turkish, in explosion at Haidar Pasha, 211; Rumanian weakness in, 162; shortage, in Italian army, 199; shortage in Russia, 4, 85–6, 109, 177; shortage of, in Gallipoli, 122; supply trains, 34–5, 37, 190; types used in trench warfare, 230–1

Muret-et-Crouttes, 59

Murmansk, supply route through, 177

Murray, Lieutenant-General Sir A. J., 31

Mus, 163

Mustafa Kemal Pasha, 121

Mustard gas, 173; see also Gas warfare

Muteau, General, 159

Mutinies

in French army, 165, 167; in German navy, 179, 236, 275

Mutzig, 26

Mwembe, Portuguese East Africa, 218

Myburgh, General, 216

Nablus, 213

Nagara, Dardanelles, 110–11

Namazieh, Gallipoli, 110–11

Nambu pistols, Japanese, 232

Nampeel, 58

Namur

airship base, 284; Belgian strategy

Namur—*contd.*
following defeat at, 60; fortifications, 16, 26, 28; relation to static Western Front lines, 17, 134; siege of, 23, 39, 42, 48–9, 51, 115
Namutoni, South West Africa, 216
Nancy, 16, 17, 30–1, 53, 134
Nanguari, Portuguese East Africa, 218
Nanichevanski, General Khan, 88–9
Nanteuil, 47, 48–9, 55–7
Nanungu, Portuguese East Africa, 218
Napier, Rear-Admiral T. D. W., 248–51
Naples, Zeppelin raid on, 285
Narrows *see* Dardanelles, Sea of Marmara
Nasiriya, 207
Naulin, General, 168
Nauroy, 168
Naval blockades, techniques, strategies, 108, 147, 177, 179, 212, 235–6
Naval guns
German ('Long Max'), shelling of Dunkirk by, 184; German long-range shelling of Verdun, 150; Hotchkiss Automatic, on British Monitors, 69; inaccuracy in trench warfare, 122; Maxims, on 'London' Class of battleships, 69; use of British 6-pounder on early tanks, 157; types used in bombardments in Dardanelles, 112, 115; 38-cm. long-range, German, 150; 4-inch, 112; 4.7-inch, 69; 6-inch, 69, 112, 115; 6.4-inch, 112; 12-inch, 69, 112; 15-inch, 115; 3-pounder, 69, 115; 12-pounder, 69, 115
Naval supremacy *see* Sea power
Nazareth, 213
Neidenburg, 90–3, 94, 96–7
Néry, 47, 48–9
Nesle, 48–9, 180, 181, 182–3
Nets, submarine losses in, 262–4
Neu-Breisach, 26, 31, 45
Neuenburg, 26
Neufchâteau, 16, 26
Neuve Chapelle, 17, 74, 76–7, 134
Neuve Chapelle, battle of, 131, 136–7
Neuve Église, 75, 186
Neuville, 169
Neuville-St.-Vaast, 144
Neuville Vitasse, 167
New York, U.S. embarkation port, 188
New Zealand, coastal minefields, 276–7
New Zealand armed forces
capture of German colonies in Pacific, 108; in battle of Messines, 165; in Gallipoli campaign, 109; *see also* Anzac forces
Newala, German East Africa, 218

Newark, air raid on, 296
Newcastle on Tyne, air raids on, 281, 287, 296
Newcastle under Lyme, air raid on, 287
Newmarket, air raid on, 296
Newport News, U.S. troops embarkation point, 188
Newton Pippin rifle grenades, British, 230
Ngaundere, Cameroon, 217
Ngomano, Portuguese East Africa, 218
Nibrunesi Beach, Gallipoli, 123
Nibrunesi Point, Gallipoli, 119
Nicaragua, Bryan-Chamorro Treaty with, 214
Nicholas, Grand Duke, 85–6, 147
Nicholas II, Tsar, 147, 177
Nieppe, 75, 76–7
Nieumunster, air base, 293
Nieuport
battle for, 66, 68, 69; inundation of, 13–15, 70–1, 83; relation to static Western Front lines, 17
Nieuport 17 C.1 French aircraft, 302
Nigeria, Allied advance into Cameroon from, 217
Nikolaiev, naval construction yards at, 272
Nivelle, Robert Georges, 159, 165, 166
Nivelles, 16
Nixon, General Sir J. E., 207
Nonsard, 192, 193
Noord Vaart Siphon, 71
Nordenburg, 87, 88–9
Nordholz, airship base, 282, 286, 290–1
Noreuil, 182–3
Norfolk
air raids on, 286, 296; naval bombardment on coast of, 296
Norroy, 192, 193
North Africa *see* Africa, North
North Sea
contestants' naval strategies in, 235–6, 255, 256, 275; Franco-British agreement on naval supremacy in, 2, 3; German access to, 5, 21; minefields, 236, 246, 249, 256, 259, 268, 276; U-boats in, in 1914, 246; *see also* Sea, War at, Submarine warfare, *and individual battles*
North Weald Bassett, fighter airfield, 295
Northampton, air raid on, 296
Northern Rhodesia, advance on German East Africa from, 218
Norwich, air raids on, 287, 296
Nottingham, air raid on, 296
Novo-Georgievsk, 18, 91, 100, 135

Noyon, 16, 17, 47, 48–9, 58–9, 134, 167, 180, 181, 182–3, 197
Nungesser, Lieutenant Charles E. J. M., 300
Nun's Copse, Ypres, 80
Nurlu, 182–3
Nyamirue, Portuguese East Africa, 218
Nyasaland, advance into German, Portuguese East Africa from, 218
'Nymphe' class of protected cruisers, 245

Oberleutnant, rank of, equivalents, 300
Oblong Farm, Ypres, 138
Obrégon, Alvaro, 214
Observation balloons, 152–3
Odessa, bombardment of, 272, 273
Offenburg, bombing of, 298
Oil
contestants' strategies for securing of supplies, 177, 199, 206, 210; use of burning, in trench warfare, 219
Oise River, region, 16, 17, 52, 53, 190
Oisy, 47
Old Contemptibles, 13–15
Oliezy, 182–3
Olleris, General, 81–2
Omaruru, South West Africa, 216
Omecourt, 158
Oostakker, air base, 292
Oostaverne, 173
Oostniewkerke, 75
Oranovski, General, 88–9
Orkanie, Dardanelles, 110–11, 112–14, 119
Ornes, 148–50
Ortelsburg, 90–1, 95–7
Oscillating mines, 279
Ossowiec, 87
Ostend
Allied bombardment of, 68; battles for, 181, 197; British attempt to block harbour, 236, 274; minefield laid outside, 68; relation to Western Front lines, 17; strategic importance, 66, 68, 172; submarine base at, 268
Osterode, 96–7
Ostrolenka, 87, 90, 91
Otranto, 236, 271
Ottoman Empire *see* Turkey
Ouchy, Treaty of, 7
Oudenarde, 197
Ouderdom, 141
Ourcq, River, 16, 54–7
Ourthe, River, 16, 52
Ovillers la Boisselle, 154–5, 156, 158

Pacific Ocean, area
German squadron in, 108, 238; loss of German colonies in, 108

328

Armed Forces Index *

AUSTRO-HUNGARIAN FORCES

ARMY

Armies, Army Groups
First, 32, 100–2, 104, 161
First Isonzo, 202
Second, 32, 99, 100, 104, 161, 176
Second Isonzo, 202
Third, 32, 100–2, 160, 176, 202
Fourth, 32, 100–2, 104, 161
Fifth, 32, 99
Sixth, 32, 99
Seventh, 161, 176
Tenth, 202
Eleventh, 202
Kövess Group, 100–2
Kummer Group, 100–2
Südarmee, 176
'Balkan' *see* Second, Fifth, Sixth armies

Corps
I, 101
II, 101
V, 101
VI, 101
VIII, 99
IX, 101
X, 101
XIII, 99
XVII, 101
XVIII, 195
Kummel, 32

NAVY

Szent Istvan, 271
Viribus Unitis, 271
Wien, 271

BELGIAN FORCES

ARMY

Divisions
1, 30, 60, 62, 64–5, 66, 67, 83
2, 30, 60, 62, 63, 64–5, 66, 67
3, 30, 40, 60, 62, 64–5, 66, 67, 83
4, 30, 42, 60, 62, 64–5, 66, 67, 83
5, 30, 60, 62, 64–5, 66, 67, 83
6, 30, 60, 62, 64–5, 66, 67, 75, 83, 139, 140

1 Cavalry, 30, 60, 62, 64–5, 66, 67, 75, 83
2 Cavalry, 30, 64–5, 66, 67, 83

Brigades
1, 67
15, 40

Regiments
4 Line, 69
9, 40
11, 40
12, 40
14, 40
29, 40
31, 40
32, 40
34, 40

BRITISH ARMED FORCES

ARMY

Armies, Army Groups
First, 169, 180, 182–3, 186, 194
Second, 165, 171, 172, 173, 180, 186, 194
Third, 169, 174, 180, 182–3, 194, 196
Fourth, 152–3, 172, 194
Fifth, 109, 172, 180, 182–3, 196
B.E.F., 23, 30–1, 38–9, 46, 48–9, 51, 53, 54–7, 58–9

Corps
I, 46, 47, 48–9, 51, 54–7, 58–9, 65, 78–82, 83, 145, 169, 170
II, 38–9, 46, 47, 48–9, 54–7, 58–9, 64–5, 66, 72–4, 75, 76–7, 139, 196
III, 47, 48–9, 54–7, 58–9, 64–5, 66, 72–4, 75, 76–7, 78–9, 81–2, 83, 174, 182–3, 191
IV, 75, 78–82, 83, 136–7, 145, 174, 182–3
V (Plumer's Force), 139–42, 169, 182–3
VI, 169, 182–3
VII, 169, 174, 182–3
VIII, 124–5, 128
IX, 129, 171
X, 171, 196
XI, 196
XV, 196

XVII, 169, 170, 182–3
XVIII, 182–3
XIX, 182–3, 196
XX, 213
XXI, 213
Cavalry Corps, 65, 66, 75, 78–82, 83
Chaytor's Force, 213
Desert Mounted, 213

Divisions
1, 47, 56, 57, 78–82, 83, 145
2, 46, 47, 56, 57, 78–82, 83, 145
3, 46, 47, 50, 56, 57, 64–5, 72–4, 75, 76–7, 78–82, 145
4, 47, 48–9, 50, 56, 57, 75, 76–7, 78–82, 83, 142, 143
5, 46, 47, 50, 56, 64–5, 72–4, 139, 142, 143
6, 74, 75, 76–7, 83
7, 64–5, 66, 67, 75, 78, 136–7, 145
8, 136–7
9, 145
10, 123
11, 123, 128
13, 128, 129
15, 145
16 (Irish), 171
19, 171
23, 171
25, 171
27, 139–40, 142, 143
28, 139–40, 142, 143
29, 120, 129
36 (Ulster), 171
41, 171
46 (North Midland), 139
47, 145, 171
50, 143
52, 129
Royal Naval, 13–15, 62, 116–17, 120, 121, 129
1 Cavalry, 64–5, 75, 78–80, 81, 142, 143
2 Cavalry, 78–82, 82, 128, 143
3 Cavalry, 64–5, 67, 75, 83, 142, 143
4 Cavalry, 80
5 Cavalry, 213
Cavalry Division, B.E.F., 38–9

Brigades
2 Infantry, 46
3 Infantry, 46
4 Infantry, 46

* Prepared by Mrs Brenda Hall, Society of Indexers.

334